THE CRAFT OF CRITICISM

With contributions from thirty leading media scholars, this collection provides a comprehensive overview of the main methodologies of critical media studies. Chapters address various methods of textual analysis, as well as reception studies, policy studies, production studies, and contextual, multi-method approaches, like intertextuality and cultural geography. Film and television are at the heart of the collection, which also addresses emergent technologies and new research tools in such areas as software studies, gaming, and digital humanities. Each chapter includes an intellectual history of a particular method or approach, a discussion of why and how it was used to study a particular medium or media, relevant examples of influential work in the area, and an in-depth review of a case study drawn from the author's own research. Together, the chapters in this collection give media critics a complete toolbox of essential critical media studies methodologies.

Contributors: Cynthia Baron, Ron Becker, Mary Beltrán, Patrick Burkart, Jeremy G. Butler, Cynthia Chris, Norma Coates, Eric Freedman, Rosalind Gill, Jonathan Gray, Mary L. Gray, Timothy Havens, Matt Hills, Michele Hilmes, Nina B. Huntemann, Victoria E. Johnson, Michael Kackman, Mary Celeste Kearney, Bill Kirkpatrick, Amanda Ann Klein, Shanti Kumar, Suzanne Leonard, Jessa Lingel, Madhavi Mallapragada, Daniel Marcus, Todd McGowan, Jason Mittell, Ted Nannicelli, Diane Negra, Matthew Thomas Payne, Miriam Posner, Jacob Smith

Michael Kackman is Associate Teaching Professor in the Department of Film, Television, and Theatre at the University of Notre Dame, Indiana, USA, where he teaches courses in the history and criticism of U.S. television, Cold War cultural history, nationhood and political culture, and history and memory practices in everyday life. He is the author of *Citizen Spy: Television, Espionage, and Cold War Culture* (University of Minnesota Press, 2005), and co-editor of *Flow TV: Television in the Age of Media Convergence* (Routledge, 2010).

Mary Celeste Kearney is Director of Gender Studies and Associate Professor of Film, Television, and Theatre at the University of Notre Dame, Indiana, USA. She is author of *Girls Make Media* (Routledge, 2006) and *Gender and Rock* (Oxford University Press, 2017). She is editor of *The Gender and Media Reader* (Routledge, 2011) and *Mediated Girlhoods: New Explorations of Girls' Media Culture* (Peter Lang, 2011), as well as co-editor (with Morgan Blue) of *Mediated Girlhoods'* second volume (Peter Lang, 2018). She is academic editor of the book series Routledge Research in Gender, Sexuality, and Media, and serves on the boards of several academic journals.

THE CRAFT
OF CRITICISM

CRITICAL MEDIA
STUDIES IN PRACTICE

EDITED BY
MICHAEL KACKMAN AND MARY CELESTE KEARNEY

Routledge
Taylor & Francis Group

NEW YORK AND LONDON

First published 2018
by Routledge
711 Third Avenue, New York, NY 10017

and by Routledge
2 Park Square, Milton Park, Abingdon, Oxon OX14 4RN

Routledge is an imprint of the Taylor & Francis Group, an informa business

© 2018 Taylor & Francis

Library of Congress Cataloging in Publication Data
A catalog record has been requested for this book

ISBN: 978-0-415-71629-1 (hbk)
ISBN: 978-0-415-71630-7 (pbk)
ISBN: 978-1-315-87997-0 (ebk)

Typeset in Amasis
by Swales & Willis Ltd, Exeter, Devon, UK

CONTENTS

FIGURES

TABLES

ACKNOWLEDGMENTS

First and foremost, our sincere thanks to each of our contributors. It is absolutely no exaggeration to say that you would not be holding this book in your hands if not for their deep commitment to this collection and their diligent work in crafting chapters that will serve as accessible and efficient tools for many current and future scholars of media culture.

We are beyond grateful also to Dr. Morgan Blue for her expert editorial assistance. She not only lent her keen eye to every missing em dash and serial comma, she also paid close attention to each chapter's critical arguments, providing us and our contributors with insightful guidance for improvement. Thank you, Morgan, a gazillion times over.

Thanks also to the many students we have taught—and learned from—over the years in our critical media studies courses at the University of Wisconsin-Madison, the University of Southern California, DePaul University, the University of Texas at Austin, and the University of Notre Dame. You've helped us to become better teachers of the craft of media criticism and to ask better questions in our own research.

We would not be the teachers and critics we are today without the expert guidance we received in graduate school by some of the finest critical media scholars. Julie D'Acci, John Fiske, Michele Hilmes, David James, Caren Kaplan, Marsha Kinder, and Lynn Spigel welcomed us into the conversation, modeled rigorous critique, and showed us the value of a well-placed "So what?" or "Say more about that!" Thank you all.

We extend our gratitude as well to Erica Wetter, our Routledge editor, whose enthusiasm, support, and patience during our work on this project were generously offered, especially when we needed them most. We cannot think of a better shepherd for this book and for us as its editors.

Last but not least, we gratefully acknowledge the support of the University of Notre Dame. Our colleagues in the Department of Film, Television, and Theatre have created a climate of wit, rigor, and deep collegiality, and we're fortunate to teach and learn among you. Notre Dame's Institute for Scholarship in the Liberal Arts not only lent financial support during the editing process, but also hosted a conference that brought our contributors together to develop their chapters in an intimate and productive workshop environment. This collection would not be the same without their generous support.

FOREWORD

Michele Hilmes

Critical media studies is a big tent. This fine new collection of essays, populated by some of the best-known names in contemporary media studies, is a work focused not on setting boundaries but on laying out the contours of a very lively and inclusive field. And how rapidly it has grown!

In the early 1980s, a field that we might recognize as "media studies" began to emerge. Out of a tangle of communications, film, literature, journalism, cultural history, technology studies, sociology, political science, and a number of other disciplines, a central core of concerns began to cohere, pulling threads that eventually knit together into a complex but mutually invigorating structure of theories, methods, programs, and publications. The earliest direct reference I've been able to find to "media studies" in the context of scholarly publication is Christine Gledhill's compilation of papers from a 1979 conference entitled "Film and Media Studies in Higher Education" organized by the British Film Institute and London University School of Communication. As of late 2017, if we are to believe a website for students seeking majors called BachelorsPortal.com, there are currently 631 undergraduate degree programs in Media Studies and Mass Media in the United States. Without a doubt, it is film and television that have provoked the greatest growth in media studies over the last fifty years, with digital media gradually becoming inextricably intermixed, and with sound studies—always a vital part of media but long overlooked by scholars and critics—developing rapidly as the digital audio age emerges.

But what does it mean to add "critical" to the term? First of all, critical media studies centers on the critical analysis of *texts*—not texts in isolation, but as they are produced by industries and institutions, and received by audiences and societies. Media studies pioneered what we now call an "integrated approach" to critical study very early on, in the 1940s, linked to critical analysis of the "culture industries" made by Theodor Adorno and Max Horkheimer. More than a half century later, it is still the way in which media texts and objects are constructed and perceived—what methods are used to create meaning, how identities are represented and reinforced, what discourses are circulated, how texts intersect with legal and economic institutions, how audiences interpret and interact with texts, and how their lives are shaped by media—that remains the ongoing project at the heart of critical media studies.

Second, critical media studies focuses on *power*. It is no coincidence that the emergence of media studies as a field coincides with the growth of cultural theory in the 1980s. Drawing on the critical analysis of working-class British scholars like Raymond Williams and Richard Hoggart that began to appear in the 1950s, enhanced by the cultural theory of Stuart Hall and others at the Centre for Contemporary Cultural Studies at the University of Birmingham in the 1960s and 1970s, as well as by European post-structuralist theory, a new field began to emerge. Supported by the rise of feminist theory, critical race studies, and queer studies, the role of media in both supporting and subverting existing structures of power and authority became the dominant focus of critical media scholarship and media studies education. Issues of ideology, representation, and patterns of discourse, all fundamentally concerned with the way that power plays out in the production and reception of media texts, continue to inform the field and give it continuing relevance as new media technologies are introduced and work to affect society in the deep ways that their predecessors have.

Finally, critical media studies inherently *resists disciplinarity*. Rather than seek to draw lines around what counts as appropriate objects or approaches, the emphasis is on inclusion. The present volume is an admirable expression of that openness, reflecting theories and methods drawn from across a multitude of scholarly disciplines, and offering analyses that cut across existing categories and objects to reach out to new ones. It marks how far the field has come and gives indications of the many directions it may take in the future.

INTRODUCTION, OR HOW TO COOK AN ARTICHOKE

Mary Celeste Kearney

Imagine that you're on a hillside somewhere near the Mediterranean Sea sometime in the distant past, before human beings invented agriculture. You're with a small group of people who are looking for edible vegetation for yourselves and your families. You're hungry, but the land is dry and doesn't offer up much by way of food. So you have to make do with what you can find. Eventually you see a plant in the distance that's about waist-high with large, arching, frond-like leaves, and ask each other: *What is this? Is it edible?* Upon closer inspection, you realize that the plant has several green, flower-like bulbs a bit larger than a fist. You bend near one, notice its faint, fragrant smell, and attempt to bite into it. But you can't get past the tough petals. Rather than turn away empty-handed, your hunger prompts another question: *How might we cook it?*

In reality, developing effective methods for cooking an artichoke must have taken considerable trial and error, for the plant's most edible and flavorful parts—the heart and choke—are buried deep within its blossoms, protected by numerous tough, scale-like petals, each of which is adorned with a sharp thorn. Indeed, even after careful cultivation over hundreds of years, the artichoke remains a formidable plant for those who farm it. Yet, over that same period of time, different cooks have developed strategies for transforming artichokes into delicious food. Each of the primary methods—roasting, boiling, frying, steaming—produces different results, revealing the many different cooked artichokes that can be created from using just the raw blossoms of this strange plant.

The craft of academic criticism—the subject of this book—entails a process similar to the one the first artichoke gatherers likely undertook: Scholars search for interesting objects or people or concepts about which we have questions, and we must determine the best strategy of analysis, or **methodology**, that will help us to answer those questions and produce significant results.

The Craft of Criticism introduces readers to the diverse set of methodologies used in **critical media studies**, a broadly international and interdisciplinary field that encompasses research related to film, television, radio, games, popular music, and the Internet. Critical media scholars understand **media culture** as encompassing not just the world of media texts (e.g., songs, websites, television programs), but also the realms of media production and media consumption. More specifically, the field of critical media studies includes scholarship on the content, style, and meanings of media texts; the artistic and business practices of producers and industries that create those texts; and audience members' interactions with such texts in their everyday lives.

Many critical media scholars focus their attention on mainstream/commercial media culture, which is the most dominant globally. However, a significant number investigate independent/non-commercial forms of media instead. This alternate arena has been especially important to scholars interested in marginalized groups long overlooked by the media industries, such as women, people of color, the disabled, the working class, and members of the LGBTQI community. While numerous media scholars focus on current media culture, others engage in historical analyses by exploring older media texts as well as older systems of media production and reception. Yet even researchers who focus on today's media are historians, in the sense that such work requires critical reflection on the contemporary sociopolitical moment to understand the full meaning of the objects, people, or concepts being studied.

A primary goal of this collection is to provide readers with a plentiful toolkit of methods that can be used when developing your own studies and interpretations of media culture. As such, this volume is organized primarily by method rather than by medium to emphasize the adaptability of these research strategies to different sites in our expansive mediascapes. Each chapter addresses a particular method and is written by an established scholar who both teaches in that area and conducts research using that approach. Each contributor demonstrates the application of that method via their discussion of a case study from their own scholarship. The methods outlined in this volume draw from critical traditions related to aesthetics, literature, technology, philosophy, economics, sociology, linguistics, psychology, history, anthropology, and geography. The study of film and television are at the heart of many of the discussions included here, but this collection also covers methods used by scholars who research sound, games, popular music, and other forms of media. In turn, this book includes several chapters that explore the particular challenges faced by researchers of emergent technologies, such as digital media.

Each method outlined in this volume has its own intellectual history and thus conceptualizes media culture's various objects, players, practices, and institutions in a distinct way. Yet the broader field of media studies is grounded upon interlocking and overlapping critical literacies built up over time. Thus, many of the methods covered here have intellectual histories that converge with the development of other approaches to analyzing media culture. Meanwhile, several chapters included in this collection focus on complex research topics, such as media history, that are best served by a multi-method approach.

By including twenty-seven research methods in this collection, we hope to disabuse readers of the notion that there is only one way, or a small number of ways, to study media culture. Instead, we want to expose you to the breadth of methodologies in our field and to encourage you to think creatively and expansively about the strategies that might work best in your own media research. Moreover, we hope that this volume works as a companion that helps you to make sense of methods employed in other scholarship you are reading.

What Is Research? Where Do I Begin?

Research is the common umbrella term for those activities focused on gathering information to advance knowledge. Research involves the systematic study of some object, person, institution, practice, or concept, and often entails developing solutions to problems. At its most basic, research involves asking a question, gathering data or evidence, analyzing that information, and answering the question. Yet most research projects involve many other steps on the path to knowledge discovery, insightful explanations, and innovative applications. Moreover, there are many forms of research, spanning from those that are experimental and performed in laboratories to those that are analytical and require little more than the researcher and a singular object. Most critical media scholarship falls into this second category.

All research begins with an **object of study**, the thing being analyzed. In critical media studies, objects of study are often (but not always) individual units of a particular medium, such as a film, website, or television series. Critical media scholars commonly refer to such objects as **texts,** a term borrowed from literary studies. When analyzing media texts, a key issue for us is understanding the tensions that exist between **medium specificity** and **media convergence**. That is, we must balance the idea that each medium has its own particular formal properties, conditions of production, institutional structures, and associated cultural practices (e.g., film as different from radio) with an awareness that an increasing number of media properties are produced for consumption across a variety of media platforms (e.g., comics, games, and television). Media convergence is largely due to contemporary culture's dominance by **media conglomerates**, which own multiple companies involved in the production of virtually all forms of popular entertainment and communication, including film, broadcasting, music, games, publishing, and the Internet.[1]

The range of objects studied by critical media scholars is much broader than the various media texts produced by the culture industries, however. As demonstrated by the case studies discussed in this collection, that range spans from the material to the abstract, from, say, subway ads for new television series to governmental regulations related to the electromagnetic spectrum. Moreover, the range of objects analyzed by critical media scholars is expansive both temporally and spatially, encompassing texts, institutions, practices, and practitioners associated with media cultures past and present as well as local and global.

While many reasons exist for why a critical media scholar might focus on specific research topic, that decision is often determined, at least in part, by which objects are readily accessible. After all, most students and many professors are unable to conduct research out of town at either archives or media companies due to cost and accessibility. Fortunately, the Internet has made many media texts available to us in our own homes. But the Internet is not a complete archive of every media text ever made as it is limited by human interest as well as time and money. Many other worthy objects of study are available to media scholars, however, in local libraries, archives, museums, and bookstores, without requiring too much time or expense to access. We encourage you to be creative when surveying the field of potential objects of study and to consider focusing on those that have received little scholarly attention thus far in order to expand the larger pool of knowledge about media culture.

Good research, like all good writing, begins with curiosity, and for many media scholars, our curiosity about certain aspects of media culture is related to our identities, experiences, tastes, and literacies. Your initial interest in an object or topic will likely be multiplied many times over as you conduct more research on it, and that interest will sustain you through what might be a long, challenging period of study. The point is not to select an object because it is deemed worthy or appropriate by other people. Indeed, the field of critical media studies has largely been developed by scholars who have resisted dominant academic tastes and risked their professional reputations by studying such "lowly" media texts as soap operas, horror films, video games, pop hits, and reality TV shows, not to mention the producers and fans of such media. Fortunately, you have a wide swath of objects to choose from, particularly if you remember that it's not just media texts that critical media scholars study, but also the practices and practitioners of media production and reception.

One of the challenges of conducting media research is that media are ubiquitous in contemporary society, so much so that many of us cannot conceive of life without them. We regularly consume media throughout the day from technologies that are readily at our fingertips, whether that's playing games on our tablets, participating in social media on our smart phones, listening to songs on our car radios, or watching movies on our TV sets. Because media culture is so much a part of our daily lives, and because we often spend a great deal of time talking about it with others, its various objects, practices, and players (if not institutions) often seem very familiar to us. Yet that familiarity can blind us to how those various aspects

of media culture might appear to others, as well as to how our own values, literacies, and preconceptions have made our own media tastes and practices seem natural and universal. Therefore, the critical analysis of media culture requires us to challenge our initial assumptions about it and to view its different components with fresh eyes so that we can be open to understanding them in new ways.

Every object of study is an artichoke—a thorny, difficult challenge that requires particular tools to make manageable. The most essential tools you can use in this process are the questions you have about your object. Once you have determined your object of study, you must consider what **research questions** arise from it, or in relation to it, and decide which you're most interested in pursuing further. Many research questions can be related to one object of study, and scholars often brainstorm to determine what all of the potential questions might be before moving forward with their study. Nevertheless, the questions that emerge from a singular object of study are not infinite but instead limited by the place and time, or **sociohistorical context**, in which it appears. For example, to return to our story of the artichoke, the food gathers' interest in that plant and the questions posed by them about it were constrained by their particular geographic and historic location, that is, the Mediterranean during pre-agricultural times. If a similar group of hungry people encountered an artichoke plant in 2018 Chicago, they would likely ignore it altogether and go to a grocery store to obtain food. Indeed, the presence of artichoke plants in urban environments today is more often for aesthetic than gastronomic purposes.

Primary sources can elicit questions about the object of study also. A **primary source** is a document that is closely related to the object being analyzed and was produced at approximately the same time that it was created. Primary sources are the raw materials out of which you build an initial portrait of your object of study. For example, in a study of the audience of a particular television series, letters from audience members to the production company would function as primary sources. In a study about a media celebrity, an autobiography or diary would be considered a primary source. Primary sources are especially important when an object of study has received little scholarly attention and when a researcher wants to question or refute the official or common-sense story about the object under analysis.

Another important frame to consider with regard to narrowing research questions is the scope of your interests in your object. For example, in our artichoke story, the people who encountered the plant had basic needs that impacted their interaction with it. In other words, their hunger led them to approach it in a certain way, and that framing limited the questions they had about it. They likely knew from previous experience that many plants with fruit are edible. So, when they happened upon the artichoke plant and saw its blossoms, they perceived it as potential food. Hence, they didn't ask, "Can we write with it?" or "How do we make shoes from it?" Instead, they asked, "Is it edible?" and hoped that it was. Similarly, the interests of scholars can provide additional contextual frames that limit and direct the questions we ask of our object of study. Indeed, your personal investment in an object can influence the pleasure you have interacting with it, which in turn can lead you to question, for example, why you and others enjoy it and why some people do not.

One way scholars consciously limit their research questions is by conducting a **literature review** of prior research or public commentary about their object of study or similar objects. Such research projects serve as the scholar's **secondary sources**, that is, work that helps to contextualize your own object of study. These sources can include non-academic materials, such as film reviews from the popular press, yet more typically involve academic scholarship. The bibliographies and endnotes of familiar academic books and articles can be rich sources for ideas about additional research materials; they can also help you to map the larger critical conversations in which those scholars are engaged. Researchers typically rely as well on electronic databases, such as Google Scholar, to find other scholarship related to their objects of study, as such databases can offer an expansive view of research on a particular topic. Once you have determined which studies are most similar to and important for your own, you make notes of common themes and arguments, which helps in determining your questions and narrowing the scope of your research to something innovative yet manageable. Given the breadth of information contained in databases today, not to mention the interdisciplinary nature of critical media studies, the biggest challenge for researchers is often not finding scholars who have explored their object of study, but determining the threads of debate that connect the particular types of research related to it.

After you have selected your object of study, conducted your literature review, and determined your research questions, you must select a strategy, or set of strategies, for analysis that will help you to produce answers to those questions. In research, we call these strategies **methodologies**, or "methods" for short. To clarify what a method is, let's return again to our artichoke story: Once our hungry food gatherers failed at eating the raw artichoke, they had to determine what type of cooking might work best to produce something edible. Given the pre-agricultural time period, the gatherers likely roasted the artichoke on a long stick over an open fire, which softened the leaves and exposed the tender heart and choke. After hundreds of years, humans have advanced significantly with cooking technology, and we now have several methods to choose from when determining how to prepare a raw artichoke for eating.

Bringing this all back home to critical media studies: Every movie that catches our eye, every pop song that expresses our feelings, every game that keeps us striving to reach the next level, every TV show that makes us wonder about just who else is watching … is an artichoke. We find an object; it captures our curiosity and inspires questions; we poke it and ask more questions; maybe it pokes back. Eventually, however, we have to figure out how to cook it.

Methods in Critical Media Studies

Scholars have a wide array of methodologies from which to choose when determining how to analyze their objects of study. The broader field of such methods is typically divided into two types: **quantitative** approaches, which are scientific in orientation and involve mathematical or computational techniques; and **qualitative** approaches, which involve interpretation supported by **critical theories**, that is, speculative explanations developed from research studies conducted by other scholars. While quantitative data can offer answers to such questions as "How much?" or "Of what kind?" and thus help scholars to paint a general picture of a media text, its production, or reception, qualitative media scholars pursue such questions as "How?" "Why?" and "What's at stake?"

The vast majority of critical media scholars gravitate toward this second category, qualitative analysis, as we seek to understand and offer informed interpretations of specific qualities or aspects of media culture. Yet we are also committed to broadening knowledge beyond those objects of study by offering theoretically informed insights on how they impact the larger realms of art, culture, commerce, politics, and society.[2] This is why we use the word "critical" in the title of our field. That tradition traces back to the early part of the twentieth century and such scholars of media culture as Sergei Eisenstein, who developed theories of cinematic form, and Max Horkheimer and Theodor Adorno, who first analyzed the culture industries.[3] Nevertheless, many critical theories used by media scholars are not specific to media culture, the arts, or commerce; a vast array of critical theories has been developed in disciplines across the humanities, fine arts, and social sciences that are useful in the study of media culture. It is through our careful questioning and analysis of media culture using established critical theories that we produce strong, convincing arguments that encourage other people to see it anew and to understand its relation to larger society. One of the challenges for each critical media scholar is determining which theories best align with our project and can best support our argument.

Let's consider an example of critical media analysis: Perhaps you are interested in studying the first fictional television series to feature a Japanese girl as the protagonist. You might be interested in this show because no studies have been conducted to determine its specific artistic and commercial qualities and how they might relate to other media texts involving Japanese girlhood and girls in general. Thus, the research questions that might be used to direct this study include, "In what kind of story does the Japanese girl appear?" and "How is this character portrayed?" Such questions are related to the broad field of critical methods known as **textual analysis**, approaches that involve the close study of particular qualities of individual literary or artistic objects to determine their meaning. More specifically, the two research questions raised above in relation to the Japanese girl TV show are associated, respectively, with narrative and representational forms of textual analysis. As demonstrated in Chapters 3 and 8 of this collection, many scholars have formulated critical theories related to the practices of storytelling and representation. Therefore, as the researcher, you would need to review the literature not only on this TV show, Japanese broadcasting, and girls' television series, but also scholarship on narration and representation to determine which theories might work best for your particular analysis. (This series' narrative and representational strategies are not the only textual elements that you could study, however. As other chapters in this volume demonstrate, you could also analyze, for example, the discursive themes, sound style, or performance strategies associated with this particular TV show.)

Other qualitative approaches beyond textual analysis could also be used to interpret the first television series featuring a Japanese girl. For instance, if you were interested in how this particular TV show was created, you might ask questions related to the people who worked on the show and the practices involved in its production. Such questions might include, "How are the creator's identity and experiences related to those of the protagonist?" and "What type of actors were considered when casting the lead character?" This method is referred to as **production analysis**. Critical studies of media producers have long been a part of our field, as authorship has been a primary focus of film, television, and popular music studies, all of which have antecedents in older disciplines, like literature, theatre, and art, where artists have been important sites of inquiry. Nevertheless, authorship and artistry are just two of the topics scholars of media production can study. As Chapter 22 of this volume demonstrates, a growing number of scholars have been researching the media industries and their practices of creation, distribution, exhibition, and marketing, using theories from various disciplines, including economics and business. In turn, our field has seen an increase in policy analysis, the topic of Chapter 11, which focuses on the relationship between governmental regulations and media culture.

Another possible way of analyzing this Japanese girl television series relates to its audience. Questions that might inspire this type of study include, "How did girls in Japan engage with this series, either alone or in groups?" and "How did girls outside Japan react to this show?" A research project employing this methodological frame would be labeled a **reception study**. While many scholars have employed psychoanalytical theory to speculate on the processes of media reception (see Chapter 12), other media scholars, particularly those whose work is informed by cultural studies, sociology, and anthropology, have used ethnographic analyses to understand the practices and pleasures of media audiences (see Chapters 14 and 15).

Sociohistorical context is relevant in each of these potential studies, for context always impacts meaning. For example, with regard to conducting a textual analysis of the television series featuring the first Japanese girl protagonist, the place and time depicted in the show have specific implications for its meaning. Consider, for example, the difference between Japan in the 1910s versus Japan in the 1980s. In turn, the place and time of the show's production also contribute to its meaning—for example, consider a Japanese series made in the 1960s in comparison to an Australian series from the early 2000s. The place and time of viewers' engagement with the show are important to consider as well. Indeed, the same person could interact with this TV series at two different points in their life, say the 1950s and the 1990s, and develop two different interpretations of it based on changes in their literacies, tastes, and identities.

Cultural Studies and the Integrated, Multiperspectival Approach

Attention to sociohistorical context is crucial for critical media scholars, and this is largely due to the significant impact on our field by **cultural studies**, an interdisciplinary approach to analyzing popular culture developed by British researchers in the second half of the twentieth century.[4] A key concern among cultural studies scholars is to develop methodological strategies in our research that produce richly contextualized and nuanced interpretations of our objects of study, or what anthropologist Clifford Geertz, in a different context, labeled "thick descriptions."[5] For media scholars trained in cultural studies, this means attending to the social, historical, political, and economic contexts of our objects of study in order to answer the hows, whys, and so whats of critical qualitative analysis. According to Lawrence Grossberg, cultural studies' argument for the significance of contextuality in cultural analysis is that "[n]o element can be isolated from its relations." Rather,

> the identity, significance, and effects of any practice or event . . . are defined only by the complex set of relations that surround, interpenetrate, and shape it, and make it what it is. . . . Any event can only be understood relationally, as a condensation of multiple determinations and effects.[6]

Ideally, all critical media research projects will touch upon all three sites of media culture—texts, production, and reception—while respecting the blurred boundaries between them and also attending to sociohistorical context. Yet doing so is quite difficult, especially if your time and resources are limited, as is particularly the case for many students and contingent faculty members. Julie D'Acci's pathbreaking book *Defining Women: Television and the Case of* Cagney & Lacey is one of the few projects to have attended successfully to the media culture of which this television text was part.[7] She offers critical insights not only about *Cagney & Lacey*, but also its producers and strategies of production, as well as

its various interpretive communities, including fans, critics, and activists. D'Acci describes this methodological strategy as an **integrated approach** to understanding the **circuit of media study**.[8] Douglas Kellner describes a similar approach and refers to it as **multiperspectival**.[9] Most critical media scholars today find that attending to two sites in media culture (say, a text and its production, or a text and its audience) is adequate for any one study, as long as you also engage in sociohistorical contextualization and are conscious that the third, unstudied site of media culture might have relevance to your interpretations as well.

Cultural studies' turn toward popular culture helped to legitimate as worthy objects of study not only films and television, but also magazines, games, comics, popular music, the Internet, and many other forms of popular entertainment. Moreover, by taking seriously those elements of media culture that have long been considered inappropriate for academic attention, media scholars informed by cultural studies have foregrounded the mechanisms of **pleasure** at work in consuming media.

Such commitments to reclaim "low" forms of media culture and their audiences are connected to cultural studies' deep investment in the analysis of **power**, an intellectual legacy formed by such critical theorists as Karl Marx, Antonio Gramsci, and Michel Foucault.[10] Thus, political economy, ideology, and discourse—each the subject of an individual chapter in this collection—have been at the heart of many critical media studies projects. Media scholars informed by the cultural studies approach readily investigate the workings of power in media culture, attempting to bring greater understanding to systems of categorization, dominance, and oppression as well as to strategies of resistance, self-determination, and survival. This political project has been further emboldened through media scholars' influence by **poststructuralist theories**, which challenge us to think outside traditional frameworks of meaning and to understand reality as socially constructed through language, media, and other forms of signification.[11] In turn, critical media scholars' attention to power can be seen through our adoption and application of theories developed in feminist and queer studies, critical race studies, subculture studies, postcolonial studies, and disability studies. As new media forms emerge, critical media scholars build from this rich legacy to develop innovative theories about how power and pleasure work in media culture.

Ongoing Conversations

The chapters collected here are organized into three major parts. The first, Primary Methods, articulates those research methodologies that lie at the heart of critical media studies, including narrative, style, and discourse analysis. These approaches are among the oldest and most popularly used by critical media scholars today. The book's second part, Synthetic and Multiperspectival Methods, articulates the mixed methodologies that inform such areas of critical media inquiry as genre, history, production, and globalization. Finally, the Emergent and Challenging Objects part broadens the collection's scope to discuss the particular methodological challenges that arise when researching new and complicated media forms, such as games, software, and Internet-based cultures.

As each contributor to this book demonstrates, every research methodology associated with critical media studies has a long and complicated history, as new scholars rework old approaches, often formulated in other academic fields, to develop new strategies for exploring and understanding their objects of study. In addition to outlining the intellectual development of a particular method and a discussion of why and how it emerged, each chapter offers relevant examples of influential work in that area, as well as an in-depth review of a case study drawn from the author's own scholarship. Additionally, each chapter includes a discussion of the method's current and future applicability in a field that increasingly employs multi-method research to explore texts and cultural processes that cross the boundaries between traditional media forms. Each author has also included recommended readings if you would like to dig deeper into a particular method or topic.

An important reminder before you proceed further, however: Qualitative analyses produce speculations about objects of study, not truth. While scholars using qualitative methods amass evidence, just as quantitative scholars do, such evidence is not gathered and quantified in order to make statistical generalizations about a broad number of media texts, practices, players, or institutions. Instead, it is gathered and analyzed via the application of critical theories in order to offer informed interpretations that can be utilized by other scholars in their own studies. Thus, qualitative researchers are not interested in offering the one true, definitive meaning of their objects of study. Instead, we understand that each object is **polysemous** (i.e., has numerous potential

meanings), and that each person who interacts with it brings their own knowledge, values, and identities to their comprehension of it. As a result, qualitative research is an ongoing enterprise involving numerous people, with scholars entering into critical conversations that began well before we were born and will continue long after we die. Literary scholar Kenneth Burke uses a productive analogy to describe this process:

> Imagine that you enter a parlor. You come late. When you arrive, others have long preceded you, and they are engaged in a heated discussion, a discussion too heated for them to pause and tell you exactly what it is about. In fact, the discussion had already begun long before any of them got there, so that no one present is qualified to retrace for you all the steps that had gone before. You listen for a while, until you decide that you have caught the tenor of the argument; then you put in your oar. Someone answers; you answer him; another comes to your defense; another aligns himself against you, to either the embarrassment or gratification of your opponent, depending upon the quality of your ally's assistance. However, the discussion is interminable. The hour grows late, you must depart. And you do depart, with the discussion still vigorously in progress.[12]

To engage meaningfully in qualitative research, it is important for scholars to first understand the basic rules and norms of the conversations in which we immerse ourselves, as well as their longer histories. That principle aligns well with the main objectives of this collection: to equip you with the knowledge not only of the methods you can use to interpret media culture, but also of the history and intellectual traditions of those approaches. We hope that this helps you to be a better reader of critical media scholarship, to make informed and creative choices as you proceed with your research, and to participate confidently in the conversations in our parlor. Put in your oar.

Notes

1. See Henry Jenkins, *Convergence Culture: Where Old and New Media Collide* (New York: New York University Press, 2006).
2. Because of the strong connection of method and theory in qualitative media studies, it is sometimes difficult to determine which is which. For example,

psychoanalytic media criticism involves the application of theories developed within the field of psychoanalysis to media texts; the method and the theory are closely entwined. As a result, in some areas of critical media studies, scholars have not articulated and discussed methods as much as theories.

3. Sergei Eisenstein, *Film Form: Essays in Film Theory*, ed. and trans. Jay Leyda (1949; New York: Houghton Mifflin Harcourt, 2014); Max Horkheimer and Theodor W. Adorno, *Dialectic of Enlightenment*, ed. Gunzelin Schmid Noerr, trans. Edmund Jeffcott (1944; Stanford: Stanford University Press, 2002).
4. For a brief history of cultural studies, see Simon During, "Introduction," in *The Cultural Studies Reader*, 3rd edition, ed. Simon During (New York: Routledge, 2007), 1–30.
5. Clifford Geertz, "Thick Description: Toward an Interpretive Theory of Culture" in *The Interpretation of Cultures* (New York: Basic Books, 1973), 3–30.
6. Lawrence Grossberg, *Cultural Studies in the Future Tense* (Durham: Duke University Press, 2010), 20.
7. Julie D'Acci, *Defining Women: Television and the Case of* Cagney & Lacey (Chapel Hill: University of North Carolina Press, 1994).
8. Julie D'Acci, "Cultural Studies, Television Studies, and the Crisis in the Humanities," in *Television after TV: Essays on a Medium in Transition*, eds. Lynn Spigel and Jan Olsson (Durham: Duke University Press, 2004), 418–42.
9. Douglas Kellner, "Cultural Studies, Multiculturalism, and Media Culture," in *Gender, Race, and Class in Media: A Text-Reader*, eds. Gail Dines and Jean M. Humez (Thousand Oaks: Sage Publications, 1995), 5–17.
10. Karl Marx, *Capital* (1867; London: George Allen and Unwin, 1948); Antonio Gramsci, *Selections from the Prison Notebooks*, ed. and trans. Geoffrey Nowell Smith (1971; New York: International Publishers, 1997); Michel Foucault, *The History of Sexuality, Volume I: An Introduction*, trans. Robert Hurley (1976; New York: Vintage Books, 1990).
11. See Chapter 9 for a discussion of poststructuralist theory.
12. Kenneth Burke, *The Philosophy of Literary Form* (Berkeley: University of California Press, 1941), 110–11.

PART I

PRIMARY METHODS

1.
IDEOLOGY
Ron Becker

Ideology refers to a way of thinking about the world that emerges from and reinforces a specific social order. The concept—a cornerstone of critical approaches to media—assumes that societies are structured by economic, cultural, and political systems that separate people according to their position in those systems (e.g., by economic class, racial identity, gender identity, sexual orientation, age, national origin, able-bodiedness). Such systems also work to privilege certain groups at the expense of others, distributing power, resources, and status unevenly to individuals according to their positions in those groups. From this perspective, societies are structured by systemic inequities and antagonistic social relations. Yet most societies, especially modern, capitalist societies, remain *relatively* stable. Disadvantaged groups do challenge the status quo, but they rarely revolt in ways that overturn the systems that work against them. Why not? The concept of ideology helps explain the relative stability of societies structured by such systems of domination and provides options for thinking about the possibilities of social change.

To examine ideology, then, is to examine how the ideas, assumptions, and logics through which we make sense of reality and live in the world help justify and reproduce systems like capitalism, patriarchy, heteronormativity, ableism, or white supremacy. A dominant ideology—a web of beliefs that underpins a specific system of domination at a specific moment— works to make certain social arrangements, practices, and behaviors that promote the interests of some people over and against others' *seem* neutral or universal. A dominant ideology can make unequal social relations that are culturally constructed and historically specific *seem* natural and inevitable. It can make highly politicized ways of seeing and living in the world *seem* commonsensical and arguments against the established social order *seem* illogical or impractical. When most successful, then, a dominant ideology makes the way a society operates appear inescapable, even when it isn't and makes it difficult to imagine how else our society could be organized.

The concept of ideology fuels many scholars' interest in studying media and plays an important role in a diverse range of research agendas, including many of those you will encounter in this volume. Its most obvious impact has been to provide justification and strategies for analyzing the vast array of media texts produced by the culture industries. Critical attention to popular culture's texts, including those widely denigrated as artless or ephemeral, is warranted when they are reframed as artifacts through which one can glimpse a society's ideologies. When those texts, backed by the distribution and marketing power of media institutions, are consumed by millions of people, they might not merely reflect, but also shape, reinforce, or challenge ideologies. Ideological criticism is often equated with close textual analyses that link texts' ideas to wider systems of domination; my case study connecting family-makeover reality TV shows to the logics of neoliberalism and heteronormativity is an example of this mode.

Ideology is not only relevant to the study of media texts, however. The people and practices involved in creating, consuming, and regulating media are also deeply influenced by ideologies, making ideological analysis relevant to many other modes of criticism such as production/industry studies, ethnography, and policy. Finally, ideological analysis has implications for every mode of media criticism. Since the concept focuses our attention on the relationship between the ways we understand reality and the dynamics of social power, it can always be turned back onto our own work as critics, leading us to ask how our own motivations, methods, and analyses are shaped by ideologies and entangled with the dynamics of unevenly distributed social power.

Intellectual History of the Concept

To offer a relatively straightforward definition of ideology as I do above is a necessary starting point but also misleading, since the concept is among the most contested in the field. The evolution of the concept has not followed a straight line or even a circuitous path. It is better to think of its history as a vast river delta with multiple converging and diverging streams of development. The result is a concept that has evolved within different intellectual traditions and acquired many different shades of meaning. Debates over its proper definition have been so intense because the concept serves as an entry point for understanding things that matter enormously. It lies at the nexus of fundamental philosophical, sociological, and moral questions involving the nature of reality and humans' understanding of it; the origins of a person's consciousness; the nature of social power; the possibilities for social change in complex societies; and competing visions of a just society. These issues rarely have objective answers, yet the stakes involved in them are extremely high. It isn't surprising that scholars have struggled over the concept for more than 200 years.

Rather than sketch out a chronological account, I have organized this section around three points of divergence. I map out how different definitions of ideology have intersected with questions of **determination** (what factors shape a society), **epistemology** (what is the nature of people's understanding of reality), and **textuality** (how do ideologies operate within media texts). I am less interested in adjudicating among the diverse uses of the concept than in identifying what insights the different theories and the tensions among them offer. I also hope to avoid a reductive progress narrative that implies older, misguided definitions were superseded by more accurate or sophisticated ones. Some debates have led to valuable reformulations, yet there are many points of divergence that remain. They persist less because of a failing of one theory or another and more because the issues involved are, in the end, unresolvable. Below, I provide an overview of the terrain by mapping two streams of thought that diverge around each topic.

A major point of divergence arises from competing opinions about the role ideology plays in shaping a society. One perspective gives causal priority to economic forces and sees ideology as supplementary. From this perspective, a society's economic system—the historically specific conditions within which people pursue their most basic *material* needs like food, clothing, and shelter—is its defining feature; it serves as the base for everything else that happens in society and sets the conditions of human thought and existence. This **historical materialist perspective** emerged out of efforts in the nineteenth century to understand how societies were transformed by a new kind of economy: commodity capitalism (i.e., a system where most people meet their material needs by buying products with money they earn by selling their labor to a smaller group of people who make their money by selling the fruits of the first group's labor). Following Karl Marx, whose critique of capitalism established the parameters within and against which most subsequent theories of ideology developed, historical materialism argues that to understand modern capitalist societies we must first recognize that this economic system divides people into classes by the way they make money and creates inequality by systematically channeling more resources to owners and less to workers. Secondly, we must trace how this economic system has a determining effect on other social institutions (e.g., systems of government, schools, family structures, religious institutions, the media).[1] A historical materialist analysis then tries to reveal how such institutions and the ideology they circulate reflect the underlying economic base and help maintain it and the unequal class relationships it generates. Here, ideologies play a role in shaping society, but one that is secondary to the economy.

Such analyses have been questioned by scholars who argue that economic forces, while important, are not the only or sometimes even the most salient determining factor. From such **culturalist perspectives**, a society is defined by the complex intersection of the economic with ideological systems like nationalism, patriarchy, white supremacy, and heteronormativity as well as socio-cultural institutions like the family, religion, and the media. The internal dynamics of these systems and institutions also divide people into groups and channel resources to them unevenly. This tradition emerged out of the work of twentieth-century scholars like Antonio Gramsci, Ernesto Laclau, and Chantal Mouffe who adapted Marx's arguments to the conditions of increasingly complex and media-saturated Western capitalist societies.

Whereas historical materialism tends to analyze ideological systems as the epiphenomena of an underlying economic base (as growing out of or reinforcing rather than intersecting or conflicting with it), culturalism insists that ideological systems have their own logics and histories. It acknowledges that ideologies may (perhaps even usually) evolve over time to align with an economic system, but it also insists that such alignments are not guaranteed—that ideologies have their own internal mechanisms (e.g., the operations of language) and their own impacts on a society's development. Thus, an economic system might evolve in response to ideological forces. From a culturalist perspective, ideologies are no less important than economic practices. In fact, some culturalist scholars insist that ideologies shouldn't be understood as only *ideas* about reality but also as the *material* reality that emerges from those ideas (e.g., arguing that segregated drinking fountains and the use of them are as much a part of white supremacist ideology as ideas about racial difference).

At times, the gap between historical materialist and culturalist perspectives seem merely to rest on subtle disagreements over which factor is *more* important; historical materialism, after all, acknowledges that ideological systems like patriarchy matter. Tensions persist, however, because of deeply held investments. Critics in the historical materialist tradition give analytic priority to the economic system in which people struggle with and against each other to meet their needs for basic physical survival, because they believe it involves matters of life and death and therefore is the place where those who want to create a better society should focus their efforts. Critics in the culturalist tradition, in contrast, argue that humans don't survive by bread alone but have other needs—the need to communicate, develop a sense of self, build community, create order in a chaotic world, find meaning in the fragility of human existence. For culturalist critics, ideologies are the systems through which people struggle with and against each other to meet these existential needs; as such, they involve matters of life and death and thus are places where those who want to create a better society should focus their efforts.

These two perspectives fuel diverging agendas in media criticism. Culturalist assumptions have legitimated the close analysis of media texts and focused attention on a broad range of ideologies, especially those related to race, gender, and sexuality. Given the degree of causal force they accord ideologies, culturalist scholars see critical engagement with media

representations as a politically valuable enterprise. Historical materialist assumptions, on the other hand, have fostered doubt about the political payoff of engaging with media texts. Scholars influenced by this perspective stress how the production and consumption of culture have been fully co-opted by market forces. As a result, they argue, media texts serve the economic system as commodities that channel money into the coffers of media corporations; seductive appeasements that distract viewers from the exploitative nature of their working conditions; and delivery-vehicles for consumerist values that naturalize commodity capitalism. Given their notion of economic determination, the best way to challenge bourgeois ideology and inequality is to analyze media ownership structures and promote media production outside the market system.

A second major point of divergence in theories of ideology is rooted in a deep philosophical tension between, on the one hand, confidence that human reason can provide an objective understanding of reality and an ethical path for social progress and, on the other, a countervailing skepticism that insists that our knowledge of reality and our ethical priorities will never be complete or objective.

For the confident tradition, ideology is a way of thinking that serves the interests of a dominant social group by distorting or obscuring aspects of reality. The point of ideological critique, here, is to use reason to expose ideology's distortions and reveal the true, exploitative nature of unequal social systems. Emerging out of the eighteenth-century Enlightenment project, this tradition is confident in the power of rationality.

Marxism, for example, argued that capitalist societies were defined by an underlying form of economic exploitation: the lower workers' wages were, the higher factory owners' profits would be. The exploitative and conflict-ridden essence of capitalism, however, could be difficult for both owners and workers to see, because bourgeois ideology worked to hide or distort it by framing capitalist practices in terms of ideals like freedom, individualism, and equality. Through this ideological lens, wage labor appeared to be a fair and neutral system: each "individual" worker entered the labor market on "equal" terms with the employer (i.e., he wasn't a slave or a serf) and was "free" to negotiate the wage for which he was willing to trade his labor. Much of this account is not a lie exactly (ideologies rarely lie in any narrow sense of the term), but it does frame the dynamics of the labor market in specific ways and entirely ignores, and thus ends up hiding, core aspects of the *reality* of wage labor (e.g., workers' and owners' interests are in conflict; a worker's "freedom" to reject a certain wage is limited by the fact that if no other job is available, she could die from starvation).

In this tradition, ideological criticism is a form of revelation. When those disadvantaged by the system understand reality and their own position in it through ideology (e.g., when the working class think of the wage labor system as acceptable or even desirable), this tradition argues, they are living in **false consciousness** and don't challenge that system. The critic's goal is to enlighten them about reality's underlying truth, with the hope of stirring them to take political action to create a better society. Here, the critic is part scientist (using methods of critical inquiry to access the true essence of things beneath surface-level appearances) and part prophet (leading the way to a new, moral future). In the context of media analysis, the critic is a passionate observer armed with penetrating insights, reading against the ideological grain of media texts, searching for hidden truths.

This confident tradition defines ideology narrowly and pejoratively as the "false" ideas that support a dominant class and oppressive system. In contrast, a second tradition defines ideology broadly and neutrally as an inevitable facet of human social existence. For the latter, ideology isn't something to be overcome in order to see reality accurately, but rather the medium through which humans experience reality and the means by which they define it. From this perspective, a Marxist critique of bourgeois ideology is not objective truth operating outside of ideology, but rather a competing ideology—one that reflects the experience and serves the interests of the working class. What the first tradition defines as ideology, here becomes **dominant ideology** and is juxtaposed against the **subordinated ideologies** of less powerful groups.

This broader concept of ideology emerged from various twentieth-century critiques of the Enlightenment. Karl Mannheim's sociology of knowledge, which attempted to show how all knowledge is shaped by social conditions, undercut the Enlightenment principle of objectivity.[2] Frankfurt School theorists, shaken by the rise of fascism and the atrocities of the Holocaust, came to see the growing power of science and instrumental rationality as a threat to humanity, not the path to clear understanding and liberation.[3] Psychoanalytic theories of the unconscious problematized the idea of the rational subject who could be brought out of false consciousness

in any straightforward sense.[4] And perhaps most significantly, the linguistic theory of semiotics argued that the very language we use to think and communicate isn't a neutral tool that corresponds to reality in any direct way but a biased system that defines how we understand and experience reality.[5] If the confident tradition rests on the belief that human reason can, with effort, come to know the objective truth of reality; the second tradition has been guided by a deep skepticism about that very assumption.

Such skepticism creates a conundrum for those critics who turn to the concept of ideology in order to challenge unjust systems. How does one do that if all knowledge of the world, including one's own, is circumscribed by ideology—if there is no privileged place outside of the power dynamics of social existence from whence one can measure ideological distortion? For some, this erosion of epistemological certitude also erodes moral certitude; if our knowledge of the world is always socially contingent, is the same true of our definitions of justice? Critics in the skeptical tradition have responded to these thorny questions by redefining what counts as political engagement through ideological criticism. The point of ideological critique, here, is not to reveal the truth as a path to the just society, but to reveal the contingency of all knowledge (though especially of dominant ways of seeing the world) and to question the possible injustice of all ethical agendas (though especially dominant definitions of morality). Neither scientist nor prophet, the ideological media critic here serves as a freelance devil's advocate anxious to point out the blind spots that inevitably exist in any worldview offered by a media text and in any vision of the just society.

The tension between the confident and skeptical traditions can run high. To advocates of the first, the latter can serve as the path to moral relativism and political nihilism and as such betray the goals of ideological analysis. To advocates of the second, the first can fail to understand that the self-evident truths a critic might use to expose dominant ideologies could very well be the source of inequity to others. This tension is both inevitable and useful. The confident tradition reminds us that facts can be distorted by power, that justice matters, and that both are worth fighting for; the skeptical tradition reminds us that what we see as facts can be more complicated than we think and that our better future could be critiqued by someone else as an unjust system of domination. Even though scholars debate the existence of an objective ethical truth, in the end most agree that we can and must dissect how ideologies operate. While skeptical scholars may bristle at the notion of false consciousness and the implication that an unproblematic truth awaits to be revealed by the wise critic, in practice they acknowledge that cognitive distortions and logical fallacies can support inaccurate understandings of the world and that an ideology can be "false" when it recognizes only part of social reality or presents something as natural when it is not.

A third point of divergence in theories of ideology is evident in distinct approaches to the analysis of ideology in media texts. Some scholars focus on texts as delivery systems for dominant ideologies. Others focus on texts as sites where competing ideologies exist in tension and approach the consumption of texts as a process of negotiation between the viewer and a text's ensemble of competing ideologies.

The first approach has been influenced by efforts to explain how societies remain relatively stable despite being structured by antagonism and inequalities. Nineteenth-century Marxist criticism, for example, had suggested revolution would be inevitable once the working class came to understand the exploitative nature of wage labor. By the middle of the twentieth century, however, capitalism endured, leaving scholars to explain why. Their answers would often implicate the ideological power of media. Theodor Adorno and Max Horkheimer, for example, experiencing the complacency of post-World War II U.S. consumer society, argued that the oppositional potential of the working class had been stifled by a newly ubiquitous culture industry.[6] Rampant advertising-supported media instilled consumerist desires and destroyed people's ability to imagine alternatives. Louis Althusser, responding to the failed French student revolts of the late 1960s, provided a structuralist theory informed by psychoanalysis that ascribed ideologies enormous power to determine our thoughts and desires. For Althusser, our consciousness is not simply fooled by ideology but is actually a product of it.[7]

At times, such work proposed a totalizing theory in which all social institutions are tightly coordinated, each playing a role in ensuring the reproduction of the wider system. Here, the highly centralized, corporate-owned, and advertiser-supported mass media industry is understood to be part of a wider socio-cultural-economic complex, delivering a narrow range of news and entertainment that promotes ways of thinking that align with the interests of the most powerful classes (whether they be economic, racial, gendered, etc.). To use Althusser's term, media texts **interpellate** viewers—address and position us through specific frames and logics. When we buy into a sitcom's narrative, root for a film's hero, or agree with a news report's framing of events, our thoughts and desires can fall in line with their ideologies and become part of the system reproducing the status quo. By identifying how dominant ideologies get encoded into media texts, the ideological critic can, by extension, understand how those ideologies are written into viewers' subjectivities.

A second body of work defines media texts and viewers' relationships to them in terms of **contingency** rather than certainty. Instead of functionalist visions of a rigid, static, unified social order, this second approach theorizes societies and by extension the media texts produced in them as complex amalgams of independent parts (economic forces, social practices, ideological systems, human agents) that move in different directions and at different speeds. While some forces (e.g., commodity capitalism, patriarchy) may have great power to draw other elements into closer alignment with their priorities at certain moments, complete fusion of the parts is never achieved; tensions and contradictions remain, and as a result, social change is always possible.

This approach grew from Antonio Gramsci's notion of **hegemony**—the theory that the position of a dominant class is not guaranteed, but is the result of a continual process of struggle and negotiation to win the consent of subordinate groups.[8] It also grew from Raymond Williams' historicist response to Althusser's structuralism. Williams argued that a social order's dominant ideology always exists alongside residual ideologies from past eras and emergent ideologies that could be the thin edge of a new social order.[9] It was also influenced by Stuart Hall, who argues that ideologies should not be understood as rigid worldviews to be escaped or replaced, but rather as the terrain where the ongoing process of social life and political struggle takes place, where different class factions fight to connect or **articulate** concepts in ways that serve their interests.[10]

In this approach, media texts are not analyzed as delivery mechanisms for dominant ideology but as **sites of negotiation** where various ideologies might co-exist. They are understood as the result of production processes that occur at the intersection of multiple forces. The economic and ideological imperatives of a capitalist industry shape the stories and information that get circulated, but so do an array of other factors (e.g., genre conventions, ideologies of race in the minds of writers, ideals of creative freedom, technological constraints). The audiences that consume texts are also embedded in such complex dynamics; our identities are socially constructed by multiple ideologies, not simply determined by dominant ideology. As a result, our relationship to media texts is complicated; the goal of ideological textual criticism here is to analyze the ideologies in a text, not in order to *know* how audiences will be interpellated by it but to map the terrain in which a socially positioned viewer engages with it. What ideologies are present in the text? How does the text position or privilege them in relationship to each other?

Both the totalizing and contingent approach offer useful insights for media scholars. The first reminds us that revolutions rarely happen and that media texts can work to keep certain ideologies firmly in place. The second reminds us that meaningful social change can occur even if there isn't a revolution and that media texts can be imbricated in those changes. The first draws our attention to the deep structures that might shape us in ways we aren't aware of, guiding us down a path that we wrongly experience as the path we freely chose. It makes us think about how media texts we consume might sometimes determine how we think about the world. The second reminds us that even within such structures—or perhaps because of the complex intersection of multiple structures—we have a degree of agency; we may not be able to see all possible paths, but we can choose among those

we do see. It encourages us to think about how media texts can sometimes offer insights into the contradictory nature of the social system and of our own positions in it.

Together these approaches challenge us to think about ideologies as simultaneously rigid and flexible. Figure 1.1 lays out a sample of ideological assumptions drawn from contemporary U.S. society on a continuum from those that are most hegemonic (i.e., held by most Americans) to those that are highly contested, as well as ideologies that are so residual as to be essentially defunct. In Figure 1.2, I provide a rough diagram of an **ideological formation** or web of ideas linked or articulated across two dimensions to underscore that certain ideas often depend on lower-level assumptions, and to point out that, even if certain assumptions change, others might remain firmly in place.

Despite the varied approaches that spring from these three points of divergence, there is an underlying core perspective all ideological criticism shares: social reality is the result, in large part, of human actions, and we should therefore strive to push it in the directions we think best. From that shared foundation, of course, arise intense debates over what path society should take, how difficult it is to change, and what the targets of our efforts should be. For many scholars, one useful target of ideological criticism is the production and consumption of a society's media texts.

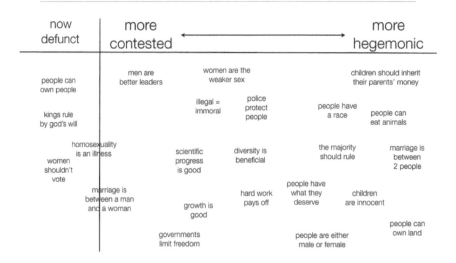

Ideological Assumptions

now defunct	more contested		more hegemonic

people can own people

men are better leaders

women are the weaker sex

children should inherit their parents' money

kings rule by god's will

illegal = immoral

police protect people

people have a race

people can eat animals

homosexuality is an illness

women shouldn't vote

scientific progress is good

diversity is beneficial

the majority should rule

marriage is between 2 people

marriage is between a man and a woman

hard work pays off

people have what they deserve

children are innocent

growth is good

governments limit freedom

people are either male or female

people can own land

Figure 1.1 Chart of ideological assumptions

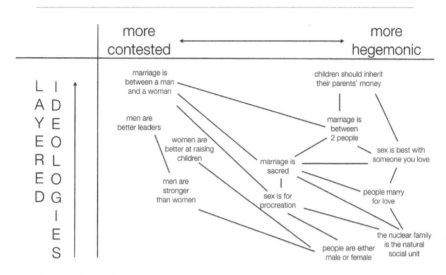

Figure 1.2 Chart of an ideological formation

Method and Major Terminology

For media scholars, the concept of ideology serves as the basis for a way or (given the debates mapped above) ways of thinking about media and its relationship to society, rather than as the basis for a rigid set of methodological protocols. Scholars draw upon many of the methodological traditions covered in this volume, especially the analysis of discourse, narrative, visual style, representation, genre, intertextuality, and ethnography. Nevertheless, there are specific approaches rooted in ideological criticism, and I highlight some of them below, using my case study as a point of reference.[11] The rest of this chapter reveals my position in the different streams of thought I mapped above. My perspectives tilt toward culturalist, skeptical, and contingent approaches, and I urge you to identify how such biases shape the rest of this chapter.

To start, it is worth emphasizing that ideological media criticism is an act of interpretation. As such, the critic does not uncover the objective truth of a media text, but rather constructs an argument in an effort to get her audience to think about the relationship between a media text and its social reality. To do so, critics draw on two sources of expertise: our training in the kind of concepts and methods this chapter and volume provide, and our social experience as people positioned by systems of domination. Like fish trying to understand what water is, it can be difficult to get a critical perspective on the ideologies that shape us and the media we study. Having said that, there is always some gap between our everyday experience of the world and the ideological messages we encounter. That gap is likely smaller for those who benefit from a system than those who are disadvantaged by it, but no ideology can perfectly match up to our experience of reality. I mention this to underscore that as ideological critics, we are embedded in the very processes we interrogate, and our criticism is both hindered and enabled by our being so. My analysis of *Supernanny* and *Nanny 911*, for example, is shaped by my training as a media scholar and by my experience as a middle-class, white, able-bodied, coupled, childless, gay, American man with a split relationship to the romanticized ideology of the autonomous, heterosexual, nuclear family; I grew up in the kind of stable, middle-class family the series normalize, yet as a gay man I simultaneously felt (because I legally was) excluded from it. Someone with a different social identity and historical experience might offer a different interpretation of the series.

Ideological criticism, however, is not just personal reflection, but an argument aimed at convincing a reader that your interpretation provides a meaningful perspective on how a text reflects or shapes its socio-political context. Thus, the object of study isn't a media text *per se*, but rather a text's relationship to a wider ideological dynamic. The evidence you marshal to support your argument should reflect that. Careful textual analysis is necessary, but so too is evidence linking the text's ideologies to a wider context. In my article, I provide such evidence through my choice of sources. I link *Supernanny* and *Nanny 911* to each other and to other primary sources like an Applebee's commercial, the gay marriage debate, and Bush's family policies, and I use secondary sources to provide broader evidence of our historical constructions of the nuclear family and their relationship to economic forces. Since ideological criticism typically challenges assumptions your reader may believe to be common sense (including assumptions about the triviality of popular culture), building a persuasive argument can be challenging. Unconvinced readers may dismiss your argument as "reading too much into the text" or "making a mountain out of a mole hill." If you were not convinced by my argument, it is worth pondering whether different evidence could persuade you.

Now to a crucial question: in what ways can a text operate ideologically? Below I describe a few of the heuristics you might use to think about media texts through the lens of ideological criticism.

A text can reproduce a myth. In ideological criticism, a **myth** is a powerful story through which a historically specific and socially constructed idea or practice is made to feel like an eternal or quasi-spiritual truth.[12] According to Terry Eagleton, myth exists as a particular "*register* of ideology, which elevates certain meanings to numinous status."[13] Wrapped in the guise of myth, an idea or practice can seem to exist in a realm beyond the social or political life and immune to rational analysis. A myth can reduce the messy, antagonistic dynamics of social struggle and the vast diversity of human experience to a simple, powerful storyline. In these ways, a myth can legitimate an exploitative social system.

The American Dream—the optimistic narrative where hard work results in the happy ending of middle-class prosperity—is a powerful myth that serves the interests of American nationalism and capitalism. It edits out the brutal vagaries of market forces and the experiences of millions of people who work hard yet never get ahead. We often talk about *believing* in the American Dream and to question it can feel like blasphemy. As the Horatio Alger novels, the *Cosby Show*, and countless Hollywood movies suggest, myths and media have a mutually beneficial relationship. Myths like the American Dream serve as valuable material for media producers looking for stories that will resonate with audiences, and media texts can deepen viewers' "faith" in a myth.

Although I don't use the term, in arguing that *Supernanny* and *Nanny 911* tap into a "romanticized ideology" of the autonomous nuclear family, I am analyzing the operation of a powerful myth that casts the heterosexual nuclear family as the natural, eternal foundation of society. A key goal of my argument is to counter that myth, to reveal that this conception of the nuclear family is not natural or universal, but rather historically and culturally specific, and to argue that the myth serves the interests of a neoliberal political agenda. The extent to which you resist my argument, look askance at my evidence, and think to yourself, "Yes, but the nuclear family is the natural way for people to have and raise kids," might indicate the power of that myth.

A text can try to manage systemic tensions. As mentioned earlier, social systems are inevitably riddled with conflicts. In their effort to sustain a system of domination, ideologies try to manage or contain them. They may, for example, translate socio-economic antagonisms into personal dilemmas, displace political anxieties onto scapegoats, or offer imaginary resolutions to unresolvable tensions. The goal of the ideological media critic is to explain how a text that presents itself as simply about one thing, might actually be about something else.

Supernanny and *Nanny 911* worked to contain the class conflicts and anxieties circulating in a climate where social support systems were being rolled back in the name of smaller government. In dealing with these families in crisis, the shows never address the fact that the neoliberal makeover of America shifts economic resources to upper-class families (through reduced tax obligations) and away from working-class families (through reduced government subsidized services). Instead, the problems these families face are unruly children. In this way, the programs translate wider socio-economic conflict into the personal plight of each family. They displace working- and middle-class fears about eroding public schools and cuts to Head Start programs onto ineffective parenting. They also provide an **imaginary resolution** in the guise of the nannies who magically arrive just in time like Mary Poppins. By the end of each episode, as far as the show allows us to know, the nannies' work is successful and the crisis ends. Left unacknowledged and unresolved, of course, are the economic challenges many families face. Through such **displacements** and happy endings, these shows might work to contain working- and middle-class resentment over and political mobilization in response to neoliberal policies. At the very least, they don't explicitly draw attention to them.

The act of linking *Supernanny* and *Nanny 911* to neoliberal class conflicts exemplifies the way ideological media criticism involves a creative act of interpretation (or re-articulation, to use Hall's term)—an analytical move that demands some ability to think beyond the world of the text. That doesn't mean it involves making things up. After all, I don't make up the fact that the shows are about rehabilitating dysfunctional families, that government policies helped construct a vision of the ideal family, or that neoliberal advocates call for ending government programs that help economically struggling families. If the reader feels I am making things up, that suggests my evidence and argument are not up to the task of offsetting the power of neoliberal and heteronormative ideologies to hide their operations.

A text can establish narrow frames. Ideologies channel the ways we think about reality down paths that serve dominant interests and limit our ability to imagine possibilities that would challenge those interests. One way they can do this is to establish the **frames** within which we understand an issue. Frames actively exclude alternative ways of thinking, but because they are often set before we encounter the topic, it can be hard to appreciate the ways they affect our thinking. Frames rationalize the paths taken and make the conclusions reached seemed commonsensical.

Ideological media criticism exposes how texts operate in this manner. Frame analysis reveals the various ways news reports can set the parameters for how readers think about a topic; by deciding which experts to quote as representatives of "both sides of a story," journalists define the nature of a debate. If news reports didn't quote climate change deniers, the debate would likely shift from whether man-made climate change is real to how society should respond to it. In fictional television series, many decisions about what can happen on a show are determined by the genre or the series' founding premise; although it seems as if anything can happen on unscripted reality TV series, the producers dictate much of what takes place through the rules of the game or the establishing dynamic (not to mention later editing). On *Big Brother*, for example, there isn't going to be a same-sex "showmance" if only one gay, lesbian, or bisexual houseguest is cast.

Supernanny and *Nanny 911* establish very narrow frames with important ideological consequences.

The highly formulaic programs feel hermetically sealed within a problem-cause-solution logic in which out-of-control children caused by bad parenting call for parental re-training. When viewers are hooked by this logic, when they think, "Yes, those parents are horrible," root for the nanny to whip them into shape, and feel satisfaction when the family gets its act together, Althusser would say they have been interpellated. Even skeptical viewers who doubt the family's transformation might remain trapped within the series' frames: they may doubt the success of the solution without rejecting the diagnosis of the problem or cause. The ideological critic, however, could propose a series with alternative frames—e.g., a reality series in which diverse teams of psychologists, marriage counselors, and labor activists assess families' problems. Noticing that one mother works long hours in stressful conditions to save for her children's private school, the team may decide to organize a union to negotiate better pay and working conditions for the mother and a school-levy ballot initiative to raise money to improve the community's public schools.

A text can shape ideologies. Media texts don't create ideologies, as much as they tap into and channel them. In the process, media texts can shape ideologies, pushing them in certain directions, helping them evolve over time. They can also bring conflicting ideologies together, creating contradictions. This happens, in part, because media production is a process driven by multiple forces and media texts are complex constructions built from polysemous codes and conventions. Thus, for the ideological media critic, a text doesn't reflect an ideology as much as it serves as a site where ideologies get negotiated. Understanding how media industries and texts operate (through the methods and concepts you will encounter in this volume) is an important element for the craft of ideological media criticism.

Supernanny and *Nanny 911* don't simply reflect neoliberal ideology as much as they adapt it to the conditions of a prime-time network reality series. While neoliberal arguments for rolling back government programs idealize the autonomous nuclear family, the programs present images of intensely dysfunctional families. Sensationalistic footage of kids swearing at their mother serves producers' strategic needs to create drama and stand out in the crowded prime-time arena, but it also generates a contradiction between a neoliberal agenda that claims families don't need help and these families that clearly do. The makeover narrative and the "magical" British nannies can only attempt to resolve this tension in favor of neoliberalism.

When I wrote the essay at the end of the series' first seasons, every family featured on both shows conformed to a strikingly narrow household form—married, heterosexual parents with children. As the series progressed, however, a wider range of families was featured, including blended families and families with gay parents, separated parents, parents and children with disabilities, adopted children, and extended family members as caregivers. Although the traditional able-bodied, two-parent, heterosexual family remained dominant, one could argue that the series didn't reinforce heteronormative ideologies in exactly the same way they did at the start. Given the complex dynamics of series production, various factors could explain the shift. For instance, to stay on air for multiple seasons, producers may have felt the need to make tweaks to keep the program fresh. A production studies research project would be needed to test this hypothesis.

At this point, you might return to Figure 1.1 to consider how different media products relate to the ideological assumptions noted there. How, for example, do cop shows like *Law & Order* relate to the idea that police protect the public? How might video games like *Farmville* or *Diner Dash* shape how we think about the payoff of work? How might a film like *The Avengers* intersect with ideas about diversity?

A text and reality can verify each other. Ideologies don't simply distort our understanding of the world we live in but also help to create that world. In other words, we think in ways that align with the society we construct and construct a society that aligns with the ways we think. Thus, ideologies become true—in a certain sense of the word at least. They remain false, however, when they blind us to the fact that we could construct society differently. One way to be in false consciousness, then, is to forget that things don't have to be the way they are.

For example, it is a commonsense assertion today that children are better off being raised by two parents. Given the way we have organized society, that could be true. However, that doesn't mean that it's inherently true. If we organized society differently—encouraged living in multi-generational households, promoted less rigid gender norms, created universal access to quality daycare, offered extensive parental leave, strengthened public school systems—children could be as well or maybe better off with one parent. Neoliberal and heteronormative ideologies about the sanctity of the autonomous, heterosexual, nuclear

family keep many of us from imagining and thus building such a reality.

Ideological media messages about the American family like those in *Supernanny* and *Nanny 911* make sense—seem perfectly logical—because we live in a world where families are increasingly told to solve their problems on their own. And we live in a world where families are increasingly left to their own devices, in part, because such shows (along with many others) circulate messages that idealize the sanctity of the autonomous, heterosexual, nuclear family. Challenging the ideologies circulated by media texts, then, can be difficult because it often requires challenging reality itself (and facing the possibility of social exclusion and threats of violence that can result from doing so). It is also difficult because it requires being able to imagine alternatives—something a mutually self-verifying ideology and reality work to thwart. Yet the fact that many people do raise children in alternative households reminds us that people escape, resist, or negotiate dominant ideologies, and the legalization of same-sex marriage in the U.S. ten years after these series debuted demonstrates that people can change reality.

Conclusion

At its best, ideological media criticism involves participating in an ongoing conversation about how we understand the world we live in and how we can make it better. It is an important but difficult enterprise. As a critic of contemporary media culture, both you and your audience are embedded in the very reality and ideological processes under scrutiny. Ideally, the craft of ideological media criticism is a practice of self-reflection about your experience in those processes—of acknowledging your social position within multiple systems of domination, of using that position as a springboard for seeing reality differently while also identifying your ideological blind spots, of developing the kind of imagination your social position might otherwise thwart.

Such self-reflection requires help—not only help from the kind of theory and tools introduced here, but also help from people positioned differently in society than you. We share our ideological interpretations of media texts (or their production and consumption) with someone to help her think about those texts and practices, the social reality they support, and her own assumptions about the world from a different perspective. We need to be open to learning from other people's interpretations as well. In doing ideological media criticism, John Thompson points out, "we are re-interpreting a pre-interpreted domain and thus engaging in a process which can, by its very nature, give rise to a conflict of interpretations."[14] Such conflict requires us to justify our interpretations with evidence and be humble enough to take others' interpretations seriously, to ask how their perspectives might help us discover our own ideological blind spots and imagine a better world. No interpretation or political prescription for a just society is ever the final word, but always an opening for more conversation, debate, or struggle.

Returning to Figure 1.1, for example, I must note that determining the extent to which a specific ideological assumption is contested isn't a science; it is an interpretation and thus involves the critic's subjective experience. Has the idea that marriage is between a man and a woman, for example, become defunct or not? What role has a series like *House Hunters*, which includes same-sex couples looking for their "forever home" alongside straight couples, played in that ideological change? Is that change a good thing? Ideological media criticism can't offer definitive answers to these questions, but it can promote productive conversations.

Unfortunately, some conventions of ideological media criticism work at cross purposes with this ideal. The traditional formats of the single-authored essay and book are stubbornly monologic. Without the give-and-take of a conversation, the critic's effort to justify an interpretation can acquire the aggressive conviction of a scientific proof. My own essay, I fear, suffers from this weakness. While "conversation" can occur across academic publications and at conferences and even more so in the classroom, that shouldn't keep us from developing our craft so we write in ways that open up rather than close down debate. Stuart Hall addressed a similar issue regarding the craft of critical theory:

> I don't want to prescribe, but I want to draw your attention to the problem of courtesy.... Because there is a kind of competitive way in which intellectuals live with their tensions in which they can only do so by climbing on the backs of those people whose positions they're trying to contest.... We have a lot to learn about the manners of a genuinely dialogically critical engagement.[15]

Conversations rarely take place on equal footing, and the most disempowered don't always have the luxury for a certain generosity of manners. So like Hall, I am hesitant to prescribe, but as you hone your skills as an ideological media critic, I urge you to consider the opportunity you have to engage with others—especially those whose experiences of social life differ from yours.

I also want to identify some limits of ideological analysis. If a goal of our analyses is to help us understand how social systems reproduce themselves in order to intervene in the organization of social life, the concept of ideology and the analysis of media texts will get us only so far. People help reproduce the status quo for many reasons beyond the ideologies through which they understand reality. Apathy, habit, the threat of violence, "the dull compulsion of economic relations,"[16] and the dazzling sensations of embodied pleasures are only a few. Ideological analysis, for example, may help us understand the romanticized ideology of the family as a myth, but it doesn't actually explain that myth's persistent emotional appeal. And if we ever want proof that knowing better doesn't always lead to people doing better, we need only look at the way most U.S. citizens, even those who believe that human activities are causing climate change, continue to engage in practices that threaten humanity's long-term existence. Ideological analysis may be necessary, but it is also insufficient.

I want to conclude by identifying some future directions for ideological media criticism. The ever-changing dynamics of media industries have important consequences for the craft. Media critics were first drawn to the concept of ideology in the 1970s at a time when most media production was highly centralized, industrialized, nationally oriented, and driven by a mass-marketing mindset. Such conditions helped justify ideological analyses of mass media. Recent developments (e.g., digitization, narrow- and microcasting, mobile media technologies, global media flows) have transformed how media texts are produced, distributed, and consumed. Such changes certainly don't make the concept of ideology irrelevant, but they do require us to adapt to these new contexts. Given the relative fragmentation of cultural production and consumption, for example, critics should reassess the strengths and limitations of analyses like my case study that focus on only a few media texts. To better understand and perhaps intervene in the media's role in the reproduction of social systems, we may now benefit more by using the concept of ideology to drive ethnography, production, and policy studies. The growth in video games and social media makes it increasingly difficult for ideological criticism to sidestep questions of affect and embodied sensations; we need to better understand how the ways we think are entangled with the ways we feel. And the widespread use of irony in a culture that some people allege is post-feminist, post-racial, or post-national (i.e., somehow beyond those systems of domination) requires critics to engage with theories of humor as well as contemporary political theories. I urge the reader to consider how the insights and methods raised in the other chapters in this volume can help advance the craft of ideological criticism.

Notes

1. Karl Marx and Friedrich Engels, *The Marx-Engels Reader* (New York: Norton, 1978).

2. Karl Mannheim, *Ideology and Utopia: An Introduction to the Sociology of Knowledge* (New York: Harcourt Brace Jovanovich, 1985).

3. Max Horkheimer and Theodor W. Adorno, *Dialectic of Enlightenment* (Stanford: Stanford University Press, 2002).

4. Sigmund Freud, *Civilization and Its Discontents* (New York: W.W. Norton, 1962).

5. Ferdinand de Saussure, *Course in General Linguistics* (New York: McGraw Hill, 1966).

6. Horkheimer and Adorno, "The Culture Industry: Enlightenment as Mass Deception," in *Dialectic of Enlightenment*, 94–136.

7. Louis Althusser, "Ideology and Ideological State Apparatuses," in *Lenin and Philosophy and Other Essays* (New York: Monthly Review Press, 1971), 127–86.

8. Antonio Gramsci, *Prison Notebooks* (New York: Columbia University Press, 1991).

9. Raymond Williams, *Marxism and Literature* (Oxford: Oxford University Press, 1977).

10. Stuart Hall, "Signification, Representation, Ideology: Althusser and the Post-Structuralist Debates," *Critical Studies in Mass Communication* 2 (1985), 91–114; Stuart Hall, "The Problem of Ideology: Marxism Without Guarantees," in *Stuart Hall: Critical Discourses in Cultural Studies*, ed. David Morley and Kuan-Hsing Chen (New York: Routledge, 1996), 25–46.

11. Ron Becker, "'Help Is on the Way!' *Supernanny, Nanny 911*, and the Neoliberal Politics of the Family," in *The Great American Makeover: Television, History, Nation*, ed.

12. Roland Barthes, *Mythologies* (New York: Hill and Wang, 2012).

13. Terry Eagleton, *Ideology* (London: Longman, 1994), 189.

14. John Thompson, *Ideology and Modern Culture: Critical Social Theory in the Era of Mass Communication* (Stanford: Stanford University Press, 1990), 22–23.

15. Stuart Hall, "Cultural Studies and Its Theoretical Legacies," in *Cultural Studies*, eds. Lawrence Grossberg, Cary Nelson, and Paula Treichler (New York: Routledge, 1992), 291.

16. Nicholas Garnham, "Political Economy and Cultural Studies: Reconciliation or Divorce?" *Critical Studies in Mass Communication* 12 (1995), 66.

Dana Heller (New York: Palgrave Macmillan, 2006), 175–91.

Further Reading

Battles, Kathleen, and Wendy Hilton-Morrow. "Gay Characters in Conventional Spaces: *Will and Grace* and the Situation Comedy Genre." *Critical Studies in Media Communication* 19 (2002): 87–105.

Gitlin, Todd. *The Whole World Is Watching: Mass Media and the Making & Unmaking of the New Left*. Berkeley: University of California Press, 1980.

Gledhill, Christine. "Pleasurable Negotiations." In *Female Spectators: Looking at Film and Television*, edited by E. Deidre Pribram, 64–89. London: Verso, 1988.

Gray, Herman. "Television, Black Americans, and the American Dream." In *Television: The Critical View* (5th Edition), edited by Horace Newcomb, 176–87. Oxford: Oxford University Press, 1994.

Jameson, Fredric. "Reification and Utopia in Mass Culture." *Social Text* 1 (Winter 1979): 130–48.

Larrain, Jorge. "Stuart Hall and the Marxist Concept of Ideology." In *Stuart Hall: Critical Discourses in Cultural Studies*, edited by David Morley and Kuan-Hsing Chen, 47–70. New York: Routledge, 1996.

Malešević, Sinšia, and Iain MacKenzie, eds. *Ideology after Poststructuralism*. London: Pluto Press, 2002.

Žižek, Slavoj. "The Specter of Ideology." In *Mapping Ideology*, edited by Slavoj Žižek, 1–33. London: Verso, 1994.

2.
DISCOURSE
Rosalind Gill

Overview

Discourse analysis is the name given to a variety of approaches that take language and social constructions as their object of study. **Discourse** means all forms of talk and text—it includes media texts of all kinds, as well as interview data and naturally occurring conversation. Strictly speaking, there is no single "discourse analysis," but many different styles of analysis which all lay claim to the name. What these perspectives share is a rejection of the realist notion that language is simply a neutral means of reflecting or describing the world, and a belief in the central importance of language and representations in constructing social life. Discourse analysis became a popular approach in media and communications studies from the 1990s onwards, reflecting a wider "turn to language" across the humanities and social sciences, along with the influence of poststructuralist ideas. Types of discourse analysis used in studying media include Foucauldian discursive analysis, critical discourse analysis (CDA) and conversation analysis. Discourse analysis has close intellectual connections to ideological and narrative analysis, as well as to broad thematic analysis and qualitative approaches more generally.

This chapter is structured as follows. First, it will provide a brief intellectual history of discourse analysis, situating it in relation to other methodologies in media studies. It will examine a range of different approaches to analyzing discourse and introduce their key terms and concepts. Next it will discuss one particular approach to discourse analysis that I have used in a variety of types of research, including studies of media organizations, analyses of media texts, and interview-based audience research. To illustrate the nature of the approach and the kinds of findings/knowledge it generates, I will focus on one case study, analyzing sex and relationships advice in women's magazines. I will conclude by reflecting on the challenges and dilemmas of using this approach in media and communications research.

History and Intellectual Context

The extraordinarily rapid growth of interest in discourse analysis in recent years is both a consequence and a manifestation of the "turn to language" that has occurred across the arts, humanities, and social sciences in the wake of the influence of structuralism, poststructuralism, and postmodernist ideas. Discourse analysis belongs to a group of approaches that are sometimes called **social constructionist**. Key features of these perspectives include:

1. a critical stance towards taken-for-granted knowledge, and a skepticism towards the view that our observations of the world unproblematically yield its true nature to us (a perspective known as **positivism**);
2. a recognition that the ways in which we commonly understand the world are historically and culturally specific and relative;
3. a conviction that knowledge is socially constructed—that is, our current ways of understanding the world are not determined by the nature of the world itself but by social processes;
4. a commitment to exploring the ways that knowledges—the social construction of people, phenomena or problems—are linked to actions.[1]

The terms "discourse" and "discourse analysis" are contested. To claim that one's approach is a discourse analytical one, therefore, does not necessarily tell anybody much. Instead, it may be helpful to identify some different approaches to discourse analysis and to connect them with distinct intellectual traditions. Here, I discuss three contrasting traditions of discourse analysis that have been used in media research.

First, there is the variety of positions known as **critical linguistics**, **social semiotics**, or **critical discourse analysis**.[2] Compared with many types of discourse analysis, this tradition has a close association with the discipline of linguistics, but its clearest debt is to semiotics and structuralist analysis. The central semiotic idea is that a word's sense derives not from any inherent feature of the relationship between that word and the thing it represents—the signifier and signified—but from the system of oppositions in which it is embedded. This idea posed a fundamental challenge to "word-object" accounts, which viewed language as a process of naming. This insight has been developed in recent critical linguistic work, which has an explicit concern with the relationship between language and power. The critical linguistic tradition is also well-represented in media studies, particularly in research on news, and has highlighted—amongst other things—the ways in which particular linguistic forms can have dramatic effects upon how an event or phenomenon is understood—not simply the choice of individual terms (such as "terrorist" versus "freedom fighter") but also distinctions between active and passive voice, or agent deletion, e.g., the difference between "Police shoot dead demonstrators" versus "Demonstrators shot dead". The critical linguistic approach has a strong interest in **ideology**[3]—understood as the ways in which power and meaning intersect[4]— and has been popular amongst feminist media researchers,[5] as well as anti-racist scholars and those who are interested in critical race theory. Most recently it has been developed within the field of communication studies into a broader approach known as **multimodal analysis** that allows the researcher to look not just at language but at sound and image, too, attempting to offer a systematic approach to analyzing meaning in media texts such as television programs or Facebook pages.[6] Although not referred to as multimodal, this approach to discourse analysis has a longer tradition within film, television, and game studies, where audiovisual media are central objects of study.

A second broad tradition of discourse analysis is that influenced by **speech act theory**, **ethnomethodology**, and **conversation analysis**.[7] These perspectives stress the functional or action orientation of discourse and are interested in looking in detail at the organization of social interaction. The approach emerged out of micro-sociology and has made a significant contribution to understanding how sense and meaning are produced out of the everyday messiness of talk—punctuated as it is by hesitations, false starts, deviations, "ums," and "ers." Conversation analysis offers insights into how we "do" things with words, e.g., make excuses, apologize, offer an invitation, practice sarcasm. It has been taken up in media and communications studies to research mediated interactions such as radio phone-ins or talk shows.[8]

The third body of work that sometimes identifies itself as discourse analysis is that associated with **poststructuralism**. Poststructuralists have broken with realist views of language and rejected the notion of the unified coherent subject, which has long been at the heart of Western philosophy. Among poststructuralists, Michel Foucault is notable for characterizing his genealogies of discipline and sexuality as discourse analyses. In contrast to most discourse analysis, this work is not interested in the details of spoken or written texts, but in looking historically at discourses. Foucault's methodology has had a significant influence on some media analysts. His work rejected mono-causal explanations, and he attempted to write "histories of the present" that disrupt the obviousness of the way things are. As he put it, "the genealogist tries to rediscover the multiplicity of factors and processes which constitute an event in order to disrupt the self-evident quality ascribed to events through the deployment of historical concepts and the description of anthropological traits."[9] A good example of this approach in media studies is Sean Nixon's genealogy of the development of new sexualized ways of representing the male body, which showed how emergent representational practices for signifying masculinity had multiple points of origin (e.g., in fashion, advertising, magazines) and were not the outcome of one single change.[10] To do a discursive analysis in this Foucauldian sense, then, is to be interested in reading how new masculinities materialized across multiple mediated sites, in other words, how fashion photography or the music industry literally brought new constructions of manhood into being.

Foucault was critical of the notion of "ideology," often understood as "falsehood," versus science or truth. Unlike Marxists, he did not think it was possible to divide up representations between the true and the false but was more interested in what he called "truth effects" and their relationship to power—that is, what discourses do by dint of constructing the world in a particular way. Moreover, rather than seeing science as "truthful" and "innocent" he was precisely interested in the ways in which the sciences—and particularly the emerging human and social sciences—were themselves enmeshed in power relations through the production of new subjects and categories of experience, for example, the hysteric, the schizophrenic, or the homosexual. He called this idea the "power-knowledge" nexus, and it has been central to much media and communications research because of the way it directs our attention to what representations and stories *do* rather than comparing them with an assumed "reality." We come back to this point in the case study.

Having looked briefly at a number of different discourse analytic traditions, in the next section, I will turn to elaborating the approach I have used in my own media research.

Elaborating Discourse Analysis

The approach to be elaborated here draws on ideas from each of the three traditions outlined above, as well as from the growing field of rhetorical analysis.[11] Developed initially in work in the sociology of scientific knowledge and social psychology, it has now produced analyses in fields as diverse as gender studies, social policy, technology studies, and is a valuable addition to approaches in media and communications studies.[12] It constitutes a theoretically coherent approach to the analysis of talk and texts.

It is useful to think of discourse analysis as having five main themes. First, it takes *discourse itself* as its topic. As noted already, the term discourse is used to refer to all forms of talk and texts, including naturally occurring conversations, interview material, and written or spoken texts of any kind—from blogs to TV programs to SMS messages. Discourse analysts are interested in texts in their own right, rather than seeing them as a means of "getting at" some reality that is deemed to lie behind the discourse—whether social or psychological or material. Instead of seeing discourse as a pathway to some other reality, discourse analysts are interested in the content and organization of texts. Thus if a discourse analyst were looking at a news broadcast, she would not be interested in comparing the news representation with "reality" (indeed she would not believe that there exists some ultimate,

unmediated, non-discursive reality), but might rather be concerned with exploring how the broadcast was organized to produce a sense of truth and coherence, to make its version of events persuasive, to generate a sense of "liveness" and authenticity, to accord authority to the host, and so on.

The second theme of discourse analysis is that language is constructive. Jonathan Potter and Margaret Wetherell argue that the metaphor of construction highlights three facets of the approach: It draws attention to the fact that discourse is built or manufactured out of pre-existing linguistic resources; it illuminates the fact that the "assembly" of an account involves choice or selection from a number of different possibilities; and it emphasizes the fact that we deal with the world in terms of constructions, not in a somehow "direct" or unmediated way; in a very real sense texts of various kinds *construct* our world.[13] The constructive use of language is a taken-for-granted aspect of social life. The notion of construction, then, clearly marks a break with traditional "realist" models of language, in which it is taken to be a transparent medium, a relatively straightforward path to "real" beliefs or events, or a reflection of the way things really are. All media show this constructed quality—for example, social media like Instagram or Facebook are often centered on presenting people in a positive light, adverts are designed to offer persuasive communications, and news broadcasts aim to construct an authoritative version of events.

The third feature of discourse analysis that I want to stress here is its concern with the "action orientation" or "function orientation" of discourse. That is, discourse analysts see all discourse as *social practice*. People use discourse to *do* things—for example, to offer blame, to pay compliments, or to present themselves in a positive light. To highlight this is to underline the fact that discourse does not occur in a social vacuum. As social actors, we are continuously orienting to the interpretative context in which we find ourselves and constructing our discourse to fit that context. This is very obvious in relatively formal contexts such as hospitals or courtrooms, but it is equally true of all other contexts too. To take a crude example, you might give a different account of what you did last night depending upon whether the person inquiring was your mother, your boss, or your best friend. It is not that you would deliberately be being duplicitous in any one of these cases (or at least not necessarily) but simply that you would be saying what seems "right" or what "comes naturally" for that particular interpretative context. Discourse analysts argue that all discourse is, in this sense, "occasioned" or produced for a particular audience or context.

Even the most apparently straightforward, neutral sounding description can be involved in a whole range of different activities, depending upon the interpretative context. Take the following sentence: "My cell phone is not working." This sounds like a straightforwardly descriptive sentence about an object. However, its meaning can change dramatically in different interpretative contexts:

- When said to a friend who has been waiting for you in a restaurant for an hour, it may be the beginning of an excuse or mitigation.
- When said to the person or store who sold you the phone only a few days earlier, it may be part of an accusation, a blaming.
- When said to a stranger, approached in the street, it may be an implicit request to borrow his or her phone in order to make a call.

One way of checking your analysis of the discourse is to look at how the participants involved responded, as this can offer valuable analytical and contextual clues. For example, if the phone sales person responded by saying, "Well, it was working fine when I sold it to you," this indicates that the sentence was heard as an accusation—even though no explicit accusation was made. It is important to note that the person to whom one is speaking does not have to change in order to alter the interpretative context. Think about how a question like "Are you going out tonight?" can have multiple meanings when said by someone to their partner, depending on mood, history, and so on. The key point here is that there is nothing "mere" or insubstantial about language: Talk and texts are social practices, and even the most seemingly trivial statements are involved in various kinds of activities. Aims of discourse analysis include identifying the functions or activities of talk and texts and exploring how they are performed.

This brings me to the fourth point: Discourse analysis treats talk and texts as *organized rhetorically.*[14] Unlike conversation analysis, discourse analysis sees social life as being characterized by conflicts of various kinds. As such, much discourse is involved in establishing one version of the world in the face of competing versions. This is obvious in some cases—politicians, for example, are clearly attempting to win people around to their view of the world, and advertisers are attempting to sell us lifestyles, dreams, and products, but it is also true of other discourse. The emphasis on the rhetorical nature of texts directs our attention to the ways in which discourse is organized to make itself persuasive. Discourse analysis teaches us to approach all discourse critically—from the *Big Brother* contestant to the talk show confession, the tweet to the DJ's patter—to see it as attempting to construct particular versions of the world.

As well as examining the way that language is used, discourse analysts must also be sensitive to what is not said, to silences. This, in turn, requires a significant awareness of the social, political and cultural trends and contexts to which our texts refer. As I have argued elsewhere, without this broader contextual understanding:

> [W]e would be unable to see the alternative version of events or phenomena that the discourse we were analysing had been designed to counter; we would fail to notice the (sometimes systematic) absence of particular kinds of account in the texts that we were studying; and we would not be able to recognize the significance of silences.[15]

Finally, discourse analysis involves identifying patterns in discourse, being able to highlight recurrent themes or ideas or tropes—particularly when looking across a corpus of data—whether this is in newspapers or interviews. Discourse analysts call these patterned features of discourse **interpretative repertoires**. Their common features may be content or they may be marked by particular metaphors or figures of speech. Sometimes they encode particular ideological positions. For example, terms such as "community" or "responsible citizens" or "hardworking families" seem to come ready-evaluated in contemporary discourse, always already presented as a *good thing*. Recently, British political discourse has been marked by a shift from the phrase "this country" to "our country," with potent ideological effects.

To offer an example: In my research on women and radio[16], I was interested in the reasons radio station managers and program controllers put forward for the very small number of female broadcasters compared to males, particularly in music programming. Using a discourse analytic approach to analyze my interviews, I identified six interpretative repertoires used in interviews to account for the lack of women in presenting roles. These were

- women just do not apply (for the role of presenter);
- the audience prefer male presenters;
- women don't have the right skills for radio presentation;
- women who want to become broadcasters all go into journalism;
- women's voices are wrong;
- daytime radio is targeted at housewives so it is better to have a male presenter.

The broadcasters all drew on and combined these different repertoires, moving between accounts when it felt right to do so. Thus, one moment, they might assert that the reason for the lack of women at the station was that no women applied; the next, they would regretfully explain that actually the issue was audience objections or the fact that women's voices did not sound appealing on radio. Rather than taking any of the accounts at face value, the analysis looked at the patterning, organization, and action orientation of the discourse. That is, the force of the analysis as a critique of sexist ideology or practice lay not in comparing the accounts with a taken-for-granted reality (e.g., the assertion that women do apply), but in looking at how the accounts worked together to justify the lack of women at the radio stations in question.

One of the things that attention to the fine detail of discourse was able to show was how carefully these accounts were constructed, despite being part of the fast cut and thrust of an interview conversation. They were, for example, full of disclaimers about sexism (such as "I'm not being sexist but …") and other rhetorical devices designed to head off potential criticisms of their own sexual politics or the equal opportunities practices of the radio station. The interviews were also characterized by multiple strategies to make the radio bosses' accounts persuasive, for example, the use of scientific terms to lend credibility and objectivity or the deployment of "extreme case formulations."

What the analysis showed, in sum, was the subtlety and the detail of the way that discrimination was practiced: At no point did any one of the interviewees say that they did not think women should be employed as radio presenters. On the contrary, they were keen to stress their positive attitude to female presenters and to suggest that they were (to quote one) "looking hard" to appoint women. However, what they produced were patterned accounts that justified the exclusion of women, whilst simultaneously protecting themselves against potential accusations of sexism.

Method and Major Terminology

In order to more fully flesh out the principles of discourse analysis discussed above and its use as an approach within media and communications research, I am going to discuss my development of this approach to examine sex and relationship advice in a top-selling women's magazine. This is reported fully in my article, "Mediated Intimacy and Postfeminism: A Discourse Analytic Examination of Sex and Relationships Advice in a Women's Magazine."[17] *Glamour* is the United Kingdom's best-selling monthly magazine, targeted at upwardly mobile women in their 20s and 30s and gaining (at the time of the analysis) 8 million hits on its website each month. Articles about sex and relationships are a key part of its success, along with fashion, beauty and celebrity news. Each month sees this fare prominently displayed on the cover with headlines such as "How good are you in bed? Men tell you what your partner won't," and "We're coming to your sexual rescue: never be bored in bed again." The aim of the analysis was to understand the kinds of messages about sex and relationships that were presented in the magazines, asking questions about sex, gender, and sexuality. Other research looking at similar magazines (e.g., *Cosmopolitan*) had highlighted themes of "naughtiness" and transgression, alongside the notion that the "fun, fearless female" must ultimately be focused on pleasing the man, rather than herself.[18] Pantea Farvid and Virginia Braun argued that such sex advice draws on the "male sex drive" discourse, which depicts the man as "needing" lots of great sex and the woman as having to develop sexual skills in order to satisfy him and prevent him from straying.[19] In their research, carried out in New Zealand, men were presented as easily aroused and satisfied, whilst women's orgasms were depicted as difficult to achieve, building into a his 'n' hers, Mars and Venus notion of gender complementarity and heteronormativity.[20] My research set out to extend these studies, looking in detail at sex and relationship advice in *Glamour* magazine.

The study could be seen as a type of ideological analysis or critique in that it examines a cultural artifact—sex and relationship advice in a magazine—as a means of understanding and illuminating the ideological notions that run through it. In this sense, as Ron Becker puts it in Chapter 1 of this volume, it connects "close textual analysis" with "wider systems of domination."

The analysis also bears resemblance to some Weberian approaches, which are interested in the rationalization of modern life, or what George Ritzer has called its "McDonaldization"[21]—its standardized, homogenized and commodified nature. Eva Illouz's work on "emotional capitalism" is pertinent, particularly her incisive critique of Internet dating sites.[22] She documents how these push people towards very particular ways of relating in which oneself and all potential partners must be advertised and apprehended as competing products in a marketplace of intimacy.

My case study is also informed by a Foucauldian interest in "technologies of the self" and an attentiveness to the way the magazines incite us to become entrepreneurs, even in this most intimate of domains.

In reality, then, it is striking to note the varied and hybrid intellectual influences on this project; it is not a "pure" discourse analysis (whatever such a thing might be) but benefits from a range of scholarly traditions.

Sampling

The first challenge for most researchers is in building a sample of material that will offer reliable—and in some cases generalizable—findings whilst working with a volume of data that is manageable. I started my research with a corpus of three years' worth of editions of *Glamour*—that is 36 issues, each one averaging around 380 pages—around 150,000 pages in total. This is a huge volume of data for a single researcher to work with—though might be suitable for a small team or two or three people working together. In order to manage it, I selected two issues at random from each year. However, I had to be careful that they were spread across the year, as Christmas issues, summer issues, and (in the Northern hemisphere) the famous September issue, which launches new fashion collections, all have a distinct flavor and tone.

Having selected a more manageable number of magazines to examine in detail, the next dilemma was to think about how to develop rigor in my sampling within the magazines. Given the focus of *Glamour* upon beauty, fashion, and celebrity, it was quite difficult to draw the boundaries in a principled way around those articles that could be considered sex and relationship advice articles and the mass of the rest of the magazine. Inevitably, articles about hairstyles, skin care regimes, or new makeup techniques often touched upon sex or sexiness, whilst those about celebrities frequently discussed relationships. How was I to narrow down my sample?

In order to do this, I read and re-read the magazines in detail and identified a recurring set of **article types** or **genres** that took as their main focus intimate relationships or sex. These included the survey report articles which described the results of new research (often commissioned by the magazine) (e.g., *Glamour*'s sex survey and a survey about sexual fantasies); the "men's voice" article which discusses what men do/want/think/fantasize about when "you" (the assumed heterosexual female reader) are not there; the "how to" article, which explicitly sets out to educate you on how to be a better lover or how to get a man to commit; the quiz in which you can find out what sort of lover you are, how shy or forward you are in bed; and the feature article, which focuses on a group with a particular relationship to sex or intimacy (e.g., women who learned sex tips from porn stars, women who are determined to marry within six months of a first date, men who are sex addicts). Focusing on these types of articles, all of which explicitly take intimate relationships as their primary focus, yielded more than 20 full-length articles to examine and this became my data corpus.

Identifying Patterns and Themes in the Data

As discussed above, one of the aims of discourse analysis is to identify patterns in a corpus of data in order to be able to say something meaningful about it. The key concept here is the **interpretative repertoire,** which is a unit of analysis that allows researchers to go beyond individual or discrete expressions to begin to identify themes, consistencies, and patterns across and between texts and to connect these to wider contexts and social formations. In some discursive traditions, these are known as "discourses," and researchers may speak of "consumer discourse" or "environmental discourse" or "legal discourse" and so on. However, rather than assuming that each domain—law, medicine, environment—has its own associated discourse that can be readily identifiable and which maps directly onto it, the notion of interpretative repertoire allows for more flexibility and dynamism, recognizing that any one phenomenon or text may be constituted by multiple intersecting discourses, some of which may be contradictory. Magazines are the example par excellence and have always been discussed as sites of intense contradiction yet somehow able to hold together competing discourses in a pleasurable whole, e.g., injunctions to love your body alongside articles about dieting;

stories about cheating husbands alongside articles about wedding planning.[23]

In beginning to identify interpretative repertoires, different researchers take different approaches. Wetherell and Potter, in their important work on the dynamics of new forms of racism, discuss the need to look out for common or recurrent themes or figures of speech and to be attentive to the repeated use of particular metaphors, similes or tropes.[24] In my own analysis, the focus is more on particular ideas or arguments. Whichever approach is taken, central to all discourse analytic approaches is what Potter has called "the spirit of **skeptical reading**."[25] This involves the suspension of belief in the taken for granted. It is analogous to the injunction by anthropologists to "render the familiar strange." It involves changing the way that language is seen in order to focus upon the construction, organization, and functions of discourse rather than looking for something behind or underlying it. As Potter and Wetherell have pointed out, academic training teaches people to read texts for gist, but this is precisely the wrong spirit in which to approach analysis:

> If you read an article or book the usual goal is to produce a simple, unitary summary, and to ignore the nuance, contradictions and areas of vagueness. However, the discourse analyst is concerned with the detail of passages of discourse, however fragmented and contradictory, and with what is actually said or written, not some general idea that seems to be intended.[26]

By contrast to our normal practices of reading, doing discourse analysis involves interrogating our own assumptions and the ways in which we habitually make sense of things. It involves a spirit of skepticism and the development of an "analytic mentality," which does not readily fall away when you are not sitting in front of a transcript.[27] You need to ask of any given piece: Why am I reading this in this way? What features of the text produce this reading? How is it organized to make itself persuasive? In my opinion, discourse analysis should carry a health warning, because doing it fundamentally changes the ways we experience language and social relations—much as studying media and communications more broadly can radically shift our perspective and experience of everyday experiences and media.

In this phase of the analysis, I might try out multiple ways of coding or parsing, trying to make sense of the data. A key point, which I will return to later, is to be able to account for the **variability** in the data. It is no good coming up with a way of understanding magazine sex advice that leaves out several types of argument or theme because they don't fit the schema. The analysis must be able to lend coherence and understanding to the whole data set, not just the "juiciest" quotes or the parts we find most interesting. For me, this stage involves multiple notes and different ways of trying to code the data. The magazine research involved a very untidy work environment that was a hive of activity: magazines spread out everywhere, marked with sticky notes; piles of paper; detailed notes made on the computer. It is, as Beverley Skeggs has noted, inevitably a "messy" process that often gets cleaned up, smoothed over and sanitized in the process of writing up in a way that obfuscates the difficulties and the hard work, the frustration and dead-ends, the false starts and abandonments of notions.[28]

The Analysis

This complicated, at times frustrating, process is difficult to write up honestly and authentically. It is much easier to explain the key themes of discourse analysis than it is to explain how actually to go about analyzing texts. Pleasing as it would be to be able to offer a cookbook style recipe for readers to follow methodically, this is just not possible. Somewhere between selecting the data and writing up, the essence of doing discourse analysis seems to slip away; ever elusive, it is never quite captured by descriptions of coding schemes and analytical schemas. However, just because the skills of discourse analysis do not lend themselves to procedural description, there is no need for them to be deliberately mystified and placed beyond the reach of all but the cognoscenti. Discourse analysis is similar to many other tasks: Journalists, for example, are not given formal training in identifying what makes an event news, and yet after a short time in the profession their sense of "news values" is hard to shake. There really is no substitute for learning by doing. This is how I learned to analyze discourse.

In the magazine study, after going through the process described above, I finally identified three interpretative repertoires that helped to make sense of the sex and relationship advice being offered, whilst also offering a new—and hopefully productive— way of thinking about how articles about intimate life were connected to a broader postfeminist sensibility operating across popular culture. The repertoires I identified were what I called the *intimate entrepreneurship repertoire*, which was based on a language of goals, plans, and strategies, a "professionalization" of intimate life; *men-ology* organized around the idea that women need to study and learn about men's needs and desires; and *transforming the self* which exhorted women to "makeover" not simply their bodies and sexual practices, but their emotional lives too—in order to become confident and adventurous sexual subjects. I will say a little about each repertoire in order to highlight their key themes.

Intimate Entrepreneurship

In this repertoire, relationships are cast as work, using analogies and metaphors from the worlds of finance, management, science, and military campaigns. Finding a satisfying intimate relationship is portrayed as having little to do with fate and more to do with careful planning and strategy. Women are advised to build a detailed checklist of what they want in a partner and to "go out and find him" and market themselves to suitable partners. Even sex is treated as an entrepreneurial activity, best approached in a rational, quasi-scientific manner. As one article put it: "Forget spontaneity—if it's passion you're after, you need to plan for it. Here we tell you what to eat, the exercises to boost your libido, and the tricks that will guarantee sex worth waiting for."[29]

Men-ology

The name I gave this repertoire is designed to draw attention to two things: the emphasis it places upon learning and studying and its focus on men as the subjects of this intense pedagogic activity. Whereas women were depicted as smart and go-getting in the intimate entrepreneurship repertoire, in this repertoire they appear naïve and unworldly, requiring guidance about every aspect of intimate relationships and particularly how to please men. Women are exhorted to study men closely, to learn about how they like to be seen and to offer compliments that fit with this perceived self-image, to familiarize themselves with men's interests, to mirror their speech patterns, and to ensure that they reassure and affirm what is presented as an extremely fragile male ego at all times—but especially during difficult sexual encounters. The asymmetry of the emotional labor required in relationships is striking, albeit obfuscated through a discourse of "good communication" (which turns out to mean women's communication).

Transforming the Self

This third repertoire also focuses on the work women are required to do in relationships, but differs from the two others in that it involves a profound "work on the self." This repertoire helped to make sense of articles that were neither about planning and goal setting to get a man or a good sex life, nor about learning to please men, but—perhaps more fundamentally—necessitated a transformation of subjectivity. In this repertoire, women were advised to "love your body," "banish neediness," work on their attitudes so that they are confident and adventurous, having rid themselves of any body "hang-ups" or sexual repression.

What this brief summary has shown, I hope, is that sex and relationships were constructed in three very different and quite contrasting ways across the body of data found in *Glamour*. Considering them now, these interpretative repertoires may have taken on the status of a certain kind of obviousness. This is partly because they capture and express well the main thematics of contemporary sex and relationship advice targeted at young, middle-class women. In practice, however, these repertoires did not come "ready identified" but were entangled within the magazine articles—sometimes all three repertoires might be mixed up together in the space of two or three sentences. The quotation below demonstrates this vividly:

> You just have to give sex the same priority you do to everything else in your life which you cherish. Educate yourself, try out new things, and, above all, have the right attitude. Try anything (within reason) once, put some effort into planning, but also don't worry if nothing goes to plan. Great sex stems from sexual confidence and if you feel sexy and believe in yourself, your body and your own ability, you really will be better at everything in bed.[30]

Here, then, we see a mash-up of all three repertoires: the focus on planning and prioritizing sex, the emphasis upon education, and the injunctions to "have the right attitude" and "believe in yourself". The repertoires give us a way to understand and unpack the different discourses at work in extracts like this and in the magazines in general. This constitutes the main work of analysis, offering a fresh yet rigorous take. However, for me, what is interesting is not to stop at the identification of the different repertoires but to explore how these patterned ways of talking about intimate relationships connect back to larger social contexts and cultural shifts and sensibilities. In the analysis fore-grounded here, I did this by situating them within the neoliberalization and postfeminization of culture.[31]

A Critical Evaluation of Discourse Analysis

One of the questions asked of research findings generally is: Are they representative? Can they, in other words, tell us something beyond the specifics of the particular analysis? This is a good question and an important one for scholars, pushing us to be careful about the status of the claims we want to make. In the case of discourse analysis, much of the time researchers are less interested in **representativeness**—let alone in the generalizability of their findings—than in the richness of their research, the ways it may offer insights into the structure and organization of everything from a TV talk show to advice pages. Looking back on my own research on *Glamour* magazine, however, I would make a bolder claim: By careful sampling I attempted to generate a representative set of articles to analyze. I think it is fair to claim that my analysis is representative of the kinds of discourses about sex and relationships circulating in a particular kind of magazine, in a particular historical and geographical context. Clearly my analysis is not true of *all* magazines at *all* times. Indeed, it is striking how different sex and relationship advice is in otherwise similar men's magazines such as *GQ* or *Men's Health*. My research does, I think, offer something that goes beyond an analysis of the particular editions of *Glamour* that came under my forensic gaze.

Another important set of questions concerns the **reliability** and **validity** of research. How can we judge this? How do we know, in other words, which research to take seriously and to trust? Discourse analysts have been extremely critical of many existing methods for ensuring reliability and validity. In psychology, for example, much experimental and qualitative research depends upon the suppression of variability, or the marginalization of instances that do not fit the story being told by the researcher.[32] Potter argues that discourse analysts can make use of four considerations to assess the reliability and validity of analyses:[33]

1. Deviant case analysis—that is, detailed examination of cases that seem to go against the pattern identified. This may serve to disconfirm the pattern but it may help to add greater sophistication to the analysis.[34] This step was part of the process of coding in my research—trying out new ways of organizing the material until I could make sense of all the data, not just some of it.

2. Participants' understanding. As I noted earlier in the chapter, one way of checking whether a piece of discourse analysis holds water is to examine how participants responded. This is most relevant, of course, in records of interaction, but in media research like mine, magazine letters pages and online comments can provide useful ways of checking how (other) readers responded.

3. Coherence. Discourse analytic research is building increasingly upon the insights of earlier work. For example, we know from many types of discursive analysis that certain forms of speech and writing are especially effective and persuasive rhetorically. This includes three-part lists, contrast structures, extreme case formulations, and disclaimers. As Potter argues, there is a sense in which each new study provides a check upon the adequacy of earlier studies.[35]

4. Readers' evaluations. Perhaps the most important way for the validity of the analysis to be checked is by presentation of the materials being analyzed, in order to allow readers of the research to make their own evaluation and, if they choose, to put forward alternative interpretations. Where academic publishers permit it, discourse analysts present full transcripts of their materials to readers, but this is more common in Ph.D. research, where raw data may be presented in appendices. When this is not possible, extended passages will be presented. In this way, discourse analysis is more open than almost all other research practices, which often present data "pre-theorized" or, as in ethnographic or psychoanalytic research, ask us to take observation and interpretations on trust.

Limitations and Drawbacks

In all these ways, discourse analysis offers a principled, rigorous approach to researching media and communications. Three limitations or drawbacks are perhaps worth mentioning. Firstly, discourse analysis is not an ideal approach for analyzing large data sets. It is much better at telling us "a lot about a little" than producing broad and sweeping findings. Secondly, the labor-intensiveness of the approach is another key point to note. Compared with a simple thematic analysis, a proper discourse analysis will require significantly greater investment of time, concerned as it is with the organization, action orientation, and rhetorical functions of texts as well as their thematic content. Finally, a third limitation of discourse analysis, including the case study presented here, is its inattention to the visual and audiovisual dimensions of the text. In this sense, discourse analysis requires further elaboration for use in moving image research in communication studies—as some scholars are now attempting with "multimodal (discourse) analysis."[36]

If I were doing this study again today, I would make some changes to the design of the research. My focus would probably be on online sex and relationship forums or blogs, or even smartphone apps, since these are displacing the former prominence of the printed word. Laura Favaro has produced a fascinating study of English- and Spanish-language forums concerned with both editorial and peer-to-peer advice using a broadly discourse analytic method.[37] If I were to do a similar study, it would also be important to analyze how audiences take up, negotiate, and resist the ideas offered in sex and relationship advice; clearly, people are active in their engagement with these texts.

In a further development of the work, Meg-John Barker, Laura Harvey, and I have examined constructions of intimacy across many different media, looking at how consent, desire, and pleasure are presented, and interrogating how media depict gender and sexual normality.[38] This work extends and develops the analysis of a single magazine discussed here, and is also notable for its focus upon diverse texts from sex apps to You Tube videos, to self-help books and television documentaries.

Conclusion

Ultimately, discourse analysis, like much other media and communications research, involves an individual or research team making a reading or interpretation. Discourse analysts put forward their take on a particular phenomenon, "showing their working" and presenting as much information as possible to allow others to make alternative interpretations. In the case

of media texts such as *Glamour* magazine, their ubiquitous nature makes it easy for others to contest or challenge the findings. At the end of the day, analyses stand or fall by the extent to which they illuminate a contemporary phenomenon, such as the changing nature of sex and relationship advice, and become part of an ongoing conversation about how to understand a world that is increasingly mediated. In this chapter, I hope to have shown how I have used the approach to aid in our understanding of the changing ways in which intimate life is mediated in a popular cultural text.

Discourse analysis is an enduringly popular method for media studies. It is "low budget" (i.e. relatively economical to carry out) and produces rich qualitative findings. Challenges for future research in communication studies of discourse involve integrating visual and moving image data and using discourse analytic approaches to analyze bigger data sets.

Acknowledgment

I would like to thank Yvonne Ehrstein and Danielle Bikhazi for their careful assistance in editing and formatting this chapter.

Notes

1. Vivien Burr, *An Introduction to Social Constructionism* (London: Routledge, 1995).
2. Roger Fowler, Robert Hodge, Gunther Kress, and Tony Trew, *Language and Control* (London: Routledge, 1979); Gunther Kress and Robert Hodge, *Language as Ideology* (London: Routledge, 1979); Robert Hodge and Gunther Kress, *Social Semiotics* (Cambridge: Polity Press, 1988); Norman Fairclough, *Language and Power* (Harlow: Longman, 1989).
3. See Chapter 1 in this volume.
4. John B. Thompson, *Studies in the Theory of Ideology* (Berkeley: University of California Press, 1984).
5. For example, Michelle M. Lazar, ed., *Feminist Critical Discourse Analysis: Gender, Power and Ideology in Discourse* (London: Palgrave, 2005); Lia Litosseliti, *Gender and Language: Theory and Practice* (London: Hodder Arnold, 2006).
6. David Machin, "Multimodality and Theories of the Visual," in *The Routledge Handbook of Multimodal Analysis*, ed. Carey Jewitt (London: Routledge, 2009), 181–90; Gunther Kress and Theo van Leeuwen, *Multimodal Discourse: The Modes and Media of Contemporary Communication* (London: Arnold, 2001).

7. Harold Garfinkel, *Studies in Ethnomethodology* (New Jersey: Prentice-Hall, 1967); Harvey Sacks, Emanuel A. Schegloff, and Gail Jefferson Sacks, "A Simplest Systematics for the Organisation of Turn-Taking in Conversation," *Language* 50, (1974): 697–735; Malcolm Coulthard Coulthard and Martin Montgomery, eds., *Studies in Discourse Analysis* (London: Longman, 1981); John Heritage, *Garfinkel and Ethnomethodology* (Cambridge: Polity Press, 1984); J. Maxwell Atkinson and John Heritage, *Structures of Social Action: Studies in Conversation Analysis* (Cambridge: Cambridge University Press, 1984).

8. See, for example, Andrew Tolson's collection, *Television Talk Shows: Discourse, Performance, Spectacle* (Mahwah: Lawrence Erlbaum, 2001).

9. Lois McNay, *Foucault and Feminism: Power, Gender and the Self* (Cambridge: Polity Press, 1992), 15; see also Michel Foucault, *The History of Sexuality*, trans. by Robert Hurley (London: Pelican, 1981); Michel Foucault, *Discipline and Punish: The Birth of the Prison*, trans. by Alan Sheridan (Harmondsworth: Penguin, 1977).

10. Sean Nixon, *Hard Looks: Masculinities, Spectatorship and Contemporary Consumption* (London: UCL Press, 1996); see also Rosalind Gill, "Power and the Production of Subjects: A Genealogy of the New Man and the New Lad," in *Masculinities and Men's Lifestyle Magazines*, Sociological Review Monographs, ed. Bethan Benwell (Oxford: Blackwell, 2003), 34–56.

11. Michael Billig, *Arguing and Thinking: A Rhetorical Approach to Social Psychology* (Cambridge: Cambridge University Press, 1987); Michael Billig, "Methodology and Scholarship in Understanding Ideological Explanation," in *Analysing Everyday Explanation: A Casebook of Methods*, ed. Charles Antaki (London: Sage, 1988), 199–215; Michael Billig, *Ideology and Opinions: Studies in Rhetorical Psychology* (Cambridge: Cambridge University Press, 1991).

12. Jonathan Potter and Margaret Wetherell, *Discourse and Social Psychology: Beyond Attitudes and Behaviour* (London: Sage, 1987).

13. Ibid.

14. Billig, *Arguing and Thinking*; Billig, *Ideology and Opinions*.

15. Rosalind Gill, "Discourse Analysis: Practical Implementation," in *Handbook of Qualitative Research Methods for Psychology and the Social Sciences*, ed. John Richardson (Leicester: British Psychological Society, 1996), 147.

16. Rosalind Gill, "Justifying Injustice: Broadcasters' Accounts of Inequality in Radio," in *Discourse Analytic Research*, eds. Erica Burman and Ian Parker (London: Routledge, 2000), 79–93.

17. Rosalind Gill, "Mediated Intimacy and Postfeminism: A Discourse Analytic Examination of Sex and Relationships Advice in a Women's Magazine," *Discourse & Communication* 3, no. 4 (2009): 345–69.

18. David Machin and Joanna Thornborrow, "Branding and Discourse: The Case of Cosmopolitan," *Discourse and Society* 14 (2003): 453–71.

19. Pantea Farvid and Virginia Braun, "'Most of Us Guys Are Raring to Go Anytime, Anyplace, Anywhere': Male and Female Sexuality in *Cleo* and *Cosmo*," *Sex Roles* 55 (2006): 295–310. See also Wendy Hollway, *Subjectivity and Method in Psychology: Gender, Meaning and Science* (London: Sage, 1989).

20. Farvid and Braun, "'Most of Us Guys.'" See also Annie Potts, "The Science/Fiction of Sex: John Gray's *Mars and Venus in the Bedroom*," *Sexualities* 1 (1998): 153–73.

21. George Ritzer, *The McDonaldization of Society 6* (Thousand Oaks: Pine Forge Press, 2011).

22. Eva Illouz, *Cold Intimacies: The Making of Emotional Capitalism* (Oxford: Polity Press, 2007).

23. Janice Winship, *Inside Women's Magazines* (London: Pandora, 1987); Rosemary Ballaster, Margaret Beeton, Elizabeth Fraser, and Sandra Hebron, *Women's Worlds: Ideology, Femininity and the Women's Magazine* (London: Macmillan Education, 1991); David Machin and Joanna Thornborrow, "Branding and Discourse: The Case of Cosmopolitan," *Discourse and Society* 14 (2003): 453–71.

24. Margaret Wetherell and Jonathan Potter, *Mapping the Language of Racism: Discourse and the Legitimation of Exploitation* (Hemel Hempstead: Harvester-Wheatsheaf, 1992).

25. Jonathan Potter, *Representing Reality: Discourse, Rhetoric and Social Construction* (London: Sage, 1996).

26. Potter and Wetherell, *Discourse and Social Psychology*, 168.

27. Jim Schenkein, "Sketch of the Analytic Mentality for the Study of Conversational Interaction," in *Studies in the Organisation of Conversational Interaction*, ed. Jim Schenkein (New York: Academic Press, 1978), 1–6.

28. Beverley Skeggs, ed., *Feminist Cultural Theory: Process and Production* (Manchester: Manchester University Press, 1995), 2–3.

29. "All day foreplay for your sexiest night ever," *Glamour*, March 2006, cited in Gill, "Mediated Intimacy and Postfeminism."

30. Tracy Cox, "Six ways to be better at everything in bed," *Glamour*, Nov. 2005, cited in Gill, "Mediated Intimacy and Postfeminism."

31. See Gill, "Mediated Intimacy and Postfeminism."

32. See Potter and Wetherell, *Discourse and Social Psychology*.

33. Potter, *Representing Reality*.

34. See J. Maxwell Atkinson and John Heritage, eds., *Structures of Social Action* (Cambridge: Cambridge University Press, 1984); Jonathan Potter, "Discourse Analysis and Constructionist Approaches: Theoretical

Background," in *Handbook of Qualitative Research Methods for Psychology and the Social Sciences*, ed. John Richardson (Leicester: British Psychological Society, 1996), 125–40.

35. Potter, "Discourse Analysis and Constructionist Approaches."

36. Ibid.

37. Laura Favaro, "Porn Trouble," *Australian Feminist Studies* 30, no. 86 (2016): 373–85.

38. Meg-John Barker, Rosalind Gill, and Laura Harvey. *Mediated Intimacy: Sex Advice in Media Culture* (Cambridge: Polity Press, 2017).

Further Reading

Billig, Michael, Susan Condor, Derek Edwards, Mike Gane, and Dave Middleton. *Ideological Dilemmas*. London: Sage, 1988.

Fairclough, Norman. *Media Discourse*. London; New York: E. Arnold, 1995.

Gill, Rosalind. *Gender and the Media*. Cambridge: Polity Press, 2007.

MacDonald, Myra. *Exploring Media Discourse*. London: Hodder, 2003.

3.
NARRATIVE
Jason Mittell

Most media tell stories. This truism applies to nearly every genre, from the obviously narrative forms of horror films and television soap operas, to factual documentaries and unscripted reality television shows, and even the compressed storytelling found in 30-second advertisements or the interactive narrative form of videogames. Most media embrace storytelling as a default, whether in the still images captured in a photograph or the tales of love and lust commonly found in pop music. No single method or approach would be adequate to understanding narrative media in full, as nearly every other chapter in this book offers insights relevant to analyzing stories in their various incarnations. This chapter considers the study of narrative as an approach itself, where the central object of analysis is storytelling form and structure, not primarily the content of a story.

As a theoretical field, the study of storytelling is often termed **narrative theory**, or sometimes the more technical term *narratology*. The core question that motivates most narrative theory is "How does storytelling work in a particular medium, genre, body of work, or example?" Sometimes a narrative analysis will examine an overarching trend, such as the use of flashbacks in primetime television dramas, or take a comparative perspective, such as contrasting character construction in novels versus comic books or videogames, or drill down into a specific text, such as the nested storyworlds in the film *Inception* (2010). In all such studies, the analysis is interested less in the specific meanings of a text than in the broader structures and forms that enable meanings to be made. In other words, a narrative analyst doesn't ask "What does this story mean?" as much as "How does this story make meaning?" Certainly, the formal insights

of narrative analysis can be applied to other methods and approaches, helping to explain how stories perpetuate ideologies, influence cultural representations, or shape viewer experiences, but these questions are usually secondary to a narrative theorist who is looking at the structures of storytelling themselves.

One of the common tendencies of narrative theory is to provide distinctions between categories, often leading to a **taxonomy** of narrative concepts, techniques, and structures. Nearly all narrative analyses depend on a central distinction: the differences between narrative story, discourse, and medium. The concept of story seems obvious, as it is such a common term, but it holds a particular meaning for narrative theory—the **story** consists of the characters, setting, and events that occur within a narrative. When we imagine what is happening within a narrative, we are constructing the story within our minds. Thus, for the classic fairy tale "Cinderella," the story consists of a girl who is condemned to servitude by her evil stepmother, but with the help of her fairy godmother, she manages to attend a ball and capture the heart of a prince, who rescues and marries her. As with most folk tales, there are numerous variations and adaptations that can change the story elements: Cinderella's father is sometimes dead and sometimes in cahoots with her stepmother, the prince might find Cinderella by a glass slipper, a bracelet, or a ring, or she may be helped by a wishing tree or magical item rather than a fairy godmother. A narrative analysis might examine such variations to see how they emerge over time and what core patterns and elements remain within the story across retellings.

A story is only accessible to us through a specific instance of storytelling, usually called the **narrative**

discourse. The same story can be told in countless different ways, which greatly impacts what sense we make of a narrative. We could tell "Cinderella" solely from her perspective, providing insight into her thought processes and limited by her knowledge and experiences, or it could include the experiences of other characters by representing the attitudes and experiences of the prince, the stepmother, or others. It could narrate the story chronologically, or jumble the timeframe by starting with Cinderella's wedding to the prince, flashing back to her earlier story. A telling might take a long time to portray the prince's hunt for his beloved to create suspense and interest, or simply skip over his process in a single sentence or film edit. In these various versions, the story remains the same, as the same characters have the same experiences in the same setting, but the storytelling changes dramatically by altering the narrative discourse. One of the crucial aspects of narrative theory is outlining the various ways that a single story might be told via very different techniques of narrative discourse, and understanding the impact of such storytelling changes.

The third main category of any narrative is its **medium**, or the format that the particular storytelling takes. The same story can be told in a wide range of different media, from print to comic book to live-action film to animated film to videogame—all of which have seen adaptations of the "Cinderella" story. One common tenet of narrative theory is that storytelling is medium independent, meaning that narrative structures and techniques can be used across different media. This is certainly true to a degree, as a flashback could be used in a comic book just as easily as a film. However, there are some techniques that are much more tied to a specific medium, such as a first-person perspective, which takes on a far different effect when we can read a character's internal thoughts in a novel than visually representing their experiences in a film. Likewise, a videogame creates an interactive experience where both narrative discourse and story can change in reaction to a player's actions, a facet of storytelling that is not easily translatable to non-interactive media like television or comics. Thus narrative theorists are split as to whether medium shapes storytelling to the point that it requires more medium-specific approaches, or whether medium independence can still guide analysis. Regardless, the analysis of any narrative needs to consider how it is shaped by its medium and what elements might be understood more fully by thinking across media forms, a perspective that becomes more by thinking about the intellectual history of narrative theory.

Intellectual History

The earliest narrative theory does not account for videogames, television, films, or even novels. Arguably the first work of narrative theory is one of the oldest works of aesthetic philosophy that has survived: Aristotle's *Poetics*.[1] Aristotle was writing about the two main storytelling media of ancient Greece, poetry and drama, which were designed to be performed orally. Unlike most of the theorists discussed in this book, Aristotle was not writing for an audience of other academics to provide a better critical understanding of narratives; instead, Aristotle was writing what we might call **practical theory** to inspire an audience of storytellers to create better narratives. *Poetics* introduced many key concepts that still are used today, including the different genres of tragedy, comedy, and epic; the importance of a well-balanced plot and goal-driven protagonists; and the emotional impact of pathos and catharsis. These concepts were presented to make an argument, aimed at poets and dramatists who valued certain forms of storytelling over others, as Aristotle believed that particular narrative techniques were more effective than others and that writers should embrace those elements in their plays and poems. Even though its audience was storytellers, *Poetics* has since been a cornerstone of narrative theory as written by academics.

Practical theory has survived as a popular thread of narrative analysis, typically featuring successful storytellers sharing their insights into their craft. We can see such a tradition in the literary criticism of Henry James and Annie Dillard, the comics criticism of Will Eisner and Scott McCloud, and the game design writings of Katie Salen and Eric Zimmerman, all of which provide a set of critical concepts that emerge from the writers' own creative work but also have influenced the academic analysis of their respective media. The most common form of practical narrative theory today are screenwriting manuals, which are widely read by aspiring film and television writers and taught in screenwriting courses. Manuals by writers like Syd Field or Robert McKee not only influence the way that films and television series are written, but they provide a vocabulary for both critical analysis and everyday discussion, popularizing concepts like the three-act structure and inciting incidents.[2]

While practical theory can have tremendous influence amongst narrative creators, scholars have developed their own body of **critical theory**, writings that seek primarily to analyze and understand existing narratives, not guide storytellers to create new ones. The modern academic study of narratives emerged in the first half of the twentieth century within literary criticism in a number of related schools of thought —so-called Russian Formalists focused their attention on the norms and conventions that could be found across various literary forms and first posited the distinction between story and discourse, while the rise of New Criticism in the United States emphasized close analysis of literary texts rather than focusing on authorial biography or literary history. Out of these approaches to close textual analysis, the subfield of narratology developed in the 1960s under the influence of **structuralism** as a broader academic trend in both America and Europe. The structuralist turn in the humanities emphasized how cultural forms like narratives share common underlying norms and patterns, emphasizing both ahistorical universals and a systematic, almost scientific approach to categorizing culture through taxonomies and binary oppositions. **Narratology** is the systematic analysis of narratives, seeking underlying structures and norms that transcend historical moments, genres, and even media incarnations.

Some structuralist narratology focuses on story, looking for overarching patterns in the plots of common narratives; for instance, Vladimir Propp was a Russian scholar who analyzed dozens of folktales to deduce a common structure of narrative events and character functions. Although Propp wrote his major book *Morphology of the Folktale* in 1928, it became influential only when translated into English in the late-1950s and was integrated into the structuralist theories of Claude Lévi-Strauss, Roland Barthes, and Tzvetan Todorov.[3] Propp's approach was extended to film in the 1970s, with Will Wright's analysis of Westerns as structured by shared plots and character functions in a manner that emphasizes the underlying cultural conflicts between nature and civilization. Similarly, the mythological analysis of Joseph Campbell demonstrates the underlying "monomyth" of the hero's journey that he claims functions as a cultural universal structuring all storytelling; he became particularly influential in screenwriting practical theory of the 1970s and beyond, influenced by George Lucas's use of Campbell's theory as inspiration for *Star Wars* (1977).[4] While structuralist accounts of story can be influential to creators looking to tap into widespread tropes and myths, as an analytic approach it tends to focus too broadly on generalities, ignoring textual differences and cultural specificities that other approaches emphasize.

The most influential structuralist narratology within academia focuses on narrative discourse, looking to categorize the various ways that a story can be told. Such scholarship, innovated in the 1960s and 1970s by Barthes, Todorov, Gérard Genette, Jonathan Culler, Gerald Prince, Meir Sternberg, and Mieke Bal, among others, provides a comprehensive vocabulary for the various storytelling techniques that can be found in narratives across media. In many ways, these structuralist narratologists sought to create a grammar of storytelling, comparable to the taxonomic efforts of linguistics, which was an important influence on structuralism as an academic movement. This formative narratology provided the basis of most narrative analysis to come, with key concepts outlining the dimensions of temporality, narrative perspective, characterization, narration, and narrative tense. Although these narratologists were generally interested in devising a storytelling grammar that transcended any specific medium, they were almost exclusively focused on literature and the prose fiction forms of the novel and short stories, rather than concerned with visual and sonic forms of storytelling.

Film studies emerged in the academy in the 1960s under the influence of structuralism, with a focus on semiotic approaches to the construction of meaning, as discussed in this volume's chapter on representation. The two most influential works of film narratology came in the late-1970s and 1980s; the first was by Seymour Chatman, who explored how to apply and adjust concepts from literary narratology to the study of film, including perspective, narration, and authorship.[5] David Bordwell built upon Chatman's work to offer a more comprehensive model of the formal techniques of storytelling specific to the film medium, along with two other important innovations.[6] First, Bordwell was not interested in timeless, universal structures, but rather understanding specific storytelling practices that emerge at a particular time in relation to industrial, technological, and cultural contexts, an approach he terms **historical poetics**. Second, Bordwell explored how viewers make sense of a story through a theory of **narrative comprehension** that builds upon emerging insights in cognitive psychology to posit an active spectator posing questions and making hypotheses to construct the story within their mind as they view a film; this approach is discussed in more depth in Chapter 13 of this volume. Chatman and Bordwell laid the groundwork for many studies of film narrative and established influential analytic models for moving-image storytelling that would be extended to other media.

Even though storytelling is a crucial aspect of television in many genres and formats, media scholars have been less interested in exploring television narrative form until recently. The major exception is Robert Allen's work on soap operas in the 1980s, as he added another key element to historical poetics: a focus on viewing practices.[7] For Allen, the interaction between a text and its consumer, whether a prose reader or television viewer, is the site where narrative comes into being; thus, he proposes a **reader-oriented poetics** to consider how the storytelling strategies of a text can be engaged with by a consumer. In studying soap operas, Allen considers the crucial form of **seriality** as a continuing narrative broken into installments, and explores how viewers incorporate such storytelling into their everyday lives and social interactions, a topic that Robyn Warhol has extended by looking at the intersections of narrative form and gender as a social category.[8] In more recent years, media scholars have been more attentive to narrative form as a key aspect of the television medium, emphasizing new blends between episodic and serial form, and considering how television viewers incorporate new technologies of viewing and social networking to extend their engagement with series.

Emerging forms of media storytelling have grappled with narrative theory as well. Videogames have fast developed into a central entertainment medium in recent decades; while they seemingly can be seen as a narrative form, many scholars in game studies have questioned the applicability of narratology to the medium. As discussed in Chapter 25 on games/gaming, many so-called ludologists view the core facet of videogames as gameplay, regarding the characters, settings, and narrative events as mere window-dressing on top of the central interactive practices and designed structures that are unique to games. Games certainly challenge the medium-independent approach to narratology, as the variability of both story and discourse in response to reader activity has few precedents in other media; however, scholars like Janet Murray, Henry Jenkins, Marie-Laure Ryan, and Jesper Juul have all shown how narratives are important aspects of videogames and have developed some medium-specific theories. A new type of narrative analysis focuses on **transmedia storytelling**, a term coined by Jenkins to explore narratives that extend into an array of different media rather than focused on a single core medium with potential auxiliary paratexts.[9] Narratology is well-suited to consider new media, as its categorical emphasis allows scholars to apply its terms to new forms, either demonstrating cross-media continuities or developing new concepts to account for emerging practices.

Major Modes and Concepts

There is no universally accepted definition of a narrative, but there is general consensus about the elements that comprise a narrative. Any narrative consists of *a sequence of events involving characters that takes place in a particular setting*—thus the first step to understanding narratives is clarifying the concepts of characters, events, and setting. For most media narratives, a **character** is a person who does things in a story, but as always with such categories, there are exceptions. Sometimes a character need not be a person, as with the animated animals in many cartoons, or even a living being, like the droids in the *Star Wars* franchise; the most memorable character in *2001: A Space Odyssey* (1968), the computer HAL, does not even have a physical presence. In some instances, a character is completely passive for much of a story, such as the comatose love interest Peter in *While You Were Sleeping* (1995), or might even be deceased throughout the narrative, like Bruce Wayne's parents who were memorably murdered in Batman's backstory. But in all of these instances, these figures are more clearly characters than "extras" who appear in a crowd scene to function more as part of the setting than as distinct characters.

Characters can serve a number of different narrative functions, with one key variable being the relative prominence of any character within the story. **Primary characters** are those who are central to the narrative, both in terms of their importance to the core story and their proximity to the audience in terms of time spent on-screen and the amount of access viewers have to their goals, thoughts, and experiences. Usually primary characters are those that viewers spend the most time with, although at times a character can be central to the plot but appear little on-screen, as with Harry Lime in *The Third Man* (1949), who is central to the plot but appears only briefly. Primary characters can be framed explicitly as protagonists or antagonists, especially in genres with clear heroes and villains, or might be more ambiguous in terms of their morality or audience allegiance. **Secondary characters** work to support the main plot, often appearing less frequently on-screen or revealing less of their own goals or beliefs than the main characters do. However, narratives can often be distinguished by the quality of their secondary characters; for instance, *Casablanca* (1942) is renowned for its great central romance and political plots, but much of its charm comes from the engaging secondary characters, including Louis, Ferrari, Sam, and Carl. Finally, **tertiary characters** are marginal figures that rarely exhibit little more than plot functionality or obstacles for primary characters. In long-form serialized narratives, like television or comics, one of the interesting ways that stories develop can be through shifting constellations of character functions, as marginal tertiary characters shift to the center or main protagonists are killed off, as in the television series *Game of Thrones* (HBO, 2011–).

Scholarship on characters explores how a narrative can imbue certain figures with a sense of interior life, motivation, and emotional depth to create empathy for audiences and generate the connections that engage viewers. For performance-based media like film and television, the study of characters has clear overlap with the analysis of acting, as performers create characters through their collaborations with directors, writers, and other production personnel, as discussed in Chapter 7 on acting. Some scholars have suggested that characters are much more central in serialized media, such as television and comics, as audiences establish relationships with such fictional people that override plot as the primary point of engagement, while stand-alone narratives, such as feature films, rely more on plots and events than elaborated characters. For both stand-alone narratives and ongoing series, relationships between characters can be a major drive for viewer pleasure, with some viewers forging their own connections to some pairings that may be either represented or hoped for in a text.

The concept of **narrative event** seems obvious, as it is simply something that happens in a story, but there are more complications to understand. One important distinction is between major or minor events, where a major event is essential to the narrative while minor events are more optional—every telling of "Cinderella" must include her meeting and falling in love with the prince (or it would constitute a revisionist take on the tale), but the fairy godmother changing a pumpkin into a carriage is a minor event that could be left out without changing the core story. The distinction between major and minor events typically depends on a crucial element of storytelling: **causality**. If one event causes a future event to happen, it's usually a major element in the plot as, typically, stories present a series of events in a cause and effect relationship. Events always occur chronologically within the story, as

that is how characters experience them (except for rare instances of time travel), but can be shifted in the discourse through techniques discussed below. Events are so central to a narrative that when we tell a story to someone else, we typically recount the major events over anything else.

The final essential narrative element is **setting**, where and when a story takes place. Setting can be defining for genres, such as for Westerns and science fiction, or the key element that distinguishes a single text, as with *Mad Men*'s (AMC, 2007–15) 1960s New York or Middle Earth in the *Lord of the Rings* (2001–03) series. For genres like fantasy and science fiction, the setting also includes various rules and possibilities of the fictional universe that diverge from real life, as with the different rules that vampires must follow or how they can be killed in various texts like *Dracula*, *Buffy the Vampire Slayer* (WB/UPN, 1997–2003), and *True Blood* (HBO, 2008–14). Sometimes an adaptation can significantly revise a story by changing its setting, as is common with both theatrical and film versions of Shakespeare plays. For the interactive medium of videogames, the ability to explore and navigate a setting is an appealing innovation of the form, especially when a game is adapted from a preexisting narrative text or franchise that players might already know. For instance, wandering the virtual city of Springfield is a chief appeal for *The Simpsons* (Fox, 1989–) videogames. Scholars have extended the concept of setting to a broader notion of **storyworld**, meaning the full story universe conveyed by a narrative comprising the setting, characters, and events—a storyworld is never fully presented by the discourse, as viewers fill in gaps to imagine a full coherent universe that is only presented selectively by a narrative. For an ongoing series, one crucial variable is the cumulative coherence of the storyworld, as many texts embrace full continuity across episodes while others assume that events will be forgotten across installments, even though they take place in the same setting with the same characters. One of the initial tasks of any narrative is to establish both the storyworld and the storytelling rules that it will follow in presenting the story.

Such rules of storytelling can be understood as norms that may or may not be shared by other texts. Every text establishes its own particular **intrinsic norms**, storytelling rules that are particular to its own storyworld and narrative discourse. The television series *Lost* (ABC, 2004–10) follows intrinsic norms of its storyworld, as with how time travel works on its mystical island, and norms unique to its narrative discourse, as with its patterned use of flashbacks within its episodic structure. Additionally, a shift in established norms can be an exciting moment in a narrative, as with *Lost*'s surprising shift from flashbacks to flash-forwards at the end of its third season. Narratives also rely upon **extrinsic norms** that surpass the bounds of any single text; genres are a key source of extrinsic norms, as with the horror film's character of the monster, the use of voiceover narration in *film noir*, and withholding essential narrative information in mysteries. Extrinsic norms can also be tied to a historic trend, as with the rise of so-called puzzle films since the 1990s; an industrial practice, as with U.S. premium cable channels presenting television series without commercial breaks; or a technological development, as with the emergence of sound films allowing specific musical cues to signal emotional reactions. While many narrative analyses focus on a single text, it is always crucial to remember that texts are always created in a broader context of industries, technologies, and other texts that can help shape how any single story is told.

One central task of any narrative is to manage information. Some **narrative information** is within the storyworld, as some characters know different things about past events than other characters, a distinction that is essential to the mystery genre where the discovery of story information is the main narrative goal. Viewer knowledge can align or diverge from characters in various ways, as sometimes we wonder what a particular character is hiding, while other times we share their secrets and can understand what other characters cannot. Thus in *The Sixth Sense* (1999), viewers learn about the secrets that Cole is hiding only when Malcolm discovers them, allowing us to rethink everything we have seen once the film reveals its final twist. Information management and knowledge differentials can be particularly challenging in serial narratives, as viewer memories can fade and some viewers might not have seen every episode; producers use strategies like internal redundancies and retellings, as well as paratextual "previously on" recaps and written synopses to remind viewers of previous events and relationships.

Differences in narrative information can be a main storytelling drive for viewers and their emotional engagement. When viewers lack information about the storyworld's past or present, it prompts **curiosity** about what might have previously happened. Such curiosity can be tied to mysteries—who killed Marion Crane in *Psycho* (1960)?—or underlying character motivations—why does Livia Soprano treat her son

Tony so badly on *The Sopranos* (HBO, 1999–2007)? Even if the narrative discourse proceeds chronologically forward, we still watch in hope that the backstory will be revealed and our curiosity will be sated. Most narratives focus primarily on revealing subsequent story information, answering the question "What will happen next?", driving viewers' **anticipation** of what is to come. Sometimes a narrative is designed to prompt anticipation of a future event that is particularly undesirable, as when a time-bomb is ticking or a hero is in peril—such anticipation of unwelcome events is called **suspense**, and it can prompt some of the most compelling emotional responses, even when savvy viewers know full well that the hero must survive for future episodes or sequels. Finally, some new information can be completely unanticipated, prompting **surprise** with a narrative twist or stunning revelation—while surprise seems like an important emotional reaction to storytelling, critics and creators have both suggested that it is actually a shallower and less powerful experience than coupling anticipation and curiosity to set-up story revelations and generate suspense. Narrative analysts can look at how stories manage narrative information and prompt audience reactions to succeed or fail in achieving their emotional goals.

One of the crucial storytelling elements integral to engaging readers and viewers is **temporality**, or the use and manipulation of time. Every narrative has multiple layers of temporality that corresponds to the three categories of story, discourse, and medium. **Story time** is the temporality as it occurs within the storyworld, which is typically linear and chronological (unless time travel is an intrinsic norm). **Discourse time** is the temporal sequence, duration, and choices as presented in the storytelling, not as it is experienced by the characters. In the film *Pulp Fiction* (1994), discourse time is nonlinear, jumping around between episodes and perspectives with some repetition and a flashback. However, story time is straightforward, commencing twenty years before the main action in a flashback to Butch's childhood when he received his father's gold watch and ultimately concluding with Butch and Marcellus escaping captivity—these two scenes are presented back-to-back in the middle of the movie, highlighting the film's atemporal sequence. While on first viewing *Pulp Fiction* offers a jumbled chronology in its narrative discourse, a viewer does attempt to piece together a coherent storyworld that fits together logically in their mind; rewatching the film encourages even more coherence in recognizing patterns and continuities to draw connections and map chronologies.

One of the main distinctions between literature and screen-based media like film and television is how they treat temporality in the third level of medium. The time it takes to consume a book is quite variable and idiosyncratic to particular readers, as we all read at different paces and might sometimes reread sections or take lengthy pauses between chapters. Films and television are much more uniform in how we consume them, leading to particular norms of **screen time** structured by the medium. Film traditionally has been consumed with a strict chronology, scheduled by cinema screenings and running straight through from start to finish. Television episodes can be even more restricted in screen time, as the broadcast schedule mandates that a given episode might only ever air at a single prescribed time; likewise, in U.S. television, commercial breaks often disrupt the narrative at specific moments that may or may not have been planned by the producers. The rise of DVDs, DVRs, and streaming in the 2000s has transformed the norms of screen time, as viewers now can watch films and television episodes on their own schedules, as well as pausing, rewatching, and skipping around in a manner more comparable to reading than traditional cinema or broadcast television. However, screen media are still more regimented by length, with norms of episode and feature film duration: Sitcom episodes typically last 22–24 minutes (without ad breaks), drama episodes run around 42–46 minutes, and feature films usually run between 90 and 150 minutes, all of which are much narrower ranges than the time it takes to read a novel.

Another major aspect of screen time involves the narrative structure of **seriality**, when a story is broken up into installments and released with intervening gaps between episodes. Television is certainly the most prominent serial medium, with nearly every program broken into episodes presented in daily or weekly installments, creating a screen-time pattern that structures the overall narrative design. With daytime soap operas, the screen time creates a daily ritual that defines the cultural experience of the genre as part of viewers' everyday lives; for primetime series, the weekly schedule can create so-called "appointment television" with viewers eager to tune in to satisfy their anticipation and curiosity. Netflix has popularized the "full-drop season," with all of a season's episodes released at once, leading to a very different mode of narrative consumption that many term "binge watching." Seriality and its various modes of distribution and consumption all raise interesting research questions beyond temporality,

ranging from the industry's strategies for building ongoing franchises with committed audiences across media, to the various methods that audiences use to fill gaps between episodes via theorizing, paratextual consumption and production, and other forms of participatory fandom.

Such viewing practices point to a significant research area for narrative scholars: studying the reception and comprehension of narratives. As discussed in other chapters, media scholars cannot assume how viewers will make sense of or engage with a narrative by analyzing the text alone; instead we have to look at actual reception practices to understand the multiple ways that viewers might consume a text. For narrative analysis, one useful method is to examine **paratexts** that surround a text, like reviews and previews, and those that encourage discussion between viewers, like comment threads and wikis, or fan productions, like remix videos or fan fiction, all of which are discussed more in Chapter 17 of this volume. By exploring such sites, we can get a sense of the various ways that viewers make sense of a narrative beyond just the apparent design of the producers, as such reception research typically demonstrates the breadth of viewer responses and practices, rather than one singular norm of consumption. We can also use theoretical models like cognitive studies or psychoanalysis that point to possible ways that viewers might comprehend, engage with, and be absorbed by a narrative, but such potential experiences can never be assumed to match real viewing practices without studying actual audiences or their paratextual traces.

As noted earlier, the question of **medium specificity** has been debated amongst narrative scholars. While many elements of narrative analysis pertain to every medium, such as the division of story and discourse or variations of temporality, it is vital to see how the specific incarnations of such elements adapt to different media. Narrative scholars need to attend to the technological features and institutional practices that help shape a medium's storytelling possibilities, and consider how such elements change in the wake of media transformations. For instance, the screen-time structures of series television are undergoing major shifts as a result of new digital modes of distribution, with storytelling techniques changing in reaction to the rise of on-demand streaming or boxed-set viewing as new alternatives to the broadcast schedule. The rise of transmedia storytelling further complicates the notion of medium specificity, as a narrative may be divided across numerous formats and platforms, each of which has its own typical norms and possibilities—since this form is still emerging, scholars can approach transmedia with an evaluative eye to look at how each segment fits with its medium strengths, and how the pieces coalesce into an effective whole. One common transmedia trend that invites narrative analysis is the prevalence of tie-in videogames based on existing storyworlds from film, comics, and television, as the shift into an interactive game form demands shifts in narrative strategies that highlight the norms of each medium.

One of the common critiques of narratology is that it is overly focused on formal elements as isolated from cultural politics and historical contexts, but narrative analysis has broadened in scope to include such issues as developed within cultural studies since the field's structuralist origins. Amongst literary scholars, **feminist narratology**, as led by Susan Lanser and Robyn Warhol, challenges the universal assumptions of structuralism, highlighting how gender can often shape perspectives about emotional response, authorship, and other underlying issues in narrative. For screen media, work on melodrama by Christine Gledhill and Linda Williams emphasizes how narrative structures are embedded in gendered assumptions, Theresa de Lauretis analyzes how the Oedipus plot frames desire in starkly gendered terms, and Warhol explores sentimentality as a gendered emotional response triggered by narrative forms in a range of different media.[10] Scholars have employed such political approaches to explore other axes of difference or power relations as well, including how characterization helps reinforce racial divisions, how default heterosexuality is embedded in many plot structures, and how other dominant ideologies might be structured by narrative forms. In all such instances, formal analyses of narrative can help us better understand the political and social issues that motivate many media scholars, as explored in many other chapters of this book; likewise, the insights of other approaches can make sure that narratological analyses consider historical and cultural contexts, rather than just treating forms as universal and ahistorical.

Case Study: *Veronica Mars*'s Pilot in Slow-Motion

More than with many theories and approaches, narrative analysis demands application to specific examples in order to be understood, as it does not make much sense as abstract philosophy or theory. The case study I have chosen to discuss is a section from my book, *Complex TV: The Poetics of Contemporary*

Television Storytelling.[11] The book develops television-specific narrative theories and concepts, as applied to examples from contemporary prime-time series, with particular focus on issues like characterization, narrative comprehension, paratexts, authorship, and the gender politics of serial melodrama. This case study concludes the chapter on "Beginnings," which explores the poetics of television pilot episodes and culminates in the close analysis of the pilot of *Veronica Mars* (UPN/The CW, 2004–06). After reviewing some of the concepts from the longer chapter, I outline how I approached the case study and how such analysis might be further extended.

Pilots are unusual episodes of television, as they serve a variety of functions and are addressed to different audiences. First and foremost, they target an industrial audience of network executives who must be convinced that the script is promising enough to fund production of a pilot, and then that the produced episode is of sufficient quality and potential appeal to audiences to schedule as a series. For comedies, a pilot needs to establish the situation and cast of characters, but most producers and many audiences understand that a comic ensemble can take time to gel, meaning that most great television comedies do not find their rhythm until later in their first season or beyond. For serialized dramas, the pilot must launch an ongoing storyline, establish setting, characters, and relationships, and create a hook that interests viewers enough to keep them watching week after week. Thus any pilot must be evaluated within that context, as the strategies aimed at convincing executives to pick up the series might be different from what might inspire audiences to continue viewing a series.

Another central goal of a pilot episode is to effectively teach viewers how to watch the series, establishing intrinsic and extrinsic norms appropriate to the text. This includes identifying the program's genre category making relevant connections to other narratives, establishing any ongoing episodic or seasonal patterns, and iterating the narrative devices that the series will typically use. Every narrative in any medium uses the beginning of its storytelling to teach its readers or viewers what to expect and how to consume the text. A film's opening establishes its intrinsic norms, typically in a condensed fashion to move onto the meat of the story, while the opening pages of a written novel or comic book teach readers what to expect moving forward. Probably the most elaborated opening sequences are in videogames, which frequently use early tutorial levels to literally teach players how to move forward in the game by establishing norms of controller use, spatial navigation, avatar features, and other elements of both the storyworld and gameplay. Although not as explicitly framed as tutorials as in videogames, pilot episodes similarly offer an introduction to the storyworld and its storytelling that provides guidance for viewers moving forward.

With these elements of pilot episodes in mind, why did I choose *Veronica Mars* as a case study for my book? As with any research project, there are numerous reasons for such choices. For one, it is both an exceptional pilot and an ordinary one—it is a quite effective 43 minutes of screen storytelling, covering a remarkable amount of plot and character information while also establishing a distinctive tone that sets it apart from many other pilots. At the same time, it is more typical than many pilots, as it aired on a commercial broadcast network, UPN, without the highbrow ambitions of cable dramas from HBO or AMC, and it embraces genre norms from both teen dramas and detective stories, two commonplace types of television programming. It is thus both a more interesting and complex example than many pilots but also more typical of how television works than other more exceptional pilots, like those for *Deadwood* (HBO, 2004–06), *Dexter* (Showtime, 2006–13), or *Breaking Bad* (AMC, 2008–13).

The *Veronica Mars* pilot is also relevant to many of the issues explored in my book, and thus the case study resonates across other chapters. It features the balance between episodic and serial forms that I discuss throughout *Complex TV*, it embraces self-conscious storytelling devices like flashbacks and voiceover, it foregrounds characterization and moral ambiguity, and it centers on a female protagonist with links to serial melodrama as a narrative form, all of which echo arguments developed throughout the book. When developing a long-form scholarly argument in a book manuscript, finding examples that resonate across multiple chapters and ideas is an efficient way to reinforce ideas and build continuity across what can be many pages of scholarship. The example fit well with some of the important established scholarship I wanted to bring into the discussion, especially David Bordwell's work on the opening moments of films teaching viewers how to watch and Robert Allen's study of the reader-oriented poetics of serial television. Finally, the *Veronica Mars* pilot is a personal favorite, which both reinforces ideas about evaluation explored elsewhere in the book and makes the research process of repeatedly viewing and analyzing an episode enjoyable, an aspect of

scholarship that should not be overlooked in charting out research projects.

Methodologically, most narrative scholarship centers on close reading of media texts, and this chapter is no different—most of the analysis involves watching, describing, categorizing, and illuminating the elements found in the episode. When the primary source material is a media text, there is still some research involved in determining what version is appropriate to analyze, and whenever possible, it is useful to gather production documents to provide insight into the making of the text. For *Veronica Mars*, the question of version is crucial: as discussed in the chapter, the original script and produced version of the pilot are different from the episode as broadcast on UPN, and later the original-produced version was released on DVD. Most differences were minor, but the crucial change was in the opening scene: the script and producer cut started *in media res* (mid-story) with a noir-esque scene of Veronica doing surveillance before flashing back to an earlier moment, while the UPN version begins at that earlier moment in a sunny high school parking lot with no framing flashback, establishing a distinctly different initial genre, mood, and attitude. Since the opening moments of any story teach us how to watch, understanding the significance of these different openings is essential to a narrative analysis. To understand these differences, I analyzed the various versions, compared them with the script (as found on creator Rob Thomas's website), and read interviews with Thomas to understand why the changes were made, highlighting how looking at a finished media text alone is insufficient to detailed analysis.

As I analyzed the episode, I tried to chart the visual and aural cues in the text that would lead a first-time viewer to make sense of the unfolding storyworld. The goal of this type of analysis is to understand the multi-faceted formal systems necessary to simply ensure viewer comprehension, especially of a newly established narrative universe. While I would not claim that the producers consciously designed the episode to make every single element aid viewer comprehension, there are many choices that must be made in staging, camerawork, editing, and sound that all work together to create a coherent narrative experience. Many of these cues and norms are understood intuitively by both producers and viewers, such as the shift in space signaled by an edit or the establishment of narrative perspective cued by a voiceover. But by slowing down the comprehension process to analyze each of these devices in practice, we can

Figures 3.1 and 3.2 The original producer version of *Veronica Mars* pilot introduces Veronica in a *film noir* style stakeout, while the UPN broadcast edit (aired September 22, 2004) reveals her in a more typical high school setting.

better understand the strategies employed to tell a story and appreciate both the craft of production and complexity of meanings offered by a seemingly simple television episode. As a case study, my primary goal was to analyze how pilots work as a form of television storytelling, and thus my analysis aimed to highlight the historical poetics of this particular pilot as an example of broader techniques and trends.

Although my primary approach to *Veronica Mars* was formal narrative analysis, I was still interested in pointing toward relevant cultural questions of gender central to both the episode and the series as a whole. Because the series is a genre mixture of the more masculinist detective story with the more feminized mode of teen drama, I highlight how the character of Veronica both draws upon and challenges gender norms for a teenage girl, and the entire constellation of characters reverses many typical gender and genre assumptions. If we were to extend this analysis more fully, we could consider how the gender norms impact the program's reception, looking to audience reactions to the series and trying to understand the differences between male and female viewing reactions and appeals. We could also consider other axes of difference by analyzing the clashing class politics explicitly raised by the series and its "town without a middle class," as well as the less explicit racial politics raised by its multiethnic ensemble but with a white family clearly at its center. Narrative analysis can highlight how the story structures power differences and representations by giving varying levels of focus and agency to different characters or groups, as well as by charting how particular storylines or characters are granted more emotional centrality that might promote greater viewer empathy with some characters over others.

Other narrative research could extend beyond the pilot analysis as well. As suggested above, a pilot is a distinct and atypical episode, so it would be interesting to compare the pilot with future episodes of the series—what intrinsic norms change and what remains the same? How might future episodes both welcome new viewers and build on assumptions that viewers had seen previous installments? We could also look at the first episode of the second and third seasons, each functioning as a mini-pilot to launch new story arcs and welcome new viewers but also assuming that returning fans are eager to catch up with old characters. The third season of *Veronica Mars* differed from the first two in being set in college instead of high school, so comparing those narrative norms would be particularly interesting to understand how new settings are established. One of the challenges of close analysis of a series is that the portion of the text that you choose to analyze is always going to be atypical in some ways, so it is important to acknowledge how an analysis of one episode might differ from looking at other episodes.

Finally, we might consider the unusual production history of *Veronica Mars*—it aired for two seasons on UPN, before that network merged with The WB to form The CW, which retained the series for one more season under a somewhat different serial narrative structure. The CW canceled it due to lagging ratings, but Rob Thomas proposed a form of "reboot" to flash forward to after Veronica graduated college and was in training in the FBI Academy—Thomas produced a brief "pitch video" for that new setting, which circulated widely online among fans. It was unsuccessful and the series was dormant for seven years, until Thomas launched a historic Kickstarter campaign to produce a film version, which was released in 2014. The film ignored the FBI plot line, jumping forward years from where the television series left off. An interesting narrative analysis could examine how the film employed similar or different storytelling norms and techniques from the television show, attempting to account for any changes as related to the shift in medium or what had changed in production

techniques over the seven-year gap. Another interesting question is how the film addresses multiple types of viewers, ranging from those brand-new to the storyworld, to television viewers who had not watched the series for many years, to dedicated fans who had rewatched episodes in recent years—such differentials in viewer knowledge lead to multiple levels of address, requiring patience for both redundancy and confusion, while teaching viewers how to make sense of this new medium and multiyear gap.

This chapter has aimed to outline the key questions, methods, and possibilities of narrative analysis. One strength of narrative analysis is that it meshes well with other approaches outlined in this book, as there are no innate conflicts between narrative theory and other theoretical models. Some topics are readily apparent in their overlap, such as cognitive theories of narrative comprehension or the study of narrative genres or paratexts. Others might be less obvious but are still compatible, such as considerations of how narrative structures build upon notions of desire and pleasure discussed by psychoanalytic theory, or how fan studies can help us make sense of how viewers engage with narrative structures. Narrative theory is also well poised to consider how new developments in technology, industry, and viewer practice might impact storytelling, as the concepts and norms applying to one medium or historical moment can be viewed in contrast to newer shifts; we are certainly experiencing such changes now, including the rise of full-drop streaming distribution, new formats in web series and gaming, and emerging systems of immersive interactive narrative via virtual reality. No matter what your ultimate research goal and method might be, having a clear understanding of narrative structure, forms, and terminology will make you a better media critic and allow you to make more precise and insightful analyses of the widespread practice of media storytelling.

Notes

1. Aristotle, *Poetics*, trans. Gerald Frank Else (Ann Arbor: University of Michigan Press, 1967).
2. Syd Field, *Screenplay: The Foundations of Screenwriting*, revised edition (New York: Delta, 2005); Robert McKee, *Story: Substance, Structure, Style and the Principles of Screenwriting* (New York: Regan Books, 1997).
3. Vladimir Propp, *Morphology of the Folktale*, trans. Lawrence Scott (Austin: University of Texas Press, 1968). For other key European structuralist theory, see

Roland Barthes, *Image-Music-Text*, trans. Stephen Heath (New York: Hill and Wang, 1978); Claude Lévi-Strauss, *Myth and Meaning* (Toronto: University of Toronto Press, 1978); Tzvetan Todorov, *The Fantastic: A Structural Approach to a Literary Genre*, trans. Richard Howard (Ithaca, NY: Cornell University Press, 1975).

4. Joseph Campbell, *The Hero with a Thousand Faces* (Princeton: Princeton University Press, 1973); Will Wright, *Sixguns and Society: A Structural Study of the Western* (Berkeley, CA: University of California Press, 1977).

5. Seymour Chatman, *Story and Discourse: Narrative Structure in Fiction and Film* (Ithaca: Cornell University Press, 1978); Seymour Chatman, *Coming to Terms: The Rhetoric of Narrative in Fiction and Film* (Ithaca, NY: Cornell University Press, 1990).

6. David Bordwell, *Narration in the Fiction Film* (Madison: University of Wisconsin Press, 1985).

7. Robert C. Allen, *Speaking of Soap Operas* (Chapel Hill: University of North Carolina Press, 1985).

8. Robyn R. Warhol, *Having a Good Cry: Effeminate Feelings and Pop-Culture Forms* (Columbus: Ohio State University Press, 2003).

9. Henry Jenkins, *Convergence Culture: Where Old and New Media Collide* (New York: New York University Press, 2006).

10. For an overview of feminist narratology, see Ruth Page, "Gender," in *The Cambridge Companion to Narrative*, ed. David Herman (Cambridge: Cambridge University Press, 2007), 189–202. Robyn R. Warhol and Susan S. Lanser, *Narrative Theory Unbound: Queer and Feminist Interventions* (Columbus: Ohio State University Press, 2016), collects key writings in feminist literary narratology. For film and television, see Christine Gledhill, ed., *Home Is Where the Heart Is: Studies in Melodrama and the Woman's Film* (London: British Film Institute, 1987); Linda Williams, "Melodrama Revised," in *Refiguring American Film Genres: Theory and History*, ed. Nick Browne, 1st ed. (Berkeley: University of California Press, 1998), 42–88; Teresa de Lauretis, *Alice Doesn't: Feminism, Semiotics, Cinema* (Bloomington: Indiana University Press, 1984); Robyn R. Warhol, *Having a Good Cry: Effeminate Feelings and Pop-Culture Forms* (Columbus: Ohio State University Press, 2003).

11. Jason Mittell, *Complex TV: The Poetics of Contemporary Television Storytelling* (New York: New York University Press, 2015).

Further Reading

Booth, Paul. *Time on TV: Temporal Displacement and Mashup Television*. New York: Peter Lang, 2012.

Kelleter, Frank, ed. *Media of Serial Narrative*. Columbus: Ohio State University Press, 2017.

Mittell, Jason. *Narrative Theory and* Adaptation. New York: Bloomsbury, 2017.

Ryan, Marie-Laure. *Narrative Across Media: The Languages of Storytelling*. Lincoln: University of Nebraska Press, 2004.

Williams, Linda. *On* The Wire. Durham: Duke University Press, 2014.

4.
NON-FICTION MEDIA
Daniel Marcus

The study of **non-fiction media** has traditionally been based on **documentary** film and television, and television news and journalism. More recently, scholars also have focused attention on the varied forms of reality television; talk shows have occasionally been studied, and sports programming has been an area of increased attention in recent years. The approaches to these subjects each have their own histories, concerns, and questions, but they have also overlapped in their methods and conclusions. The growing hybridity of forms in contemporary television is reflected in the increasingly shared concerns of critics and historians of non-fiction media.

Media are considered to be non-fictional when they pertain to the world as it exists outside of the screening venue, rather than a world created by artistic imagination. Non-fiction media purport to show real people taking action in the world as is, though their methods to do so have varied over time; they seek viewers' attentions on the basis of the depicted events' impacts on our lives and world. This chapter will concentrate on documentary film, television, and new media, and will also briefly address journalism and reality programming. The chapter begins by reviewing the intellectual foundations of the inquiries into documentary, before addressing the specific concerns and debates inspired by them. Finally, it offers a case study investigating the relationship between documentary producers and their subjects and allies, and the innovations in distribution and exhibition of politically charged documentaries.

Documentary Studies

The Intellectual Foundations of Documentary Studies

The study of documentary took initial shape in the period between the two world wars. Films became classified as documentaries when they presented information on one topic at some length, using audio and visual materials primarily gathered from the real world. They represented real events and situations but with greater depth or more subjective perspectives than conventional news reports. Initially, the primary influences on documentary criticism were the discussion of poetics and aesthetics by literary theorists such as Cambridge professor I. A. Richards; humanism in studying narratives as espoused by another Cambridge professor, F. R. Leavis, and other literary critics; Marxist aesthetics and social concerns inspired by the Russian Revolution; and theorization about public opinion and the responsibility of the press by American journalist Walter Lippmann.

Richards and other literary theorists systematized the study of modern literary style in the 1920s and 1930s. They sought to trace the creation of meaning in artistic works by their structural forms and aesthetic devices. Such critical notions as rhythm, language, and metaphor held obvious applicability to both fictional and documentary film texts. Leavis's early work focused on how literary works' formal characteristics related to their cultural values, and the role of texts in telling stories of individuals in social context. Leavis's work promoted a humanist framework that prized the relevance and dignity of the individual, within a Western cultural tradition.

Film critics looking at documentary could use Leavisite precepts to explain the use of characters to impart the themes and meanings of early productions, a practice which has continued to be a major strain of criticism in the popular press to the present day. Analysis was centered on discussing the characters and events on-screen as real people and experiences. The idea that the events were part of a filmic representation dropped away, and the content of the film was related without complication to broader political, social, and cultural issues. The film became the entry point to a discussion of social problems and human struggles that transcended immediate circumstances. This was in accordance with documentary's claims to special access to reality.[1]

The work of Marxist theoreticians and practitioners (who were primarily one and the same) contributed another strain of early thought on documentary, to highlight the filmic constructions that Leavisite criticism largely ignored. Sergei Eisenstein's promotion of montage and other formalist devices in the creation of Russian revolutionary cinema inspired Dziga Vertov's paeans to the possibilities of film, especially documentary, to inspire new ways of literally and figuratively envisioning life.[2]

Walter Lippmann's work also addressed media's relevance in new mass society, but with more doubtful conclusions about its role in empowering civic participation than those arrived at by filmmakers in thrall to the Russian Revolution. Lippmann feared that democratic publics would fail in their civic responsibilities without major and unlikely improvements in public education and the quality of public discussion in the press. The influential documentary theorist and producer John Grierson sought to answer Lippmann's pessimism about participatory democracy by using film's ability to reach mass publics; inspired by the Russians' optimism, Grierson argued that film could become a key educational resource not just in revolutionary societies, but in nations invested in democratic reforms.[3]

Documentary Studies after World War II

The post-World War II era saw the beginning of canon formation in documentary studies, as critics looked at the trajectory of individual producers' contributions to the field. Much of this was inspired by Leavis's highly influential work on the canon of British literature, augmented by **auteur theory**, associated with the French film journal *Cahiers du Cinéma* and the American feature-film critic Andrew Sarris. Auteur theory analyzes films as expressions of the

personal styles and themes of their primary directors or producers, placing individual films in the context of their other productions.[4] Writing on documentary centered on reviews of individual works by significant figures in the field, given the small number of works made and available to be seen. Chroniclers of the field often functioned as cheerleaders for a commercially marginal corner of the film world that had yet to earn intellectual respect in academia and other circles. Documentary criticism often has seemed tied more closely to concurrent innovations in its subject field than have other areas of media criticism. New currents in theory and analysis have tended to follow closely upon what was going on in documentary production itself. In the 1960s, discussion of documentary was spurred by the rise of **cinéma vérité** and **direct cinema**, two movements that prized spontaneity, immediacy, and, in the case of the latter, a rigorous ethos of non-interference in the events depicted. Filmmakers within these movements (primarily French in the former and American in the latter) asserted the need to strip documentaries of any artifice, including reenactments of unfilmed events using actors and, in the case of direct cinema, the disavowal of interviews and framing voiceovers. These innovations led documentary criticism to become obsessed with questions of objectivity and proximity to the real.[5]

Of course, in other areas of media and film studies, scholars have responded to whatever was new in their respective time periods, but this tendency seems particularly striking in documentary studies. *Cinéma vérité* and direct cinema dominated discussions of documentary from the early 1960s to the mid 1970s, as producers heralded a new era and scholars followed behind in response, creating a critical insularity even as these new styles of productions contributed to the cultural ferment of the 1960s and led documentaries to enjoy new levels of public visibility and popularity.

In the 1970s, the intellectual incursions of feminism, social history, and anti-colonialism all influenced documentary studies. Feminist critiques of patriarchy highlighted the exclusion of female participation in public debate, the formal characteristics of texts that favored male points of view, and Lacanian and other psychoanalytic insights into personal and social identity formation.[6] Feminism shared emphases with the emerging movement in social history on revising ideas about the past to include female experiences and in the celebration of previously marginalized voices. Documentary production became a significant outlet for social history, as filmmakers presented research into past political movements and social phenomena by combining archival footage, interviews with participants and witnesses, and academic experts on hidden corners of U.S. and global history. Concurrently, the field of **anthropological ethnography**, the study of structures and practices of daily life in Third World societies that had created its own branch of fact-based filmmaking, came under attack for perpetuating neo-colonialist relations and silencing voices from the Global South. Ethnographic filmmakers had to grapple with questions of their own positioning in the production of knowledge and the ethics of presenting other people's lives on-screen. The interest in marginalized voices and their opportunities for truly representative expression converged with public sphere theory, as articulated by Jürgen Habermas, Oskar Negt and Alexander Kluge, and Nancy Fraser, with its interest in media's role in serving the communication needs of what Fraser dubbed "counterpublics," or groups outside of the main mechanisms of social power.[7]

Structural semiotics, post-structuralism, and postmodernism, associated with the work of French theorists such as Roland Barthes, Jean Baudrillard, and Gilles Deleuze, became firmly established as significant intellectual approaches to culture in the last quarter of the twentieth century, to account for the surge in image production and the complexities of identity in contemporary society. Documentary scholarship, with its penchant for valuing grounded and sober senses of reality, lagged in embracing theories that emphasized the questionable and constructed status of reality, the proliferation of surface imagery, the playfulness of meaning, and issues of subject positioning and subjectivity. These concepts finally entered significantly into documentary discussion when Bill Nichols and Michael Renov introduced them in the mid 1990s.[8] Explorations of the meaning and practices of new media and other technological innovations across the humanities have only recently been introduced into documentary scholarship, as documentary producers are catching up to other cultural producers in using the Web and social media as sites of production and distribution.

Major Modes of Documentary Studies

Certain themes have recurred throughout much of the study of the genre: documentary's claims to reality and special knowledge of its subjects; the value of realism as a presentational mode; the form's ability to represent marginalized perspectives; producer–subject relations and the ethics of production; and the role of technology in determining documentary form.

The Truth and Realism Debates

John Grierson was the dominant figure in early theorizations of documentary as a distinct form. He argued that documentary was the "creative treatment of actuality."[9] Grierson's statement offers an emblematic tension between documentary's claim to special access to the reality of human experience, and recognition that documentary functions through representation, which involves the creativity and artistry of a maker, thereby reducing its claim to objective truth. Scholars have grappled since Grierson's time with documentary's relationship to reality. They have debated questions such as:

1. What kind of truth claims can producers comfortably make?
2. What are the best practices to ensure accuracy in production?
3. Does documentary require realism as a style in presenting truth claims? Are other styles acceptable, or even preferable?

Some discussants have come down strongly on the side of the accessibility of truth to documentary producers, as long as they follow certain techniques and ethical practices.[10] In particular, direct cinema practitioners and supporters argued that their policy of non-interference in the actions they depicted was the royal road to truth. Direct cinema producers such as Richard Leacock and Frederick Wiseman banished such textual elements as narration, post-production music, and elaborate editing, and, in their most successful productions, they relied on persistence to accumulate revelatory moments and signs of deeper patterns of behavior. Critics of direct cinema such as Bill Nichols, Thomas Waugh, and Brian Winston saw this position as naïve, in obscuring the editorial decisions made by any producer in choosing a topic, picking what to shoot and from what angles, and cutting a mountain of raw footage into a final product. They also doubted that the performance by subjects could be undisturbed or uninfluenced by the presence of a camera and attendant crew.[11]

Analysts writing from within leftist traditions had a further critique of **realism**, a style that emphasized unobtrusive camera movements and editing, long takes, plainly observable behavior by subjects, and coherent narratives and explanations of meanings.

In the 1920s, the Russian Marxists Sergei Eisenstein and Dziga Vertov sought to penetrate the veil of appearances that might obscure the underlying structures and true workings of society. A new society needed audiences who would make intellectual connections among far-flung phenomena and new understandings of patterns of social behavior, which could be accomplished through innovative positioning of the camera, elaborate editing schemes, and unusual combinations of aesthetic elements that would need active thinking by audiences to achieve coherence. Two generations later, feminist theorists Claire Johnston and Elaine McGarry argued that realism merely reinforced accepted patriarchal ideas about society, and a disruptive aesthetics was necessary to represent feminist critiques of oppressive social structures and practices.[12]

Other feminist scholars such as E. Ann Kaplan and Annette Kuhn rallied around the idea that realism could bring marginalized voices to the public in accessible ways. This argument paralleled the position of social historians who often favored a straightforward presentation of previously silenced voices, seeing power in an unadorned style that highlighted the subjects' experiences and opinions rather than the presenter's talents or personality.[13]

Critical Theory advocates, influenced by German playwright Bertolt Brecht and French filmmaker Jean-Luc Godard, argued for self-reflexive work that acknowledged the power relations within the production process and the social positioning of cultural producers. Some documentary producers began to increase visibility of their own actions within their productions.[14] Errol Morris with *The Thin Blue Line* (1988) and Michael Moore with *Roger & Me* (1989) attained new levels of popularity and attention for theatrical documentaries in the 1980s by being both entertaining and self-reflexive. Their success propelled the realism discussion into the direction of postmodernism, with its emphases on sophisticated audiences, hybridity, playful strategies of signification, and hyperconsciousness of media practices.[15]

Given these debates, what methods can a critic employ when assessing documentary work? Textual analysis can be used to determine the narrative structures and aesthetic styles of pieces. How might the style relate to the subject and the aims of the producer? How does the producer establish the credibility and authenticity of the material? What are the work's sources of knowledge and authority, such as action captured by the camera, eyewitness testimony, opinions by established experts, or an appealing narrator? Is the work self-reflexive, explicitly pointing to its status as the product of particular individuals, organizations, or social perspectives? Does it interrogate or throw into doubt its own truth claims?

It is important to note that for most documentary producers, claiming to be accurate or truthful is not the same as being objective. A specific point of view and motivation for making the work is usually assumed. Making a documentary can be arduous and time-consuming, with little promise of monetary reward. Producers are often motivated to make a piece to advance an argument or highlight a theme, and many feel no need to present all sides in a debate or believe that this is even possible. Only producers working for established news organizations who follow professionalized codes of practice may want to claim to be objective or balanced; following the example of Grierson, Vertov, and other early documentarians, the rest use their personal investment in their subject to differentiate themselves from conventional reporters whose role is to cover assigned stories impersonally.

While documentary studies discarded the objectivity vs. subjectivity debate decades ago, for popular audiences it remains the most discussed controversy about documentary production, showing that for much of the public, there is no substantive difference between conventional news reporting by large media organizations and long-form documentary work by individuals and various forms of production collectives. This discrepancy between audience and scholarly expectations of objectivity persists despite many of the most renowned documentaries of the last few decades being clearly partisan or subjective in their approaches.

Personal and Local Knowledges

Feminist critics also initiated considerations of autobiography and memory as important elements of documentary production. Feminism introduced the idea that "the personal is political," and women filmmakers often organized their work around issues of personal identity, asserting the need to introduce women's private experiences into public discussion. These film- and videomakers used autobiography, memory, and fantasy to construct personal, emotional truths around individual perceptions of experience.[16] Concurrently, the anti-colonialist critique of anthropology was making itself felt in the realm of ethnographic film. Critics of ethnographic practices argued against the right of Western filmmakers to represent the experience of non-Western groups and societies, and against the viewing practices of Western audiences who gained a sense of epistemological mastery over subordinated peoples.[17] A movement began by indigenous groups to make their own media, documenting their lives through their own social and cultural perspectives.[18] Feminist and anti-colonialist interventions provoked a new set of questions for documentary studies, including:

1. What are the power relations between producers and subjects?
2. What responsibilities do producers have to their subjects?
3. How can subjects be empowered in the process of production, or become producers themselves?
4. How does personal story telling by subjects convey different truths than traditional producer-led documentary practices?
5. How can subjective and interiorized states of mind be represented in an audiovisual medium?

The first three questions can be addressed by research into production histories and practices of specific producers and the study of the development of ethical codes of conduct within the field.[19] Political economic analysis can also assist in addressing the third question, to trace the dispersal of production resources and the terms of access to distribution for producers operating outside of traditional centers of the documentary industry. The last two questions call for research into the cultural contexts from which indigenous productions emerge, and the employment of textual, narrative, and genre analysis. Insights gleaned from psychology and memory studies can further the understanding of the roles that subjectivity and memory play in personal identity. Feminism, critical race theory, class analysis, and queer theory can inform discussion of work by producers who seek to represent marginalized experiences.

The Social Functions of Documentary

What are documentaries for? Public sphere theory rose in prominence to explain the need for communication in complex societies. Theorists such as Nick Couldry, James Curran, and Nicholas Garnham examined the ownership structures of modern media, government policies toward public discussion of issues, and media's ability to convey and circulate the perspectives and demands of social groups.[20] Documentaries could raise significant issues and contribute to public debate. Questions inspired by these concerns include:

1. Who has access to the resources needed to produce successful documentaries, and what are the terms of such access?
2. What political organizations are available to assist documentary producers, and what are their interests and priorities?
3. How have documentaries started or intervened in public debate of important issues?
4. How do distribution and exhibition systems affect documentaries' impact?

Researchers of these questions look at production histories, government records, and economic analyses of media industries. They also have written on efforts by producers to create institutions within the field to support production and distribution, and their attempts to obtain government support. Scholars have done analyses of documentary institutions and trends in different countries, tracing histories of production within varying political, economic, and cultural contexts.[21]

Low-budget alternative media have garnered attention relating to public sphere, post-structuralist, and cultural studies concerns with the diffusion and decentralization of sources of communication, and the spread of video technologies in the 1980s and 1990s.[22] In the age of cell phone cameras and YouTube, amateur mediamakers have emerged as historically important participants in and witnesses to major political struggles, from the Arab Spring to controversies over police brutality in the United States.[23] Political economy and public sphere theories have been used to assess the importance of alternative media; textual analysis, genre theory, and new media theory can elucidate its forms. Organizational histories are central to the study of a movement that privileges collective activity. Feminist, postcolonial, critical race theory, and queer theory approaches are often relevant to its content.

Questions of distribution, exhibition, and reception gain prominence when studying the impacts of documentary, yet until recently there had been little actual research in these areas—which means that important and illuminating work remains to be done. Records relating to documentary as an industry are widely scattered and hard to access. Given documentaries' traditional limits as profit-generating commodities, scholars attracted to study documentaries evince more interest in political meanings, producer biographies, production histories, and stylistic innovations than in business strategies and histories. Documentaries have been distributed through theatrical exhibition, broadcast and cable television, home video, and streaming services. Critics and researchers have rarely paid attention to venue, and emphasize individual works over series. Public Broadcasting System (PBS) series such as *Frontline* (1983–) and *NOVA* (1974–) could be studied for their thematic and stylistic consistencies, and their roles in mediating political controversies and contexts, but most documentary research has been on single productions. A few PBS producers, particularly Ken Burns and Frederick Wiseman, have garnered critical attention, but their use of PBS as a distributor of their work has not been addressed significantly, and their works are organized as either personally branded series (by the former) or stand-alone productions (by the latter).

Critical hierarchies that privilege work by independent producers and non-profit institutions, however, are now being challenged by commercial cable channels with adventurous programming, often made by significant figures in both non-fiction and feature production. Series such as ESPN's *30 for 30* (2009–) offer new templates for study by combining corporate branding with explorations of diverse subjects by well-known filmmakers and reporters.[24] ESPN has expanded its work in serious sports documentary, offering the eight-hour series *OJ: Made in America* in 2016. Netflix is increasingly replacing its emphasis on extensive offerings of previously released documentaries with original productions such as Ava DuVernay's *13th* (2016). These developments may inspire new examinations of the relationships between producers and exhibitors, as well as brand, genre, and discourse analyses of networks, series, and social contexts. In addition, documentary's beginnings in film and its scattershot patterns of exhibition slowed scholars' embrace of reception studies associated with television research. With platforms multiplying and interactivity being built into some new media documentaries, however, questions of exhibition and reception are finally being addressed in the literature.

The Contemporary Scene

Interest in documentaries has burgeoned in the last two decades, catalyzed by the work of directors such as Ken Burns, Barbara Kopple, Spike Lee, Michael Moore, Errol Morris, and Werner Herzog. Scholarship has also grown, in accordance with the form's higher visibility and the incursion of new insights inspired by postmodernism, cultural studies, and new media studies. Questions that have arisen in recent years include:

1. How has documentary responded to the explosion of media products and technologies over the last thirty years?

2. What new forms and practices of documentary have emerged?
3. What kinds of truth and knowledge claims are being made in response to the critique of absolute knowledge by contemporary social theory?

Considerations of semiotics, post-structuralism and postmodernism have brought focus back to specific textual and formal elements, while relating them to continued concern with truth claims, and structured relations between producer and subject within the text. Increased volume in production of any medium inspires attempts to make new information manageable by the creation of systematized categories based on similarities in provenance, style, or purpose. In documentary studies, the most influential typology has been suggested by Bill Nichols, whose schema is based on the variety of producer–subject relations and the mix of materials used to convey authority and meaning.[25] Hybridity is a growing hallmark of current documentary. Works that include documentary content or values can also include fictional interludes and elements difficult to classify. The establishment and commercial and critical acceptance of animated documentaries such as *Waltz with Bashir* (2008) makes clear the breakdown of old categories and aesthetic strategies as absolutes. Recent experiments in new media formats have complicated the typology of documentary even further.[26]

Journalism Studies

The discipline of journalism studies began by studying print publications but quickly included radio programming in its considerations, given the importance of the medium in the 1930s and 1940s. It was thus well positioned to study television once the new medium developed significant non-fiction productions. Scholars of print and electronic non-fiction media continue to inform each other's work, and some analysts have written on both. Most of the issues and questions raised within the field pertain to all modern media, though considerations of regulatory policy have concentrated on the more heavily regulated electronic media. Such questions include:

1. How do ownership structures of corporate media influence coverage of politics, economics, and other subjects?
2. How do government regulation and deregulation affect news programming, coverage, and tone?

3. How well do reporting organizations represent diverse perspectives, especially those of marginalized groups? What is excluded from significant coverage?
4. What textual devices are used to express the values and points of view that the media represent?
5. How do the news media foster political participation in society?

Journalism studies has had four main currents: political economy of media organizations and the study of relationships with financial and governmental elites, in the Marxist tradition; hegemony theory and its tracing of how the values and interests of competing groups are used to create and contest social consensus, which is also a goal of discourse analysis; questions of the role of the press in democracy, based on Walter Lippmann's critique in the 1920s and public sphere theory; and occupational and popular notions of fairness, objectivity and subjectivity, and professionalism that still pervade popular concerns about media's roles in society and the truth claims of both news reports and documentaries.

Political economy, hegemony theory, and discourse analysis are discussed in other chapters in this book. Scholars working in these areas share concerns with public sphere theory, in their examinations of the opportunities for social groups to use media to communicate within their communities and to the broader social whole. The news media can be studied from within these traditions for its promotion of values, characterizations of political struggles, depictions of social identities, and provision of access to marginalized groups and opinions.

Story selection has always been a concern of journalism studies, which has sought to show what kinds of issues attract media attention and the reasons for editorial decisions. Is story selection tied to corporate agendas, governmental action, elite audience interest, or pressure from social movements? The Internet's use of formal links between stories adds an important dimension to studies of story selection, as researchers can now more clearly trace information flows and connections among various media sources.

Equally important is **frame analysis**, which asserts that a specific perspective on events is inherent in news stories. No story is read without a broader context of understanding to which the story refers. Frame analysis is a journalistic variant of the analysis of articulation in hegemony theory, which asks which concepts are brought together in culture, to appear to be naturally or inevitably connected. These webs of meaning are the contexts from which individual news stories emerge and to which they implicitly refer. How do stories reinforce these contexts, and how do they negotiate among different perspectives and positions when established contextual meanings are challenged by new social movements?[27] Perhaps the most crucial periods for these analyses are during times of crisis, as in the beginning of war, when the mainstream media often coalesce in support of the national government and restrict access by dissenting voices.[28]

Journalism scholars have also done sociological studies of the culture of news organizations to explain the shaping of news stories. These studies combine an analysis of power hierarchies within the industry with ideological analysis of how news professionals see themselves and their responsibilities. They cover such issues as the pursuit of objectivity, media-government relations, gender relations in the industry, and the influence of advertisers, pressure groups, and media critics on coverage of controversial stories. Sociological investigators pursue detailed chronicles of how stories are selected and framed, and how reporters choose sources of information.[29]

Popular discussions of journalism are now dominated by the impact of the Internet on news practices. The industry's financial model, especially as it pertains to print publications, has been strongly challenged by the free flow of information trumpeted by Web enthusiasts. The number of people providing news coverage, analysis, and opinion has increased vastly; the incursion of amateurs, and experts from other fields, through the use of blogs, amateur video, and on-line magazines has put into question the professionalized codes of conduct that journalists use to establish their credibility and ward off competition from outsiders. The impact of new media on journalistic values, financing, and performance has become a prime subject of study, with traditionalists decrying the decline in adherence to professionalized codes, and insurgents celebrating the decline in the gatekeeping functions of media institutions.[30]

The postmodern conflation of news and entertainment, and the relaxation of boundaries between political and cultural spheres, have extended beyond officially defined news programming into reality TV formats and the "fake news" comedy shows *The Daily Show* (Comedy Central, 1996–), *The Colbert Report* (Comedy Central, 2005–15), *Last Week Tonight with John Oliver* (HBO, 2014–), and *Full Frontal with Samantha Bee* (TBS, 2016–), which have mixed comic routines with sharp appraisals of both global politics and its attendant media coverage.[31] Their use of popular entertainment forms has attracted cultural studies scholars interested in the use of popular culture in expressing political perspectives. These critics deploy industrial histories, rhetorical analysis, and audience studies to address the series' interventions into public controversies.[32]

Reality Television Studies

Reality television has emerged as a super-genre within television only in the last fifteen years, so it may be expected that its study would be intellectually thinner than that of documentary studies. Because reality TV takes so many forms, however, and hybridizes so readily, scholars investigating the phenomenon have called upon a wide range of theories and methods to explore it. With a subject that stretches from the globe-spanning competition series *The Amazing Race* (CBS, 2001–) to the psychodramas of the *Real Housewives* franchise (syndicated, 2006–) to the political concerns of *30 Days* (FX, 2005–08), scholars of many different media forms have been able to contribute to its study. As reality TV series have proliferated globally, they have become an important part of television and cultural studies. Major questions that have been explored include:

1. Why have reality TV shows become so pervasive in the twentieth-first century?
2. How truthful are reality TV shows, and does it matter?
3. How should reality TV shows be distinguished from documentary and other non-fiction forms?
4. What is the range of social representations within reality shows, and how do they matter in contemporary political contexts?

Reality TV research shares most of its foundations with its precursors in non-fiction media studies. Leavisite ideas about the transmission of cultural values are relevant to a field that has generated social controversy about proper behavior and individual ethics. Feminism, multiculturalism, critical theory, and queer theory are used to study the social identities of reality TV participants, and postmodern theories of the contemporary elision between reality and fiction are readily applied to much of its programming. Documentary debates on producer–subject power relations and the ethics of production hold clear relevance to reality shows that offer intimate portraits of their subjects. Political economy has contributed to the study of network strategies in programming reality shows and the financial underpinnings of reality production, as well as in investigating exploitative labor practices within the industry.[33] Questions of the realness of reality programming repeat *ad infinitum* old debates that have pervaded documentary studies.

Not surprisingly, reality TV scholarship also borrows from studies of entertainment programming that are discussed elsewhere in this book. Approaches from the study of ideology, genre, and narrative have been used to analyze reality shows. Industrial strategies have been central to reality TV scholarship, and audience studies have played a much larger role in reality TV studies than in documentary studies.

Case Study: Documentary and Video Activism

Looking at my process of researching and writing "Documentary and Video Activism" can elucidate some of the contours of criticism of non-fiction forms.[34] I will recount the considerations of subject, resource materials, and critical approaches during the writing of the piece.

The book in which my chapter appears is a collection that covers the documentary field since the late 1980s, and particularly looks at works since 2000. As the book's editors, Selmin Kara and I wanted to include a chapter on alternative media and video activism—explicitly political work that takes advantage of the diffusion of low-cost technologies to intervene against corporate elite domination of media. We also wanted the book to direct attention to questions of distribution and exhibition, areas that have historically been given short shrift in documentary scholarship. Tracing the distribution methods of alternative productions could contribute to the discussion of documentary's political and social efficacy in the digital era. I also wanted to look at documentary makers' relationships with political activist groups, which have rarely been significant and successful despite shared interests, but which have attained greater senses of coordination and cooperation in some recent ventures.

Subjects that mark shifts in historical direction or lay the groundwork for other efforts in the field have always seemed especially important to chronicle and analyze. I decided to focus on two projects that marked new relationships between producers and activists and new uses of technology and organizational resources: the Gulf Crisis TV Project (GCTV), which gathered videos from many sources to distribute anti-war television series via satellite during the first Persian Gulf War in 1991; and Robert

Greenwald's Brave New Films (BNF), which distributes its documentaries on contemporary politics and foreign affairs through both the Web and house parties. BNF worked in conjunction with groups such as left-leaning activist website MoveOn.org, the American Civil Liberties Union, and the Center for Democratic Progress, a liberal Washington think tank. The combination of these two projects traces video activism from its pre-Web embrace of camcorders and satellite technology, through its increasingly sophisticated use of Internet distribution, to the surprising return of in-person, group exhibition and new forms of activism. It also traces the growth of coordination between producers and activist organizations. GCTV had been chronicled many years ago, but no reconsideration of the project had been made since the rise of BNF, so a comparison between them seemed useful. Greenwald and BNF had also received significant critical attention, but their innovations in distribution and exhibition had not been thoroughly discussed. Also, I had been a participant in the GCTV and had knowledge and an informed perspective that I thought would prove particularly useful and worthy of inclusion in our book. Finally, the GCTV and BNF, while producing work with strong political opinions, were each more innovative in their distribution and exhibition strategies than in their textual techniques or political stances, and thus our desire for the chapter to emphasize the former within the overall plan of the book was also appropriate to both subjects.

The case study was centered on the organizational histories of the projects, a form of analysis that most closely aligns with the traditions of political economic research. It also borrowed from traditional documentary scholarship emphasis on the intentions of producers and their relation to a greater political context, and public sphere theory on cultural interventions into political controversies. Technology studies, which is just beginning to become an important field in documentary criticism, could also be relevant to these projects. However, because there has been little significant research on distribution and exhibition of documentaries, the critical canon was not going to be very helpful for this specific topic. The major source of information and discussion about contemporary distribution comes from the Center for Social Media, affiliated with American University in Washington, DC, which has published several useful articles and guides on the new opportunities for distribution of political documentaries. Looking at distributors' websites was also useful in getting a sense of the efforts today to use the Internet and other resources. Reviewing the history of

documentary also helped to confirm the hypothesis that, while producers have often had political intent and some worked in government units for that purpose, direct working relationships between producers and non-governmental activists had been scattershot and relatively undeveloped.

The most relevant published literature lay mainly in the field of alternative media, particularly articles written by or featuring interviews with producers. Because the alternative media community is concerned with the political efficacy of its productions and is highly conscious of the use of the media to make political points, participants tend to be articulate and self-aware about their process and results. Several articles by GCTV participants and interviews featuring Robert Greenwald provided solid information and insight about their work processes and results.

Personal interviews conducted by me filled out the picture, with two types being particularly helpful. Because I wanted to trace the coordination of projects with activist groups, getting an interview with leaders of anti-war groups that worked with the Gulf Crisis TV Project helped me to understand the extent of the groups' involvement and reasons why it was limited. Articles about GCTV had focused on the process of gathering material, the content of specific episodes, and the political maneuvers of GCTV personnel. Hearing from the activist camp provided me with complementary explanations of what worked and what did not, as anti-war groups and GCTV scurried to respond to events happening on a global scale. Crucially, while the events described in the interviews took place twenty-five years ago, my conversations with activist leaders had occurred just a few years after GCTV's activities, allowing recollections to be fairly fresh and detailed. The other interview took place during my research for the chapter, when I was able to speak with BNF's Education Outreach director about a new campaign by the company to reach college audiences. This provided me with very up-to-date information that had not been published anywhere else. The major claims of the article became:

1. Despite many claims of documentary as a political form, collaborations between producers and activist organizations have been rare historically in the United States, and often have been problematic.
2. There have been new ventures that stress coordination between producers and activists, with some success that has aided both sides.
3. In an era of surging production possibilities, producers who aim for political efficacy must

concentrate on developing successful distribution and exhibition models.

4. New technologies have spurred new forms of collaboration and alternative media, but one of the most significant sources of political documentary in recent decades mixes digital distribution with group screenings that recall earlier eras of political organizing.

It is the fourth point that makes the case study particularly valuable. It is the most specific argument, and intervenes in a contemporary controversy about political activism. As the Internet and the World Wide Web developed, supporters claimed that they would usher in a new era of heightened political participation in digital societies and the weakening of hierarchies based on possession of communication resources. Activist groups have used the Internet to publicize their causes, keep in touch with membership, distribute video and other media, organize petition drives, survey public opinion, and provide forums for discussion of issues. Within the last few years, however, a criticism of Web-based activism has emerged, taking aim at "clicktivism," the simplification of activist impulses that ultimately may lead to passivity, top-down hierarchies within activist groups, and the substitution of consumption of information for real political participation. The clicktivism critique is most associated with Micah White, one of the initiators of Occupy Wall Street, whose model of political work was based much more on embodied activity and physical presence than digital networking and response.[35]

Greenwald's Brave New Films project combines using its website to publicize and distribute video productions, YouTube to display works as well, and house parties organized by local activists around the country in conjunction with activist groups. Thus, BNF uses both digital resources and the emotional pull of physical presence in its organizing. Greenwald and his allies use the lure of watching a BNF production to get like-minded people together in the same place at the same time, during which they can meet each other, learn about local political organizing, and volunteer for more activities. This model has attracted millions of viewings of Greenwald productions and created real-time opportunities to reach the Holy Grail of political documentary: to spur further civic action by its audience. This is the strongest point I wished to make in the case study.

What more can be researched about documentary and video activism? What important areas have I left untreated in my case study? First, both of my examples are based in the United States, and there are many documentaries around the world that promote social and political causes. Human rights groups have launched projects such as Witness, EngageMedia, and video4change to provide production equipment and outlets for exhibition to chroniclers of human rights struggles globally. Indigenous communities have also embraced video as a means of communicating their political claims and preserving cultural traditions. Finally, there are activist groups such as Anonymous and Wikileaks that have pioneered the use of new media for new forms of activism. All of these campaigns have and should continue to inspire research and exploration.

In addition, while the article looked at distribution methods, the moment and consequence of exhibition remained outside its sphere of attention. Documentary studies has done almost none of the audience-response research that has marked the last generation of television studies. GCTV audiences were out of reach, impossible to contact twenty-five years after the fact. I did not talk to any BNF audiences about the impact viewings had on them. Organizers of house parties have reported success in keeping audiences involved in local issues after screenings, but more research needs to be done on the processes of the activation of interest, emotional investment, and participation that are the explicit goals of BNF and its allies. With the increased complexity of exhibition models, all areas of study of non-fiction media need to attend to questions of audience response.

Conclusion

Scholarship on non-fiction media usually follows closely upon contemporary developments. As the media change, new directions and techniques for critical exploration will emerge as well. As documentary has enjoyed a renaissance of production, popularity, and social relevance in recent decades, documentary studies appears to be entering a period of energetic critical exploration of its innovations. Documentary producers are finally engaging with the Internet and digital media in all phases of their work, creating new narrative structures, innovative avenues for participation by many contributors, and new distribution and exhibition strategies. Consequently, documentary scholarship is borrowing from and reformulating insights by new media researchers. Journalism studies is grappling with the vast changes in the business and technological landscape of its subject, and a persistent sense of crisis about journalistic ethics and relevance. Reality TV studies enjoyed a surge of interest as its subject became a dominant televisual form. Both the entertainment super-genre and its attendant criticism now face the challenge of maintaining interest as their novelty has worn off, though both are going strong in many niches of the media sphere. With the current political polarization in many countries and attendant controversies about the control of media, truthfulness of news, and use of social media, scholars of non-fiction media have the opportunity to affect public discussion of crucial issues inspiring high levels of public visibility. Non-fiction media will continue to take many forms, and the need for informed and insightful criticism based on a mix of approaches will continue as well.

Notes

1. Early examples of documentary criticism can be found in Lewis Jacobs, ed., *The Documentary Tradition*, 2nd ed. (New York: W. W. Norton & Company, 1979).

2. Sergei Eisenstein, *Film Form: Essays in Film Theory* (New York: Harcourt, 1969); Dziga Vertov, *Kino-Eye: The Writings of Dziga Vertov* (Berkeley: University of California Press, 1985).

3. John Grierson, *Grierson on Documentary* (London: Faber and Faber, 1966).

4. Andrew Sarris, *The American Cinema: Directors and Directions 1929–1968* (New York: E. P. Dutton, 1969).

5. For direct cinema and declarations of its practitioners and theorists, see Stephen Mamber, *Cinema Verite in America: Studies in Uncontrolled Documentary* (Cambridge: MIT Press, 1974); and Louis Marcorelles, *Living Cinema* (New York: Praeger, 1973).

6. Luce Irigaray, *The Sex Which Is Not One*, trans. Catherine Porter with Carolyn Burke (1977; Ithaca: Cornell University Press, 1985); for application of some of these concepts to fiction film, see Laura Mulvey, "Visual Pleasure and the Narrative Cinema," *Screen* 16, no. 3 (1975): 6–18, reprinted in Laura Mulvey, *Visual and Other Pleasures* (Bloomington: Indiana University Press, 1989).

7. Craig Calhoun, "Introduction: Habermas and the Public Sphere," and Nancy Fraser, "Rethinking the Public Sphere: A Contribution to the Critique of Actually Existing Democracy," both in *Habermas and the Public Sphere*, ed. Craig Calhoun (Cambridge: MIT Press, 1992), 1–48; 109–42.

8. See Bill Nichols, *Representing Reality: Issues and Concepts in Documentary* (Bloomington: Indiana University Press, 1991); Michael Renov, *The Subject of Documentary* (Minneapolis: University of Minnesota Press, 2004).

9. John Grierson, "The Documentary Producer," *The Cinema Quarterly* 2, no. 1 (1933): 8.

10. Alan Rosenthal, "Introduction," in *New Challenges for Documentary*, ed. Alan Rosenthal (Berkeley: University of California Press, 1988), 11–19; James Blue, "One Man's Truth: An Interview With Richard Leacock," in Jacobs, *The Documentary Tradition*, 406–19.

11. Thomas Waugh, "Beyond *Verité*: Emile de Antonio and the New Documentary," and Bill Nichols, "The Voice of Documentary," in *Movies and Methods, Vol. II*, ed. Bill Nichols (Berkeley: University of California Press, 1985), 233–57; 258–73.

12. Claire Johnston, "Women's Cinema as Counter-Cinema," in *Notes on Women's Cinema* (London: SEFT/BFI, 1973), 24–31; Elaine McGarry, "Documentary, Realism, and Women's Cinema," *Women & Film* 2, no. 7 (1975): 50–59. For discussions of the strengths and weaknesses of semiotic and psychoanalytic critiques from feminist perspectives, see E. Ann Kaplan, "Theories and Strategies of the Feminist Documentary," in Rosenthal, *New Challenges for Documentary*, 78–102; and Janet Bergstrom, "Rereading the Work of Claire Johnston," in *Feminism and Film Theory*, ed. Constance Penley (New York: Routledge/BFI, 1988), 80–88.

13. For nuanced defenses of realism, see E. Ann Kaplan, "The Realist Debate in the Feminist Film" in *Women and Film: Both Sides of the Camera* (New York: Methuen, 1983), 125–41, and Annette Kuhn, "Real Women" in *Women's Pictures: Feminism and Cinema*, 2nd ed. (London: Verso, 1994), 127–50. For a discussion of documentary as social history, see Pat Aufderheide, "*The Good Fight*," in Rosenthal, *New Challenges for Documentary*, 488–94. For an extensive discussion of the major trends in feminist criticism, see Janet Walker and Diane Waldman, "Introduction" in *Feminism and Documentary*, ed. Diane Waldman and Janet Walker (Minneapolis: University of Minnesota Press, 1999), 1–35.

14. Jay Ruby, "The Image Mirrored: Reflexivity and the Documentary Film," in Rosenthal, *New Challenges for Documentary*, 64–77.

15. Linda Williams, "Mirrors without Memories: Truth, History, and *The Thin Blue Line*," in *Documenting the Documentary: Close Readings of Documentary Film and Video*, eds. Barry Keith Grant and Jeannette Sloniowski (Detroit: Wayne State University Press, 1998), 379–96; Paul Arthur, "Jargons of Authenticity (Three American Moments)," in *Theorizing Documentary*, ed. Michael Renov (New York: Routledge/AFI, 1993), 108–34. For varying critical perspectives on Moore, see Matthew Bernstein, ed., *On Michael Moore: Filmmaker, Newsmaker, Cultural Icon* (Ann Arbor: University of Michigan Press, 2010).

16. See Michelle Citron, "Fleeing from Documentary: Autobiographical Film/Video and the 'Ethics of Responsibility'," in Waldman and Walker, *Feminism and Documentary*, 271–86; Kaplan, "Theories and Strategies of the Feminist Documentary."

17. A survey of the varieties of interactions and representations in anthropological mediamaking can be found in Faye D. Ginsburg, Lila Abu-Lughod, and Brian Larkin, eds., *Media Worlds: Anthropology on New Terrain* (Berkeley: University of California Press, 2002).

18. Pamela Wilson and Michelle Stewart, eds., *Global Indigenous Media: Cultures, Poetics, and Politics* (Durham: Duke University Press, 2008).

19. The most influential writing on documentary ethics has been Cal Pryluck, "Ultimately We Are All Outsiders: The Ethics of Documentary Filmmaking," in Rosenthal, *New Challenges for Documentary*, 255–68.

20. Nick Couldry and James Curran, eds., *Contesting Media Power: Alternative Media in a Networked World* (Lanham: Rowman & Littlefield, 2003), and Nicholas Garnham, "The Media and the Public Sphere," in Calhoun, *Habermas and the Public Sphere*, 359–76.

21. For analyses of many national documentary scenes, see Brian Winston, ed., *The Documentary Film Book* (Basingstoke, Hampshire: Palgrave Macmillan/ BFI, 2013). For an in-depth analysis of one nation's recent experience with documentary, see Chris Berry, Lu Xunyu, and Lisa Rofel, eds., *The New Chinese Documentary Film Movement: For the Public Record* (Hong Kong: Hong Kong University Press, 2010).

22. For a history of important antecedents, see Deirdre Boyle, *Subject to Change: Guerrilla Television Revisited* (New York: Oxford University Press, 1997). For surveys of alternative media projects, see Kate Coyer, Tony Dowmunt, and Alan Fountain, eds., *The Alternative Media Handbook* (London: Routledge, 2007); John Downing, et al., *Radical Media: Rebellious Communication and Social Movements* (Thousand Oaks: Sage, 2001).

23. For new forms of political activism in media, see Megan Boler, ed., *Digital Media and Democracy: Tactics in Hard Times* (Cambridge: MIT Press, 2008), and Leah A. Lievrouw, *Alternative and Activist New Media* (Cambridge: Polity Press, 2011). For the influence of the Internet and other recent trends, see Kate Nash, Craig Hight, and Catherine Summerhayes, eds., *New Documentary Ecologies: Emerging Platforms, Practices and Discourses* (New York: Palgrave Macmillan, 2014).

24. Thanks to Victoria Johnson for suggesting this point.

25. Bill Nichols, *Introduction to Documentary*, 2nd ed. (Bloomington: Indiana University Press, 2010).

26. See Daniel Marcus and Selmin Kara, eds., *Contemporary Documentary* (London: Routledge, 2016).

27. For a liberal activist orientation in discussing contemporary framing of issues, see George Lakoff, *Moral Politics: How Liberals and Conservatives Think*, 2nd ed. (Chicago:

University of Chicago Press, 2002), and George Lakoff, *Don't Think of an Elephant: Know Your Values and Frame the Debate* (White River Junction: Chelsea Green Publishing, 2004). For a conservative activist orientation, see Frank Luntz, *Words That Work: It's Not What You Say, It's What People Hear* (New York: Hyperion, 2007).

28. Douglas Kellner, *The Persian Gulf TV War* (Boulder: Westview, 1992.)

29. Herbert J. Gans, *Deciding What's News* (New York: Pantheon, 1979); Maxwell McCombs, *Mass Media and Public Opinion*, 2nd ed. (Cambridge: Polity Press, 2014).

30. Arguments on each side are reviewed in Bill Kovach and Tom Rosenstiel, *The Elements of Journalism*, 3rd rev. ed. (New York: Three Rivers Press, 2014). See also Boler, *Digital Media and Democracy*.

31. Jonathan Gray, Jeffrey P. Jones, and Ethan Thompson, eds., *Satire TV: Politics and Comedy in the Post-Network Era* (New York: New York University Press, 2009).

32. Kees Brants and Katrin Voltmer, eds., *Political Communication in Postmodern Democracy: Challenging the Primacy of Politics* (Basingstoke, UK: Palgrave Macmillan, 2011).

33. For a variety of approaches, see both editions of Susan Murray and Laurie Ouellette, eds., *Reality TV: Remaking Television Culture* (New York: New York University Press, 2004; 2009). For a rare audience-centered study, see Annette Hill, *Reality TV: Factual Entertainment and Television Audiences* (London: Routledge, 2005).

34. Daniel Marcus, "Documentary and Video Activism," in Marcus and Kara, *Contemporary Documentary*.

35. Micah White, "Clicktivism Is Ruining Left Activism," *The Guardian*, August 12, 2010, accessed October 23, 2017, www.theguardian.com/commentisfree/2010/ aug/12/clicktivism-ruining-leftist-activism.

Further Reading

Anderson, C. W., Leonard Downie, Jr., and Michael Schudson. *The News Media: What Everyone Needs to Know*. New York: Oxford University Press, 2016.

Curran, James. *Media and Democracy*. London: Routledge, 2011.

Marcus, Daniel, and Selmin Kara, eds. *Contemporary Documentary*. London: Routledge, 2016.

Nichols, Bill. *Introduction to Documentary*, 2nd ed. Bloomington: Indiana University Press, 2010.

Ouellette, Laurie, ed. *A Companion to Reality Television*. Malden: Wiley Blackwell, 2014.

5.
VISUAL STYLE
Jeremy G. Butler

The analysis of **visual style** in media texts suffers from an abundance of meanings commonly associated with the term "style." Auteurist critics, as discussed in Chapter 9, use it to identify a director's often ineffable identity inscribed in his or her television programs and films—e.g., Joss Whedon's style across *Buffy the Vampire Slayer* (The WB and UPN, 1997–2003), *Firefly* (Fox, 2002–2003), and *The Avengers* (2012). Some aesthetic critics employ it to refer to a decorative flourish, which may be absent entirely or may be distractingly excessive and stylized. For a style-less text, see an Adam Sandler film and for a style-full text, see the extravagant visual effects in *Game of Thrones* (HBO, 2011–). Style can even be thought of as a function of an actor's on-screen/off-screen persona. We might say that Beyoncé has *style* while the average human does not. Mostly, however, style is simply glossed over. Many academic scholars, media bloggers, and journalistic critics neglect to write about style in any capacity. For some, style is too ephemeral to pin down. For others, the topic seems too arcane. And many, simply enough, lack the necessary analytical tools to comfortably discuss style. Stylistic criticism is a craft that few are taught in school.

The first challenge in this chapter is to winnow down this abundance of definitions. One common way to begin this definitional task is to conceive of style as the *how* that produces the *what* of media texts. The preceding chapters of this book have centered on that "what." To wit, they have examined the meanings and stories that we derive from media texts. In contrast, this chapter will pose a set of questions built on media texts' "how": How does lighting tell us something about a character? How does editing juxtapose symbolic objects? How does camera framing influence our understanding of a setting? How might style define a genre or a director's work? To answer questions such as these, a working definition of style in media texts must be adopted, and, for that, I turn to David Bordwell, the cinema's premiere analyst of style. In his work, style refers to the "*patterned* use of a medium's techniques" to communicate plot and theme and to generate affect.[1] Thus, style is not just a matter of isolated instances of lighting design, editing, or framing, but, rather, refers to meaningful patterns of those techniques in media texts. A search for such patterns in 1980s television is what drew me to *Miami Vice* (NBC, 1984–1990), the focus of this chapter's case study.[2] The program was hailed during the 1980s as a remarkably *stylized* program whose visual design was inspired by a notably stylized genre, film noir. *Miami Vice*'s patterned use of film/TV techniques thus seemed to cry out for analysis.

Armed with a working definition of style, we can begin to understand what is involved in its analysis—an academic discipline commonly known as "**stylistics**." The actual work of most stylisticians centers on either the interpretation of style or the description of style from a particular time period and a consideration of how it has evolved. I will begin, therefore, with an examination of how style is interpreted in media studies and then explain how the history of style is charted. I will not address aesthetic questions related to the evaluation of style, however, because stylistic aesthetics remains a highly contentious area of media studies. Recently, authors such as Christine Geraghty, Jason Jacobs, and Greg Smith have vociferously lobbied for the aesthetic analysis of film and television, but, as of yet, no model of aesthetic evaluation is generally agreed upon.[3]

Interpreting Style

Media stylisticians identify patterns of film/TV techniques in **texts**—using the term liberally to refer to films, television programs, video games, and so on—and then interpret the meanings and significance of those patterns. As Bordwell argues, "Style is the tangible texture of a film, the perceptual surface we encounter as we watch and listen, and that surface is our point of departure in moving to plot, theme, feeling—everything else that matters to us."[4] Thus, stylisticians examine the sometimes elusive connections between style and meaning. Bordwell's point makes sense in the abstract, but, when we are crafting media criticism, how do we get from a text's perceptual surface to its narrative, meaning, and affect? The key lies in Noël Carroll's "functional theory of style" in the cinema: "*the form* [or style] *of an individual film is the ensemble of choices intended to realize the point or the purpose of the film.*"[5] In other words, we analyze style by examining the functions that it serves in a media text. This definition will carry us toward understanding how style can communicate and affect viewers.

In Bordwell's *Figures Traced in Light: On Cinematic Staging*, he identifies four stylistic functions in narrative cinema, all of which can also be found in other media's narrative texts, too; but his functions are insufficient to account for additional aspects of style that are characteristic of media other than the cinema.[6] Expanding Bordwell's functions with four more, I arrive at the following list, where style can be said to:

1. denote
2. express
3. symbolize
4. decorate
5. persuade
6. hail or interpellate
7. differentiate
8. signify liveness and/or verisimilitude.

Let us briefly consider each of these functions. As we shall see, many of them are exemplified in my case study of *Miami Vice*.

When stylisticians examine how visual style can **denote** aspects of narrative setting and character, they are looking at its most basic function. Borrowing from the study of semiotics (which is explained further in Chapter 8 on representation), it may be theorized that a sign's denotation is the rudimentary meaning conveyed by its signifier. It is that which is communicated to a listener or viewer before connotations

are attached to the signifier through cultural implications. In the English language, the word "dog" *denotes* the simplest notion of a canine. And, within Western culture, "dog" further *connotes* additional meanings such as loyalty. In an episode of *Boardwalk Empire* (HBO, 2010–2014), a scene begins with a long shot of a man, Eddie (Anthony Laciura), alone in a room, seated on a chair (Figure 5.1). Stylistic choices establish or denote narrative elements in this scene. The set design establishes that it is a deserted room, with peeling paint and chairs discarded in the corner. The framing, a long shot showing the entire room, reveals that Eddie is alone. The costume design, as in the rest of the program, helps set up the time period as 1920s America. This is all very basic diegetic information that director Timothy Van Patten, cinematographer David Franco, and the rest of the creative personnel communicate to us through stylistic choices.

Bordwell's second function is style's **expressive** quality, which, for him, is specifically its emotional aspect. Style both can signify an emotion and it can elicit an emotion in the viewer—two distinct qualities in Bordwell's view. He explains, "We can distinguish between style *presenting* feelingful qualities ('The shot exudes sadness') and *causing* feelings in the perceiver ('The shot makes me sad')."[7] The expression of feelingful qualities by the text "can be carried by light, color, performances, music, and certain camera movements."[8] The shot of Eddie in *Boardwalk Empire* presents his feelings of fearful anxiety as he waits to be interrogated. His tension is communicated through actor Anthony Laciura's performance style (sitting rigidly in the chair) and the composition of the shot, which makes him look small and vulnerable in the enormity of the decaying room. Depending upon the viewer's emotional connection with Eddie, the shot might also cause feelings in the viewer. Bordwell prefers to analyze style's presentation of emotions and does not spend much time analyzing the emotional responses of the viewer that are caused by style, but there is a sizeable body of empirical experiments surrounding media style's emotional impact, especially when it comes to television texts such as the commercial. Advertising agencies and academic researchers alike often expose a subject to a visual stimulus and then record his or her heart rate, skin conductance, and/or other physical signifiers of emotional impact. Such research is much less common in film studies than in conventional mass-communication research, but it does occasionally surface.

Bordwell's third stylistic function addresses the **symbolic** meanings that may be inferred from

Figure 5.1 The denotation of this image establishes a scene's decaying setting and a man seated alone on a chair ("Erlkönig," *Boardwalk Empire*, HBO, October 6, 2013)

film and television techniques. This raises stylistic techniques to the level of connotation. When a technique suggests a meaning to a viewer, then we have achieved this symbolic function. Editing techniques, for example, have been used to construct abstract meanings since the silent era and are still used in contemporary media. When, in *Lucy* (2014), Luc Besson cuts from shots of a cheetah stalking its prey to threatening gangsters approaching Lucy (Scarlett Johansson), the abstract meaning is clear: "Lucy is being hunted like prey." This meaning does not exist in the individual shots on their own and is not indicated in dialogue but is conveyed only through the juxtaposition of images through the technique of editing. Hence, style symbolizes meaning for the viewer.

Bordwell's final function of style in narrative cinema is **decoration**. Here is style for the sake of style itself, with no attempt at denotation, emotional expression, or symbolism. It does not *mean* anything or provoke a response beyond an aesthetic pleasure. When viewers appreciate a text's quirky visual flourishes, but can discern no denotative, expressive, or symbolic function for them, then they are engaging with its decorative function. They might, for example, find pleasure in the simple, but precisely symmetrical, framing of the shot from *Moonrise Kingdom* (2012) where Suzy's (Kara Hayward) dress harmoniously matches the color of the lighthouse metalwork and the top rail neatly separates sea and sky, highlighting picturesque clouds in the upper two-thirds of the image (Figure 5.2).

Many critics dismiss decorative visual style as decadent or the result of a cinematographer's self-indulgence, but the argument has been made that decorative style can encourage a postmodern sense of play, of messing with signifiers for the pure pleasure of disrupting conventional approaches to technique. Inspired by Mikhail Bakhtin's notion of **carnival**, John Fiske proclaims, "In the postmodern world, style performs many of the functions of carnival. It is essentially liberating, acting as an empowering language for the subordinate."[9] For Bakhtin, the carnivalesque subverts social conventions and, for Fiske, this subversion can be found in stylistic elements that refuse to serve conventional functions—such as signifying meaning or eliciting emotion.

My remaining four stylistic functions are less common in narrative cinema than in the related medium of television. To start, consider the **persuasive** function of style. Narrative cinema, unless it is an outright propaganda effort, does not bluntly attempt to persuade the viewer to do something or believe a particular idea, but the television commercial exists solely for that purpose. Style of sound and image is one of the principal tools advertisers use to convince the viewer to go buy a product or service. Consider how enticing lighting can make a hamburger look delicious or how fast cutting renders a car dynamic and speedy. Since commercials have a very short period of time to work their wiles, their stylistic elements are very carefully wrought in order to maximize their persuasive impact.

Commercials are also the preeminent examples of the **hailing** function of style. The concept

Figure 5.2 A shot from *Moonrise Kingdom* (Focus Features, 2012) encourages the viewer to indulge in the visual pleasures of director Wes Anderson's very precise aesthetic

of hailing comes from Marxist philosopher Louis Althusser who contends, "[A]ll ideology hails or interpellates concrete individuals as concrete subjects."[10] He argues that **hegemonic ideology**—a dominant class's set of values and beliefs—hails or calls on members of society, pulling them into acceptance of those values. In Althusser's hailing process, dominant ideology virtually shouts, "Hey, you!" and attempts to earn your acquiescence to its beliefs. In today's media landscape, there are many screens shrieking for our attention—televisions in our living rooms and computer monitors on our desks, laptops, smartphones, tablets, televisions in public places, and on and on. Each visual medium must compete for our attention, must figure out how to secure our attention. Sound style is particularly effective at hailing viewers. A sudden bump in volume or the explosion of a laugh track can divert our attention to a video text. And visual style can also hail viewers. Visually dense imagery, such as the elaborately detailed 1960s set design in *Mad Men* (AMC, 2007–2015), calls out for our attention (Figure 5.3). If we wish to get the most pleasure out of that program, we must gaze at the screen intently. Sound and image style thus hail us to pay attention to a particular text.

Once commercials and other texts have lured us to them, they must then **differentiate** themselves from other texts. Just as the products advertised in commercials must establish their brand identities and separate themselves from similar items in order to earn sales, so must movies and television programs develop a strategy that makes them stand out from the rest of the texts clamoring for our attention. Style can assist in these strategies. When *ER* debuted on NBC in 1994 it had to find a way to distinguish itself from other hospital dramas, including *Chicago Hope* (1994–2000), which CBS programmed against it in the same time slot. There were differences in narrative structure and theme between the two shows, but what was most striking about *ER* was its liberal use of a Steadicam to achieve fluid camera movements and long takes of characters moving through elaborate sets that had been constructed with four walls so that the camera could spin 360 degrees. *ER* was among the first television programs to use the Steadicam to such an extreme extent, a technology that would later be adopted by producer Aaron Sorkin for shows such as *The West Wing* (NBC, 1999–2006). Thus, *ER*'s visual style differentiated it from contemporaneous television programs.

The final function of style, to **signify liveness** and/or **verisimilitude**, is not shared equally among all mass media. Rather, it is one of television's distinctive characteristics. In the early, post-World War II years of television as a commercial medium, it distinguished itself from the cinema by its ability to transmit sports, newscasts, game shows, inaugurations, royal coronations, political conventions, theatrical productions, and, later, state funerals and humans walking on the moon—all at the same time that the events actually occurred. Aside from television's progenitor,

Figure 5.3 The dense set design of an office in *Mad Men* ("Public Relations," AMC, July 25, 2010) establishes its time period in intricate detail and rewards the attentive viewer

radio, no other mass medium could match television's immediacy, its ability to bring the world into your living room, its distant sight (from the Greek *tēle* and the Latin *visio*). Elements of style came to be associated with these live broadcasts: haphazard framing and clumsy editing, low-resolution black-and-white video, handheld camerawork, inadequate lighting, poorly recorded audio, and so on. Taken together, these stylistic elements comprise a conventionalized code of liveness, which evolves as the technology of live broadcasting evolves. These elements were originally associated with programs that actually are live, but they can be employed by programs that are not broadcast live but still wish to signify liveness. *The Daily Show* (Comedy Central, 1996–) and *The Colbert Report* (Comedy Central, 2005–2015), for instance, give the appearance of live news broadcasts through their studio lighting and newscast-like camera positions and editing; but they are recorded hours before their transmission—a fact at which their hosts occasionally poke fun.

Closely related to this fake liveness is the fake documentary, which also relies on conventionalized stylistic codes. Ever since *The Office* (U.K. version, BBC, 2001–2003; U.S. version, NBC, 2005–2013), there have been numerous television mockumentaries—programs that use the code of documentary verisimilitude but are not genuine documents of nonfiction reality. In Figure 5.4, for example, a shaky, handheld shot captures Kelly (Mindy Kaling) in an "awkward" framing, with a cubicle divider in the foreground, that

director Stephen Merchant and cinematographer Matt Sohn chose to replicate the look of a documentary. Brett Mills and Ethan Thompson refer to this subgenre of the sitcom as *comedy vérité*.[11] A similar tradition exists in the cinema where films use the stylistic conventions of documentary filmmaking to create fiction films. *This Is Spinal Tap* (1984) is among the most amusing fake documentaries while *The Blair Witch Project* (1999), *District 9* (2009), and *Cloverfield* (2008) use stylistic conventions to build very effective horror films. Significantly, these films do not present themselves as transmitting live events. Rather, as in the "found" footage of *Cloverfield*, they suggest that we are watching events that have already happened. But their style does suggest that they are actual recordings of real events. Their claim to verisimilitude can be so strong that some moviegoers even mistake them for authentic documentaries. For the stylistician, the most interesting aspect of fake liveness, *comedy vérité*, and the inauthentic documentary is how they can disengage the stylistic conventions of liveness and documentary from texts that are genuinely live and authentic documentaries. Fiske and others might argue that the ability to counterfeit verisimilitude is a sign of a postmodern semiotic apocalypse, but I would maintain that most viewers can recognize these counterfeits as such and engage with them in a manner that might well be carnivalesque.

In sum, there are many routes that a stylistician can take toward the interpretation of patterned

Figure 5.4 *The Office* ("Customer Survey," NBC, November 6, 2008) imitates documentary style by awkwardly framing its actors and allowing foreground objects to block our view—such as this cubicle wall

techniques in film, television, and other media, but all of them rely on a presumption of those techniques' functions in the text—whether that text be a feature-length film, a sitcom, a newscast, a commercial, or, by extension, a video game or a podcast. Style can be found to signify and to have an effect through these functions.

Historicizing Style

The stylistic patterns that researchers identify in films and television programs do not exist in a vacuum. The media texts of a particular time tend to look similar, to share stylistic aspects. Consequently, to understand properly the function of style in a specific text, one must know the historical context of media style. There are four factors that govern the historical evolution of style: **economics**, **technology**, **industry standards**, and **aesthetic codes**. Let us expand for a moment how each of these affects style.

The budget of a film or television program can affect style in a variety of ways. Creative personnel often complain about the limiting function of budgets. For example, a director might want a scene with a thousand extras, but the studio will only pay for a hundred. But another way to think of economic restraints is that they force creative personnel to be, well, *creative*—to figure ways to turn budgetary limitations into creative potential. During the 1940s, for example, color film was too costly for low-budget productions of crime dramas. The directors of such dramas, however, could use black-and-white film to

maximize the shadowy contrast of their films, as can be seen in Jacques Tourneur's *Out of the Past* (1947), among many others (Figure 5.5). If Tourneur had had the budget to shoot in color, it would have diminished the low-key lighting style of this film noir. And thus an economic restraint resulted in a stylistic opportunity during a specific time period.

Color film can also be used as an example of how technology has an impact on visual style. There were experiments with color film early in the history of the cinema, but it wasn't until the mid-1930s that a process known as three-color Technicolor could create a pleasing, plausible reproduction of the color spectrum found in nature. And the same could be said about color television, which had a particularly tortured and complicated history that led to its eventual adoption in the late 1960s. The obvious point to be made about visual style and technologies such as color film/TV is that media texts can be created only with the technology available to them at the time they are made. However, it is very important to recognize that the opposite point is not always true. One cannot say that just because a technology exists at a certain point in time, it will *necessarily* be used. It must first win over the media practitioners. For instance, the technology for zoom lenses was available, albeit in primitive form, in the 1930s, but cinematographers did not begin using them on a regular basis until the 1960s.

I have already discussed how color film was not available to film noir cinematographers because of economic concerns, but availability and cost are not the only aspects governing the adoption

Figure 5.5 Black-and-white cinematography emphasizes the contrast between light and shadow framing Jeff (Robert Mitchum) in *Out of the Past* (Jacques Tourneur, RKO Radio Pictures, 1947)

of technology, in particular, and the history of style, in general. A third crucial aspect is industry standards—the conventionalized practices of film and television production. I must return to Bordwell to explore this topic:

> I propose that we can fruitfully analyze and explain the historical dynamic of film style by inferring, *on the basis of the films and what we know about their making*, some pertinent craft traditions. The *traditions preserve favored practices*, practices that are the result of choices among alternatives. In choosing, filmmakers exercise their skill and judgment, thereby replicating, revising, or rejecting options supplied by their predecessors and peers.[12]

What Bordwell calls "**craft traditions**" are the rules or the code, one might say, that media practitioners accept, modify, or spurn as they choose to make media one way and not another. For example, the technological shift from film stock to digital recording of movies in the early twenty-first century was slowed by cinematographic customs. Even after digital recording technology became the virtual equal of film recording in terms of image quality, there were still many cinematographers who resisted change,

sticking with the older technology out of loyalty to a shooting tradition. Thus, there was no significant technological reason to snub digital recording, but there were substantial craft traditions blocking its adoption.

Craft traditions often have their roots in an aesthetic, not a technological, concern, which is the fourth of our historical style factors. Directors, cinematographers, set and costume designers, soundtrack composers, and other creative personnel all work under assumptions of what looks good or functions best in film, television, video games, and so on. Sometimes they are inspired by the visual composition of a work of art, as when director Christopher Nolan and cinematographer Wally Pfister drew inspiration from the work of M. C. Escher when they designed the look of the puzzle worlds of *Inception* (2010).[13] It is easy to see how aesthetics affected that film in very direct ways. And such a choice does not rely on economics or technology. A long shot does not cost more than a close-up; a special lens is not necessary to shoot one framing or the other. Rather, the selection of framing is at least partially governed by what a director thinks looks good. And, notably, standards change over time. In the 2010s, close-ups tend to be framed tighter than they were in the 1930s, for example. Another example is editing pace in television. In the 1950s, the average length of a shot in a television program was approximately eight seconds, and some live programs had considerably higher average shot lengths. Today the average shot length is much closer to four seconds. Different eras have different stylistic schemas that are conventionalized in their films and television programs.

Historicizing the Study of Style (Stylistics)

When investigating a critical method, it is often inviting to dive right into it. And I hope that this chapter has inspired you to become a bit of a stylistician and to attempt your own stylistic analyses. But it can also be useful to pause before engaging a critical method and consider how that method evolved and its major modes and terminology. The history of stylistics goes back at least 90 years. Outlining its evolution can help us better understand the nuances of this critical endeavor and the debates it has sparked. Of course, this is but a brief and necessarily incomplete survey of media stylistics. At the end of the chapter, I will have some suggestions for further reading that I hope this survey will entice you to explore.

The study of style was central to the birth of film theory in the 1910s and 1920s. Soviet filmmakers Lev Kuleshov and Sergei Eisenstein, among others, were at the forefront of early attempts to theorize what made the cinema unique. They were keen to identify what separated it from earlier art forms and came to the realization that it was a stylistic element that was crucial to the young medium. They argued that the technique of film editing or **montage**, as they called it, was the essence of the cinema. Kuleshov, in particular, had strong ties with the mode of literary criticism known as Russian formalism. The formalists emphasized how artistic technique—for example, film editing—could and should provoke viewers/ readers, slapping them in the face with its artfulness. They reasoned that film and literary techniques could thereby stimulate fresh perspectives on everyday objects, could *defamiliarize* them. Thus, as Kuleshov and Eisenstein were writing the first film theories, they were also writing the first academic stylistic analyses.

The formalists' emphasis on style was challenged in the late 1940s and 1950s by the post-World War II era's most influential film critic and journal editor, André Bazin, a co-founder of the highly influential magazine *Cahiers du Cinéma* in 1951. Like the formalists, Bazin was also fascinated with the relationship between film and reality, but he was less interested in how film technique could distort reality than he was intrigued by how film technique could replicate human perception. He reasoned that the cinema was rooted in still photography's ability to render the physical world in lifelike fashion.[14] Where the formalists strove to manipulate or even manufacture reality through style, Bazin sought techniques that would imitate human perception. Specifically, he was a proponent of **deep-focus** cinematography (where images in the foreground and background are equally in focus) because he felt it more closely resembled how the human eye views the world than shallow focus does.

Deep focus also encourages an active viewing experience where spectators can more easily choose where they direct their attention within the frame. One of Bazin's most famous examples is from *The Best Years of Our Lives* (1946), directed by William Wyler with cinematography by Gregg Toland (Figure 5.6).[15] In a bar scene, Homer (Harold Russell), a war veteran and amputee, plays piano in the foreground with Butch (Hoagy Carmichael) while Al (Fredric March) watches. In the middle ground can be seen two men sitting at the bar. What's particularly notable about Wyler and Toland's deep-focus composition is that it makes visible a man in a phone booth at the extreme rear of the frame (Fred [Dana Andrews]). Fred and Al have just had an altercation and Fred is now phoning Al's daughter to break off their relationship. By composing the image in depth, Bazin argues, Wyler and Toland allow viewers either to watch the foreground action or to let their attention stray to the action in the distant background—just as one can when sitting in a bar in real life. Bazin contrasts with the formalists in terms of the functions he believes style should serve, but both Bazin and the formalists ground their theories of the cinema in aspects of style. Thinking back to our eight functions for analytical stylistics, Bazin may be put in the category of style signifying liveness and/ or verisimilitude, while the formalists fit into several categories but were most interested in how style can denote and symbolize.

Bazin's *Cahiers du Cinéma* played an important role in the next stage of cinematic stylistics. The magazine provided a significant forum for rabble-rousing young critics who wished to mount an assault on the French film establishment. The virtual manifesto for their cause was an essay by director-to-be François Truffaut titled, "A Certain Tendency in the French Cinema," which appeared in the January 1954 issue.[16] Truffaut took issue with the "tendency" of prestigious

Figure 5.6 Deep-focus cinematography in *The Best Years of Our Lives* (William Wyler, RKO Radio Pictures, 1946) allows the viewer to select where to look: the men playing piano in the foreground or the man in the phone booth in the background

French films produced as part of the "tradition of quality." His argument with them was that their directors merely took established classics from French literature and translated them into films, without adding any of their own personal vision to the original texts. In short, the directors of the tradition-of-quality films were not investing their own personalities in their films. In place of the tradition of quality, Truffaut demanded in an article the following year, should be a *"politique des auteurs,"* a "policy of the authors," where directors express themselves as personally on film as an author does in a novel.[17] Directors should, as suggested by critic Alexandre Astruc, employ the camera-as-pen or *"caméra stylo."*[18]

At the heart of Truffaut's passionate argument is the notion that the most important part of a film is that which the director controls and orchestrates. Cameras' and actors' positions and movements, lighting, set design, costume design, and so on are all under his or her command and, as you may have already surmised, all of them are aspects of visual style. Truffaut's original phrase, *politique des auteurs*, eventually morphed into the half-French, half-English phrase, the **"auteur theory"** and sparked some of the liveliest critical debates of the 1950s and 1960s—as

are chronicled in Chapter 9 on authorship. Not all auteurist critics were focused on visual style, however. Many, as a matter of fact, were more concerned with narrative structure. But those that were obsessed with visual style often referred to is as ***mise-en-scène***, a theatrical term that has inspired myriad meanings in media studies, almost all of which come down to elements of visual style and the director's implementation of them. Some auteurist critics, drawing on the Byronic tradition of Romanticism, see *mise-en-scène* as an ineffable, unknowable quality of a director's divine spark, his or her creative genius. Others, such as Bordwell and Kristin Thompson, take a more mundane tack—identifying *mise-en-scène* as the patterning of all elements in front of the camera: set and costume design, lighting, and actor positioning and movement. Whether the result of a director's brilliance or just a workaday instance of film-technique's functions, *mise-en-scène* is derived from presumptions about style.

In reaction to the impressionistic excesses of auteurist critics, 1970s film criticism and theory sought a more reasonable and systematic approach to style and its meanings/functions. Christian Metz, perhaps the most significant film theorist of this time, championed the use of **semiotics** to analyze film.[19]

But what did he mean by semiotics? Simplifying, it may be said that semiotics studies how texts in the broadest sense of that term—including sentences, books, street signs, movies, fashion, paintings, and so on—communicate meaning through signs and their organization in systems and codes. Semiotics grew from the linguistic theories and philosophies of Charles Sanders Peirce and Ferdinand de Saussure late in the nineteenth century, but it had no meaningful application to media until Metz's work—shaking up French film and literary theory in the 1960s and then influencing English-language media theory in the 1970s, once it was translated. Metz's own analyses spend little time on visual style, but his approach opened up film theory to close readings of cinematic texts—where a critic might spend an entire article deconstructing a single scene. Such rapt attention to minuscule details invariably led to analyses of style's functions in cinematic texts, as could be seen in the pages of *Screen*, the (British) journal that defined film theory in the 1970s.[20]

Just a few years later, Bordwell and Thompson began advocating for a **poetics** of cinema—with Bordwell relying on cognitive psychology while Thompson considered the ramifications of neoformalism. Although Bordwell's and Thompson's solo efforts took slightly divergent paths, their co-authored textbook, *Film Art*, authoritatively established how to analyze style in a systematic fashion and, starting in 1979, it has influenced legions of film students.[21] Bordwell has been particularly dogged in his pursuit of poetics. In *Ozu and the Poetics of the Cinema* (1988), he clarifies how he understands that term, using words shaped by semiotics even though he would not call himself a semiotician: "'Poetics' refers to the study of how films are put together and how, in determinate contexts, they elicit particular effects."[22] Semiotics has been criticized for being "just" about the text and thereby ignoring cultural context, the historical facts of how texts are produced, and reader's/viewer's responses. Bordwell, in contrast, has been attentive to how industry changes affect style and, through cognitive psychology, how the viewer responds to the text. The former is the focus of a magisterial study of style and the film industry that he mounted with Thompson and Janet Staiger: *The Classical Hollywood Cinema: Film Style and Mode of Production to 1960*.[23] Although 30 years old, it remains the most comprehensive book ever published on film style.

The reader may reasonably wonder how the study of style in television evolved while there was all this activity in the stylistics, semiotics, and poetics of the cinema. In point of fact, the analysis of television style has lagged far behind that of the cinema. In part, this was due to condescending aesthetic presumptions that early television—that is, in the decade following the end of World War II—was visually bland, a tiny, blurry imitation of the cinema, whose only distinctive feature was the simultaneity it offered during its broadcasts of sports, inaugurations, parades, and other major cultural events. Television studies, as a discipline, had not gelled yet and television style was considered an object unworthy of study. John Fiske and John Hartley were among the first to explore ways to critically analyze television and its style. In 1978, they included a close semiotic analysis of a five-shot portion of the documentary *Cathy Come Home* (BBC, 1966) in their short book, *Reading Television*.[24] Fiske continued his attention to television style in his most extensive consideration of the medium, 1987's *Television Culture*.[25] He contends that television texts such as *Miami Vice* and music videos featuring performers like Madonna offer the viewer an intense postmodern pleasure: images untethered from the necessity of making meaning so that they might stimulate pure, liberating joy. A few years later, John Caldwell made a similar claim for *Miami Vice*, including it as an example of "excessive style," which defined his category of "**televisuality**." Television texts that exemplify televisuality are ones that use style to serve the "picture effect": "*The new television does not depend upon the reality effect or the fiction effect, but upon the picture effect.*"[26] In terms of style's functions that I enumerate above, I can say that Caldwell rejects style that functions to establish liveness or verisimilitude ("reality effect") or to denote a story ("fiction effect") and enthusiastically extolls its ability to decorate ("picture effect").

Thus, both Caldwell and Fiske view television style as a postmodern pleasure unto itself. This pleasure was sparked by television texts that were markedly stylized at a time, the 1980s, when most television style was still rather attenuated and television productions such as soap operas employed a pedestrian style. The texts Caldwell and Fiske favored were often said to be more "cinematic" than the rest of television—meaning that they incorporated stylistic conventions and practices similar to those of the cinema. The blurring of the line between cinema and television style has only increased in recent years. As media have converged, so have stylistic practices—to the point that a program such as HBO's *True Detective* (2014–) looks and sounds very much like a contemporary theatrical release. As a consequence, we have also seen increasing overlap among all media's stylistics and poetics. There are certainly distinctions to be made among theatrical film, television, and other visual media such as video games, but many of the critical tools that were once the sole province of cinema studies have found their way into the toolboxes of scholars analyzing other media.

A Case Study of Stylistic Analysis

When *Miami Vice* debuted as a two-hour pilot episode on September 16, 1984, I was among those who were astonished that such a visually rich program had been created for television and not for release to theaters. As is so often the case in academic media research, I was initially drawn to it as a fan or, as Henry Jenkins might say, an **aca/fan**—"a hybrid creature which is part fan and part academic."[27] I must confess that my decision to analyze *Miami Vice* was not part of a carefully plotted academic research agenda, but, rather, it was a result of my dabbling in television analysis after having earned a doctorate in film studies just a few years before. I was not alone in this regard. During the 1980s, television studies was emerging as a distinct discipline, and some of its most vocal advocates were expatriates from film studies—as can be seen in Robert C. Allen's groundbreaking television-studies anthology, *Channels of Discourse*, which has numerous contributors, including Allen himself, who were trained in film studies.[28] *Miami Vice* was a perfect match for my research interests of that time because of its crossover style—a television program that borrowed so much of its sound and image style from the cinema. *Miami Vice*'s style was particularly notable because early-1980s television craft practices were dominated by attenuated, purely functional visual style. As a *Miami Vice* reviewer in *Film Comment* explained, "It's hard to forbear saying, every five minutes or so, 'I can't believe this was shot for *television*!'"[29] Today, some thirty years later, the division between the two media has become less distinct, but in 1984 the boundary between them seemed unassailable.

My key, fairly obvious revelation, thus, was that *Miami Vice* spliced film style onto a television program. The challenge was to develop this common insight into systematic academic research. The approach I took was adopted from genre studies. Film noir was well established as a genre that relied heavily upon visual style for its defining characteristics. There were clear visual similarities between films noirs and *Miami Vice* episodes, but what were their differences? How was a film genre renovated to suit the particular properties of the television medium? These questions structured my approach to the program and provided a larger justification for restricting my study to a single television show. Merely pointing out the noir aspects in *Miami Vice* would have had fairly limited import, but ruminating upon how the program highlights essential characteristics of television itself made the study more compelling as it gave it greater significance beyond a single television show. Media studies often proceeds this way. Investigation of a specific instance is used to make broader claims about a program, a genre, even an entire medium.

At the moment that *Miami Vice* arrived, scholarship on film noir was burgeoning. Hundreds of articles, books, Master's theses, and Ph.D. dissertations have been devoted to the topic since the mid-1980s—leading film noir to become the genre most written about in academic circles. One of the commonplace assumptions about film noir is that its visual style disrupted the monotonous craft practices of 1930s classical cinema. For my purposes, an essay by J. A. Place and L. S. Peterson was the clearest catalogue of "Some Visual Motifs of *Film Noir*" (1974) that broke with classical film traditions.[30] Place and Peterson's work inspired my own essay because I saw a clear parallel between noir's "antitraditional" film style, as they call it, and *Miami Vice*'s rejection of conventional 1980s television style. Thus, noir's reliance on visual style for its definition attracted me to it initially, and then its disruptive qualities cemented my interest in the genre's intersection with *Miami Vice*.

Genre study, in general, and film noir scholarship, in particular, were the two most significant theoretical resources underpinning my essay, but when it was expanded and reprinted in 2010, I also relied upon concepts that had developed since the essay's original publication. Specifically, Fiske's and Caldwell's enthusiastic valorization of stylistic excesses gave further credence to my argument that the character of *Miami Vice*'s style was strongly antitraditional. And I also incorporated Bordwell's related idea of **intensified continuity**, which holds that 1980s film amplified the techniques of the classical continuity system without utterly breaking the system entirely.[31] Similarly, I found that *Miami Vice disrupted* 1980s television craft practices, but it did not wholly *destroy* them.

Building upon a theoretical/methodological foundation incorporating (1) genre study, (2) film noir scholarship, (3) carnivalesque visual pleasure/televisuality, and (4) intensified continuity, this essay arrives at four major claims:

1. Style has meaning; film noir's visual style conveys the genre's themes and its conventional narratives (stylistic functions: to denote and to symbolize).
2. Genres may cross over from one medium to another, but they must be modified to account for medium specificity. Film noir elements may be identified in the television program *Miami Vice*, but they have been modified to suit the television medium—particularly in terms of signifying narrative and theme.
3. 1980s television favored a tedious, attenuated visual style that was disrupted by *Miami Vice*'s intensified style (stylistic function: to differentiate).
4. Unlike much television (and film, for that matter), *Miami Vice* offers moments of pure visual pleasure, where the image is not laboring in service to narrative or theme (stylistic function: to decorate).

These claims matured as this essay went from an initial publication in *The Journal of Popular Film and Television* to a reprinting in *Film Noir Reader* and a final reworking in *Television Style*, but they still do not exhaust what there is to say about *Miami Vice* and film noir.

Conclusion: Whither Style in the Age of Streaming Video?

Perhaps the main limitation of my essay, like many stylistic studies, is that it lacks any specific theory of emotional effect, of how style catalyzes a viewer's emotions and has an impact on the viewer. The ability of style to express and provoke emotion, as I discussed above, is often thought to be one of its most significant functions, but without engaging in empirical research on actual human subjects, it is extremely difficult to assess emotion. Cognitive (or another) psychology might conceivably be applied to the viewing of *Miami Vice*, but I have yet to find a satisfactory solution to this problem. Another, not unrelated, limitation to this study is that it requires further consideration of *Miami Vice*'s sound design. Music is one of the program's defining features, and it is also an elusive, emotionally potent stylistic element—notoriously difficult to analyze (see the next chapter on sound). The essay offers a few thoughts on music, but there are definitely opportunities to do more with it.

This case study gestures toward other possible opportunities for further research. Narrative continuity style in visual media has grown ever more intensified

since the 1980s—incorporating accelerated editing, extravagant visual effects, baroque lighting design, and so on. One might profitably track how intensified style functions in today's television narrative programs, films, sports/news coverage, and commercials. Examples could include television shows like *Game of Thrones* and *Breaking Bad* (AMC, 2008–2013) or films like *Moonrise Kingdom* and *Inception*. New craft practices have emerged as new distribution venues have evolved; particularly significant is online streaming, as provided by services such as Netflix, Amazon, and Apple. Style continues to serve the same functions as articulated above, but it has a very different impact when a film or television show is viewed on a tiny smartphone screen, a 50-inch home monitor, or a large screen in a theater. Stylisticians need to account for the functioning of style in a period of media convergence. Another related, but narrower, research topic that could jump off from the current study would be to examine how directors and producers function within the strictures of this media crossover. Executive producer and director of *Miami Vice*, Michael Mann, is a particularly interesting example because he has worked so extensively in both film and television. Thus, an auteurist analysis of Mann might chart the position of *Miami Vice*'s style within the stylistics of his other work—helping to understand how a director can travel between television and film.

Notes

1. David Bordwell, *Figures Traced in Light: On Cinematic Staging* (Berkeley: University of California Press, 2005), 32. Emphasis added.
2. Jeremy G. Butler, "Stylistic Crossover in the Network Era: From Film to Television," in *Television Style* (New York: Routledge, 2010), 70–108.
3. Christine Geraghty, "Aesthetics and Quality in Popular Television Drama," *International Journal of Cultural Studies* 6 no. 25 (2003): 25–45; Jason Jacobs and Steven Peacock, eds., *Television Aesthetics and Style* (London: Bloomsbury, 2013); Greg M. Smith, *Beautiful TV: The Art and Argument of Ally McBeal* (Austin: University of Texas Press, 2007).
4. Bordwell, *Figures Traced in Light*, 32.
5. Noël Carroll, "Film Form: An Argument for a Functional Theory of Style in the Individual Film," in *Engaging the Moving Image* (New Haven: Yale University Press, 2003), 141. Emphasis in the original.
6. Bordwell, *Figures Traced in Light*, 33–34.
7. Ibid., 34.
8. Ibid.
9. John Fiske, *Television Culture* (New York: Methuen, 1987), 249.

10. Louis Althusser, "Ideology and Ideological State Apparatuses," in *Lenin and Philosophy and Other Essays*, trans. Ben Brewster (New York: Monthly Review Press, 1970), 174.

11. Brett Mills, "Comedy Vérité: Contemporary Sitcom Form," *Screen* 45, no. 1 (2004): 63–78; Ethan Thompson, "Comedy Vérité? The Observational Documentary Meets the Televisual Sitcom," *Velvet Light Trap* no. 60 (2007): 63–72.

12. Bordwell, *Figures Traced in Light*, 265. Emphasis added.

13. Blogger Nick DeSantis points out this and nine other connections between art and film in "The Paintings Behind the Films: When Fine Art and Filmmaking Collide," *Film.com*, July 12, 2013, accessed July 17, 2014, www.film.com/movies/pacific-rim-painting.

14. André Bazin's essays have been anthologized as *What Is Cinema? Volumes 1 and 2*, ed. and trans. Hugh Gray (Berkeley: University of California Press, 1967, 1971).

15. André Bazin, "William Wyler, or the Jansenist of Directing," in *Bazin at Work: Major Essays and Reviews from the Forties and Fifties*, ed. Bert Cardullo, trans. Alain Piette and Bert Cardullo (New York: Routledge, 1997), 1–22.

16. François Truffaut, "Une Certaine Tendance du Cinéma Francais," *Cahiers du Cinéma* 31 (January 1954): 15–29. Reprinted and translated as "A Certain Tendency of the French Cinema," in *Movies and Methods, Vol. I*, ed. Bill Nichols (Berkeley: University of California Press, 1974), 224–37.

17. François Truffaut, "*Ali Baba* et la 'Politique des Auteurs,'" *Cahiers du Cinéma* 44 (February 1955): 45–47.

18. Alexandre Astruc, "The Birth of a New Avant-Garde: La Caméra-Stylo," in *The New Wave*, ed. Peter Graham (Garden City, NY: Doubleday, 1968) 17–23. Translated from Alexandre Astruc, "Naissance d'une nouvelle avant-garde: la caméra-stylo," *L'Écran Français* 144 (30 March 1948) 5–6.

19. Christian Metz, *Film Language: A Semiotics of the Cinema*, trans. Michael Taylor (Chicago: University of Chicago Press, 1974, 1991). His "*Le Cinéma: Langue ou Langage?*" ("The Cinema: Language or Language System?") is included in *Film Language*. It originally appeared in *Communications* 4 (1964) and might well be the earliest attempt to apply semiotics to film.

20. For more, see John Gibbs, *The Life of Mise-en-scène: Visual Style and British Film Criticism, 1946–78* (Manchester: Manchester University Press, 2014).

21. David Bordwell and Kristin Thompson, *Film Art: An Introduction*, 11th ed. (New York: McGraw-Hill, 2017).

22. David Bordwell, *Ozu and the Poetics of Cinema* (Princeton: Princeton University Press, 1988), 1, accessed March 2, 2018, https://quod.lib.umich.edu/c/cjs/0920054.0001.001/--ozu-and-the-poetics-of-cinema-david-bordwell?view=toc.

23. David Bordwell, Kristin Thompson, and Janet Staiger, *The Classical Hollywood Cinema: Film Style and Mode of Production to 1960* (New York: Columbia University Press, 1985).

24. John Fiske and John Hartley, *Reading Television* (New York: Methuen, 1978), 55–58.

25. John Fiske, *Television Culture* (London: Routledge, 1987).

26. John Thornton Caldwell, *Televisuality: Style, Crisis, and Authority in American Television* (New Brunswick: Rutgers University Press, 1995), 152. Emphasis in the original.

27. Henry Jenkins, "Who the &%&# Is Henry Jenkins?" *Confessions of an Aca-Fan*, n.d., accessed July 22, 2014, http://henryjenkins.org/aboutmehtml.

28. Robert C. Allen, ed., *Channels of Discourse: Television and Contemporary Criticism* (New York: Routledge, 1987). A second edition, *Channels of Discourse, Reassembled*, was released five years later, but there have been no further editions. Consequently, its claim to "contemporary" criticism is becoming increasingly dated.

29. Richard T. Jameson, "Men over Miami," *Film Comment* (April 1985): 66.

30. J. A. Place and L. S. Peterson, "Some Visual Motifs of *Film Noir*," *Film Comment* (January-February 1974): 30–35. Reprinted as J. A. Place and L. S. Peterson, "Some Visual Motifs of *Film Noir*," in *Movies and Methods*, ed. Bill Nichols (Berkeley: University of California Press, 1976), 325–38.

31. Bordwell, *Figures Traced in Light*, 23.

Further Reading

Bordwell, David. *Poetics of Cinema*. New York: Routledge, 2008.

Burnett, Colin. "A New Look at the Concept of Style in Film: The Origins and Development of the Problem-Solution Model." *New Review of Film and Television Studies* 6, no. 2 (2008): 127–49.

Butler, Jeremy G. *Television: Visual Storytelling and Screen Culture*. 5th ed. New York: Routledge, 2018.

Carroll, Noël. *Engaging the Moving Image*. New Haven: Yale University Press, 2003.

Doucet, Ron. "The Cinematography of *The Incredibles*." *Flooby Nooby*. December 9, 2013. Accessed July 7, 2014. http://floobynooby.blogspot.com/2013/12/the-cinematography-of-incredibles-part-1.html.

Eisenstein, Sergei. *Film Form: Essays in Film Theory*. Edited and translated by Jay Leyda. New York: Harcourt, 1969.

Heath, Stephen. "Film and System: Terms of Analysis, Part I." *Screen* 16, no. 1 (1975): 7–77.

Kuleshov, Lev. *Kuleshov on Film: Writings*. Edited and translated by Ronald Levaco. Berkeley: University of California Press, 1974.

Zettl, Herbert. *Sight Sound Motion: Applied Media Aesthetics*. 8th ed. Belmont: Wadsworth, 2016.

6.
SOUND

Jacob Smith

Sound Studies has emerged as a vital field of academic research that exists at the crossroads of a number of disciplines. Jonathan Sterne defines Sound Studies as "the interdisciplinary ferment in the human sciences that takes sound as its analytical point of departure or arrival." Scholars working in this field analyze sonic practices, discourses, and institutions, with the goal of better understanding "what sound does in the human world, and what humans do to the sonic world." The sonic world—which includes musical practices but is not confined to them—can be an object of study, but sound can also provide a method. That is, turning one's attention to sound—activating what Sterne calls the **sonic imagination**—can be a way to ask "big questions" about culture, society, and experience.[1]

The strength of Sound Studies lies in the range and diversity of the voices it sustains, as well as the excitement that comes from the possibility of new insights and discoveries. At the same time, the "interdisciplinary ferment" of Sound Studies can intimidate scholars who feel they must become conversant in musicology, the anthropology of sound, architectural design, noise abatement policy, psychoacoustics, the history of the senses, the politics of deafness, the artistry of the cinematic soundtrack, and the history of radio broadcasting. My chapter aims to demonstrate that, though Sound Studies can come across as a rather cacophonous enterprise on first listen, most of its participants are working from the same score.

In a 2005 essay, Michele Hilmes wrote that Sound Studies threatened to be an "emerging field" that never quite materialized; one that was "always emerging, never emerged."[2] In the decade since Hilmes' comment, a number of edited volumes have been published that map the terrain of Sound Studies, academic journals dedicated to sonic culture have been launched, university courses on the topic have been designed and taught, international conferences on sound have been held, and major museum exhibitions have been devoted to sound art. All of this activity makes it an exciting time for students of the sonic world, but it is also a time when much seems to be at stake. How can sound scholars balance the security of institutional recognition with the desire to prolong the field's "revolutionary moment," when "unanticipated zones of possibility" might be discovered?[3] Mikhail Bakhtin, a particularly sound-minded theorist, might say that Sound Studies is experiencing an acute tension between a centripetal pull to unify around core texts and principles, and a centrifugal pull to celebrate the field's **heteroglossia**—that is, its many voices.[4]

I want to keep those forces in productive tension throughout this chapter, by providing the reader with an overview of the field's disciplinary history and some of its major themes, authors, and concepts, while at the same time, acknowledging its continuing emergence and fostering the sense of its open-ended possibilities. Hoping to strike a balance between establishing a canon and enabling future scholarship, I offer a number of "research-generating terms": the words or phrases that have become prominent features in the intellectual terrain of Sound Studies.[5] Think of these terms as a set of riffs that constitute a repertoire of standard melodies, while also serving as a resource that a new generation of scholars might re-accentuate, re-voice, and re-mix. I conclude with a discussion of how some of these standard melodies played out in one of my own essays.

Sound Among the Senses

Numerous scholarly trajectories have fed into Sound Studies, one of which is a tradition of work on "oral poetry" in Folklore and Anthropology. Albert Lord's *The Singer of Tales* (1960) built upon the earlier research of Milman Parry to make an argument about the specificity of poetic composition in cultures that made relatively little use of writing. The tendency to demarcate "oral" and "literate" modes of expression spread to broader arguments about the relationship between media, culture, and sensory experience in the decade that followed. The next key figure, of course, is Marshall McLuhan, who wrote about the differences between visual and acoustic space, and made corresponding contrasts between pre- and post-literate people.[6] McLuhan's student, Walter Ong continued this line of argument, making observations on the nature of sound, the "psychodynamics of orality," and the "secondary orality" brought about by audiovisual media.[7] McLuhan and Ong's writing tended to be nostalgic for an acoustic lifeworld that was understood to be more authentically co-present than a print-based visual one, and they pulled against an "ocularcentrism" in Western culture later diagnosed by scholars like Martin Jay.[8]

The work of McLuhan and Ong made an important contribution to the theorization of sound, but it is problematic to the extent that it is marked by technological determinism, creates a "great divide" between oral and literate cultures, and reinforces what Sterne has called an **audiovisual litany** that posits essential differences between hearing and vision. "The problem with the litany," Sterne argues, is that "it elevates a set of cultural prenotions about the senses (prejudices, really) to the level of theory."[9] Subsequent ethnographic work on sonic experience in various cultural contexts has added much-needed nuance to the discussion, such as Ruth Finnegan's *Literacy and Orality* (1988). The anthropologist Stephen Feld has done much to define an anthropology of sound, and he uses the term **acoustemology** to describe the ways in which sound is "a modality for knowing and being in the world." The influence of Feld's approach to the cultural specificity of sonic practices can be felt in Tia DeNora's sociological study of the functions of recorded music in everyday life, in Charles Hirschkind's ethnographic examination of the cassette sermon in Islamic culture, and in Ana Maria Ochoa Gautier's work on the politics of the voice in nineteenth-century Latin America and the Caribbean.[10]

Just as scholars have rejected the stark divide between oral and literate cultures, they have also rejected a strict division of sensory experience. For many of its proponents, the goal of Sound Studies is not to place sound at the top of a reordered hierarchy of the senses, but rather to prompt a better understanding of what Steven Connor calls the "fertility of the relations" between the senses.[11] Constance Classen writes of the various "sensory meanings and values" that might be espoused by a given society.[12] Her notion of a "sensory model," as well as work on the anthropology of the senses by scholars such as David Howes and Paul Stoller, reveals the senses to be a "domain of cultural expression" and stresses the functional interdependence of sensory modalities.[13] Nina Sun Eidsheim's work on singing and listening as multisensory, "intermaterial vibrational practices" represents one way in which Sound Studies scholars continue to explore the fertility of the relations between the senses.[14]

Several concepts taken from the work of the French film theorist Michel Chion—a prolific creator of research-generating terms in the field—illustrate how a Sound Studies method can result in insights extending beyond the auditory. Chion approaches film as an inherently multisensory aesthetic form in which sound and image work together to create meaning. "Instead of saying that film sound is subservient to the image, or reversing the equation," he writes, "couldn't we just say that sounds and images both devote themselves to the constitution of narrative cinematic space-time?"[15] Chion refers to **synchresis** as the "weld produced between a particular auditory phenomenon and visual phenomenon when they occur at the same time," and describes dynamics of **spatial magnetization** whereby sounds are understood in relation to images on the screen.[16] In the book *Audiovision* (1994), Chion shares some of the classroom techniques that he uses to illustrate these ideas, such as a "masking" exercise in which a sequence is played with image only or sound only and then with sound and image together. Another technique is "forced marriage," in which a film clip is paired with different musical pieces.[17] Chion's exercises have been extremely productive in my own introductory film classes, where I have often shown a film clip without the sound and then asked students to work in groups to create a plan for the sound design they think would be most effective. Without fail, we are all surprised at the remarkable variety of ideas generated by the different groups and impressed by how each design changes the overall meaning of the scene.

Rendering is another important concept from Chion's oeuvre, and it refers to the translation of "one order of sensation into another."[18] Because filmmakers must render a situation through audio and visual channels alone, sound is often called upon to compensate. For example, the sound of a punch in a Hollywood film is typically exaggerated in order to convey "a rush of composite sensations and not just the auditory reality of the event."[19] The concept of rendering begins with sound, but asks us to think in terms of sensory admixture, as does Chion's oft-cited discussion of the **acousmetre**: a character in a film narrative whose voice we hear but whose body we either do not see, or only partially see; for example, Norman Bates' mother in *Psycho* (1960) or the computer HAL in *2001: A Space Odyssey* (1968). In his short but remarkably dense chapter on the *acousmetre*, Chion shows how the careful calibration of sound and image has been an expressive resource for filmmakers, and, like his work in general, it shows that sound can become a productive research method. That is, Chion's work demonstrates that thinking through sound does not mean limiting the object of study to auditory experience but serves as a means to apprehend the totality of multisensory media experience in a new way.

Chion's corpus is only one example of how the sonic imagination can be mobilized to explore the intersensory experience of the media. Other authors have examined how the sounds of radio were coupled with the visual design of the receiver; or how phonograph records can become the subject of visual attention; or how bass frequencies are felt in the body; or how sounds become a military weapon used to induce pain.[20] One area of research explores dynamics of **sonification**: the techniques by which non-sonic data is made audible.[21] Sonification is the aural equivalent of information visualization, and sonic analogues to the pie chart and bar graph include sonar technology, Geiger counters, metal detectors, auditory displays of seismic or volcanic activity, and visual-to-auditory sensory substitution devices. A stunning example of sonification can be found in the work of the First Sounds organization, a group of audio historians, recording engineers, and archivists whose aim is to make audible the earliest known sound recordings and inscriptions.[22] First Sounds made international headlines when they sonified written inscriptions of sound waves made by Édouard-Léon Scott de Martinville's phonautograph. These experiments effectively pushed back the history of audio playback to decades before Thomas

Edison's invention of the phonograph. In the process, this endeavor brings up intriguing questions about the plasticity of the senses, what kind of technologies should be considered a sound medium, and what counts as "sound" in Sound Studies.[23]

First Sounds have allowed us to listen to the earliest known recorded sounds, and historians have allowed us to hear even further back in time. This extends to the first evidence of human culture in the field of "archaeoacoustics." David Hendy describes archaeological research that suggests that prehistoric cave paintings are found in places where the acoustics are unusual, such that "wherever a cave *sounds* most interesting, you are also likely to find the greatest concentration of prehistoric art."[24] Moving forward in time to the nineteenth century, Alain Corbin's *Village Bells* (1998) is a fascinating analysis of the intricate social functions performed by bells in the French countryside, which Corbin argues worked to organize the "temporal architecture" of the community.[25] A number of texts on auditory history were published in the decade after Corbin's book: Mark M. Smith's *Listening to Nineteenth-Century America* (2002) and *Hearing History* (2004); John Picker's *Victorian Soundscapes* (2003); Richard Cullen Rath's *How Early America Sounded* (2005); and Gary Tomlinson's *The Singing of the New World: Indigenous Voice in the Era of European Contact* (2009).[26] That decade also saw the publication of Emily Thompson's influential *The Soundscape of Modernity* (2004), which, along with the work of Jacques Attali and Karin Bijsterveld, stands as a key text in the investigation of **noise**. This scholarship reveals the various discursive histories of noise through the development of noise abatement legislation and anxieties about changing notions of public and private space in the era of modernity.[27]

From work on auditory history, we move to the related investigation of sound's role in popular memory. Scholars have examined the "technonostalgia" displayed by collectors of vintage musical gear and "residual" sonic forms like vinyl records.[28] Cultural historians have done ethnographic studies of **ear-witnessing**: the experience of past events through sound, as in the role of air raid sirens in remembering World War II bombing attacks.[29] Air raid sirens are an example of a historically significant **earcon**, a sonic event that contains "special symbolic meaning not present in the sound wave."[30] The literature on sound and memory suggests that Walter Benjamin might have been correct to question whether the term "déjà vu" was well chosen: a more appropriate metaphor would be taken from "the realm of acoustics," he wrote, since it is "a word, a tapping, or a rustling that is endowed with the magic power to transport us into the cool tomb of long ago, from the vault of which the present seems to return only as an echo."[31]

Sonic Spaces

It is perhaps not surprising that research on sound's relationship to history and memory has proliferated, given the fact that hearing has often been understood in relation to the experience of time. Common statements in the audiovisual litany include claims that sound exists only when it is "going out of existence," or that we cannot freeze a sound in the way we can freeze an image, or that sound is inherently concerned with movement. In aesthetics, this tendency is expressed in arguments that contrast music and poetry as temporal arts with painting and sculpture as spatial arts.[32] The desire to pull against the grain of this litany has spurred scholars to consider the spatial investigation of sound. Georgina Born notes that recent years have seen "a veritable avalanche of scholarship devoted to the interconnections between sound and space."[33]

A fundamental term in the investigation of sound and space is R. Murray Schafer's notion of **soundscape**, which Emily Thompson has defined as "an aural landscape that is both a physical environment and a way of perceiving that environment; including not only sounds, but the material culture of sound, ways of listening, and the listener's relationship to that environment."[34] Schafer's work been criticized for its nostalgic tendencies and a certain anti-urban bias, but it has provided students of sound with a rich vocabulary for describing the lived environment and has inspired not only academic work, but a burgeoning sub-genre of sound art based upon **field recordings**.[35] Thompson's work is suggestive of how the study of the soundscape can involve both the analysis of architectural design and the spaces of film exhibition. Scholars of film sound have developed a vocabulary for the spatial experience of the soundtrack. Chion names the space created by sound as the **superfield** and explains that it fills the room beyond the "physical boundaries of the screen."[36] In my own work, I have drawn upon Bakhtin's concept of the **chronotope** (the intrinsic connectedness of time and space as expressed in literature) to say that a **sonotope** is the generic representation of a particular nexus of sound and space.[37] There is more work to be done on the connection between the lived environment and modes of sonic representation, on the

practices of field recording, and on the use of sound to create a sense of immersion in media texts.

Paying attention to sound and space has also prompted the investigation of the increasing mobility of sound via portable media devices. Unencumbered by an electronic display, sound media are eminently portable, and the experience of their playback is conducive to movement through and engagement with the world, as is evidenced by the cultural history of the portable phonograph, transistor radio, portable cassette player, iPod, satnav device, and museum audioguide. Scholars of sound have examined mobility and portability primarily in relation to devices like the Apple iPod and the Sony Walkman, often asserting that portable music creates a personalized "soundtrack to the city."[38] Jean-Paul Thibaud describes that experience in terms of "visiophonic knots": the points of convergence between mediated sound and the visible environment.[39] Portable sound practices are an excellent way to explore the "augmented spaces" that are created when digital technologies "place layers of data over the physical space." Notably, Lev Manovich points to Janet Cardiff's **audio walks**—a form of sound art in which the listener is given prerecorded audio that guides them through a landscape—as "the best realization" of augmented space, due to their power to create "interactions between the two spaces—between vision and hearing … and between present and past."[40] The recent publication of two volumes of the *Oxford Handbook of Mobile Music Studies* (2014) indicates the interest in this area of media culture.

Record Machines

The Walkman and iPod show the importance of specific technologies in the history of auditory experience, and sound devices have played a prominent role in research on the cultural history of media technology. Theodor Adorno's critical essays on the popular music industry are well known, but he also wrote about the materiality of phonograph records.[41] German media theorist Friedrich Kittler grants the gramophone a special place in his analysis of modern media technologies, and, more recently, Jonathan Sterne, James Lastra, and Lisa Gitelman have published cultural histories that situate sound technologies in relation to the simulation of the human ear and throat, discourses of reading and writing devices, and the cultural construction of "new media."[42]

Some of the most generative work on sound technology emerges from the study of cinema, perhaps because the arrival of the "Talkies" in the late

1920s was such a decisive event in the history of the medium. Rick Altman is a pioneer in the study of film sound, and among his contributions is a critique of the **reproductive fallacy** in previous discussions of sound in film theory. This fallacy assumes that, while the image is carefully rendered, the soundtrack simply reproduces a faithful version of the original sonic event. Altman's corrective is to show that, through microphone placement, mixing, and a host of other factors, "recordings do not reproduce sound, they represent sound."[43] Altman's work has been extended and developed by scholars such as Lastra, who adds an insightful analysis of the debate among Hollywood sound engineers that shaped the conventions of the soundtrack. There are numerous genre-specific studies of film sound: Robert Spadoni on horror; Jane Feuer, Steven Cohan, and Jean Ma on the musical; Britta Sjogren on melodrama; Daniel Goldmark on animated cartoons; and William Whittington's study of science fiction.[44]

In a classic essay, Altman describes the soundtrack of Orson Welles' *Citizen Kane* (1941) as a site where the aesthetics of Hollywood and radio broadcasting merge.[45] Until recently, Altman's essay was a rare instance of dialogue between Film Studies and Radio Studies, the latter being another scholarly field that intersects with Sound Studies. Rudolf Arnheim embodies the potential for crosstalk between film and radio, since he is both a seminal film theorist and the author of an early analysis of radio aesthetics. Arnheim wrote that radio used sound, voice, and music to create an "amazing new unity out of pure form and physical reality."[46] Neil Verma updates Arnheim's spatial poetics of radio through his discussion of **audioposition**: "the place for the listener that is created by coding foregrounds and backgrounds."[47] Verma posits two dominant formulas used by radio directors of the 1930s to create a sense of auditory space: an "intimate" mode in which the listener is positioned alongside a "carefully selected character for the duration of the drama" and a **kaleidosonic** mode that creates the feeling of a "shifting sonic world" by aurally leaping from place to place. Verma's description of an intimate mode of radio narrative resonates with historical work on the ways in which radio microphones shaped new modes of political speech (as in Franklin D. Roosevelt's "fireside chats") and popular singing (in the case of the "radio crooners").[48]

Radio history has been a burgeoning area of inquiry in recent years, partly due to television scholars' realization that radio is more than a footnote to TV history; indeed, it is a crucial foundation for broadcasting styles, formats, and industrial practices. Michele Hilmes' work has been particularly generative in the new wave of radio history, and many scholars have been inspired by her analysis of daytime and nighttime programming, the synergies between Hollywood and broadcasting, and the dynamics of female radio stardom.[49] Given the growth of podcasting and claims for a new "Golden Age" of radio in the form of popular series such as *This American Life* (Chicago Public Media, 1995–present), *Radiolab* (WNYC, 2002–present), *Serial* (WBEZ, 2014–present), and *S-Town* (WBEZ, 2017), it is safe to assume that scholarly work on radio will continue to gain momentum.

Listening Publics and Talking Bodies

One of the benefits of research on radio is that it prompted scholars to ask "big questions" about the broader category of "listening." Susan Douglas catalogs what she refers to as radio's "repertoire of listening," while David Goodman focuses on the "distracted" radio listener.[50] Kate Lacey makes a distinction between "listening in" to a specific media text, and a **listening out** that involves an openness to others in the act of listening that is a precondition for political action. The latter kind of listening "constitutes a kind of *attention* to others (and otherness) . . . that is the prerequisite both of citizenship . . . and of communicative action."[51] Lacey defines listening as the "active direction of the sense of hearing to discern meaning from sound," and she stresses that it is an active endeavor that is shaped by culture.[52]

The emphasis on agency in the act of listening in this definition is an important counter to the common trope that, since "we have no ear lids," we cannot control what we hear. Here is another version of the audiovisual litany, which assumes that vision is a conscious, rational act, while hearing is somehow pre-conscious, irrational, and pre-modern. Sterne provides another antidote to such assumptions in his account of how telegraph operators and the users of stethoscopes embodied an **audile technique** that was characterized by "logic, analytic thought, industry, professionalism, capitalism, individualism, and mastery."[53] Mara Mills makes a crucial intervention in the field by bringing it into dialogue with Disability Studies, complicating our understanding of terms like "reading" and "listening," and revealing the close connection between the development of sound technologies and devices for deaf and blind communities.[54]

All of this talk about ears and listening can make one forget that Sound Studies is also concerned with throats, mouths, and voices. The great theorist of the voice is Bakhtin, who had a predilection for metaphors like voice, dialogue, accent, and polyphony, making him a key thinker for the field. In fact, the film scholar Robert Stam suggests that Bahktin's sonic metaphors argue for "an overall shift in priority from the visually predominant logical space of modernity . . . to a 'post-modern' space of the vocal," as a way of "restoring voice to the silenced."[55] Sound students might follow Bakhtin's influence into the field of sociolinguistics and the micro-sociology of Erving Goffman, who often drew his examples from the modern media and wrote a long essay on the subject of "radio talk."[56]

Jacques Derrida's work on speech and writing has been a touchstone for many studies of the voice that are concerned with questions of authenticity, presence, and identity.[57] Scholars have been drawn to vocalizations at the margins of speech such as laughter, moans, shouts, and the expressive possibilities of vocal timbre. The ur-text here is Roland Barthes' essay on the "**grain of the voice**," which manifests "something which is directly the singer's body."[58] Interest in the voice and the body has continued, as in Steven Connor's discussion of the "vocalic body," which he calls "a surrogate or secondary body, a projection of a new way of having or being a body, formed and sustained out of the autonomous operations of the voice."[59]

The voice has been studied as an important signifier of race. Lindon Barrett and Alexander Weheliye write about ideologies of race as embodied in the distinction between a "singing voice" that enacts "blackness [and] embodiment," and a "signing voice" of Euro-American alphabetical literacy that has signaled whiteness and disembodiment.[60] Alice Maurice explores similar dynamics in regards to the ways in which African-American voices were used to promote early sound films.[61] In a trenchant essay, Gus Stadler calls for more work in Sound Studies that acknowledges "that our understanding of sound is always conducted, and has always been conducted, from within history, as lived through categories like race."[62] Recent publications by Jennifer Stoever on the "sonic color line" and Shilpa Davé on the racial performance of "brown voice" show promising developments in that area.[63]

Scholars have also listened closely to how gender is performed by the voice. Along with Altman, Mary Anne Doane is a crucial figure in the early study of film sound, and her essay "The Voice in the Cinema,"

along with Kaja Silverman's *The Acoustic Mirror* (1988), did much to draw attention to the gendered ideologies shaping norms of sound–image synchronization in the cinema.[64] Sjogren is the most recent feminist critic to engage with the topic of **voice-off**—when a character speaks from offscreen—focusing on classic Hollywood melodramas of the 1940s.[65] The voice has been an important way in which scholars have understood the embodied dynamics of film stardom, as in Richard Dyer's classic studies of Judy Garland and Paul Robeson, and Shane Vogel's work on Lena Horne.[66] Neepa Majumdar's work on the voices of female playback singers in the Indian film industry, and Jean Ma's book on female singers in Chinese cinema show the importance of moving this analysis beyond European and American contexts.[67] More work needs to be done at the crossroads of Queer Theory and Sound Studies, to build upon Wayne Koestenbaum's pioneering book on queer experience and the recorded voices of opera stars.[68]

The Sound of Music / The Music of Sound

In 2005, Hilmes complained that the "various venues of academic work on sound phenomena so rarely speak to or take heed of each other, and equally as rarely do they attempt to systematically theorize across medium-specific practices."[69] That shortcoming has been particularly troubling in the relative lack of dialogue between work on sound in Media Studies and Musicology (for more on popular music studies, see Chapter 23). As Georgina Born observes, "musicology and the burgeoning literatures on sound and auditory cultures have proceeded largely in isolation from each other."[70] Douglas Kahn and Brandon LaBelle are notable exceptions, publishing influential work that encompasses the history of radio, phonography, avant-garde musical practices, and sound art.[71] Music video has been a somewhat peripheral genre in Television Studies, but it is a rich site of intermedial connection. The work of Robert Walser and, above all, Carol Vernallis has done much to map its aesthetic possibilities.[72] Sound Studies and Musicology also coexist in a growing body of literature on the role of music, dance, and sound design in video games.[73]

Another point of intersection between Sound Studies and Musicology can be found in work on the history of the record industry by David Suisman, William Howland Kenney, Susan Schmidt Horning, David Morton, Michael Chanan, Patrick Feaster, Tim Anderson, and Mark Katz.[74] In a recent book, Michael

Denning brings a global scope to the history of phonography, describing how vernacular musics during the era of electrical recording such as hula, tango, samba, and blues, which "emerged on the edges and borders of the empires of global capitalism," circulated along an "archipelago of colonial ports," and became the soundtrack to decolonization.[75] Scholars such as Paul Gilroy, Tricia Rose, Daphne Brooks, Murray Forman, and Michael Veal remind us of the importance of African-American musical styles in the history of popular music, as well as media culture more broadly.[76] We might refer here, to Manovich's claim that "electronic music" serves as one of the "key reservoirs of new metaphors for the rest of culture today."[77] When we consider that Manovich is talking about terms like mashups, sampling, remixes, and dub, it becomes clear that this is a reservoir not only of electronic music, but more specifically, of black electronic music.

Finally, popular music provides a vivid example of the intertwining of sound and memory; as Tia DeNora writes, "music reheard and recalled provides a device for unfolding, for replaying, the temporal structure of past moments . . . This is why, for so many people, the past 'comes alive' to its soundtrack."[78] It is certainly true that the past comes alive to its soundtrack when we think of film soundtracks of recent years. Jeff Smith makes this point in his analysis of the ways in which films like *Boogie Nights* (1997) use popular recordings to register the past.[79] More recent films like *Guardians of the Galaxy* (2014) and *Baby Driver* (2017) show the continued importance of the soundtrack to signify the past and of popular music to function as an "earcon" that connects the audience to a shared sense of history.

I hope that the depth and range of the scholarship that I have touched upon in this overview illustrates that Sound Studies has indeed emerged and that it remains a zone of possibility. Research-generating terms such as acoustemology, synchresis, *acousmetre*, sonification, earwitness, soundscape, listening out, audioposition, audile technique, voice-off, and mashup have mobilized research and forged new interdisciplinary conversations. Enough traction has been gained that scholars can move beyond diagnosing a "visual bias" in a given field to embark upon dedicated studies of sound on its own terms, developing their sonic imagination in order to think across sounds, media forms, and disciplinary boundaries. In the next section, I will offer a case study from my own research as an example of such an approach.

Case Study: Tearing Speech to Pieces

My article, "Tearing Speech to Pieces: Voice Technologies of the 1940s," appeared in the journal *Music, Sound, and the Moving Image* in 2008. The journal was founded in 2007, one of several that helped to establish Sound Studies as a robust field. My article began as a spin-off from an earlier study of children's phonograph records, and came into its own as I accumulated research materials indicating how a particular sound technology was being mobilized in various contexts. The project gained momentum as I discovered what I considered to be significant interventions in scholarly discussions having to do with the history of sound technology, the voice in cinema, the genre of melodrama, and radio advertising. The article can thus stand as an example of how a "sonic imagination" can facilitate listening across sounds, media forms, and cultural practices, and so provide a fresh historical narrative.

I begin the paper at the Bell Telephone exhibit at the 1939 World's Fair in New York, where a female operator manipulated the complex interface of a device in order to produce a simulated voice. This talking machine was known as the Voder, and was one of several voice technologies of the 1940s. My first move is to place these mid-century devices in a history of sound technology that draws on the work of scholars like Sterne, Gitelman, and Lastra, and shows how the Voder exhibit recalls earlier demonstrations of talking machines such as Joseph Faber's nineteenth-century "Euphonia." Scholars have tended to end the story of talking machines with Edison's phonograph or the cinematic soundtrack, suggesting a teleological understanding of technological development. The talking machines of the 1940s complicate that history and make an implicit claim about the benefits of taking a Sound Studies approach rather than a medium-specific one.

The argument's structure is provided by Altman's "crisis historiography," which is described in his book, *Silent Film Sound* (2007). I discuss the multiple, and sometimes conflicting, definitions of these new speaking devices, concentrating on several applications of the Sonovox. Gilbert H. Wright's Sonovox fed sound recordings into two hand-held speakers that were placed on each side of the throat. Whatever sounds were on the recording were transmitted to the larynx, so that they came out of the throat, as if produced there, and could then be shaped into speech by articulating the desired words. This strange device, with its hybrid simulation of both mouth and ear, became a way for me to engage with the embodied dimensions of sound and voice, and so make a small contribution to the history of technologically-enhanced speech.

The Sonovox found one of its most lucrative implementations in the field of radio advertising, and I situate the device in the history of radio advertising, specifically, the introduction of spot advertisements. Radio ads used the Sonovox to make objects speak, and I compare these with television ads of the 1950s that presented dancing cigarettes and beer bottles, and the streamlined logos and stylized lettering found on billboards. These comparisons are intended to clarify the sonic object under consideration and to show the relevance of sound culture to other media histories.

Radio advertisers were addressing what they considered to be a largely female radio audience, which becomes one plank in an argument about gender and the uses of postwar voice technologies. Press accounts described how the Sonovox was typically operated by female "enunciators" or "articulators," which was similar to the configuration of female operator and speaking machine at the 1939 World's Fair. I explore the figure of the female enunciator as a way to think about how discourses of gender shaped voice technologies of this era, on radio as well as film. Sonovox "articulators" who were featured in radio ads also did work on Hollywood films such as the Joan Crawford star vehicle, *Possessed* (1947), a prestigious example of the postwar "woman's film." In one scene from that film, the Sonovox functions as an aural equivalent to a subjective camera shot.

The Sonovox was also featured in *Letter to Three Wives* (1949), which concerns Addie Ross, a character that we never see but whose voice we hear. Ross leaves town, sending a letter to three friends saying she has run away with one of their husbands. The letter prompts each woman to reconsider her marriage, which the film presents through flashback sequences that are initiated by a sound bridge utilizing the Sonovox. I argue that Wright's talking machine had the ability to combine mise-en-scène and voice-off narration, which made it a particularly salient tool for film melodrama. An approach that began with the sonic imagination allowed me to discover a new point of entry to the discussion of the voice-off and film melodrama.

The practice of the Sonovox bridged postwar radio and film, the two most popular sources of narrative fiction at that time. The Sonovox gets Film Studies and Radio Studies talking to each other, and it reveals a dialogue between film and broadcasting that goes beyond more familiar case studies such as Orson Welles and film noir. Altman's crisis historiography helped me to acknowledge the female operators behind these voice technologies and provided me with a method for organizing what otherwise might have been an unwieldy and disparate set of historical cases. In that way, the article serves as an example of how I managed the potentially overwhelming interdisciplinary scope of Sound Studies.

There are certainly gaps and omissions in my article. The argument about gender and technology could have been developed through an engagement with the work of scholars such as Jennifer Light and Ruth Oldenziel. I might have elaborated on how vocal technologies can disrupt gender performance and expanded upon the "queer sounds" of the Sonovox through recourse to Queer Theory. More could be said about the Sonovox as multiply-authored media performance, with comparisons to digital motion capture, body doubles, stunt performance, voice actors, and puppetry. Further research remains to be done as well on the public demonstration of new technologies as a mode of performance and a source of historical information about sound culture.

Conclusion

My article was published at a time when Sound Studies was coming into its own as an academic field of study. Now, a decade later, Sound Studies is poised at an exciting moment for the next generation of scholars, who will have the benefit of a field-specific academic infrastructure as well as considerable latitude to shape and define the field. Future research should strike a balance between deepening the dialogue with long-standing disciplinary interlocutors and opening up new scholarly conversations. The field needs to cultivate work that explores the sonic dimensions of social difference and encompasses a global scope. Students of sound should take a prominent role in the digital humanities, through experiments in the sonification of data and the communication of academic work through audio platforms like podcasting. Listening publics and the politics of the voice will continue to be key components of social life, and will require further study. The scope of sound art continues to expand, and will best thrive in conversation with theory and history. Sound Studies has opened our ears, and we are just beginning to realize how much there is to hear.

Notes

1. Jonathan Sterne, "Sonic Imaginations," in *The Sound Studies Reader*, ed. Jonathan Sterne (London: Routledge, 2012), 2.

2. Michele Hilmes, "Is There a Field Called Sound Culture Studies? And Does It Matter?" *American Quarterly*, vol. 57, no. 1 (2005): 249–59.

3. Robert B. Ray, *How a Film Theory Got Lost* (Bloomington: Indiana University Press, 2001), 46, 53. Ray is writing about the emergence of Film Studies.

4. M.M. Bakhtin, *The Dialogic Imagination* (Austin: University of Texas Press, 1981), 270, 272. Robert Stam, *Subversive Pleasures* (Baltimore: The Johns Hopkins Press, 1989), 19.

5. Ray, *How a Film Theory Got Lost*, 51

6. See discussion of McLuhan in Kate Lacey, *Listening Publics* (Cambridge: Polity, 2013) 5–6.

7. Walter Ong, *Orality and Literacy* (London and New York: Routledge, 1982), 32, 71.

8. Martin Jay, *Downcast Eyes* (Berkeley: University of California Press, 1994).

9. Sterne, "Sonic Imaginations," 9.

10. Steven Feld, "A Rainforest Acoustemology," in *The Auditory Culture Reader*, eds. Michael Bull and Les Back (New York: Berg, 2003), 226. See also, Steven Feld, *Sound and Sentiment* (Philadelphia: University of Pennsylvania Press, 1982); Tia DeNora, *Music in Everyday Life* (Cambridge: Cambridge University Press, 2000); Charles Hirschkind, *The Ethical Soundscape* (New York: Columbia University Press, 2006); Ana Maria Gautier Ochoa, *Aurality* (Durham: Duke University Press, 2014); David W. Samuels, Louise Meintjes, Ana Maria Ochoa, and Thomas Porcello, "Soundscapes: Toward a Sounded Anthropology," in *Annual Review of Anthropology*, vol. 39 (June 21, 2010): 329–45.

11. Steven Connor, "Edison's Teeth: Touching Hearing," in *Hearing Cultures*, ed. Veit Erlmann (Oxford: Berg, 2004), 154. See also Don Ihde, *Listening and Voice* (Albany: State University of New York Press, 2007), 13.

12. Constance Classen, "Foundations for an Anthropology of the Senses," *International Social Science Journal*, vol. 153 (1997): 402.

13. David Howes, *Sensual Relations* (Ann Arbor: University of Michigan Press, 2003), xi. David Howes, ed., *The Varieties of Sensory Experience* (Toronto: University of Toronto Press, 1991), 3; David Howes, ed., *Empire of the Senses* (Oxford: Berg, 2005); Thomas Porcello, Louise Meintjes, Ana Maria Ochoa, David W. Samuels, "The Reorganization of the Sensory World," in *Annual Review of Anthropology*, vol. 39 (June 14, 2010): 51–66.

14. Nina Sun Eidsheim, *Sensing Sound* (Durham: Duke University Press, 2015), 3.

15. Michel Chion, *Film, A Sound Art* (New York: Columbia University Press, 2009), 228.

16. Michel Chion, *Audio-vision* (New York: Columbia University Press, 1990), 63, 70.

17. Ibid., 187–8.

18. Ibid., 112–3.

19. Ibid. 112–3.

20. Philip Auslander, "Looking at Records," in *Aural Cultures*, ed. Jim Drobnick (Toronto: YYZ Books, 2004), 153.

21. See, for example, Gregory Kramer, Bruce Walker, Terri Bonebright, Perry Cook, John Flowers, Nadine Miner, John Neuhoff, "Sonification Report: Status of the Field and Research Agenda." This paper was prepared by an interdisciplinary group of researchers gathered at the request of the National Science Foundation in the fall of 1997 in association with the International Conference on Auditory Display (ICAD), accessed October 18, 2017, www.icad.org/websiteV2.0/References/nsf.html.

22. See www.firstsounds.org.

23. See Jonathan Sterne and Mitchell Akiyama, "The Recording That Never Wanted to Be Heard and Other Stories of Sonification," in *The Oxford Handbook of Sound Studies*, eds. Trevor Pinch and Karin Bijsterveld (Oxford: Oxford University Press, 2011). See also David Howes, "Cross-talk Between the Senses," *Senses and Society*, vol. 1, no. 3 (2006): 383.

24. David Hendy, *Noise* (New York: HarperCollins, 2013), 4–5.

25. Alain Corbin, *Village Bells* (New York: Columbia University Press, 1998), 110.

26. See Mark M. Smith, "Making Sense of Social History," *Journal of Social History*, vol. 37, no. 1 (Autumn 2003): 165–186; Mark M. Smith, *Listening to Nineteenth Century America* (Chapel Hill: University of North Carolina Press, 2001); Richard Cullen Rath, *How Early America Sounded* (Ithaca: Cornell University Press, 2003).

27. Karin Bijsterveld, *Mechanical Sound* (Cambridge: MIT Press, 2008), 94; John M. Picker, *Victorian Soundscapes* (Oxford: Oxford University Press, 2003), 44.

28. See essays in *Sound Souvenirs*, eds. Karin Bijsterveld and Jose van Dijck (Amsterdam: Amsterdam University Press, 2009).

29. Carolyn Birdsall, "Earwitnessing: Sound Memories of the Nazi Period" in *Sound Souvenirs*, eds. Karin Bijsterveld and Jose van Dijck (Amsterdam: Amsterdam University Press, 2009).

30. Barry Blesser and Linda-Ruth Salter, *Spaces Speak, Are You Listening?* (Cambridge: MIT Press, 2007), 82.

31. Walter Benjamin, *Reflections* (New York: Schocken Books, 1978), 59.

32. See discussion in W.J.T. Mitchell, *Iconology* (Chicago: University of Chicago Press, 1986).

33. Georgina Born, "Introduction," in *Music, Sound and Space*, ed. Georgina Born (Cambridge: Cambridge University Press, 2013), 4.

34. R. Murray Schafer, *The Tuning of the World* (New York: Knopf, 1977); Emily Thompson, *The Soundscape of Modernity* (Cambridge: MIT Press, 2002), 3.

35. For a critique of Schafer, see Ari Y. Kelman, "Rethinking the Soundscape," in *Senses and Society*, vol. 5, no. 2 (2010): 212–34. On field recording, see *In the Field: The Art of Field Recording*, ed. Cathy Lane and Angus Carlyle (Axminster: Uniformbooks, 2013).

36. Chion, *Audio-Vision*, 150. See also Rick Altman's discussion of a sound's "signature," which is the "testimony provided by every sound as to the spatial circumstances of its production" (Rick Altman, "Afterword," *Sound Theory/Sound Practice*, ed. Rick Altman [New York: Routledge, 1992], 252).

37. Jacob Smith, "Sound and Performance in Stephen Sayadian's *Night Dreams* and *Café Flesh*," in *Peep Shows: Cult Visual Erotica*, eds. Ernest Mathijs, and Xavier Mendik (New York: Columbia University Press, 2012), 41–56.

38. See Iain Chambers, "The Aural Walk," in *Audio Culture: Readings in Modern Music* eds. Christoph Cox and Daniel Warner (New York: Continuum, 2010), 98–101. For a different take, see David Beer, "Tune Out: Music, Soundscapes and the Urban Mise-en-Scène," in *Information, Communication and Society*, vol. 10, no. 6 (2007): 846–66.

39. Jean-Paul Thibaud, "The Sonic Composition of the City," in *The Auditory Culture Reader*, eds. Michael Bull and Les Back (New York: Berg, 2003), 337.

40. Lev Manovich, "The Poetics of Augmented Space," in *New Media: Theories and Practices of Digitextuality*, eds. Anna Everett and John T. Caldwell (New York: Routledge), 78, 81.

41. Theodor W. Adorno, *Essays on Music* (London: University of California Press, 2002).

42. Friedrich Kittler, *Gramophone, Film, Typewriter* (Stanford: Stanford University Press, 1999); Lisa Gitelman, *Scripts, Grooves and Talking Machines* (Stanford: Stanford University Press, 2000).

43. Rick Altman, "Four and a Half Film Fallacies," in *Sound Theory Sound Practice*, ed. Rick Altman (New York: Routledge, 1992), 39–40.

44. William Wittington, *Sound Design and Science Fiction* (Austin: University of Texas Press, 2007); Robert Spadoni, *Uncanny Bodies* (Berkeley: University of California Press, 2007); Britta Sjogren, *Into the Vortex* (Urbana: University of Illinois Press, 2006); Steven Cohan, ed., *The Sound of Musicals* (London: BFI, 2010); Daniel Goldmark, Lawrence Kramer, and Richard Leppert, eds., *Beyond the Soundtrack: Representing Music in Cinema* (Berkeley: University of California Press, 2007); Jane Feuer, *The Hollywood Musical* (Bloomington: Indiana University Press, 1993); Jean Ma, *Sounding the Modern Woman: The Songstress in Chinese Cinema* (Durham: Duke University Press, 2015).

45. Rick Altman, "Deep Focus Sound: *Citizen Kane* and the Radio Aesthetic," in *Perspectives on* Citizen Kane, ed. Ronald Gottesman (New York: Simon & Schuster, 1996), 94–121.

46. Rudolf Arnheim, *Radio: An Art of Sound* (1936: New York: Da Capo Press, 1972), 15, 120.

47. Neil Verma, *Theater of the Mind* (Chicago: University of Chicago Press, 2012), 63, 68, 35.

48. Jason Loviglio, *Radio's Intimate Public* (Minneapolis: University of Minnesota Press, 2005); Allison McCracken, *Real Men Don't Sing* (Durham: Duke University Press, 2015).

49. Michele Hilmes, *Radio Voices* (Minneapolis: University of Minnesota Press, 1997).

50. Susan Douglas, *Listening In* (Minneapolis: University of Minnesota Press, 2004); David Goodman, "Distracted Listening: On Not Making Sound Choices in the 1930s," in *Sound in the Age of Mechanical Reproduction*, eds. David Suisman and Susan Strasser (Philadelphia: University of Pennsylvania Press, 2010), 15–46. For an overview of "modes of listening," see Pinch and Bijsterveld, *The Oxford Handbook of Sound Studies*, 14.

51. Lacey, *Listening Publics*, 165.

52. Ibid., 22.

53. Jonathan Sterne, *The Audible Past* (Durham: Duke University Press, 2003), 95.

54. See Mara Mills, "Deaf Jam: From Inscription to Reproduction to Information," *Social Text*, vol. 102 (Spring 2010): 35–58; Mara Mills, "On Disability and Cybernetics: Helen Keller, Norbert Wiener, and the Hearing Glove," *differences*, vol. 22 (Summer–Fall 2011): 74–111; Mara Mills, "Do Signals Have Politics? Inscribing Abilities in Cochlear Implants," in *The Oxford Handbook of Sound Studies*, eds. Trevor Pinch and Karin Bijsterveld (Oxford: Oxford University Press, 2011), 320–46; Mara Mills, "Deafness," in *Keywords in Sound*, eds. David Novak and Matt Sakakeeny (Durham: Duke University Press, 2015), 45–54.

55. Robert Stam, *Subversive Pleasures* (Baltimore: The Johns Hopkins Press, 1989), 19.

56. Erving Goffman, *Forms of Talk* (Philadelphia: University of Pennsylvania Press, 1981).

57. Jacques Derrida, *Speech and Phenomena* (Evanston: Northwestern University Press, 1973); Mladen Dolar, *A Voice and Nothing More* (Cambridge: MIT Press, 2006); Adriana Cavarero, *For More Than One Voice* (Stanford: Stanford University Press, 2005); Jacob Smith, *Vocal Tracks* (Berkeley: University of California Press, 2008).

58. Roland Barthes, *The Responsibility of Forms* (Berkeley: University of California Press, 1985), 270.

59. Steven Conner, *Dumbstruck* (New York: Oxford University Press, 2000), 35.

60. Alexander G. Weheliye, *Phonographies* (Durham: Duke University Press, 2005), 37; Lindon Barrett, *Blackness and Value* (Cambridge: Cambridge University Press, 1998); Louis Chude-Sokei, *The Last "Darky"* (Durham: Duke University Press, 2004); Daphne Brooks, *Bodies in Dissent* (Durham: Duke University Press, 2005); Fred Moten, *In the Break* (Minneapolis: University of Minnesota Press, 2003).

61. Alice Maurice, "Cinema at its Source," in *Camera Obscura*, vol. 17, no. 1 (2002): 1–71.

62. Gus Stadler, "On Whiteness and Sound Studies," July 6, 2015, accessed October 1, 2017, https://soundstudiesblog.com/2015/07/06/on-whiteness-and-sound-studies/.

63. Jennifer Lynn Stoever, *The Sonic Color Line* (New York: New York University Press, 2016); Shilpa Davé, *Indian Accents* (Urbana: University of Illinois Press, 2013); also see Josh Kun, *Audiotopia* (Berkeley: University of California Press, 2005).

64. Kaja Silverman, *The Acoustic Mirror* (Bloomington: Indiana University Press, 1988); Mary Ann Doane, "The Voice in the Cinema," *Yale French Studies*, no. 60 (1980): 33–50.

65. Sjogren, *Into the Vortex*, 4, 9–10.

66. Richard Dyer, *Heavenly Bodies* (London: Routledge, 2003); Richard Dyer, *In the Space of a Song: The Uses of Song in Film* (London: Routledge, 2011); Shane Vogel, *The Scene of Harlem Cabaret* (Chicago: University of Chicago Press, 2009).

67. Neepa Majumdar, *Wanted Cultured Ladies Only!* (Urbana: University of Illinois Press, 2009).

68. Wayne Koestenbaum, *The Queen's Throat* (New York: Da Capo, 2001), 47.

69. Hilmes, "Is There a Field Called Sound Culture Studies?", 249.

70. Georgina Born, "Introduction," in *Music, Sound and Space*, ed. Georgina Born (Cambridge: Cambridge University Press, 2015), 5.

71. Douglas Kahn, *Noise, Water, Meat: A History of Sound in the Arts* (Cambridge: MIT Press, 2001); Brandon LaBelle, *Background Noise: Perspectives on Sound Art.* (London: Bloomsbury, 2015).

72. Carol Vernallis, *Experiencing Music Video* (New York: Columbia University Press, 2004); Carol Vernallis, *Unruly Media: YouTube, Music Video, and the New Digital Cinema* (New York: Oxford University Press, 2013), 127–54; Robert Walser, *Running with the Devil* (Wesleyan University Press, 1993).

73. Kiri Miller, *Playing Along* (Oxford: Oxford University Press, 2012); Kiri Miller, *Playable Bodies* (Oxford: Oxford University Press, 2017); William Cheng, *Sound Play* (Oxford: Oxford University Press, 2014); Michael Austin, ed., *Music Video Games* (New York: Bloomsbury, 2016).

74. See, for example, Mark Katz, *Capturing Sound: How Technology Has Changed Music* (Berkeley: University of California Press, 2010); William H. Kenney, *Recorded Music in American Life* (Oxford: Oxford University Press, 2003); David L. Morton, *Sound Recording: The Life Story of a Technology* (Baltimore: Johns Hopkins University Press, 2004); David Suisman, *Selling Sounds* (Cambridge: Harvard University Press, 2012); David Suisman and Susan Strasser, eds., *Sound in the Age of Mechanical Reproduction* (Philadelphia: University of Pennsylvania Press, 2010).

75. Michael Denning, *Noise Uprising* (London: Verso, 2015), 38.

76. Tricia Rose, *Black Noise* (Middletown: Wesleyan University Press, 1994); Michael Veal, *Dub: Soundscapes and Shattered Songs in Jamaican Reggae* (Middletown: Wesleyan University Press, 2007); Paul Gilroy, *The Black Atlantic* (Cambridge: Harvard University Press, 1993).

77. Lev Manovich, "What Comes After Remix?" Winter 2007, accessed October 1, 2017, http://remixtheory.net/?p=169.

78. Tia DeNora. *Music in Everyday Life* (Cambridge: Cambridge University Press, 2000), 67.

79. Jeff Smith, "Popular Songs and Comic Allusion in Contemporary Cinema," in *Soundtrack Available*, eds. Pamela Robertson Wojcik and Arthur Knight (Durham: Duke University Press, 2001).

Further Reading

Altman, Rick. *Silent Film Sound.* New York: Columbia University Press, 2004.

Barlow, William. *Voice Over: The Making of Black Radio.* Philadelphia: Temple University Press, 1999.

Beck, Jay and Tony Grajeda. *Lowering the Boom.* Urbana: University of Illinois Press, 2008.

Brady, Erika. *A Spiral Way.* Jackson: University Press of Mississippi, 1999.

Bull, Michael. *Sound Moves: iPod Culture and Urban Experience.* New York: Routledge, 2008.

Chion, Michel. *The Voice in Cinema.* New York: Columbia University Press, 1999.

Daughtry, J. Martin. *Listening to War.* Oxford: Oxford University Press, 2015.

Erlmann, Veit. *Reason and Resonance.* Cambridge: MIT Press, 2010.

Gopinath, Sumanth. *The Ringtone Dialectic*. MIT Press, 2013.

Gracyk, Theodore. *Rhythm and Noise: An Aesthetics of Rock*. Durham: Duke University Press, 1996.

Helmreich, Stefan. *Sounding the Limits of Life*. Princeton: Princeton University Press, 2015.

Jacobs, Lea. *Film Rhythm after Sound*. Berkeley: University of California Press, 2014.

Kane, Brian. *Sound Unseen*. Oxford: Oxford University Press, 2016.

Kahn, Douglas. *Earth Sound, Earth Signal*. Berkeley: University of California Press, 2013.

Lastra, James. *Sound Technology and the American Cinema*. New York: Columbia University Press, 2000.

Novak, David and Matt Sakakeeny, eds. *Keywords in Sound*. Durham: Duke University Press, 2015.

Pinch, Trevor and Karin Bijsterveld, eds. *Oxford Handbook of Sound Studies*. Oxford: Oxford University Press, 2012.

Schmidt, Leigh. *Hearing Things*. Cambridge: Harvard University Press, 2000.

Smith, Jacob. *Eco-Sonic Media*. Berkeley: University of California Press, 2015.

Smith, Jeff. *The Sounds of Commerce*. New York: Columbia University Press, 1998.

Sterne, Jonathan. *MP3*. Durham: Duke University Press, 2012.

Tompkins, Dave. *How to Wreck a Nice Beach: The Vocoder from World War II to Hip-Hop*. Chicago: Stop Smiling Books, 2010.

7.
ACTING AND PERFORMANCE
Cynthia Baron

One could ask, what is the difference between acting and performance? Put simply, **acting** involves the portrayal of fictional characters, whereas **performance** is a wider category that includes acting (embodiment of character) and appearances as oneself or a generic type.

Film and media scholars ground their more inclusive vision of screen performance on work in **performance studies**, a field of research that emerged in the 1960s due to contributions by anthropologist Victor Turner, theatre scholar Richard Schechner, and others. Performance studies scholars see performance as any behavior a person learns, rehearses, and performs. The field examines human performance in countless aesthetic and social contexts, including theatre, dance, music, sports, rituals, and daily life. This chapter on acting and performance narrows that range to focus on film and media performances, but it retains performance studies' vision that screen performance is (1) prepared in some way, and (2) framed or displayed in some fashion.

Studies of screen performance primarily analyze the physical and vocal details in leading actors' embodiment of fictional characters. Yet film and media studies also consider many other dimensions of performance. Researchers investigate the way background extras help to establish the reality or mood of a scene. They analyze documentary interviews and performances by news anchors, reality TV contestants, and talk show guests. Scholars examine both acting and performance because a media text can include acting and performance more broadly defined. For example, musicals have some scenes when performances convey character and other scenes that highlight performers' singing or dancing abilities. Similarly, action films devote entire sequences to audiovisual spectacle, yet they also depend on moments when actors' expressive voices and faces establish emotional connections between characters and audiences.

Despite the importance of screen performance, twentieth-century scholars and critics often paid more attention to directors and show-runners. Given this, the next section discusses academic and popular perspectives that once suggested screen performances are of little importance. It also describes reassessments that have made screen performance a burgeoning area of study, for film and media scholars now recognize that the telling details of performers' physical and vocal expression contribute to audience interpretations in much the same way that framing, editing, music, and production design choices do.

The subsequent section outlines useful ways to examine screen performances. It highlights the value of asking, for example, how do genre conventions shape performances and audience expectations about them? The discussion covers terms and concepts developed by scholars and acting professionals. It closes with a look at Prague School scholarship, which provides an effective foundation for analyzing screen performances. Prague theorists lead scholars to ask questions such as, When performers use recognizable social signs (a handshake), how do the details of the performers' gestures convey the meaning of that moment? How do the changing details of a performer's physical and vocal expression communicate the evolving thoughts and feelings of the person or fictional character?

The penultimate section analyzes performances in **postmodern** media productions. The term "postmodern" can describe postindustrial global capitalism, a critical stance that challenges monolithic

modernist perspectives, or aesthetic strategies spanning various art forms. In film and media discussions
of postmodern aesthetics, scholars often reference
films such as *Blue Velvet* (Lynch, 1986), *Blade Runner*
(Scott, 1982), *Pulp Fiction* (Tarantino, 1994), and the
films of Wong Kar-wai and John Woo, who both
began their careers in Hong Kong. These productions
are seen as postmodern because they are highly stylized, include media culture references, and feature
rapid shifts in tone, often from comedic to dramatic
or horrific. Scholars also find postmodern aesthetics
in television. For example, *The Sopranos* (HBO 1999–
2007) has been described as postmodern because
its "self-reflexive, multidimensional and subjective
form [reflects] the social inconsistencies and moral
uncertainties of a 'postmodern' world."[1] In addition
to seeing the stylistic choices in these examples as
emblematic of postmodern productions, film and
media scholars also consistently identify postmodern aesthetics with visual and narrative choices that
include "a faster tempo ... hand-held camerawork,
elliptical editing, unusual shot transitions, montages,
fantasy sequences, and surreal inserts."[2]

Building on film, media, and performance studies,
the emerging work on screen performance highlights
the fact that postmodern aesthetics shape not only
visual and narrative elements but the details of screen
performances as well.[3] The new scholarship shows
that postmodern performances involve noticeable
shifts in tone and a sampling from disparate genre
conventions and acting traditions. The research finds
that performers' contributions are essential to postmodern productions, because they provide emotional
contact amidst the cacophony of audiovisual elements and the multilayered, sometimes fragmented
narratives.

The chapter's penultimate segment thus looks at
postmodern performances in different types of media
productions. The chapter concludes by revisiting my
analysis of postmodern performances in John Woo's
film *The Killer* (1989), which became the first Hong Kong
release since Bruce Lee's *Fists of Fury* (Wei Lo, 1971)
to have international critical and commercial success.[4]
Analyzing *The Killer* leads to important insights about
postmodern aesthetics and performance because the
film fuses trends in modernism and realism in ways
that are beholden to neither Western tradition. The
film causes one to think globally about performance
and postmodernism, for its quintessential postmodern strategies display the influence of Chinese
theatrical traditions that make characterization and
logical plot development secondary to flamboyant

performance and audiovisual elements that have
the potential to create both reflection and emotional
impact.

Screen Performance: Misconceptions and Reassessments

In the early twentieth century, scholars and critics
believed that real acting could occur only on stage.
Performers in prestigious stage productions were
seen as skilled actors. By comparison, screen actors,
while prized as stars that embodied idealized cultural
values, were thought to have little training or agency.
While listed "above the line" along with writers, producers, and directors, leading screen actors were
seen as charismatic people who essentially played
themselves in every role. Since their performances
were mediated and worked in concert with framing, editing, sound, and design choices, film actors
were essentially considered "below the line" labor-
ers supervised by creative professionals, and screen
acting became associated with non-intellectual labor
with little significance.

Vsevolod Pudovkin's widely circulated account
of the "Kuleshov test" seemed to confirm the theatre–
screen hierarchy and greatly influenced film-media
scholarship. Pudovkin claimed that Lev Kuleshov's
experiment of intercutting the image of an actor's
face with three images (a bowl of soup, a woman in
a coffin, and a child playing with a toy bear) proved
that screen actors' contributions are irrelevant. Yet
Kuleshov himself concluded that the experiment
simply showed that connotations conveyed by combinations of images are variable. Moreover, other
experiments, and a lifetime of work as a teacher who
sought to develop actors able to work well in film, led
Kuleshov to value actors' creative labor and to see
silent film stars Charles Chaplin, Lon Chaney, and
Mary Pickford as exemplifying the expressive clarity
needed in screen performances. As Kuleshov's belatedly translated writings find wider circulation, they
have overturned Pudovkin's interpretation.[5]

The equation between real acting and legitimate
theatre, and the related idea that screen performances
are produced by technology and the decisions of other
people also influenced work in **cine-semiotics**.
These studies drew on psychoanalysis to posit that
audience responses to shot-reverse-shot sequences
(featuring over-the-shoulder close-ups of performers'
facial expressions) are unrelated to seeing embodied
human emotion. Cine-semiotics instead proposed that
audience responses depend on media productions'

correspondence to psychic experience, with continuity editing mirroring the process in which subjectivity arises as an effect of being sutured into language and culture. This line of scholarship deterred researchers from analyzing actors' facial and vocal expression as a component of film and media.

Mid-twentieth-century commentary about **Method acting** by critics and scholars supported the misconception that screen acting does not involve legitimate training. Such thinking became possible because of ambiguities surrounding the Method, which refers to Lee Strasberg's approach to acting, and Method acting, which is a style associated with certain performances in mid-twentieth-century dramas. For example, critics and scholars mistakenly saw a connection between Strasberg's Method and the intense style of Marlon Brando's portrayal in *A Streetcar Named Desire*. In reality, Brando used Stella Adler's script-centered Modern acting approach to create his performances, and Elia Kazan, who directed the play and subsequent film, rejected Strasberg's focus on emotional memory. Yet the myth that the new acting style depended on performers' use of personal experiences fit the era's misconceptions that screen acting involved little training and that stars played themselves. The idea that screen actors relied on personal associations became even more widely circulated after Marilyn Monroe started working with Strasberg in 1955. Publicity about Strasberg and Monroe solidified the fallacy that screen acting involved essentially psychotherapy sessions between an all-knowing teacher/director and a performer with little agency.

As a teacher and erstwhile director, Strasberg would demand "true emotion" from his actors, "often evoking . . . it himself, then judging the truthfulness of its expression."[6] He believed he could "cure" actors' "problems" by exposing their fears and inhibitions, and he consistently used women as "examples to illustrate psychological, emotional, and behavioral problems" he could "fix."[7] Strasberg thought that directors/teachers should interpret a script and then lead actors through performances, explaining the character's actions at each step and suggesting personal substitutions the actor should use to realize the vision of the director/teacher. In his view of acting, the director/teacher is the author of the performance. Strasberg's highly publicized ideas obscured the reality that screen actors, like other members of a production, use their training, aesthetic sense, and craft experience to contribute to the production as a whole.

Scholars and acting professionals have largely rejected Strasberg's approach, seeing it as something marred by manipulation. Highlighting the opposition to the Method that crystallized in the 1970s and 1980s, Richard Hornby even argues that Strasberg's insistence that actors use associations from their own experiences to build and execute performances led to a decline in American acting.[8] Since the 1980s, feminist scholars have also criticized the gender-bias that has valorized "the 'matrix' of Method practice" with its (white) male-centered norms in actor training, acting theory, scripts, casting, and direction.[9] Clarifying the historical record, Sharon Carnicke has disentangled the Method from the multifaceted **System** developed by Konstantin Stanislavsky.[10] As she demonstrates, Stanislavsky experimented briefly with emotional memory but turned to physical and vocal training, script analysis, and improvisation because they proved to be more reliable and artistically stimulating for actors. Similarly, *Modern Acting: The Lost Chapter of American Film and Theatre* shows that the psychologically-based Method was not the primary approach to acting in the twentieth century and that instead actors depended on script analysis and physical and vocal training.[11] After decades of practitioners and theorists calling its efficacy, politics, and history into doubt, the Method is now taught at only a handful of conservatories. This development is important for studies of acting, because it leads scholars to avoid speculation about the psychology of actors or directors and to focus instead on analyzing performers' physical and vocal expression.

The many reassessments of the Method have coincided with other evolving perspectives on performance. Traditional views about the performing arts once made written texts superior to embodied productions, directors more significant than performers, and theatre performances more legitimate than those that are mediated. Yet these biases began to change in the 1960s as video art, installation pieces, and other unscripted performance art projects challenged aesthetic hierarchies. In addition, as postmodern theorists dismantled modernism's opposition between esteemed high art and disparaged mass culture, scholars reimagined mediated performance. They found that both stage and screen performances reflect cultural-aesthetic trends, and that screen performances acquire meaning the same way stage performances do—through interrelationships with other formal elements in the production, dramatic facts established by previous scenes, and audiences' extra-textual associations. Current research on acting builds on Sergei Eisenstein's writings about montage, identifying the selection and combination of vocal/physical details as elements in performance montage.[12] Contemporary studies also set aside the language-based semiotics of Ferdinand de Saussure and Charles Sanders Peirce[13] and instead use Prague semiotics, which provides tools for analyzing the temporal and spatial sign-complexes in composite art forms (theatre, film, television, video, and performance art) that employ culturally specific material signs (types of postures, laughs, costumes, etc.).[14]

Analyzing Screen Performance: Terms and Concepts

To explore the myriad types of screen performance, it is useful to remember that performances exist on a spectrum, where some are subsumed into the narrative while others highlight performers' mastery of singing, martial arts, or other non-acting skills. Before the influence of performance studies, scholars ranked acting—**integrated performances** that convey character psychology—higher than **autonomous performances**, which offer interest independent of the narrative. Today, scholars value both modes of performance, analyzing them on their own merits. Acting (integrated performance) lends itself to questions about representation, invisibility, disguise, and plausibility, whereas performance broadly defined (autonomous performance) tends to warrant questions about presentation, visibility, spectacle, and display of non-acting skills (dancing, use of weapons).[15]

Referring to television, David Marc sees the same spectrum of performance, which ranges from a **representational mode** of acting/integrated performance to a **presentational mode** of autonomous performance. He explains that in the representational mode, a performer "dons the mask of a frankly fictional character," whereas in the presentational mode, performers play themselves, addressing "the audience within the context of the theatrical space."[16] Noting that Jack Benny would employ both modes within a single program, Marc explains that Benny would open the show "in front of the curtain doing stand-up and discussing the week's 'show' in the presentational manner of Carson opening *Tonight*."[17] However, after the first commercial, he would be "miraculously transported into a sitcom in which he remained 'Jack Benny' while an actor named Eddie Anderson played his valet, Rochester."[18]

Performance studies offers additional concepts for analyzing the various registers of screen performance.

Michael Kirby identifies a series of points on a performance continuum.[19] **Non-matrixed performing** is when people engage in non-acting tasks in a theatrical environment, as when crewmembers reset stage furniture between scenes. Then there are performances arising from a **symbolized matrix**, as when a costume suggests a character or character type; here, performers do not limn the thoughts or feelings of fictional characters, but character traits can arise because audiences make inferences. The next step on the continuum involves **received acting**, where performers do mundane things that generate meaning, but their behavior takes on meaning because it belongs to a performative event, as when extras provide background action. The next step to **simple acting** marks a shift into the realm of acting because a performer does something to represent a character or convey an emotion that fits the scene. It can also involve a person selecting and projecting their beliefs or emotions to an audience. Next, in **complex acting**, performers portray changing emotions and incorporate additional elements into their representation of character. Here, the performer might convey "emotion (fear, let us say), physical characteristics (the person is portrayed as old), place (there is bright sun)."[20]

Kirby's outline is a reminder that even non-fiction media texts involve performance. News programs, commercials, talk shows, and reality programs feature both received acting (where people's behavior takes on meaning because it belongs to a television program) and simple acting (where people perform a thought or feeling for an audience). Acting choices by ostensibly amateur performers warrant analysis, particularly because reality television "has developed an appetite for the 'type' of 'ordinary' people [who] can guarantee something close to a semi-professional performance."[21] Amateur performances in film or television must seem spontaneous. Yet to maintain audience interest, they are often highly expressive (full of emotion), and, to avoid audience discomfort, they are focused (devoid of personal tics) and well suited to the conventions shaping the entire film or program.

The fact that screen performances conform to certain conventions has led scholars to explore ways that genre expectations influence screen performances. Richard deCordova made early contributions to this area of study. In the 1980s, he called for "a general account of performance and its role within an economy of genres" and kick-started the research by showing how noir films, melodramas, and westerns "circumscribe the form and position of performance" in distinctive ways.[22] Christine Cornea's *Genre and Performance: Film and Television* continues the work on **genre-specific performances**. The volume has chapters on biopics, noir films, science fiction, sitcoms, docudramas, serial dramas, and news parody programs.[23] To explore other genre-specific performances, one could consult Jeremy Butler's discussion of acting in soap operas, Su Holmes's research on quiz show performances, or Andrew Tolson's anthology on television talk show performances.[24]

Doug Tomlinson has amplified this line of research by examining performance in relation to larger aesthetic movements. For example, discussing **modernist performances** in Robert Bresson's films, Tomlinson shows that performers tend to suppress physical and vocal expression of emotion, and that performance details are one of many meaningful cinematic and mise-en-scène elements. Analyzing **realist performances** in Jean Renoir's films, Tomlinson explores a different set of cinematic and performance strategies in which simple, understated filmic choices enhance audience access to actors' highly communicative gestures and expressions.[25]

Scholarship by deCordova, Tomlinson, and others illuminates the integral connection between performance choices and narrative demands that arise from genre conventions or the priorities of aesthetic movements. Actors, directors, and acting teachers have developed especially powerful tools for understanding links between narrative demands and performance. Thus, just as craft terms (close-up, jump cut) clarify discussions of cinematography or editing, terms from the craft of acting facilitate studies of performance. Crucial terms for analyzing performance come from the script-centered principles of **Modern acting**, which developed in response to the demands and opportunities created by the wave of lifelike domestic dramas that transformed Euro-American theatre at the turn of the twentieth century. The dramas' intense, underlying subtexts required exhaustive script study, and to create the minute changes in expression that conveyed the characters' unspoken thoughts or implicit meaning, actors had to do the close study themselves. **Script analysis** was integral to the System Stanislavsky developed. It was an essential aspect of actor training at Hollywood studios in the 1930s and 1940s and institutions such as the American Academy of Dramatic Arts in New York, first established in 1884. Script analysis concepts were also a key feature of the information Stella Adler shared with fellow members of the Group Theatre in

1934 after studying with Stanislavsky. She would continue to focus on script analysis when teaching at the New School for Social Research during the 1940s, at her New York studio starting in 1949, and at her Los Angeles studio starting in 1985.

An emphasis on script analysis makes actors independent of directors. Instead of using personal experiences to produce emotion, actors depend on script analysis and research to develop and perform characterizations. Adler and other Modern acting teachers ask actors to concentrate not on themselves but on their characters' circumstances, beliefs, and experiences. The focus leads actors to analyze the specific social, political, and economic circumstances that shape individual characters. Script analysis helps actors "score" performances. This involves identifying series of **actions** (amuse, flatter, denounce, overpower) to play in each scene; importantly, actions are distinct from **stage business** (pouring a drink, packing a suitcase). Actors develop their score of actions by analyzing the facts in the script that reveal how their character would answer questions such as, who are you? What is your action? When is it happening? Where is this happening? And, most importantly, why are you there—what are you there to do?[26] In Adler's conception of acting, performers have a great deal of agency. Their direct, intellectual connection with the script makes them authors of their performances. In the view of Adler and other Modern acting teachers, actors' creative labor in preparing and executing performances does not depend on an outside authority. Actors use their research and imagination to reach beyond the limits of their personal experiences. Their creative labor allows them to be independent agents empowered to collaborate with fellow artists.

The principles of script analysis that Stanislavsky clarified for Adler greatly facilitate analyses of screen performances, for scholars can study completed performances the way actors study scripts, considering, for example, distinctions between surface activities (or stage business) and the dramatic actions that reveal what the characters are really thinking and feeling. For instance, to analyze a scene with characters having a cup of coffee (stage business), one must examine the qualities infusing the actors' body language and vocal expressions (loose, tense). From there, one begins to see what actions they are performing (flattering, challenging). Actors know that the actions they perform make their characters' thoughts and feelings visible. Put another way, the selection and combination of their goal-directed actions allow audiences to make inferences about their characters. Highlighting the centrality of goal-directed actions, acting teacher Doug Moston explains, "If your objective is to propose marriage to your lover, your first beat might be to impress, then to charm, then to tease, then possibly to seduce."[27]

Script analysis can be useful when studying performances, because the basic terms—**given circumstances**, **objectives**, **actions**, and **units of action** (or **beats**)—can capture and clarify the meaning of performers' physical and vocal details. When using script analysis to examine completed performances, one asks four questions: What are the given circumstances for each character in the scene? What is each character's objective in the scene? What are the actions each character uses to achieve that objective? And, what physical and/or vocal changes convey shifts from one unit of action to another? Whether studying a script to build a characterization or analyzing performances in a completed scene, key questions include, how do characters try to reach their respective objectives? And, what goal-directed actions do they use to create a change in the other character?

Moston emphasizes that these questions drive both dramatic and comedic performances. He clarifies that "acting is doing [and what] to do comes from your character's objective, that is, what you want from the other character(s)."[28] Writing specifically about comedy, Scott Sedita argues that identifying what characters want is the first and most important step in building a performance. As he explains,

> Every character in every scene "wants" something. They usually want it desperately and are determined, against all odds, to get it. How they go about getting it and the obstacles that get in their way are the basis for the situation comedy.[29]

Goal-directed actions are especially visible in superhero films like *Wonder Woman* (Jenkins, 2017) and *Guardians of the Galaxy Vol. 2* (Gunn, 2017) in which characters/actors use spectacular physical behavior to achieve their objectives. Yet goal-directed actions are also integral to performances in non-fiction settings. Studies of news anchors and acting manuals for sports, weather, business, and entertainment reporters illuminate the goal-directed dimension of news coverage performances.[30] Journalist Nancy Reardon explains that before reading "a news story, or asking questions," reporters rehearse the "subtext or intention" that will color their words.[31] She highlights the need to practice lines using different active verbs

(cajole, needle, invite) as the subtext, and to annotate scripts (news stories) to help vocal inflections reflect script analysis. Voice-acting manuals also emphasize that script analysis allows one to develop the actions and objectives of the imaginary figures who give life to advertising copy, documentaries, and voiced characters. In any context, to convey meaning, voice actors must know and embody "the who, how, what, when, where and why of a script" and the character to be portrayed.[32]

Goal-directed actions are even central to talk shows that involve the Oprah Winfrey social problem/personal perspective approach or the Jerry Springer trash talk format. While talk shows might feature "different types of performance," the hosts consistently guide the public interaction to achieve a particular end.[33] For instance, Winfrey often employs actions that secure confessions that generally confirm "the existence of a shared moral-ethical code."[34] Goal-directed actions are equally important in dating and makeover shows, because contestants generate drama as they move from given circumstances such as loneliness or unattractiveness to socially sanctioned goals.[35] Contestants' actions and objectives are also crucial to quiz shows, game shows, and the many subgenres of reality television.[36] Thus, when studying any genre or type of media text, script analysis terms (given circumstances, objectives, actions, and units of action) provide an extremely useful lens for examining performances.

Additional terms and concepts developed by practitioners can also facilitate studies of screen performance. For example, **Laban Movement Analysis** offers effective vocabulary for describing connotations in performers' passing physical/vocal expressions and coordinated goal-directed actions. In studies of screen performance, it can illuminate the spatial, temporal, strength, and energy qualities in performers' behavior. Collaborating with other leaders in modern dance, Rudolf Laban found that in daily life or scripted performance people's physical and vocal expressions exist on a series of continua. He determined that any gesture, movement or facial/vocal expression tends to be **more direct or more flexible**, **more sudden or more sustained**, **stronger/ weighted or lighter**, and **more bound or free flowing**. Picture a sharp angry slap on the face: it will be direct, sudden, strong, and tightly bound. Consider a chaste kiss on the cheek: it can seem sweet because it is a light, direct, and sudden dab of intimate contact. Imagine how shifts in physical/vocal expression communicate changes in goal-directed actions, as when quicker, sharper/stronger intonations convey a move from persuading to demanding.[37] **Conversation Analysis** represents a useful, academic complement to Laban Analysis. It also clarifies how the simplest detail in a person's physical/vocal expression discloses background, intention, and emotion. This approach employs transcription conventions (for intakes of breath, stressed words, etc.) to analyze scripted or unscripted speech. Scholars have used it to study interviews, sports commentary, and talk shows. They analyze the formal language of experts, informal language of audiences, and hosts' roles as mediators and instigators of conflict.[38]

Prague semiotics provides perhaps the most comprehensive tools for analyzing screen performance. The belatedly translated work of Prague School theorists establishes that performances—in daily life and performance frames like media texts—involve **gesture-signs** (conventional gestures such as waves of hand, nods of the head) and **gesture-expressions** (individual enactments of those recognizable gestures).[39] Prague theorists such as Jan Mukařovský explored a performance-based variation of the linguistic distinction between langue (language system) and parole (individual speech acts). They found that any gesture-expression sustains, amplifies, or contradicts the thought or feeling associated with culturally specific gesture-signs for greetings, farewells, condolence, and so on. Prague semiotics clarifies the value of analyzing how performers utilize recognizable gesture-signs, because it shows that the physical and vocal qualities in their individual gesture-expressions contain crucial information about characters.

The intensely social dimension of humor means that attention to performers' individual gesture-expressions facilitates studies of comedic screen performances. Consider, for instance, how Alfonso Riberio's performance in an episode of *The Fresh Prince of Bel Air* (NBC 1990–1996) highlights the ways that both humor and representations of social identity depend on individual gesture-expressions. In the episode, Riberio sets aside the repertoire of gestures that distinguish Carlton, the nerdy cousin. As Carlton, Riberio always "carried himself with straight-A posture," but to show that Carlton adopts a new persona, C-Note, during a visit to the rough neighborhood of Compton, Riberio "moves casually, with rounded shoulders and a suddenly broad, muscular back."[40] The shift in performance details suggests that performed signs of social identity warrant close analysis. The new performance choices also show that Carlton is more capable that expected

and that Riberio's regular embodiment of Carlton involves choices based on script analysis.

Along with highlighting the need to examine culturally recognizable gestures, Prague semiotics clarifies the value of analyzing how media texts combine audiovisual choices and performers' gestures and expressions. As guidelines, Prague theorists highlight the idea that audiovisual details extend, support, or counterbalance impressions conveyed by performance details. For example, they prompt one to see that, in a scene, harsh lighting and somber music would support the connotations conveyed by the drooped shoulders of a performer, whereas warm lighting and a lively musical score might create a potentially comedic counterbalance.

Prague semiotics is especially important to studies of screen performance because it frames all aspects of a text as elements that function together as a whole. Thus, the light but sustained quality of an elderly woman's frail, clasping and unclasping hands is a meaningful element on a par with the tight framing of the long take that draws attention to her hands. The glazed expression in the eyes of a young man portraying a character out of his depth is a meaningful detail of equal importance to the camera's movement when it pans slowly past him. The sudden rising inflection in a youngster's voice works in tandem with the cut to a close-up of the child's wide-eyed expression. The interplay among audiovisual and performance elements leads scholars of screen performance to analyze performers' expression together with framing, editing, and sound/production design choices.

In addition to fostering comprehensive textual analysis, Prague semiotics facilitates analysis of performance and aesthetic influences. This is because Prague theorists highlight the importance of studying **performers' expressivity** (the degree to which performers display or communicate characters' thoughts and feelings through physical and vocal expression) and **cinematic or media expressivity** (the way in which audiovisual elements enhance, truncate, or otherwise mediate access to performance details). As the subsequent section on postmodern performances reveals, productions' use of performers' and cinematic/media expressivity are integrally connected, with all production details colored by an identifiable aesthetic tradition.

Analyzing Postmodern Performances

Postmodern media texts depend on certain narrative and audiovisual strategies (media culture references, montages, surreal inserts). Yet they also feature what

Maitland McDonagh has called "bizarrely stressed acting" where "performers slip back and forth between low-key naturalism and exaggerated theatricalism."[41] To picture postmodern performances, one might think of *Only God Forgives* (Refn, 2013), which includes performances by Ryan Gosling and Kristin Scott Thomas that swing from minimalistic to highly expressive. Alternatively, one might consider *Jane the Virgin* (The CW, 2014–present) starring Gina Rodriquez, which features performances that fluctuate between plausible, lifelike realism and stylized performative excess.

In postmodern film and media, performances sometimes involve minimalistic modernist portrayals that intermittently feature highly expressive but conventional melodramatic choices. Sometimes postmodern performances mix pared-down, minimalistic performance details with expressive but plausible naturalistic choices. Bizarrely stressed postmodern performances can contribute to films with different ideological orientations. The performances sometimes suture audiences into the narratives by giving them fleeting but essential emotional connection with the characters. In other instances, postmodern performance choices help to create a critical distance from the story and characters in productions that challenge the status quo.

Some independent films use postmodern performance strategies to facilitate audience reflection. Echoing an approach used in performance art, their stylistic collage can require actors to "skip blithely from arch parody to . . . fleeting moments of startling sincerity."[42] *Do the Right Thing* (Lee, 1989) illustrates this type of postmodern tonal shift. Late in the film, a casual, lifelike conversation at the pizzeria counter between Sal (Danny Aiello) and Mookie (Spike Lee) suddenly transitions to a tense, highly stylized scene in the cramped pizzeria storeroom. The heightened performance style highlights the symbolic significance of the argument that Pino (John Turturro) and Vito (Richard Edson) have about black–white relations. As the overhead light swings back and forth, the intense physicality of the performances transforms the verbal debate between Pino and Vito into a virtual wrestling match. Then, a cut to the blasting boom box of Radio Raheem (Bill Nunn) underscores the tension in the content and form of the brothers' argument. The unexpected juxtaposition of disparate performance styles disrupts the narrative flow. The portrayals illuminate characters' subjective experiences, yet because they shift from lifelike to highly stylized, they also invite analysis of the characters. Illustrating a key aspect of some postmodern texts, the performances'

tonal fluctuations highlight the narrative's artifice and create a distance from the characters.

Postmodern performances also contribute to mainstream films that feature dazzling cinematic effects and emotion-grabbing characterizations by star performers. For example, *Man on Fire* (Scott, 2004) reveals that Denzel Washington's powerful poses, gestures, movements, and facial expressions anchor the meaning of certain scenes. Washington plays a retired CIA assassin hired as a bodyguard for an American child living in Mexico City. A scene with his character alone and reflecting on his self-imposed isolation opens with a chaos of noise/music fragments and shots that cut from one to another unexpectedly. Importantly, Washington's highly expressive gestures and facial expressions cut through the audiovisual barrage. His eyes fill with tears. His mouth turns down in an exaggerated expression of sorrow. He rubs his hand across his forehead, then covers his eyes with his outstretched fingers. The cuts and camera movement slow down; Washington stands and tries several times to load and aim his gun. Cuts and camera movements return to a frenetic pace. They feature another series of intense facial expressions: Washington furrows his eyebrows, covers his face with his hands, bares his lower teeth, breaks into a tight-lipped grin, and then flinches just before putting the gun to his head. The gun fails to fire. In close-ups, Washington takes deep breaths, pauses, and then infuses his movements with quiet purpose as he lowers the gun and checks the bullet. The details of his performance convey the fact that this is a turning point for the character.[43]

Washington's performance is emblematic of mainstream postmodern performances that communicate engaging emotion in intermittent moments. These performances feature alternating expressive modes to suit the overall design of explosion-heavy action films, which themselves have irregular rhythms and hyperbolic shifts in tone. Mainstream postmodern performances do not follow conventions of realism, but instead include intensely expressive moments that would be out of place if combined with the seamless filmic choices in, for example, romantic comedies.

Case Study: Considering Postmodern Performances from a Global Perspective

My interest in the surprising amalgamation of aesthetic strategies in postmodern media texts led me to write "Suiting Up for Postmodern Performance in John Woo's *The Killer*," published in *More Than a Method: Trends and Traditions in Contemporary Film Performance*. When *The Killer* received its international release, North American critics described the film's stylistic choices in ways that echoed comments about work by David Lynch, who is known for such highly stylized, postmodern films as *Blue Velvet* as well as the television show *Twin Peaks* (ABC 1990–1991). Highlighting *The Killer*'s self-reflexive postmodern media allusions, James Wolcott discussed the "cool" surface of Woo's blood opera, suggesting that Woo's film made him "the most exciting cult-icon director from overseas since Sergio Leone put Clint Eastwood in a poncho."[44] Calling attention to the film's postmodern moments of intense human and cinematic expressivity, J. Hoberman focused on its "hot" emotionality, proposing that *The Killer* suggested "nothing so much as *Magnificent Obsession* remade by Sam Peckinpah."[45]

I thus set out to see how *The Killer* presents performances (enhancing or minimizing viewers' access to performers' expressivity), and how its interplay between filmic and human expression creates meaning and emotional effects. My approach recognized that individual performances reflect specific conceptions of character and narrative design, and that differing styles of performance are not simply deviations from one set of norms (realist conventions). I asked, what are some distinguishing features of postmodern performances? How do they differ from modernist or naturalist performances? How do physical and vocal elements contribute to meaning in this postmodern production?

My investigation revealed that there is a connection between *The Killer*'s performances and its postmodern conception of character. I found that the film departs from **modernist texts** (where minimalist performances coincide with the idea that identity involves ostensibly universal abstract traits) and **naturalistic texts** (where lifelike performances reflect the view that characters are shaped by social environments and personal histories). Taking a third path, *The Killer*'s **postmodern** performances quote from popular images in the same way that postmodern art and social identity depend on sampling options offered by media-saturated society. I found that the film's postmodern aesthetic informs the vocal and physical aspects of the actors' portrayals. It shapes the tone, volume, rhythms, intonations, and inflections of the actors' vocal performances that illuminate characters' goals and inner experiences. *The Killer*'s complete postmodern aesthetic colors how the actors' expressions, gestures, postures, and gaits contribute to the inferences audiences make about the characters.

I discovered that in *The Killer*, setting, lighting, costumes, props, and performances address audiences as global consumers. Significantly, Chow Yun-Fat's Armani-suited body serves as the stable and anchoring public norm in the film's spectacular audiovisual display. In addition, Chow's depiction of Jeffrey, the gentle hired assassin, belongs to the film's larger audiovisual design. The film's postmodern presentation of character creates a cool, distanced identification that allows audiences to engage with its spectacular visuals as much as with the characters. Camera and editing choices suture viewers into the protagonists' perspectives, but *The Killer* also fosters viewers' pleasure that results from negotiating the shifting rhythms, moods, and levels of emotional engagement with the characters. The film's aesthetic choices reflect postmodernism's interest in the play of signifiers and its drive to wring meaning out of surface details. Significantly, *The Killer* also reveals the influence of Peking Opera's striking combination of florid emotionality and codified gesture, movement, and costume.

Chow Yun-Fat's performance coordinates with those of Sally Yeh (Jenny, the innocent songstress he protects after she loses her sight), Chu Kong (Sydney, an aging assassin and Jeffrey's oldest friend), and Danny Lee (Inspector Lee, a detective who admires Jeffrey's moral code and becomes his ally). As my study reveals, the actors' cool, often truncated physical and vocal expressivity suggests a comparison with modernist acting. However, their performances break with modernist tradition in moments when the actors' project intense emotion, and the film goes beyond realism as it amplifies their expression of emotion through overheated sound-image combinations.

In my study, I examined how the film's performances depart from both modernist and realist traditions, considering, for example, that they often feature gestures and poses drawn from advertising imagery. The overtly commercial images in key dramatic moments create distance from the narrative. However, the strangely familiar material also creates avenues for emotional contact, as one accesses the characters' pivotal experiences through and in terms of the gestures, poses, and vocal expressions one would find in glossy ads for expensive clothing, liquor, or travel destinations. Similarly, the film's use of lowbrow aesthetic traditions can be surprisingly engaging. For example, echoing soap opera conventions, in an important scene where Jeffrey and Jenny are physically separate but emotionally intimate, hidden lavalier microphones and close-miked

Figure 7.1 Postmodern productions feature moments when actors' expressive performances create emotional connections with audiences (*The Killer*, 1989, Golden Princess Amusement Company)

Figure 7.2 Postmodern productions also engage audiences by presenting characters in settings made familiar by advertising (*The Killer*, 1989, Golden Princess Amusement Company)

post-production dialogue recording allow Chow Yun-Fat and Sally Yeh to use hushed tones. This intensifies the emotion conveyed as the actors use breathing and intonation more than volume and rhythm to communicate the characters' intermingling feelings of hope and despair.

The distinguishing features of the postmodern performances in *The Killer* became clear when I saw how they transform the modernist choices in *Le samouraï* (Melville, 1967). This precursor to Woo's film features a pared-down, minimalist style where actors project little emotion and camera-editing choices keep audiences at a physical and emotional distance from the characters. The qualities that make performances in *The Killer* postmodern also became more visible when I compared them to the portrayals by Chow Yun-Fat and Jodie Foster in *Anna and the King* (Tennant, 1999). In this Hollywood film, even scenes that depict strong emotion discreetly and "realistically" parcel out details of the actors' expressive hands and faces as the scene builds slowly and then gradually lowers in intensity. By comparison, echoing Bruce Lee's portrayal in *Fists of Fury*, performances in *The Killer* exemplify global postmodern aesthetics as they bounce between cool minimalism and exaggerated theatricalism.

I believe that my study of *The Killer* effectively applies Prague semiotics, for it thoroughly analyzes performance details in relation to surrounding cinematic choices. I think it clarifies the postmodern dimension of the performances through comparisons with the modernist performances in *Le samouraï* and the conventions of realism in *Anna and the King*. My analysis also successfully illustrates *The Killer*'s roots in Chinese theatrical traditions by identifying similarities with performance rhythms in *Fists of Fury*. Yet my study would benefit from a more thorough discussion of the ways in which Chow Yun-Fat's performance captures a vision of Hong Kong masculinity that must honor the code of *yi* (brotherhood) and strive to maintain the proper place of *qing* (emotive feeling) in relation to *li* (reason) and *jing* (cleverness to survive). One could perhaps illustrate the romantic quality of the film's vision of Hong Kong masculinity by contrasting performances in *The Killer* with those in comparable American films of the period, such as the hitman film *Cohen and Tate* (Red, 1989) or the gangster film *The Untouchables* (De Palma, 1987). I would like to have demonstrated connections between character and performance by using script analysis terms to examine the interplay between two characters' given circumstances, objectives, and actions in one or more scenes. The study ends by highlighting the need to consider postmodern aesthetics and performance in an international light, and I would like to have addressed more fully how close analysis of performance can contribute to larger studies of representation.

Conclusion

The range of scholarship considered in this chapter does not exhaust the ways to analyze screen performances. Studies of performance tend to be most effective when combined with other forms of textual, cultural, and material analysis. Star studies, archival research, and industry studies often contribute to effective discussions of screen performance. Looking ahead, scholarship on the eroding boundaries between film and television should generate nuanced studies of media performance. Continued research on motion-capture, animated, and videogame performances will further illuminate the range and complexity of screen performances.[46] Attention to insights by actors and acting teachers will enhance critical vocabularies and shed light on the creative labor behind complex performances. Similarly, film and media scholarship supported by work in performance studies should continue to break new ground in cross-cultural research.

Notes

1. Glen Creeber, *Serial Television: Big Drama on the Small Screen* (London: British Film Institute, 2004), 14–15.
2. Lez Cooke, *British Television Drama: A History* (London: British Film Institute, 2003), 178.
3. See Cynthia Baron, Diane Carson, and Frank P. Tomasulo, eds., *More Than a Method: Trends and Traditions in Contemporary Film Performance* (Detroit: Wayne State University Press, 2004); Cristina Degli-Esposti, ed., *Postmodernism in the Cinema* (New York: Berghahn Books, 1998).
4. See Cynthia Baron, "Suiting Up for Postmodern Performance in John Woo's *The Killer*," in Baron et al., *More Than a Method*, 297–329.
5. See Lev Kuleshov, *Kuleshov on Film: Writings*, trans. and ed. Ronald Levaco (Berkeley: University of California Press, 1974); Lev Kuleshov, *Lev Kuleshov: Selected Works*, trans. Dmitri Agrachev and Nina Belenkaya (Moscow: Raduga, 1987).
6. Rosemary Malague, *An Actress Prepares: Women and "the Method"* (New York: Routledge, 2012), 48.
7. Ibid., 26.
8. See Richard Hornby, *The End of Acting: A Radical View* (New York: Applause Theatre Books, 1992).
9. Malague, *An Actress Prepares*, 25.
10. See Sharon Carnicke, *Stanislavski in Focus: A Master for the Twenty-First Century* (New York: Routledge, 2009).
11. Cynthia Baron, *Modern Acting: The Lost Chapter of American Film and Theatre* (London: Palgrave Macmillan, 2016).
12. See Sergei Eisenstein, *Film Form: Essays in Film Theory* (New York: Harcourt, Brace & World, 1949); Cynthia Baron, "Acting Choices/Filmic Choices: Rethinking Montage and Performance," *Journal of Film and Video* 59, no. 2 (2007): 32–40.
13. See Chapter 8 in this volume for further information about semiotics.
14. See Jan Mukařovský, *Aesthetic Function, Norm and Value as Social Facts*, trans. Mark E. Suino (Ann Arbor: University of Michigan Press, 1970); Michael L. Quinn, *The Semiotic Stage: Prague School Theater Theory* (New York: Peter Lang, 1995). Prague theorists find that composite art forms use iconic signs (e.g., photographs), indexical signs (weather vanes), symbolic signs (written/spoken language), and ostensive signs (gestures, vocal intonations, objects on stage/in the scene). They see distinctions between character, actor, and performance details, and show that audiences

make inferences about characters due to the observable qualities in performance details and social and institutional factors (from publicity to audiences' cultural and personal experiences).

15. Richard Maltby, *Hollywood Cinema*, second edition (Malden: Blackwell, 2003), 389.

16. David Marc, *Demographic Vistas: Television in American Culture*, revised edition (Philadelphia: University of Pennsylvania Press, 1996), 99.

17. Ibid., 100.

18. Ibid.

19. See Michael Kirby, "On Acting and Not-Acting," *The Drama Review* 16, no. 1 (1972): 3–15. The article also appears in *Acting (Re)considered: Theories and Practices*, second edition, ed. Philip Zarilli (New York: Routledge, 2002), 40–52.

20. Kirby, "On Acting and Not-Acting," 9.

21. Su Holmes, *The Quiz Show* (Edinburgh University Press, 2008), 118.

22. Richard deCordova, "Genre and Performance: An Overview," in *Film Genre Reader*, ed. Barry Keith Grant (Austin: University of Texas Press, 1986), 138.

23. See Christine Cornea, ed., *Genre and Performance: Film and Television* (New York: Manchester University Press, 2010).

24. See Jeremy Butler, "'I'm not a doctor, but I play one on TV': Characters, Actors, and Acting in Television Soap Opera," in *To Be Continued . . . Soap Operas Around the World*, ed. Robert C. Allen (New York: Routledge, 1995), 145–63; Holmes, *The Quiz Show*, Andrew Tolson, ed., *Television Talk Shows: Discourse, Performance, Spectacle* (Mahwah: Lawrence Erlbaum Associates, 2001).

25. See Doug Tomlinson, "Studies in the Use and Visualization of Film Performance: Alfred Hitchcock, Robert Bresson, Jean Renoir" (PhD diss., New York University, 1986). Before his premature death, Tomlinson edited *Actors on Acting for the Screen* (New York: Garland, 1994).

26. Malague, *An Actress Prepares*, 99.

27. Doug Moston, *Coming to Terms with Acting: An Illustrative Glossary* (New York: Drama Books, 1993), 19.

28. Ibid., 2.

29. Scott Sedita, *The Eight Characters of Comedy: A Guide to Sitcom Acting and Writing*, second edition (Los Angeles: Atides Publishing, 2014), 322.

30. See Kimberly Meltzer, *TV News Anchors and Journalistic Tradition: How Journalists Adapt to Technology* (New York: Peter Lang, 2010); Nancy Reardon, *On Camera: How to Report, Anchor and Interview* (Boston: Focal Press, 2006).

31. Reardon, *On Camera*, 204.

32. Bernard Graham Shaw, *Voice-Overs: A Practical Guide* (New York: Routledge, 2001), 15.

33. Louann Haarman, "Performing Talk," in *Television Talk Shows: Discourse, Performance, Spectacle*, ed. Andrew Tolson (Mahwah: Lawrence Erlbaum Associates, 2001), 31–32.

34. Haarman, "Performing Talk," 53.

35. See Judith Lancioni, ed., *Fix Me Up: Essays on Television Dating and Makeover Shows* (Jefferson: McFarland, 2010).

36. See Su Holmes and Deborah Jermyn, eds., *Understanding Reality Television* (New York: Routledge, 2004); Beverly Skeggs and Helen Wood, *Reacting to Reality Television: Performance, Audience and Value* (New York: Routledge, 2012).

37. See Eden Davies, *Beyond Dance: Laban's Legacy of Movement Analysis* (New York: Routledge, 2006); John Hodgson, *Mastering Movement: The Life and Work of Rudolf Laban* (New York: Routledge, 2001); Jean Newlove, *Laban for Actors and Dancers* (New York: Routledge, 1993). Laban also identified eight "efforts" underlying physical/vocal expression: press, thrust, wring, slash, glide, dab, float, and flick; for variations see Newlove.

38. See Paddy Scannell, ed., *Broadcast Talk* (London: Sage, 1991).

39. See Jan Mukařovský, "An Attempt at a Structural Analysis of a Dramatic Figure (1931)," in *Structure, Sign, and Function: Selected Essays by Jan Mukařovský*, trans. and ed. John Burbank and Peter Steiner (New Haven: Yale University Press, 1978), 171–77.

40. Kristal Brent Zook, *Color by Fox: The Fox Network and the Revolution in Black Television* (New York: Oxford University Press, 1999), 20.

41. Maitland McDonagh, "Action Painter John Woo," *Film Comment* 29, no. 5 (1993): 48.

42. Jacob Gallagher-Ross, "Image Eaters: Big Art Group Brings the Noise," *TDR: The Drama Review* 54, no. 4 (2010): 54.

43. See Cynthia Baron, "The Modern Entertainment Marketplace, 2000–Present," in *Acting*, eds. Claudia Springer and Julie Levinson (New Brunswick: Rutgers University Press, 2015), 143–67.

44. James Wolcott, "Blood Test," *New Yorker*, August 23, 1993, 63.

45. J. Hoberman, "Hong Kong Blood and Guts," *Premiere*, August 1990, 33.

46. See Lisa Bode, *Making Believe: Screening Performance and Special Effects in Popular Cinema* (New Brunswick, NJ: Rutgers University Press, 2017); Cynthia Baron, "The Temporal Dimensions of Screen Performances: Exploring Expressive Movement in Live Action and Animated Film," in *Acting and Performance in Moving Image Culture: Bodies, Screens, Renderings*, eds. Jörg Sternagel, Deborah Levitt, Dieter Mersch (Piscataway: Transaction Publishers, 2012), 303–20; and Sharon Marie Carnicke, "Emotional Expressivity in Motion Capture Technology," in Sternagel et al., *Acting and Performance in Moving Image Culture*, 321–38.

Further Reading

Baron, Cynthia and Sharon Marie Carnicke. *Reframing Screen Performance.* Ann Arbor: University of Michigan Press, 2008.

Benedetti, Robert. *Action! Acting for Film and Television.* London: Longman, 2006.

Bernard, Ian. *Film and Television Acting: From Stage to Screen*, second edition. New York: Routledge, 2016.

Butler, Jeremy, ed. *Star Texts: Image and Performance in Film and Television.* Detroit: Wayne State University Press, 1991.

Hogg, Christopher and Tom Cantrell, eds. *Exploring Television Acting.* London: Bloomsbury, 2018.

Lovell, Alan, and Peter Krämer, eds. *Screen Acting.* New York: Routledge, 1999.

Naremore, James. *Acting in the Cinema.* Berkeley: University of California Press, 1988.

Tucker, Patrick. *Secrets of Screen Acting*, third edition. New York: Routledge, 2015.

Weston, Judith. *Directing Actors: Creating Memorable Performances for Film and Television.* Studio City: Michael Wiese, 1999.

Wojcik, Pamela Robertson, ed. *Movie Acting: The Film Reader.* New York: Routledge, 2004.

8.
REPRESENTATION
Mary Beltrán

A **representation** is a visual, written, or audio depiction of something or someone. This term also refers broadly to what images and texts *mean,* the meanings that they potentially convey, and how they come to take on those meanings. With respect to the focus of this volume, representation refers to the meanings associated with mediated images and narratives, such as television episodes, films, and music videos. We can also think more specifically of the **politics of representation**, or how representation *matters* for social groups and for society as a whole. This chapter will trace the major theories and methods of criticism in the humanities that have focused on both of these lines of inquiry, understanding how media images and narratives convey meaning, and studying media texts with an eye to how specific social groups, such as women and girls, Muslims, or gay men and lesbians have been portrayed in the entertainment media. While the study of mediated representation can't tell us about every audience member's interpretation of a media text (Chapter 15 in this volume expands on this complexity), it can illuminate some of its potential meanings.

Given the many diverse ways media critics understand representation, it can be a difficult concept to pin down and define. At the same time, representation has been a (if not *the*) primary area of focus driving media studies as a whole. Before media studies existed as we know it today, scholars such as Ferdinand de Saussure and Roland Barthes conducted pioneering work exploring and mapping how language (in the case of Saussure) and popular images and narratives (in the case of Barthes) conveyed meanings; the aim to understand how language and symbols *signify* motivated the work of these two scholars.[1] This line of inquiry was subsequently one of

the catalysts of the birth of film and television studies, and it remains central to media criticism today. Scholars and critics who explore the symbolic meanings and the narrative impact of aesthetic elements of a film, television episode, or other media text, or who explore how ideas about gender, race, sexual orientation, and other social categories are conveyed in that text are all engaging in studies of representation.

Differing theoretical understandings of representation and how and why it matters have spurred the development of diverse and at times oppositional threads of media studies in the humanities. As is explained in more detail below, this has included the growth of structuralist and later post-structuralist understandings of media texts and meaning, the study of the politics of representation in conjunction with the rise of cultural studies, feminist studies, critical race studies, queer studies, and other identity-based studies, and also postmodern and postcolonial studies. **Image analysis**, an approach to studying representation that examines media images in relation to questions of equity, is one of the primary research methods discussed in this chapter. Scholars studying representation often use and may combine other methods, such as **stylistic or formalist analysis** (the study of aesthetic choices and how they lend meaning), **narrative analysis** (the study of stories in media texts), and/or **ideological analysis** or **discourse analysis** (the study of ideological messages or discourses embedded in media texts). These approaches have been utilized extensively by media scholars to explore how particular social groups have been and are represented and to study representation in film, television, and mediated culture more generally. I take up several of these methods as my critical tools in my case study, which I discuss later in this chapter.

A Brief History of the Study of Representation

The study of how media representations convey meaning has its roots in philosophy, linguistics (the study of language), and literary analysis. American philosopher Charles Sanders Peirce and Swiss linguist Ferdinand de Saussure are among the scholars credited with the invention of **semiotics**, a term coined by Peirce in 1867 to describe the study of symbols or **signs** and the logic of how they convey meaning.[2] Saussure, in research on language and how words and their arrangement make meaning, termed the study of these dynamics **semiology**.[3] The arrangement of words in this sentence, for instance, is an illustration of how structure is tied to meaning. These ideas were further developed by scholars viewed as **structuralists**. These scholars analyzed narratives, language, and elements of popular culture with respect to the impact of structures of meaning. **Structuralism** builds on the assumption that words, images, objects, and behavior within cultural systems have singular meanings, derived through their relationship with other objects within the system in a discernable structure. For instance, meanings were believed to result from binary oppositions (such as good/bad, light/dark, and sacred/profane) creating meaning through contrasts.

Scholars such as anthropologist Claude Lévi-Strauss and literary theorist Roland Barthes popularized structuralism within their respective disciplines. Lévi-Strauss pioneered structuralist anthropology in studies of kinship and popular folk tales in remote regions of the world.[4] He argued that a universal system of meaning, including structuring binaries such as heroism and cowardice, informed the repeated character types and narratives he found in vastly different cultures. Barthes, in turn, brought structuralism to popular journalism and to literary studies. In his writing, he explored seemingly trivial objects and events of mid-1950s French culture—ranging from margarine, to film stars, to cereal boxes—as inscribed with linked cultural meanings and what he termed **myths**, reinforcing popular ideologies of the time.[5] For instance, in "The World of Wrestling," Barthes underscored the appeal of professional wrestling. Examining this performative style of wrestling through a structuralist lens, he described it as the spectacular staging of showdowns between good and evil, with wrestlers portraying exaggerated versions of heroic figures and villains who ultimately received a satisfying comeuppance for their dastardly acts.[6] To provide another illustration, we might consider Mattel's Barbie® Doll, with its always made-up face and bust–waist–hip proportions that in real life would measure an extraordinary 35–22–32 inches. Despite its role as children's toy, this doll also arguably served to endorse an ideal of thin, busty, and blonde beauty upon its introduction in U.S. culture in 1959. As these examples demonstrate, Barthes' conceptualization of myth links representation to **ideology**, systems of normative ideas and social values. His theory of mythology also usefully overlaps with the concept of **hegemony**, as conceived by Karl Marx and expanded upon by social theorist Antonio Gramsci to describe a ruling group's struggle for dominance, in part through control of representation and thus of social norms and values.[7] Myths as described by Barthes are elements of **hegemonic** influence, endorsing ideas and values of dominant groups within a society.

Structuralism was challenged in the 1960s and 1970s by scholars such as philosopher Jacques Derrida, theorist Michel Foucault, and literary and psychoanalytic scholar Julia Kristeva.[8] These scholars are often described as **post-structuralists**, although they did not always embrace the term. This disparate group was influential in bringing to the study of representation ideological critique, **psychoanalytic theory** (a conceptualization of personality organization and development that guides psychoanalysis), and, in the case of Foucault, consideration of social and historical context and its influence on the multiple meanings potentially attached to representations. Some structuralists, such as Barthes and Foucault, later became post-structuralists as they began to reconsider assumptions of totalizing social structures lending meaning to images and narratives. Barthes' 1967 essay "The Death of the Author," for instance, expressed his newfound belief that the ultimate meanings of a text rested in its readers' interpretations rather than in the text itself.[9] Among its differences from structuralism, **post-structuralism** builds on the assumption that there is no underlying structure of relationships that provides singular or set meanings to social phenomena. Post-structuralism also overlaps with postmodern theory, discussed below, particularly in challenging "**grand narratives**." This term, coined by theorist Jean-François Lyotard, refers to narratives that historically have influenced social relations, cultural memory, and public interpretations of meanings, such as the former belief in an "American melting pot" that gave all Americans equal status.[10] Derrida argued for scholars to engage in **deconstruction,** the analysis of representation from a post-structuralist critical stance.

Put simply, deconstruction involves reading a text against the grain in order to examine the many ambiguities inherent in its history, linked meanings, and embedded ideologies. For example, Jordon Peele's 2017 horror film *Get Out,* about an African American young man who faces life-threatening dangers when his white girlfriend takes him home to meet her parents, smartly deconstructs Hollywood paradigms. To do so, it builds on its audience's knowledge of the typical marginalization of African Americans in horror films to build tension and to prompt humor and surprise (Figure 8.1). Deconstruction carried to its fullest extent by Derrida and other scholars considered **high post-structuralists** ultimately finds meaning itself so ambiguous that it is impossible to pin down, a theoretical stance that most media scholars have not found useful as a critical tool.

The study of representation also includes a long tradition of critique of how various social groups and **identities** have been represented in the media and popular culture more broadly. This scholarship informs and is part of the disciplines of **feminist studies**, **critical race studies**, **queer studies**, **postcolonial studies**, **class studies**, and **disability studies**, which approach representation with a primary focus on gender, race and ethnicity, sexual orientation, colonization and its aftermath, class, and ability, respectively. The broadening of film and television studies to include a focus on representation in relation to these axes of identity coincided in the late 1960s and early '70s with the rise of **identity politics**, or identity-based consciousness and activism. Women, people of color, LGBTQ people, and working-class people were among the groups actively reflecting on the impact of their identities on their status and opportunities and agitating for better treatment in society.

Critiques of representation in film and television with respect to identity and marginalization also entered public conversation through the forum of the popular press. This included books and magazine articles by feminist writers such as Betty Friedan, who wrote *The Feminine Mystique* in 1963, and Molly Haskell, whose *From Reverence to Rape: The Treatment of Women in the Movies* was published in 1974, who made a major impact in raising public consciousness regarding sexism embedded in popular culture.[11] Authors who similarly engaged in early writing about race and sexual orientation in media representation included James Baldwin and Donald Bogle, who wrote about how African American characters and stars were represented in Hollywood film and publicity, and Vito Russo, who wrote *The Celluloid Closet,* the first extensive survey of the treatment of gay and lesbian characters in Hollywood film.[12]

The first scholars of the politics of representation engaged in image analysis, often studying **stereotypes**, images of a social group that are misleading, denigrating, and/or homogenizing. George Gerbner and Gaye Tuchman, for instance, pioneered the study of what Gerbner termed **symbolic annihilation**.[13] Tuchman broke this concept down into three separate dynamics—omission, trivialization, and condemnation—in her study of how women were misrepresented and often excluded from films and television in the early 1970s.[14] Questions of **realism**, or of whether media portrayals accurately reflect real life, at times entered these critiques. Feminist critics, for instance, challenged representations that posited women and girls as the "frailer sex," pointing to how this construction inaccurately **naturalized** supposed differences between women and men as innate. In connection with this work,

Figure 8.1 The film *Get Out* (dir. Jordan Peele, Universal Studios Home Entertainment, 2017) engages in post-structuralist stance in its deconstruction of common patterns of representation for African American characters in horror films

some activist writers urged their groups to demand more "positive" images and to take up the tools of production to counter Hollywood's patterns of representation. Over time, media advocacy groups, such as the National Association for the Advancement of Colored People (NAACP), the National Hispanic Media Coalition (NHMC), and the Gay and Lesbian Alliance Against Defamation (GLAAD), began to take up these charges, while scholars shifted to more nuanced and theoretically grounded studies of representation.

Scholars who were part of this next wave of scholarship included but were not limited to Laura Mulvey, bell hooks, Richard Dyer, Edward Said, and Charlotte Brunsdon.[15] Scholars with theoretical grounding in postcolonial studies and cultural studies such as Said and Stuart Hall engaged in study of what they called **Othering**, dynamics by which marginalized groups in a society are constructed through their representations in popular culture as potential threats or as in need of guidance and control.[16] With a similar focus but in the realm of feminist studies, Mulvey and Brunsdon were among the pioneering scholars studying women's images and how feminist perspectives were often absent or distorted in film and television.[17]

With scholarly grounding in film studies and ethnic studies, Dyer's *White*, in turn, was the first comprehensive study of the privileging of whiteness in Hollywood film,[18] while scholars such as Jacqueline Bobo, Jane Gaines, and bell hooks broke new ground in analysis of African American women's media representation and how they negotiated limitations in representation through their viewing practices.[19] This and other scholarship on the representation of various ethnic groups ultimately was foundational to what is now called **critical race studies**, the application of critical theory and scholarship in various disciplines to study links between race and social power in society. Bobo, Gaines, hooks, and others also modeled **intersectional analysis,** or study with attention to elements of identity, such as gender and race, along more than one axis. **Intersectionality** was championed by African American feminist theorists such as Kimberlé Crenshaw and Patricia Hill Collins, who challenged white feminist scholars to consider how their conceptualization of "women" often left out women of color and pointed to the need for analyses that instead focused on multiple axes of identity.[20]

Cultural studies, an approach developed in part at the University of Birmingham in the UK in the 1960s, also made a major contribution to the study of representation. Combining theory and methods from a wide variety of disciplines, including sociology, feminist studies, anthropology, history, and art/literary criticism, it focuses in particular on the dynamics of hegemony, social power, and audiences' negotiations with what they consume in the media. The work of Antonio Gramsci, described above in relation to his conceptualization of hegemony, also influenced cultural studies scholars' ideas of agency and **resistance**, or counter-hegemonic activity, in audience responses to hegemonic popular culture.[21] Cultural studies scholars and theories have been important to studies of media representation of marginalized individuals and social groups, particularly youth and subcultures (e.g., the work of Dick Hebdige), people of color (such as in the work of Stuart Hall and Paul Gilroy), and girls and women (as in Angela McRobbie's and Charlotte Brunsdon's scholarship).[22] Hall in particular was influential for building on Gramsci's understanding of hegemonic culture. In doing so, he emphasized the **polysemy** (multiple meanings) of media texts and how audiences actively engage with what they consume in the media.[23] His theory of **encoding** and **decoding** was foundational in this regard.[24]

Postcolonial studies also was influential in the development of the study of representation, particularly in relation to global hegemonies. Postcolonial studies examines the impact of **colonialism** and **imperialism**, the long-term subjugation of entire countries and of colonized people and cultures, and how this oppression has influenced cultures and their systems of knowledge. In the mid to late twentieth century, influential postcolonial studies scholars included literary scholar Homi K. Bhabha, psychiatrist Franz Fanon, who studied the dynamics of dehumanization experienced by colonized people, and cultural theorist Edward Said, who is best known for his explication of **Orientalism**, a concept linked to the dynamics of Othering.[25] Said posits Orientalism as the dynamic by which Western scholarship and literature on the East have reified global structures of power and imperialism through reinforcing notions of an East–West binary. Through this binary, Western cultures are seen as intellectual, rational, and stable, and Eastern cultures and people as primitive, irrational, and weak.

Finally, scholars of **postmodernism**, such as Jean Baudrillard and Fredric Jameson, have stressed that representation and identity are not fixed and in fact can be hybrid, fluid, and performative.[26] Postmodernism is defined in multiple and, at times, diverging ways by scholars. Most broadly it is described as an aesthetic or worldview that breaks from and questions the master narratives of the past and is related to an era in which culture is increasingly fragmented, media driven, and hybrid. The concepts of hybridity and performativity, which derive from postmodern and postcolonial studies, will be described in further detail below.

Reading Representation: Concepts and Terms for Your Critical Tool Box

Media scholars from differing theoretical orientations use distinct terms and concepts, and indeed may disagree regarding the most constructive objects of study and the questions to ask when it comes to studying representation. It is useful to learn about as many of these modes and concepts as possible in order to understand their overlaps and distinctions. In this section, we'll review a number of commonly used concepts, terms, and approaches that may be useful for your own critiques of representation in entertainment media texts and for articulating your conclusions.

In semiotics, the study of representation begins with a focus on a narrative unit that is rarely but occasionally considered in media criticism, the **sign**. Signs are units of meaning that are further broken down into two parts, the **signifier** and the **signified**. The signifier is the material part of the sign, while the signified refers to the social meanings attached to that signifier. For example, a heart-shaped container of chocolates given to another person is both a container filled with candy (the sign's signifier) and a symbol of love for one's sweetheart (what is signified).

Two other terms that derive from semiotics that are often used by other scholars exploring representation are **denotation** and **connotation**. A study of representation in a film, television episode, or other media text typically begins with focus on denotation, an assessment of the material image and narrative and their most manifest, external qualities. This would entail a focus on aesthetic elements, or a **stylistic analysis** of a media text. The media critic would then move on to discern the connotative, or submerged, meanings of these style choices—the linked cultural meanings, ideologies, and myths. Such meanings are not simply attached to a particular image but are culturally constituted in relation to the particular era and place in which a representation circulates. For example, in an episode of the television sitcom *The Big Bang Theory* (TBS, 2007–), about a group of nerdy male friends in the contemporary United States, Sheldon, the most socially awkward of the group, has to be schooled regarding the semiotics of his housemate's tie hung outside their locked apartment door while romantic music plays inside (Figure 8.2). The connotation that he finally understands is that the tie is a warning to stay away because his housemate is inside with a woman with whom he hopes to get amorous. While on its face it's just a tie (its denotative meaning), with respect to its connotative meaning in contemporary culture, it is telling Sheldon, "Do not disturb!" The two meanings of the tie illustrate how

Figure 8.2 Sheldon is schooled in how to read the semiotics of his housemate's tie on their front door in *The Big Bang Theory*, "The Hamburger Postulate" (CBS, October 21, 2007)

representation can be fruitfully analyzed in relation to denotative and connotative meanings as understood within a social and cultural context.

The related concepts of **ideology** and **discourse** also are useful to understanding representation in relation to linked meanings and social impact. Ideology refers to systems of beliefs and ideals, particularly those that undergird the dominant politics and social values in a society, such as capitalism and patriarchy in the United States. As noted above, Barthes was one of the first scholars to imply that representation is inherently ideological. The overlapping term discourse refers to socially sanctioned ways of thinking that define what can be said about a topic and how it is represented. Discourse thus also can be understood as hegemonic in function. Michel Foucault most notably illustrated how discourses are both discernible in popular culture and powerful in their impact in his in-depth examinations of how discourses of knowledge and of power have been shaped by and have profoundly shaped Western societies. For example, in *History of Sexuality,* he examined how past and current discourses of sexuality have maintained laws and taboos that support the societal structure of the family as we know it.[27]

The concept of **stereotyping,** while limited in what it illuminates, was useful as an early springboard to the study of representation. The term has disciplinary roots in philosophy, psychology, and sociology. As cognitive psychologists note, we make sense of the world through categorizing objects and people into **types**, in a process that becomes negative with the addition of **xenophobia**, the fear or dislike of people we deem different from our own group. When these ideas become integrated into media narratives, mediated **stereotypes** can take the form of stock characters that come to falsely stand in for a group. Walter Lippman is credited with coining the term in 1922.[28] A public intellectual focused on issues of democracy, Lippman argued that stereotypes about marginalized groups were being disseminated through the new medium of that era, newspapers. The subsequent rise of film, radio, and television similarly prompted attention from scholars in the social sciences to their integration of cultural stereotypes and the impact on audiences. A 1930s study that was a part of the Payne Fund studies, for instance, found that the 1915 film *Birth of a Nation* reinforced denigrating stereotypes of African Americans and ultimately encouraged white youth who watched it to form strongly negative opinions of them.[29]

In an overlapping approach grounded in the humanities, Hall described historical patterns of Othering non-white groups as **racialized regime(s) of representation**, similar to Said's explication of Orientalism.[30] Ella Shohat and Robert Stam usefully expand on this previous work in exploring what they term **Eurocentrism**, historical patterns of representation in film that have privileged the Western world, whiteness, and patterns of global oppression.[31] Contemporary studies of **gendered** or **racialized** images similarly examine those images in relation to historical patterns of representation for a gender or for a specific racial or ethnic group.

The concept of **the gaze**, in turn, emphasizes these dynamics in production practices. The **male gaze**, a term coined by Laura Mulvey, describes the dynamics of **objectification** in relation to female characters in film. As Mulvey notes in relation to the male gaze, female characters in film were (and often still are) constructed primarily as passive objects to be looked at, in other words, as damsels in distress or one-dimensional love interests, in contrast with male characters, who have more often been constructed as active subjects in film.[32] The concept of the gaze also highlights imbalances experienced by women in the media industries with respect to having less power and agency to write, produce, or "green light" media texts. Manthia Diawara and bell hooks built on this scholarship to address parallel imbalances for African Americans inherent to what they termed the **white gaze**, while E. Ann Kaplan, described the **imperial gaze** as a way of seeing evident in media texts linked to global histories of colonization.[33]

In addition, two concepts help scholars address nuances in the social dynamics related to representation: hybridity and performativity. The concept of **hybridity**, as developed by Homi K. Bhabha, Gloria Anzaldúa, Nestor García Canclini, and others, calls attention to and describes the mixed and fluid identities and cultures that often form within postcolonial and postmodern societies such as the contemporary United States.[34] Hybridity also serves to challenge essentialism in scholarship on social categories, identity, and representation. **Performativity** refers to individuals' construction and performance of identities, which are based in part on social discourses that also influence how those identities are perceived. Judith Butler, Teresa de Lauretis, and Werner Sollors are among the scholars that have written about the performativity and fluidity of social categories such as gender (in the case of Butler and de Lauretis) and race

(Sollors' focus).[35] Such scholarship reminds us that representation itself should not be taken for granted, that identity categories can be permeable, unstable, and complex, and that the media play a role in the construction of our ideas of social categories.

It also is helpful to have an understanding of three terms that claim to address contemporary representation but that have been contested by media scholars, **post-racialism**, **postfeminism**, and **post-queer**. **Post-racial** is a term that has been used particularly by conservative pundits to describe U.S. society as having transcended race and racism. Perhaps unsurprisingly, it began to appear in journalistic writing in 2008 as mixed-race President Barack Obama took office. Since then, it has been deployed at times to describe media texts, particularly those that feature themes and aesthetics linked to multiculturalism, such as the *Fast and Furious* franchise. In media studies, post-racialism has been critiqued by scholars such as Ralina L. Joseph and Catherine Squires for inaccurately implying that patterns of racial representation have substantially changed.[36] Postfeminism and related aesthetic and thematic trends in representation have similarly been debunked by scholars. Cultural theorists Rosalind Gill and Angela McRobbie have described **postfeminist** representation in media culture as a sensibility that often repudiates feminism, even while it paradoxically may rely on feminist discourse and aesthetics.[37] In other words, postfeminist media representations suggest that sexism has been overcome and that gender equality exists. As an ideological style of representation, postfeminism involves the presentation of women and girls as independent and confident to a degree, but also as traditionally feminine and/or anti-feminist. For example, a nearly naked Miley Cyrus performing "Wrecking Ball" in her 2013 music video could be viewed as a postfeminist celebrity image, in light of the contradictions she embraces in her performance as a strong, independent woman while also making her body the object of sexual display. Finally, the term **post-queer** has been defined in two distinct ways. In popular writing, post-queer (or similarly, post-gay or post-lesbian) has referred to a belief that sexual orientation no longer matters because of progress achieved in LGBTQ rights, witnessed, for example, in the greater numbers of gay, lesbian, bisexual, and trans celebrities choosing to be out. This belief has been challenged by scholars such as Michael Warner, who argue that U.S. social institutions continue to naturalize heterosexuality as the preferred social norm.[38] In an overlapping area of debate, post-queer refers to a push by some queer theory scholars to move beyond an emphasis on subjectivity and categories of sexual orientation in order to be able to study heteronormativity as a broader social force.[39]

A Case Study in Interpreting Representation: *Macha* Latinas

As this overview illustrates, the divergent ways in which representation has been understood and studied are nothing if not complex. How might a media critic incorporate these approaches and concepts in exploration of one example of media representation? This is very much up to you, in relation to own your research questions and goals, as well as your object of study. In this section, I explore a case study from my own work as a model of media criticism with a focus on representation.

In "Más Macha: The New Latina Action Hero," I analyze how Latina protagonists in several late 1990s and early 2000s films were represented and to what end, with respect to their possible linked meanings and significance.[40] My objects of study consisted of roles played by Jennifer Lopez and Michelle Rodriguez in five films. These included Lopez's characters in the films *Out of Sight* (1998), *Angel Eyes* (2001), and *Enough* (2002)—roles as police officers and as an abused ex-wife who learns to fight back—and Rodriguez's characters in *Girlfight* (2000) and *Resident Evil* (2002), a troubled high school student who finds confidence in the world of boxing and a futuristic soldier fighting zombies and other dangers. In each film, the protagonists were notable for moments in which they demonstrated physical capabilities and bravery.

What spurred my interest in exploring these characters further was that they were markedly different from their white counterparts in earlier action films, such as Sarah Connor, played by Linda Hamilton in the first two *Terminator* films (1984 and 1990); Ripley, played by Sigourney Weaver in four *Aliens* films (1979–1997); and Samantha Caine/Charly Baltimore, played by Geena Davis in *The Long Kiss Goodnight* (1996). As Yvonne Tasker detailed in a study of 1990s female action protagonists, these characters underwent a dramatic transformation, becoming noticeably tougher, less traditionally feminine, and, particularly in the case of Sarah Connor, more muscular.[41] In Tasker's analysis, semiotics proved useful: the characters she analyzed had shed the visual trappings of Hollywood-defined femininity. It would seem that only after these transformations did these characters possess the physical toughness and the emotional stoicism needed to take up the mantle of the action heroine and face the villain or conflict, whether it was a monster, a bad guy, or another calamity.

The films featuring Latinas didn't follow this trajectory, however. For example, Lopez's characters Karen Sisco in *Out of Sight* and Sharon Pogue in *Angel Eyes*, and Rodriguez's Diana Guzman in *Girlfight* did not undergo a physical transformation or eschew hegemonic markers of femininity, such as long hair, high-heeled shoes, or lipstick, as they steeled themselves to take on the challenges ahead. Diana Guzman, for her part, did dress as and take on the persona of a boxer as she trained, but she didn't cut her hair short to do it. Why were these characters represented so differently from their unambiguously white counterparts? To answer this question, I needed to better understand how these characters were represented within their respective films. To do so, I conducted textual analysis rooted in the principles of semiotics, in conjunction with **genre criticism** with attention to Latinas and the evolution of the action genre. My critique also entailed historical analysis grounded in cultural studies as I considered these representations in relation to the regime of representation that Latinas had experienced in Hollywood films. To illuminate how I went about this work, let's turn back to *Out of Sight*.

In the romantic thriller *Out of Sight*, Karen Sisco is a federal marshal who ends up ambushed and unwittingly sharing a car trunk with Jack Foley (George Clooney), a thief she had been charged with bringing to prison. She ultimately falls for Foley; her full intentions are unclear as she follows the escaped criminal and his crew, who are competing with a more hardened group of criminals trying to steal some diamonds. Despite being fooled once, she is portrayed as a woman not to be messed with. In contrast to white female action protagonists, such as Ripley or Sarah Connor, Sisco is feminine by Hollywood standards, and her appearance does not change in the course of the narrative. In addition, while I noted in my analysis that Karen Sisco is ethnically ambiguous, I interpreted her as Latina in my reading of the film. Why might this be the case? In this instance, I felt Jennifer Lopez's star image as Latina, particularly after playing beloved Mexican American singer Selena in the eponymous *Selena* (Gregory Nava, Warner Home Video, 1997), had a strong influence. My interpretation highlights how a critic's response, particularly to a star's history, can play a role in representation analysis.

In exploring Karen Sisco's character with respect to denotation, I noted that she is slim (but curvaceous) and is always professionally but femininely attired. She wears perfect, glossy lipstick, even on the job, and does not sport noticeable biceps. She comports herself with confidence and speaks perfect, unaccented English in a slightly husky voice. In the scene in which Sisco faces the most clear physical danger, during an interview with a menacing African American informant in his own home, she handily uses a retractable police baton to put the informant in his place without a trace of hesitation or fear. At the time, Sisco is clothed in a tight leather skirt and top that has simultaneous connotations of "badass," "classy" (it appears to be an expensive designer outfit), and "overtly feminine" in the visual lexicon of American popular culture (Figure 8.3). Her spoken dialogue to the man is tough, to the point, and betrays a touch of confident humor: "You said you wanted to tussle. We tussled." My semiotic analysis honed in on the signifiers of traditional femininity and fierceness that are combined in the construction of Sisco, and their connotative meanings: strength, resilience—*and* sexiness.

To further illuminate the meanings attached to Lopez's and Rodriguez's characters in the films I studied, I also engaged in genre criticism with a focus on racial and gendered representation in the evolution of action films and television. Traditionally a white and male-centered domain with roots in the Western, the action films of the 1980s emphasized a powerful, muscular, and typically white male body as a symbol of the capabilities of the hero, as noted by scholars such as Yvonne Tasker, Susan Jeffords, and Richard Dyer.[42] Female characters, if they did appear, were usually relegated to the roles of damsel in distress and love interest. Increasing genre hybridity and film budgets in the 1990s led to changing narrative expectations and the desire for a broader and more diverse audience with respect to gender and ethnicity, however. The combination of action and science fiction genres, for instance, meant that women's physical capabilities might be included within a narrative at the safe remove of fantasy.[43] These shifts encouraged the entrance of action protagonists of color and female action heroines, among them characters played by Wesley Snipes, Angela Bassett, and Lucy Liu. By the late 1990s and early 2000s, this led to openings for a few Latinas. By this period, the slippage of the borders between the action genre and other genres had fully called into question who could be described as an action hero.

Exploring this history helps us to understand the casting of Lopez and Rodriguez in their respective

Figure 8.3 Karen Sisco, as played by Jennifer Lopez in *Out of Sight* (dir. Steven Soderbergh, Universal Studios, 1998), is depicted as both feminine and fierce

films, but does not fully explain the choices made regarding the development of their characters. At this point, I found it useful to explore the regimes of representation experienced by Latinas in Hollywood film more broadly. As Charles Ramírez Berg and other historians of Latina and Latino cinematic representation have documented, femininity was often racially coded in studio-era Hollywood films, to the detriment of Latina characters.[44] In a classic example, the Western *High Noon* (1952), Amy Fowler, the white newlywed Quaker wife of Marshal Will Kane played by Grace Kelly, is white, blonde, and impeccably clothed and groomed, an idealized feminine beauty. She also is sheltered, passive, and presumably chaste. In contrast, the Mexican American saloon owner Helen Ramírez (Katy Jurado) is not considered a worthy marriage partner by the white men of the town, despite the fact that several had past romances with her. Notions of race and class play into this narrative; the two characters embody constructed ideals of the "feminine" white woman and "transgressive" Latina. This was not unusual for the time: Latina characters historically were constructed in opposition to hegemonic constructions of idealized (and white) femininity. As actress Rita Moreno has noted in relation to her career in the 1950s and 1960s, if Latina actors were cast as love interests during this era, it was only as temporary love interests, to be dropped when more suitable (white) marriage partners arrived on the scene.[45] Both in Hollywood films and in American social life in the 1950s, white females also were commonly associated with the domestic sphere and roles as wives and homemakers.

In contrast, Latinas were more likely to have to work outside the home. Some also were, by necessity or choice, as Rosa Linda Fregoso puts it, "*pachuca-chola-homegirls*" who knew how to handle themselves outside the protection of the domestic sphere.[46] This cinematic history clarifies why Karen Sisco and the other Latina action protagonists didn't need Sarah Connor biceps or a more androgynous appearance in order to be viewed as physically capable and unafraid; based on the racialized regimes of representation that Latinas experienced in film and popular culture, they arguably were already viewed as ready to take on the challenges ahead, as able to be believably strong, brave, and also beautiful.

My study concludes with an unanswered question regarding these characters and the hegemonic meanings implied for physically capable Latinas. Are these examples of empowered women or of stereotypically aggressive women? Is this a progressive opening of Latina representation to new possibilities of representation or simply more of the usual? Multiple and potentially contradicting meanings can be gleaned from the construction of Karen Sisco and the other Latina action heroines for each reader.

As a media critique focused on representation, this study of Latina action protagonists reflects my own subject position and knowledge of regimes of representation. Like any such study, it has limitations, however. In retrospect, I would add further consideration of whether the always-feminine Latina is a progressive construction in relation to the white male dominance of Hollywood film behind the scenes and on screen, as manifest in patterns of representation and in the white and male gaze. In addition, I believe it would be useful to explore whether these Latina characters might have been linked to postfeminist representational trends in 1990s media culture. Like Xena and high school cheerleader-turned-vampire slayer Buffy Summers, also popular during this decade, Karen Sisco and the other Latina action heroines could be viewed as 1990s postfeminist figures who were strong, silent about their views on feminism, and also conventionally feminine and pretty.

Representation as Critical Focus: Final Thoughts

While we are less likely to see obviously racist, sexist, or otherwise xenophobic images or media narratives today, social inequities and the stigmatization of some groups still are manifest in a variety of ways in films, television, and other entertainment media. For this reason, a focus on representation can help media scholars gain valuable insights regarding the construction and significance of media images and narratives, particularly regarding associations that media texts may reinforce or challenge about the groups being represented. For example, some groups, including but not limited to women, Latina/os, and people of Arab and Middle Eastern descent, continue to be less visible in the entertainment media as protagonists and as storytellers behind the scenes, and to often be represented in a manner that symbolically denies their worth to society. If we want to be able to critique these dynamics, it is vital to possess the critical tools and language with which to scrutinize and better understand media texts through a focus on representation. This is especially important in our contemporary environment, in which complex media texts can appear to signal that discrimination and oppression no longer exist.

The field of media representation studies thus is still robust, with sub-disciplines such as Middle Eastern and Islamic media studies and feminist media studies flourishing. Recent scholarship is grappling with the complexity of contemporary media texts and ideologically diverging approaches to the politics of representation, as in media criticism that has challenged modern myths that we have become a post-racial, postfeminist, or post-queer culture. Contemporary scholarship with a focus on representation tends to combine this focus with other critical approaches, moreover, such as through an emphasis on ideology, genre, stardom, industry studies, or on

how audience members are interpreting, responding to, or even creating their own media texts. For readers of this chapter, your future endeavors to critique films, television, and other media will similarly benefit from taking up multiple methods as a part of your work.

Notes

1. For an overview of their contributions, see Ferdinand de Saussure, *Course in General Linguistics*, eds. Charles Bally and Albert Sechehaye with Albert Reidlinger, trans. Wade Baskin (New York: Philosophical Library, 1959); Roland Barthes, *Elements of Semiology* (New York: Hill and Wang, 1968) and *Mythologies* (New York: Hill and Wang, 1972).

2. The most complete collection of Charles S. Peirce's essays on semiotics is *Peirce on Signs: Writings on the Semiotic,* ed. James Hoopes (Chapel Hill: University of North Carolina Press, 1994).

3. Saussure, *Course in General Linguistics.*

4. See, for example, Claude Levi-Strauss, *The Structural Study of Myth, Vol. I* (New York: Basic Books, 1963), *The Structural Study of Myth, Vol. II* (New York: Basic Books, 1976), and *The Savage Mind* (Chicago: University of Chicago Press, 1996).

5. See, for example: Barthes, *Elements of Semiology* and *Mythologies.*

6. Barthes, "The World of Wrestling," *Mythologies,* 15–25.

7. Antonio Gramsci, *The Prison Notebooks,* ed. and trans. Joseph Buttegeig (New York: Columbia University Press, 1992).

8. Jacques Derrida, *Of Grammatology,* trans. Gayatri Spivak (Baltimore: Johns Hopkins University Press, 1976) and *Writing and Difference,* trans. Alan Bass (Chicago: University of Chicago, 1978); Michel Foucault, *The Foucault Reader,* ed. and trans. Paul Rabinow (New York: Pantheon Books, 1984); Julia Kristeva, *The Kristeva Reader,* ed. Toril Moi, trans. León S. Roudiez (New York: Columbia University Press, 1987).

9. Roland Barthes, "The Death of the Author," trans. Richard Howard, *Aspen* 5–6 (1967): 3 of 28 numbered items, n.p.

10. Jean-François Lyotard, *The Postmodern Condition: A Report on Knowledge,* trans. Geoffrey Bennington and Brian Massumi (Minneapolis: University of Minnesota Press, 1984).

11. Betty Friedan, *The Feminine Mystique* (New York: W.W. Norton, 1963); Molly Haskell, *From Reverence to Rape: The Treatment of Women in the Movies* (Chicago: University of Chicago Press, 1974).

12. Their writing on representation includes but is not limited to James Baldwin, *The Devil Finds Work,* 1st Vintage

international ed. (New York: Vintage Books, 2001); Donald Bogle, *Toms, Coons, Mulattoes, Mammies and Bucks: An Interpretive History of Blacks in American Films,* 4th ed. (New York: Bloomsbury, 2001); Vito Russo, *The Celluloid Closet: Homosexuality in the Movies,* rev. ed. (New York: Harper & Row, 1987).

13. George Gerbner, "Violence in Television Drama: Trends and Symbolic Functions," in *Television and Social Behavior, Vol. 1, Media Content and Control,* eds. George A. Comstock, Eli Abraham Rubinstein, and John P. Murray (Washington, DC: U.S. Government Printing Office, 1972), 28–187; Gaye Tuchman, "Symbolic Annihilation of Women by the Mass Media," in *Hearth and Home: Images of Women in the Mass Media,* eds. Gaye Tuchman, Arlene Kaplan Daniels, and James Benet (New York: Oxford University Press, 1978), 3–38.

14. Tuchman, "Symbolic Annihilation of Women by the Mass Media."

15. Their relevant publications include but are not limited to Laura Mulvey, "Visual Pleasure and Narrative Cinema," *Screen* 16, no. 3 (1975): 6–18; bell hooks, *Ain't I a Woman? Black Women and Feminism* (Boston: South End Press, 1981) and *Black Looks: Race and Representation* (Boston: South End Books, 1992); Stuart Hall, "The Work of Representation," in *Representation: Cultural Representations and Signifying Practices,* ed. Stuart Hall (London: Sage, 1997), 13–74; Richard Dyer, *The Matter of Images: Essays on Representation* (London: Routledge, 1993) and *White: Essays on Race and Culture* (London: Routledge, 1997); Edward Said, *Orientalism* (New York: Pantheon, 1978); Charlotte Brunsdon, *Screen Tastes: Soap Operas to Satellite Dishes* (London: Routledge, 1997).

16. Edward Said, *Orientalism* (New York: Penguin, 1978/2003); Stuart Hall, "The Spectacle of the 'Other,'" in *Representation: Cultural Representations and Signifying Practices,* ed. Stuart Hall (London: Sage, 1997), 223–79.

17. Mulvey, "Visual Pleasure and Narrative Cinema"; Brunsdon, *Screen Tastes: Soap Operas to Satellite Dishes.*

18. Dyer, *White.*

19. Jacqueline Bobo, *Black Women as Cultural Readers* (New York: Columbia University Press, 1995); Jane Gaines, "White Privilege and Looking Relations: Race and Gender in Feminist Film Theory," *Cultural Critique* 4 (Autumn 1986): 59–79; hooks, *Black Looks.*

20. Kimberlé Crenshaw, "Traffic at the Crossroads: Multiple Oppressions," in *Sisterhood is Forever: The Women's Anthology for a New Millennium,* ed. Robin Morgan (New York: Washington Square Press, 2003), 43–57 and "Demarginalizing the Intersection of Race and Sex: A Black Feminist Critique of Antidiscrimination Doctrine, Feminist Theory, and Antiracist Politics," *University of Chicago Legal Forum,* 1, no. 8 (1989): 13–67; Patricia Hill Collins, *Black Feminist Thought: Knowledge,*

Consciousness, and the Politics of Empowerment* (New York: Routledge, 1990).

21. Gramsci, *The Prison Notebooks.*

22. Their relevant publications include but are not limited to Dick Hebdige, *Subculture: The Meaning of Style* (London: Routledge, 1979); Stuart Hall, "New Ethnicities" in *ICA Documents 7: Black Film, British Cinema,* ed. Kobena Mercer (London: Institute for Contemporary Arts, 1988), 27–31, "Gramsci's Relevance for the Study of Race and Ethnicity," *Journal of Communication Inquiry,* 10, No. 2 (1986): 5–27, and *Representation;* Paul Gilroy, *There Ain't No Black in the Union Jack: The Cultural Politics of Race and Nation* (London: Hutchinson, 1987) and *The Black Atlantic: Modernity and Double Consciousness* (London: Verso, 1993); Angela McRobbie, "Jackie: An Ideology of Adolescent Femininity," *CCCS Stenciled Papers* (Birmingham: Birmingham Centre for Contemporary Cultural Studies, 1978) and her edited collection *Zoot Suits and Second-Hand Dresses: An Anthology of Fashion and Music* (Boston: Unwin Hyman, 1988); Brunsdon, *Screen Tastes: Soap Opera to Satellite Dishes* and *The Feminist, the Housewife, and the Soap Opera* (London: Oxford University Press, 2000).

23. Hall, "The Work of Representation."

24. "Encoding and Decoding in Television Discourse," *CCCS Stenciled Paper No. 7* (Birmingham: University of Birmingham Centre for Contemporary Cultural Studies, 1973).

25. For a sampling of their relevant scholarship, see Homi Bhabha, *The Location of Culture* (London: Routledge, 1994); Franz Fanon, *The Wretched of the Earth,* trans. Constance Farrington (New York: Grove Weidenfeld, 1963) and *Black Skin White Masks,* trans. Charles Lam Markmann (New York: Grove Press, 1967); Said, *Orientalism.*

26. Jean Baudrillard, *Simulacra and Simulation,* trans. Sheila Glaser (Ann Arbor: University of Michigan Press, 1994); Fredric Jameson, *Postmodernism, or, the Cultural Logic of Late Capitalism* (Durham: Duke University Press, 1991).

27. Michel Foucault, *History of Sexuality, Vol. 1.,* reissued ed., trans. Robert Hurley (New York: Vintage, 1990).

28. Walter Lippman, *Public Opinion* (New York: Harcourt, Brace, and Co., 1922).

29. Ruth C. Peterson and L.L. Thurstone, *Motion Pictures and the Social Attitudes of Children* (New York: Macmillan, 1933).

30. Hall, "The Spectacle of the Other," 225–79.

31. Ella Shohat and Robert Stam, *Unthinking Eurocentrism: Multiculturalism and the Media* (London: Routledge, 2013).

32. Mulvey, "Visual Pleasure and Narrative Cinema."

33. Manthia Diawara, "Black Spectatorship: Problems of Identification and Resistance," in *Black American Cinema,* ed. Manthia Diawara (New York: Routledge,

1993), 211–20; bell hooks, *Black Looks*; E. Ann Kaplan, *Looking for the Other: Feminism, Film, and the Imperial Gaze* (New York: Routledge, 1997).

34. Bhabha, *The Location of Culture*; Gloria Anzaldúa, *Borderlands/La Frontera: The New Mestiza* (San Francisco: Aunt Lute Books, 1987); Nestor Garcia Canclini, *Hybrid Cultures: Strategies for Entering and Leaving Modernity*, trans. Christopher Chiaparri and Sylvia L. Lopez (Minneapolis: University of Minnesota Press, 1995).

35. Judith Butler, *Gender Trouble: Gender and the Subversion of Identity* (New York: Routledge, 1990); Teresa de Lauretis, *Technologies of Gender: Essays on Theory, Film, and Fiction* (Bloomington: Indiana University Press, 1987); Werner Sollors, *Beyond Ethnicity: Consent and Descent in American Culture* (Oxford: University of Oxford Press, 1986).

36. Ralina L. Joseph, "Tyra Banks is Fat: (Post-) Racism and (Post-) Feminism in the New Millennium," *Critical Studies in Media Communication* 26, no. 3 (2009): 237–54; Catherine Squires, *The Post-Racial Mystique: Media and Race in the Twenty-First Century* (New York: New York University Press, 2014).

37. Rosalind Gill, "Postfeminist Media Culture: Elements of a Sensibility," *European Journal of Cultural Studies* 10, no. 2 (2007): 147–66; Angela McRobbie, *The Aftermath of Feminism: Gender, Culture, and Social Change* (Thousand Oaks: Sage Publications, 2009).

38. Michael Warner, *The Trouble with Normal: Sex, Politics, and the Ethics of Queer Life* (Cambridge: Harvard University Press, 2000).

39. See, for example, Adam Isaiah Green, "Gay But Not Queer: Toward a Post-Queer Study of Society," *Theory and Society* 31, no. 4 (2002): 521–45; Karen E. Lovaas, John P. Elias, and Gust A. Yep, "Shifting Ground(s): Surveying the Contested Terrain of LGBT Studies and Queer Theory," *Journal of Homosexuality* 52, no. 1–2 (2006): 1–18; David V. Ruffalo, *Post Queer Politics* (London: Routledge, 2009).

40. Mary Beltrán, "Más Macha: The New Latina Action Hero," in *The Action and Adventure Cinema*, ed. Yvonne Tasker (London: Routledge, 2004), 186–200.

41. Yvonne Tasker, *Working Girls: Gender and Sexuality in Popular Cinema* (London: Routledge, 1998).

42. Tasker, *Working Girls* and *Spectacular Bodies: Gender, Genre, and the Action Cinema* (London: Routledge, 1993); Susan Jeffords, *Hard Bodies: Hollywood Masculinity in the Reagan Era* (New Brunswick: Rutgers University Press, 1994); Richard Dyer, "Action!" in *Action/Spectacle Cinema*, ed. José Arroyo (London: British Film Institute, 2000), 17–21

43. Carol M. Dole, "The Gun and the Badge: Hollywood and the Female Lawman," in *Reel Knockouts: Violent Women in the Movies*, eds. Martha McCaughey and Neil King (Austin: University of Texas Press, 2001), 78–105.

44. Charles Ramírez Berg, *Latinos in Film: Stereotypes, Subversion, and Resistance* (Austin: University of Texas Press, 2002).

45. Mary Beltrán, *Latina/o Stars in U.S. Eyes: The Making and Meanings of Film and TV Stardom* (Urbana: University of Illinois Press, 2009).

46. Rosa Linda Fregoso, "Homegirls, Cholas, and Pachucas in Cinema," *California History* 74, no. 3 (1995): 317–27. Fregoso is referring to terms used to describe young Latinas who chose to be proudly visible in U.S. urban public culture in the 1930s and '40s (pachucas), in the 1970s and '80s (cholas), and in the present day (homegirls).

Further Reading

Alsultany, Evelyn. *The Arabs and Muslims in the Media: Race and Representation after 9/11*. New York: New York University Press, 2012.

Becker, Ron. *Gay TV and Straight America*. New Brunswick: Rutgers University Press, 2006.

Davé, Shilpa. *Indian Accents: Brown Voice and Racial Performance in American Television and Film*. Urbana: University of Illinois Press, 2013.

Gray, Herman. *Watching Race: Television and the Struggle for "Blackness."* Minneapolis: University of Minnesota Press, 1997.

Grindstaff, Laura. *The Money Shot: Trash, Class, and the Making of TV Talk Shows*. Chicago: University of Chicago Press, 2002.

Haggins, Bambi. *Laughing Mad: The Black Comic Persona in Post-Soul America*. New Brunswick: Rutgers University Press, 2007.

Levine, Elana and Lisa Parks, eds. *Undead TV: Essays on "Buffy the Vampire Slayer"* (Durham: Duke University Press, 2007).

Molina-Guzmán, Isabel. *Dangerous Curves: Latina Bodies in the Media*. New York: New York University Press, 2010.

Studlar, Gaylyn. *This Mad Masquerade: Stardom and Masculinity in the Jazz Age*. New York: Columbia University Press, 1996.

9.
AUTHORSHIP AND AUTEURISM
Cynthia Chris

André Bazin's essay "On the *Politique des Auteurs*" begins with an epigraph from the Russian novelist Leo Tolstoy's diary:

> Goethe? Shakespeare? Everything they put their name to is supposed to be good, and people rack their brains to find beauty in the silliest little thing they bungled. All great talents, like Goethe, Shakespeare, Beethoven, Michelangelo, created not only beautiful works, but things that were less than mediocre, quite simply awful.[1]

It is easy to recast the quip with the names of film directors adulated in the pages of the influential French film magazine *Cahiers du Cinéma*, which Bazin co-founded in 1951: Alfred Hitchcock, Fritz Lang, Howard Hawks, Nicholas Ray. But cinema is not the only medium that recognizes individuals as **authors**. In television, Norman Lear, Joss Whedon, Shonda Rhimes, and Mark Burnett may be our "Goethe, Shakespeare, Beethoven, Michelangelo." They are creators of "beautiful works" as well as some run-of-the-mill fare. For example, most would agree that Whedon's *Dollhouse* pales in comparison to *Buffy the Vampire Slayer*. Even "great talents" don't make masterpieces every time. Still, from the perspectives of media scholarship, popular criticism, and the industry's marketing machines, recognizing the author of a creative work, whether that author is an individual, a team, or a corporation, is widely considered to be an intelligible indicator of quality.

The convention of acknowledging individual **authorship** is widespread, but not uniform, throughout mass media. It may elevate particular authors with large, coherent bodies of work over others who may be just as prolific but are, for various reasons, less acclaimed. Consider the names already dropped above, some of the best-known **directors** and **showrunners** of their generations. It is no coincidence that men outnumber women on these lists, given that the film and media industries suffer a real dearth of women in leadership positions.[2] As well, historical institutional racism plays a role in the underrepresentation of people of color throughout media industries.[3] Nevertheless, and recalling these distortions, the concept of authorship and authorship theory are tools that can illuminate the dynamics of conditions of production, the extent of creative sovereignty, the legal rights of authors, and the marketing strategies of industry.

Further, studying the authorship framework reveals junctures and disjunctures between film and media studies. What can each area of study learn from the other? What have they learned from other disciplines? Film criticism has both scholarly and popular modes with strong traditions of aesthetic analysis, alongside literary, theatre, and art criticism, all of which recognize authorial primacy. In contrast, media studies emerged from early- and mid-twentieth century projects in the sociology, psychology, and economics of communication, which were preoccupied with the effects of rapidly proliferating electronic media on individuals and society. Accordingly, media studies has attended relatively sparsely to authorship as an analytical category. In recent decades, however, new approaches have influenced authorship studies among scholars challenged to understand authorial practices in a range of media. Accordingly, in this chapter, I explore the history, applications, and critiques of a variety of theories of authorship.

Who Is an Author?

One of the driving questions of film and media scholarship regards how we understand the designation of individuals as "authors" for cultural productions that are almost invariably **collaborative**. In different media, different individuals may be designated as primarily responsible for creative aspects of a production. The practice did not take hold in cinema in its earliest years, when personnel on both sides of the camera went largely **uncredited**.[4] Eventually, directorial authorship became a feature of the Hollywood studio system, codified in rules regarding credits, which are governed by the **Directors Guild of America** (DGA). It is easy to see why posters for *Knocked Up* (2007) and *This Is 40* (2012) labeled these films as "From Judd Apatow," given his prior success with *The 40-Year-Old Virgin* (2005); he produced, wrote, and directed all three films. The DGA calls this way of billing a director "**possessive**" or "**possessory credit**." It is a privilege reserved for those who "are acclaimed by critics . . . or have established a signature style of filmmaking . . . or a substantial body of work."[5] Similarly, *Bridesmaids* (2011) was advertised as "From the producer of *Superbad*, *Knocked Up*, and *The 40-Year-Old Virgin*." While Apatow was not named, which might have violated DGA guidelines reserving possessory credit for directors, this tagline associated the film, which was directed by Paul Feig, with the Apatow **brand**.[6]

This cinematic model does not necessarily translate across media. *Orange Is the New Black* is recognized as executive producer Jenji Kohan's project, even though Kohan shares writing credits with Piper Kerman, whose memoir inspired the series. In television, the producer (or executive producer, now commonly known as the showrunner) creates a series, may facilitate its production, and is generally considered its author. But not all mass media have strong traditions of individual authors. For videogames, individual authors may be less emphasized in promotional material (such as advertising and packaging), but industry insiders, the trade press, and avid fans recognize key creative agents. A casual user may understand the *Uncharted* game series as a product of the company Naughty Dog, but those most engaged with the line are aware that Amy Hennig was long its creative director and lead writer.

Analysis of a group of works by a single author allows us to observe thematic, aesthetic, and stylistic choices across a body of work. If this approach overvalorizes individual authors, recent developments shift authorship studies' focus away from singular genius. Production studies brings alternative methodologies to the study of authorship, and theories of collective authorship, corporate authorship, and massively collaborative authorship provide new frameworks through which to understand both "old" media, such as film, and newer forms, such as videogames or social media, with interactive elements that require fresh theorization. Each of these innovations is discussed later in this chapter.

What Is an "Auteur"?

Not long after the end of World War II, influential considerations of film authorship started to appear in *Cahiers du Cinéma*. These ideas were not without precedent, but crystallized forcefully in its pages.[7] One key precursor is Alexandre Astruc's "The Birth of a New Avant-Garde: La camera-stylo" (1948), which observed that "the cinema is quite simply becoming a means of expression, just as all the other arts have before it."[8] But **auteur theory** began, in many ways, with "A Certain Tendency of the French Cinema" by François Truffaut, published in 1954, five years before his directorial debut *The 400 Blows* (1959). Truffaut attacked French cinema's "tradition of quality," finding it plagued by stagnating aesthetics and values he considered retrograde. As well, he objected to the apparent centrality of *scenarists*—screenwriters—rather than "men of the cinema" such as Max Ophuls, Jacques Tati, and Robert Bresson.[9] If he did less to outline the agenda of the "*auteur's* cinema,"[10] the preferences of like-minded critics became clear in the writings of Jacques Rivette, Éric Rohmer, and others who, like Truffaut, soon turned to filmmaking. While there were differences of opinion among *Cahiers* writers, most admired Jean Renoir, Roberto Rossellini, Federico Fellini, and Michelangelo Antonioni. Among those working in Hollywood, according to Rivette, "we've chosen to defend directors like Hitchcock rather than [William] Wyler, and [Anthony] Mann, rather than [Fred] Zinnemann, because they are directors who actually work on their scenarios."[11] In other words, *Cahiers du Cinéma* advocated for cinema in which directors are the singular creative force rather than collaborators with screenwriters or producers—and for directors whose signature stylistic motifs and thematic preoccupations are expressed throughout their bodies of work.

Eventually, Bazin attempted to rein in *auteurism*. In "On the *Politique des Auteurs*," Bazin argues that his colleagues overstated the inextricable unity of author and authored works, as well as the unity of any authored body of work. He also lamented that the *auteurists* commit "criticism by beauty" in which it is "a good method to presuppose that a supposed weakness in a work of art is nothing other than a beauty one has not yet managed to understand," a method that is hardly criticism at all.[12] In this essay, Bazin hands us many of the tools required to account for authorial practices in our present media environment.

To begin, Bazin reminds us that the notion of the author is subject to "historical and social contingencies," such as the relative value of **originality** and the robustness of economic and legal apparatus that enable the author to profit from the work. Further, he insists, "the cinema is an art which is both popular and industrial."[13] That is, its mode of production has more in common with architecture than with literature or painting because of industrialized techniques as well as economic, spatial, and social relationships between the medium and its audience. Bazin doesn't abandon the author as a productive organizing principle for criticism, scholarship, or the industry itself. Rather, he recognizes the author as situated within powerful and complex conditions of production. This groundwork foreshadows later scholarly approaches to authorship.

Still, *auteurism* remained a preferred theory of film authorship in some quarters. Andrew Sarris promoted *auteur* theory to American film critics in "Notes on the Auteur Theory in 1962." He codifies *auteurism* as a three-part test consisting of "technique ... personal style, and ... interior meaning," and insists that "the auteur theory emphasizes the body of a director's work rather than isolated masterpieces"—even if an occasional masterpiece is expected from an *auteur*.[14] A year later, in "Circles and Squares," Pauline Kael dismisses his criteria as pretentious and vague ("is 'internal meaning' any different from 'meaning'?"), suggesting that what Sarris identified as signature themes in a director's body of work may be only tedious repetition, and suspecting the whole approach to be a misguided attempt to create an elite canon.[15]

British film scholars reworked *auteur* theory for their own, arguably more nuanced, purposes. Geoffrey Nowell-Smith jettisoned the idea of the author as the sole agent with "direct and sole responsibility" for all aspects of a film, as well as use of the term as a title to bestow only on directors achieving at a uniformly high level of quality throughout their *oeuvre*. Instead, drawing on parallel developments across the humanities—such as anthropology and literary studies—Nowell-Smith and others took a "**structural approach**," offering authorship "as

a principle of method, which provides a basis for a more scientific form of criticism than has existed hitherto."[16] Structural criticism would favor systematic, taxonomic analyses of cultural works and language itself, both internally and as parts of larger sociocultural systems. (For more on structuralism, see the chapter "Narrative" by Jason Mittell in this volume.) According to Nowell-Smith, *auterist* theory has usefully emphasized that "the defining characteristics of an author's work are not always those that are most readily apparent."[17] Even so, structural analysis has "problems of its own. It narrows down the field of inquiry almost too radically. ... In doing so it is in danger of neglecting two other equally basic factors. One is the possibility of an author's work changing over time ... the other is the importance of the nonthematic subject-matter and of sub-stylistic features of the visual treatment."[18] That is, Nowell-Smith insisted, against the *auteurists*, that oppositions and anomalies are key components through which to understand an author's output.

Peter Wollen also rejected what he regarded as the imprecision of *auteur* theory, its preoccupation with constancy, and its "critical extravaganzas" (which included the "aesthetic cults of personality" that concerned Bazin). "The structural approach," he argued, "is indispensable for the critic."[19] Wollen also recognized the complexity of the medium:

> Of course, the director does not have full control over his work; this explains why the *auteur* theory involves a kind of decipherment, decryptment. A great many features of films analysed here have to be dismissed as indecipherable because of "noise" from the producer, the cameraman [sic] or even the actors. This concept of "noise" needs further elaboration ... What the *auteur* theory does is to take a group of films—the work of one director—and analyse their structure. Everything irrelevant to this, everything non-pertinent, is considered logically secondary, contingent, to be discarded.[20]

In doing so, the *auteur* theorists could produce only partial analyses.

David Bordwell provides another model of the author as something other than a human agent with clear intention, fully knowable from traces left in the work. Drawing on the work of Boris Tomashevsky, he develops for cinema studies the "**biographical legend**," which may be understood as constructed from accumulated texts by and about the author, more "literary fact" than conventional biography or autobiography.[21] Observing that the author is more "persona" than person, Bordwell argues that evidence of an author's intentions need not be taken at face value; rather, we should examine how they contribute to the legend, which has "historical and aesthetic functions."[22] The biographical legend is a node at which social forces, conditions of production, and ambition are navigated, negotiated, and managed: "What concrete conditions confronted the filmmaker when he entered the realm of film production? . . . How does the filmmaker see his or her work as altering the historical situation, transforming standardized materials?"[23] Such a model is yet another analytical matrix through which a body of work may be examined: not as a test of right or wrong, good or bad, but as a dynamic indicator of the trajectory of a career. Writing on Carl-Theodor Dreyer, Bordwell concluded, "There is no simple congruence between legend and films. . . . Not the least interesting aspect of Dreyer for us today hangs upon the ways the films *contradict* the biographical legend."[24]

Still another notion of the author/*auteur* offers the **corporate author** as a framework accounting for the powerful influence of studios on their products. Thomas Schatz develops this model in a book drawing its title from Bazin's remark that Hollywood's individual makers are less interesting than the "genius of the system" as a whole.[25] Schatz focuses on the classic Hollywood studio era, when the output of various studios—MGM, Warner, Universal—were easily distinguished brands, an effect of the overseeing producers—Irving Thalberg, Darryl Zanuck, Louis B. Mayer—even more so than the directors they employed. Still, Schatz argues, "isolating the producer or anyone else as artist or visionary gets us nowhere," given the system's intricacies.[26] This approach, carried forward by Jerome Christensen, explores the synergistic mechanisms of industrialized production, which coalesce to reinforce a studio's brand identity.[27]

Eventually, some scholars rebelled against these critiques of *auteurism*, specifically, against their insistence that the author is a construct separable from the specific human subject. Janet Staiger, for example, points to the extent to which "the **death of the author** problem" (discussed below) may erase authoring subjects for whom the right to author has been historically difficult to obtain: "authorship does matter. It matters especially to those in non-dominant positions in which asserting even a partial agency may seem to be important."[28] Such a biographical

approach remains a validated practice in film criticism. Even so, understandings of the author like those found in Nowell-Smith, Wollen, and Bordwell—all of which distinguish the biographical author from the analyzable work—became "the reigning conceptions about authorship and intentionality,"[29] due at least in part to their relationships with influential concepts of the author in other disciplines.

The Literary Author

Debates about the author did not hail only from within film criticism. Literary and cultural theorists also interrogated the role of the author. As Martha Woodmansee summarizes, "the 'author' in its modern sense is a relatively recent invention, a product of . . . the emergence in the eighteenth century of writers who sought to earn their livelihood from the sale of their writing to the new and rapidly expanding reading public."[30] Previous writing was craft, or the result of divine inspiration—either learned skill or external intervention. It became the product of intrinsic genius. But the concept of the author/artist/genius has its limitations, among them, its capacity to set the critical stage for lauding the author rather than explicating the text.

Accordingly, in the 1940s, New Criticism sidelined the author as a principle unit of literary analysis, with its aversion to **intentionality** and its preference for Formalist textual analysis. In "The Intentional Fallacy," William K. Wimsatt, Jr. and Monroe C. Beardsley wonder how the critic is to excavate authorial intentions: "How is he [sic] to find out what the poet tried to do? If the poet succeeded in doing it, then the poem itself shows what he was trying to do. And if the poet did not succeed, then the poem is not adequate evidence, and the critic must go outside the poem—for evidence of an intention that did not become effective in the poem."[31] They advise against this latter course, taking the poem (or other work) on its own terms rather than relying analytically on biographical speculation.

In the 1960s, new formulations of the role of the literary author continued to appear. In 1961, Wayne C. Booth offered the "**implied author**" as a hypothetical, mediating figure distinct from the actual person writing the work. This implied author is recognizable in "style," "tone," and "technique"—that is, through the choices that the writer has made which result in the work.[32] For Booth, the implied author is an agent altogether apart from the living (or deceased) writer. In fact, the implied author is constructed by the reader from the work itself, knowable only from evidence located in the text. The concept of the implied author may constitute a kind of bridge between the rejection of authorial intention as a scholarly concern, and the nearly spectral reformulation of the author by subsequent theorists.

The Author, Diffused

Toward the end of the 1960s, two now-classic tracts on the author appeared, Roland Barthes' "The Death of the Author" (1967) and Michel Foucault's "What Is an Author?" (1969). Both argue that despite prior attempts to peel the text away from a determining author, the author remains a towering figure in literary criticism. To Barthes, "The Author, when we believe in him, is always conceived as the past of his own book ... Quite the contrary, the modern writer (scriptor) is born simultaneously with his text." However hyperbolic the title of Barthes' essay, he establishes that preoccupation with "the Author" has a deadening effect: "To give an author to a text is to impose upon that text a stop clause, to furnish it with a final signification, to close the writing." Barthes' project is far more radical. "[B]y refusing to assign to the text (and to the world as text) a 'secret,'" he argues, is liberating, "for to refuse to arrest meaning is finally to refuse God and his hypostases, reason, science, the law." Thus freed from the limiting "Author," the text can be understood as "a tissue of citations" that unify not at its point of origin (the author) but only at its "destination," the "birth of the reader."[33]

To Foucault, the author's name has a "classificatory function" through which discourse is commodified in a "system of ownership" that is historically contingent.[34] This **author function** is, then, a "principle by which, in our culture, one limits, excludes, and chooses; in short, by which one impedes the free circulation, the free manipulation, the free composition, decomposition, and recomposition of fiction." Within such a system, one premised on property rights that encompass fiction and other cultural forms, the author is an ideological, if luminous, tool. In the end, Foucault understands that an "absolutely free state" is a distant ideal, but it is, without a doubt, an expansive "proliferation of meanings" that he seeks in the disappearance of the author.[35]

While these landmark essays theorized the author as *function* (Foucault) or as functionally *absent* (Barthes), literary scholars were developing **reader/response theory**, to rebut the virtually authorless,

readerless New Criticism's emphasis on the text. Some reader/response theorists assumed a uniform, nonspecific reader, while others found tremendous variation among actual readers.[36] The latter set the stage for the application of empirical methods in **reception (or audience) studies** focused on mass media and popular culture.[37] (For more on audiences, see the chapter by Matt Hills in this volume.) Among the most influential, Stuart Hall's "Encoding/Decoding" model asserted the role of the viewer or reader in making meaning.[38] The text may be encoded ideologically at the point of production, but it is completed as meaningful discourse only when decoded at the point of consumption. Scholars working in this **active audience** tradition, emerging from British cultural studies, consider authorship a *process* that does not end with the author, but begins in the text and continues in the reader. While Staiger has maintained that "converting the question [of authorship] to one of reception" is a misstep that "dodges" questions of a text's causality, these approaches established some of the terms of media authorship for decades to come.[39]

Meanwhile, creative practices in some media interrogated the role of the author via implicit critiques of the valorization of **originality** over derivation. In the 1970s in New York City's South Bronx, DJ Kool Herc, Grandmaster Flash and the Furious Five, and Sylvia Robinson developed hip-hop's practices of "**sampling**." In sampling, artists incorporate passages of prerecorded music, often rhythm breaks or vocal tracks, into their own new songs. (The practice may recall Barthes's notion of the text as "a tissue of citations.") Initially, performers used samples without permission from copyright holders (but not for long, which I discuss below), and the technique of sampling was adopted throughout electronic dance music and industrial music. A corollary emerged in appropriation-based visual art by a loose group known as the Pictures Generation, which includes Richard Prince and Sherrie Levine, among many others. **Appropriation** was prefigured by Marcel Duchamp's readymades, Robert Rauschenberg's "combines," and Pop Art, all of which incorporated everyday objects, news clippings, comics, labels, and logos. The Pictures artists, whose work reproduced previously published material from fine art, advertising, and television, rejected originality as the marker of creative genius, exploring the contextual aspects of visual experience and shrugging off pedestrian concerns about copying and copyright as ethical or economic contests.[40]

Figure 9.1 *Inextinguishable Fire* by Harun Farocki (1969). Image copyright of the artist, courtesy of Video Data Bank, www.vdb.org, School of the Art Institute of Chicago

Figure 9.2 *What Farocki Taught* by Jill Godmilow (1998). Image copyright of the artist, courtesy of Video Data Bank, www.vdb.org, School of the Art Institute of Chicago

In film and video, appropriation persisted in shot-for-shot remakes such as Jill Godmilow's *What Farocki Taught* (1998), which recreated Harun Farocki's *Inextinguishable Fire* (1969).[41]

Farocki's black-and-white 16mm film uses experimental techniques to interrogate the use of napalm by U.S. troops during the Vietnam War, and Dow Chemical's role in manufacturing the incendiary weapon. Godmilow's remake, using color video, calls attention to this once-obscure film and brings its lessons about the horrors of war to new audiences. What is an author, then, after the historical romance with originality and individuality has broken up? In some media, some creative artists seemed as willing as literary and film critics to renounce traditional forms of authorship.

The (New) Media Author

Changing authorship practices in different media require new theoretical models. Lev Manovich has shown as much, noting that interactivity, remixing, sampling, and other innovations complicate and extend the definition of authorship. To Manovich, the author isn't dead: "he [sic] just looks different."[42] One result is the development of **production studies**, for which scholars have adapted interview and ethnographic methodologies already robustly applied to the audience. By shifting attention away from singularly authoritative authors to the cooperating teams that make media, production studies is uniquely situated to chart the roles played across the media industry, from manufacturing to technical, creative, and executive personnel. (See also the chapter "Production/Industry" by Timothy Havens in this volume.) According to Vicki Mayer, Miranda J. Banks, and John T. Caldwell, "We frequently come to know about media producers and their work, ironically, through the representations they make," such as "'making of' videos."[43] Production studies displaces the industry's self-mythologizing with observational fieldwork, offering empirical data through which the **collective** practices of media production can be analyzed and theorized.

Other models of television authorship have also foregrounded both complex and unique modes of production—and the key terms of reception. Drawing both on Booth's notion of the implied author and the Foucauldian model of the author function, Jason Mittell develops the concept of an **"inferred author function,"** defined as *"a viewer's production of authorial agency responsible for a text's storytelling, drawing upon textual cues and contextual discourses."*[44] Mittell also acknowledges "***authorship by origination***" in which a "singular creator" is recognized as the work's author; "***authorship by responsibility***," which acknowledges the collective efforts required by filmmaking; and "***authorship by management***," especially apt for serialized television, where multiple episodes are simultaneously in various stages of production, story arcs sprawl over multiple episodes, and teams of writers and directors work on each episode.[45] But it is the "inferred author function" that most interests Mittell as a reader-produced author who provides cues to the meaning of a text. To Mittell, especially in the most narratively complex or self-reflexive series, "it is hard to imagine how viewers might not consider issues of authorship as an active"—even "ludic"—"part of the comprehension process."[46]

Elsewhere in media studies, authorship studies are shifting attention to the viewer or user, reinvigorating reception studies. Judd Ruggill and Ken S. McAllister posit the necessity of new models of **massively collaborative authorship** for media with *interactive* components like videogames, or **user-generated content** like social media. One version of such a model is "**prosumption**," a portmanteau indicating the "conversion of the consumer into the producer."[47] Ruggill and McAllister point out that mass collaboration results in authorship is "highly complex, chance impacted (if not chance-driven), and semi-organized"—all in opposition to models of authorship that presume, or seek, evidence of purposeful control.[48] Axel Bruns' concept of **produsage** (production/usage) is similar. The "**produser**" is at once a producer and a user, operating within an established framework (YouTube, Wikipedia, Second Life), but originating content in relatively open communities with low barriers to entry, and an emphasis on ongoing processual aspects of the project rather than static end-products. According to Bruns, produsage is both "granular" (composed of many individuals' contributions) and in constant flux.[49] To Bruns, it is not the author but rather the audience that may be dead; the author is alive and well, everyone and anywhere. But, according to the law, some authors count more than others.

The Legal Author

The designation of authorship through the protective mechanism of **intellectual property (IP) law** has implications for creative control and economic gain. Throughout most of this essay, I have been exploring theories in which the designation of one entity or another as "author" is an attribution of creative, expressive, and aesthetic responsibility. But one can be an author in all but the legal sense. A credited author may not control how his or her work is distributed, if another party actually holds the **copyright** on that work. According to the U.S. Copyright Office, "If a work is made for hire, an employer is considered the author even if an employee actually created the work. The employer can be a firm, an organization, or an individual."[50] The **work-for-hire** policy is a response to the financial stakes of authoring that protects corporate interests. The rights of authorship do not only pertain to credit and recognition, but also, legally, to contractual matters such as licensing fees, royalty payments, and reprinting or resale rights. In collectively produced media such as film, television, recorded music, gaming, and social media, among others, determinations of who is an author follow each medium's conventions. These determinations have also been shaped by legislation and court decisions, and they frequently favor corporate authors over individuals who contribute creatively to media productions.[51]

While this chapter cannot fully explore the role of IP law in governing the rights of authors, it is important to observe how the law allows the rights of authors to vary from medium to medium. Compare, for example, the rights of authors in recorded music and the fashion industry. In recorded music, a string of lawsuits in the 1980s and '90s reconstituted the practice of sampling legally and economically. It became necessary to license samples to be used in commercially released recordings by means of upfront fees or shares in royalties, and to credit sampled artists as co-writers.[52] Credits for a single track can attribute "authorship" to dozens of individuals and corporations with the goal of protecting income streams flowing to copyright holders who may or may not be creative artists, since so many individuals' work is work for hire.[53] Meanwhile, couture and small-label fashion designers struggle for even minimal protection from copyists, due to a legal ellipse over clothing that opens up the field to knock-offs. Why is a fashion designer something other than an author? Do the largest manufacturers of mass-market apparel simply retain more legal clout than individual designers?[54] In this case, the law defends the interests of corporate "authors" with established trademarks and access to mass markets, bypassing the interests of individual authors where much of the creative production begins.

Case Study: The Actor, the Author, and the Animal

How can we, as scholars and critics, put theories of authorship to work in our own research and writing? To begin, our objects of analysis can point toward appropriate frameworks. The concept of the corporate author is easier to work with if you are studying a movie or TV show or other production from a major media conglomerate; it might be less relevant to a low-budget, independent film. If you are working with social media, it may be a stretch to apply *auteur* theory, while theories of massively collaborative authorship would be rich resources. We can also acknowledge that even if theorizing authorship is not our primary concern, our assumptions about authorial agency and processes structure our analyses, explicitly or implicitly.

My case study, "Subjunctive Desires: Becoming Animal in *Green Porno* and *Seduce Me*," is an essay about two series of short videos, *Green Porno* (2008–09) and *Seduce Me* (2010), which explore the mating habits of various animals.[55] Isabella Rossellini produced, wrote, and directed or co-directed each of the videos, working with a team of designers, composers, consultants, cinematographers, and editors. They are, without a doubt, collective works, but given industrial and critical conventions of designating an individual with a high degree of creative autonomy—and authority over cast and crew—as the author of a work, I understand her role in the production is, in essence, one of "authorship by responsibility," to borrow a term from Mittell.[56] Still, in writing this essay, I started from the position that authorship is a constructed claim (even if I do not explicitly state as much), one that operates as an organizing principle for an array of stakeholders, from those who stand to gain financially from a work, to its potential audiences. Authorship is a claim established through contractual agreements, critical recognition, and, importantly, the performance of the authorial role.

Rossellini's accounts of the videos' production, shared in promotional press coverage and interviews, must be recognized as contributing to the author's "biographical legend." I discuss these materials in part to glean some facts situating *Green Porno* and *Seduce Me* in terms of their conditions of production, promotion, and distribution. After all, it is a quirky project, in many ways; cable TV channels don't typically put resources into such short films. And admittedly, I explore texts produced around these works in search of clues regarding Rossellini's motivations—which is not to say that her stated intentions account fully for either how they came to be made or their meanings. That is, there is no reason to believe that the stories Rossellini tells about the project are untrue, but it is important to remember that they are *stories*: narratives that feature particular characters and develop certain themes. Foremost among those themes is this question: What's an internationally known model, actress, and daughter of filmmaking royalty (Ingrid Bergman and Roberto Rossellini) doing in an earthworm costume, anyway? As it turns out, Rossellini professes a lifelong love of animals, which has manifested in many ways, among them, her association with the Guide Dog Foundation for the Blind, which I mention in an endnote, and coursework at New York University and Hunter College in animal biology, which I do not mention.

Rossellini's didactic turn in these videos is a lovely gesture, sharing with fans her affection for non-humans and her accumulated knowledge about them. It is also what Mittell might call a ludic gesture. Rossellini plays with the genre of wildlife filmmaking, with the serious tone of most scientific work, and with her own glamorous image. She doesn't deliver lessons in animal sex as much as she acts them out: a key feature of the project is that she is not only the authorial agent but also the actor who embodies each animal, adorned in costumes of cloth and paper. As I write, she "occupies the very space in which we find the cuttlefish, the barnacle, or the whale."[57]

My primary focus in the essay, after all, is Rossellini's performance, seen through the lens of Gilles Deleuze and Félix Guattari's concept of "becoming animal." I find that her performance is intricately bound to her role as author. In fact, we observe Rossellini assert her authorial motivation in the opening lines of each video. In *Green Porno*, she wonders, "If I were . . ."; in *Seduce Me*, she asks, "Are they trying to seduce me?" These are the grammatical forms that I refer to loosely in the essay's title as "subjunctive desires," and they set up the imaginative scenes that follow. Rossellini answers each query by shifting her own role from embodied author to performing embodiment of the animal. In the end, in each of these videos, Rossellini may or may not quite "become animal," but she does become author. Just as her animal costumes are fashioned from paper and fabric, wire and string, her authorship is constructed, too, by industry conventions, by legend-building secondary texts, by theoretical paradigms, and, in this case, by performance that underscores her role as both agent and object of these works.

Conclusion

Even as critical and legal debates flourish, the answer to the question that motivates this literature—Who, or what, is an author?—is not fully resolved. Long-term trends in intellectual property law trouble the "when" of authorship, too: consider that in the original U.S. Copyright Act of 1790, a work could only be protected for 14 years before falling into public domain, so that anyone could copy, reprint, or reuse the work. Congress has extended that term several times, most recently in 1998, to its current "life of the author" plus 70 years, and some of the most urgently needed work in authorship studies is taking place in this area, to explore the impact of such restrictions on creativity

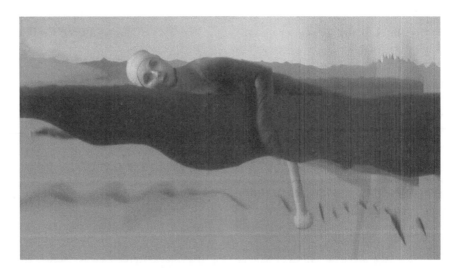

Figure 9.3 "Whale" episode of *Green Porno* by Isabella Rossellini (2009)

and cultural workers' rights.[58] In a highly conglomeratized commercial media environment, the rights of the author as a creative agent may be eclipsed by the rights of the corporate entity holding the work's copyright. This is especially apparent where participation in social media that operates on the "produsage" model is predicated on the user's tacit agreement to allow Facebook and the like to use, at will, users' content, on a "transferable, sub-licensable, royalty-free, worldwide" basis.[59] We may all be authors now, but who benefits from the rights of authorship? The work-for-hire model, in social media, becomes work-by-subscription, in which users renounce the legal rights of ownership over their texts and images, provided to corporate media conglomerates not only without compensation (other than the pleasure of participating) but at the cost of one's vulnerability to data-mining.[60] Some popular social media users are compensated through initiatives for corporate giants to share a percentage of ad revenue, and scholarship exploring the political-economic implications of these kinds of commodifying relationships is also of great current importance, especially as new media forms based on user-generated content emerge.[61]

Meanwhile, other media industries' conventions of designating—and compensating—authors remain largely intact. Authorial credit is awarded to a film's director or a television series' showrunner, despite the contributions of writers, among others. Which takes me back to where I began: Hitchcock, Lang, Hawks, Ray, Lear, Whedon, Rhimes, Burnett. These names (and many others) may be those of acknowledged *auteurs* of cinema and television. But, as collective theories of authorship—which ground, for example, production studies—have shown, those agents don't act alone. They operate within historically situated conditions of production, where corporations like Viacom, Time Warner, and Disney, as well as Netflix, King Digital Entertainment (creator of *Candy Crush Saga*), and Rockstar Games control many of the rights of ownership hypothetically associated with the author. Explorations of the corporate author can illuminate the extent and implications of that control. Who, or what, is an author? An author is an ever-shifting construct whose parameters are negotiated among creative agents, corporate entities, legal discourses, and audience expectations. As Peter Wollen surmised, "The *auteur* theory [and, I add, its many variants] leaves us, as every theory does, with possibilities and questions . . . The task which the critics of *Cahiers du Cinéma* embarked on is still far from completed."[62]

Notes

1. André Bazin, "On the *Politique des Auteurs*," in *Cahiers du Cinéma: The 1950s: Neo-realism, Hollywood, New Wave*, ed. Jim Hillier, trans. Peter Graham (Cambridge: Harvard University Press), 248. The title of this essay is frequently given with the phrase "politique des auteurs" in the original French, due to ambiguities that arise in translation. *Politique* translates literally to *politics*, or *policies*, not precisely theory.

2. See Cynthia Littleton, "Employment of Women in Film Production Dips Below 1998 Levels," *Variety*, January 14, 2014, accessed February 23, 2018, http://variety.com/2014/film/news/employment-of-women-in-film-production-dips-below-1998-levels-1201055095/.

3. Stacy L. Smith, March Choueiti, and Katherine Pieper, "Inequality in 800 Popular Films: Examining Portrayals of Gender, Race/Ethnicity, LGBT and Disability from 2007–2015." Los Angeles: Media Diversity and Social Change Initiative and Annenberg School for Communications and Journalism, University of Southern California, 2016, accessed February 23, 2018, http://annenberg.usc.edu/sites/default/files/2017/04/10/MDSCI_Inequality_in_800_Films_FINAL.pdf.

4. Jane M. Gaines, "Anonymity: Uncredited and Unknown in Early Cinema," in *A Companion to Early Cinema*, ed. André Gaudreault, Nicolas Dulac and Santiago Hidalgo (Malden, MA: Wiley-Blackwell, 2012), 443–59.

5. Director's Guild of America, Creative Rights Links, "Credits," n.d., accessed February 23, 2018, www.dga.org/contracts/creative-rights/credits.aspx. This webpage references section 8–104 of the DGA Basic Agreement of 2011.

6. The concept of branding may be familiar as the term for the symbolic languages through which manufacturers distinguish their products from others, but here I also refer to a form of **personal branding**, through which individuals market themselves, or are marketed by corporations, as recognizable commodities. For a critical discussion of contemporary branding practices, see Sarah Banet-Weiser, *Authentic™: The Politics of Ambivalence in a Brand Culture* (New York: New York University, 2012).

7. *Cahiers* grew out of the film-clubs that arose in Paris after the end of the Second World War. Members of Objectif 49 and the Ciné-Club du Quartier Latin had opportunities to reassess films unavailable during the Nazi occupation. See Peter Wollen, "The *Auteur* Theory," in *Signs and Meanings in the Cinema*, 3rd ed. (Bloomington: Indiana University Press, 1972), 73. On influences on the *auteur* critics, see John Hess, "*La Politique des Auteurs* (part one): World View as Aesthetics," *Jump Cut* 1 (May–June 1974), 19–22.

8. Alexandre Astruc, "The Birth of a New Avant-Garde: La Camera-Stylo," in *The New Wave*, ed. Peter Graham (London: Secker & Warburg, 1968), 17.

9. François Truffaut, "A Certain Tendency of French Cinema," in *Movies and Methods* Vol. 1, ed. Bill Nichols (Berkeley: University of California Press, 1976), 16.

10. Ibid., 16.

11. André Bazin, Jacques Doniol-Valcroze, Pierre Kast, Roger Leenhardt, Jacques Rivette, and Éric Rohmer, "Six Characters in Search of *Auteurs:* A Discussion About the French Cinema," in *Cahiers du Cinéma: The 1950s: Neo-Realism, Hollywood, New Wave*, ed. Jim Hillier (Cambridge: Harvard University Press, 1985), 38.

12. Bazin, "On the *Politique des Auteurs*," 256.

13. Ibid., 250–1.

14. Andrew Sarris, "Notes on the Auteur Theory in 1962," in *Film Theory and Criticism*, 6th ed., ed. Leo Braudy and Marshall Cohen (New York: Oxford University Press, 2004), 562–63.

15. Pauline Kael, "Circles and Squares," *Film Quarterly* 16, no. 3 (1963): 46.

16. Geoffrey Nowell-Smith, "*Visconti* (extract)," in *Theories of Authorship*, ed. John Caughie (New York: Routledge, 1981), 136.

17. Ibid., 137.

18. Ibid., 137.

19. Wollen, "The *Auteur* Theory," 79–80.

20. Ibid., 104.

21. See Boris Tomashevsky, "Literature and Biography," in *Readings in Russian Poetics: Formalist and Structuralist Views*, ed. Ladislav Matejka and Krystyna Pomorska (Cambridge: MIT Press, 1971), 55, cited in David Bordwell, "An Author and His Legend," in *The Films of Carl-Theodor Dreyer* (Berkeley: University of California Press, 1981), 9

22. Bordwell, "An Author and His Legend," 9–10.

23. Ibid., 10.

24. Ibid., 24, emphasis in original.

25. Thomas Schatz, *The Genius of the System: Hollywood Filmmaking in the Studio Era* (New York: Pantheon, 1988), 8.

26. Ibid., 8.

27. See Jerome Christensen, *America's Corporate Art: The Studio Authorship of Hollywood Motion Pictures* (Stanford: Stanford University Press, 2012). See also Lindsay Hogan, "The Mouse House of Cards: Disney Tween Stars and Questions of Institutional Authorship," 296–313, and Catherine Johnson, "The Authorial Function of the Television Channel: Augmentation and Identity," 275–95, both in *A Companion to Media Authorship*, ed. Jonathan Gray and Derek Johnson (Malden: Wiley-Blackwell, 2013).

28. Janet Staiger, "Authorship Approaches," in *Authorship and Film*, ed. David A. Gerstner and Janet Staiger (New York: Routledge, 2002), 27.

29. Sarah Kozloff, *The Life of the Author* (Montreal: Caboose, 2014), unpag. eBook.

30. Martha Woodmansee, *The Author, Art, and the Market: Rereading the History of Aesthetics* (New York: Columbia University Press, 1994), 36.

31. William K. Wimsatt, Jr. and Monroe C. Beardsley, "The Intentional Fallacy," *The Sewanee Review* 54, no. 3 (1946): 4.

32. Wayne C. Booth, *The Rhetoric of Fiction*, 2nd ed. (Chicago: University of Chicago Press, 1983), 74. See also his concept of the "career-author," 431, 453.

33. Roland Barthes, "The Death of the Author," trans. Richard Howard, *Aspen* 5–6 (1967): 4–6.

34. Michel Foucault, "What Is an Author?", in *The Foucault Reader*, ed. Paul Rabinow (New York: Vintage, 1984), 107–8.

35. Ibid., 119.

36. See Wolfgang Iser, *The Implied Reader: Patterns of Communication in Prose Fiction from Bunyan to Beckett* (Baltimore: Johns Hopkins University Press, 1978), and C.S. Lewis, *An Experiment in Criticism* (Cambridge: Cambridge University Press, 1961).

37. See, for example, Janice Radway, *Reading the Romance: Women, Patriarchy, and Popular Literature*, 2nd ed. (Chapel Hill: University of North Carolina Press, 1991).

38. Stuart Hall, "Encoding, Decoding," in *The Cultural Studies Reader*, 2nd ed., ed. Simon During (New York: Routledge, 1999), 507–17.

39. Staiger, "Authorship Approaches," 28.

40. For discussion of the legal status of appropriation in visual art, see Nate Harrison, "Appropriation Art, Subjectivism, Crisis: The Battle for Fair Uses," in *Media Authorship*, ed. Cynthia Chris and David A. Gerstner (New York: Routledge, 2013), 56–71.

41. See Jennifer Horne and Jonathan Kahana, "A Perfect Replica: An Interview with Harun Farocki and Jill Godmilow," *Afterimage* 26, no. 3 (1998): 12–14; also, Cynthia Chris, "Girls on the Remake," *Afterimage* 28, no. 5 (2001): 11–12.

42. Lev Manovich, "Who Is the Author: Sampling/Remixing/Open Source" (2002), accessed February 23, 2014, http://manovich.net/content/04-projects/035-models-of-authorship-in-new-media/32_article_2002.pdf.

43. Vicki Mayer, Miranda J. Banks, and John T. Caldwell, "Introduction: Production Studies: Roots and Routes," in *Production Studies: Cultural Studies of Media Industries*, ed. Vicki Mayer, Miranda J. Banks, and John T. Caldwell (New York: Routledge, 2009), 1. See also Vicki Mayer, *Below the Line: Producers and Production Studies in the New Television Economy* (Durham: Duke

University Press, 2011); and John Thornton Caldwell, *Production Culture: Industrial Reflexivity and Critical Practice in Film and Television* (Durham: Duke University Press, 2008).

44. Jason Mittell, "Authorship," in *Complex TV: The Poetics of Contemporary Television Storytelling* (New York: New York University Press, 2015), 107. Emphases in original.
45. Ibid., 87–88.
46. Ibid., 108.
47. Judd Ruggill and Ken S. McAllister, "Invention, Authorship, and Massively Collaborative Media," in *Media Authorship*, ed. Cynthia Chris and David A. Gerstner (New York: Routledge, 2013), 139, 149n5.
48. Ibid., 140.
49. Axel Bruns, *Blogs, Wikipedia, Second Life and Beyond: From Production to Produsage* (New York: Peter Lang, 2008), 254.
50. "Works Made for Hire," *Circular* 9 (Washington, DC: U.S. Copyright Office, September 2012): 1, accessed June 20, 2017, www.copyright.gov/circs/circ09.pdf.
51. For more on IP law and media, see Bill Seiter and Ellen Seiter, *The Creative Artist's Legal Guide: Copyright, Trademark and Contracts in Film and Digital Media Production* (New Haven: Yale University Press, 2012).
52. Protection of sound recordings was upheld in *Bridgeport Music, Inc. v. Dimension Films* (410 F .3d 792, 6th Circuit, 2005), which involved N.W.A.'s two-second sample of a Funkadelic song. Parodies are excepted: they are protected speech. See *Campbell v. Acuff-Rose Music, Inc.* (510, U.S. 569, 1994), regarding 2 Live Crew's interpretation of "Oh, Pretty Woman" by Roy Orbison and Bill Dees.
53. For example, credits for "Otis," from the album *Watch the Throne* by Kanye West and Jay-Z, which samples Otis Redding's 1966 hit "Try a Little Tenderness," boast more than a dozen corporate authors (record labels, some of which share corporate parents) and nine co-authors, including Harry Woods, Jimmy Campbell, and Reg Connelly, who wrote the song in 1932.
54. See David Lipke, "Trovata, Forever 21 Reach Settlement in Copying Suit," *Women's Wear Daily*, October 11, 2009, accessed June 20, 2017, http://wwd.com/business-news/financial/trovata-forever-21-settle-lawsuit-2339870/; and Eric Wilson, "Designers Revisit Copyright Protection," *New York Times*, July 15, 2011, accessed June 20, 2017, https://runway.blogs.nytimes.com/2011/07/15/designers-revisit-copyright-protection/?mcubz=2.
55. Cynthia Chris, "Subjunctive Desires: Becoming Animal in *Green Porno* and *Seduce Me*," in *Animals and the Moving Image*, ed. Laura McMahon and Michael Lawrence (London: British Film Institute, 2015), 121–33. After this essay was completed, Rossellini released ten episodes of a third series, *Mamas* (2013), a co-production of Sundance Channel, Première Heure (a French film production company) and ZDF/Arte (German and French public television channels).
56. Mittell, "Authorship," 88.
57. Chris, "Subjunctive Desires," 121.
58. See Seiter and Seiter, *The Creative Artist's Legal Guide*; also, Pat Aufderheide and Peter Jaszi, *Reclaiming Fair Use: Putting Balance Back in Copyright* (Chicago: University of Chicago, 2011).
59. Facebook Statement of Rights and Responsibilities, November 15, 2013, accessed February 23, 2018, www.facebook.com/legal/terms.
60. See Mark Andrejevic, "Authoring User-Generated Content," in *Media Authorship*, ed. Cynthia Chris and David Gerstner (New York: Routledge, 2013), 123–36.
61. See, for example, Susan Murray, "Amateur Auteurs? The Cultivation of Online Video Partners and Creators," in *Media Authorship*, ed. Cynthia Chris and David Gerstner (New York: Routledge, 2013), 261–72.
62. Wollen, "The *Auteur* Theory," 113–15.

Further Reading

Film Authorship

Carringer, Robert L. "Collaboration and Concepts of Authorship." *PMLA* 116, no. 2 (2001): 370–79.

Caughie, John, ed. *Theories of Authorship*. BFI Readers in Film Studies. New York: Routledge, 1981.

Gerstner, David A. and Janet Staiger, eds. *Authorship and Film*. AFI Film Readers. New York: Routledge, 2002.

Godfrey, Nicolas. *The Limits of Auteurism: Case Studies in the Critically Constructed New Hollywood*. New Brunswick, NJ: Rutgers University Press, 2018.

Grant, Barry Keith, ed. *Auteurs and Authorship: A Film Reader*. Malden: Wiley-Blackwell, 2008.

Hess, John. "*La Politique des Auteurs* (part one): World View as Aesthetics." *Jump Cut* 1 (May–June 1974): 19–22.

Hess, John. "*La Politique des Auteurs*, 2: Truffaut's Manifesto." *Jump Cut* 2 (July–August 1974): 20–22.

Polan, Dana. "Auteur Desire." *Screening the Past* 12 (March 1, 2001): accessed July 3, 2017, www.screeningthepast.com/2014/12/auteur-desire/.

Sarris, Andrew. *The American Cinema: Directors and Directions 1929–1968*. Cambridge: Da Capo Press, 1996. First published in 1968 by Dutton.

Sellors, C.P. *Film Authorship: Auteurs and Other Myths*. London: Wallflower, 2011.

Wexman, Virginia Wright, ed. *Film and Authorship*. New Brunswick: Rutgers University Press, 2003.

Authorship in Literary Theory

Benjamin, Walter. "The Author as Producer." [1934] *New Left Review* 1, no. 62 (July–August 1970): 83–96.

Gallop, Jane. *The Deaths of the Author: Writing and Reading in Time*. Durham: Duke University Press, 2011.

Gilbert, Sandra, and Susan Gubar. "Infection in the Sentence: The Woman Writer and the Anxiety of Authorship." In *The Madwoman in the Attic: The Woman Writer and the Nineteenth-Century Literary Imagination*, 45–92. Second edition. New Haven: Yale University Press, 2000.

McGill, Meredith L., ed. *Taking Liberties with the Author: Selected Essays from the English Institute*. Cambridge: English Institute and Ann Arbor: MPublishing, 2013. eBook.

Smith, Barbara. "Toward a Black Feminist Criticism." *Radical Teacher* 7 (March 1978): 20–27.

Authorship and the Law

Coombe, Rosemary. *The Cultural Life of Intellectual Properties: Authorship, Appropriation and the Law*. Durham: Duke University Press, 1998.

Jaszi, Peter. "Toward a Theory of Copyright: The Metamorphoses of 'Authorship.'" *Duke Law Review* 2 (1991): 455–502.

——— and Martha Woodmansee, eds. *The Construction of Authorship: Textual Appropriation in Law and Literature*. Durham: Duke University Press, 1994.

Sherman, Brad, and Alain Strowel, eds. *Of Authors and Origins: Essays on Copyright Law*. Oxford: Clarendon, 1994.

Media Authorship

Chris, Cynthia and David A. Gerstner, eds. *Media Authorship*. AFI Film Readers. New York: Routledge, 2013.

Gray, Jonathan and Derek Johnson, eds. *A Companion to Media Authorship*. Malden: Wiley-Blackwell, 2013.

10.
POLITICAL ECONOMY
Patrick Burkart

Overview

This collection takes as its focus the knowledge and know-how required to participate in distinctive, lasting, and critical inquiries on many aspects of media studies. For political economy studies of media, communication, and information, the craft of criticism can take a variety of established paths and also admit trailblazers. We are fortunate to join a field that is always in the process of re-tooling and developing. My effort here is focused on providing a partial intellectual history of the approach for critical media studies researchers who may be interested in incorporating aspects of **political economy of communication** (or **critical political economy**) into their own research, or in comparing approaches. Critical political economy of communication is distinguished from liberal political economy or media economics, I am also interested in showing threads of continuity from mass communication research to digital media studies.

This chapter is organized in three parts. The first part lays out the inherited basis for critical (Marxian) political economy of communication, and discusses major influences and landmark studies in the field. The second part addresses the centrality of intellectual property rights (IPRs) to the political economic approach in media studies. The final part addresses how political economy can inform the global movement to expand communication rights in the **Information Society**, using research on digital rights activism as an example.[1] The political economic research on pirate politics, which I will review here, is unorthodox and incorporates mixed methods, but nonetheless fit for the purpose of illustrating the craft of criticism in global media studies. **Pirate politics** is the institutionalization of political parties

promoting copyright reform throughout Europe and in other parts of the world.

Critical political economy is, first and foremost, radical and normative. It seeks to get at the root of social problems by exposing the underlying power relations contributing to observable conflict. Critical political economy considers both economic and non-economic values, providing a normative basis from which to critique a broader range of social institutions including incumbent media systems, the nuclear family, the legal system, the political system, religious traditions, health, and education, among others. This approach promotes a method of analysis for providing a more just and rational course of action when confronting serious social problems related to pervasive inequalities under conditions of capitalist **globalization**. Political economists of communication tend to take media production, the production of other formats of commodified information, and international trade in media and information, as objects of critical inquiry. In contrast, **liberal political economy** is also normative, but aims to troubleshoot problems in the world economy rather than to critique inequalities, ideologies, and other root causes.

The focus on commodity makers, admittedly, discloses a productivist bias of political economy of communication, meaning that culture, audiences, texts, and the affective and aesthetic dimensions of culture in media systems are often neglected or omitted. Some critical political economists embrace it while seeking ways to acknowledge, if not compensate for, the blind spots, particularly for political cultures. For example, Robert McChesney[2] and Douglas Kellner[3] explore the impoverishment of democratic culture and news media together using political economic analysis. The perspective taken by such critical scholars is that political economy can do a fine job of accounting for the systems-side of media studies, and its ramifications for political life, while depriviliging certain fields of inquiry which are better left for cultural studies, textual analysis, and audience studies to analyze with distinctive interpretive methods.

Critical political economy of communication, as distinguished from liberal political economy or media economics, inherits a structural-functionalist orientation from Marxist sociology of capitalist production, although there are long-standing and ongoing efforts in the field to temper its functionalism with postpositivist thinking. In other words, explanations for how society works as a mechanical system have lost favor to more complex models based in part on biological models of change characterized by feedback and adaptation. Political economist Sandra Braman[4] refers to the need to develop and improve "socio-technical" research methods—those that can recognize the mutual influences of communication, information, and the economy. Elsewhere she relates the hermeneutic of political economy of communication as being social history read through the "lens of the progressive commodification of ever more types of information and informational activities."[5] This standpoint on media culture is historical, although it can provide case studies from the present day. Political economy aspires to provide analyses of how social life is affected by the capitalist **commodity form**, or the form in which wealth appears in capitalist society—historically, or in the present day.[6]

Put into practice in politics historically, political economy has informed labor, ecological, and women's movements internationally. More recently, digital rights activism is informed by a political economy of software and the Internet. Digital rights activism is an oppositional social movement that has grown up around legal conflicts over the commodification of media and software—especially in the pro-"piracy" movement. "Pirate parties" run political campaigns promoting reforms for legal file sharing and other modes of bypassing the established system of intellectual property rights protections. The creation and operation of The Pirate Bay, a notorious search engine for locating media and software on the Internet, inaugurated a protracted period of social conflict over copyright around the world. For my case study in this chapter, I use political economy to put the experiences of the Swedish and German Pirate Parties into an international perspective, showing how they implicate broader power structures and relationships, including the terms of trade in **intellectual property** (IP) between Europe and the

United States. The Pirate Bay became a political rallying point for Swedish file-sharers and "netizen geeks" worldwide after the site was targeted for closure by Swedish authorities, under considerable pressure from the U.S. State Department and U.S. Trade Representative's office.

Political economy is well suited to the study of the encroachment of market logic and commodification into everyday life, as well as to active opposition to commodification.[7] Political economy is less well suited to address some of the uses and gratifications of the Internet for access to knowledge, media, and culture, which the Pirates also explicitly thematize, and so my full treatment of pirate politics considers these aspects from other interpretive standpoints.[8] Since Dallas Smythe's elucidation of the production of **audiences as commodities** opened up aspects of media reception to political economic analysis,[9] there is more shared space than ever with cultural studies, including audience studies, screen studies, popular communication studies, and popular music studies. The notion that media companies' real "products" are the cybernetic audience ratings they produce for advertisers (in market based media systems) reoriented a great deal of political economic inquiry from the production of textual commodities to the production of audience commodities. The commodification of leisure time in consuming entertainment leads to industrial shaping of people's consciousness and a more thorough alienation of those who constitute mass media audiences. With the orientation of political economy being a general standpoint for critical media studies, then, for the purpose of this chapter, I offer a presentation of its domain of concerns and a view of its orienting landmarks. Digital networks and networking have emerged as contemporary foundations of technology practices for producing, distributing, and consuming information goods and services and audience commodities.[10] Political economists disagree about whether digitization and networking per se have altered foundationally the capitalist commodity form. For example, Dan Schiller[11] and Vincent Mosco present the case for capitalist continuity, whereas Michael Hardt and Antonio Negri[12] and Nick Dyer-Witheford[13] argue a discontinuity thesis.

Critiques of the **culture industries** since the 1940s have considered the alienation effects of mass media, the propagandistic and ideological uses of media, and other abuses of people conceived as audiences. Marxist scholarship of the celebrated "Frankfurt School" studies of radio and film in the 1940s set the tone for many subsequent studies. The scope of the political economic standpoint is inflating, as well as totalizing. Considering media production as an expression of human reason (or as "un-reason" according to the Frankfurt School) exposes a dialectical or evolving historical process, expressed in social conflict. Looking at both the "enlightenment" (as a Western representation of reason) and "mass deception" (as a perpetuation of mythological thinking)[14] functions of the culture industries has provided an ongoing critique of uncritical, orthodox approaches to media research. Critical political economy takes the standpoint of a social diagnostic, providing corrective remedies for "administrative" social science research, such as media economics, psychological media effects research, and other professions that facilitate the operation of an unreformed media system. It also challenges approaches to media studies that do not look at the realities of institutional power relationships, the empirical operation of scarcity in business, and other aspects of the more destructive side of the economic and technological changes.

Of necessity, critical political economy of communication tends to focus on the production and circulation of IP, since the outputs of the culture industries tend to be information- and knowledge-based products and services that become commodities for sale once they are copyrighted, trademarked, or in some cases, patented. Since the production and defense of IP is predicated on state action in the law and policy-making domain, political economy of communication is especially attuned to the role of the state in media commodification, especially in the many instances where the state participates in promoting free trade and common markets for IP. Directed as it is at the law and legal institutions which mystify and enshroud IPRs with an aura of legitimacy and inevitability, political economy of the culture industries is ultimately an **ideology critique** of law, for example, in unmasking IP as a hegemonic practice, or in identifying the most powerful economic interests in telecommunications policy or trade and investment treaties, such as the Anti-Counterfeiting Trade Agreement (ACTA), the Trans-Pacific Partnership (TPP), and the Intellectual Property Enforcement Directive II (IPRED II) (more below). Ideology critique in political economy is the exercise of unveiling normative practices or traditions, such as law, education, family, religion, commerce, and work routines, as being ideological or as containing coercive or powerful effects, and proposing how the practices might be freer. For example, the treaty law underpinning international free trade and copyright regimes for media receives a great deal of attention in critical political

economy as promoting the entrenched interests of powerful states and private corporations.

Since the rule of law in the liberal juridical tradition bestows legitimacy to the exercise of state power, political economy of communication is especially sensitive to state action in creating and shaping markets, or practices constitutive of **media law and policy**. Political economists are interested in explicating "how [capitalist] economic power saturates the entire policymaking process."[15] State action has been required for structuring and commercializing new electronic media platforms, such as radio, television, telephony, and data services. The state imperative to regulate markets for media and to intervene in economic crises extends also into broader fields of information policy, including intellectual property law. Policy-makers, courts, and police maintain ongoing processes of legal "harmonizations" with international standards, including cross-border enforcement of copyright infringement claims. Digital piracy has provided a reliable pretext for ongoing interventions since the early 1990s,[16] culminating with the "Uruguay Round" of World Trade Organization trade negotiations in 1994, which produced national requirements for criminal penalties for digital piracy.

Political economy of communication has targeted deregulation, privatization, and commercialization of media and telecommunications policy for criticisms, especially since Information Society programs, or public programs designed to jump-start or develop infrastructures and industries oriented toward the production and export of IP, have been modeled on the neoliberal guidelines of the New Economic Model or "Washington Consensus" reform package.[17] For developing countries, the World Bank and International Monetary Fund typically prescribe privatization of state-owned media and telecommunications enterprises, the pursuit of private financing for development, deregulation, and only light public interest regulation as preconditions for receiving loans and political support from more powerful Western countries. If not media dependency, then these institutional harmonizations with global capitalism often develop relationships of "asymmetrical interdependence."[18]

Political economic analyses of Information Society programs and institutions look for evidence of system-level contradictions in policy models as well as economic and industrial realities, especially seeking out examples of social conflicts over IP, labor, leisure, access, and distribution. Examples include **copyright maximalism**, which refers to the ever-increasing protections for private owners of IP combined with ever-diminishing rights for copyright licensees and fair use; **post-privacy**, which refers to the diminished right to privacy of personal information linked to digital media use; and **trade imbalances**, which refer to asymmetries of trade in products and services, for example, those based on royalties from IP, in a trade relationship between countries.

Intellectual History of Political Economy

As previously mentioned, studies of critical, international political economy of communication tend to disclaim positivist approaches to empirical research, preferring historically informed research methods such as case studies, and often in mixed methods approaches. Political economists start from a recognizably social scientific standpoint by emphasizing the systematic approaches to their method. Typically, political economists begin with a research question pertaining to an empirical assessment related to ownership and control of one or more aspects of media, information, or audiences as commodities. Identification and operationalization of independent and dependent variables depend upon the nature and scope of the study; for example, the directionality of certain media and information flows (or contraflows) between countries and geolinguistic regions can be analyzed with respect to the size of a language market, the market power of national producers, and international terms of trade.[19] The commodification of any audience can be analyzed using ethnographic methods[20] as well as data from broadcasting industries and ratings companies. The conversion of play and leisure time online into valuable commodities can be assessed through analyses of marketing and advertising strategies.[21]

Marxism informs the basic categories of critical political economy, and historical materialism broadly construed provides a counterpoint to the liberal tradition of political economy found in Adam Smith and David Ricardo. The **labor theory of value** underlies Marxist analysis, emphasizing the transformative power of human labor upon natural resources and capital and class agency to produce **commodities**, or useful things that are also exchangeable for other things. The labor theory of value also contributes the concept of **surplus value**, which accrues to a productive enterprise in and through productive labor, and is removed as profit from the enterprise through the force of the capitalist. Profit, rent, and interest are the surplus value created by workers. Through this

basic framework, which also provides a moral philosophy, critical political economy elaborates an analysis of labor exploitation; the critical political economy of communication and information moves this analysis to the productive realm of culture industries, media industries, and information services. Critical political economy proceeds from the perspective of the social totality, which is to say that it offers a social systems level view, proceeding from the basis of a critique of the commodity form of capitalism as a whole.[22] Classical or neoliberal economics proceeds from macro- or micro-levels of analysis, typically focusing on the firm, industry, or country level, and examining only economic value.

John Downing[23] provides an intellectual history of political economy of communication that focuses on the evolution of key debates over media ownership, concentration, and control. These early debates addressed whether there is sufficient evidence for there being concentrated media ownership, whether there is a relationship between high concentration of media ownership and risks of democratic deficits, and whether high ownership concentration of media is linked to a reduction of media diversity and competitiveness.[24] A long-standing emphasis on corporate ownership, concentration, and control over the means of production can be traced to management studies of Adolf Berle and Gardiner Means,[25] whose research distinguished control exerted by executive decision-makers from that of corporate owners. Half a century later, Graham Murdock[26] clarified and updated the relationships between ownership and control by separating economic from legal ownership, and allocative from operational control. **Allocative control** of capital expenditures happens in the corporate boardroom, while **operational control** guides the quarterly and daily routines and activities of the enterprise at the news desk, production studio, editorial office, and so forth.

As culture industries and aesthetics were the principal targets of analysis and critique by Max Horkheimer and Theodor Adorno, Marxist political economy remained mostly implicit in the work of the Institute for Social Research at Goethe University ("the Frankfurt School"). As discussed previously, mass media research informed by Herb Schiller and his contemporaries laid the groundwork for contemporary political economy of communication. But critical media studies receives regular calls to refresh its political economic analysis, especially for new varieties of labor exploitation cultivated in online environments.[27] Such criticisms tend to imply that political economy needs to adapt to new informational means and modes of production (which are qualitatively different from those of mass media), new varieties of productive work (which are qualitatively different from leisure-work), and new quanta of exchange value and surplus value. It should be possible to shed the skin of the inherited repertoire and grow into the new one. It is at this juncture where the question of the transferability of old to new models of analysis arises.

Taken alone, the critical political economy standpoint surveys social processes and structures for signs of power structures, conflict, and contradiction, but by itself can only "reach in" to make its assessments of exploitation and ideology using the interpretive method of Marxist dialectics. The "dialectical imagination"[28] in play in Frankfurt School work, for example, draws from lived experience with the capitalist mode of production and is informed by Georg Wilhelm Friedrich Hegel and his predecessors Gottfried Wilhelm Leibniz, Baruch Spinoza, Aristotle, and Epicurus.[29] History is read "backward" and symptomatically as oppositional social relations between powerful classes, driven by exchange relationships yoked to profitability and a growth impulse, while being cloaked by law, religion, and the nuclear family, among other social institutions with ideological functions.

Leaving aside the possibilities of doing "immanent critique" as a real-time examination of social relations in the present day, the empirical materials with which dialectics works are typically historical in nature. This means that evidence of an historical record should be collected and organized in a way that can be described, analyzed, measured, classified, and repeatedly cross-checked by subsequent analysts, ideographically (focusing on individual cases or events) and using hermeneutic reflection to build theories. While historical methods do not admit repeatability as a test of validity, they do admit the falsifiability test—which is to say that an historical claim can be refuted by presenting sufficient evidence to the contrary. For example, the claim that the U.S. media industries became more competitive after the passage of the 1996 Telecommunications Act can be qualified or refuted by examining increased ownership concentration, by industry sector, over time. To be sure, a variety of post-positivist and even post-Marxist approaches to historical methods compete for standing, including feminism, cultural geography, and post-structuralism. In general, these approaches tend to present a genealogical rendering of historical subjects rather than a teleological one.

Political economic work on media industries prior to the diffusion of digital platforms and computerization of media was oriented towards mass media industries, mass audiences, and the formulaic, factory-like production of texts and artifacts, from newspapers to television, film, and broadcasting, and the tendency for these media to have significant effects on audiences, much like hypodermic injections of powerful medications. Frankfurt School work on radio and film by Horkheimer and Adorno infers an ideological relationship of culture industries and their products with respect to national audiences, emphasizing the exploitability of audiences by authoritarian personalities and the reifying effects of popular culture on aesthetics, public opinion, and the social imagination. For example, they explore the psychological manipulations of Father Caughlin's depression-era political radio sermons. Adorno, especially, aimed to bring "the stars down to earth" and to emphasize the irrational aspects of political culture fed by the culture industries.[30] His essay on the *Los Angeles Times* astrology column diagnoses astrology as a media product contributing to the superstitions of alienated and mystified people learning to relate to each other only through intermediaries like astrologists. Adorno also explored early film comedy with Charlie Chaplin as a sublimation of cultural pain and traumas. Later, Dallas Smythe would address the "consciousness industries" and their use of advertising to colonize audiences' leisure time.[31]

In the 1980s, the Reagan and Thatcher administrations supervised a thorough-going reorientation of international communication systems, from a regime based on state protections of media producers and distributors, to a "free flow" approach to information and media across political borders, effected through deregulation, privatization, and free trade agreements. Continental European studies of debates surrounding a general crisis around the public broadcasting model disclosed ever-increasing pressures to promote content conforming to the needs of a "global shopping center"[32] at the expense of local cultures. Political economy expressed an early interest in computing, networking, and information processing under these conditions. Canadian political economists Vincent Mosco and Brenda Dervin recharacterized the deregulatory and privatizing pressures on national media systems as being informed by the "pay-per society," in which media goods and services are meted out individualistically and on a commercial model.[33] Mosco, for example, explored the computerization of the United Services Automobile Association in an influential case study that considered the standpoint and interests of information and media workers.[34] In the 1990s, British political economy of communication focused on the consequences of the formation of the single market for media in the European Union and anticipated future scholarship addressing a **digital divide**, or situation of permanent inequality of access to contemporary communication resources.[35] Political economists have asked whether or not Information Society projects in the European Union should not instead be oriented towards guaranteeing communication rights, rather than promoting private property rights exclusively.[36]

After the commercialization of the Internet in the United States between 1992 and 1995 and the "dot-com boom" of 1995–2000, critical political economy of communication confronted announcements of the end of media scarcity and claims that the Internet and its World Wide Web upended the economics of supply and demand.[37] Various pronouncements on the death of scarcity, death of distance,[38] and "frictionless capitalism"[39] were made in the 1990s by dot-com mythologists, who minimized or overlooked the historical function of technology hype in obscuring powerful stakeholder interests in the Internet's commercialization, or "normalization."[40] In particular, by the early 2000s, business practices began to gel that depended increasingly on a variety of "cybernetic commodification"[41] strategies built up from online surveillance, data mining, and digital rights management. The development of the **digital enclosure**[42] provided the technical and legal prerequisites for the transformation of the Internet into a general delivery platform for mass markets.

Sociological accounts of surveillance contribute to an understanding of the "panoptic sort"[43] as surplus value creation through automated classification and winnowing of personally identifying information. Surveillance can produce economic value as well as promote behavioral conformity,[44] for example, by inculcating the expectation of being observed. It serves the important role of regularizing and normalizing Internet users into predictable audiences. Surveillance and cybernetic commodification underlie the functionality of the model for digital distribution and guide the underlying operations of the so-called "Celestial Jukebox,"[45] a term used by media and telecommunications magnates to resell the original concept of David Sarnoff's "radio music box" for the policy-makers of the twenty-first century. The intertwined system of media and technology companies, its technical infrastructures and standards, and

the deregulated legal system supporting it together form the present-day Celestial Jukebox model. Near-ubiquitous broadband, online film distribution, online gaming, software delivered as a service, and cloud-based streaming music services now provide more and more commercial content for digital distribution, while monitoring user behaviors, data mining user profiles for predictive modeling, and excluding non-payers. Crucially, personalization technologies work in tandem with access control technologies to gather user data and serve content appropriate for marketing.

Critical political economy also investigates the historical and material bases of large-scale patterns of change in international communication and development communication, including perspectives focusing on north-south hemispheric relations. International political economy of communication often situates its analyses within a core-periphery model of economic flows, informed by world systems theory of Immanuel Wallerstein[46] and Christopher Chase-Dunn,[47] but also generates objections and modifications to this theory. **World systems theory** considers the economic geography of global capitalism to exhibit a core-and-periphery structure, such that the capitalist core in the Northern hemisphere exploits the peripheral South. Global media studies incorporating political economy sometimes imply a world systems theory orientation to political economy, inherited from Schiller's imperialism and cultural imperialism theses.[48] Schiller ascribes the expansionist power of global capitalism to the ideological push exerted through Hollywood and state propaganda agencies of the United States and its allies. The power geometries of world systems theory appear considerably messier and much more complicated than Schiller's "strong globalization" thesis would imply.[49] Many legal regimes now coordinate capital and information flows, and evidence of counter-flows challenging the U.S. media industries' dominance emerges from Southern hemispheric sources, such as Nigeria's "Nollywood" and India's "Bollywood."

International Political Economy of Intellectual Property Rights

Intellectual property rights law is supposed to mediate between individual self-interest and an emergent social good. But, considered historically, and from a political economic standpoint, IPRs' expansive nature in the Information Society tends to accrue to the net benefit of private interests. Political economy is uniquely suited to illuminate the power relationships and transformations around the international production, distribution, and consumption of IPRs, at macro-, meso-, and micro-levels. From the codified law policy domain to the commercial repertoires in popular communication, IPRs disclose geopolitical power dynamics as well as smaller processes.

In the mid-1990s, as the world's economies reoriented from Cold War geopolitics to unipolar hegemony by the United States and competition through regional free trade agreements, the harmonization of legal treatments of IP became an urgent matter for the net exporters of royalties-bearing copyrights and patents. The need for IPR owners to export media, software, and other protected content and services internationally, and to predict reliably the outcomes of cross-border copyright infringement lawsuits, became a major source of international coordination and negotiation in the World Trade Organization. The Uruguay Round of world trade agreements (1982–1994) completed a long cycle of consolidation of advantages for IPR owners, and set the stage for explosive growth in digital IP exports by the United States. Competition with the United States for advantage in media exports has proved extremely challenging for the European Union, which is one of the largest trading partners with the United States.

Current research and theory on intellectual property tends to emphasize the relative difficulty or ease of building "leak-proof" IP for media producers and distributors; the economic valuation and devaluation of IP; and/or the social consequences of asymmetrical media trade relationships and strong IP rights enforcement. Leak-proof IP systems are, typically, designed as closed-circuit distribution channels for copy-protected digital files and streams, where every byte of digital content is audited by the distributor within an enclosure of copy protection and personalization. Varieties of digital rights management and other technical measures for restricting access to copyrighted materials have been developed in all the culture industries. The technical specifications, business models, and usability of these systems tend to preoccupy the business and trade literature on IP, which is not reviewed here.

Scholarship on the enhanced or diminished value of particular categories or classes of IP, media "piracy," and infringement tend to fall in the domain of orthodox media economics studies. Political economy and other critical approaches to media studies, on the other hand, tend to consider IP relationally, in terms of power in trade relationships—such as imbalanced trade

relationships between national or regional importers and exporters of media, media industries as promoters of soft power, and media industries as engines for economic development. Using IP for economic competitive advantage became a foreign policy objective for countries pursuing export-led growth around the world, after industrialized countries abandoned state-led growth models and signed on to liberalized trade agreements beginning in the 1980s. In the discussion that follows, I identify the key legal frameworks by which restrictions on piracy (or infringement of IPRs more generally) are expressed as a global class interest institutionalized in law and backed by the coercive powers of the state.

The economic rents, or profits, created through IP ownership are monopolistic and typically come through royalties and licensing. The strategic value of royalties-bearing copyrights, patents, and digital content delivery classified by the Organization for Economic Cooperation and Development as "other services"[50] unifies the economic interests of the United States government and private sector. Consequently, the U.S. State Department and U.S. Trade Representative's office coordinate the promotion of a maximalist approach to IP abroad through trade negotiation—that is, the United States consistently pushes for increased protections for private IP owners, including ever-larger remedies and harsher penalties for copyright infringement. Globally, IPRs are now recognized in copyright, patent, trademark, and trade secrets, and protecting this private property is a large and growing responsibility of powerful nations and their trading blocs.

Internationally, IP law developed into a regularized system in Europe, in order to help authors, artists, and inventors pursue commercial interests in neighboring countries. During that period (mid to late 1800s) the United States pursued an isolationist IP policy, protecting only domestic creators from literary and other forms of infringement for about a century. This situation changed once the country became a net exporter of IP in the nineteenth century. The Berne Convention for the Protection of Literary and Artistic Works and subsequent iterations (1886–1979) yielded expanding protections for increasingly numerous categories of IP. Under Berne, copyright terms are set to a minimum of 50 years, with longer terms adopted by many countries. Although the United States did not ratify the Berne Convention until 1988, and did so in a limited fashion, the United States moved aggressively to achieve consistent legal treatment of IP internationally through multilateral agreements after World War II.

The 1946 General Agreement on Tariffs and Trade (GATT), together with the institutionalization of the International Monetary Fund and World Bank, further stimulated international trade in IP, governing IPRs until the establishment of the United Nations World Intellectual Property Organization (UN-WIPO) and the implementation of its Trade Related Aspects of Intellectual Property Rights (WTO-TRIPS). The TRIPS is considered to be the strongest international agreement creating obligations within member states for the protection and enforcement of IPRs. TRIPS harmonizes many aspects of IP globally and facilitates non-discriminatory treatment of foreign owned IP. In the process, TRIPS consolidates the legal powers of a transnational class of IPR owners, and provides a unified interest in defending and strengthening these powers. Besides the UN-WIPO and GATT-TRIPS obligations, another international IP agreement to which the United States is a signatory is the North American Free Trade Agreement (NAFTA). NAFTA does not bind members to Berne or WIPO, but commits the United States, Mexico, and Canada to abide by the Geneva and Berne Conventions of 1971, the Paris Convention of 1967, and international conventions on plants and agronomy.

IP infringement cases have grown organically with the explosion of IPR claims, and structurally through the extension of copyright terms and expansion of penalties for infringement. Research in law and the social sciences has queried whether maximalism, together with the uncompetitive behaviors it promotes, disturbs the reciprocity and sharing of intellectual work that was made part of the social contract in modern IP rights laws. The agglomeration and consolidation of IPRs in giant media and technology companies are frequently criticized for disrupting the balance of private and public interest and voiding the social contract, particularly by political pirates who see their own activism as a long-term corrective. Intense commercialization may well have already reached a threshold at which further creativity and participation enabled "through sharing of cultural stock"[51] is observably retarded. Some researchers have argued that the U.S. IPR regime and trade policy are mostly if not completely privatized, objectively benefitting only the interests of private property owners.[52]

The IP industries exhibit a tendency to ownership consolidation, and media deregulation in the late twentieth century also promoted the growth of media giants. While countries sign treaties to promote ostensibly pro-competitive media regulations, most do not make strong regulatory interventions against monopolies and monopolistic tendencies. Although anti-trust law was developed and strengthened after industrial-age experiences with robber barons and financial crises, it has observably failed in preventing high levels of ownership concentration to develop in media and telecommunications industries.

The trade relationship in media and entertainment between the United States and the European Union provides an example of asymmetrical interdependence of economic power in IP, where market power is shared in a lopsided trade relationship. This trade relationship lies at the heart of pirate politics. The European Union takes substantial inflows of U.S. media without becoming entirely dependent on the United States for programming, while the United States takes a smaller share of media content and services from European sources. Together they pursue an arms race of copyright maximalism, agreeing to escalate enforcement and liability provisions jointly while pursuing competitive advantage in trade in IPRs independently. The United States records the greatest trade surplus in royalties and license fees in the world (U.S.$32 billion annually), whereas European countries record their greatest trade deficits in royalties and license fees (U.S.$16 billion dollars annually). U.S. exports accrue almost half the world's royalties and license fees for patents, trademarks, and copyrights. Together, the United States and the European Union generate nearly 75 percent of the world's exports in cultural services, 32 percent coming from the United States and 42 percent from European Union countries. Within the European Union there is a regional trade imbalance as well, with only the United Kingdom, France, and Sweden achieving trade surpluses for royalties-bearing products and services.[53]

A major reason why the European Union agrees to ratchet up protections for IPR owners and penalties for infringers in cooperation with the United States is because the EU defines its own orientation to the Information Society in terms of IPRs, specifically, as a regional implementation of the WIPO Copyright Treaty. The implementation of this treaty is called the "InfoSoc Directive" (also known as the "Copyright Directive"), and is a crucial step in the creation of a common market and basis for establishing future competitive advantages over the United States. While the Copyright Directive provides important means for cross-border trade in IP and provides legal remedies for infringement of IPRs, the criminal and civil penalties for file sharing sparked resistance from some courts and all political pirates.

Case Study: Pirate Politics in the European Information Society

Political economy can illuminate pirate politics by identifying and critiquing the structural and institutional features of the media industries that have pursued an aggressive political agenda to criminalize copyright infringement by online file-sharers. The histories of the Pirate Parties of Sweden and Germany are an allegory for the ready employment of force by the informational state to regulate the Internet for the benefit of the major corporate IPR owners. The pirate politics case study employs political economy of communication as a critical standpoint, as well as historical methods. While it does not claim to access the uses or gratifications, thoughts, or beliefs of "pirates" or online file-sharers, the political economy standpoint can orient the analyst to questions about why file-sharers have come to be targeted by the culture industries with increasingly severe threats and penalties, and why their positioning as illegal subjects has informed their oppositional collective action.

For the study of the activist politics surrounding piracy or copyright infringement,[54] I used the political economic standpoint in combination with mixed methods, beginning with an historical approach to the topic area of European copyright reforms. As discussed previously, political economy is an appropriate critical perspective for research on the Information Society, especially since European countries have defined their respective paths in terms of integration into a common market for media and information commodities. The political economic standpoint leads to examination of the current legal framework to promote the detection and punishment of purported file-sharers through active, mass surveillance of Internet connections, through implementation of "graduated response" or "three-strikes" policies for cutting access to infringing users, fines, and imprisonment. As the Celestial Jukebox model of media distribution became institutionalized in Europe, the oppositional agency of the Pirates grew into a pan-European and even worldwide resistance movement, beginning in Sweden in the Pirate Bay's social milieu.

The basic research question for my book, *Pirate Politics*, is how best to explain, in the context of the escalating "copyfight" worldwide, the emergence and formal engagement of marginalized and oppositional actors with the European political system. My grand theory used for the study was Habermas's Theory of Communicative Action, which is a sociological theory of modernization based on a tension between instrumental rationality and communicative rationality played out in culture and all social institutions. The Theory of Communicative Action provides a plausible account of pirate politics as the transformation of a new social movement based in civil society into a formal political party providing demands and other inputs into the European parliamentary system. The political economy perspective offers insights into how the political and economic systems interact with the cultural lifeworld from which the Pirates operate.

The formalization of the Swedish and German Pirate Parties around 2006 can be examined as a case study of a process of political communication oriented towards preserving the communication features for which the Internet is most widely known, as political and human rights, namely, free speech, privacy, and access to knowledge. From a critical political economy standpoint, the challenges of this research project stemmed from the need to understand what was unique about the digital rights movement. The Pirates' emergence appeared to be anti-systemic; that is, its program and platform of Internet privacy, free speech online, and greater access to culture challenged the growth of commercial media companies' IPR strategies and their model of Internet regulations. The Pirates' program also exhibited reflexive and recursive characteristics common to previous new social movements such as the European Green movement and even labor politics of the twentieth century. Therefore, I developed a comparative case study, considering the mobilization of resources and identities for both the German and Swedish Pirate Parties, and related these cases to historical research on the European Greens and other new social movements.

Since the project used qualitative research, I set out to contribute to theory development, rather than to test a theory. I developed theoretical concepts on the basis of my interviews with key informants, who were (for the most part) Scandinavian researchers of communication law and policy. Since the best-quality academic research on pirate politics was being conducted in Sweden at the time, I found an opportunity to work in a communication department at a Swedish university for a year, attend academic conferences and research circles, and network with other scholars in Sweden. I also came to meet many Swedish university students, who represent the majority of the members of the Pirate Party of Sweden. I developed hypotheses after I gathered data from secondary sources (principally news reports, blogs, Wikileaks, and published research), discussed pirate politics in class with students, and compiled field notes and memos. Informants were not subjects, but were teachers for me, providing active and collaborative input in guiding me to published studies and other secondary data sources. I used triangulation in drawing from multiple key informants and sources of data, hoping to improve the reliability and validity of my findings in the process.

I sampled theoretically as my basic analysis emerged for my case studies, for example, in experimenting with accounts of political activism provided by competing new social movement theories, including perspectives from post-structuralist scholars on hegemony and from psychology scholars on relative deprivation. I settled on new social movement theories compatible with the political economy standpoint and informed by research mobilization and political identity to describe digital rights activism as a variety of "cultural environmentalism." Then the study's main concepts—spoilage and exploitation of the Internet commons by the system, imbalanced international IP trade relationships, oppositional collective social action, and legitimacy crisis—eventually reached theoretical saturation when no new information or evidence gathered changed the basic findings or arguments.

Developing and trying to refute various "null hypotheses" about my own study, by doing extra research to undermine my key claims, and then making re-assessments, provided an excellent way to improve the validity of the research findings. Political economy of communication should strive to move, hermeneutically, between improving certainties methodologically and reflecting critically on its own limits. In the case of *Pirate Politics*, an important omission was my neglect of law, policy, and technology related to **hacking** in relation to piracy. Broadly speaking, hacking involves unauthorized access to computers and databases for an instrumental purpose, and is tied historically to episodes of mass digital piracy. The project also pointed to the need for more research on the dynamics of popular communication and new social movements interacting with the fields of international relations and public diplomacy.

Conclusion

Critical political economy of media and communication is an enduring and ongoing critique of the capitalist practices of intellectual property creation, preservation, growth, and projection. Political economy considers media systems as providing a strong evidentiary basis for the potentials for cultivation and exploitation of the consciousness of media viewers, readers, and audiences. The scope of analysis for political economy expands as media and information production comes to encompass all personal and social interactions with networks, and as computer code for media enclosures becomes transposed into legal code protecting copyright and network security. Exploitation potentials can begin at the moment of surveillance by network owners and their affiliates.

The broadened scope for analysis presents conceptual challenges, but also opportunities to reconsider the subjects of analysis. Alternatives to the traditional focus on economic production of state and corporate agents as principal subjects do exist, especially where these can lose control over the constitution of audiences. Cultural studies has made much to-do about audiences as empowered "prosumers," but when these audiences increasingly resemble clusters of traces and other patterns emerging from statistical datasets of online user behaviors, audience agency and identity requires reexamination. At least nominally, media managers ascribe audience identities on the basis of algorithmically generated profiles, since they are not always discoverable through other means.

Speaking in terms of social systems and their ability to cope with change, the turn to data mining for marketing and advertising facilitated a basic differentiation of mass media audiences from new media audiences, enabled by information technologies, and also by economic and legal frameworks carefully prepared by departments of state, transnational trade blocs, and commercial interest groups. The consequences of this situation for audiences are open for debate, and the political economic position will emphasize the restrictions and limitations placed on freedom by technical and instrumental means to capitalist ends.

The intellectual history of political economy presses the critic to materialize the abstractions by providing real and continually updated cases of conflict over communication rights. The scalability of the approach makes it suitable for analyses from the macro- to the micro-levels, and especially, for connecting the levels of analysis. The constitution and reconstitution of media monopolies, of total enclosures, of work routines without escape, of life without free association or privacy are hauntings of the accumulating evidence for Horkheimer and Adorno's original proposition—of enlightenment as mass deception—or even something worse.

Notes

1. The foundational Information Society literature draws from economic sociology research on the growing proportion of value generated by information gathering, creation, and processing in advanced capitalist society since the 1970s. For example, see Daniel Bell, "The Coming of the Post-Industrial Society," *The Educational Forum* 40, no. 4 (1976): 574–9 and Marc Uri Porat, "The Information Economy: Definition and Measurement." United States Office of Telecommunications (Department of Commerce) OT-SP-77-12(1) (1977).
2. Robert McChesney, *Rich Media, Poor Democracy: Communication Politics in Dubious Times* (Champaign: University of Illinois Press, 1999).
3. Douglas Kellner, "The Media and the Crisis of Democracy in the Age of Bush-2," *Communication and Critical/Cultural Studies* 1, no. 1 (2004): 29–58.
4. Sandra Braman, "The Geopolitical vs. the Network Political: Internet Designers and Governance," *International Journal of Media and Cultural Politics* 9, no. 3 (2013): 277–96.
5. Braman, "The Geopolitical vs. the Network Political," 20.
6. Guido Starosta, "The Commodity-Form and the Dialectical Method: On the Structure of Marx's Exposition in Chapter 1 of *Capital*," *Science & Society* 72, no. 3 (2008): 295–318; Joseph D. Straubhaar, *World Television: From Global to Local* (Thousand Oaks: Sage, 2007).
7. Vincent Mosco, *The Political Economy of Communication: Rethinking and Renewal.* (Thousand Oaks: Sage, 1996).
8. Patrick Burkart, *Pirate Politics: The New Information Policy Contests.* (Cambridge: MIT Press, 2014).
9. Dallas W. Smythe, "On the Audience Commodity and Its Work," in *Media and Cultural Studies: Keyworks*, 2nd edition, ed. Meenakshi Gigi Durham and Douglas M. Kellner (Hoboken: Wiley, 2012), 185–203.
10. Nicholas Garnham, "The Political Economy of Communication Revisited," in *The Handbook of Political Economy of Communications*, ed. Janet Wasko, Graham Murdock, and Helena Sousa (Malden: Wiley-Blackwell, 2011), 52.
11. Dan Schiller, *Digital Capitalism* (Cambridge: MIT Press, 1999).
12. Michael Hardt and Antonio Negri, *Empire* (Cambridge: Harvard University Press, 2000); Michael Hardt and Antonio Negri, *Multitude: War and Democracy in the Age of Empire* (New York: Penguin Press, 2004).
13. Nick Dyer-Witheford, *Cyber-Marx: Cycles and Circuits of Struggle in High Technology Capitalism* (Chicago: University of Illinois Press, 1999).
14. Max Horkheimer and Theodor W. Adorno, *Dialectic of Enlightenment* (New York: Verso, 1997 [1947]).
15. Bill Kirkpatrick, this volume.
16. Pamela Samuelson, "The Copyright Grab," *Wired*, January 1996, 134 ff.
17. Terry Flew, *Understanding Global Media* (London: Palgrave Macmillan, 2007).
18. Straubhaar, "Beyond Media Imperialism."
19. Straubhaar, "Beyond Media Imperialism."
20. Eileen R. Meehan, "Leisure or Labor? Fan Ethnography and Political Economy," in *Consuming Audiences? Production and Reception in Media Research*, ed. Ingunn Hagen and Janet Wasko (Creskill: Hampton Press, 2000), 71–92.
21. Mark Andrejevic, "Surveillance in the Digital Enclosure," *The Communication Review* 10, no. 4 (2007): 295–317; Joseph Turow, *The Daily You: How the New Advertising Industry is Defining Your Identity and Your Worth* (New Haven: Yale University Press, 2012); Trebor Scholz, ed., *Digital Labor: The Internet as Playground and Factory* (New York: Routledge, 2012).
22. Martin Jay, *Marxism and Totality: The Adventures of a Concept from Lukács to Habermas* (Oakland: University of California Press, 1984).
23. John D. H. Downing, "Media Ownership, Concentration, and Control: The Evolution of Debate," in *The Handbook of Political Economy of Communications*, ed. Janet Wasko, Graham Murdock, and Helena Sousa (Malden: Wiley-Blackwell, 2011), 140–68.
24. Ibid., 141.
25. Adolf Augustus Berle and Gardiner Coit Means, *The Modern Corporation and Private Property* (Piscataway: Transaction Publishers, 1991 [1932]).
26. Graham Murdock, "Large Corporations and the Control of the Communications Industries," in *Culture, Society and the Media*, ed. Tony Bennett, James Curran, and Michael Gurevitch (New York: Routledge, 1982), 118–49.
27. Mark Andrejevic, "Critical Media Studies 2.0: An Interactive Upgrade," *Interactions: Studies in Communication and Culture* 1, no. 1 (2009): 35–51.
28. Martin Jay, *The Dialectical Imagination: A history of the Frankfurt School and the Institute of Social Research 1923–1950* (Berkeley: University of California Press, 1996).
29. Bertell Ollman, *Dance of the Dialectic: Steps in Marx's Method* (Champaign: University of Illinois Press, 2003).
30. Theodor W. Adorno, *The Stars Down to Earth and Other Essays on the Irrational in Culture* (New York: Psychology Press, 2001).
31. Dallas W. Smythe, "Communications: Blindspot of Western Marxism," *CTHEORY* 1, no. 3 (1977): 1–27.
32. Cees Hamelink, "The Political Economy of Dutch Public Media," *Media Culture & Society* 1, no. 3 (1979): 289–96.
33. Vincent Mosco and Brenda Dervin, *Pay-Per-Society: Computers and Communication in the Information Age* (Westport: Greenwood, 1989).

34. Vincent Mosco, *Doing it Right with Computer Communication: A Case Study of the United Services Automobile Association* (Cambridge: Program on Information Resources Policy, Harvard University, 1994).

35. Graham Murdock and Peter Golding, "Common Markets: Corporate Ambitions and Communication Trends in the UK and Europe," *Journal of Media Economics* 12, no. 2 (1999): 117–32

36. Robin Mansell, "From Digital Divides to Digital Entitlements in Knowledge Societies," *Current Sociology* 5, no. 3 (2002): 407–26; Burkart, *Pirate Politics*.

37. Patrick Burkart and Tom McCourt, *Digital Music Wars: Ownership and Control of the Celestial Jukebox* (Lanham: Rowman & Littlefield, 2006).

38. Frances Cairncross, *The Death of Distance: How the Communications Revolution Will Change Our Lives* (Cambridge: Harvard Business School Press, 1997).

39. Bill Gates, *Business @ the Speed of Thought: Succeeding in the Digital Economy* (New York: Warner Books, 1999).

40. Jonathan Zittrain, *The Future of the Internet – And How to Stop It* (New Haven: Yale University Press, 2009).

41. Mosco, *The Political Economy of Communication*, 150–51.

42. Andrejevic, "Surveillance in the Digital Enclosure."

43. Oscar H. Gandy Jr., *The Panoptic Sort: A Political Economy of Personal Information* (Boulder: Westview, 1993).

44. Patrick Burkart and Jonas Andersson Schwarz, "Post-Privacy as Ideology: A Question of Doxa and Praxis," in *Media, Surveillance and Identity: Social Perspectives*, ed. André Jansson and Miyase Christensen (New York: Peter Lang, 2014), 218–37.

45. Paul Goldstein, *Copyright's Highway: From Gutenberg to the Celestial Jukebox* (Redwood City: Stanford University Press, 2003); Siva Vaidhyanathan, "Celestial Jukebox: The Paradox of Intellectual Property," *American Scholar* 74, no. 2 (2005): 131–5; Burkart and McCourt, *Digital Music Wars*.

46. Immanuel Wallerstein, *The Modern World-System I: Capitalist Agriculture and the Origins of the European World-Economy in the Sixteenth Century, with a New Prologue*, Vol. 1 (Oakland: University of California Press, 2011).

47. Christopher K. Chase-Dunn, *Global Formation: Structures of the World-Economy* (Lanham: Rowman & Littlefield, 1998).

48. Herbert I. Schiller, "Not Yet the Post-Imperialist Era," *Critical Studies in Media Communication* 8, no. 1 (1991): 13–28.

49. Flew, *Understanding Global Media*.

50. Burkart, *Pirate Politics*, 77.

51. Robert L. Kerr, "Intellectual Property Law," in *The International Encyclopedia of Communication*, ed. Wolfgang Donsbach (Hoboken: Blackwell, 2008), 267–8.

52. Niva Elkin-Koren, "The Privatization of Information Policy," *Ethics and Information Technology* 2 (2000): 201–9.

53. Burkart, *Pirate Politics*.

54. Ibid.

Further Reading

Andersson Schwarz, Jonas. "For the Good of the Net: The Pirate Bay as Strategic Sovereign." *Culture Machine* 10 (2009): 64–108.

——— and Stefan Larsson. "The Justifications of Piracy: Differences in Conceptualization and Argumentation between Active Uploaders and Other File-Sharers." In *Piracy: Leakages from Modernity*, edited by Martin Fredriksson and James Arvanitakis, 217–39. Los Angeles: Litwin Books, 2013.

Appadurai, Arjun. "Disjuncture and Difference in the Global Cultural Economy." *Theory, Culture & Society* 7, no. 2 (1990): 295–310.

Bell, Daniel. "The Coming of the Post-Industrial Society." *The Educational Forum* 40, no. 4 (1976): 574–9.

Braman, Sandra. *Change of State: Information, Policy, Power.* Cambridge: MIT Press, 2009.

———. "The Micro- and Macro-Economics of Information," *Annual Review of Information Science and Technology* 40, no. 1 (2007): 3–52.

Burkart, Patrick. "Intellectual Property Rights." In *International Encyclopedia of Digital Communication and Society*, edited by R. Mansell and P. H. Ang. Hoboken: Wiley-Blackwell, forthcoming.

Porat, Marc Uri. "The Information Economy: Definition and Measurement." United States Office of Telecommunications (Department of Commerce) OT-SP-77-12(1) (1977). Accessed October 4, 2017. http://files.eric.ed.gov/fulltext/ED142205.pdf.

Samuelson, Pamela. "The U.S. Digital Agenda at WIPO." *Virginia Journal of International Law* 37 (1996): 369–440. Accessed July 10, 2017. http://scholarship.law.berkeley.edu/facpubs/882.

11.
MEDIA POLICY
Bill Kirkpatrick

Remember watching television as a kid? Depending on where and when you grew up, you might have spent your Saturday mornings transfixed by loud and colorful cartoons, possibly featuring Hasbro's Transformers or My Little Pony (which you could then pester your parents to buy for you). Or maybe you watched "educational" children's television— *Sesame Street* (NET/PBS/HBO, 1969–present) or *Maya y Miguel* (PBS, 2004–07)—with no ads interrupting the math and life lessons.

What you probably *don't* remember are the policy battles over these shows: Parents' groups condemning excessive violence in cartoons, cereal manufacturers claiming their products (and their commercials aimed at kids) are harmless, and grandstanding politicians vowing to protect the youth.[1]

Children may be blissfully unaware of the regulations, governmental agencies, industry groups, and other forces shaping the media; they just like watching their shows. As media scholars, however, we need to broadly understand—and often closely examine—the legal and regulatory processes that form the backdrop, or even the foreground, of media industries, texts, and practices. In this chapter, we'll look closely at what media policy is, how to study it "critically," and how these analyses can enliven our understanding of media and society.

Overview

What is Media Policy?

Media policy, broadly, is the formal and informal rules and regulations that shape or influence the production, distribution, and consumption of media. At its most basic, **media policy studies** seeks to

understand those rules, how they came about, how they have changed, why they matter, and perhaps what they *should* be.

Rules about media are everywhere, but most people think first about state or "official" media policy: the actions of governments and bureaucracies, such as the U.S. Congress and Federal Communications Commission (FCC), or the *Conseil Supérieur de l'Audiovisuel* in France. Lawmakers pass laws, regulators implement those laws, support staff provide technical advice, and so on. This official policy realm also includes the courts, who frequently make policy through their rulings and interpretations. Different countries pursue a wide range of policies, from China's censorship of the Internet to Canada's requirement that a percentage of their media must be created by Canadians.

Media policy encompasses much more than government activities, however. Media industries themselves enact policy, most notably through voluntary internal or industry-wide policies, called **self-regulation**. For example, television networks have internal censors who limit what the network may say and show, which is usually much more restrictive than what the law would allow.

In most countries, the policy arena also includes **citizens**, who play a role in media policy by writing letters to officials, working through organized activist groups to pressure politicians, and so on. One famous example of citizen action leading to policy change is 2004's "Nipplegate," when singer Janet Jackson's breast was briefly exposed during an American football broadcast. After conservative groups and half a million citizens complained to the FCC, the Commission raised fines for indecency on TV by over 1000 percent.

These three actors—the state, media industries, and citizens—together are the object of most media policy scholarship. But we can think of many more "media policymakers," such as local co-ops that build their own broadband infrastructure, school boards that have to decide whether teachers may "friend" students on Facebook, or even parents restricting the media consumption of their kids: "No TV before you've finished your homework" is, in essence, a highly localized media policy. Even more broadly, the media are influenced by environmental policy, anti-discrimination law, election law, and more. For example, laws that weaken the power of unions are normally thought of as labor policy, not media policy, yet in a highly unionized industry like film and television, such laws affect media content in profound ways.

Given this breadth, it is clear that media policy affects *you* every day, whether you are aware of it or not. Here are a few common examples (some specific to the United States, but even if you live elsewhere you'll get the idea):

- restricting movies based on age;
- deciding who gets to broadcast on which television channel;
- ensuring that every house is connected to the national telephone system;
- regulating the sexual content of books, films, magazines, and television shows;
- ensuring that radio-controlled drones don't interfere with the radios of airliners flying overhead;
- regulating speech in various ways: banning cigarette advertising, protecting individuals from libel, requiring pharmaceutical ads to mention possible side-effects, and more.

In short, where there are media (i.e., everywhere), there are rules and regulations governing those media, which means there are many potential objects of study for media policy scholars.

Studying Media Policy Critically

This chapter adopts the perspective suggested in this book's title, in the word "criticism": It's one thing to study media policy; it's another to study it *critically*.

Until recently, the tendency has been to analyze policymaking processes "on their own terms," i.e., as fairly straightforward problems of engineering or politics. In this traditional perspective, the rules of the game are set, the key players are known,

and the goal is to figure out how to solve something that has been defined as a "problem." The research question is usually, "What is the best policy?" (or, in historical analyses, "What would have been the best policy?"). The approach is rooted in positivist social science and is often heavily quantitative, measuring the costs and benefits of various options.[2] In this view, the procedures for regulating media appear fairly straightforward and technical: the issues and players are usually clearly defined, there are established procedures for making decisions, and outcomes can be measured by things like "number of channels a television viewer receives" or "box-office revenues for domestically produced films." As policy scholar Des Freedman put it, "Policy, according to this perspective, is the domain of small thoughts, bureaucratic tidiness and administrative effectiveness."[3]

To study media policy *critically*, however, is to analyze those same processes not on their own terms but as specialized microcosms of culture and society. Critical scholars understand that policymaking is political in the narrow sense, but they are also interested in policymaking as capital-P Political, revealing larger systems of power and meaning. They do not take the tidiness of decision-making procedures as a given, nor do they treat the terms and assumptions of the main actors as straightforward and transparent. The research question is not simply, "What is the best policy to solve this problem?" but also, "What does this policy dispute tell us about society and how it works?"

How might traditional and critical scholars approach the same policy issue differently? Consider the routine case of the FCC awarding a radio station license. A simplified version of the process goes something like this: The FCC determines that there is space on the dial in a given area and calculates the maximum power of the transmitter to avoid interference with other stations. Would-be broadcasters put together applications detailing the kind of content they would broadcast, how they would serve the local community, how they would finance the station, etc. The FCC awards the license to the applicant who seems to have the best combination of technical competence, public service plan, and financial wherewithal.[4] If conflicts arise, they will usually be settled by engineers or the courts; if the broadcaster does a bad job, that will usually be settled by consumers, who can "vote" by switching stations.

That description of station licensing is relatively straightforward, and, although policy analysts might suggest improvements to the process, the key terms and assumptions of the main actors are taken at face value. The primary research question is, *Who should get the license?*, or perhaps, *Is this how station licenses should be allocated?* In Freedman's terms, such an analysis involves small thoughts (i.e., which would-be broadcaster put together the best application?), bureaucratic tidiness (the FCC only needs to weigh the various factors and make a decision), and administrative effectiveness (we have institutions and procedures in place for solving problems and settling disputes).

A critical perspective would approach station licensing very differently. For example, in his book *Selling the Air*, Thomas Streeter adopts a critical perspective when he asks not, how should licenses be allocated? but rather, what led to the idea of a station license in the first place? How was the electromagnetic spectrum turned into "property" for the government to allocate to private interests? His object of study is not, "Who should get the license?" but rather, "To whom is the concept of licensing *useful?*" and, "What are the social and cultural effects of imagining radio in these terms?" In other words, he steps outside of the licensing process itself to question the very terms and assumptions that underlie it, showing how licensing enables governments to control radio speech by choosing the speaker. By turning the airwaves into property, he argues, the state more easily collaborated with private corporations to manage the powerful medium of broadcasting.[5]

We could raise other critical questions about licensing, but the point is this: to study policy critically is to question the terms and assumptions that inform policymaking in the first place, using policy to investigate larger social and cultural questions. This approach allows us to bring a wide range of theories and perspectives into dialog with media policy, such as critical race theory, feminism, political economy, or disability studies. Viewed critically, policy becomes not a technocratic exercise in problem solving but a lens through which to explore countless questions about media, power, and society.

Intellectual History of the Concept

Governments have always understood—and sought to harness—the power of communications. In the third century BCE, for example, the *Arthashastra* laid out rules for how Indian leaders should communicate with their subjects—a kind of ancient media policy. And as long as there has been media policy, there have been media policy analysts; Machiavelli's

The Prince (1532) is a study of, among other things, how monarchs should structure and control the tools of communication at their disposal.

As commonly understood in media studies, however, policy studies are a relatively recent phenomenon, rising with the mass media and initially emerging in the social sciences. An important early moment was the Payne Fund studies (1929–1932), which examined the possible psychological and behavioral effects of movies on children. Although the studies themselves were methodologically flawed, they were used to shape one of the more important policies in media history: the Hollywood Production Code, an example of industry self-regulation that dictated what the U.S. movie studios could say and show in their films.

The example of station licensing above illustrated some of the differences between traditional and critical approaches to media policy studies, but we can unpack that distinction further. What kinds of approaches are we lumping under "traditional"? What key theories and methods inform a "critical" approach?

Two main frameworks in **traditional policy studies** continue to be widely pursued today: the technological approach and the liberal-pluralist approach.

The Technological Approach

A **technological approach** focuses on how media devices work, whereby "the best policy" is seen as emerging organically and neutrally from a rational consideration of the properties of the technologies themselves. This approach emphasizes the analyses of engineers who understand the science behind the devices; it is technocratic, privileging policymaking by technical experts. For example, AM radio waves have certain properties determined by the laws of physics. They travel much farther at night, for instance, and therefore the "best" policy is to limit the transmitter power of most stations after sunset in order to minimize interference. Since skywave propagation (as it's called) is a scientific fact, one could argue that the technology itself is, in a sense, telling us what policies to implement. The technological approach is undeniably useful. If you like turning on your car radio and selecting from a number of clear, interference-free stations, thank a technocrat.

A critical policy scholar would respond, however, that one can't go very far down this road without running into politics. Take cell phones, for example.

Phone companies point out that the electromagnetic spectrum is a limited resource: only so many frequencies are available, and current cellular data networks are nearing capacity. This technological limitation seems to tell us the "best" policy: if we're running out of supply, then we should take action to curb demand. In the United States, the FCC has done exactly that by exempting cellular data carriers from certain regulations about network management and allowing them to limit the speeds at which customers get data. Presto! Thanks to these policies, cell carriers can deliberately slow down your connection to the Internet so their networks don't get overloaded, thereby solving the technological problem of spectrum scarcity.

The catch is this: spectrum scarcity is not just a technological question but also a political and economic one. For years, phone companies "squatted" on spectrum that the government had allocated to them but they chose not to use—it's more profitable to charge higher rates under conditions of scarcity than to invest in building out more capacity. No wonder one FCC insider wrote of "a big push to manufacture a spectrum crisis."[6] Furthermore, even if spectrum really is scarce, how did that spectrum get allocated in the first place? It is clearly a political decision whether to assign frequencies for civilian or military uses, whether to give those civilian frequencies to cell carriers or television broadcasters, and so on.

Regardless of where "spectrum scarcity" stands by the time you read this, the larger lesson is clear: We need engineers to help us understand technology, but we also need tools for thinking critically about what to do with that technology.

The Liberal-Pluralist Approach

Another common traditional approach to policy studies, at least in democratic societies, emphasizes the operations of **liberal pluralism**, the idea that the "best" policy emerges from the fair and legitimate processes of democratic self-governance.[7] In this view, a range of policy actors, coalitions, and interests compete within a policymaking arena that none of them completely controls. Large companies from one sector struggle against companies from another sector, public-interest groups advocate for their preferred policies, ordinary citizens call their congressperson, and so on. The goal of policy analysis is to identify possible points of consensus, overlap, or compromise—or, failing that, select the most persuasive argument.

Consider, for example, sexual content on television. A liberal-pluralist approach would tend to frame this as a problem of balancing competing interests: broadcasters' free-speech rights, the state's enforcement of public-interest obligations, citizens' tolerance of sexual content as expressed through complaints, and so on. We could weigh all these interests and come up with a range of possible policies: ban "indecent" content altogether; restrict it to certain times of the day; leave it unrestricted but require an on-screen warning; etc. In other words, the analyst seeks the optimal outcome by balancing competing interests within the existing policymaking framework.

This approach has innate appeal and common sense behind it, and it is how we've been taught that democracy works. The problem for the media scholar is that, as a way of studying policy, the liberal-pluralist framework has some gaps. First, it can't adequately account for cultures of policymaking, i.e., the ways in which policymakers decide whose voices count, grant access to some players and not others, and bring their own perspectives and interests into their decision-making. Scholars are not blind to these dynamics, of course, and various social-science approaches, such as **agenda-setting theory** (the study of how certain issues and perspectives become salient or dominant and how certain groups are able to get their interests on the agenda), have emerged to explain how policymaking can deviate from a fair and rational ideal. However, these approaches tend to understate the multiple forms of economic and social power that restrict access, limit what counts as "reasoned" debate, and produce outcomes that almost never seriously destabilize existing centers of power in society.

Second, a liberal-pluralist approach to media policy does not provide the scholar with tools for situating specific policies within larger ideological and cultural systems. By looking primarily at the established procedures of democratic decision-making, it can all too easily reinforce existing power relations and dominant perspectives in a society, rather than questioning the role of media policy in those power relations.[8]

The traditional approaches described above have at least one important advantage over critical studies, however: because they tend to analyze policy within the terms and assumptions of existing political, economic, and social frameworks, they are more likely to be considered "relevant" to actual policymaking. Of the clash between "**policy-relevant**" and critical scholarship, Ian Hunter wrote, "To travel to [the official policy sphere] is to make a sobering discovery: They are already replete with their own intellectuals. And they just look up and say, 'Well, what exactly is it that you can do for us?'"[9] The answer these busy bureaucrats want to hear is usually *not*, "Well, we can deconstruct your paradigms and disempower your legitimated stakeholders. How does that sound?"

Interpretative Policy Analysis

In contrast to the traditional approaches above, critical approaches seek to understand how policymaking fits into larger systems of culture and power. There are several such approaches, and they are largely mutually compatible.

Interpretative policy analysis (IPA) is a recent move among social-science policy scholars to introduce qualitative research into policy analyses, which as we have seen are often preoccupied with quantitative and technical data. IPA is concerned, first and foremost, with the ideological and cultural dimensions of the policymaking process itself: How do policymakers decide whom to listen to and whom to ignore? How do they define their terms? How do they decide which factors are most important? Compared to the technological and liberal-pluralist approaches, IPA is better equipped to analyze the values, meanings, and systems of power that influence how policymakers go about their work.

Imagine, for example, a local school board considering whether to censor the Internet on school computers. A traditional policy approach would tend to analyze legal questions, the costs of the filtering software, the risks of getting sued if the school board doesn't act, and so on. The range of "legitimate" voices would be clear: attorneys, accountants, technologists, and parents. Unless there is strong public outcry against censorship (rare), such analyses are going to end in a highly predictable policy decision, which is why almost every U.S. public school censors the Internet.

In contrast, an IPA analysis would question the inclusions, exclusions, and assumptions in this process, asking school board members to consider how their pre-existing beliefs and the choice of whom to consult affect the outcome of their deliberations. Chances are the board members won't think twice about filtering out pornography: the belief that children are harmed by explicit sexual imagery is currently so widespread as to be virtually unquestionable. But how much thought will they give to the non-pornographic sexual content that might get

filtered out at the same time, such as information about birth control and LGBT issues, not to mention vast swathes of art history? They will certainly talk to lawyers and the vendors of filtering software, but will they consult with youth counselors, health workers, or experts on sexual abuse? Will they even think to ask students what they think, or are the students simply persons to be spoken for? Importantly, will they question their own class, racial, and sexual privilege, which frequently blinds policymakers to the impacts of their decisions on marginalized groups? These are the kinds of questions that a scholar steeped in IPA might ask.

As Richard Freeman points out, IPA is often intensely ethnographic, meaning the scholar closely observes what those involved say and do, then tries to alert policymakers to how their biases and assumptions are shaping the process. As Freeman describes the distinction between traditional approaches and IPA:

> [IPA] is a source of reflection rather than direction or prescription. Its contribution to policy making lies in helping actors (policy makers) "learn what they do." . . . Its questions are not "What should we do?" but "What are we doing?", "How do we do what we do?" and perhaps "How do we work out what we should be doing?"[10]

Interpretative policy analysis has counterparts in other fields, such as **legal pluralism** and **science and technology studies** (see "Further Reading"). All of these approaches share a fundamental understanding that even the most rational and dispassionate of human activities are inseparable from larger political processes of meaning-making and cultural power.

Political Economy

Another important concept in critical approaches to media policy is **political economy**. Political economy is covered at length in Chapter 10 of this volume and is useful for many areas of media studies, including understanding how policy decisions are shaped by economic forces. Instead of the liberal-pluralist approach that treats economic factors as just one thread in a policy debate, presumably counterbalanced by nonprofit organizations and citizens, the political economic perspective analyzes how economic power saturates the entire policymaking process.

As the name suggests, political economy helps to identify links between politics and the economy at a broad and deep level. We're not talking solely about the political influence that money can buy, although that is real enough: when, say, the CEO of News Corp rings up a member of parliament, you can be certain that the MP gets on the phone, while *your* call to your representative is unlikely to get personally returned. However, a political economic approach goes beyond the perks of being rich to look at entire systems of money and power: how economic forces structure the terms of debate, whose voices count, how outcomes are determined as "legitimate," and more. A key difference between this approach and IPA is that the political economy perspective tends to prioritize the relationship between economics, broadly understood, and ideology at the social level, while IPA tends to privilege local processes of meaning-making and cultural difference.

For example, in the United States, politicians may vary in their policy views—this person is more liberal, that person more conservative—but they are *all* likely to fundamentally support corporate capitalism. This is, in part, because most state and national political campaigns are primarily funded by wealthy donors (i.e., people who have benefited from the corporate capitalist system). A vice president at The Walt Disney Company is unlikely to give thousands of dollars to, say, a candidate who wants to nationalize the airwaves or dramatically curtail the copyright protections that benefit Disney at the expense of the public domain. Furthermore, the corporate, advertising-driven press tends to give less sympathetic coverage to candidates running on a platform of radical reform, handing another advantage to pro-corporate politicians. Then, once those politicians are in office, major corporations use their money and political influence to ensure that their (pro-corporate) perspectives get a serious hearing in any debate. Thus the economics of the political system and the worldview of policymakers themselves tend to reinforce each other: donor-funded campaigning and corporate lobbying usually "produce" politicians and regulators who are fundamentally friendly to the corporate media.

It is much more complicated than that, of course, but the upshot is this: a political economy approach helps us explain why any policy that fundamentally undermines corporate capitalism or the private interests of media companies is, within a system such as the United States', unlikely to gain much traction, regardless of how rational and effective it might be in serving larger policy goals. This systemic perspective allows political economy to illuminate many policy outcomes that the liberal-pluralist approach struggles to explain.

Cultural Policy Studies

Cultural policy studies is perhaps a bit more difficult to explain but has become highly influential. It doesn't help that the name is so generic, but that's because it has two meanings. First, it acknowledges that the media are just one of many forms of culture—music, the arts, sports—that are subject to regulation. Media policy is thus inseparable from other policies that encourage or support certain kinds of cultural products and institutions while discouraging or limiting others. Second, it refers not just to the study of how culture itself is regulated, but also how culture is used to regulate populations. In other words, the cultural policy studies approach looks at how the object of regulation is not, in the final analysis, the cultural products themselves but rather the attitudes and behaviors of the citizens who engage with such products. It explores how cultural forms, including the media, can be deployed as tools for managing how people behave.

For example, let's return to the regulation of sexual content on television. The traditional view, discussed above, would look at the balance of interests (broadcasters, parents, etc.) and seek to come up with the "best" policy, such as banning indecency when kids might be watching. The IPA view would study the cultural factors that influenced that decision. A cultural policy view, in contrast, would ask what such policies are seeking to accomplish—not in the narrow sense of keeping TV "wholesome" but within larger systems that regulate sex in society, including age-of-consent laws, sex education in schools, dormitories segregated by gender, and many more. Taken as a whole, these systems tend to encourage and reward "good" forms of sexuality (e.g., heterosexual, married, adult, procreative) while punishing "bad" sexuality through shaming, marginalization, imprisonment, and so on. From a cultural policy studies perspective, then, policies restricting sexual content on television are doing more than "protecting children" or any of the other rationales that usually get cited; they are seeking to shape behavior by sending messages about what kinds of sexuality are appropriate, for whom, and under what circumstances. They don't just regulate the media; they try to regulate society.

We see this clearly in the movie ratings assigned by the Motion Picture Association of America (MPAA), an example of self-regulation that tends to enforce a heteronormative and patriarchal understanding of sex. As documentarian Kirby Dick has shown, the ratings board is more likely to restrict a film (through an "R" or "NC-17" rating) if it has homosexual content than if it has similarly explicit heterosexual content. If sex is depicted as pleasurable and consequence-free, the film will likely receive a stricter rating than if it's violent or if the woman is punished.[11] Such policies work to normalize certain attitudes and behaviors while stigmatizing others. Furthermore, they don't simply affect who can see which films, but also which films get made in the first place: because many theater chains refuse to show NC-17 films and many media outlets refuse to accept advertising for them, Hollywood doesn't make very many of them—they are too economically risky. At each stage, then, policy regulates sexuality in the culture by constraining what kinds of sexual speech can be produced, distributed, and consumed. From that perspective, media policies do not simply organize the media system but become integral to the workings of ideology and cultural power.

As you can tell, at this point we're well beyond simple questions like "Who should get the license?" Interpretative policy analysis, political economy, and cultural policy studies, though different in their questions, theories, and methods, all move beyond narrow, quantitative, technocratic, and outcome-oriented approaches to policy. They share an understanding of policy as a key conduit for social and economic power and a mechanism for regulating the cultural life of societies.

Major Modes and Terminology

For critical media policy analysis to go beyond the terms and assumptions of policymakers themselves, researchers must understand what those policymakers are talking about in the first place. That can be a challenging task, and media policy can vary greatly from place to place, industry to industry, and political system to political system. Nonetheless, a few broad concepts will help you think, at least in a general way, about the balance of legal, economic, and technological forces that you might need to understand.

Public Service Broadcasting, Commercial Broadcasting

In a public service broadcasting system, a nonprofit broadcaster is given privileged or even exclusive rights to produce radio and television for that country. Normally this is a governmental or quasi-governmental entity, such as the British Broadcasting Corporation (BBC) in the UK. This broadcaster is primarily funded by the state (often through a tax on television sets), and its job is to produce "quality" programs (however defined).

In a commercial system, broadcasting is dominated by private companies that, although they may be required to produce programs in the "public interest," are primarily motivated by profit. The programming is mostly paid for by advertising (although subscription models like HBO and Netflix are becoming increasingly common). Most countries initially opted for a public service system (the United States being the major exception), but today almost all have some kind of hybrid system, with a state-subsidized broadcaster competing with commercial media companies.

Markets, Market Forces, Privatization, Deregulation

Many policy analysts view the state as existing in tension with the free market, especially when it comes to commercial broadcasting. This relationship is often characterized as antagonistic, meaning that we imagine government regulations as obstacles to greater profit: if I'm a broadcaster, and the government limits how many ads I can run during children's programs, then that regulation is costing me money. This perspective has led to calls by media companies and politicians in many countries to remove such regulations, i.e., to *de*regulate the industry. Their argument is that competition and unfettered market forces will lead to better products at lower prices.

Many policy scholars have argued, however, that what appears to be an antagonistic relationship between media industries and the state is anything but. For example, Thomas Streeter has shown how broadcasters and policymakers in the 1920s and '30s actually *collaborated* through regulation: governmental policies, though often characterized as onerous burdens, in practice reduced competition and helped media companies profitably manage their markets. In other words, broadcasters were successful not despite regulation but because of it.[12] Similarly, today's era of so-called deregulation can be seen as "*re*regulation," i.e., not so much removing regulations as rewriting the rules in reaction to new technologies and market forces—usually in ways that continue to protect powerful incumbent players.

Forbidden and Compelled Speech, Censorship, Obscenity/Indecency, Libel, Fairness, Content Quotas, Language Laws

Every government regulates speech, and since the media are conduits for expression, media scholars need to understand how policymakers forbid some kinds of speech and require others. Many societies have very strict censorship, whether of political content, sexual explicitness, religiously sensitive material, or other kinds of speech that the powerful in that society wish to suppress. Other societies might have tolerant policies regarding politics or sex but strongly regulate commercial speech (e.g., banning cigarette advertising), or compel speech by requiring programming in a particular language or genre (such as public affairs programs). Another category of speech regulation involves truth and untruth. Advertisers are usually not allowed to make false claims about their products, and journalists are generally not allowed to deliberately publish lies that harm someone's reputation (libel). The point here is not to catalog all the ways that speech can be regulated, but rather to get you thinking about how such policies might affect the cases that you are researching.

Copyright, Intellectual Property, Public Domain, Fair Use/Fair Dealing

Copyright regulates speech by granting creators or authors the exclusive right to make and sell copies of their "intellectual property" for a limited time. After the copyright expires, the work enters the "public domain," making it free for anyone to copy, adapt, or rework however they choose. The idea is to incentivize creativity: we get a more vibrant culture, creators have time to earn money from their work, and after a few years we can freely build on that work to the benefit of society as a whole.

Today, unfortunately, the copyright system is broken due to policies that have dramatically expanded and extended copyright protections. In the United States, these revisions to copyright law were written by and for large corporations like The Walt Disney Company (a reminder of the value of political economy in studying policy). A 1998 act lengthened the term of copyright—originally just fourteen years—to a century or more before a work enters the public domain (i.e., becomes free to use by anyone without payment or permission). Also, the Digital Millennium Copyright Act (DMCA) gives preemptive rights to copyright holders, allowing them to boot even non-infringing videos off of YouTube, prevent consumers from refilling the ink cartridges in their printers, and more. Because of these policies, many believe that the original incentive structure at the heart of copyright is out of balance, with the public getting the short end of the stick.

Still, it is important to remember that copyright is never absolute. In addition to work in the public domain, there are exceptions allowing for "fair uses" such as scholarship, parody and satire, and transformative works. Furthermore, alternative voluntary copyright systems have emerged, such as Creative Commons, to address some of the problems with current copyright law.

Access, Universal Access, Barriers to Access, Diversity, Pluralism

Another important set of concepts relates to questions of access in a diverse society: Who has access to which technologies and content? This can be economic (e.g., how to guarantee access to communication tools for poorer citizens), geographic (how to get infrastructure to remote areas), physical (closed-caption television for d/Deaf people), or cultural (how to improve literacy and technical know-how in diverse communities). These policies are closely related to questions of power and social justice, making them ripe for critical analysis.

Globalism, Nationalism, Regionalism, Localism

Finally, media policy is created and implemented at different levels, from global standards-making bodies down to the individual, and all of those levels are interrelated. For instance, in the example above of local school boards filtering computers, such policymaking is not happening in a vacuum; instead, the U.S. government has made filtering a precondition for receiving federal educational funds. Similarly, many recent initiatives in copyright law have occurred at the global level, in particular as U.S. media companies use their influence to enact policies favorable to themselves around the world. So, we always need to be mindful of the regulatory context.

While not comprehensive, this list suggests the range of legal and cultural issues connected to media policy studies and, I hope, will help you see—and study—the media texts that interest you.

Methods

Although much of policy study is similar to research in other areas, here are a few of the key sources that policy researchers often use.

- Trade journals: These are newsletters, magazines, and websites that are written for people within a given industry (see also Chapter 22 on industry studies). Although the trades are not written for a general audience—they're the industry talking to itself—they are invaluable for understanding the ins and outs of policy. Depending on your location and the era you are studying, different publications will be helpful, so ask a research librarian for assistance.
- Government documents: In most democratic countries, government proceedings are public record, and many of these are published online. For historical research, you might need the assistance of a research librarian; you may also need to visit a library in your area that keeps paper records of legislative and administrative proceedings (called Federal Depository Libraries in the United States).
- Archives: While the trades and government documents are great research tools, many researchers find it necessary to travel to archives where an organization's records or an individual's personal papers are kept. For example, at the NBC archives in Madison, Wisconsin, are thousands of letters and interoffice memos that never made it into the public record. Government archives, such as the National Archives in the United States, keep countless documents that might be helpful.
- Ethnography and oral history: Some policy scholars, especially those using IPA, conduct ethnographies of contemporary policymaking processes. Unsurprisingly, gaining access is the challenge here; months of letter-writing and calling on your contacts may be necessary. For historical research, one possibility is oral history—interviewing people who were involved. If the folks you are writing about are still alive, it can't hurt to get in touch and see if they will share their perspectives and memories with you.

Challenges

Several things make it challenging to study policy. One is the specialized knowledge that it can require, which might be technical, legal, or economic—or all three. Since few media scholars are also engineers, lawyers, or economists, the need for specialized knowledge in these areas can seem daunting. Don't let that stop you, however: most issues quickly become clear even without an engineering or law degree. For example, in the case of station licensing above, one need not understand omnidirectional dipole antennas in order to grasp the ways that, say, a requirement like "financial wherewithal" favors well-funded corporate broadcasters over indies and nonprofits.

A second key challenge is access to information, a problem shared with media industry studies (Chapter 22). Even if you understand the issues, many relevant discussions, and often actual decisions, are made behind closed doors in the private boardrooms of media corporations, in off-the-record chats between policymakers and lobbyists, or in secret negotiations to which the public has no access. For example, the MPAA movie ratings board is famously so secretive that the public is not even allowed to know who is on it, much less why they arrived at a particular rating for any given film. Also, despite "Sunshine Laws" (such as freedom-of-information and open-meeting laws) designed to ensure public access to policy-related conversations held by government employees, it would be naïve to imagine that every relevant bit of hallway chat between regulators and industry representatives is being captured and made publicly available. Despite increasingly easy access to documents in the public record, scholars remain excluded from vast realms of important materials.

Case Study: Radio, Disability, and Media Policy

My case study, "'A Blessed Boon': Radio, Disability, Governmentality, and the Discourse of the 'Shut-In,' 1920–1930,"[13] combines two approaches discussed above, political economy and cultural policy studies, in order to understand how media policy in early broadcasting intersected with attitudes toward persons with disabilities. I got interested in this when I began to notice how often policymakers and others referred to "shut-ins" and people with disabilities when discussing radio; the obvious question was,

Why did so many regulators and industry insiders highlight people with disabilities as special beneficiaries of radio, and with what consequences for media policy?

I eventually recognized that invocations of the shut-in fit a pattern: they were used overwhelmingly in support of high-powered, expensive, national radio broadcasting. At the time, there was still a debate about whether the United States should have many low-powered local stations or just a handful of high-powered stations reaching most of the nation. The shut-in was consistently used to support the scenario with fewer national stations—which also happened to be the policy supported by rich, powerful broadcasters like RCA. In other words, ideas about disability were being used to shape media policy in the interests of corporate commercial radio.

It also became apparent that the influence went in both directions: just as disability played a role in the formation of media policy, so too did media policy play a role in changing ideas about disability. This was an era when persons with disabilities were not simply marginalized but were in fact targeted for eradication: forced sterilization, selective breeding ("eugenics"), and euthanasia were mainstream policy positions in the 1920s and '30s. Popular support for reasonable accommodations (such as requiring ramps to make buildings wheelchair-accessible) was decades off. Within this context, then, the idea that persons with disabilities might be special beneficiaries of radio had both negative and positive dimensions. It helped justify the idea that society need not enable physical and social access to public life for persons with disabilities (we can just bring public life to them in their homes via radio), but, more positively, it also subtly suggested that such individuals were worthy of inclusion in the American national community and should not be "weeded out."

Thus the major claims of my essay are:

- Disability played a key role in defining the purposes of radio in the earliest years of broadcasting.
- Discourses about people with disabilities played an important role in media policy, specifically as they were used to promote policies that benefited large corporate broadcasters.
- Simultaneously, radio helped change the meaning of disability by offering "virtual"

inclusion in public life, helping constitute people with disabilities as fuller cultural citizens.
- This virtual inclusion was positive in so far as it advanced the humanity and worth of people with disabilities at a time when eugenics enjoyed wide support, but negative in so far as it blunted calls for physical inclusion and structural/legal access.

Even from that brief description of the argument, you should be able to take away several insights for your own work:

- I'm not asking, "What would have been the best policy for shut-ins, more low-powered or more high-powered stations?" Instead, I'm asking, "What does this debate tell us about how media policy works at a cultural level, in this case in terms of how we regard persons with disabilities?" My initial research question already pointed me toward a critical approach to studying media policy.
- I'm studying how disability and radio were being thought and talked about at the time, which called for a qualitative approach. This led me to mainstream newspapers and magazines, which I mostly found in online databases; trade journals and radio enthusiast journals such as *Radio World*; archival memos, minutes, and regulatory decisions found in the National Archives; and laws and policies pertaining to people with disabilities.
- In keeping with a critical approach, I don't assume that policy debates were rational proceedings based solely on technical facts, nor that the results were the fair outcome of liberal-pluralist democratic processes. Instead, I trace the ways that corporations like RCA enjoyed a privileged position in the debate, and how the outcome depended on cultural beliefs and attitudes as well as economic power. I also explore the importance of this debate for larger systems of social regulation and control.

Given more time and unlimited resources, I would like to find stronger evidence for the policy connection between the discourse of the shut-in and the push for national, high-powered radio. I'm pretty sure I'm right, but I never found a "smoking gun" for that claim, and, realistically, one is unlikely to exist. The takeaway here is that qualitative research often results in evidence that is suggestive rather than proof-positive. People say things in passing in a letter or a newspaper interview, and scholars have to make their best guess about what that evidence is telling them. If there is a nugget of advice here, it is to research as much as you can, and always treat your arguments as invitations for further exploration rather than the final word on a topic.

Conclusion

The split between traditional and critical approaches to media policy reflects a change in media studies in the last thirty years. Ever more media studies curricula emphasize critical-cultural studies instead of traditional social-science approaches such as in journalism and mass communication programs. Through this, scholars have learned to question the neutrality of technical expertise and the fairness of mainstream consensus politics. For example, Allison Perlman has shown how streamlined procedures for renewing television station licenses—clearly the "best" policy from a traditional perspective that privileges bureaucratic efficiency and economic stability—prevent disempowered and marginalized groups from having a meaningful say in their local media. It's not that scholars in the technological or liberal-pluralist tradition could never spot the connection between license-renewal policy and social power; it's that scholars like Perlman who are trained in critical approaches start from different assumptions, ask different questions, and consult different sources, allowing them to more readily see that connection and its importance.

Through this work, policy studies are shifting away from technocratic "best solutions" toward an appreciation of the ways that "policy" is inseparable from larger cultural struggles. If there's a discernible trend here, it's that media policy will gradually become more central to *all* of media studies. For a long time, most critical media scholars treated policy, with its traditional emphasis on technology and consensus politics, as secondary to their interests in power, ideology, and identity. But as more scholars bring a critical lens to policy studies, the rest of the field is better able to see the policy implications of their own research questions. In that spirit, and without minimizing the practical challenges of researching policy, I hope you can see how media policy might be relevant to the questions and topics that *you* are interested in exploring further.

Notes

1. This example was inspired by Heather Hendershot's outstanding book, *Saturday Morning Censors* (Durham: Duke University Press: 1999).
2. For a paradigmatic example of this scholarly tradition, see Lawrence C. Soley, "An Evaluation of FCC Policy on FM Ownership," *Journalism Quarterly* 56, no. 3 (1979): 626–28. For a thorough critique of positivist and pluralist approaches to policy, with significantly more nuance than I can provide here, see Mary E. Hawkesworth, *Theoretical Issues in Policy Analysis* (Albany: State University of New York Press, 1988).
3. Des Freedman, *The Politics of Media Policy* (Cambridge: Polity, 2008), 2.
4. There can be other important considerations, such as minority ownership, though the FCC's commitment to that criterion has waxed and waned over the years.
5. Thomas Streeter, *Selling the Air. A Critique of the Policy of Commercial Broadcasting in the United States* (Chicago: University of Chicago Press, 1996).
6. Karl Bode, "FCC Insider: Spectrum Crisis 'Manufactured,'" *Broadband DSL Reports*, February 1, 2011, accessed October 7, 2017, www.dslreports.com/shownews/112526.
7. The "liberal" in liberal pluralism refers not to a liberal–conservative divide, but rather the idea that we all get to have our say in a democracy—we are free to voice our opinions and advocate for our desired policies. "Pluralism" refers to the belief that competition among all the different views will prevent any one group from dominating, which should then encourage moderation and lead to fairer policy outcomes.
8. For a good example of this, see Allison Perlman's study of how feminist organizations fought the FCC on television license renewals: part of the problem that the National Organization for Women and other activists faced was that the FCC did not see station licensing as an issue with gender implications, so feminists' voices were routinely discounted in the Commission's decisions. Allison Perlman, *Public Interests: Media Advocacy and Struggles Over U.S. Television* (New Brunswick: Rutgers, 2016).
9. Quoted in Tony Bennett, *Culture: A Reformer's Science* (London: Sage, 1998), 34.
10. Richard Freeman, "What is 'Interpretive Policy Analysis'?" *Social Science and Public Policy*, n.d., accessed October 7, 2017, www.richardfreeman.info/answer.php?id=18.
11. Kirby Dick, *This Film is Not Yet Rated,* Magnolia Home Entertainment, 2009.
12. Streeter, *Selling the Air,* Robert W. McChesney, *Telecommunications, Mass Media, & Democracy: The Battle for the Control of U.S. Broadcasting, 1928–1933* (New York: Oxford University Press, 1993).

13. Bill Kirkpatrick, "'A Blessed Boon': Radio, Disability, Governmentality, and the Discourse of the 'Shut-In,' 1920–1930," in *Disability Media Studies*, ed. Elizabeth Ellcessor and Bill Kirkpatrick (New York: New York University Press, 2017), 330–53.

Further Reading

Anderson, Chris and Michael Curtin. "Mapping the Ethereal City: Chicago Television, the FCC, and the Politics of Place." *Quarterly Review of Film and Video* 16, no. 3–4 (1999): 289–305.

Burkart, Patrick. *Pirate Politics: The New Information Policy Conflicts*. Cambridge: The MIT Press, 2014.

Chris, Cynthia. "Censoring Purity." *Camera Obscura* 27, no. 79 (2012): 97–125.

Classen, Steven Douglas. "Standing on Unstable Grounds: A Reexamination of the WLBT-TV Case." *Critical Studies in Mass Communication* 11 (1994): 73–91.

Ellcessor, Elizabeth. "Captions On, Off, on TV, Online: Accessibility and Search Engine Optimization in Online Closed Captioning." *Television and New Media* 13, no. 4 (2012): 329–52.

Heuman, Josh. "'I Don't Want to Pay for What I Don't Watch': The Cultural Politics of à la Carte Cable Television, and the Cultural Life of Communication Policy." *Communication, Culture & Critique* 4 (2011): 30–54.

Hilmes, Michele. "British Quality, American Chaos: Historical Dualisms and What They Leave Out." *Radio Journal* 1, no. 1 (2003): 13–27.

Holt, Jennifer. *Empires of Entertainment: Media Industries and the Politics of Deregulation, 1980–1996*. New Brunswick: Rutgers University Press, 2011.

Mayer, Vicki. *Below the Line: Producers and Production Studies in the New Television Economy*. Durham: Duke University Press, 2011.

Lewis, Justin, and Toby Miller, eds. *Critical Cultural Policy Studies: A Reader*. Malden: Blackwell, 2003.

O'Regan, Tom. "(Mis)taking Policy: Notes on the Cultural Policy Debate." In *Australian Cultural Studies: A Reader*, edited by John Frow and Meaghan Morris, 192–206. Chicago: University of Illinois Press, 1993.

Streeter, Thomas. "Blue Skies and Strange Bedfellows." In *The Revolution Wasn't Televised—Sixties Television and Social Conflict*, edited by Lynn Spigel and Michael Curtin, 220–40. New York: Routledge, 1997.

Tamanaha, Brian Z. "Understanding Legal Pluralism: Past to Present, Local to Global." *Sydney Law Review* 20 (2008): 375–411.

Vaillant, Derek. "Bare-Knuckled Broadcasting: Enlisting Manly Respectability and Racial Paternalism in the Battle Against Chain Stores, Chain Stations, and the Federal Radio Commission on Louisiana's KWKH, 1924–33." *Radio Journal* 1, no. 3 (2004): 193–211.

Yanow, Dvora. *Conducting Interpretive Policy Analysis*. Thousand Oaks: Sage, 1999.

12.
PSYCHOANALYTIC CRITICISM
Todd McGowan

Overview of Psychoanalytic Theory

Media texts often grip us in ways that we wouldn't expect. I might take my twins to *Inside Out* (Docter and Del Carmen, 2015) and find myself completely absorbed by the film, despite the fact that I went to it expecting to doze off for 90 minutes. Or I might flip through channels, stumble on *Paranormal Activity* (Peli, 2007), and become stricken with nightmares after seeing only a few minutes of the film. The power of media texts to attract our attention, even when we don't expect them to or even would rather not give it, leads some media scholars to psychoanalytic criticism. Psychoanalytic criticism has tended to take filmic texts as its primary concern, though this is changing in recent years. Because it focuses on the unconscious **desire** of the spectator, psychoanalytic media theory seems ready-made for addressing questions that arise when spectators respond in ways that defy their own intention or interest, when they react contrary to their conscious will.

In whatever form it manifests itself, psychoanalytic media theory necessarily foregrounds the **unconscious**. This enables us to think outside the privilege of knowledge that defines most other approaches. The major innovation of psychoanalysis in the history of thought involves Sigmund Freud's conception of subjects as desiring beings. Prior to Freud, philosophers primarily thought of human subjects as subjects of knowledge. That is, they viewed what was driving us as the impulse to know more. This belief led René Descartes to identify existence with thinking and others to posit an inherent curiosity about the world. But a major break occurred with Freud, who no longer saw knowledge as having priority. According to psychoanalytic theory, desire takes the foundational position in subjectivity that knowledge typically has. We are first and foremost desiring subjects.[1]

The privileging of desire at the expense of knowledge opposes psychoanalysis not only to the history of thought before it but also to other theories of film and media. Psychoanalytic media theory does not focus on how a text deploys knowledge (narrative or formal analysis) or on how spectators relate to what they see in terms of perception and cognition (phenomenology and cognitive analysis). It does not see media spectatorship as what David Bordwell calls

> a perceptual-cognitive activity that, informed by the logic of the film up to that point, sorts information on the basis of a stringently reduced series of possible outcomes and then bets, in rapid interaction with the flow of story cues, upon certain results.[2]

Clearly, the spectator perceives and cognizes, but this perception and cognition occurs through the distortion of desire. According to psychoanalytic theory, desire shapes our perception and knowledge so that we can never look neutrally on any text (or any object). We are always engaged with what we know, but this engagement is not just interest. Desire is always involved with a traumatic disturbance that runs counter to our interest.

For scholars working in the area of psychoanalytic theory, the central problem is how ineffective knowledge is in the face of desire. For Freud, knowledge is not only secondary, but we actively try not to know in order to continue to desire. We are constantly avoiding knowledge, especially where our desire is concerned. This is because our desire directs us toward trauma rather than away from it. Freud discovered this when he discovered the unconscious: desire is unconscious insofar as it traumatizes consciousness and is incompatible with consciousness. We can't simply bring desire to consciousness by thinking about it.

When Freud turned to repetition and the **death drive** in the 1920 work *Beyond the Pleasure Principle*, the association of desire with trauma becomes even more fully anchored in psychoanalytic thought. The death drive is not a drive to die but a desire to repeat trauma rather than avoid it. Freud discovered the death drive in soldiers who dream about their horrific war experiences, patients who don't want to be cured, and a boy who prefers losing his prized toy to finding it.[3] Freud came to see that our desire is actually drawn to traumatic events rather than being repulsed by them. Desire doesn't aim at a possible goal that would advance the interests or the good of the desiring subject but rather obtains satisfaction through its repetition of a trauma that undermines the subject's self-interest. This structure is what puts our desire in complete opposition to consciousness, which operates according to the idea of aims that would further the subject's interest. Desire is unconscious desire not because what we desire (the mother, to take the clichéd example) is traumatic for consciousness but because the nature of desire itself (its self-destructivity) is anathema to the structure of consciousness. Consciousness aims at achieving a certain good that it considers beneficial; the unconscious pushes the subject away from achieving any good. Desire manifests itself in our inability to pursue our own good, and this desire is necessarily unconscious.

The self-destructiveness of the subject's desire receives a compelling expression in the lament articulated by the figure of the Architect in *The Matrix Reloaded* (Wachowski and Wachowski, 2003). The Architect designed the matrix that keeps subjects unaware that they exist under the control of machines that use human energy to power their world. As he explains himself to Neo, who is attempting to free humanity from this control, humans are incapable of accepting a system that simply provides for their interests and produces their well-being. He states,

> The first Matrix I designed was quite naturally perfect, it was a work of art, flawless, sublime. A triumph equaled only by its monumental failure. The inevitability of its doom is apparent to me now as a consequence of the imperfection inherent in every human being.

What the Architect labels "imperfection" is nothing other than the subject's desire, a desire that refuses what would benefit the subject for the sake of what would disturb its smooth trajectory through existence. Desire is the subject's undoing, but it is also what creates a hitch in the functioning of the matrix of ideology.

From the perspective of psychoanalytic theory, we don't want to know our desire. Freud sees the fundamental status of desire as a barrier to the Socratic maxim, "Know thyself." Since desire disrupts the project of knowing, one must resort to other means than self-reflection in order to gain any insight into desire itself. This is why Freud turned to free association, dreams, jokes, and slips. These are the primary arenas of psychoanalytic inquiry because they provide a space in which unconscious desire can manifest itself in a more direct way than it does in everyday life.

As subjects of desire, we are lacking or incomplete, and this lack is the result of the individual's encounter with the **signifier** or language. (The signifier is the name that Lacan uses for language and its effects.) Language divides the subject from itself so that it can never achieve full self-identity. I am divided between my act of speaking and what I say about myself, and nothing that I say can fill this gap. Lacan calls these two positions the subject of the enunciation and the subject of the statement, and their failure to coincide leaves the subject lacking.[4] This noncoincidence of the subject with itself produces a **lack** that drives the subject to desire. This divided subject seeks the object that language seems to have taken from it. Lack is the fundamental condition of the subject, and it provides the point of departure for a psychoanalytic approach to media.

One trap that psychoanalytic theorists must constantly avoid is the idea that the subject was complete prior to its division by language. This is a retrospective illusion that the effect of the signifier creates. Loss appears as the loss of something substantial, but it is in fact the loss of nothing. When we become subjects of the signifier, we lose what we never had. We can see this same illusion functioning in the Judeo-Christian story of the fall from paradise into sinfulness. The account in Genesis 3 describes paradise in the Garden of Eden preceding the sin of eating the forbidden fruit, but this description is profoundly misleading. Paradise is simply a retrospective illusion that the Fall creates. It is the Fall that creates humanity, and humanity loses nothing with the Fall because it had nothing originally.

The fall into sin parallels exactly the way that psychoanalysis understands our emergence into language. The subject finds itself lacking, and this leads it to believe that it was once whole. This skews how subjects think about their desire. What the subject seeks is not an illusory former wholeness but the traumatic loss that causes it to emerge as a subject. This is not the loss of a positive object but of nothing, and the subject will spend its entire existence devoted to recovering this nothing in the form of an object.

The subject's lack is located in the lost object that it never had. French psychoanalyst Jacques Lacan calls this object the **objet a** (or, at times, the **objet petit a**).[5] He coined this new term instead of just calling it "the lost object" in order to avoid the implication that the subject once had the object. The lost object or *objet a* comes into existence only at the moment of its loss and thus has no substantial status. But the *objet a* orients the desire of the subject, functioning as the object that causes its desire. All the empirical objects that the subject desires—phones, friends, sexual partners, cars, and so on—stand in for the *objet a*, and they are desirable only insofar as they embody this lost object.

Lacan distinguishes between the *objet a* and the object of desire, and this is a distinction that psychoanalytic media theorists often point out because it makes clear that, although we can obtain objects, there is no way to fill the subject's fundamental lack. One can obtain an object of desire—just walk into the store and buy it, or approach a desired partner and ask her or him to have sex—but the *objet a*, which is what makes every object of desire desirable, remains constitutively out of reach. When one has it, at that instant it disappears. This distinction helps to explain why we experience dissatisfaction after obtaining what we desire. Before one purchases a car, it embodies the *objet a*, but once one owns and has total access to it, the *objet a* disappears, as the car devolves into an ordinary object that simply moves one from point a to point b.[6] One obtains an object of desire but never the *objet a* or lost object, which is what motivated the desire in the first place. In this sense, for psychoanalytic theorists, desire satisfies itself through its failure to realize itself through obtaining its object.

The point of psychoanalysis for Freud and Lacan involves grasping the structure of desire and subjectivity rather than changing the subject's desire from a failure to a success. This is a project that psychoanalytic media theory also takes up, although it does so in a completely different way—by analyzing texts rather than patients. All desire fails, but it succeeds in finding satisfaction through this failure. This is what psychoanalysis has to teach and how it informs an approach to media texts. Psychoanalysis doesn't want to cure people of their lack but to cure them of the idea of the cure. We suffer excessively because we believe that we can escape lack and achieve completion, and it is the text that promises completion that represents the gravest danger for the subject. When we watch such texts, we come to think of the impossible *objet a* as an obtainable object of desire. This is the basis for ideological **fantasies**—which promise the impossible object that always eludes the desiring subject—and the critique that psychoanalysis mounts against it is its contribution to a critique of ideology. The point is not accepting dissatisfaction but recognizing that satisfaction resides in failure rather than success.

For Lacan, the subject is not the result of ideological interpellation or hailing but what occurs because the hailing process fails. The subject is thus not ideological but a form of resistance to ideology. It is, in fact, the basis for all resistance to ideology.[7] This position distinguishes psychoanalytic theory radically from the predominant Marxist approach to ideology developed by Lacan's friend Louis Althusser, which sees the subject as the result of ideological interpellation. Althusser contends that ideology transforms concrete individuals into subjects, which means that subjectivity is just another name for ideology.[8] But for psychoanalytic theory, the subject is the subject of the signifier and thus always enmeshed in language, so it depends initially on ideology. But the signifier produces a subject divided from itself, and this division is the key to its ability to contest ideology. The unconscious is not just ideology but also the source of real opposition to ideology.

Lacan reconceives subjectivity not as a sense of agency or mastery or control. Instead, it appears in the moment of the loss of control, when we realize that we don't know what we are, or when we realize that we don't coincide with ourselves, that something is acting or speaking through us. These are the moments when we recognize ourselves as subjects of desire, and they often occur when we engage a media text. But desire is always elusive, and consciousness cannot directly access it. Desire undermines our position of mastery and control, but this is precisely what the initial incarnation of psychoanalytic film theory never fully grasped. This theory operated by translating the psychoanalytic subject of desire into a subject of power.

The History of Psychoanalytic Film Theory

Many historians of psychoanalysis have identified Friedrich Nietzsche as a precursor to Freud, as someone who anticipates the latter's theoretical insights. It is true that Nietzsche also rejected the idea of a subject of knowledge, but he replaced this not with a subject of desire but with a subject of power.[9] In contrast to Freud's position, Nietzsche's position has almost become commonsensical today due in no small part to the popularity of Michel Foucault. Foucault's genealogies of power have their inspiration in Nietzsche's philosophy, and he provides the background for much contemporary cultural analysis.[10] For Foucault (as for Nietzsche), interpretation of a cultural movement involves seeing how power silently operates within this movement.

According to this line of thought, people act as they do out of a drive for power. But this was not Freud's position. Freud saw desire as completely distinct from power. If desire were desire for power, it would not be difficult to gain self-knowledge, and there would be no unconscious. We might think of Gordon Gekko in Oliver Stone's *Wall Street* (1987): he readily admits to himself that he is trying to gain power rather than knowledge when he formulates his famous panegyric to greed ("greed . . . is good"). The search for power may be unflattering for the subject, but it is not traumatic in the way that desire is.

Though psychoanalysis has nothing to do with understanding the subject in terms of power, it is important to mention because this was the dominant way that psychoanalytic film theory initially manifested itself. Early psychoanalytic film theorists were simply not psychoanalytic at all because they took power as their point of departure. From Jean-Louis Baudry and Christian Metz in France to the theorists connected with the journal *Screen* in Britain, a massive appropriation of psychoanalysis for the sake of the analysis of power relations in the cinema took place in the late 1960s and 1970s. In her monumental attempt to refigure psychoanalytic film theory, Joan Copjec notes that "film theory operated a kind of 'Foucauldinization' of Lacanian theory."[11] That is, under the banner of Lacan, psychoanalytic film theorists interpreted film in terms of its deployment of power rather than in terms of its unleashing of desire. This is a crucial difference. Because the journal *Screen* was the site for the dissemination of much of this theory, this form of psychoanalytic film theory now goes by the name **screen theory**, and when theorists in film studies think of psychoanalytic film theory, they still tend to identify it with screen theory, which really had nothing to do with psychoanalysis except the terminology.

The primary theorist of screen theory was Jean-Louis Baudry, who wrote two influential articles entitled "Ideological Effects of the Basic Cinematic Apparatus" and "The Apparatus: Metapsychological Approaches to the Impression of Reality in Cinema."[12] In these essays, Baudry makes a decisive move for the future of psychoanalytic film theory: He aligns the cinematic experience with Lacan's **mirror stage**.[13] In the mirror stage, an infant between the ages of six and eighteen months identifies with its mirror image in order to conceive of itself as a whole despite the fragmentary nature of its bodily experience. For Baudry, this becomes the model for the ideological operation that the cinema performs, and in this way the issue of **identification** rather than desire moves to the fore of psychoanalytic film theory—and identification lends itself well to thinking about subjects in terms of power. The concept of identification aligns the subject with what it sees, whereas the concept of desire emphasizes the gap between the subject and the visual field it confronts. The identification paradigm doesn't capture the misalignment of the subject with the image.

Later, Laura Mulvey took up this emphasis on the importance of identification in her famous contribution to screen theory. Identification with the camera and identification with the male character provide the basis for cinema's role in the perpetuation of patriarchy according to "Visual Pleasure and Narrative Cinema," an essay that practically came to define the psychoanalytic approach to film.[14] Though Mulvey does include desire in her theorization of cinematic fetishism and scopophilia, these were not the aspects of her theory that had the most impact.

Screen theory's focus on power and identification ironically put it at odds with the very psychoanalytic theory that it supposedly represented. But it also made it easy fodder for attack. One could simply say that identification didn't function in this way for all spectators (as many critics did) or that the system of power had fissures in it (as many others pointed out). But the development of a genuine psychoanalytic film theory required a turn to the terrain of desire and an understanding of film as the site for the deployment of desire through a fantasy scenario akin to the fantasy scenario of the dream.

Desire is much more amorphous than power. Where power provides one with a sense of mastery, desire leaves one feeling bereft of mastery and of support for one's identity. This is why desire resists knowledge, but the dream or the film can allow us to know our desire and thus know ourselves. As Freud points out in *The Interpretation of Dreams*, "*The interpretation of dreams is the royal road to a knowledge of the unconscious activities of the mind.*"[15] For psychoanalysis, studying the cinema and media in general is of paramount importance because it allows us to know our desire in a way that would otherwise be completely impossible. Visual media analysis is like dream analysis for the society at large.

In the media text as in the dream, the power of consciousness is relaxed, and we follow rather than lead. The fact that we follow where the film leads us provides the key to understanding cinema's power, according to the new psychoanalytic film theorists. We can have an encounter with the *objet a*—that is, a point that disrupts our ideologically constructed sense of reality and sense of identity. This encounter with the *objet a*—and it can take many forms—becomes the privileged moment in the cinema.

In her essay "The Orthopsychic Subject" and later in her first book *Read My Desire: Lacan Against the Historicists*, Copjec paved the way for the privileging of the encounter with the *objet a* that has become the prevailing emphasis in psychoanalytic film and media theory.[16] Copjec attacked screen theory's reduction of the filmic screen to a mirror in which the spectator simply finds herself or himself fully represented in the imaginary space of the screen. As Copjec sees it, screen theory tends to imagine that the male spectator can identify perfectly with the camera and with the male hero driving the narrative. Though the male hero may experience lack, through the process of fetishistic disavowal this lack is displaced onto the female character that is the object of spectacle. In this way, the male spectator attains a successful ideological interpellation. The screen mirrors back to the subject the fulfillment of its own desire for mastery. Everything that would challenge that mastery—like the evidence of lack—ends up serving it. The process is ideological through and through. The **gaze**, in screen theory's conception, is the spectator's look that corresponds with the look of the camera and the hero. But Lacan's conception of the gaze is wholly different.

The problem with the emphasis that Mulvey (and screen theory in general) places on the mirror stage and mirror identification is that it erases completely what the mirror cannot capture, and this fault

in the mirror is the key point of Lacan's contribution to psychoanalysis. In his *Seminar XIII: The Object of Psychoanalysis*, Lacan specifically names the *objet a* as what remains irreducible to the mirror image, effectively refuting screen theory's theoretical turn to the mirror stage in film theory *avant la lettre*. Lacan states, "when the a appears, if there is a mirror, there is nothing reflected."[17] The *objet a* is the failure of reflection, and the *objet a* in the visual field is the gaze.

Lacan theorizes the gaze as the reverse of the mastering look. Rather than providing the subject mastery over the field of vision, the gaze disrupts the sense of mastery that the subject has over what it sees. Within every visual field (including the cinema screen), there is a point that the subject cannot see, a blot in its vision, and this blot signals the incompleteness both of the visual field and of the subject's look. This is why ideological interpellation in the cinema is never wholly successful. The gaze is not the emblem of a successful interpellation but the mark of its failure. The spectator can't just look on from a comfortable position of mastery over a visual terrain on the screen but finds itself disturbed by and involved in what it sees. The structure of the visual field is not just an open field of vision but includes traumatic disturbances within that field. The spectator doesn't overlook these disturbances; they are what arouses the desire to look in the first place. As a result, the spectator does not have a narcissistic relationship to the mirror when looking at the media screen but instead a much more complex and fraught relationship, and this is what recent psychoanalytic media theorists, beginning with Copjec, have emphasized in their deployment of the theory.

Major Modes of Psychoanalytic Theory

One of the main concerns of psychoanalytic media theory is the gaze and how it figures in the media text. The gaze, in Lacan's reckoning, is one of the objects that cause our desire, not the look of desire itself. It causes our desire not because it is attractive or appealing in any way but because it is distortion or a tear in the visual field. The gaze is not what we can see but what we can't, and that is why we look desirously at the visual field. There is something that we can't see—a traumatic absence—that draws our attention to the visual field and compels us to look. When one sees or experiences the gaze, the filmic image loses its appearance of neutrality, and one feels one's own involvement in what one sees. In this sense, the gaze is the subject manifested on the screen, not through mastery of the image but through utter submission to it. In the encounter with the gaze, it is as if the screen is looking back at you as a spectator.

Perhaps the greatest example of this in the cinema occurs when Dorothy Vallens shows up on the front lawn of Jeffrey Beaumont toward the end of David Lynch's *Blue Velvet* (1986). Dorothy appears beaten and naked in the image, and it is impossible to identify precisely when she becomes visible or where she comes from. But her presence puts a stop to everything that was going on. She stands out because she doesn't fit within the scene of the suburban neighborhood. She proclaims to Jeffrey, "You put your disease in me," right in front of Jeffrey's girlfriend Sandy. The scene disrupts not only the characters within it but also the spectators watching, and this disturbance forces spectators to recognize their psychic investment in what they see. One cannot look voyeuristically on Dorothy in this scene; instead, one confronts in her one's own gaze as the disturbance created by one's desire.

Slavoj Žižek provides another counterintuitive example of the gaze in his analysis of Alfred Hitchcock's *Psycho* (1960). According to Žižek, the gaze does not occur in the film when we see Norman Bates looking at Marion Crane in a state of relative undress and partake in his voyeuristic pleasure. Instead, it occurs after the murder of Marion, while Norman attempts to hide Marion's car in the swamp behind the hotel in order to cover up the crime.

As Norman pushes Marion's car into the swamp, Hitchcock depicts a fissure erupting in the visual field, and the desire of the spectator shows itself in this fissure. An encounter with the gaze occurs, and this encounter is traumatic because it disturbs the spectator's illusion of neutrality in front of the visual image. According to Žižek,

> when the car stops sinking for a moment, the anxiety that automatically arises in the viewer— a token of his/her solidarity with Norman— suddenly reminds him or her that his/her **desire** is identical to Norman's: that his impartiality was always-already false.[18]

As is the case with Dorothy's appearance in *Blue Velvet*, the temporary failure of the car to sink eliminates the spectator's distance from what she or he is seeing and reveals how the spectator's desire is involved in the construction of the visual field. This is an instance of the gaze.

The gaze subverts the spectator's sense of being in a transcendent position immune from any

involvement with what is transpiring on the screen. When confronting the gaze, one recognizes that the film or media text has been made to be seen, that one has an unconscious investment in what one sees. Our desire is present in the text not as a result of preview screenings or audience surveys that materially shape what we see but through the moments when the text breaks down and disturbs our spectatorship. Psychoanalytic theory contends that the traumatic disturbance of spectatorship is the condition of possibility for spectatorship itself.

Through the encounter with the gaze, the spectator recognizes that her or his desire has the effect of distorting the visual field. The gaze exposes the non-neutrality of this field. The spectator doesn't control the field through the gaze, but the gaze marks how the subject distorts this field. It is the point at which the spectator is accounted for and included. As Lacan states in *Seminar XI*, "No doubt, in the depths of my eye, the picture is painted. The picture, certainly, is in my eye. But I am in the picture."[19] The subject cannot look without distorting what it sees through the desire that informs its look, and this distortion is included in the visual field in the form of the gaze. When approaching texts for interpretation, psychoanalytic theory focuses its attention on the moments when a traumatic disturbance of seeing or hearing occurs, moments in which the text forces the spectator to confront her or his desire.

Though the gaze marks the point at which the spectator's desire is included in the text, most texts hide the gaze rather than emphasizing it, and psychoanalytic theorists spend a great deal of time analyzing texts that obscure the gaze through their use of fantasy. No text can avoid fantasy altogether because the gaze in cinema and media appears through the fantasy that each text presents. One never experiences the gaze immediately; it always manifests itself through the mediation of a fantasy. The fantasy frames the gaze and places it within a narrative structure, which both gives the gaze a form in which it can appear and domesticates its effect on the spectator. Fantasy provides temporal and spatial coordinates for the subject's desire, and it offers the subject access to its object by staging the impossible loss of this object along with the avenue for recovering it. The subject can't fantasize the recovery of the object without first fantasizing its loss, which is why fantasy has a split ideological valance. On the one hand, it highlights the absence or loss within the ideological structure, but, on the other hand, it fills in this gap with a narrative that provides an explanation for the trauma of the absence.

Once one grasps the concept of fantasy, it is tempting to dismiss texts that clearly display their investment in fantasy. But one can't just dismiss the media text for offering up a fantasy instead of reality because, for psychoanalytic theory, there is no experience of reality outside the experience of fantasy. That is not to say that everything we experience is just a fantasy but rather that fantasy informs how we perceive and judge reality. Nonetheless, the attack on film for delivering fantasy to spectators was the basic reproach articulated by screen theory, and it represents a failure to see the necessity of fantasy as inhering within the media text. One can't opt out of fantasy, and one need not constantly attempt to undermine it. Psychoanalytic theory shows us that fantasy is not necessarily ideological fantasy. The political role of fantasy depends on the relationship that the text takes up to the trauma of the gaze, and we can understand texts in terms of this relationship.

Because psychoanalytic theory deals with the concept of fantasy and its relationship to ideology, it necessarily raises the question of the relationship between aesthetics and politics, and many psychoanalytic theorists deal with this question, either implicitly or explicitly. It seems as if aesthetic and political analyses are necessarily at odds with each other. Works that try to take a political stand often fail completely as aesthetic objects, and works that strike us as aesthetically appealing often prove politically retrograde. In short, we can like films that provide us with ideological fantasies and dislike those that challenge our ideological investments. In the case of a film like D. W. Griffith's *Birth of a Nation* (1915), critics often praise its aesthetic achievement, and yet its panegyric to the Ku Klux Klan renders it one of the more politically noxious films in the history of cinema: no one denies that the film promulgates the worst racist views. When approaching the question of how to analyze a text, the problem of the relationship between aesthetics and politics comes to the fore as apparently intractable.

In order to solve this problem and to analyze media texts without ignoring either aesthetic considerations or political ones, psychoanalytic theory provides a clear path. It does not offer a ready-made formula but rather an approach that tells us where to look when we consider evaluating a text. Psychoanalytic media theory enables us to see the link between the aesthetic quality of a text and its politics, and this link centers around the role that desire plays in the fantasy that the text constructs.

Psychoanalytic theory enables us to measure the achievement of works in film and media by the relation to the spectator's desire that they set up. The significant achievements in film and media demand that spectators encounter their own desire in what they see and hear in the form of the gaze and the voice. What's more, they refuse to offer spectators a path out of this encounter. Such texts show that there is no solution to the trauma of desire and thus reveal that fantasy cannot deliver the subject or the social order from **antagonism**. This political achievement is accomplished only through the text's formal achievement and is unthinkable without it.

Media texts that utilize the gaze and voice to show the irreducibility of trauma are not typical texts. Typical texts present the trauma of desire as a soluble problem rather than an irreducible antagonism. They do so by providing the spectator a point of escape from this trauma, an ideological fantasy in which the spectator can envision the recovery of the impossible lost object and the satisfactory realization of desire. In other words, when George Lucas's *Star Wars* (1977) depicts Luke Skywalker singlehandedly destroying the Death Star through his reliance on the mystical force, the film provides the spectator with an avenue for eluding the traumatic impossibility of realizing desire. The contrast between texts that expose the lack of a solution to desire and those that fantasize such a solution offers the path to a mode of analysis that brings together aesthetics and politics and that avoids simply universalizing personal preferences, which is always the danger when one makes aesthetic claims.

Case Study: *Lost in Translation*

We could see an example of this analysis by opposing *Birth of a Nation* and a more contemporary film that also received criticism for its depiction of race—Sophia Coppola's *Lost in Translation* (2003), a film that I analyze in "There's Nothing Lost in Translation."[20] In this essay, I show how, by first establishing a fantasized image of Japan and subsequently demolishing it, Coppola's film demands that the spectator confront the impossibility of desire. By juxtaposing this film structure with that of Griffith's wholly ideological *Birth of a Nation*, we can see how psychoanalytic film and media theory offers an avenue for bringing together political and aesthetic analyses in order to understand how politics and aesthetics work together in media texts.

If *Birth of a Nation* is genuinely a political disaster—this is undeniable—then we should be able to find the indications of this disaster aesthetically as well. If we cannot, then the analysis will take place on either aesthetic or political terms but will never be able to account for their dialectical interrelation. The aesthetic indications of the disaster are visible in Griffith's dealing with the trauma of our desire. The film identifies the possibility of interracial desire, a desire that threatens the Southern social order. But the film enables the spectator to retreat from this desire through the ideological fantasy of the Ku Klux Klan, which punishes the black soldier who pursues a white woman and rescues whites threatened by other Union soldiers.

The power of white supremacy dictates the content of the film—Griffith's decision to focus on a white Southern family rather than a black Southern family, for instance—but more importantly, ideology drives the film's formal structure and limits its effectiveness. Griffith's deployment of parallel editing is commonly seen as a revolutionary development in the history of cinema. But perhaps parallel editing is not an aesthetic advance at all. This aesthetic structure that opposes black aggression to white salvation (in the form of the Ku Klux Klan) transforms the black/white antagonism that divides American society into a simple opposition that the film can resolve through the proper distribution of authority. The ideological conflicts in the film are mirrored by the parallel editing structure and then symbolically resolved by the plot. The formal structure of *Birth of a Nation* obscures the irreducibility of antagonism and, in the process, allows the spectator respite from an encounter with her or his own desire. The ideological fantasy of white supremacy locates the spectator at a secure distance from the screen. By shooting the violence against black subjects in long shots and depicting it as a fully justified response to an imminent threat, Griffith insulates the spectator from its trauma. While watching *Birth of a Nation*, one avoids moments at which one would find oneself implicated in the violence of the Klan, and yet one benefits as a spectator from this violence. When the Klan realizes the spectator's desire by saving the white family, the aesthetic structure of the film—its parallel editing that transforms irreducible antagonism into solvable opposition—lets the spectator indulge in the ideological fantasy without seeing her or his desire manifested in this fantasmatic resolution.

Of course, it is possible, as many critics have pointed out, to be a resisting spectator to the position in which *Birth of a Nation* or any other text places one. One can disinvest from the investments that the text imposes. But doing so is akin to taking conscious control of one's dream and directing the action away from trauma to what is pleasant. This turn to resisting spectatorship or conscious control of the dream represents its own form of retreat from an encounter with the trauma of one's desire. Perhaps it is necessary when viewing an ideological film like *Birth of a Nation*, but as a viewing practice, it destroys the radical possibility inherent in media spectatorship. There is no way to know ahead of time which texts to resist and which to follow. To adopt the attitude of resistance would be to guard oneself against *Lost in Translation* along with *Birth of a Nation*, and this latter film bears within it the utmost possibility of the subject's freedom. One must follow where the film leads if one is to see what it might show, which is not to say that one shouldn't be critical after seeing where it does lead.

The contrast between Griffith's and Coppola's films is stark. As I demonstrate in my essay, Coppola's film doesn't allow the retreat from desire that the form of Griffith's film facilitates, and in fact forces the spectator to confront the trauma of her or his desire in the form of the enduring **absence** that marks her film. The difference between *Birth of a Nation* and *Lost in Translation* reveals the fundamental connection between aesthetics and politics. Griffith's reactionary political position leads to a formal compromise that undermines any attempt to assert the film's aesthetic accomplishment. In other words, Griffith's aesthetic missteps parallel his political missteps, just as Coppola's aesthetic achievements in *Lost in Translation* correspond to her political insights. Where Griffith sidesteps a confrontation with desire by turning antagonism into opposition, Coppola enables such a confrontation by insisting on the trauma of the gaze through the obstacles that she places in visual field.

Coppola's film recounts the relationship between two Westerners, Bob and Charlotte, who meet while visiting Japan. Like Griffith's film, Coppola's *Lost in Translation* depicts an interracial interaction, and though Bob and Charlotte don't kill the Japanese, one might see them as distant descendants of Griffith's KKK. And if we think of how screen theory might have viewed the film, this relationship seems even more problematic.

In this sense, *Lost in Translation* provides a revelatory proving ground for the contrast between the approach of screen theory and contemporary psychoanalytic media theory. From the perspective of the earlier theory, the film offers an ideological fantasy in which the Western spectator can enjoy the image of Japan's otherness from a comfortable distance. The spectator enjoys the fantasy of Japan as an exotic realm that one can visit without ever actually engaging.

The film takes a standard Hollywood approach to the otherness of Japan and never tries to penetrate beneath the prevailing Japan fantasy. In other words, it is like Edward Zwick's *The Last Samurai* (2003) or Ridley Scott's *Black Rain* (1989), films that depict Japan as a site of inscrutable mystery. But closer attention to the film shows that this is not at all the case, and the contemporary psychoanalytic approach to the film enables us to see the complexity in its treatment of Japan.

In my essay, I argue that Coppola depicts a fantasy of Japan rather than the authentic Japan. But *Lost in Translation* uses the fantasy of Japan to comment on cultural difference and interactions between cultures, not to supply the Western spectator with a mastering look at cultural otherness. This is why the film is not an orientalist text. The key moments in the film involve the encounter with the gaze, which is what doesn't fit within the standard fantasy structure. The gaze in this film appears as an absence within the visual field, and this suggests that there is no real Japan at the heart of the Japan fantasy. Rather than providing a solution to the trauma of the desire in the way that Griffith does, Coppola demands that the spectator confront the absence of any special essence of Japan that would define its otherness for the Western look.

Though Coppola entitles the film *Lost in Translation*, the film emphasizes that there is nothing lost in translation, which isn't to say that there is no cultural difference. What is lost is nothing rather than something substantial, and this nothing or absence marks the point at which the spectator is involved in the film. It is only through the absent object, not through what we share, that interaction is possible. This works both on a personal level—between Bob and Charlotte—but also on a cultural level—between the United States and Japan. Bob and Charlotte interact through their grasp of the absence that others miss, and the film itself privileges absence formally, especially by showing interactions that occur with only a minimal amount of dialogue or none at all. The role of absence in the film acts as a barrier to identification and a stimulus to desire, and this marks its aesthetic and political achievement.

Both screen theory and psychoanalytic media theory emphasize the role of fantasy in the cinema. But only the latter sees the ambivalence that surrounds fantasy. Fantasy is often ideological, especially in media texts. But it is also a vehicle for the disruption of ideology. Through the mediated fantasy, one can have a traumatic encounter with the gaze that disturbs one's symbolic identity.

The shift in focus from identification to desire (and fantasy) represents the major shift in the terrain of psychoanalytic film theory. By highlighting desire and its inherent connection to trauma, we can see the incredible variance at work in cultural texts of all types. For a long time, theorists mobilized psychoanalysis for the critique of ideological interpellation in the cinema. But ideology doesn't work through identification, and there are many times when cultural texts work in opposition to ideology. Contemporary psychoanalytic theory demands that we look and see.

Future Directions

Most psychoanalytic media analysis has confined itself to the cinema. Psychoanalytic theorists have written little on television, video games, or the Internet, despite the decreasing cultural importance of cinema relative to these other media. This is undoubtedly due to the foundational role that the unconscious plays in psychoanalytic theory and the seemingly perfect match that occurs between psychoanalytic theory and the cinematic experience. When one watches a television program on one's phone, one is more in control of one's attention than one is in the theater, staring at a large screen with no other light sources. But if the unconscious is less readily apparent in the experience of the video game than that of the film, this does not mean that it is any less active.

Perhaps the primary challenge for psychoanalytic media theory at the present is to cease being psychoanalytic film theory. As it stands right now, psychoanalytic media theory is basically reducible to psychoanalytic film theory—this has been the only form in which psychoanalytic media theory has manifested itself—and the narrowness of its focus has limited the amount of exposure that the theory has received. Many media scholars still think of screen theory when they think of psychoanalytic criticism, and this is the result of the limited numbers of interventions that psychoanalytic theorists have made beyond cinema.

Psychoanalytic critics' lack of interaction with other media forms appears as an inability for the theory to interact with these forms. But this is simply not the case. Concepts such as desire, death drive, and the gaze do not lose their saliency when we turn from film to video games, for example. In some important sense, the medium is a matter of indifference to psychoanalysis because what matters for this theory is how aesthetic form distorts the medium, and this distortion occurs no matter what medium one experiences. Moving from medium to medium is the main challenge confronting psychoanalytic theory today. Psychoanalytic theory today has overcome its own past deviations, and now it must overcome its longtime bond with the cinema.

Notes

1. The presentation of psychoanalytic film and media theory here will focus on the contributions made on the basis of the theories of Sigmund Freud and Jacques Lacan. The influence of Freud and Lacan has far out-stripped that of all others put together. Because of their specific conception of desire (one not shared by other major psychoanalytic theorists), Freud and Lacan provide a privileged way of considering film and media texts. It should not be surprising that they have been the dominant figures in psychoanalytic film and media theory.

2. David Bordwell, *Narration in the Fiction Film* (Madison: University of Wisconsin Press, 1985), 46.

3. Freud writes *Beyond the Pleasure* in the form of a chronicle of his own gradual acceptance of the idea of the death drive. See Freud, *Beyond the Pleasure Principle*, in *The Standard Edition of the Complete Psychological Works of Sigmund Freud*, vol. 18, trans. and ed. James Strachey (London: Hogarth, 1953), 1–64.

4. For Lacan's explanation of the distinction between the subject of the enunciation and the subject of the statement, see *The Four Fundamental Concepts of Psychoanalysis*, trans. Alan Sheridan (New York: Norton, 1978), 136–48.

5. There is much argument about when Lacan actually invented the *objet a*, but there is no doubt that the most thorough initial elaboration of the concept came in Lacan, *Le Séminaire, livre X: L'angoisse, 1962–1963* (Paris: Seuil, 2004).

6. The loss of the new car smell provides a synecdoche for the phenomenon of the disappearance of the *objet a* when one obtains the object of desire. As this smell goes away, the car ceases to be a desirable object that one treasures and changes into being simply a mode of transportation.

7. Slavoj Žižek is responsible for clarifying Lacan's position on the subject and distinguishing it from that of Louis Althusser, who views subjectivity as the endpoint of the process of ideological interpellation. Žižek first articulates this correction of the interpretation of Lacan in his initial English-language book, *The Sublime Object of Ideology* (London: Verso, 1989).

8. See Louis Althusser, "Ideology and Ideological State Apparatuses (Notes Toward an Investigation)," in *Lenin and Philosophy and Other Essays*, trans. Ben Brewster (New York: Monthly Review Press, 1971), 127–86.

9. In *The Gay Science*, Nietzsche articulates his critique of the subject of knowledge. He states, "Look, isn't our need for knowledge precisely this need for the familiar, the will to uncover under everything strange, unusual, and questionable something that no longer disturbs us? Is it not *the instinct of fear* that bids us to know? And is the jubilation of those who attain knowledge not the jubilation over the restoration of a sense of security?" Nietzsche, *The Gay Science*, trans. Josefine Nauckhoff (Cambridge: Cambridge University Press, 2001), 300–1.

10. See, for example, Michel Foucault, *Discipline and Punish: The Birth of the Prison*, trans. Alan Sheridan (New York: Vintage, 1995).

11. Joan Copjec, *Read My Desire: Lacan Against the Historicists* (Cambridge: MIT Press, 1994), 19. Despite the incisiveness of Copjec's critique of psychoanalytic film theory as it had been practiced, few scholars in film and media studies have paid attention to her work. For example, when David Bordwell attacks what he calls "Grand Theory" (an amalgam of psychoanalysis, Marxism, and structuralism) in his contribution to *Post-Theory*, he fails to mention Copjec's psychoanalytically informed corrective, despite evincing knowledge of her work in the essay. See Bordwell, "Contemporary Film Studies and the Vicissitudes of Grand Theory," in *Post-Theory: Reconstructing Film Studies*, eds. David Bordwell and Noël Carroll (Madison: University of Wisconsin Press, 1996), 3–36.

12. See Jean-Louis Baudry, "Ideological Effects of the Basic Cinematographic Apparatus," trans. Alan Williams, *Film Quarterly* 28, no. 2 (1974–1975): 39–47; and Baudry, "The Apparatus: Metapsychological Approaches to the Impression of Reality in Cinema," trans. Bertrand Augst, *Camera Obscura* 1, no. 1 (1976): 104–26.

13. Given the deleterious effect that the mirror stage essay had not just on film studies but also on the theory of ideology, it would have been better if Lacan had simply never written it. But if one must look for oneself, see Jacques Lacan, "The Mirror Stage as Formative of the *I* Function," in *Écrits: The First Complete Edition in English*, trans. Bruce Fink (New York: Norton, 2006), 75–81.

14. It is telling (and to her credit) that Mulvey doesn't identify herself completely with psychoanalysis but rather openly admits that she is appropriating it as an implement for assaulting patriarchy. She says, "Psychoanalytic theory is thus appropriated here as a political weapon, demonstrating the way the unconscious of patriarchal society has structured film form." Laura Mulvey, "Visual Pleasure and Narrative Cinema," *Screen* 16, no. 3 (1975): 6.

15. Sigmund Freud, *The Interpretation of Dreams* (II), in *The Standard Edition of the Complete Psychological Works of Sigmund Freud*, vol. 5, trans. and ed. James Strachey (London: Hogarth, 1953), 608 (Freud's emphasis).

16. See Joan Copjec, "The Orthopsychic Subject: Film Theory and the Reception of Lacan," *October* 49 (1989): 53–71; and Copjec, *Read My Desire: Lacan Against the Historicists.*

17. Jacques Lacan, *Le Séminaire, livre XIII: L'objet de la psych-analyse, 1965–1966,* unpublished manuscript, session of January 5, 1966.

18. Slavoj Žižek, "'In His Bold Gaze My Ruin Is Writ Large,'" in *Everything You Always Wanted to Know about Lacan (But Were Afraid to Ask Hitchcock),* ed. Slavoj Žižek, (London: Verso, 1992), 223.

19. Jacques Lacan, *The Seminar of Jacques Lacan, Book XI: The Four Fundamental Concepts of Psychoanalysis,* trans. Alan Sheridan (New York: Norton, 1978), 96 (transla-tion corrected). Alan Sheridan's translation of the final sentence reads, "But I am not in the picture." There is no precedent in the French text for this magical appear-ance of the word "not," which completely transforms the meaning and pushes Lacan in the direction of screen theory. One is tempted to blame the emergence of screen theory on this mistranslation, but unfortunately its originators were native French speakers (and conceived their theory before the translation of *Seminar XI* in 1978).

20. Todd McGowan, "There's Nothing Lost in Translation," *Quarterly Review of Film and Video* 24, no. 1 (2006): 53–64.

Further Reading

Friedlander, Jennifer. *The Feminine Look: Sexuation, Spectatorship, Subversion.* Albany: SUNY Press, 2008.

McGowan, Todd. *The Real Gaze: Film Theory After Lacan.* Albany: SUNY Press, 2007.

Neroni, Hilary. *The Violent Woman: Femininity, Narrative, and Violence in Contemporary American Film.* Albany: SUNY Press, 2005.

Žižek, Slavoj. *The Fright of Real Tears: Krzysztof Kieslowski Between Theory and Post-Theory.* London: British Film Institute, 2001.

Žižek, Slavoj. ed. *Everything You Always Wanted to Know about Lacan (But Were Afraid to Ask Hitchcock.* New York: Verso, 1992.

Zupančič, Alenka. *The Odd One In: On Comedy.* Cambridge: MIT Press, 2008.

13.
COGNITIVISM
Ted Nannicelli

Overview

The term **cognitivism** describes an approach to the study of media that is characterized both by methodological assumptions and research foci. The latter primarily consist of the perceptions, cognitions, conations, and emotions we experience when we engage with various media and how these are elicited. Thus, cognitivism tends to focus its inquiry on the general mental operations of viewers and the individual media works that cue them.

The methodological features characteristic of cognitivism (though by no means exclusive to it) are (1) a dedication to the highest standards of reasoning and evidence in media studies and other fields (including, but not limited to, empirical data from the natural sciences), (2) a commitment to stringent intertheoretical criticism and debate and, thus, a dialectic model of knowledge building, and (3) an acceptance of **naturalism**. In this context, "naturalism" refers to the idea that, because we are part of the natural world and employ the same faculties we depend upon to perceive and understand the natural world in order to perceive and understand media artifacts, the natural sciences will play a role in explaining the latter just as they do the former. Implicit in this account is also a dedication to and dependence on interdisciplinarity, which, as we shall see, has been a feature of cognitivism since its inception. Because of cognitivism's emphasis on reasoning, argumentation, and naturalism and its focus on the mental world of media users, its closest ties in the academy are to analytic philosophy and the psychological sciences.[1]

Based on this brief sketch, readers may justifiably wonder why the approach is called cognitivism—a term that would seem to indicate an exclusive or, at least, strictly circumscribed focus on cognition and its constitutive hallmarks like attention, comprehension, and memory. The explanation lies in the approach's historical ties to cognitive science, which the next section will explore. And, to be sure, some cognitivist scholarship *does* investigate the ways in which media users attend to, comprehend, and remember, say, film and television narratives. However, it is important to emphasize that, as the preceding characterization indicates, contemporary cognitivism's purview extends beyond cognition per se, and, in relation, it has interdisciplinary links not only with cognitive psychology, but also communications, linguistics, literary studies, narratology, neuroscience, phenomenology, philosophical aesthetics, philosophy of mind, and videogame studies. As such, cognitivism does not refer to a specific method and the cognate term, cognitive theory, does not pick out a particular theory. Rather, cognitivism is best understood more generally as an approach, a stance, or a research program.

Close analysis or criticism, then, is just one sort of research project undertaken by cognitivists. Cognitivists of a more philosophical orientation, such as Noël Carroll and Malcolm Turvey, may examine the concepts and logical consistency underlying theories advanced by other cognitivists or media scholars who adopt other approaches. Cognitivists of a more empirical orientation, such as Torben Grodal and Ed Tan, may either conduct experimental work themselves or draw upon empirical findings to propose general explanations of various mental phenomena elicited by media. And, of course, many cognitivists wear several hats, critiquing or proposing general explanations in some contexts, while offering close analyses in others.

A cognitive approach to close analysis may be taken in two ways, broadly speaking. One option is to take a top-down perspective. In this case, the analyst encounters the media work with some specific hypothesis or principle in mind, which she may either test or explain by closely analyzing the work. Here the work functions as evidence that may undermine or support the hypothesis or theory. The top-down approach is clearly susceptible to confirmation bias (in which case the analyst simply finds the evidence to support her preferred hypothesis or theory) and demands extreme care. The close analysis of a single media work may severely undermine a general hypothesis or theory.

For example, analyzing the generation of comic amusement in a movie full of sight gags (think *Playtime* [1967]) may prove devastating to a superiority theory of cinematic comic amusement. That is, the enumeration of, say, visual puns in such a film would constitute a counterexample to the idea that comic amusement is essentially a matter of laughing contemptuously, from a position of superiority, at the expense of someone else. (Note that such a critique could still be a positive contribution to research insofar as it helps us improve our theories.) However, the reverse is not true: the analysis of comic amusement in such a movie would not be sufficient to demonstrate the general truth of an incongruity theory of cinematic comic amusement, according to which "what is key to comic amusement is a deviation from some presupposed norm—that is to say, an anomaly or an incongruity relative to some framework governing the ways in which we think the world is or should be."[2] Instead, one would have to marshal much more evidence, analyzing films across historical periods, national boundaries, and cultural milieux. Some cognitivists pursue this sort of research—most notably David Bordwell, whose pioneering work has traced connections between "contingent universal" features of human culture and the development of particular stylistic norms across a number of film-historical contexts. At this point, though, we are no longer talking about a top-down approach, but a "middle-level" approach.

Alternatively, one could pursue a bottom-up cognitivist analysis of a media work. Arguably, this is the more popular strategy among cognitivist analysts and, perhaps, the more promising one. In this case, the research aim is not to test a general hypothesis or explanation but to answer a particular question about a given work and how it likely engages its audience. Consider, for example, the question, how do serialized television comedies like *Arrested Development* (Fox 2003–06; Netflix 2013–) generate comic amusement?

or, in what ways are serialized television dramas like *Breaking Bad* (AMC 2008–13) able to generate and sustain suspense?

These sorts of research questions make clear that cognitivism differs from many prominent approaches to the study of media (and TV, in particular) with respect to its tacit supposition that there is a significant degree of cooperation and convergence in the way media users respond to particular works. Even more worrisome for some media scholars, these questions tacitly assume that there are at least broadly drawn ways in which media users *should* engage particular works inasmuch as the questions imply that "normal viewers" ought to feel comic amusement when they watch comedies and suspense when they watch thrillers. Such assumptions are part and parcel of cognitivism's commitment to naturalism, to be discussed further presently. But cognitivism's ability to deal with normative matters is an open question, and it is arguable that cognitivists also need to account for the heterogeneous media engagement documented by audience researchers and cultural studies scholars.

Intellectual History

Sketching this approach's emergence in media studies also goes some way to explaining how the name cognitivism stuck. In the 1980s, a number of critical methods—most notably structuralist semiotics, Lacanian psychoanalysis, Althusserian Marxism, and post-structuralist textual criticism—collectively petrified as a grand theoretical paradigm that dominated a number of humanities disciplines in the Anglo-American academy. By the mid-eighties, small groups of scholars in several fields, including literary studies, television studies, and film studies, began to push back against this "Theory," according to which viewers were merely "positioned subjects"—unwitting ideological dupes. In film studies, this resistance came primarily from scholars who objected to the model of viewers' mental activities posited by subject-position theory and the loose, associational reasoning often employed by its advocates. Because these scholars emphasized, in contrast, the active mental activity of viewers, and because they drew support for their claims from the interdisciplinary field of cognitive science, their approach came to be known as cognitivism.

Thus, from its emergence, cognitivism was both critical and constructive. For example, in a landmark paper published in 1985, a year that roughly marks the inception of cognitivism, Noël Carroll implicitly rejected the central assumptions of subject-position theory in an analysis of the accessibility and appeal of popular, commercial cinema in terms of its ability to engage "the *cognitive* faculties of the audience." "Only by focusing on cognitive capacities," Carroll wrote, "especially ones as deeply embedded as pictorial recognition, practical reason, and the drive to get answers to our questions, will we be in the best position to find the features of movies that account for their phenomenally *widespread* effectiveness." Why? Because, he reasoned, "cognitive capacities ... seem the most plausible candidate for what mass-movie audiences have in common."[3] In this essay, Carroll cited some pioneering cognitive psychological research on pictorial perception, but his argument—essentially an inference to the best explanation—pointed to the need for further empirical work without explicitly invoking "the cognitive revolution."

Also in 1985, David Bordwell published the first book to take a cognitive approach to the study of media—*Narration in the Fiction Film*. Bordwell's volume used an analysis of cinematic narration to argue that films engage a number of shared cognitive processes that make our perception and comprehension of narrative films possible. Like Carroll's account, this view of the spectator as mentally active was underpinned by an inference to the best explanation, but it also made more extensive and detailed use of number of findings in cognitive science. In particular, Bordwell drew upon research emerging out of the New Look school of psychology pioneered by Jerome Bruner, Irwin Rock, R.L. Gregory, and others, which emphasized the *constructive* nature of mental activities such as perception. The result was a sustained, empirically supported argument, outlined in a chapter titled "The Viewer's Activity," according to which, "A film ... does not 'position' anybody. A film cues the spectator to execute a definable variety of *operations*."[4] Four years later, in his ground-breaking essay, "A Case for Cognitivism," Bordwell offered a summative statement of what a cognitive approach to the study of film might involve and a sustained account of the literature informing this emergent research program.[5]

To be sure, 1985 did not mark the first occasion researchers had ever thought of media users as active or investigated the cognitive processes underlying media use. Somewhat ironically, something like the cognitivist approach can be traced back to what is arguably the first work of film theory: the psychologist and philosopher Hugo Munsterberg's *The Film: A Psychological Study*, published in 1916. For example, he wrote of cinematic motion: "The movement ... is

superadded, by the action of the mind."[6] Closer in temporal proximity to contemporary cognitivism, experimental psychologists working in communications departments in the United States in the 1970s and 1980s steadily churned out empirical research in the vein of what can be roughly called the media effects tradition (although this tradition itself has a much longer history).[7] For example, a relatively unknown edited collection from 1980, *The Entertainment Function of Television*, includes papers with titles like "The Power and Limitations of Television: A Cognitive-Affective Analysis," "Entertainment as Vicarious Emotional Experience," "Anatomy of Suspense," and "Humor and Catharsis: The Effect of Comedy on Audiences."[8] Nevertheless, a variety of institutional and disciplinary factors impeded sustained collaboration between this latter research program and the cognitive approach that emerged in film studies. Most notably, academic film studies was born out of literary studies and was initially steered by the current trends and interests of its parent discipline—trends and interests, which, in the 1960s and 1970s, did not include the empirical, psychological study of the audience (readers or viewers).

In addition, however, it is worth emphasizing that cognitivism was never merely the study of viewer psychology undertaken under different disciplinary auspices. Rather, cognitivism was informed by two other significant research fields: film studies and philosophy (in the Anglo-American tradition). First, it is crucial to emphasize that cognitivism has always been fundamentally grounded in film studies, where it originated. The work of Bordwell, his colleagues (most notably Kristin Thompson), and his students figures centrally here because it established an essential tie between cognitivism and the careful, formal and historical analysis of films themselves. The historical poetics of film initiated by the so-called Wisconsin Project constituted an important complement to cognitivism, grounding the latter's more general claims in the detailed study of individual films and film history.[9] As one would expect given film studies' descent from literary studies, historical film poetics was, in turn, deeply influenced by particular research traditions in literary studies. Of special importance in this regard is Russian formalism, which is why the historical poetics of film was initially (and still sometimes is) called neoformalism. Neoformalism and cognitivism share a central research question: How does the design of a film elicit particular perceptual and cognitive effects in its viewers?[10] Moreover, they tend to approach the question in distinct but complementary ways, which is one of the reasons cognitivism's home has remained in film studies.

The third significant research field informing cognitivism is philosophy as it is practiced in the analytic or Anglo-American tradition. Again, there are both distal and proximate reasons for this. In part, it is because the cognitive science that developed in the 1980s was itself deeply interdisciplinary, involving work in philosophy of mind being conducted by scholars with a naturalist orientation such as Daniel Dennett, Jerry Fodor, and John Searle. So cognitivism would have likely been somewhat philosophically informed regardless of the particularities of its development in film studies. More proximately, however, cognitivism's philosophical inflection can be traced to Noël Carroll's work in the 1980s, which was mentioned previously. Importantly, Carroll was formally trained in both film studies and philosophy—a unique combination that lent itself to sustained philosophical reflection on film and the nature of film viewing for its own sake rather than in the service of some broader philosophical agenda. Somewhat later, another philosopher, Gregory Currie, made an additional significant contribution to this stream of cognitivism with a careful, interdisciplinary monograph entitled *Image and Mind: Film, Philosophy, and Cognitive Science*.[11] Currie lodged a series of devastating objections to the then orthodox views that film is language-like in terms of how it represents and how viewers comprehend it and that the film viewing experience involves cognitive illusions, whereby viewers mistake fiction for reality.[12] Drawing on contemporary work in cognitive science and philosophy of mind, Currie emphasized the centrality of imagination to our engagement with cinema.

These three central strands of early cognitivism—empirical psychology, film studies, and analytic philosophy—have given rise to a rich, deeply interdisciplinary research program. For some time, cognitivism's positive research contributions were overlooked by mainstream film and media studies. Whether this was because the field bristled at the criticism cognitivism advanced or the (sometimes) polemical terms in which that criticism was couched is a question that is beyond the scope of the present essay. But it is worth mentioning one often-overlooked feature of Bordwell and Carroll's edited collection, *Post-Theory*—for better or worse the book most commonly associated with cognitivism because of its sharp censure of the field and its uncompromising tone.[13] *Post-Theory* offers an illuminating look at the interdisciplinary formation of cognitivism described above. The volume comprises sections entitled "Film

Theory and Aesthetics," "Psychology of Film," and "History and Analysis," and includes work from film scholars, philosophers, and psychologists. Not all individual contributors take a cognitive approach, let alone focus on cognition in a narrow sense, but these essays collectively illuminate cognitivism's interdisciplinary constitution.

It was around the time *Post-Theory* was published—the mid-1990s—that cognitivism really gained steam, since which it has continued to thrive. Initially, it was common to see research monographs, such as Murray Smith's *Engaging Characters* and Ed Tan's *Emotion and the Structure of Narrative Film*, grounded in one discipline (film studies and psychology, respectively), incorporating research from the other.[14] Today this is still the case, but it is equally common to see edited collections, such as Arthur Shimamura's *Psychocinematics*, Carl Plantinga and Paisley Livingston's *Routledge Companion to Philosophy and Film*, and Ted Nannicelli and Paul Taberham's *Cognitive Media Theory*, initiated in any of cognitivism's constitutive disciplines and including contributions from scholars in all three.[15] Moreover, as indicated previously, cognitivism's purview has expanded far beyond "cognition," narrowly construed as conscious, rational, mental operations, and beyond film. The next section will chart some of the central questions and topics that cognitivism has addressed in the past and is currently addressing today.

Major Modes and Concepts

As indicated above, one of the features that unites cognitivist research is a commitment to naturalism. "Naturalism" is a notoriously vague term, which refers to a cluster of views with somewhat varied ontological and methodological commitments. In other contexts, it would be important to delineate those commitments and specify which of them one sought to endorse. Indeed, cognitivists who adopt a naturalistic perspective, broadly construed, sometimes vehemently disagree amongst themselves about the role of scientific inquiry within film and media studies. So, the naturalism to which cognitivists are committed is rather broad in scope. As Murray Smith has helpfully summarized the view, naturalism is

> the project of explaining human behaviour based on the assumption that the human species is part of the natural world, and that consequently the methods and knowledge of the natural sciences will play a central role in such an explanation.[16]

Yet the natural sciences' precise role in the study of moving images and our engagement with them is a matter of some debate within cognitivism. Given the heterogeneous nature of research questions posed by film and media scholars (within and outside of the cognitivist program), it seems implausible that the natural sciences will provide the appropriate tools for answering *all* of them. Rather, as Smith points out, "The questions we ask about film [and other media] are of very different sorts—ontological, epistemological, ethical, and aesthetic. Each of these perspectives will call upon different methods, indeed probably different *mixes of method*."[17] This is an important point both for the purposes of understanding cognitivism's underlying methodological pluralism (remember, it is an approach rather than a method per se) and for appreciating the wide variety of research projects under the broad banner of cognitivism.

As described above, cognitivism initially developed in film studies because of dissatisfaction with the account of spectatorship offered by "Grand Theory," so an initial research question was, how does the design of a film elicit particular perceptual and cognitive effects in its viewers? As a result, one early strand of cognitivism focused on the processes underlying perception, comprehension, and interpretation, and drew heavily upon contemporary cognitive psychology accordingly. I have already discussed Bordwell's *Narration in the Fiction Film* and "A Case for Cognitivism," but there are two more key works in this research cluster that bear mentioning. First, in *Making Meaning*, Bordwell expanded his cognitivist account of the active viewer to include her interpretive activity. He summarized his central claim in this oft-cited passage: "The sensory data of the film at hand furnish the materials out of which inferential processes of perception and cognition build meanings. Meanings are not found but made."[18] Less quoted are the two lines that follow, which should have dispelled from the outset the erroneous idea that cognitivism excludes the realm of the social from its purview: "Comprehension and interpretation thus involve the *construction* of meaning out of textual cues. In this respect, meaning-making is a psychological and social activity fundamentally akin to other cognitive processes."[19] Second, in *Narrative Comprehension and Film*, Edward Branigan elaborated upon Bordwell's initial work on narrative comprehension, making further use of schema theory in particular. Thus, by 1992, one initial set of research questions regarding perception, comprehension, and interpretation had been established and investigated.

There is a clear mesh between cognitivism's initial research project and the cognitive science literature of the period, which saw the mind in largely computational terms and focused centrally on "cold cognition," or, information-driven mental processes. More specifically, the accounts of perception, comprehension, and interpretation offered by Bordwell and Branigan were indebted to **constructivist psychology**. In Bordwell's words, "According to Constructivist theory, perceiving and thinking are active, goal-oriented processes ... Sensory stimuli alone cannot determine a percept, since they are incomplete and ambiguous. The organism *constructs* a perceptual judgment on the basis of nonconscious inferences."[20] On this view, inference-making occurs in either a bottom-up or top-down fashion. In the former case, the inference is formed primarily on the basis of perceptual input; Bordwell suggests color perception is a good example of bottom-up inference-making. In the latter, the inference is formed against a background of expectations and hypotheses; Bordwell's example here is scanning the faces in crowd in search of a friend. "Both bottom-up and top-down processing are inferential," Bordwell claims, "in that perceptual 'conclusions' about the stimulus are drawn, often inductively, on the basis of 'premises' furnished by the data, by internalized rules, or by prior knowledge."[21] Another key concept in constructivist psychology is the "schema" (pl. schemata), which is, in Branigan's words, "an arrangement of knowledge *already possessed* by a perceiver that is used to predict and classify new sensory data."[22] That is, schemata are structures of prior knowledge that guide the hypothesis-making involved in top-down processing. In navigating the public transportation system in a new city, for example, one draws upon a schema comprising information one has acquired from previous experiences with public transportation. One hypothesizes, for example, that a metro card or, at least, loose change is probably necessary to board a rush-hour bus. Thus, for Bordwell and Branigan, schemata figure centrally in the comprehension of film narrative, since they involve the viewer's knowledge of genre, story structure, and other sorts of narrative conventions.

One important reaction to the early focus on inference-making and hypothesis-forming, both in cognitive science and film and media cognitivism, was to supplement this constructivist-oriented work with new research initiatives focused on "hot cognition," or affect-driven mental processes. Perhaps the first major book to offer a substantive analysis of emotion in the cinema was Carroll's *The Philosophy of Horror*, which subtly analyzed both the paradox of fiction (we feel emotions about things we know are not real) and the paradox of horror (we take pleasure in being scared) in cognitive terms.[23] By the mid-1990s, pioneering studies such as Smith's *Engaging Characters*, Tan's *Emotion and the Structure of Narrative Film*, and Torben Grodal's *Moving Pictures* indicated the establishment of a distinct research project on the relationship between film, cognition, and emotion, the various strands of which are well represented in Carl Plantinga and Greg M. Smith's edited collection, *Passionate Views: Film, Cognition, and Emotion*.[24] An important feature of this work is the understanding of **emotion** not as unconscious, irrational, or opposed to cognition, but as deeply intertwined with it. Although the term "emotion" has multiple meanings just as "naturalism" does, cognitivists typically reserve it to refer to a process by which feelings (including changes to one's physiological state *and* what one feels in a subjective, consciously felt sense) arise from cognitive appraisals and result in apposite behavior. So, for example, having lost sight of my son in a crowd, my heart races and my palms sweat; I immediately start scanning the scene around me and shouting his name: I am overcome with fear.

This moderate cognitive account of emotion still recognizes the importance of non-cognitive **affect**. Indeed, affect, understood in a broad sense described by Carl Plantinga as "any felt bodily state … including emotions, moods, reflex actions, autonomic responses, mirror reflexes, desires, pleasures, etc.," has been of topic of recent interest to cognitivists.[25] Greg M. Smith's *Film Structure and the Emotion System* draws upon research in neuropsychology to investigate the ways in which films cue general moods, which, in turn, orient viewers for the purposes of eliciting specific emotions.[26] Plantinga's own *Moving Viewers* offers a broad theory of "affect-elicitation" in the cinema, which includes responses such as affective mimicry and emotional contagion as well as emotion in the narrower sense of the term.[27] Roughly, affective mimicry and emotional contagion describe the phenomena of "catching" the affective states of others in an automatic, preconscious fashion. It is worth noting here that such automatic, preconscious affective dimensions of film viewing, which also include, for example, the startle response, are not beyond the purview of cognitivism when *cognition* is understood in a sufficiently inclusive sense—neither necessarily opposed to emotion nor necessarily involving consciousness or higher-order rationality.

As Plantinga argues, "Cognition is not separate from affect and bodily processes; rather, affect and bodily processes are aspects of cognition."[28] Indeed, few contemporary cognitivists would deny that cognition is fundamentally embodied.

Cognitivists' recent interest in preconscious affective phenomena like emotional contagion has coincided with greater attention to the part of the body thought to be primarily responsible for them—namely, the brain. In film studies, Grodal's *Embodied Visions* represents the most extended engagement with neuropsychology, but cognitive theorists increasingly cite relevant literature in the brain sciences, and neuroscientists themselves have sought to collaborate with film scholars on projects such as Shimamura's *Psychocinematics*.[29] This trend is, of course, not specific to film and media studies, but can be seen across the humanities and popular culture. The debate about whether developments in neuroscience will generate an unprecedented understanding of human life, practices, and values, or will merely fan the flames of "neuromania" is one in which important subtleties are often lost, but it does have an important parallel in contemporary cognitivism. Given the broad ways in which I have characterized cognition and the cognitive approach, it is perhaps unsurprising that the film and media scholars do not always agree with the psychologists, who do not always agree with the philosophers about what role research in each of these respective fields ought to play in answering a given research question.

But perhaps what is most promising about contemporary cognitivism is its ability to "triangulate" the evidence presented by each sort of inquiry—an idea advanced by Murray Smith. As Smith explains,

> At the heart of triangulation is the principle that at the outset of enquiry we take seriously … three levels of analysis with their attendant types of evidence … that we have at our disposal with respect to mental phenomena: the phenomenological level (what, if anything, if feels like when we undertake some mental act), the psychological level (what sorts of psychological capacities and functions our minds seem to possess), and the neurological level (what seems to be happening in the brain when we exercise these capacities).[30]

In this passage, Smith is discussing aesthetic experience, but it is easy enough to see how this approach would be applied to a mental phenomenon involved in film viewing. Elsewhere I have suggested

Margrethe Bruun Vaage's work on character engagement serves as a good example. As Vaage's work attests, explaining the elicitation of, say, sympathy for an ostensibly evil television character like Walter White from *Breaking Bad* plausibly involves triangulating three different sorts of inquiry, types of evidence, and levels of explanation: we need the psychological level to account for how we recognize and build emotional affinities with Walter, we need the neurological level to understand some of the low-level, automatic ways in which we "catch" Walter's emotions (even when we know that, rationally, we should not sympathize with him), and we need an account that respects the phenomena that we set out to explain—namely, how we can, in a qualitative sense, *feel* so sympathetic towards a fictional character (and a deeply morally flawed one at that).[31] Finally, it is worth noting that, as Vaage's work attests, contemporary cognitivism has expanded its purview to a broader range of media objects including television, videogames, (still and moving) digital photography, and so forth.

Case Study: Long-Running Gags in Serial Television Comedy

As suggested by the preceding discussion, there are a number of ways one could take a cognitive approach to the analysis of a particular media object depending on one's disciplinary background and the research question one is trying to answer. Because I tend to take a philosophical approach to the study of media, the sort of cognitivist analysis I do is very different from that which might be performed by a trained psychologist doing empirical research. Yet because cognitivism is often identified solely with the latter activity, there may be value in emphasizing the former in this context.

In my recent book, *Appreciating the Art of Television: A Philosophical Perspective*, I take up a number of broad theoretical questions about what is involved in appreciating television as an art form.[32] One immediate question is, of course, whether television is an art form at all. Answering "yes" need not commit one to the implausible thesis that *all* instances of television are art; rather, the thesis I advance is that *some* instances of television are artworks of a particular, appreciative kind distinctive from works of film. (It is relatively uncontroversial to suppose what I am claiming for television is also true of film; film is an art form not because all instances of film are art—they're not—but because instances that are art constitute a distinct, appreciative category.)

I advance my argument by first asserting an underlying premise regarding the conditions that need to be satisfied to show that television is an art form and then working through three sorts of examples that I claim demonstrate that they are indeed satisfied. The premise is borrowed from the philosopher of film Berys Gaut, who puts it this way: "For a medium to constitute an art form it must instantiate artistic properties that are distinct from those that are instantiated by other media."[33] I don't argue for this claim; I simply assume it is *prima facie* plausible. (I do argue that television is a medium in a particular sense of that term, but I won't rehearse that argument here.) I then describe three ways in which the medium of television is able to instantiate distinctive (from film, that is) artistic properties in virtue of its particular temporality.

The medium of television can be understood as distinct from the medium of film partly in virtue of a "standard" feature I call temporal prolongation. "Standard" here is used in the sense first articulated by the philosopher Kendall Walton in his ground-breaking essay, "Categories of Art."[34] By categorizing properties as "standard," "variable," and "contra-standard" relative to a particular category of art, Walton offers a way for us to conceive of relative categorical differences without falling prey to the errors of essentialism—that is, the view that media or art forms are defined in virtue of a timeless unchanging essence constituted by a unique property or cluster of properties. "Temporal prolongation" is a term from music theory connoting a temporally unfolding yet organically unified structure. I use it to refer to the various ways in which a television work's temporal boundaries may be diffuse and expansive. So, the idea here is that temporal prolongation is a standard feature of the television medium that differentiates it from the medium of film, but this need not commit us to medium essentialism.

In *Appreciating the Art of Television,* I argue that comedy is one context in which we can observe temporal prolongation instantiating artistic features and eliciting artistic effects that distinguish television from film. Temporal prolongation furnishes comedy series with a particular pairing of artistic device and artistic effect—the running gag and the comic amusement it elicits. More specifically, temporal prolongation provides television series with the ability to foreshadow gags far in advance, sometimes on multiple occasions, to keep gags running over extended periods of time, and to interweave running gags. In what follows, I elaborate upon this argument, attempting to add a bit of detail and support to the version of it published in my book.

However, I need to head off an immediate objection. Of course, it is not the case that running gags are unique to television comedy. One classic example from film, mentioned in Steve Neale and Frank Krutnik's *Popular Film and Television Comedy*, involves Groucho and Harpo Marx on the motorbike and side-car in *Duck Soup* (1933). In the first two iterations of the gag, Groucho is sitting in the sidecar and Harpo speeds away on the motorcycle. The third time, Harpo gestures Groucho towards the sidecar, but the latter protests: "Oh, no you don't. I'm not taking any more chances." Harpo hops into the sidecar and Groucho mounts the motorcycle. But after he revs the engine, it is the sidecar that accelerates, leaving Groucho behind once again. Furthermore, Neale and Krutnik accurately note that in many Buster Keaton pictures, including *The General* (1926) and *College* (1927), part of the humor derives from the fact that "gags and situations are systematically repeated, but the second time round they are symmetrically inverted or reversed so as to result in triumphant success."[35] And one could enumerate many more examples.

While this objection might have force against a medium essentialist who claims that running gags are unique to television, it does not imperil my more moderate thesis that the differential feature of temporal prolongation allows television to instantiate running gags that appear to be structurally different from running gags in film Here one might wonder what this putative structural difference amounts to in terms of artistic effects. It would be specious, I think, to suggest that the structural difference makes running gags in television funnier than running gags in film *tout court*. However, I think the structural difference of running gags in television generates at least one more artistic effect that is modest yet distinctive; such gags afford cognitive pleasure of a different order than that provided by running gags in film.

The cognitive pleasure afforded by running gags in television is *not*, to be sure, entirely dissimilar to the pleasure afforded by the simple set-up–payoff structure that is ubiquitous in film comedy. Both sorts of pleasures fall under the broader category of comic amusement or mirth—an emotional state characterized by pleasure and laughter.[36] The term "emotional state" is used here in a semi-technical sense to indicate that pleasure and laughter associated with comic amusement arise from the perception and cognition of some object or event. This is because, according to many emotion researchers, emotions involve both the perception of some object and the cognitive appraisal of its relationship to one's goals or well-being.[37] Somewhat more technically, Carroll claims,

> comic amusement is an emotion that is aimed at particular objects ... which meet certain criteria, where such appraisals then eventuate in enjoyment and an experience of levity which itself correlates with increased activation of the reward network of the limbic system in the brain.[38]

For example, the comic amusement furnished by the ending of *Caddyshack* (1980) stems from the cognitive pleasure we take in seeing the golf course blown up (thus inching a short putt forward just enough to win the game for our heroes) as a result of Carl Spackler's increasingly intemperate attempts to rid the grounds of gophers, which we have tracked since early on in the film. Similarly, the comic amusement elicited at the end of a Buster Keaton film like *The General* involves a kind of cognitive pleasure derived from our observation that "the symmetrical structure of the plot" creates parallels between gags in the first half of the film (which result in pratfalls) and gags towards the end of the film (which, incongruously, allow our hero to demonstrate his competence).[39]

In contrast to these film comedy structures, television's temporal prolongation allows for both set-up and payoff to be distributed over more time and repeated on multiple occasions. In part, this is because television series are created progressively such that the writing staff can devise new ways to work old gags into additional episodes and, more interestingly, can concoct gags with set-ups that are only established post-hoc—i.e. gags that initially served as set-ups for *other* gags or that were not initially conceived as set-ups at all.

All of this has consequences for our appreciation of television comedy. My contention is that identifying a gag as set up by a series of events, which occur on several different occasions over an extended period of time, deepens the cognitive pleasure it affords. So, too, I think, does the fact that the payoff comes not once—at a more or less expected point in the narrative such as the ending—but over and over again at unexpected moments and in unexpected ways. If one accepts the plausible claim that comic amusement "comes about in virtue of *cognition* of [some object],"[40] then it is a short step to concluding that objects that furnish deeper or greater cognitive pleasure will tend to elicit deeper or greater comic amusement. Here we can draw upon recent scientifically grounded philosophical work on humor that posits a close connection between mirth and problem-solving or discovery: Matthew Hurley, Daniel Dennett, and Reginald Adams characterize mirth as "the pleasure in unearthing a particular variety of mistake in active belief structures."[41] In other words, there is reason to think that what underlies comic amusement is not merely the cognition of an object, but a pleasure afforded by the cognitive achievement of solving a kind of problem or puzzle. In the case of television comedy, this amounts to tracking and recognizing complex and temporally diffuse running gags—an activity that plausibly involves more of a cognitive workout than following running gags in film and thus results in more of a payoff: deeper comic amusement.

Consider, first, a structurally simple example: one of the better-known gags from *Curb Your Enthusiasm* (HBO, 2000–) is Larry's stare-down of people he (erroneously) believes have lied to him. As a helpful chart by Sean Petranovich demonstrates, the stare-down originated in season two, as a stand-alone gag, when Larry deployed it against his acupuncturist in an attempt to discern whether orchids are a traditional Japanese gift from a man.[42] However, in the ninth episode of season three, the gag is revisited and amplified. Accompanied by a non-diegetic musical motif, Larry stares down not one but three people—not coincidentally, all of whom are in low-wage service jobs: a waiter, his landscaper, and his housekeeper. Thereafter, the gag appears at least once in every season and, in all but one case, in multiple episodes in each season. Part of the cognitive pleasure of the gag, then, derives from its longevity, but also from the various ways in which it is able to

be instantiated thanks to the temporal prolongation of television. In "The Larry David Sandwich," from the fifth season, Larry's stare-down of his own father is funny in its own right, but a special cognitive pleasure—and, arguably, deeper comic amusement—is available to viewers who recall that, characteristically, Larry deploys the stare-down against people to whom he imagines himself superior. In season seven, the gag is inverted such that Larry *receives* the stare-down from Mr. Takahashi in one episode and Jerry Seinfeld in another. Again, the gag here is funny in its own right, but a special cognitive pleasure is furnished by the way in which it is inverted after we have seen it run for such a long period of time.

Turning to *Arrested Development* will allow us to see how television's temporal prolongation can be used to devise running gags of more structural complexity, which, again engenders cognitive pleasures not available from film comedy. Let's start with the running gag of Buster's back rubs, which is established in the pilot episode. Arguably, there's nothing particularly funny about this gag, which is first repeated in the third episode, beyond Buster's general social awkwardness—even around his family members. Starting in the fourth episode, the gag is amplified with a catchphrase involving Buster's tendency to refer to people by their relationships to him rather than by their names (for example, "Hey, brother!").

Perhaps surprisingly, these few basic gags are enough to make things very interesting after some additional narrative development afforded by temporal prolongation. Apparently unrelatedly, we are

Figure 13.1 Jerry returns Larry's stare-down in "Seinfeld," the season finale of season seven of *Curb Your Enthusiasm* (HBO, original airdate November 22, 2009)

introduced to J. Walter Weatherman in the tenth episode and Oscar Bluth in the twentieth episode. Weatherman, who only has one arm, was enlisted by George Bluth to teach his children various "important" lessons by pretending to lose his arm as a result of their various oversights such as "forgetting to leave a note." Weatherman's "loss" of his arm becomes important later. So too does episode twenty's introduction of Oscar Bluth, the twin brother of George Bluth and the (apparent) uncle of the Bluth children—Michael, G.O.B., Lindsay, and Buster. In this episode, Buster's backrub and catchphrase gags are repeated and, in a sense, amplified by Oscar greeting Michael with "Hey, nephew!" and a backrub. But the payoff comes later, when we discover that Oscar is Buster's biological father (hence the similarity of behavior), which, as one can imagine becomes its own running gag from this point forward. However, once *all* of these gags have been established, a further payoff for the initial backrub gag is achieved in one brilliant moment in the second season episode "Hand to God." After having his hand bitten off by a seal, Buster is fitted with a hook. Attempting to give Oscar a backrub, Buster accidentally impales him with the hook. "I'm a monster!" he screams later.

The point here is that part of the cognitive pleasure—and thus comic amusement—afforded by television comedies like *Arrested Development* is only possible due to the differential feature of temporal prolongation. The cognitive pleasure we get from gags like those described above stems from the ways in which the temporal expansion of a series

allows television comedies to devise payoffs for running gags on multiple occasions and in multiple ways. In particular, after the initial payoff of a running gag, the gag may be interwoven with others to realize an additional, amplified payoff down the line. There is a particular cognitive pleasure in perceiving how such gags are interwoven, catching moments where the set-up seems to be established, anticipating how the payoff will be implemented, and, once the payoff has been realized, reflecting back on the structural choices made to set it up.[43]

Conclusion

As I hope the preceding discussion has indicated, cognitive media analysis can be conducted at any number of levels of specificity depending upon a scholar's background training and her research questions. In my own philosophically inflected work, I tend to explore broad theoretical questions from a cognitivist perspective in two senses: (1) My work proceeds from cognitivist assumptions regarding the naturalistic understanding of the mental operations of viewers—including the frequent convergence of viewers' cognitive and emotional responses; and (2) I draw upon empirical research by psychologists and empirically based work by film theorists to support my claims when appropriate. However, cognitivism, broadly construed, comprises all three of these research strands—work that is oriented towards analytic philosophy, the psychological sciences, and film/media studies. The cognitivist

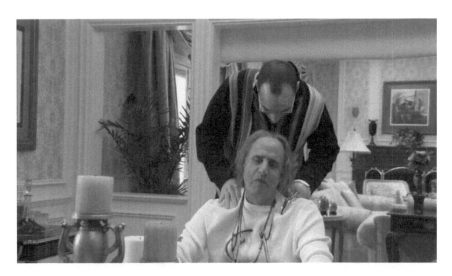

Figure 13.2 Buster forgets about his hook and tries to give Uncle Oscar a back rub in "Hand to God," episode twelve of season two of *Arrested Development* (Fox, original airdate March 6, 2005)

analysis of media may use any of the methods characteristic of these fields depending on the nature of the research question posed.

The future of cognitivism is therefore tied to the ways in which these three research strands will be further integrated (or not). One increasingly visible research program within cognitivism draws upon neuroscientific research. Encouragingly, at least some neuroscientists, like Shimamura and Vittorio Gallese, are also actively working with film and media scholars so that the flow of knowledge and understanding moves both ways.[44] Perhaps surprisingly, this interdisciplinary exchange has also put cognitivism in closer dialogue with work in film and media studies that is heavily influenced by philosophy in the Continental tradition—in particular, work by Maurice Merleau-Ponty, Henri Bergson, and Giles Deleuze.[45] Another recent research area that has brought cognitivism and Continentally oriented film and media studies together is ethics.[46] This is particularly interesting because perhaps the biggest unanswered question about cognitivism's future direction is whether it can (or should) inform out understanding of axiological questions—that is, questions about value—and, if so, how.

Notes

1. Ted Nannicelli and Paul Taberham, "Introduction: Contemporary Cognitive Media Theory," in *Cognitive Media Theory*, eds. Ted Nannicell and Paul Taberham (New York: Routledge, 2014), 4.
2. Noël Carroll, *Humour: A Very Short Introduction* (Oxford: Oxford University Press, 2014), 17.
3. Noël Carroll, "The Power of Movies," reprinted in *Theorizing the Moving Image* (1985; Cambridge: Cambridge University Press, 1996), 92.
4. David Bordwell, *Narration in the Fiction Film* (Madison: University of Wisconsin Press, 1985), 29.
5. David Bordwell, "A Case for Cognitivism," *Iris* 9 (1989): 11–41.
6. Hugo Münsterberg, *The Photoplay: A Psychological Study* (New York: Dover, 1970), 29.
7. It is also worth noting that British media studies scholars were pushing back against subject-position theory at this time, albeit in rather different ways. In 1973 Stuart Hall published the first version of what came to be an influential theoretical account of the receiver's negotiation of meaning in media products, which in turn informed a number of qualitative audience studies in the 1980s. See Stuart Hall, "Encoding and Decoding in Television Discourse," *University of Birmingham Centre for Contemporary Cultural Studies Stenciled Occasional Paper Series* no. 7 (Birmingham, 1973), accessed July 31, 2017, www.birmingham.ac.uk/Documents/college-artslaw/history/cccs/stencilled-occasional-papers/1to8and11to24and38to48/SOP07.pdf; Charlotte Brunsdon, *Everyday Television—'Nationwide'* (London: BFI, 1978); and David Morley, *The 'Nationwide' Audience: Structure and Decoding* (London: BFI, 1980).
8. Percy H. Tannenbaum, ed., *The Entertainment Functions of Television* (1980; New York: Psychology Press, 2014).
9. See David Bordwell, "Poetics of Cinema," in *Poetics of Cinema* (New York: Routledge, 2008), 11–55.
10. See Kristin Thompson, *Breaking the Glass Armor: Neoformalist Film Criticism* (Princeton: Princeton University Press, 1988).
11. Gregory Currie, *Image and Mind: Film, Philosophy, and Cognitive Science* (Cambridge: Cambridge University Press, 1995).
12. See, for a paradigmatic expression of this sort of view in film studies, Stephen Health, *Questions of Cinema* (London: Macmillan, 1980).
13. David Bordwell and Noël Carroll, ed., *Post-Theory: Reconstructing Film Studies* (Madison: University of Wisconsin Press, 1996).
14. Murray Smith, *Engaging Characters: Fiction, Emotion, and the Cinema* (Oxford: Oxford University Press, 1995); Ed Tan, *Emotion and the Structure of Narrative Film: Film as an Emotion Machine* (Mahwah: Lawrence Erlbaum Associates, 1996).
15. Arthur P. Shimamura, ed., *Psychocinematics: Exploring Cognition at the Movies* (Oxford: Oxford University Press, 2013); Paisley Livingston and Carl Plantinga, eds., *The Routledge Companion to Film and Philosophy* (New York: Routledge, 2009); Nannicelli and Taberham, *Cognitive Media Theory*.
16. Quoted in Nannicelli and Taberham, *Cognitive Media Theory*, 8.
17. Quoted in Nannicelli and Taberham, *Cognitive Media Theory*, 9
18. David Bordwell, *Making Meaning* (Cambridge: Harvard University Press, 1989), 3.
19. Ibid.
20. Bordwell, *Narration in the Fiction Film*, 31.
21. Ibid.
22. Edward Branigan, *Narrative Comprehension and Film* (New York: Routledge, 1992), 13.
23. Noël Carroll, *The Philosophy of Horror, or Paradoxes of the Heart* (New York: Routledge, 1990).
24. Smith, *Engaging Characters*; Tan, *Emotion and the Structure of Narrative Film*; Torben Grodal, *Moving Pictures: A New Theory of Film Genres, Feelings, and Cognition* (Oxford: Oxford University Press, 1997); Carl Plantinga and Greg M. Smith, eds., *Passionate Views: Film, Cognition, and Emotion* (Baltimore: The Johns Hopkins University Press, 1999).
25. Carl Plantinga, "Emotion and Affect," in Livingston and Plantinga, 87.

26. Greg M. Smith, *Film Structure and the Emotion System* (Cambridge: Cambridge University Press, 2003).

27. Carl Plantinga, *Moving Viewers: American Film and the Spectator's Experience* (Berkeley: University of California Press, 2009).

28. Carl Plantinga, "Putting Cognition in its Place: Affect and the Experience of Narrative Film," in *Current Controversies in Philosophy of Film*, ed. Katherine Thomson-Jones (New York: Routledge, 2016), 131–147.

29. Torben Grodal, *Embodied Visions: Evolution, Emotion, Culture and Film* (Oxford: Oxford University Press, 2009); Shimamura, *Psychocinematics*.

30. Murray Smith, "Triangulating Aesthetic Experience," in *Aesthetic Science: Connecting Minds, Brains, and Experience*, eds. Arthur Shimamura and Stephen Palmer (Oxford: Oxford University Press, 2013), 83. Smith borrows the triangulation metaphor from Owen Flanagan, *Consciousness Reconsidered* (Cambridge: MIT Press, 1992).

31. See Nannicelli and Taberham, *Cognitive Media Theory*, 15–17. Also see, Margrethe Bruun Vaage, "Blinded by Familiarity: Partiality, Morality, and Engagement with Television Series," in Nannicelli and Taberham, 268–54; and Margrethe Bruun Vaage, *The Antihero in American Television* (New York: Routledge, 2016).

32. Ted Nannicelli, *Appreciating the Art of Television: A Philosophical Perspective* (Routledge, 2017).

33. Berys Gaut, *A Philosophy of Cinematic Art* (Cambridge: Cambridge University Press, 2010), 287.

34. Kendall Walton, "Categories of Art," reprinted in *Marvelous Images* (1970; Oxford: Oxford University Press, 2008), 195–219.

35. Steve Neale and Frank Krutnik, *Popular Film and Television Comedy* (London: Routledge, 1990), 59.

36. Although the concept of comic amusement (or mirth) is contested, this characterization is intended to be fairly neutral. It is especially influenced by Jerrold Levinson, "The Concept of Humor," in *Contemplating Art* (Oxford: Oxford University Press, 2006), 389–99.

37. See, for a popular scientific account, Antonio R. Damasio, *Descartes' Error: Emotion, Reason, and the Human Brain* (New York: Grosset/Putnam, 1994), 127–64. For an alternative, empirically informed philosophical account of emotions, see Jesse J. Prinz, *Gut Reactions: A Perceptual Theory of Emotion: A Perceptual Theory of Emotions* (Oxford: Oxford University Press, 2004). As the subtitle of Prinz's book indicates, he breaks with Damasio and other researchers who maintain emotions have a cognitive component.

38. Carroll, *Humour*, 5.

39. Noël Carroll, *Comedy Incarnate: Buster Keaton, Physical Humor, and Bodily Coping* (Malden: Blackwell, 2009), 170.

40. Levinson, "The Concept of Humor," 396.

41. Matthew M. Hurley, Daniel C. Dennett, and Reginald B. Adams, Jr., *Inside Jokes: Using Humor to Reverse-Engineer the Mind* (Cambridge: MIT Press, 2011), 117.

42. Sean Petranovich, "How to Philosophize with a 5 Wood," in *Curb Your Enthusiasm and Philosophy*, ed. Mark Ralkowski (Chicago: Carus Publishing, 2012), 184–85.

43. In the case of particularly long-running and/or self-aware television comedies, this latter process may be extensive indeed: National Public Radio hosts just one of the websites devoted to mapping out the set-ups and call-backs to *Arrested Development*'s diverse array of running gags. In relation to the gags I discussed above, one might note that prior to Buster's loss of his hand, there are a variety of ways in which the incident is foreshadowed, even though they are too subtle to constitute part the of set-up. Thus, viewers are afforded additional cognitive pleasure by recalling what appeared to be inconsequential moments from much earlier in the series, such as Buster saying, "This party is going to be off the hook," and a camera pan to a shot of Buster during a television news report of seal attack. See Jeremy Bowers et al., "Previously, On Arrested Development," *NPR.org*, May 18, 2013, accessed July 31, 2017, http://apps.npr.org/arrested-development/.

44. In addition to Shimamura, *Psychocinematics*, see Vittorio Gallese and Michele Guerra, "Embodying Movies: Embodied Simulation and Film Studies," *Cinema: Journal of Philosophy and the Moving Image* 3 (2012): 183–210, accessed February 23, 2018, http://cjpmi.ifil-nova.pt/3-contents.

45. See the additional essays comprising the above-cited 2012 special issue of *Cinema: Journal of Philosophy and the Moving Image*, which is devoted to "Embodiment and the Body" and edited by Patrícia Silveirinha Castello Branco, as well as *Cinéma & Cie: International Film Studies Journal* 22–23 (Spring/Fall 2014), which is a special issue dedicated to "Neurofilmology: Audiovisual Studies and the Challenge of Neuroscience" and edited by Adriano D'Aloia and Ruggero Eugeni.

46. See Robert Sinnerbrink, *Cinematic Ethics: Exploring Ethical Experience Through Film* (New York: Routledge, 2016); and Carl Plantinga, *Screen Stories: Emotion and the Ethics of Engagement* (Oxford: Oxford University Press, 2018).

Further Reading

Anderson, Joseph. *The Reality of Illusion: An Ecological Approach to Cognitive Film Theory*. Carbondale: Southern Illinois University Press, 1996.

Carroll, Noël. *Engaging the Moving Image*. New Haven: Yale University Press, 2003.

Hogan, Patrick Colm. *Cognitive Science, Literature, and the Arts: A Guide for Humanists*. New York: Routledge, 2003.

Smith, Murray. *Film, Art, and the Third Culture: A Naturalized Aesthetics of Film*. Oxford: Oxford University Press, 2017.

14.
ETHNOGRAPHY
Jessa Lingel and Mary L. Gray

This chapter considers the value of ethnographic approaches to media studies. It sets up a working definition of **ethnography** as both a methodological practice and analytic framework. Through discussion of a case study looking at queer youth and their media engagements, we demonstrate how ethnography can offer media scholars a way to expand the field. We argue that ethnography is well-suited to addressing a specific tension between a push for objective neutrality in reporting human activity and a pull to produce grounded research that engages with the holistic experiences of participants.

Overview

What is ethnography and why use it as a mode of media analysis? This chapter reflects on how theories of production and media effect change when we consider people's engagements with media, beyond a moment of creation or reception. Research driven by observation and participation, a long-standing practice in anthropology and qualitative sociology, generates interpretations of not only the media texts in question but also the ebb and flow of how those texts are taken up in people's daily lives and their pleasures with media, including disagreements and disregard for scholarly takes on their experiences. The chapter also makes a case for why communication scholars might benefit from the ethical dilemmas and contingencies that come with engaging living, breathing humans as a way to understand the everyday experiences and material conditions of media production, consumption, and circulation.

One way to define ethnography is by what it does *not* do. Ethnographic approaches are decidedly not about "getting the facts on the ground" or finding out "what's really going on" in a particular social setting. As Tom Boellstorff, Bonnie Nardi, Celia Pearce, and T. L. Taylor argue, ethnography is an approach best suited to generating theory through interpreting people's expressed experiences of the world.[1] Janet Staiger notes that ethnographic methods are essentially textual analysis of human cultural practices.[2] Ethnography assembles and interprets interviews, field notes from observations of media production and consumption, popular discourse about our objects of study, and our participation in cultural practices. For most questions, ethnography cannot be done rapidly. Its value comes from the slow boil of looking at several moving targets—people, interactions, texts—to see how they collude and collide. Time is crucial to ethnography because only time's passing shuffles circumstances enough to provide a sense of the norms surrounding people's engagements with media and what is taken for granted one moment to the next. Ethnography requires time, but it also requires space or, in fact, multiple spaces; ethnography, to riff on renowned linguistic anthropologist Keith Basso, cannot easily sit in one place.[3] An individual's effort to make sense and meaning rarely happens in one locale, in the absence of others, or thoughts of the world around us. Our own sense of ethnography is indebted to its anthropological roots and sensibilities. We see ethnography as both a framework and set of practices for investigating how people make sense of their world and place in it through a co-produced, reflective archive of shared conversations, silences, and exchanges. We value ethnography for its capacity to create a shared index of what we, otherwise, ignore or dismiss in the quotidian passing of time.

As Mary Beltrán argues in Chapter 8 of this collection, representations reflect the confluence of larger social histories, systems of privilege, and hegemonic norms defining what or who counts as "typical." Ethnography uniquely equips media scholars to move beyond stylistic or moral evaluations of "good" or "bad" representations. Ethnographic materials offer researchers an analytical framework for media's cultural meanings—to consider what individuals "do" with media representations under different conditions and over time. Ethnographic studies of media, then, offer the field a chance to rethink the complexities of core debates, from cultivation theory[4] to theories of uses and gratifications[5] and media's role in formations of notions of the self. Media ethnographers turn to the people caught up in processes of media representation to ask, who is being represented here, with what authority and with what possibilities for revision? From these assessments, the ethnographer builds theory to generate new questions about how the world works in relation to media cultures. The ethnographer can then suggest possibilities for new ways of occupying the world that better account for the mediation that shapes and is shaped by us.

The most pressing discussions and productive disagreements that shape how scholars conduct ethnographic work come from ongoing debates about what counts as ethnographic study and what ethnography offers us beyond descriptive narratives. What are the benchmarks of this approach? How can we bring ethnography in as an interpretive, critical approach to expand how we understand (and improve) the world through media studies? We offer some reflections on Mary Gray's research, illustrating the strengths and challenges of ethnography as framework and practice. We use these reflections to suggest how to shape a future of critical ethnographic praxis—an interweaving of positionality, practice, and theory—in media studies. We argue that ethnographically grounded media studies require, first and foremost, de-centering media as the unit of analysis. Focusing on media as the central object or core text can quickly obscure the key elements that drive ethnographic inquiry, namely the interactions and social processes among people, technologies, and their contexts that give meaning to media. Ethnography allows media studies to move beyond a specific moment of engagement in production or consumption to consider how media become meaningful, and the political, social, and historical conditions that prime media as sites of cultural exchange and power.

Intellectual History of the Concept

Several fields claim ethnography as a primary methodological practice, particularly the humanistic social sciences of anthropology and qualitative sociology. Ethnography stands as a defining feature and core element of not just the methodological toolkit of these intellectual traditions but also as their analytic framework. Ethnography's critical forebears saw this method as a way to salvage cultural practices that appeared to be vanishing in the wake of colonialism[6] or had been rendered invisible because they were seen as the deviant acts of a social underworld.[7] Even disciplines that are somewhat removed from "field science" approaches to social and cultural behavior, such as psychology and human computer interaction, have recently adopted elements of ethnography.[8] The most relevant voices with something to teach media scholars and others interested in drawing on ethnographic sensibilities hail from anthropology and qualitative sociology. They would argue that ethnography must involve a transparent effort to engage individuals as theorists with whom we collaborate rather than passive texts or subjects we study from a distance. Ethnography is at its finest when its practitioners (1) contend with the role of the researcher/reflexivity debates, by sharing how their presence shapes what can be known about the practices under analysis; (2) define their relationship to activism and research vs. practice debates by explicitly telling readers the actionable lessons offered through their analysis; and (3) address methodological debates about empirical value by holding the scholarship to the demands of systematic, longitudinal observation and participation, while at the same time accepting that no body of evidence is ahistorical or outside of the power dynamics that produce it.

Contemporary ethnography, as an interpretative praxis, resonates with poststructuralist critiques of power offered by, among others, Antonio Gramsci[9] and the Frankfurt School.[10] These critiques challenge epistemologies that make universal truth claims by drawing clear lines between cause and effect. They presume that power dynamics and tensions among institutional, social, and historical forces continuously collide, pool, ebb, and flow, shaping and being shaped by individuals and their cultural milieu along the way. As such, ethnography resists fact-checking how things "really are." Instead, its practitioners strive to build theories about how groups of people see the world and come to understand their place and possibilities in it. Ethnographers come to their conclusions through close attention and interrogation of the histories, goings-on, and prognostications encountered as they navigate the day-to-day with research participants.

Attention to the circulations of power, and hierarchies that fracture and billow out from them, pushes ethnography into interdisciplinary conversations that draw on sociology, postcolonial studies, gender studies, anthropology, and science and technology studies. Ethnography disrupts a model of media flows that assumes the intentions of a producer or author make it to the consumer, audience, or end user in a hermetically sealed box. It defies presumptions that media can, in and of themselves, produce predictably uniform effects on those who engage it. Media scholars, with the notable exceptions referenced above, have not widely adopted ethnography's analytical framework or its attending commitments to participant observation and the temporal and spatial dimensions of media engagement.

Major Modes and Terminology

As a method, ethnography is well-suited to studying both media producers and media consumers. Regarding the former, ethnographic practice allows for inquiry into the different means and practices underlying the technical operations of producing, circulating, and interpreting media. If we see media production as the work of a community of practice, meaning a group of people bound together by a shared understanding of how to do something, ethnography allows a researcher to understand how people live with and through media artifacts as well as how individuals value those artifacts within a specific context. For example, the early work of Hortense Powdermaker stands as one of the first (and only) ethnographies of the Hollywood studio system and the power of media moguls to control mainstream representations.[11] John T. Caldwell is perhaps best known in media studies for his pioneering, multi-sited ethnographic studies of television and film production and labor conditions that shaped content and scheduling in those industries.[12] Katherine Sender's critical analysis of the advertising and marketing strategies that gave rise to the coherency of a gay and lesbian audience and media market hinged on her deft use of ethnography to map the interplay between professionals in the marketing industry and their own identities as gay men and lesbians.[13] Ethnography is also well-suited

to the project of understanding media consumption, such as Ellen Seiter's early work exploring women's complex relationships to one-dimensional female stars in soap operas and children's creative reworking of stereotypical gender roles in cartoon characters.[14] More recently, Bonnie Nardi's ethnography of the video game, *World of Warcraft*, involved more than three years of playing this massively multi-player online role playing game (MMORPG), which included Nardi learning game-specific vocabulary and norms, as well as learning how to contribute to group activities like raids and barter exchanges.[15] Note that in the cases above, the specific media content is less important than how media are constructed, valued, and interpreted by those who create and interact with it. On a core level, for an ethnographer, the question is rarely, "What counts as media?" or "What different forms of media exist?" but rather, "What do particular groups of people call out as meaningful forms of media engagement?" "What makes these different forms important in these specific contexts of use?" and "How can we use relationships to media to understand larger issues and values of a group's practices and boundaries?"

A strength of ethnography as a method is its flexibility, in that the researcher shapes her methodological approach to fit her site of inquiry. There are, however, some key staples that are vital to any ethnographic practice. **Fieldwork**, or being "in the field," refers to time spent sharing space with one's participants. Crucially, this is time spent learning about one's participants and their surroundings, rather than time spent reading about related research or writing up results. Fieldwork builds a base of participants who will serve as the key theorists informing the ethnographer's arguments. **Participant observation** is the second core task of ethnographic work and involves bringing the researcher's careful attention to the actions, conversations, and habits of a particular group of people through their connections with the people they meet. This deep embodiment of the setting demands reflection on one's own engagements with those encountered through fieldwork. It is through participant observation that we learn what it means to participate in and be in relationship to groups of people for an extended period. Through it, we come to understand the values and ethics of the people we encounter as a series of operations and practices. A third core task of ethnography involves interviews, and more specifically, **open-ended interviews**. In contrast to highly-structured interviews or survey instruments, open-ended interviews follow the interview participant's lead in contesting how to interpret a given social phenomenon. Ethnographers ask the interviewee to probe and reflect on their understanding of a phenomenon's social and cultural meaning. Whether conducting fieldwork, participant observation, or open-ended interviews, an ethnographer produces and, ultimately, relies on **field notes** as a means of detailing what she experiences, organizing her observations and developing early-stage theories of her findings. Together, these different ethnographic lenses provide a holistic understanding of the everyday interactions that constitute a particular field site.

More quantitatively oriented researchers may harbor concerns that privileging the perspectives of participants limits the applicability of ethnographic work. We would make two points to address this concern of generalizability. First, rather than thinking of how generalized the findings of ethnography can be, we would do better to think of transferability, which refers to making connections between groups or subject positions. Ethnography as method and analytic framework demonstrates a way of making connections that extend beyond a particular research site, offering opportunities to generate new questions and build theories and hypotheses rather than land on generalizable results. Second, the question of generalizability belies a particular approach to academic inquiry that does not fit many of the meta-theoretical assumptions governing ethnography. Ethnography is polyvocal rather than universal, striving for the inclusion of multiple voices, experiences, and perspectives that cannot necessarily be rolled up into a set of generalizable claims about human behavior.

Perhaps most beguiling, ethnographic approaches come with distinct methodological expectations. We must commit to participants and locations, deeply investing in the time that it takes for media texts to seep into people's day-to-day. This commitment can conflict with media studies' predilections for quantifiable findings from a discrete moment of media consumption and formalist criticism of a text that can ignore how those interpretations square with people's quotidian media engagement. In the case study we discuss below, interdisciplinarity created a cross-epistemological dialogue needed to plumb the question, what difference do media representations make in a particular time and place?

Some immediate and pragmatic questions around doing ethnographic work include, how much time should one spend doing ethnographic fieldwork? Does one need to be physically present for all facets of the research? What does presence mean in the case of digital media studies? To start with the issue of how much time to spend in the field, while there's no magic number that works for every project, as we argued earlier, a sustained commitment to one's field site is crucial for the in-depth and holistic understanding at the root of all ethnographic work. In anthropology, twelve months is the conventional period of time to spend doing fieldwork—although in some cases it may be possible to conduct rigorous ethnographic work in a shorter time frame, it is difficult for us to imagine an ethnography with fewer than six months in the field. In many cases, ethnography demands time for one simple reason: it takes time to build the trust and rapport that one needs with participants to ask sensitive or complicated questions and delve into the meanings embedded in participants' responses. The less familiar the field site to the researcher, the more time an ethnographer likely needs to understand it. Often there are practical considerations that shape the ability to conduct fieldwork—a grant may expire, and there isn't enough money to stay in the field; demands of taking care of family members may take precedence over conducting additional research; the site being studied may change in some way that makes further research impossible. Leaving these important practical matters aside, **saturation** is the best way to determine when it's appropriate to transition from fieldwork to writing. Saturation refers to a kind of recursion or repetition in qualitative work broadly. When the same themes begin to emerge from interview after interview, when observation begins to feel predictable in terms of patterns and habits, a researcher becomes increasingly confident that she can begin the process of writing up her results. It's important to note that saturation is not the same thing as completion—it's impossible to craft a complete picture of any social phenomenon, and there will always be some unknown factors in a field site. Rather than a complete picture, saturation means that a researcher has come to understand the field so thoroughly that she has a multi-faceted understanding of her surroundings, an understanding that is saturated by the views and perspectives of many different stake-holders and subject positions. She can imagine whom she might have missed in her efforts to know who inhabits the terrain of her fieldwork.

Research on digital media presents some particular issues for what it means to be "present" in the field. Presence means spending time with one's participants, seeing what they see, hanging out where they hang out. As media studies researchers have turned their attention to online phenomena, they have encountered challenges related to planning research that encompasses both online and offline interactions. For researchers investigating "in world" digital communities—such as Boellstoerff's ethnography of *Second Life*[16] or Nardi's ethnography of *World of Warcraft* mentioned above[17]—researchers may never meet their participants in real life and all of their observations and interviews will be conducted online. For projects that seek to understand how online platforms are connected to offline life, or for researchers whose questions address real-life factors, such as one's physical surroundings and embodied reality, it may be necessary to spend time both online and offline. For example, both Pearce and Taylor[18] conducted ethnographies of online communities, but also went to in-person meet-ups, which provided important insights into how online norms and practices translated (or not) offline. At the other end of the spectrum, researchers may spend the majority of their fieldwork with participants in offline contexts, while also interacting with participants in online forums, or they might use participants' blogs and social media profiles as media artifacts that shape interview questions and analytical themes.[19] These different scenarios reveal a spectrum of how much time in the field is spent online versus off, but it is essential to understand that conducting part or all of one's fieldwork online should not be seen as an easier or less time-intensive form of ethnography. Researchers who conduct "in world" ethnographies are still beholden to the same standards of being present, which requires logging hundreds of hours in the field. We should also note that, as mobile technologies become increasingly popular as a means of accessing the Internet, the distinctions between online and offline practices are even more difficult to delineate.

Deciding how to situate oneself as an ethnographer in relation to a media platform (or indeed, several media platforms) brings us to an important consideration of positionality. Ethnographers approach research projects with specific investments in the field sites that we identify as rich or meaningful for empirical inquiry. Ethnographers have a long tradition of conducting work in places far removed from the researcher's home or lived experience. The conventional image of a researcher traveling to a distant land and returning from the field with insights of a distant people and culture is still pervasive. Throughout the late twentieth century, this trope shifted towards conducting ethnographies at sites much closer to a researcher's own experience, or even to studying one's own community. Whether one is conducting fieldwork in a far-off location or in one's own backyard, it is important to be explicit about one's investment in a particular field site.

Beyond acknowledging our positionality in terms of our investment in a research site, it is important to be reflexive and intentional about how we deploy our identities in fieldwork. Identifying oneself as connected to the group being studied can be an important gateway for establishing rapport and gaining participants' trust. At the same time, by virtue of the fact that ethnographers are approaching a community and place as a researcher, it is paramount that ethnographers also recognize that there is always a gap between ourselves and the people we study, even if we identify with them in significant ways. Ethnography traditionally conceptualizes this issue in terms of "going native," which refers to feeling so connected to a community that one loses a sense of distance from the people and sites being studied. This is one of the trickiest dilemmas of conducting ethnographic work: On the one hand, learning to see the world as our participants do is a hallmark of sustained engagement in the field, and it means that we have likely succeeded in learning how a community functions and identifying its key norms and values. On the other hand, every ethnographer eventually has to leave the field and return to an academic setting to write up her results, which requires an analytical distancing from the field. And, in fact, throughout the process of conducting fieldwork, ethnographers are always, to some degree, removed from their participants precisely because their primary reason for engaging with a range of individuals and communities is not participation as an end unto itself, but rather to gain an ethnographic understanding of the worlds her participants inhabit. The key to resolving this tension of belonging yet not belonging, seeing like a participant while being an ethnographer, is to remain reflexive and self-aware about one's relationship to what one is studying. One way to make sure that this process of self-evaluation is baked into the ethnographic process is to think of field notes as a consistent check-in process of one's positionality. Some ethnographers use a template for field notes that includes a section for reflecting on how the researcher has experienced any changes in relationships to participants,[20] effectively setting up a longitudinal process of reflexivity that can be used to trace positionality throughout the course of fieldwork.

Case Study: Media Ethnography in Practice

Gray's ethnographic studies of young peoples' engagements with media consider the material difference that location makes in the cultural uptake of media representations. How do LGBTQ-identifying youth in southeast Appalachia make sense of the queer representations that they see and when, how, and why do those representations matter to them? Gray studied the particular value of rural young people's digital and popular media consumption and production as sites that circulate representations and experiences of queer life that are not part of the mainstream discursive construction of "the good gay life" found in popular media. Core questions guiding this work included,

- What difference do media make to youth negotiating "queer" senses of sexualities and genders in the rural United States?
- How do young people do "queer identity work" vis-à-vis a range of interlocking media?
- How is queer identity work placed, aged, gendered, classed, and raced differently in the rural United States?
- How are rural queer youth identities organized vis-à-vis media in a cultural moment that demands/expects social legibility/visibility for political recognition/efficacy?

These research questions developed in relationship to an interdisciplinary set of frameworks and concepts. For example, asking how young people rework pop culture, messages from peers and local resources, and digital media to "queer" identities fits within a media-studies framing of audiences, active reception, and media effects. Asking how the politics of age, place, gender, class, and race shape digitally mediated queer identity work dovetails with key questions from queer theory and sexuality studies. Examining what difference digital inequalities make to youth negotiating a queer sense of sexuality and gender, particularly in the rural United States, challenges the cisheteronormativity that dominates research in geography and rural sociology.

In keeping with what we mentioned above about the need for both sustained spatial and temporal commitments, this project involved 19 months of fieldwork with rural youth in Kentucky and its border states. For Gray, fieldwork included participant observation among youth and their support agencies, peer networks, and LGBTQ youth advocates. Gray's previous research

with queer youth activists in California and her own experiences as an "aged-out" queer-identifying political organizer gave her access to a network of LGBTQ activists willing to connect her to LGBTQ support services in the region. Across these different sites, Gray conducted open-ended interviews and unstructured participant observation with 34 youths, ages 14–24. Given that Gray's questions were tied to issues of representation and identity work, open-ended interviews were crucial in gaining a complex, rich account of the role of media in the lives of queer rural youth. To supplement these interviews, Gray conducted informal interviews with over 100 youth and LGBTQ advocates, who provided different understandings of the everyday lives of queer rural youth. Beyond interviews and participant observation, Gray analyzed websites, blogs, and message boards, hosted by LGBTQ-identifying non-profit groups as well as sites generated by individual account holders for imagined audiences of friends and families, created for or by rural LGBTQ youth and allies. She used thematic coding to identify patterns in the language and images used across the sites, noting common elements and outliers to establish a sense of the organizational rhetoric young people might encounter online.

A challenge of ethnographic work is that once a researcher starts investigating the worlds of her participants, an incredible array of media sites and threads for analytical inquiry come rushing to attention. Education, religion, family dynamics, economics—these are all vantage points that emerge with sustained interaction in a given place, and any one or combination of these dynamics could easily constitute its own investigation. We use "emergence" rather than "discovery" of vantage points here to underscore the power of ethnography as an interpretative process rather than a fact-finding endeavor. Although attentive to these (and other) research avenues, Gray's project was fundamentally invested in understanding the role of media in the lives of queer and rural youth, including popular media representations of LGBTQ life in film, television, and the press as well as representations of young people's use of digital media. The historical moment of her research (before the mainstream explosion of social media, like Facebook and Twitter) and rural young people's limited access to the Internet dictated the parameters of the most salient media texts: the research focused on primarily web-based, pre-social media platforms and young people's use of and participation in web-based and email-circulated media.

Earlier we argued that ethnography is not only a methodological commitment, it is also an analytical approach. By spending time with participants and understanding their lived realities, the ethnographer becomes a "co-producer" of data. When an ethnographer first enters the field, she often struggles to understand what's important and what's not. This uncertainty is more complicated than the project of identifying norms and traditions within a given community—it is a matter of coming to terms with what components of the world she has encountered and how those facets give shape and coherent meaning to participants' lives. As a result of sustained time in the field, open-ended inquiry with participants, and participant observation across a range of settings, Gray developed a series of theories related to queer rural youth and their relationship to media. These themes developed through a process of co-construction with her participants; this process of co-construction, or making sense of what an ethnographer sees through a dialectic exchange with participants, led to the following analytical claims:

- Intimate senses of self are always mediated through media representations and social interactions.
- Queer senses of self aren't (just) discovered, they work through and across boundaries, including boundaries between places, times, and politics. Moreover, these processes of sense-making are always mediated, even when explicitly queer representations seem invisible.
- Media representations of queer subjectivities position urban queer organizing and identity formation as the (only/best) path to self-understanding, which can create acute tensions or gaps for people outside urban areas.
- Related and in contrast to the above, media representations of queer rural life are positioned as backward, lacking, and endemically hostile.
- Different degrees of media access (often called the "digital divide") distribute queer centers and margins of cultural/political production. In other words, financial, cultural, and social capital can pool and consolidate in urban centers in ways that they historically have not in rural communities. The infrastructure, tax base, and historical weight of a city's gay and lesbian enclaves consolidate the representational power of urban-based queer media-makers and those with the means to fund them.

As a method, ethnography requires sustained interactions in a field site in order to understand the everyday lives and experiences that give rise to a particular social phenomenon. Analytically, the relationships that ethnographers build with participants and their environment become part of the critical process of developing claims and theories.

Time is perhaps the most valuable resource an ethnographer must manage, particularly if she has a finite amount of it. While time constraints may be frustrating, what strains most ethnographic fieldwork is the dilemma of choosing among myriad possibilities of where to spend one's energy. There are as many options as there are encounters in a day. More collaborative approaches to ethnography, particularly those that invite participants to become co-investigators, can expand the number of interviews and observations generated through fieldwork. Gray's research could have benefited from more longitudinal analysis, allowing her to see how the rise of social networking sites, like Facebook and Twitter, made their way through the youth networks she came to know. And, certainly, further ethnographic study of other regions, youth populations, countries, and media experiences could further complicate and challenge what Gray's work has to offer. For better and for worse, ethnographic fieldwork requires accepting what Haraway dubbed the "partial truths" of situated knowledge.[21] No matter the number of collaborators, ethnography still produces rather than discovers a sense of the world, and that sense-making can never account for all the dynamics that go into a single moment in time.

Along the way, Gray faced several research obstacles that shaped her arguments. The two that posed the greatest challenges are common to most ethnographic research, namely, the fallout of losing key participants who no longer wish to take part in the research and navigating the ethical minefields that come with being intimately connected to people, particularly people historically marginalized because of their identities. Midway through Gray's fieldwork, a group of young women asked to have their interviews deleted and references to them removed from the study. One of the young women feared that her father, a prominent politician in her small town, might kick her out of the house after he found an email on her computer referencing one of the meetings Gray had organized for other LGBTQ youth in the region. Out of concern for their friend's safety, others in this close-knit circle of bisexual and lesbian-identifying young women also withdrew from the study. Gray had not met enough other young women in other towns to fully grasp young queer and questioning women's experiences of their rural communities, limiting the strength of her arguments. In turn, as many ethnographers have experienced, interviews and fieldwork can often lead to difficult or uncomfortable conversations. Good interviewing requires gaining participants' trust and eliciting open responses, but, as Gray discovered, sometimes it is precisely this openness that can generate difficult or emotionally intense moments, from disclosures of abuse to panicked and immediate requests for a safe place to stay. What we take away from these experiences is an earnest reminder that every ethnographic encounter is a moment to assess what one can offer in exchange for the time and trust participants give to us. While the major obstacles to rigorous ethnographic research may feel like time and funding to bring more than one researcher to the field, often it is the managing of the time and relationships that one has that proves most challenging.

Ethnography and Media Studies: Lessons Learned and Challenges Ahead

Like any method, ethnography comes with limitations. It is limited by having to "name" and draw boundaries around groups or phenomena under investigation, which means foreclosing who doesn't identify. Gray's focus on LGBTQ and questioning youth meant excluding people who don't identify with those terms, but who are still bound up in queer media and identity. A common criticism of ethnography is its lack of representativeness, meaning that the findings of an ethnography cannot easily be generalized to speak for a larger group of people. Gray's project speaks to the experiences of queer rural youth that she met in her extensive fieldwork, but to what extent can these findings be "scaled up" to reflect American queer rural youth more broadly?

Ethnography is fundamentally about plumbing people's worldviews. Rather than asking if all queer rural youth experience the same anti-rural bias that Gray identified in her fieldwork, we can ask whether the experiences of queer youth in rural southeast Appalachia also speak to other rural areas, or other places that drop out of a sociological mindset that privileges the urban as the locus of culture. For example, do youth of color in the suburbs experience similar feelings of being left out of dominant media discourses of what it means to be queer? Similarly, we can ask if other groups of people besides queer and questioning youth feel left out of mainstream media depictions of queerness, such as older lesbians, gays, bi, or trans-identifying people. In this sense, ethnography is largely resistant to purporting objective claims about the people and places informing ethnographic work. Put another way, objectivity is not the goal of ethnographic inquiry, making generalizability a problematic end-game of ethnographic analysis. In light of this relationship to interpreting ethnographic results, the ethical value of ethnography is in sharing and exploring the meanings of texts with others, particularly our participants. Methodologically and interpretively, ethnography is a creative project. Indeed, we might call ethnography a process of rigorous creativity that is moreover a collective process of learning from and exchanging with participants. Ethnography as a praxis—a way of moving in the world to test out our theories of it—calls on us to be part of the process of sense-making. Doing right by participants in describing their lives, practices, and worldviews is a way of doing justice to the complexity and multi-faceted nature of everyday human life.

Today's media scholars must take on understanding the value, meanings, and power of commercially generated, DIY, and other forms of cultural representation that asymmetrically spiral, ricochet, and career rather than channel through narrowly broadcasting systems. Ethnographies of media, from Jessa Lingel's current work on the historical and contemporary experiences of peer-to-peer barter of goods and services to Gray's collaborations with computer scientists to understand lived experiences of digital labor, present new opportunities for ethnographic practitioners to re-evaluate basic premises of the practice. Shifting technological landscapes have introduced new debates (as well as returned us to old debates) around gathering data and protecting participant privacy, provoked by questions of how to integrate massive data sets of people's digital traces and what it means for an individual to consent to levels and degrees of surveillance that exceed their single vantage point. It is both an exciting time to be a media ethnographer and a daunting prospect, with important challenges and opportunities for thinking about the complex ways that technology and media are increasingly bound up in everyday life.

Notes

1. Tom Boellstorff et al., *Ethnography and Virtual Worlds: A Handbook of Method* (Princeton: Princeton University Press, 2012).
2. Janet Staiger, *Media Reception Studies* (New York: New York University Press, 2005).

3. Keith H. Basso, *Wisdom Sits in Places: Landscape and Language Among the Western Apache* (Albuquerque: University of New Mexico Press, 1996).

4. First conceptualized by George Gerbner and Larry Gross in 1976, cultivation theory attempts to make sense of media effects by situating itself in a higher order empirical site: the TV drama itself. See, George Gerbner and Larry Gross, "Living with Television: The Violence Profile," in *Journal of Communication* 26, no. 2 (1976): 172–99; George Gerbner, Larry Gross, Michael Morgan, Nancy Signorielli, and Marilyn Jackson-Beeck, "The Demonstration of Power: Violence Profile" in *Journal of Communication* 29, no. 10 (1979): 177–96.

5. Also in the subfield of effects research, uses and gratifications research examines individual use of media, taking for granted that individuals make judgments on media content to fulfill needs. See, Paul Felix Lazarsfeld and Frank Stanton, *Radio Research* (New York: Duell, Sloan and Pearce, 1944); Herta Herzog, "What Do We Really Know about Daytime Serial Listeners?" In Paul Felix Lazarsfeld, ed., *Radio Research* (London: Sage, 1944), 3–33.

6. Franz Boas, *Anthropology and Modern Life* (New York: W. W. Norton, 1962).

7. William Foote Whyte, *Street Corner Society: The Social Structure of an Italian Slum* (Chicago: University of Chicago Press, 1943).

8. Paul Dourish and Victoria Bellotti, "Awareness and Coordination in Shared Workspaces," in *Proceedings of the 1992 ACM Conference on Computer-Supported Cooperative Work*, CSCW 1992 (New York: ACM, 1992), 107–14; Jonathan Grudin, "Why CSCW Applications Fail: Problems in the Design and Evaluation of Organizational Interfaces," in *Proceedings of the 1988 ACM Conference on Computer-Supported Cooperative Work*, CSCW 1988 (New York: ACM, 1988), 85–93; Edwin Hutchins, *Cognition in the Wild* (Cambridge: MIT Press, 1995).

9. Antonio Gramsci, *Selections from the Prison Notebooks of Antonio Gramsci*, ed. Quintin Hoare and Geoffrey Nowell-Smith (New York: International Publishers, 1971).

10. Martin Jay, *The Dialectical Imagination: A History of the Frankfurt School and the Institute of Social Research, 1923–1950* (Berkeley: University of California Press, 1996).

11. Hortense Powdermaker, *Hollywood, the Dream Factory: An Anthropologist Looks at the Movie-Makers* (Boston: Little, Brown, 1950).

12. John Thornton Caldwell, *Production Culture: Industrial Reflexivity and Critical Practice in Film and Television* (Durham: Duke University Press, 2008).

13. Sender, *Business, Not Politics: The Making of the Gay Market* (New York: Columbia University Press, 2005).

14. Ellen Seiter, Hans Borchers, Gabriele Kreutzner, and Eva-Maria Warth, *Remote Control: Television, Audiences, and Cultural Power* (New York: Routledge, 1989); Ellen Seiter, *Sold Separately: Children and Parents in Consumer Culture* (New Brunswick: Rutgers University Press, 1995).

15. Bonnie Nardi, *My Life as a Night Elf Priest: An Anthropological Account of "World of Warcraft"* (Ann Arbor: University of Michigan Press, 2010).

16. Tom Boellstorff, *Coming of Age in "Second Life": An Anthropologist Explores the Virtually Human* (Princeton: Princeton University Press, 2008).

17. Nardi, *My Life as a Night Elf Priest*.

18. Celia Pearce, *Communities of Play: Emergent Cultures in Multiplayer Games and Virtual Worlds* (Cambridge: MIT Press, 2011); T. L. Taylor, *Play Between Worlds: Exploring Online Game Culture* (Cambridge: MIT Press, 2006).

19. Jessica Lingel, "Ethics and Dilemmas of Online Ethnography," in *CHI '12 Extended Abstracts on Human Factors in Computing Systems*, CHI EA '12 (New York: ACM, 2012), 41–50; Jessa Lingel and danah boyd, "'Keep it secret, keep it safe': Information Poverty, Information Norms, and Stigma," *Journal of the American Society for Information Science and Technology* 64, no. 5 (2013): 981–91.

20. Virginia Eubanks, *Digital Dead End: Fighting for Social Justice in the Information Age* (Cambridge: MIT Press, 2011).

21. Donna Haraway, "Situated Knowledges: The Science Question in Feminism and the Privilege of Partial Perspective," *Feminist Studies* 14, no. 3 (1988): 575.

Further Reading

Allen, C. "What's Wrong with the "Golden Rule"? Conundrums of Conducting Ethical Research in Cyberspace." *The Information Society* 12, no. 2 (1996): 175–87.

Askew, Kelly Michelle, and Richard R. Wilk, eds. *The Anthropology of Media: A Reader*. Malden: Blackwell, 2002.

Association of Internet Researchers. "Ethical Decision-Making and Internet Research: Recommendations from the AoIR Ethics Working Committee," 2012. Accessed January 23, 2016. http://aoir.org/reports/ethics2.pdf.

Bauman, Richard, and Joel Sherzer. *Explorations in the Ethnography of Speaking*. 2nd ed. New York: Cambridge University Press, 1989.

Baym, Nancy K. "Introduction: Internet Research as It Isn't, Is, Could Be, and Should Be." *The Information Society* 21, no. 4 (2005): 229–32.

Baym, Nancy K. *Tune In, Log on: Soaps, Fandom, and Online Community (New Media Cultures)*. Thousand Oaks: Sage Publications, 2000.

Beemyn, Brett, ed. *Creating a Place for Ourselves: Lesbian, Gay, and Bisexual Community Histories*. New York: Routledge, 1997.

Best, Amy L. *Representing Youth: Methodological Issues in Critical Youth Studies*. New York: New York University Press, 2007.

Binnie, Jon, and Gill Valentine. "Geographies of Sexuality— a Review of Progress." *Progress in Human Geography* 23, no. 2 (1999): 175–87.

Boellstorff, Tom, Bonnie Nardi, Celia Pearce, and T. L. Taylor. *Ethnography and Virtual World: A Handbook of Method*. Princeton: Princeton University Press, 2012.

Brekhus, Wayne. *Peacocks, Chameleons, Centaurs: Gay Suburbia and the Grammar of Social Identity*. Chicago: University of Chicago Press, 2003.

Briggs, Charles L. *Learning How to Ask: A Sociolinguistic Appraisal of the Role of the Interview in Social Science Research*. Cambridge: Cambridge University Press, 1994.

Burke, Susan. "In Search of Lesbian Community in an Electronic World." *CyberPsychology and Behavior* 3, no. 4 (2000): 591–604.

Burrell, Jenna. "The Field Site as a Network: A Strategy for Locating Ethnographic Research." *Field Methods* 21, no. 2 (2009): 181–99.

Cavanagh, Allison. "Behavior in Public? Ethics in Online Ethnography." *Cyberpsychology* 6 (1999). Accessed March 9, 2018. www.cybersociology.com/files/6_2_ ethicsinonlineethnog.html.

Clifford, James, and George E. Marcus, eds. *Writing Culture: The Poetics and Politics of Ethnography*. Berkeley: University of California Press, 1986.

Coleman, Gabriella. "Am I Anonymous?" *Limn*, no. 2 (2012). Accessed July 30, 2017. http://limn.it/am-i-anony mous/.

Correll, Shelley. "The Ethnography of an Electronic Bar: The Lesbian Cafe." *Journal of Contemporary Ethnography* 24, no. 3 (1995): 270–98.

Driver, Susan. "Beyond 'Straight' Interpretations: Researching Queer Youth Digital Video." In *Representing Youth: Methodological Issues in Critical Youth Studies*, edited by Amy L. Best, 304–24. New York: New York University Press, 2007.

Duggan, Lisa. "Making It Perfectly Queer." *Socialist Review* 22, no. 1 (1992): 11–31.

Epstein, Steven. "Gay Politics, Ethnic Identity: The Limits of Social Constructionism." *Socialist Review* 93–94 (1987): 9–54.

Gallo, Marcia M. *Different Daughters: A History of the Daughters of Bilitis and the Rise of the Lesbian Rights Movement*. New York: Carroll & Graf Publishers, 2006.

Gamson, Joshua. "Gay Media, Inc.: Media Structures, the New Gay Conglomerates, and Collective Sexual Identities." In *Cyberactivism: Online Activism in Theory and Practice*, edited by Martha McCaughey and Michael D. Ayers, 255–78. New York: Routledge, 2003.

Geiger, R. Stuart, and David Ribes. "Trace Ethnography: Following Coordination through Documentary Practices." 44th Hawaii International Conference on System Sciences. IEEE *Xplore*, February 22, 2011. Accessed July 30, 2017. http://ieeexplore.ieee.org/ document/5718606/.

Gray, Mary L. *Out in the Country: Youth, Media, and Queer Visibility in Rural America*. New York: New York University Press, 2009.

Haag, Anthony M., and Frankling K. Chang. "The Impact of Electronic Networking on the Lesbian and Gay Community." In *Rural Gays and Lesbians: Building on the Strengths of Communities*, edited by James Donald Smith and Ronald J. Mancoske, 83–94. Binghamton: The Harrington Park Press / The Haworth Press, Inc., 1997.

Heath, Deborah, Erin Koch, Barbara Ley, and Michael Montoya. "Nodes and Queries: Linking Locations in Networked Fields of Inquiry." *American Behavioral Scientist* 43, no. 3 (1999): 450–63.

Herring, Susan. "Content Analysis for New Media: Rethinking the Paradigm." In *New Research for New Media*. Ithaca: Cornell University, 2004.

Hine, Christine., ed. *Virtual Methods: Issues in Social Research on the Internet*. New York: Bloomsbury Academic, 2005.

Hirsch, E. "Bound and Unbound Entities: Reflections on the Ethnographic Perspectives of Anthropology vis-a-vis Media and Cultural Studies." In *Ritual, Performance, Media*, edited by F. Hughes-Freeland, 208–28. London: Routledge, 1998.

Jones, Steve. *Doing Internet Research: Critical Issues and Methods for Examining the Net*. Thousand Oaks: Sage, 1998.

Katz, Elihu, and Paul Felix Lazarsfeld. *Personal Influence: The Part Played by People in the Flow of Mass Communications*. New Brunswick: Transaction Publishers, 1955.

Kendall, Lori. *Hanging Out in the Virtual Pub: Masculinities and Relationships Online*. Berkeley: University of California Press, 2002.

Kennedy, Elizabeth Lapovsky, and Madeline D. Davis. *Boots of Leather, Slippers of Gold: The History of a Lesbian Community*. New York: Routledge, 1993.

Kirkey, Kenneth, and Ann Forsyth. "Men in the Valley: Gay Male Life on the Suburban-Rural Fringe." *Journal of Rural Studies* 17 (2001): 421–41.

Lave, Jean, and Etienne Wenger. *Situated Learning: Legitimate Peripheral Participation*. New York: Cambridge University Press, 1991.

Lederman, Rena. "The Perils of Working at Home: IRB 'mission Creep' as Context and Content for an Ethnography of Disciplinary Knowledges." *American Ethnologist* 33, no. 4 (2006): 482–91.

Lewin, Ellen, and William L. Leap, eds. *Out in Theory: The Emergence of Lesbian and Gay Anthropology*. Urbana: University of Illinois Press, 2002.

Leyshon, Michael. "On Being 'in the Field': Practice, Progress and Problems in Research with Young People in Rural Areas." *Journal of Rural Studies* 18, no. 2 (2002): 179–91.

Lievrouw, Leah A., and Sonia M. Livingstone, eds. *Handbook of New Media: Social Shaping and Social Consequences of ICTs*. 2nd ed. Thousand Oaks: Sage, 2006.

Livingstone, Sonia. *Young People and New Media: Childhood and the Changing Media Environment*. Thousand Oaks: Sage, 2002.

Lyman, Peter, and Nina Wakeford. "Going in the (Virtual) Field." *American Behavioral Scientist* 43, no. 3 (1999): 359–76.

Mann, Chris, and Fiona Stewart. *Internet Communication and Qualitative Research: A Handbook for Researching Online*. Thousand Oaks: Sage, 2000.

Marcus, George E. "Ethnography in/of the World System: The Emergence of Multi-Sited Ethnography." *Annual Review of Anthropology* 24, no. 1 (1995): 95–117.

Marcus, George E., and Michael M. J. Fischer. *Anthropology as Cultural Critique: An Experimental Moment in the Human Sciences*. 2nd ed. Chicago: University of Chicago Press, 1999.

Markham, Annette N. "The Methods, Politics, and Ethics of Representation in Online Ethnography." In *The Sage Handbook of Qualitative Research*, 3rd ed., edited by Norman K. Denzin and Yvonna S. Lincoln, 793–820. Thousand Oaks: Sage, 2005.

Miller, Daniel, and Don Slater. *The Internet: An Ethnographic Approach*. New York: Bloomsbury Academic, 2000.

Morley, David, and Kevin Robins. *Spaces of Identity: Global Media, Electronic Landscapes and Cultural Boundaries*. New York: Routledge, 1995.

Paccagnella, Luciano. "Getting the Seats of Your Pants Dirty: Strategies for Ethnographic Research on Virtual Communities." *Journal of Computer-Mediated Communication* 3, no. 1 (1997): 1–16.

Panelli, Ruth. "Young Rural Lives: Strategies Beyond Diversity." *Journal of Rural Studies* 18, no. 2 (2002): 113–22.

Papacharissi, Zizi. "The Virtual Sphere: The Internet as Public Sphere." *New Media and Society* 4, no. 1 (2002): 9–27.

Raffo, Susan. *Queerly Classed*. Boston: South End Press, 1997.

Reid, Eric. "Informed Consent in the Study of Online Communities: A Reflection of the Effects of Computer-Mediated Social Research." *The Information Society* 12, no. 2 (1996): 169–74.

Rybas, Natalia, and Radhika Gajjala. "Developing Cyber-ethnographic Research Methods for Understanding Digitally Mediated Identities." *Forum: Qualitative Social Research* 8, no. 3 (2007). Accessed July 30, 2017. www.qualitative-research.net/index.php/fqs/article/view/282.

Schatzman, Leonard, and Anselm Leonard Strauss. *Field Research: Strategies for a Natural Sociology*. Englewood Cliffs: Prentice Hall, 1973.

Schuetz, Alfred. "The Stranger: An Essay in Social Psychology." *American Journal of Sociology* 49, no. 6 (1944): 499–507.

Seiter, Ellen. *The Internet Playground: Children's Access, Entertainment, and Mis-Education*. New York: Peter Lang, 2005.

Sender, Katherine. "Sex Sells: Sex, Taste, and Class in Commercial Gay and Lesbian Media." *GLQ: A Journal of Lesbian and Gay Studies* 9, no. 3 (2003): 331–65.

Shibutani, Tamotsu. *Society and Personality; an Interactionist Approach to Social Psychology*. Englewood Cliffs: Prentice-Hall, 1961.

Silver, David, and Adrienne Massanari, eds. *Critical Cyberculture Studies*. New York: New York University Press, 2006.

Skelton, Tracey, and Gill Valentine, eds. *Cool Places: Geographies of Youth Cultures*. New York: Routledge, 1998.

Smith, Barbara. "Narrative Versions, Narrative Theories." In *On Narrative*, edited by W. J. Thomas Mitchell, 209–32. Chicago: University of Chicago Press, 1981.

Spitulnik, Debra. "Mobile Machines and Fluid Audiences: Rethinking Reception through Zambian Radio Culture." In *Media Worlds: Anthropology on New Terrain*, edited by Faye D. Ginsburg, Lila Abu-Lughod, and Brian Larkin, 337–54. Berkeley: University of California Press, 2002.

Star, Susan Leigh. "The Ethnography of Infrastructure." *American Behavioral Scientist* 43, no. 3 (1999): 377–91.

Strathern, Marilyn, ed. *Audit Cultures: Anthropological Studies in Accountability, Ethics and the Academy*. New York: Routledge, 2003.

Strauss, Anselm. *Continual Permutations of Action*. New York: Aldine, 1993.

———— and Juliet M. Corbin. *Basics of Qualitative Research: Techniques and Procedures for Developing Grounded Theory.* 2nd ed. Thousand Oaks: Sage, 1998.

Taylor, T. L. *Play between Worlds: Exploring Online Game Culture.* Cambridge: MIT Press, 2009.

Thomas, Jim. "When Cyberresearch Goes Awry: The Ethics of the Rimm 'Cyberporn' Study." *The Information Society* 12, no. 2 (1996): 189–98.

Valentine, Gill. *From Nowhere to Everywhere: Lesbian Geographies.* New York: Harrington Park Press, 2000.

Waskul, Dennis. "Considering the Electronic Participant: Some Polemical Observations on the Ethics of On-Line Research." *The Information Society* 12, no. 2 (1996): 129–40.

Wenger, Etienne. *Communities of Practice: Learning, Meaning, and Identity.* Cambridge: Cambridge University Press, 1998.

Wysocki, Diane. "'Growing up Gay in Rural Nebraska' or a Feminist Relocates to the Midwest." *Sexuality and Culture* 4, no. 3 (2000): 57–64.

PART II

SYNTHETIC/MULTIPERSPECTIVAL APPROACHES

15.
AUDIENCES
Matt Hills

Overview

A significant amount of media criticism has involved the empirical study of audiences, predominantly film and TV viewers given that this mode of scholarship arose in the 1970s. The "audience turn" then developed in the 1980s and 1990s, being aligned, in part, with the rise of cultural studies. Perhaps the most important conceptual framework was a strong challenge that emerged to notions of the "ideal" audience. In the case of the ideal reader, audience readings of media texts were assumed to be identical to academics' expert interpretations—one could simply interpret from a text how audiences would respond to it or be positioned by it. Versions of this projected audience were present in **Screen Theory** of the 1970s (a body of work on spectatorship linked to the journal *Screen*), and in the **media effects** work linked to communication studies, which assumed that audiences were "affected" by media texts.

But conceptualizing audience activities as patterned in sociological ways—i.e., related to social and cultural identities such as their age, level of education, class, ethnicity, gender, and so on—called for a specific method. Audience studies has often been based around broadly **ethnographic approaches**, meaning that audience members are observed *in situ*,[1] invited to participate in focus groups, or interviewed in-depth. As Ann Gray has observed of such work:

> the most interesting points in ... interviews are the "inarticulate" moments, the fumbling for words, ... for these are moments when people are trying to find words for what they do and what they feel about their lives. Those areas for which there are no "ready made" descriptions or terms or concepts are thus being rendered "speakable." This is [an] ... example of the ... dialogic character of this kind of intensive interviewing ... [and] can provide new ways of looking at the world.[2]

Such methodology is qualitative rather than quantitative, aimed at generating rich rather than generalizable data. However, a number of researchers would go on to challenge this binary by combining qualitative and quantitative audience studies.[3]

Any overview of **audience studies** operates, though, as a kind of shorthand narrative. Nick Abercrombie and Brian Longhurst note that "Typically, histories of audience research in the media divide up that history into phases, or periods."[4] I have already suggested a before and after of effects research versus audience ethnographies, for instance, but this can be complicated by thinking about how at least some qualitative audience studies have retained a concept of media "influence."[5] Also, work that reads audience responses from media texts has not been entirely superseded by audience ethnography; textual analysis has continued as one form of trained academic expertise, especially in film studies,[6] drawing on a range of theories from psychoanalysis to cognitive philosophy (see chapters on these approaches in this volume), which make very different assumptions about audiences and whether they unconsciously relate to media texts or consciously figure out media meanings. Where empirical audience study can be interested in the "inarticulate" moments when actual audiences struggle to make sense of their experiences, these text-centered approaches produce a kind of academic mastery, asserting that they know how media audiences will (or should) behave.

The question of understanding audience activities remains important for the media industries just as much as for scholars, with digital technologies, especially the Internet and streaming platforms, leading to new models of audiencehood and new ways of calculating ratings for TV, as well as new methods of algorithmically predicting the tastes of subscribers to online services such as Netflix.[7] Audiences are surveyed and shaped by the agendas of media institutions here.[8] Indeed, Ien Ang has argued that "knowledge produced from the institutional point of view" tends to construct the television audience,[9] that is, audiences are reduced to mere numbers, represented through specific market research and its questions, or tracked via proprietary data. For Ang, it is not only the institutionally recorded audience that is a kind of construction: "No representation of 'television audience,' empirical or otherwise, gives us direct access to any actual audience."[10] And if this is equally true for qualitative ethnographies, industry statistics/ratings, and "ideal" readers implied in rival scholarly theories, then we might wonder whether any given representation of the audience is a better fabrication than any other. One possible way out of this conundrum is implied in Ann Gray's rationale for cultural-studies-indebted audience study—namely, that it "can provide new ways of looking at the world."[11] This involves challenging forms of "common sense" and cultural power. For example, one emergent form of audience activity may commonly be thought of as "binge-watching," implying a pathological addiction.[12] But rather than devaluing ordinary audience practices, ethnographic analysis can offer alternative ways of seeing:

> Although the popular press uses the negatively connoted phrase "binge-watching," I employ the more comprehensive and complimentary phrase "media marathoning." Rather than viewing these media experiences as mindless indulgences, "media marathoning" connotes a conjoined triumph of commitment and stamina. The phrase also captures viewers' … engrossment … and sense of accomplishment.[13]

Discourses linked to empirical audience study—even if they cannot present the ultimate truth of any audience—can have value in terms of how they contest what might otherwise be culturally powerful (and reductive) images of media audiences. Such dominant images include "affected" audiences, "bingeing" audiences, and audiences rendered as numerical blocs via box office figures or TV ratings. All too often, audiences are subordinated to political anxieties that aim to pathologize certain media consumers, such as horror fans or videogame players; to industrial agendas that seek to monetize their activities; and to academic theories that seek to infer their activities without speaking to or studying actual audience members. In each case, forms of cultural power and prestige are (re)produced out of the figure of the audience, rather than audiences' struggles to make meaning being taken seriously.

Audiences are more visible now than ever before—they can be directly accessed today via online forum postings, Facebook groups, Twitter hashtags, and all manner of comment threads.[14] Recent scholarly work has thus begun to address the "networked audience"[15] in relation to social media usage. Some critics have even questioned whether the term "audience" is still a useful one[16] in the era of what's been termed amateur **produsage**[17] (i.e., a new phase of media creation and distribution when Internet users and content producers blur together via the activity of the "produser," who might be a blogger, a meme-maker, or a digital artist/photoshopper). This is a curious development: just as media audiences supposedly become more able to give clearer voice to their own concerns, then "the audience" allegedly dissolves into new forms of digital-cultural production, hence no longer acting merely as an audience. However, I will suggest that the "audience" concept remains extremely useful to the shaping of media criticism. This is so for three reasons:

1. There are different kinds of audience—some being physically co-present, some being part of a "mass" experience, and some consuming in socially atomized ways via "on-demand." Interactions between different types and categories of audience continue to be a significant part of our contemporary media culture;

2. Production of the "produsage" type is linked to audience identities and cultures, e.g., this is typically true in fan cultures;[18]

3. Media content often remains privileged within social media activities such as commenting and sharing, e.g., live-tweeting event TV or posting links to movie trailers. And hence **spreadable media**—which means all those bits of content that produsers share online and distribute outside the channels of official media distribution—is often still official content, e.g., publicity.[19]

Having provided a brief overview of the concept and key methods of audience studies, I will now move on to consider relevant intellectual histories and terminologies in greater detail, before concluding with an examination of one case study taken from my previous work.

Intellectual History of the Concept

As Kate Lacey has pointed out, the notion of being part of a collective group is essential to the concept of "the audience":

> "Audience," according to the OED, refers to the action, state, condition or occasion of hearing, or an "assembly of listeners." The modern idea of an audience certainly retains that notion of a collectivity ... "Audience" is a collective noun for the activity of listening that has been assimilated for other activities, precisely because no parallel nouns existed that gave the same sense of collectivity.[20]

Given this "inescapable collectivity suggested by the word 'audience,'"[21] the term's history has been one of various pathologizations, denigrations, and celebrations. When it has failed to behave as a rational public of informed citizens, then "the audience" has supposedly been made up of threateningly hysterical individuals, whose identity has allegedly been lost in the mass, or it has been figured as a culturally dangerous "crowd."[22] More recently than such pathologizing trends, and partly in reaction to them, "the audience" has been celebrated in sectors of cultural studies' work for its "active" nature,[23] or viewed as part of the democratization of cultural production linked to Web 2.0.[24] The audience has thereby acted as a kind of cultural Rorschach test, having political anxieties and hopes projected onto it. As Martin Barker has observed, consequently it is important to ask the following:

> How are "audiences" defined and understood, both broadly in a period, and locally around a particular moment? What claims are made and circulating about who "they"/"we" are ...? What models of influence are at work, both overtly and implicitly? And how do all these permeate actual audiences' engagements ...? What real, imagined, and hoped-for communities result from the interpenetration of all these ...? Only with this broad agenda in mind do we ... know how to "listen to people."[25]

Audiences have sometimes been positioned as passively "vulnerable" to media "messages," e.g., images of the "affected" audience have been mobilized by political elites to justify media censorship. In the 1970s an opposing academic tradition—still drawn on by some scholars today—called "Uses and Gratifications" sought to understand what audiences did with media rather than what it (allegedly) did to them. However, this approach has been criticized by cultural studies scholars for its overly individualizing bent. They argue that people's psychological "needs" are socially shaped and sociologically meaningful rather than simply emerging within individuals.[26]

Audiences have also been placed in broader intellectual, philosophical currents such as the transdisciplinary emergence of "post-structuralism" in the academy during the 1970s and 1980s. Following influential work, such as literary theorist Roland Barthes' "The Death of the Author,"[27] which emphasized how readers could make their own meanings via the intertextual possibilities circulating around and through a text, the stage was intellectually set for a turn to readers and audiences. This move away from authorial "intent" or authority and towards audiences' activations of meaning was far from universally followed, however: film studies had strongly attempted to legitimate its newfound position in the academy by adopting text-based protocols from more traditional literary and artistic approaches. As such, Screen Theory retained a strongly "structuralist" tone, in which textual structures were assumed to impact ideologically on audiences, suturing them into an acceptance of the cultural status quo. Just as cultural studies had critiqued "Uses and Gratifications" for being individualistic and lacking in sociological context, it attacked Screen Theory for its "entirely text-centred" approach,[28] which lacked a sense of sociological contexts and audience activities.

As the **active audience** was debated,[29] some cultural studies scholars began to feel that ideas of audience "agency" (the audience's capacity to follow their own agenda such as communal reinterpretation) had been overstated, while textual structures and media power had been downplayed.[30] This is sometimes referred to as the "structure-agency" debate, where each side captures part of the truth of the matter. Political economists, who emphasize how capitalist ownership of the media can limit its range of representations, especially displacing radical or "non-mainstream" politics,[31] have found themselves partly in agreement with critics of excessive audience agency.

The "audience turn" which had emerged in TV studies also gradually found a place in film studies. It was sometimes marginalized there by a text-based tradition, which moved on from Screen Theory, and its psychoanalytic debts, to new master theorists and theories. Against these periodic reinvigorations of textual determinism, film audiences have been studied in a range of important ways: Jackie Stacey's *Stargazing*[32] innovatively used a form of psychoanalysis in empirical work on women who had been fans of movie stars in the 1950s; Annette Kuhn analyzed audiences' life-long memories of cinema-going;[33] Martin Barker, Jane Arthurs, and Ramaswami Harindranath have explored "unsettled" audiences who aren't sure what to make of controversial arthouse movies like David Cronenberg's *Crash* (1996),[34] and Thomas Austin has empirically explored how audiences make sense of Hollywood blockbusters and their hype.[35] By contrast, work on television audiences has clustered around certain genres, e.g., the interest in soap opera or reality TV audiences.[36] Other strands of audience research have been less concerned with reclaiming devalued and feminized culture and more concerned with celebrating "quality" TV legitimated as "complex,"[37] although this kind of move has been contested by those in the cultural studies tradition aiming to show how valued and "masculinized" TV culture often shares the melodramatic qualities of supposedly trashy and feminized TV.[38]

But if "the audience" has perhaps followed a slightly less coherent trajectory within film studies than in TV studies—being differently placed in relation to more dominant text-based paradigms in the cinematic case—then notions of audience "collectivity" have remained central across media. Different kinds of audience grouping can be analyzed, and Abercrombie and Longhurst term these three types "simple," "mass," and "diffused" audiences.[39] Simple audiences are co-present in a cinema theater or in front of a TV screen; mass audiences watch something at the same time but are dispersed across space (usually a nation-state); and diffused audiences are both asynchronous and spatially dispersed, corresponding less clearly to a "broadcast" or "release window" model and instead resembling an "on-demand culture"[40] where mobile media can be consumed at any time in line with audiences' interest.

For Abercrombie and Longhurst, the rise of the diffused audience calls for a new paradigm of analysis— the **Spectacle/Performance Paradigm** (SPP).[41] This is a key development, as it moves away from debates over structure and agency or media power[42]

and instead focuses on how audiences perform their audience role not only when they are engaged in watching film or TV, but also at a series of other moments, "diffusing" audience identities into culture and society more widely. When we tweet about a (dis)liked movie, blog about a TV series, or plan to "media marathon" a show, we are engaged in being part of an audience, just as we are when we consume ancillary products. Abercrombie and Longhurst's approach was itself partly prefigured by work in cultural studies and fan studies,[43] although they sought to distinguish the SPP from earlier models of audience (and fan) activity. Within the SPP, audience affiliations are performed culturally rather than merely in the moment of viewing, as people anticipate, critique, remember, and re-watch. Of course, sometimes our "ordinary" engagements with media will be fleeting and forgettable.[44] And sometimes we will tune out certain trailers, advertisements, or texts.[45] But these moments of non-audiencing, where some media are unimportant or ignored, occur against the backdrop of audiences displaying their investments in highly visible ways.

The relevance of the SPP has been strengthened by the emergence of Web 2.0 and "user-generated content," as audiences can now perform themselves, potentially becoming a version of "the show"[46] by starting YouTube channels, blogging, tweeting, and interacting online. It can be argued that these are no longer audience activities, as these consumers are acting as cultural producers or "prosumers" in their own right, engaging in media produsage. But much produsage occurs in relation to official media texts and products—it is derivative and/or transformative of media content—as audiences perform themselves for other audiences. It is surprising that despite textual analysis having long had a model of intertextualities (relations between texts), to date there has been little sustained analysis of "inter-audiences," as audiences relate in a range of ways to other audiences (though analysis of **anti-fans**, those who detest certain genres or texts and by association denigrate their audiences, has made a good start[47]). We also need to think about audiences not merely as falling into one part of an intellectual taxonomy, focusing instead on how these different categories can interact.[48] Platforms such as Twitter, Facebook, and Instagram can enable the experiences of "simple" audiences—being there at a premiere or convention—to be stretched into a "mass" realm, whilst the "diffused" nature of much audience interaction can also be brought back into a communal and "mass" arena via the likes of YouTube or Twitter, where timely performances of audience-hood can possess currency. Far from "simple" and "mass" audiences being superseded by the "diffused" audience, the mass audience has instead been reconfigured in cultural/technological terms.

I have necessarily introduced some key terminology already, but in what follows I want to focus more directly on major modes of audience study—oriented around interpretation and identity—and their scholarly terms such as contextualism, decoding, everyday life, fandom, and transcultural consumption.

Major Modes and Terminology

Major modes of audience studies have tended to focus on audiences' interpretations and identities. And although these dimensions are often interwoven in complex ways, I want to separate them analytically, in order to examine some key terms involved in theorizing media audiences.

The focus on audiences' interpretations has its roots in the **encoding/decoding model** set out by Stuart Hall in a much-applied essay.[49] This model was important because it argued that there was no necessary or determining link between how media texts were constructed to carry meaning, or how they were "encoded," and how audiences made meaning from them, or "decoded" or interpreted them. This enabled Hall to argue that media effects, as well as media propaganda, could never be assumed merely on the basis of studying textual encodings. Instead, the encoding/decoding model indicated that it remained an empirical, open question as to how audiences would interpret news and entertainment.[50] Hall posited the existence of three possible decoding positions: audiences might produce "preferred" decodings that were closely aligned with encoded meaning, but on the contrary they could also create "oppositional" readings which thoroughly rejected the terms of a media text, or they could fall somewhere between these positions by carrying out "negotiated" readings that agreed with aspects of textual encoding but disputed others.

This was a very flexible model, and it proved to be highly productive in terms of understanding audience interpretations. Hall's work led audience researchers to think sociologically about how interpretations might be correlated with identities such as class and ethnicity. The encoding/decoding model has also been challenged in a variety of ways: How might audiences' responses vary in line with the cultural experience they have of depicted issues?[51] Does "decoding" pay insufficient attention to audiences' emotions?[52] Is the "preferred" reading an artifact of the text itself or is it constructed by the academic analyst?[53] Furthermore, Jonathan Gray argues that the encoding/decoding model needs a sense of "re-decoding"[54] since it implies that audiences encounter something once, in a single moment. What about the situation where audiences re-view media texts? Our understanding of the same text can shift when we re-watch it, interpreting it in the light of new social circumstances.

The focus on audience interpretations became linked not only to debates around encoding/decoding, but also to discussions of **contextualism**, which meant addressing how texts were integrated into the everyday lives of audiences. In turn, this meant analyzing moments of media consumption—where, when, and how were media texts encountered? Contextualist scholars were interested in the domestic sphere (in relation to TV especially[55]), and in the practices of everyday life that framed audiences' meaning-making, also including non-domestic contexts.[56] In some cases, contextualism even undermined the prevalent emphasis on "interpretation," as in Joke Hermes' work on women's magazines. Hermes argued that there was a "fallacy of meaningfulness" in much audience analysis that presumed audiences "decoded" meaning.[57] But in certain cases—such as killing time by glancing at a magazine, or carving out a sense of "one's own time" during a day of housework—it was the context of media use that was more significant than any specific decoding. Some media, Hermes concluded, were utilized by audiences in ways that had little to do with interpreting meaning and more to do with blending media products into the duties and obligations of everyday life.[58]

One major subset of audience studies has been **fan studies**; the analysis of textual interpretations carried out by especially dedicated, loyal, and emotionally committed viewers who form part of media fandom.[59] Some have argued that too much attention has been paid to fans. As they are only one kind of audience, we would do well to also analyze "anti-fans" (those who viscerally detest a genre, franchise, or text) as well as "non-fans" (those whose media consumption may be much more casual and less intense).[60] Fandom has been over-represented in audience criticism, but this is no accident: it has been important for particular reasons. By making fan audiences more visible, it has enabled the existence of **interpretive communities** to be studied—audience groups that share the ways in which they make sense of media texts, characters, and "golden ages" of a TV show, or entries in a movie franchise. This doesn't mean that all fans will read in the same way, but it does mean that fan communities tend to generate favored fannish interpretations and rankings, with newbies being socialized into the "right way" of reading.[61] And fandom has been important for emphasizing how viewers can be selectively resistant to producers' interests, making meanings—such as **slash** fiction and other forms of art (videos, etc.) where male lead characters are depicted as being in homosexual relationships[62]—which are strongly opposed to "preferred" or encoded meanings.[63] Such audience resistance has offered a crucial way of understanding how audience groups can challenge the authority of media producers over "their" texts, and in ways that can be progressive, i.e., expanding the potential meanings and politics of media representations in unpredictable ways. Fandom demonstrates very well how interpretations can be used to sustain audience identities, with fan identities being bolstered via the production of fan fiction, fan art, and fan videos (fanvids) at the same time that communal readings are developed. Slash fiction has become something that media producers are distinctly aware of—as well as becoming just one of the many subgenres of fan fiction produced by fans—demonstrating how audiences and producers can operate in a kind of feedback loop. The U.S. TV show *Supernatural* (WB, 2005–06; CW, 2006–), for example, has repeatedly "broken the fourth wall" (the imaginary wall separating the show's storyworld from its audience) by self-reflexively acknowledging fandom and its activities in the program itself.[64] In one sense, this brings recognition to fan audiences, but, in another sense, fan activities are co-opted and commodified. The relationship between fan communities and mainstream culture has thus sometimes been uneasy, as in the case of the bestselling *Fifty Shades of Grey* that began life as *Twilight* fan fiction.[65] But if commercial culture can sometimes reward and recognize fandom, and at other times appropriate or monetize it, fans remain a co-creating as well as consumer audience.[66] Whether through crowdfunding, social media buzz, or fan fiction, fans contribute to the economic lives and cultural meanings of the franchises and texts they love. As co-creators of popular culture, fans demonstrate how audience and producer identities have begun to blur together, even as media institutions ultimately retain forms of economic and cultural power as rights-owners and official creators and distributors.

If the field of fan studies has combined work on audience interpretations and identities, then other major modes of audience studies have focused more on the latter rather than the former. Audience identities have been linked to citizenship, with "good" audiences being those who perform their citizen identity via media consumption, participating in the "public sphere" of political debate.[67] Audience identities have also been performed and studied as collectors of merchandise[68] and as savvy consumers who navigate the hype of media culture.[69]

Audiences perform their identities through the tastes they display and the media texts they value.[70] At the same time, audiences classify themselves and others through their tastes. Sociological audience studies offer much evidence for such tastes being articulated with what John Fiske has called "semantic discourses," i.e., discourses of age, gender, class, etc.[71] These patterns of consumption, according to theorists who follow and apply the work on *Distinction* by French sociologist Pierre Bourdieu,[72] suggest that media audiences construct appropriate cultural identities via their media tastes. For instance, we might distinguish between "classy," "mainstream" horror films, described as "gothic chillers," and "gorefest" splatter flicks that are "hardcore" and appropriate for subcultural, underground horror fans. Whilst the former will tend to connote feminized horror, the latter are more likely to be aligned with "tough," masculinized, challenging horror. Or we might distinguish between HBO TV series such as *The Wire* (2002–08) or *Game of Thrones* (2011–)—these being culturally positioned as "quality" TV dramas linked to social realism, novelistic plotting or world-building, and politics—and network TV soap operas felt to be lacking in televisual style and complex subject matter.[73] Such **taste culture** values tastes that are aligned with middle-class or white-collar preferences over cultural forms that are more accessible to a wider audience. Soaps have historically been linked to a female audience and hence continue to be feminized, as is much reality TV.[74] Audiences can thus perform their levels of education, their class, and even implied gendering through the texts they choose to embrace.

Performed identity is not only a matter of demographics here; audiences can also align themselves with national groupings, diasporic identities, or transnational/transcultural affiliations via the media that matter to them. Some viewers, e.g., of Japanese horror or anime, can align themselves across national and linguistic boundaries. And **informal distribution** (i.e., Web piracy or illicit downloading or streaming)[75] can enable audiences to keep up with films and TV shows that have not yet been officially released in their national territory,[76] whilst some fans can use their language skills to "fansub" texts, that is, to create unofficial subtitles for a foreign language film or TV show. National identity may remain important within (un)official transnational flows of media, such as in the case of Americans identifying as Anglophile viewers, or U.K. audiences marking out their cultural distinction by following a U.S. quality TV program that has not been broadcast in the United Kingdom and is barely known there. But in other cases, national identity becomes less significant to these flows of media, with audiences instead becoming **transcultural** viewers[77] for whom national affiliations are not as important as cross-cultural interpretive communities, e.g., being a fan of *Sherlock* (BBC One / PBS, 2010–) in Japan or a fan of *Doctor Who* (BBC One, 1963–89; 2005–) in Germany.

Despite these explorations of audiences' interpretations and performed identities, the audience has become less important to certain kinds of media criticism, as the pendulum of critical thinking has swung away from empirical audience study and back towards text-based forms of academic expertise that audience studies originally reacted against. Certain studies of affect, which one might expect to involve the empirical understanding of audience emotion, have sometimes argued that affect is pre-subjective and non-conscious,[78] therefore philosophically deeming it irrelevant or impossible for audiences to have anything to say about affective processes—i.e., the ways in which media texts can be disliked, loved, circulated, imitated, or otherwise invested in. Such a philosophically underpinned retreat from audiences to texts occurs, ironically, just when audiences are most visible (in terms of Web 2.0), but also at a point when Institutional Review Boards (IRBs) in the U.S. academic system—responsible for overseeing the ethical conduct of work with human subjects— may feel restricted by an increasingly litigious social context, potentially creating unhelpful obstacles for critical audience studies.

"Viral" metaphors have appeared in philosophical work on affect,[79] suggesting that affect can be "transmitted" from person to person in a manner analogous to an infection. However, this language of contagion has been strongly disputed by scholars of fans and audiences from the cultural studies tradition. For example, Jenkins, Green, and Ford reject any "viral" discourse, which they view as downplaying or disregarding empirical audiences' agency and activity.[80] It seems curious that the affective would be defined in a way that leaves non-academic

audiences with no possibility of being heard as cultural agents—such representations of audiences as wholly subordinated to academic discourse strike me as highly problematic if not elitist and potentially reactionary. Here, it is academic criticism that produces its own institutionalized audience as an object.[81]

A similar problem has recurred in debates around TV aesthetics. Scholars have again implied that it is not really important what forms of knowledge non-academic audiences have, as only properly "tutored" subjects (i.e., the scholars themselves) can adequately analyze "good" or "quality" television.[82] Writers in the cultural studies tradition have opposed this derogation of audience interpretations and identities, countering it with an ethnographic interest in "popular aesthetics," i.e., seeking to study how fans and audiences value the artistic attributes of different media and genres.[83] Akin to work on affect, the turn to television aesthetics seems intent on restoring "tutored" academic superiority over other media audiences.

The crafting of media criticism can hence be enacted in different ways: as a dialogue between academic and non-academic audiences, where "lay" audiences are given a voice and where theoretical presumptions are challenged or complicated; or as the exercising of "good" knowledge over "bad" others, whose alleged misunderstandings or non-understandings are subordinated. As I argued in *How To Do Things With Cultural Theory*, scholarly criticism has all too often positioned itself as a form of knowledge metaphorically "above" alternative ways of knowing.[84] Against this, media criticism can aim instead to be relational, i.e., to work in relation to other cultural discourses in circulation. Here, the activity of criticism involves challenging assumptions and absences in previous scholarship. Ethnography (see Chapter 14) offers one method for carrying out these creative challenges, though if we get caught up in old binaries, such as sociology versus psychoanalysis, then there's a danger of placing academic commitments above the commitment to representing audiences as subjects rather than objects. If we fall into this trap, then audiences can become institutionalized and objectified in scholarship just as much as they are in the ratings/monetizing of media institutions.

Case Study: Psychoanalytic Ethnography and Cyclical Fandom

In my journal article, "Patterns of Surprise: The 'Aleatory Object' in Psychoanalytic Ethnography and

Cyclical Fandom,"[85] I draw on a number of primary materials. These include the self-reported memories and self-narratives of one respondent, Shaun (not his real name), produced ethnographically through a series of semi-structured interviews conducted weekly. I use a case-study format to explore, in detail, the texture and characteristics of one person's media consumption. Rather than defining my respondent as a fan of any specific film or TV show, I am interested in his wider range of tastes as part of the "diffused" audience. This involves asking about particularly intense media-related experiences and memories, and soliciting a kind of "media biography," with self-defined chapters of the life course being discussed in relation to changing pop-cultural interests.

Although case studies have sometimes been criticized for being too detailed, or for lacking generalizability,[86] a single case study can have different uses. It can provide the space for a highly reflexive encounter between researcher and researched,[87] where each can reflect on what is generated in the interview setting. And despite being a "project on a small scale,"[88] even a single case study can generate responses to open-ended questions that enable the scholar to complicate or critique established theories. Furthermore, for anyone attempting audience study for the first time, I would say that the individual case study can be incredibly useful, allowing new researchers to pilot and test their interviewing abilities with friends or family before branching out. Students sometimes imagine that audience research has to involve hundreds of questionnaires, making it a tough ask for an assignment or even a dissertation. But audience ethnography can start with an audience of one, given that as individuals we perform our contemporary audience identities in relation to an array of texts, other audiences, and assorted moments of productivity within everyday life and via social media.

In terms of secondary literature, my work was in dialogue with ethnography as well as the "object-relations" tradition of **psychoanalysis**, which is interested in how people internalize and fantasize their relationships with what are termed "objects" (i.e., other people, aesthetic experiences, and so on). But my work also related partly to sociological analyses of taste and fan studies' work, seeking to combine sociological and psychoanalytic readings into **psychosocial analysis**.

The article makes a number of claims:

1. That we need to look beyond text-centered audience work which aims to isolate out responses to one TV show or singular media product, instead examining the repertoire of people's consumption and how a variety of texts are felt to matter.

2. That characteristic and personalized or individualizing engagements can be discerned in people's media use, as well as socially and culturally predictable patterns of value and meaning being present. Questionnaires and focus groups may be more likely to access the socially predictable, precisely because participants are aware of what is culturally normative and feel happier performing this for a researcher. In contrast, more detailed, semi-structured interviews carried out repeatedly and over a period of time may be more successful in accessing the textures and idiosyncrasies of media consumption that are felt to be more personal, less culturally normative, and less "easy" to talk about as they don't always fit culturally dominant discourses of audience activity.

3. That the researcher can be understood in the same way as the researched. Far from being an objective and expert audience for my respondent's performances of audiencehood, I was also reflexively part of the exchange of ideas. And the central psychoanalytic concept that I drew on—the "aleatory object" that arrives in our life by chance and transforms us by evoking a sense of belonging or speaking to us—was applied both to myself and my interviewee. Rather than psychoanalytic reading being some sort of zero-sum game where the academic analyst is somehow all-knowing and the audience member under analysis is said to be driven by unconscious processes or to lack self-knowledge,[89] I instead posited a scenario where self and other were equally open to being surprised by media texts and "objects."

However, there were also some notable omissions in my psychosocial case study. Partly as a result of when it was written, and partly because the broader research project that this single case study was taken from involved asking people to look back on their media-related lived experience, I tended to focus on "old media," meaning that the wider data gathered perhaps did not focus sufficiently on audiences' online and "new media" practices. But the analysis also lacked an explicit focus on transmedia consumption and performances of audience identity. Although media scholarship has frequently been oriented around particular forms—film studies, TV studies, digital media studies, etc.—subsequent research has argued that as audiences' investment in a narrative increases, their concern with its specific medium decreases.[90] As audiences become immersed in story-worlds that are extended via transmedia storytelling, they read through media: the particular medium becomes almost invisible. This challenge to theories of medium specificity implies that media are less significant to invested audiences than the pop-cultural world they're intently following. However, by allowing participants in the study to discuss their media consumption in terms of memories of favored and intensely experienced popular culture, my data did at least allow people's accounts to implicitly and tacitly range across different media.

I should also have reflected more carefully on the contradiction between drawing on an ethnographic rationale—that of being "surprised" by new data such as the "cyclical fandom"[91] that Shaun discusses—and the fact that I was simultaneously using a particular theoretical framework based on object-relations psychoanalysis. To employ such a framework means conceptualizing self-identity in a very particular way. Hence, rather than my journal article offering up an ethnographic encounter whereby the researcher and researched truly enter into dialogue, one could argue that I have already constructed (or narrated and objectified) my audience respondent via theoretical discourses. This tension between challenging established theories and yet also drawing on versions of them at the same time indicates that there can be no "pure" audience ethnography. Despite textbooks sometimes arguing that we have moved from "ideal" readers to "empirical" audiences, both of these concepts still involve projecting theoretical assumptions onto the figure of "the audience." "Actual" audiences don't stop being objects of theoretical projection, even if some of these projections can enable audiences to represent their own lived experiences whilst others disqualify nonacademic discourses.

An additional omission is related to the fact that I frame my case study as widening the scope of theorized activities—bringing into focus a kind of fandom that had not been studied at that point, and looking at culturally individualizing audience discourses rather than community-based practices. I don't adequately consider how these culturally individualized audience discourses might resonate with consumer culture. Shaun may spend time waiting for the next cultural object that will have a major impact on him, but he seems to have no doubt that this event will transpire. His cyclical pursuit of the next media "hit" accords with John Tomlinson's argument that "contemporary consumption is characterized by the expectation of *delivery* [of goods and experiences] rather than of satisfaction."[92] As Tomlinson puts it, "'Delivery' ... becomes the *telos* of consumption,"[93] where "to expect ongoing 'delivery' is to imagine consumption as a 'life process,' as linear ... [and] as something strung out across a biography,"[94] which is exactly the process recounted and described by Shaun in my data.[95] It would therefore be possible to argue that this audience data could itself be subjected to further critique, with Shaun's "cyclical fandom" not only positively representing a challenge to accounts of fandom dominant in academia at the time of writing, but also displaying a consumerist discourse that calls out to be ideologically questioned.

Conclusion

I have argued that audiences are institutionally *and* theoretically shaped. But media criticism can critically challenge these constructions. This can change how we view the world, amplifying the voices of audiences rather than accepting images of them that may be highly derogatory (the vulnerable; the addicted) and linked to forms of cultural elitism and power that assume they can speak on behalf of audiences (e.g., "media effects" and censorship arguments). Audience studies can also challenge kinds of grand theory and theoretical ventriloquism whereby audiences are rigidly objectified, spoken for again, and defined as lacking in self-knowledge. "The audience" is an ever-developing concept: it is no longer linked to moments of viewing, although the "mass" audience continues to be significant via social media as well as broadcasting. Media criticism has evolved too, and the mode of analysis I've been advocating—linked to cultural studies—aims to perform qualities of *reflexivity* (reflecting on one's own position of analysis), *equality* (treating and theorizing respondents as one would hope to be theorized/treated), and *originality* (challenging outmoded theories, binaries such as psychoanalysis/sociology, and reductive understandings).

Where might media audience studies be headed? Well, as corporations accumulate ever greater stores of "big data" about audiences' practices, audience studies could respond with an emphasis on neoquantitative analysis, aiming to generate "open data" that could be shared across researchers. At the same time, how audiences access streaming media content through interfaces and via algorithmic protocols calls for further study, as do the ongoing roles of cultural context (e.g., everyday life and self-identity). And the cultural presence of produsage, where productive audiences have their own audiences, also certainly calls for additional research.[96] Furthermore, the influential "encoding/decoding" model needs to be updated and retooled with a view to properly theorizing co-decoding, as we increasingly respond to media through and in relation to a filter of others' responses, whether these are tweets, blogs, forum posts, or Facebook comments.

Notes

1. David Morley, *Family Television* (London: Comedia/ Routledge, 1986).
2. Ann Gray, *Research Practice for Cultural Studies* (London: Sage, 2003), 100.
3. For example, Philip Schlesinger, Rebecca Dobash, Russell Dobash, and C. Kay Weaver, *Women Viewing Violence* (London: BFI, 1992).
4. Nick Abercrombie and Brian Longhurst, *Audiences: A Sociological Theory of Performance and Imagination* (London: Sage, 1998), 4.
5. For example, Jenny Kitzinger, *Framing Abuse: Media Influence and Public Understanding of Sexual Violence Against Children* (London: Pluto Press, 2004).
6. David Bordwell, *Making Meaning* (Cambridge: Harvard University Press, 1989).
7. Chuck Tryon, *On-Demand Culture: Digital Delivery and the Future of Movies* (New Brunswick: Rutgers University Press, 2013).
8. Philip M. Napoli, *Audience Evolution* (New York: Columbia University Press, 2011), 3.
9. Ien Ang, *Desperately Seeking the Audience* (London: Routledge, 1991), 32.
10. Ibid., 34–35.
11. Gray, *Research Practice*, 100.
12. Richard Butsch, *The Citizen Audience* (London: Routledge, 2008), 133.
13. Lisa Glebatis Perks, *Media Marathoning* (Lanham: Lexington Books, 2015), ix.
14. Joseph M. Reagle, *Reading the Comments* (Cambridge: MIT Press, 2015).
15. Alice E. Marwick, *Status Update: Celebrity, Publicity and Branding in the Social Media Age* (New Haven: Yale University Press, 2013), 213.
16. John L. Sullivan, *Media Audiences* (London: Sage, 2013), 245.
17. Axel Bruns, *Blogs, Wikipedia, Second Life and Beyond* (New York: Peter Lang, 2008), 215.
18. Henry Jenkins, *Textual Poachers* (New York: Routledge, 1992); Matt Hills, *Fan Cultures* (London: Routledge, 2002).
19. Henry Jenkins, Sam Ford, and Joshua Green, *Spreadable Media: Creating Value and Meaning in a Networked Culture* (New York: New York University Press, 2013).
20. Kate Lacey, *Listening Publics: The Politics and Experience of Listening in the Media Age* (Cambridge: Polity Press, 2013), 13–14.
21. Ibid., 14.
22. Butsch, *Citizen Audience*.
23. John Fiske, "Moments of Television: Neither the Text nor the Audience," in *Remote Control: Television, Audiences and Cultural Power*, ed. Ellen Seiter, Hans Borchers, Gabriele Kreutzner, and Eva-Maria Warth (New York: Routledge, 1991), 56–78.
24. David Gauntlett, *Making is Connecting* (Cambridge: Polity Press, 2011).
25. Martin Barker, "Crossing Out the Audience," in *Audiences*, ed. Ian Christie (Amsterdam: Amsterdam University Press, 2012), 190.
26. David Morley, *Television, Audiences and Cultural Studies* (London: Routledge, 1992), 88.
27. Roland Barthes, *Image-Music-Text* (London: Fontana, 1977), 142–48.
28. Thomas Austin, *Hollywood, Hype and Audiences. Selling and Watching Popular Film in the 1990s* (Manchester: Manchester University Press, 2002), 13.
29. Nicholas Garnham, *Emancipation, the Media, and Modernity* (Oxford: Oxford University Press, 2000), 126.
30. Morley, *Television, Audiences*, 38.
31. Robert W. McChesney, *Digital Disconnect* (New York: The New Press, 2013).
32. Jackie Stacey, *Stargazing: Hollywood Cinema and Female Spectatorship* (London: Routledge, 1994).
33. Annette Kuhn, *An Everyday Magic: Cinema and Cultural Memory* (London: I.B. Tauris, 2002).
34. Martin Barker, Jane Arthurs, and Ramaswami Harindranath, *The Crash Controversy: Censorship Campaigns and Film Reception* (London: Wallflower Press, 2001), 127–28.
35. Austin, *Hollywood, Hype*.
36. Charlotte Brunsdon, *The Feminist, the Housewife, and the Soap Opera* (Oxford: Clarendon Press, 2000); Beverley Skeggs and Helen Wood, *Reacting to Reality Television* (London: Routledge, 2012).
37. Jason Mittell, *Complex TV: The Poetics of Contemporary Television Storytelling* (New York: New York University Press, 2015).
38. Michael Kackman, "Quality Television, Melodrama, and Cultural Complexity," in *Flow*, October 31, 2008, accessed June 11, 2017, www.flowjournal.org/2008/10/ quality-television-melodrama-and-cultural-complexity %C2%A0michael-kackman%C2%A0%C2% A0university-of-texas-austin%C2%A0%C2%A0/; Michael Z. Newman and Elana Levine, *Legitimating Television: Media Convergence and Cultural Status* (New York: Routledge, 2012).
39. Abercrombie and Longhurst, *Audiences*, 159; Sonia Livingstone, "On the Relation between Audiences

and Publics," in *Audiences and Publics: When Cultural Engagement Matters for the Public Sphere*, ed. Sonia Livingstone (Bristol: Intellect, 2005), 26.

40. Tryon, *On-Demand Culture*.

41. Abercrombie and Longhurst, *Audiences*, 179.

42. Nick Couldry, "The Extended Audience: Scanning the Horizon," in *Media Audiences*, ed. Marie Gillespie (Maidenhead: Open University Press, 2005), 183–222.

43. Fiske, "Moments"; Jenkins, *Textual Poachers*.

44. Sullivan, *Media Audiences*, 246.

45. Nick Couldry, *Inside Culture* (London: Sage, 2000), 73.

46. Annette Hill, *Paranormal Media: Audiences, Spirits and Magic in Popular Culture* (London: Routledge, 2011), 151.

47. Jonathan Gray, "New Audiences, New Textualities: Anti-Fans and Non-Fans," *International Journal of Cultural Studies* 6, no. 1 (2003): 64–81.

48. Abercrombie and Longhurst, *Audiences*, 177–78.

49. Stuart Hall, "Encoding/Decoding," in *Culture, Media, Language*, ed. Stuart Hall, Dorothy Hobson, Andrew Lowe, and Paul Willis (London: Hutchinson, 1980), 128–38.

50. Hall, "Encoding/Decoding," 135–36.

51. Abercrombie and Longhurst, *Audiences*, 20.

52. Morley, *Television, Audiences*, 126–27.

53. Stuart Hall, "Reflections upon the Encoding/Decoding Model: An Interview with Stuart Hall," in *Viewing, Reading, Listening: Audiences and Cultural Reception*, ed. Jon Cruz and Justin Lewis (Boulder: Westview Press, 1994), 266.

54. Jonathan Gray, *Watching with The Simpsons* (New York: Routledge, 2006), 35.

55. See Lynn Spigel, *Make Room for TV* (Chicago: University of Chicago Press, 1992).

56. Anna McCarthy, *Ambient Television* (Durham: Duke University Press, 2001).

57. Joke Hermes, *Reading Women's Magazines* (Cambridge: Polity Press, 1995), 12–17.

58. Ibid., 144.

59. Cornel Sandvoss, *Fans: The Mirror of Consumption* (Cambridge: Polity Press, 2005); Mark Duffett, *Understanding Fandom* (London: Bloomsbury Academic, 2013).

60. Gray, "New Audiences."

61. Lucy Bennett, "Tracing *Textual Poachers*: Reflections on the Development of Fan Studies and Digital Fandom," *Journal of Fandom Studies* 2, no. 1 (2014): 13.

62. Although "slash" has been used as a term in fandom and scholarship to refer to male–male pairings, "femslash" fan fiction focuses on relationships posited between female characters.

63. Jenkins, *Textual Poachers*.

64. Lynn Zubernis and Katherine Larsen, *Fandom at the Crossroads* (Newcastle: Cambridge Scholars Publishing, 2012), 143–74.

65. Abigail De Kosnik, "*Fifty Shades* and the Archive of Women's Culture," *Cinema Journal* 54, no. 3 (2015): 122.

66. Ian Condry, *The Soul of Anime: Collaborative Creativity and Japan's Media Success Story* (Durham: Duke University Press, 2013), 111.

67. Butsch, *Citizen Audience*; Livingstone, "On the Relation."

68. Lincoln Geraghty, *Cult Collectors* (London: Routledge, 2014).

69. Jonathan Gray, *Show Sold Separately* (New York: New York University Press, 2010).

70. Audiences' "performativity" has therefore merited a far greater research focus; for key work on this concept, see Judith Butler, *Gender Trouble* (London: Routledge, 2006).

71. John Fiske, "Ethnosemiotics: Some Personal and Theoretical Reflections," *Cultural Studies* 4, no.1 (1990): 86.

72. Pierre Bourdieu, *Distinction* (London: Routledge, 1986).

73. Newman and Levine, *Legitimating Television*.

74. Christine Gledhill, "Speculations on the Relationship between Soap Opera and Melodrama," *Quarterly Review of Film and Video* 14, no. 1–2 (1992): 103–24; Skeggs and Wood, *Reacting to Reality Television*.

75. Ramon Lobato, *Shadow Economies of Cinema: Mapping Informal Film Distribution* (London: BFI Publishing/Palgrave Macmillan, 2012).

76. Elizabeth Evans, *Transmedia Television: Audiences, New Media and Daily Life* (London: Routledge, 2011), 166.

77. Bertha Chin and Lori Morimoto, "Towards a Theory of Transcultural Fandom," *Participations* 10, no.1 (2013): 92–108.

78. Brian Massumi, *The Power at the End of the Economy* (Durham: Duke University Press, 2015).

79. Anna Gibbs, "Affect Theory and Audiences," in *The Handbook of Media Audiences*, ed. Virginia Nightingale (Malden: Wiley Blackwell, 2014), 264.

80. Jenkins, Ford and Green, *Spreadable Media*, 21.

81. Ang, *Desperately Seeking*, 34–35.

82. Sarah Cardwell, "Television Aesthetics: Stylistic Analysis and Beyond," in *Television Aesthetics and Style*, ed. Jason Jacobs and Steven Peacock (London: Bloomsbury Academic, 2013), 23–44.

83. Matt Hills and Amy Luther, "Investigating '*CSI* Television Fandom': Fans' Textual Paths through the Franchise," in CSI: *Crime TV Under the Microscope*, ed. Michael Allen (London: I.B. Tauris, 2007), 208–21.

84. Matt Hills, *How to Do Things with Cultural Theory* (London: Hodder-Arnold, 2005), 150; see also Brunsdon, *The Feminist* on feminist criticism's "us versus them" approach to women audiences.

85. Matt Hills, "Patterns of Surprise: The 'Aleatory Object' in Psychoanalytic Ethnography and Cyclical Fandom," *American Behavioral Scientist* 48, no. 7 (2005): 801–21.

86. Jo Whitehouse-Hart, *Psychosocial Explorations of Film and Television Viewing: Ordinary Audience* (London: Palgrave Macmillan, 2014), 63.

87. Gray, *Research Practice*, 95–96.
88. Kristyn Gorton, *Media Audiences: Television, Meaning and Emotion* (Edinburgh: Edinburgh University Press, 2009), 154.
89. Fiske, "Ethnosemiotics," 90.
90. Barker, "Crossing Out."
91. The process of discovering a fan object and becoming immersed in it before seeming to exhaust the topic, then rapidly moving on to a whole new fandom.
92. John Tomlinson, *The Culture of Speed: The Coming of Immediacy* (London: Sage, 2007), 138.
93. Ibid., 139.
94. Ibid., 140.
95. Of course, it could be argued that this expectation has a longer history stretching back at least to the serialized fiction of Charles Dickens. The difference here lies in the extent to which this expectation has been internalized as part of a biographical "life process" of consumerism.
96. Ranjana Das and Brita Ytre-Arne, ed., *Audiences, towards 2030: Priorities for Audience Analysis* (Surrey: CEDAR, 2017).

Further Reading

Brooker, Will and Deborah Jermyn, eds., *The Audience Studies Reader* (London: Routledge, 2003).

Carpentier, Nico, Kim Christian Schrøder, and Lawrie Hallett, eds., *Audience Transformations* (New York: Routledge, 2014).

Robinson, M.J., *Television on Demand: Curatorial Culture and the Transformation of TV* (New York: Bloomsbury Academic, 2017).

16.
GENRE
Amanda Ann Klein

Overview

The aim of **genre studies** is to bring order, structure, and stability to a group of texts sharing similar characteristics—including characters, plots, themes, and settings—so that these texts can be studied collectively and comparatively. **Genre** has been described through multiple metaphors: as a blueprint or structure on which a text is built; as a label for marketing a product to the audience; as a contract or viewing position established among the text, its producer, and the audience consuming it; and as a language, or shared set of signs, that allows audiences to make sense of the text. Rick Altman, whose scholarship has been some of the most prominent and influential in the field of genre studies, argues that genres not only open up meanings, they also limit them: "Rather than seeing genres as structures helping individual texts to produce meaning, we must see genres as restrictive, as complex methods of reducing the field of play of individual texts."[1] Steve Neale, another influential genre scholar, argues that genres do not consist only of texts; a genre is also defined by "specific systems of expectation and hypothesis that spectators bring with them to the [text]" and that interact with the text during the viewing process.[2] For example, viewers of the realist police drama, *The Wire* (HBO, 2002–08), would be shocked if Stringer Bell began singing a pop version of "Don't Stop Believin'" in the middle of Baltimore. However, if a character in the musical television series, *Glee* (Fox, 2009–15), did the same thing, fans would not question it because breaking into song is a convention of the musical.

At the heart of genre studies is the belief that new meanings can be unlocked when a text is studied in relation to other texts that have similar **iconography** (settings, characters, and images), **conventions** (a small, relatively separate unit of action within the film), plot **formulas**, and **themes**. While, for example, the classic gangster film, *Little Caesar* (1930) is, with the exception of Edward G. Robinson's charismatic performance, a fairly unremarkable film on its own (static direction, trite action sequences, and a wooden script), it becomes a more meaningful text when understood in the context of the larger gangster genre. When scholars watch *Little Caesar as* a gangster film and *in conversation* with other gangster films released around the same time, like *Underworld* (1928), *Public Enemy* (1931), and *Scarface* (1932), certain details begin to take on a new resonance: (1) How, in pre-Code Hollywood, there was a public interest in stories about outlaw immigrants who take what they want; (2) How the basic tension at the heart of the American Dream is between the desires of the individual and the needs of society as a whole; and (3) How most of the classic gangster films were made at Warner Bros. studios due to its interest in realist, "ripped from the headlines," stories. Here, genre studies acts as a lens, revealing a world of meanings and connections not readily visible when a text is read in isolation. It is not necessary to have seen other gangster films to appreciate and enjoy *Little Caesar*, but the viewer's experience of the film is enhanced by having had previous encounters with gangster films, as illustrated above.

Although genre is a useful analytical tool, a fundamental issue in the field is that there is no litmus test for determining when a text might be usefully categorized as belonging to one genre or another, or whether a text is part of multiple genres, or any genres at all. In this way, as Andrew Tudor writes, "Genre is what we collectively believe it to be."[3] A movie like *Guys and Dolls* (1955), for example, *looks* like a gangster film, but it *functions* like a musical. A movie like *Shaun of the Dead* (2004) is both a horror film *and* a comedy. How we interpret these films will shift depending on the generic framework in which we analyze them. This is the inherent slipperiness of genre studies. No matter how careful the methodology, a theory of genres will never neatly line up with its material history. Indeed, if there is one consistency to be found throughout the history of genre studies, it is this tension between history and theory, between how audiences understand and consume a genre, and how critics and producers define a genre.

It's also important to keep in mind that the lens of genre is not the *only* method for categorizing media texts. For example, David Bordwell argues that the labels **art film** and **classical narrative cinema** are useful ways to sort and analyze films.[4] Jeffrey Sconce uses the label **paracinema** to group films together based on similarities in aesthetics (bad), budgets (low), audience (juvenile, marginalized), and subject matter (sensational).[5] Media industries scholars might categorize a film based on whether it was produced by a major studio or a small, independent collective, whether it has a wide theatrical release or limited release, or whether it was released directly to DVD. Television scholars might use terms like soap opera, sit-com, and police procedural to provide ways of grouping together television series based on shared characteristics. Terms like broadcast, cable, and subscription streaming services also serve as useful explanatory labels for various television series. Of course, the rise and increasing cultural cachet of digital streaming platforms means that the student of television might be well served by categorizing contemporary streaming TV based on its mode of production (cable, streaming, network) or even by its platform (Hulu, Netflix, Amazon).[6] These conceptual categories are useful but function differently from generic categories. The explanatory power of genre studies is in its ability to trace a common story, character, or theme across a variety of media texts, over the course of decades, in order to see how that story, character, or theme is translated and communicated at different times, in different ways, for different audiences and purposes.

Intellectual History of the Concept

The concept of genre dates back, as so many literary concepts do, to Aristotle's *Poetics* (c.335 BCE), wherein the philosopher argues that it is possible to categorize certain poems by their "essential qualities,"

and by impact of these codified qualities on their audience. While Aristotle's work argues for the existence of genres, Horace's *Ars Poetica* (The art of poetry), written in 19 BC, takes their existence for granted.[7] Of interest to genre scholars is Horace's belief that specific forms of poetry require specific writing styles and diction. For example, he writes that tragedy should not "prate forth trivial verses . . . [l]ike a matron commanded to dance on the festival days."[8] Aristotle and Horace thus established the roots of the neoclassical approach to the study of literary genres, taken up again in the seventeenth century by neoclassical poets like John Dryden and Alexander Pope, who were primarily concerned with identifying discrete genres and naming their characteristics. By contrast, the Romantics of the nineteenth century were more interested in questioning the concept of "pure" genres, noting how easily generic borders break down when the critics looks too closely. This was also the same time period in which genre theory became heavily influenced by the work of evolutionary scientists, like Charles Darwin, who aimed to classify and sort organisms into discrete categories.[9] So while genre studies was a field first located in theories of fine art, genre scholars began to rely on science to bolster its claims for order and reason. In *The Order of Things* (1966), French philosopher, Michel Foucault, argues that this need to taxonomize the world is a recurring theme in human history. Of particular interest to the field of genre studies is the fact that this need to order things into categories is often taken as natural, when in reality, it is always a human construct.[10]

In the twentieth century, critics like Benedetto Croce argued against the notion that all literature can be located within the boundaries of genre, whether pure or mixed.[11] Croce saw genres as one approach to writing and in opposition to writing that is innovative and actively seeking to be different than what came before it. Hence genre became a way to impugn a text as being less creative or less original (a trend that continues today with the critical disdain for sequels, remakes, and reboots). In *Anatomy of Criticism* (1957), Northrop Frye identifies four archetypal generic plots, or **mythoi**: romantic, tragic, comic, and ironic. He also identifies five basic modes of fiction characterized by the relationship between the plot's protagonist, supporting characters, and/or the environment.[12] Less than 15 years later, Tzvetan Todorov published *The Fantastic: A Structural Approach to a Literary Genre* (1970), which is both a case study of a single genre—fantasy—and an examination of genre theory itself. Todorov faults

Frye for not distinguishing between what he sees as theoretical genres, which are formulated through and by literary theory (i.e., produced by critics), and historical genres, which result from studying what texts actually exist (i.e., produced by history).[13] Here the question of where genres come from—do they exist out in the world (the historical approach to genres) or only in the words of critics (the theoretical approach to genres)—takes its modern form.

Prior to the late 1950s, most American film critics were in agreement with Theodor Adorno and Max Horkheimer's critique of the popular culture industry, which they believed bred mindlessness and compliance among its consumers.[14] American genre films, like Westerns, gangster films, and musicals, were largely viewed through this culture industry lens as simple, mass-produced, studio products that catered to the lowest common denominator. The cinema clubs that popped up in the United States in the 1950s and 1960s often centered on films imported from France, Sweden, and Italy—the so-called European art cinema—because American cinema was thought to be too commercial and, therefore, crass. But with the development of *auteur* theory, first pioneered by the critics-turned-directors who wrote for *Cahiers du Cinéma* in the 1950s, like Francois Truffaut,[15] and later by American critics like Andrew Sarris, the study of American cinema earned more cultural capital and critical cachet.[16] **Auteur theory** is the idea that the film's director is the text's sole "author," even (and especially) during the reign of the Hollywood studio system when directors were generally given a set budget, cast, and crew; auteurs working under these limited rules nevertheless managed to lend each film their unique vision. However, cinema studies' focus on auteurs—and determining who fitted into this rarefied category—ignored one of the key precepts that would be foundational to genre studies: structure. Genre criticism argues that the larger meaning of a work (or a body of work) comes not from the meanings of its individual elements, but from how they interrelate within a "formal system."

In the 1980s, Vivian Sobchack was one of the first scholars to apply structuralism to the study of film.[17] She relies on the work of anthropologist Claude Levi-Strauss, who uses structural linguistics (taken from the work of Ferdinand de Saussure), to better understand the laws and beliefs governing human rituals. Of interest to Sobchack is Levi-Strauss' analysis of how myths are deployed across cultures to provide concrete explanations for resolving unresolvable human conflicts. Indeed, genre films often present problems

as conflicts between two opposing poles, or binary oppositions, which are impossible to resolve in real life but which can be resolved on screen. As Thomas Schatz, another important figure in the field of genre theory, explains, "The sustained popularity of any genre indicates the essentially unresolvable, irreconcilable nature of those oppositions."[18] Westerns reveal the American audience's conflicted views of how American civilized society was established (would we have been better off without laws?) while horror films highlight the individuals or forces in society that we see as a threat to the Self (i.e., the "Other" or monster). This **structuralist approach** to genre also reveals how we—the audience—are interested in seeing these conflicts addressed and negotiated over and over again on screen. Arguing that genre films were part of the enduring, deep structures of human storytelling also offered a patina of respectability to the new field of film studies.

The work of French Marxist philosopher Louis Althusser was integral in the development of an **ideological approach** to studying genres, which is often contrasted with the structuralist approach discussed above. Althusser contends that the media are powerful examples of ideological state apparatuses that interpellate their viewers and transform them into compliant subjects.[19] Judith Hess Wright applies this theory to genres, arguing that a central feature of generic texts is their ability to address social conflicts and resolve them in simplistic and reactionary ways. (See also Chapter 1 in this anthology.) She explains that American genre films, namely Westerns, science fiction films, horror films, and gangster films, help to reinforce the status quo by "produc[ing] satisfaction rather than action, pity and fear rather than revolt."[20] Unlike the **structuralist approach** to genre, which argues that genre films were developed to satisfy a human need to hear certain stories over and over again, this **ideological approach** to genre argues that genre films tell audiences how to think, feel, and act. In the former, genres are at the service of audiences; in the latter, audiences are programmed how to think by the genres they consume.

In the late twentieth century, there was a move away from a strictly theory-based approach to media studies. Scholars began to return to the archive and to attend to questions of history and use. Innovative genre studies like Rick Altman's *Film/Genre* (1999) and Steve Neale's *Genre and Hollywood* (2000), aimed to reevaluate the foundations of genre theory by questioning how generic structures have been traditionally defined and understood. Both studies rely heavily on historical evidence to complicate otherwise neat generic categorization. *Refiguring Film Genres: Theory and History* (1998), an anthology edited by Nick Browne, also investigates how our understanding of genre changes when history is consulted.[21] Thus, in the late 1990s, the study of film genres was once again a flourishing discipline, reanimated by this return to history.

Much as the field of film studies initially borrowed its language of genre theory from the already-established field of literary studies, the field of television studies initially based its terminology and approaches to genre on film studies. As Jason Mittell notes, this approach does not account

> for many of the specific industry and audience practices unique to television (such as scheduling decisions, commonplace serialization, habitual viewing, and channel segmentation), as well as for the mixture of fictional and nonfictional programming that constitutes the lineup on nearly every TV channel.[22]

Jane Feuer's essay on sitcoms, "Genre Study and Television" (1992), offers one of the earliest attempts to apply genre theory to the medium of television. Feuer argued that genres were necessary in the early history of the television industry as a surefire way to predict audience interest in a new medium but that the television industry also works to redefine the audience for its own ends. Thus, the scholar of television genres must ask medium-specific questions such as, "What caused the TV industry to redefine the audience at certain points?" and "To what extent does this correspond to material changes in culture?"[23]

Another unique feature of TV genres is that television programs do not operate as discrete texts to the same extent as movies; before the development of the DVR and streaming television, there was **flow** from one program to the next, and programs were interrupted at regular intervals by commercial advertisements.[24] Mittell expands on Feuer's work in his monograph *Genre and Television: From Cop Shows to Cartoons in American Culture* (2004), arguing that classifying TV genres based primarily on the textual components of a series is unstable.[25] For example, a series like *Laguna Beach: The Real O.C.* (2004–06), which may have been categorized as a reality show capitalizing on the success of a scripted series like *The O.C.* (2003–07) at the time of its release, may later be "regenrified" as part of a larger trend of reality programming on MTV that focuses on micro slices

of youth identities. This cycle of reality programming would dominate MTV's programming for more than a decade, leading to successful series, such as *The Hills* (2006–10), *Teen Mom* (2009–present), and *Jersey Shore* (2009–12). Furthermore, applying genre studies to a television series that runs for years or even decades (like *The Simpsons* [Fox, 1989–present]) can be more challenging than working with a single two-hour film with a defined beginning, middle, and end. A television series will change from its pilot episode to its series finale, possibly becoming a different genre, or appealing to a completely different audience. Scholars of television genres must therefore always be aware of the medium of analysis and its formal and industrial particularities.[26]

The consolidation of TV networks, film studios, music studios, and print media into just a handful of large conglomerates means it is has become increasingly difficult to discuss media platforms as discrete industries. Many different media forms exist today, made by different industries, and yet, the structure of the texts, their budgets, and audiences are deeply intertwined. As Jennifer Holt writes: "[A]ny industrial analysis, particularly those focused on more contemporary periods, must view film, cable *and* broadcast history as integral pieces of the same puzzle, and parts of the same whole."[27] Critics tend to separate film genres from TV genres (and TV genres from literary and theatrical genres), but it's far more useful to consider these media all together when discussing genre. To be sure, this was true even before the era of media deregulation and consequent media conglomeration (1980–96). For example, when discussing a genre like the Western, it is challenging to articulate the distinctions between serialized, 1930s B Westerns, like those starring Gene Autry and Roy Rogers, and the Western TV series of the 1950s, like *Bonanza* (NBC, 1959–73). The television Western cannot be detached from its B Western predecessors, and B Westerns owe *their* origins to a variety of sources: folk music celebrating the life of cowboys on the open range, Indigenous American captivity narratives which were told and shared from the late seventeenth century until the close of the Unites States' frontier late in the nineteenth century, the Wild West shows performed along the East Coast after the Civil War, late-nineteenth century dime novels celebrating (and exaggerating) the derring-do of gunfighters and "savage Indians," and even the work of American painter, Fredric Remington, whose work was published in *Harper's Weekly* and widely distributed as a "realistic" rendering of life in the West.

Given the way that media texts influence, borrow, steal, and replicate the stories, characters, and images found across the cultural spectrum, it is a fool's errand to segregate genre studies by medium. In order to usefully consider texts from different media forms as belonging to the same genre, the media scholar must find a common language for reading signs stemming from two different sign systems (e.g., **semiotic systems**). For example, in the early 1990s, the politicized antiestablishment lyrics and accompanying music videos by rappers like N.W.A. and Tupac Shakur were translated into the imagery of the highly successful but controversial ghetto action film cycle (i.e., *New Jack City* [1991] and *Boyz N the Hood* [1991], *Menace II Society* [1993], among others), which was later replicated in (equally controversial) video games like *Grand Theft Auto* (Rockstar Games, 1997). Although the semiotics of a rap lyric are words and notes, and the semiotics of a film are image and sound, the concept of the urban, criminalized, black male easily flows across platforms.

Major Concepts

One of the first questions a student of genre faces is that of establishing the **corpus,** or the body of texts, which compose a genre. When a media scholar begins to study a genre, she can go about it in one of two ways. She can first identify the genre itself (e.g., the musical) and its characteristics (e.g., characters burst into song), or she can locate a group of texts that share certain characteristics and *then* determine a generic category. Does one begin with the chicken or the egg? This quandary, which Tudor calls **the empiricist's dilemma**, points to the often-arbitrary nature of defining genres as well as to the fundamental role played by the critic in deciding which texts and characteristics "count" as part of a particular genre. He writes that the body of texts considered to be part of a genre "can only be isolated on the basis of the 'principal characteristics,' which can only be discovered from the films themselves after they have been isolated."[28] Janet Staiger also rejects these methods because they work in service of a "purity thesis" in genre studies; it is a standard no genre can live up to.[29]

Genres are generally defined as groups of texts that share the same iconography, conventions, plot formulas, and themes. But this definition is more complicated than it appears. A film like *Oklahoma!* (1955) has the iconography of the Western—ranchers, cowboys, gun fights, and barn dances—but the central theme of *Oklahoma!* is the opposition between the rational world in which people live their lives and the fantastical world in which they can sing and dance about their feelings, a theme central to the musical genre. So where do we place *Oklahoma!?* Does it belong under the heading of the Western or the musical? The first reading above categorizes *Oklahoma!* as a Western because of its **semantics**, or the repeated iconography, conventions, and plot formulas of the genre. When using a **semantic approach** to genre, critics focus on the surface structure of the genre and the characters, plots, and settings that they all share. The second reading categorizes *Oklahoma!* as a musical because of its **syntax**, or its deep thematic structure. When using a syntactic approach, critics focus on the basic conflict at the heart of the genre. The gangster genre's conflict is the individual versus society, the horror text is centered around the Self versus the Other, and the unchanging conflict around which every Western is centered is civilization versus savagery. No matter when a genre film is released and no matter what stories it tells, its central thematic core remains static.

Schatz compares the concepts of syntax and semantics to theories of language, by borrowing from the work of linguist Ferdinand de Saussure.[30] Schatz argues that a generic syntax is the *langue*, "a system of rules of expression and construction," while a genre's semantics represent an individual utterance or *parole*, a "manifestation of these rules."[31] In the Western, the conflict between civilization and savagery (its syntax) represents the rules (or *langue*) of that genre, while each individual Western is another attempt to resolve this conflict, another manifestation (or *parole*) of the Western's rules. Critics who define a genre only by its semantic elements will find they have created a corpus that is broad and inclusive but lacks explanatory power. By contrast, critics who define a genre only by its syntax will create a more limited exclusive corpus that opens up meanings in the text but is often an ahistorical view of the text.

Rick Altman usefully solves this problem with his **semantic/syntactic approach** to genre studies, an approach that ties these two methods of genre analysis into a single system. He argues: "[G]enres arise in one of two fundamental ways: either a relatively stable set of semantic givens is developed through syntactic experimentation into a coherent and durable syntax, or an already existing syntax adopts a new set of semantic elements."[32] This approach unites theory (a syntactic approach) with history (a semantic approach). Years after he first developed his semantic/syntactic approach to genre,

Figure 16.1 Is *Oklahoma!* a musical or a Western? (1955, RKO Radio Pictures)

Altman added a third methodology that factors in the uses of a genre, or its **pragmatics**. A **semantic/syntactic/pragmatic approach** argues that scholars of genre view genre films, not just as sets of images and themes, but as texts that are *used*—by audiences, producers, exhibitors, and even cultural agencies.[33] This approach to corpus building has also been employed by music and television scholars.[34]

Building a genre's corpus is also complicated by **modes** like *film noir* or melodrama. A **mode** is a visual style of production that can be applied to a wide range of media texts. For example, *High Noon* (1952) is a Western, *The Day the Earth Stood Still* (1951) is science fiction, and *Veronica Mars* (UPN, CW, 2004–07) is a teen TV series, but all three texts can *also* be classified as *noir* due to their reliance on *chiaroscuro* (the dramatic use of light and shadow) and their sense of fatalism and moral ambiguity. **Modes** are not genres but rather cut *across* generic lines, bringing together media texts from different genres.

Generic evolution is the idea that media texts will undergo a predictable development over time. This idea of the evolution of art forms was first addressed by Henri Focillon in the book *The Life of Forms in Art* (1948), which argues that cultural forms have a predictable life span, moving from a period of experimentation, to equilibrium, and then on to increasingly self-conscious forms.[35] As an explanatory tool, the evolutionary model is ahistorical—it is able to account for certain media texts only at certain moments in time. In reality, genres do not experience a linear model of change; they go through periods of self-reflexivity and periods of earnestness or conservatism, and these periods can recur throughout

the life of a genre (as opposed to moving through these stages in a linear fashion).[36] Furthermore, the term "evolution" implies that later examples of a genre will somehow be "better"—more intelligent, more complex, more self-aware—than earlier, more "naïve" examples. Because the evolutionary model of generic change is ahistorical, historians like Tag Gallagher argue that a genre's history is best understood in terms of **cycles**.[37] Cycles are a series of texts associated with each other due to shared images, characters, settings, plots, or themes. However, while genres are primarily defined by the repetition of key images (their semantics) and themes (their syntax), cycles are primarily defined by how they are used (their pragmatics). In other words, the formation and longevity of media cycles are more directly tied than genres are to their immediate financial viability as well as the public discourses circulating around them, including reviews, advertisements and trailers, social media discourse, and media coverage. A cycle will form only if its originating text—the text that establishes the images, plot formulas, and themes for the entire cycle—is financially or critically successful. Genres may be composed of discrete cycles (like the gangster film), and cycles can also stand alone as their own structure (the torture porn cycle of the early 2000s).[38]

In light of the ever-increasing way in which texts move from page to screen to tablet to video game and back again, it is all the more pressing that scholars find cohesive ways for discussing transgeneric groupings, and theorizing the complicated ties between medium, text, audience, industry, and culture. As Henry Jenkins notes, "**Transmedia** storytelling represents a process where integral elements of a fiction get dispersed systematically across multiple delivery channels for the purpose of creating a unified and coordinated entertainment experience."[39] For example, Tasha Oren and Sharon Shahaf argue that it is important to consider the industrial and cultural consequences of our global entertainment landscape.[40] Their anthology, *Global Television Formats,* studies the way certain television series, like reality television franchises, are repackaged for different global audiences. Likewise, Barton Palmer and I coined the term **multiplicities** as a way to categorize media texts that consciously repeat and exploit images, narratives, or characters found in previous texts. Within this category we include cycles, but also modes, sequels, trilogies, series, remakes, and reboots. Perhaps the most central trait of multiplicities is that they lack an end: "they can be constantly told, retold, reconfigured, and spread across platforms, no matter how many times the monster is defeated or the world is saved."[41] Although film and television seem to be dominated by multiplicities at the moment, it is a production strategy that dates back to the earliest era of filmmaking; the repetition, continuation, and retelling of stories has always been a feature of mass media.[42] For example, *Dead End* (1937) was part of a larger cycle of social problem films addressing economic and social inequality in America produced by Warner Bros. in the 1930s. The group of boys who starred in *Dead End* were featured widely in public discourses surrounding the film, and they soon went on to star in a series of social-problem films centering on their exploits in the city, including *Angels with Dirty Faces* (1938), *Hell's Kitchen* (1939), and *Angels Wash Their Faces* (1939). The success of the "Dead End Kids" as a concept led to these young actors to being cast in three additional cycles of films, all of which were primarily comic, not tragic. Images that provoked pity in the original cycle, like a starving boy stealing food, became the basis for a comic chase scene in later series like the "East Side Kids" and the "Bowery Boys." Here we can see how a story told in a film like *Dead End* can become something very different after it is repeated across dozens of films over the course of several decades.

A **sequel** is a text that continues a story that was begun in a previous text. As Carolyn Jess-Cooke notes, "Deriving from the Latin verb *sequi,* meaning 'to follow', a sequel usually performs a linear narrative extension, designating the text from which it derives as an 'original' rooted in 'beforeness'."[43] A sequel is explicitly tied to the text that precedes it and may

even repeat the title of the first film. (See, for example, *Breakin'* [1984] and its sequel, *Breakin'2: Electric Boogaloo* [1984].) A **trilogy** is a text that appears in a set of three, such as *The Lord of the Rings* trilogy (2001, 2002, 2003) and the *Matrix* (1999, 2003, 2003) trilogies. As Claire Perkins and Con Verevis explain,

> These trilogies function as planned, tripartite exercises, where the designation is a specific prop in the films' production and marketing. Each set of films was initially promoted as a three-part series to build a sense of structure and anticipation designed to translate into box office returns upon the release of the first and second sequels.[44]

Generally speaking, a trilogy tells a complete story that has an "end."

A **series** is a group of texts that continues a story, and follows its characters across four or more films, along with the possibility to go on infinitely (as long as there is audience interest or demand). As Verevis and Perkins explain, "[S]equels operate in a linear fashion to pick up the thread of their characters' lives, whereas each entry in a film series offers a new adventure for the characters in a temporally indistinct manner."[45] A **remake** is a text that retells the same story with the same characters, rather than continuing a story that was started in a previous text (i.e., a sequel). Remakes are texts that "to one degree or another *announce* to us that they embrace one or more previous texts."[46] For example, *The Dukes of Hazzard* (2005) is a cinematic remake of the television series (CBS, 1979–85), relying on the same settings and characters in both media platforms. A **reboot** is a text that retells the same story with the same characters, but which also "attempts to disassociate itself textually from previous iterations while at the same time having to concede that it does not replace—but adds new associations to—an existing (serial) property."[47] For example, *The Dark Knight* (2008) and *Batman* (1989) feature the same character, the same origin story, and the same villains, but Nolan's Batman is a reboot of Burton's film (and the *Batman* series released in 1992, 1995, and 1997) because it was made with a desire to revive the entire franchise with a new aesthetic and new actors, and, thus, make the films appealing to a new generation of moviegoers.

All of these categories—genres, cycles, modes, sequels, series, trilogies, remakes, and reboots—are specific examples of ways to group films that consciously repeat the semantics or syntax of a previous text. The semantics and the syntax of one genre film may be repeated in other films of that genre, or in a stand-alone cycle. Likewise, a genre film may be part of a trilogy (like *The Godfather* films [1972, 1974, 1990]), or remade or rebooted (like *Scarface* [1932, 1983]). But not *all* trilogies, remakes, and reboots are genre films, even though they, by definition, repeat the images, plots, and characters found in other films. It is also important to note that a non-genre film, a film that lacks an interrelated semantics and syntax, can still produce a sequel (*The Color of Money* [1986]), be part of a trilogy (*The Three Colors Trilogy* [1993, 1994, 1994]), or be remade or rebooted (e.g., the planned remake of *Jacob's Ladder* [1990]). In summary, a genre is more concerned with reusing the same thematic conflict, a cycle is more concerned with reusing the same imagery and topic, a sequel is more concerned with reusing the same characters experiencing the same story, and a reboot is repetition with a difference. Genres, cycles, sequels, trilogies, series, remakes, and reboots are all different manifestations of media multiplicities, a production strategy central to all mass media texts, from film to television to video games to YouTube videos.

Case Study: The Kissing Cycle

As with any scholarly theory, the study of genre is best understood in the practical application of the theory. This case study comes from a chapter I wrote for the anthology I co-edited with R. Barton Palmer entitled *Multiplicities: Cycles, Sequels, Spin-Offs, Remakes and Reboots.*[48] The anthology was based on our interest in bringing together the many ways in which films that replicate each other have been labeled and categorized over time and across media platforms.[49] My contribution to this anthology was a cultural and industrial history of a group of silent films that were released around the same time (circa 1896–1906) and shared the same semantics: a woman who is kissed, a man who performs the kiss, and the aftermath of this kiss, which varies depending on whether the kiss is welcomed or unbidden. Almost all of these films feature similar public settings like parks, sidewalks, alleys, and train cars. When kissing-themed films were discussed and analyzed by film historians, they were often lumped together as part of a general trend in early silent cinema, described by Tom Gunning as "the cinema of attractions."[50] Gunning argues that early silent cinema was characterized as a "cinema of instants," rather than a cinema of developing characters and plots. Kissing films fit neatly into Gunning's framework because of their focus on

the spectacle of kissing and the chance to see a sex act close up.

As I began to watch the many examples of films featuring heterosexual kissing from this period in film history, it became apparent that these films were doing more than simply serving as a spectacle; they also shared a syntax. I noticed that early entries in the kissing cycle's corpus, like *The May Irwin Kiss* (1896), depict consensual kissing and base their appeal on the spectacle of witnessing sexual intimacy, but in later kissing films women are kissed unwillingly or they play a trick on the man who tries to kiss them. Were these later films providing a commentary on one of the big moral panics in turn-of-the-century America, namely the beginning of street harassment? Did these films have something to say about the changing relationships between men and women at this time in U.S. history?

Researching the cultural history and public discourse around moral panics can illuminate the syntax attached to the cycle's semantics. Cultural historians like Patricia Cohen, argue that the creation of new commercial travel systems (railroads, steamships, canal boats) and the movement of the American population into crowded cities impacted the previously established rules of conduct between men and women.[51] Cohen claims that the presence of women moving about public spaces unaccompanied by male escorts necessitated "cultural improvisation," or a rewriting of the rules of engagement between the genders. One manifestation of this cultural improvisation was the figure of the "masher," a white, upper-class male who takes social and sexual liberties with the unaccompanied women he encounters in train cars or on sidewalks. Cohen's work illuminated how the lecherous men who appeared in kissing films were, in fact, meant to be seen as mashers, even though the films' titles never label them as such. A search in my university library's online database of historical newspaper articles from the late 1800s and early 1900s for the term "masher" revealed a slew of articles, editorials, and letters to the editor which alternately complained about the mashers ("Flirting Is a Crime: District Code Designates It So on the Streets") or celebrated the heroics of the women who fought them off ("Girl Fells Two Mashers: Swings Her Umbrella So Forcibly that One Goes to Hospital"). The masher's transgressions ranged from saying "Good evening" to an unaccompanied woman to sexual assault. One article, titled "Warring on Mashers," explains how a mother and daughter "of some prominence" were insulted by a man who approached the daughter and said, "Hello kid: want to take a walk?"[52]

Turn-of-the-century kissing films, it turns out, were about more than just spectacle; they were conduits through which contemporary American audiences managed their fears about changing gender relations in the United States' burgeoning urban centers. For example, several kissing films feature moments of resistance and revenge on the part of the women. In *A Frontier Flirtation* (1903), a masher tries to kiss a young woman seated in the park. He lifts the veil that covers her face only to find she is wearing a monkey mask! When the terrified masher runs off, the woman laughs, as this had been her plan. In *Kiss Me* (1904) a man stops in an alleyway to ogle theatrical posters featuring images of showgirls. When he approaches one of the posters, the woman in the image leans forward, puckering up her lips for a kiss. She visibly startles the man and gets him in trouble with his nagging wife. These films were reflections of the many stories appearing in newspapers of the time featuring women who fought back against their male attackers with umbrellas and hat pins, or, as in the case of the aforementioned films, a disguise or subterfuge. Indeed, one 1906 article recounts how an unaccompanied woman fought back against two men who harassed her on her walk home from work.[53] Reading these articles illuminated for me how films

Figure 16.2 Turn-of-the-century newspapers articles featured stories about women who defeated their mashers ("Girl Gives Her Masher Hearty Thrashing," *The Philadelphia Inquirer*, Oct. 28, 1906, 3)

like *Kiss Me* and *A Frontier Flirtation* represent female resistance to male harassment, rather than just the spectacle of the kisser getting a kiss.

Another interesting aspect of the kissing cycle is that many of the films in its corpus took place inside train cars, like *The Kiss in the Tunnel* (1899) and *Love on a Railroad Train* (1902). Given filmmakers' aversion to financial risk, it makes sense that two popular cycles of early silent films—kissing films and train films—would eventually be combined. A common plot involves a young couple who takes advantage of the darkness that engulfs the frame once the train car enters a tunnel so that they may indulge in a furtive kiss. In later examples of these kissing films, the figure of the masher became a feature in train cars, highlighting how the danger of sexual assault was often present for women who traveled alone.

However, the racialized aspect of the masher—and the way in which this threat is only ever understood in terms of white women's chastity—did not become apparent until I watched *What Happened in the Tunnel* (1903). In this film, a white woman and her black maid are seated on a train. A masher seated behind them attempts to engage the white woman in conversation until the train enters a tunnel, thus turning the entire screen black. When the black screen fades back into an interior shot of the train car, the masher, a white man, finds himself pressing lips with the black maid. He is outraged and curses the women for tricking him into kissing the maid instead of her lady. As in *A Frontier Flirtation*, the clever women laugh over the success of their ruse. As so often happens with historical studies of media texts, one reading of the film comes to stand in as the primary (or only) reading. In this case, *What Happened in the Tunnel*'s inclusion of an interracial kiss is the main aspect of the film that is discussed and highlighted by film historians.[54]

However, analyzing this film in the context of a larger cycle of films about mashers attempting to kiss women (and the revenge that these women take upon the men who try to kiss them), reveals the raced nature of this moral panic. Much as the mask is used to punish the masher in *A Frontier Flirtation*, the black maid is used (by her white boss) to teach the masher a lesson and punish him for taking liberties. The replicated plot—a seemingly vulnerable woman successfully defeats a masher—only works by denying the humanity of the black maid, who, unlike her white mistress, is *not* saved from the dastardly advances of the lecherous masher. But there was no label—nor any punishment—for a white man who bothered black women. Thus, *What Happened in the Tunnel*, when read

through the lens of kissing films, is a reminder that black women were too frequently at the sexual mercy of white men as well as white women. Viewing this film in the context of a cycle that has its own history and origins (both in other film cycles but also real life), demonstrates that studying a film as part of a group (in this case, a cycle), rather than in isolation, can reveal previously hidden aspects of the text.

When I discovered the concept of the masher, and his prevalence in newspaper accounts of women imperiled in the American city, I connected the images found in kissing films to public discourses surrounding street harassment. But a major gap in this research was my failure to consider *where else* these narratives might appear. Though the turn-of-the-century mediascape is not the multiplatform, pop culture mélange that contemporary American consumers experience, there were still many other media platforms working together to build, circulate, and articulate discourses around heterosexual mixing beyond newspapers and motion pictures. For example, the jokes and images at the center of the popular early silent film called *The Whole Dam Family and the Dam Dog* (1905), were borrowed from a souvenir postcard series containing the same images. Were there also postcards in the early 1900s featuring heroic women fighting off their lecherous mashers? Is the masher's race highlighted or further obscured when rendered in a postcard caricature? If I ever return to this study of kissing films—and the moral panic it addressed—I plan to search through popular turn-of-the-century lithographs, and postcards, as well as vaudeville acts and newspaper cartoons to see if and how the figure of the masher is represented on those media platforms.

Conclusion

This chapter has overviewed the intellectual history, central questions and methods, and key terminology of studying media texts which are linked by their conscious (and sometimes unconscious) replication of images, characters, settings, and themes. While media scholars have historically referred to this field as genre studies, I hope this chapter has demonstrated that the simple term genre does not always fully or usefully encompass the ways in which media texts are replicated, and the purposes, uses, and meanings of these replications. As mentioned earlier, the term genre can be limiting since it refers only to texts which repeat a thematic core, or syntax, tied to a defined set of semantic elements. The student of genre should therefore also consider the relationship between different *kinds* of multiplicities, including cycles, modes, sequels, trilogies, remakes, and reboots, both within *and* across media platforms in order to account for all the ways in which repetition occurs in media, and how to usefully analyze those texts as a group.

It's also important for genre scholars to perpetually be aware of the stakes of their studies. When performing genre work, it is easy to fall into the trap of categorization for the sake of categorization. Scholars enjoy drawing generic battle lines and defending them, and many a viral thinkpiece has lived and died by the strawman of unavailing generic categories. As I remind my students when they get bogged down in the minutiae of a debate over, for example, whether *Aliens* (1986) is actually a horror film or a science fiction film, "How is the deployment of *this* generic category at *this* moment in *this* context useful to your understanding of the text?" A student writing a paper about the ways in which *Aliens* dramatizes contemporary American fears about technological changes in the 1980s will best be served by viewing the film as science fiction. However, students who wish to compare the various "Others," or monsters, of the 1980s American psyche should read the film as part of the horror genre. All of the approaches outlined above—from generic evolution to semantic/syntactic/pragmatic approaches to transmedia studies—have their uses, depending on the needs of the scholar.

Of course, it is precisely the fluid nature of this field that creates one of its biggest challenges: creating and maintaining a shared language. Because the field of media studies works with texts that are consumed, enjoyed, and even analyzed by non-experts (unlike say, the field of genetics or astrophysics), there are many conflicting terms—and definitions for those terms—circulating throughout popular discourse. Film reviews, fan community discourse, and social media conversations about films, TV series, and other popular media texts often borrow terms from the field of genre studies, only to deploy those terms incorrectly. For example, fans often refer to superhero films as a genre, even though superhero films do not share a core syntax. Likewise, the perceived uptick in remakes and franchise series over the last decade has led to many misinformed essays about Hollywood's seeming lack of creativity, despite the fact that repetition is, and always has been, central to popular culture production. This is why creating and maintaining a clear, shared language about genres, cycles, sequels, and other screen multiplicities remains an important task for the media studies scholar.

Notes

1. Rick Altman, *Film/Genre* (London: British Film Institute, 1999), 5.
2. Steve Neale, *Genre and Hollywood* (London: Rutledge, 2000), 46.
3. Andrew Tudor, "Genre," in *Film Genre Reader*, ed. Barry Keith Grant (Austin: University of Texas Press, 1986), 7.
4. David Bordwell, "The Art Cinema as a Mode of Film Practice," in *Film Theory and Criticism: Introductory Readings*, 5th Edition, ed. Leo Braudy and Marshall Cohen (New York: Oxford University Press, 1999), 717.
5. Jeffrey Sconce, "Trashing the Academy: Taste, Excess and an Emerging Politics of Cinematic Style," *Screen* 36, no. 4 (1995): 372.
6. See Chuck Tryon, *On-Demand Culture: Digital Delivery and the Future of Movies* (New Brunswick: Rutgers University Press, 2013).
7. Aristotle, *On the Art of Poetry*, trans. T.S. Dorsch, *Classical Literary Criticism* (London: Penguin Books, 1965).
8. Horace, "*Ars Poetica*," trans. C. Smart and by E. H. Blakeney, October 13, 2009, accessed October 1, 2017, www.poetryfoundation.org/articles/69381/ars-poetica.
9. Altman, *Film/Genre*, 6.
10. Michel Foucault, *The Order of Things* (1966; London: Routledge, 1989).
11. Benedetto Croce, *Aesthetic as Science of Expression and General Linguistic*, trans. Douglas Ainslie (London: Peter Owen, 1909).
12. Northrop Frye, *Anatomy of Criticism* (Princeton: Princeton University Press, 1957).
13. Tzvetan Todorov, *The Fantastic: A Structural Approach to a Literary Genre* (Cleveland: Case Western Reserve University Press, 1973).
14. See Theodor Adorno and Max Horkheimer, *Dialectic of Enlightenment*, trans. Edmund Jephcott (Stanford: Stanford University Press, 2002).
15. Francois Truffaut, "A Certain Tendency of the French Cinema," in *Movies and Methods, Vol. I*, ed. Bill Nichols (Berkeley: University of California Press, 1974).
16. Andrew Sarris, *The American Cinema: Directors and Directions: 1929–1968* (Cambridge: DaCapo Press, 1996).
17. Vivian Sobchack, "Genre Films: Myth, Ritual and Sociodrama," in *Film/Culture: Explorations of Cinema in its Social Context*, ed. Sari Thomas (Metuchen: The Scarecrow Press, 1982), 147–67.
18. Thomas Schatz, *Hollywood Genres: Formulas, Filmmaking and the Studio System* (New York: Random House, 1981).
19. Louis Althusser, *Lenin and Philosophy and Other Essays*, trans. Ben Brewster (New York: Monthly Review Press, 2001).
20. Judith Hess Wright, "Genre Films and the Status Quo," in *Jump Cut: A Review of Contemporary Media, no. 1 (1974): 1.*

21. Nick Browne, preface to *Refiguring American Film Genres: Theory and History,* ed. Nick Browne (Berkeley: University of California Press, 1998), xii.

22. Jason Mittell, *Genre and Television: From Cop Shows to Cartoons in American Culture* (New York: Routledge, 2004), 1.

23. Jane Feuer, "Genre Study and Television," in *Channels of Discourse: Television and Contemporary Criticism,* ed. Robert C. Allen (Chapel Hill: The University of North Carolina Press, 1987), 127.

24. Jane Feuer, "Genre Study and Television," in *Channels of Discourse: Television and Contemporary Criticism,* ed. Robert C. Allen (Chapel Hill: The University of North Carolina Press, 1987), 127.

25. Mittell, *Genre and Television,* 7.

26. Ibid., 10.

27. Jennifer Holt, *Empires of Entertainment: Media Industries and the Politics of Deregulation, 1980–1996* (New Brunswick: Rutgers University Press, 2011), 7.

28. Andrew Tudor, "Genre," in *Film Genre Reader,* ed. Barry Keith Grant (Austin: University of Texas Press, 1986), 3–10.

29. Janet Staiger, *Interpreting Films: Studies in the Historical Reception of American Cinema* (Princeton: Princeton University Press, 1992).

30. Ferdinand de Saussure, *Course in General Linguistics,* eds. Charles Bally and Albert Sechehaye, trans. Roy Harris (La Salle: Open Court, 1983).

31. Schatz, *Hollywood Genres,* 19.

32. Altman, *Film/Genre,* 222.

33. Ibid., 210.

34. See Simon Frith, *Performing Rites* (Cambridge: Harvard University Press, 1996); Jason Mittell, *Complex Television: The Poetics of Contemporary Storytelling* (New York: New York University Press, 2015).

35. Henri Focillon, *The Life of Forms in Art* (New York: Wittenborn, Schultz, 1948).

36. Altman, *Film/Genre,* 22.

37. Tag Gallagher, "Shoot-Out at the Genre Corral," in *Film Genre Reader III,* ed. Barry Keith Grant (Austin: University of Texas Press, 2003), 262–76.

38. Amanda Ann Klein, *American Film Cycles: Reframing Genres, Screening Social Problems, and Defining Subcultures* (Austin: University of Texas Press, 2011).

39. Henry Jenkins, "Transmedia 202: Further Reflections," *Confessions of an Aca/Fan,* August 1, 2011, accessed October 20, 1997, http://henryjenkins.org/2011/08/defining_transmedia_further_re.html.

40. Tasha Oren and Sharon Shahaf, eds., *Global Television Formats: Understanding Television Across Borders* (New York: Routledge, 2012).

41. Amanda Ann Klein and R. Barton Palmer, "Introduction," in *Cycles: Sequels, Spin-Offs, Remakes, and Reboots:* *Multiplicities in Film and Television,* ed. Amanda Ann Klein and R. Barton Palmer (Austin: University of Texas Press, 2016), 1–21.

42. See also Mary Celeste Kearney, "Recycling Judy and Corliss: Transmedia Exploitation and the First Teen-Girl Production Trend," *Feminist Media Studies* 4, no. 3 (2004): 264–95.

43. Carolyn Jess-Cooke, *Film Sequels: Theory and Practice from Hollywood to Bollywood* (Edinburgh: Edinburgh University Press, 2009), 3.

44. Claire Perkins and Constantine Verevis, "Introduction: Three Times," in *Film Trilogies: New Critical Approaches,* eds. Claire Perkins and Constantine Verevis, (Houdsmills: Palgrave Macmillan, 2011), 4.

45. Ibid., 2.

46. Andrew Horton and Stuart Y. McDougal, "Introduction," in *Play It Again, Sam: Retakes on Remakes,* eds. Andrew Horton and Stuart Y. McDougal, (Berkeley: University of California Press, 1998), 3.

47. Constantine Verevis, "The Cinematic Return," *Film Criticism* 40, no. 1 (2016): n.p., accessed February 23, 2018, http://dx.doi.org/10.3998/fc.13761232.0040.134.

48. Amanda Ann Klein and R. Barton Palmer, eds., *Cycles: Sequels, Spin-Offs, Remakes, and Reboots: Multiplicities in Film and Television* (Austin: University of Texas Press, 2016).

49. Ibid., 1.

50. Tom Gunning, "As Aesthetic of Astonishment: Early Film and the (In)Credulous Spectator," in *Viewing Positions: Ways of Seeing Film,* ed. Linda Williams (New Brunswick: Rutgers University Press, 1997), 114–33.

51. Patricia Cline Cohen, "Safety and Danger: Women on American Public Transport, 1750–1850," in *Gendered Domains: Rethinking Public and Private in Women's History,* eds. Dorothy O. Helly and Susan M. Reverby (Ithaca: Cornell University Press, 1992), 109–22.

52. "Warring on Mashers: Women Must Be Guarded, Says Maj. Sylvester," *Washington Post,* May 25, 1911, n.p.

53. "Girl Fells Two Mashers: Swings Her Umbrella So Forcibly that One Goes to Hospital," *Washington Post,* Sept. 15, 1906, n.p.

54. See Jane Gaines, *Fire and Desire: Mixed-Race Movies in the Silent Era* (Chicago: University of Chicago Press, 2001), 54–55.

Further Reading

Browne, Nick, ed. *Refiguring American Film Genres: Theory and History.* Berkeley: University of California Press, 1998.

Grant, Barry Keith, ed. *Film Genre Reader.* Austin: University of Texas Press, 1986.

Lavigne, Carlen and William Proctor, eds. *Remake Television: Reboot, Re-use, Recycle.* Plymouth: Lexington Books, 2014.

17.
INTERTEXTS AND PARATEXTS
Jonathan Gray

The promise of "close" textual analysis is alluring: sit down in solitary congress with a text and emerge later with a definitive understanding of its meaning. This, however, is a fiction, for **textuality** (the "being-ness" of a text) is messy, and one can never truly isolate any given text. Thus, while close textual analysis is vital if we are to appreciate how meaning in any text works, ultimately meaning is only ever produced in interaction, relation, and concert with other texts and meanings. This process—the fundamental interreliability of texts upon each other for the construction of their meaning—is called **intertextuality**. An intertextual approach to studying media is one that is always aware of textual histories, connections, and resonances.

Sometimes intertextuality will take obvious forms, as when an episode of *The Simpsons* (FOX, 1989–) appropriately titled "Rosebud" mimics *Citizen Kane* (1941), when audiences' regard for a character is framed by their knowledge of the actor's past roles, or when *The Daily Show* requires an understanding of the news as genre to appreciate much of its humor. But intertextuality is always at work, as we make sense of every image, sound, name, word, plot, and character in terms of our textual histories and the expectations, hopes, concerns, and meanings that they have willed to us. This chapter will therefore examine how we can operationalize intertextuality in the analysis of media, arguing that the textual world is full of ghosts, resonance, and residue that demand to be studied. In doing so, it is connected to numerous other chapters in this collection, for genre, celebrity, and authorship—to name three—are all intrinsically intertextual, and it will also discuss paratextuality, as a form of intertextuality that warrants particular consideration. Central to the chapter's argument is the idea that texts never end. Even stories we heard as children can change meaning in our minds decades later, for meaning is always up for grabs, always at least potentially contested or contestable. And when texts are always open, they and their meanings will often continue in and through other texts. The intertextual analyst's task is to track these meanings and to chronicle how meaning develops.

First, this chapter will chart the intellectual history of intertextuality as a concept. To say that intertextuality is everywhere, though, and to say that it leaves all texts open, is to introduce no small amount of chaos into the task of criticism. The chapter will therefore next offer several ways to find order in the chaos of intertextuality and to study it meaningfully. Since one of these ways is to study paratextuality, the chapter will then focus specifically on paratexts.

An Intellectual History

"Intertextuality" as a term relies upon the concept of **the text**, and thus any story of intertextuality must begin as a story of what texts are and how scholars have studied them. Though statements about texts can be found in Western culture as far back as Ancient Greece, I begin our story here in early nineteenth-century England with the "Romantic" poets, for it is their concept of art, text, and culture that influenced much of the next two centuries' worth of textual analysis, and that was eventually institutionalized as the form of textual analysis taught pervasively in schools and universities worldwide. Three of the Romantic poets in particular—William Wordsworth, Samuel Taylor Coleridge, and Percy Bysshe Shelley—wrote not only poems but treatises on art and poetry. To them, the poet was a special individual, endowed with a pseudo-divine power to encapsulate Beauty and Nature, translating them for the reader into Meaning. This act of self-aggrandizement certainly had its precedents, with Ancient Greeks' discussion of artistic "inspiration" and muses, but it settled into a clearly stated theory of art *and of the text* with the Romantics. If poets spoke the sublime so that we mortals could hear it, after all, texts were their medium, and texts were posed as almost otherworldly entities of significant power. We might note the Romantics' quasi-religious overtones, wherein God was replaced by a looser notion of Nature and the sublime, and texts were the new holy books that spoke godliness to the world.

In the Victorian era, Matthew Arnold would then take up this notion of textuality and institutionalize it. Arnold's mission for the humanities, and one that was adopted widely in England and exported to the world, sought to turn Art and Culture into the new religious texts of our time. In his wake, two literature professors at Cambridge, F. R. Leavis and I. A. Richards, innovated what they called "Practical Criticism," or close textual analysis. They encouraged a radically decontextualized mode of study whereby all "external" information was denied to the analyst, so that one's focus could be entirely upon the text in and of itself. It is their fetishized notion of the text as totem, standing alone and speaking itself to any who could burrow deep enough into its core, that would in time inform most high school curricula. Think here, therefore, of how you were likely introduced to Shakespeare or Dickens, with the notion of Universal Truths unequivocally existing "in the text," there to be found, where the goal of studying their texts was to locate this meaning.

In the latter half of the twentieth century, literary theorists attacked this idea, motivated in part by a profoundly different idea of what textual studies should be. If, before, texts were studied to learn from their wisdom, then literary theory was motivated by an interest in what ideological work texts did in society. Inspired by Saussurean linguistics and the notion that language is never neutral and is constitutive of meaning rather than simply a recording of meaning (see this volume's chapter on representation), many theorists studied what roles texts play in this process. If, for instance, the meaning of "manly" or "just"—or even the Romantics' beloved "sublime" or "beauty"—will change over time and in different cultural contexts, theorists became fascinated with how texts variously shifted those meanings, or upheld and maintained them. This was a key move towards

re-theorizing the text and what it is, for whereas prior modes of analysis consulted the text as if it were an oracle, and whereas they therefore romanticized its distinctness from the world around it, a text was now to be consulted precisely as engaged and involved in the workings of the world around it. This new project required an intertextual view of meaning.

Roland Barthes was prominent amongst these literary theorists, due to his interest in what he called **mythologies**—deep meanings developed across multiple texts that set up the ideological apparatus of a society. Barthes drew an important distinction between what he called **the work** and the text. Writing about books, he saw the work as that which could be held in the hand—the object, the collection of words on a series of pages. The text, by contrast, was how the work came alive and what it *meant* to its readers, extending beyond the work at hand and "*experienced only in an activity of production*" by the reader.[1]

Barthes eventually discussed intertextuality explicitly, but he was preceded by Julia Kristeva, who is widely regarded as having coined the term and who was in turn working with (and translating) the writings of Mikhail Bakhtin and Valentin Volosinov. Volosinov's theory of linguistics is intertextual to the core. He wrote of "the social character of meaning," arguing that "A sign can be illuminated only with the help of another sign," since any word "presents itself not as an item of vocabulary but as a word that has been used in a wide variety of [other] utterances."[2] Bakhtin applied this idea to texts and novels in particular, writing of how texts inevitably drew upon each other to create meaning. By way of simple illustration, consider a rose. Should this appear in a text, it may have symbolic meaning, whether intended or not. But this symbolic meaning precedes the text at hand, as any given reader will come to the text with a sense of what a rose is and what it means gleaned from other texts. Or not: perhaps some readers will never have encountered a rose in their textual travels, and hence will have no frame of reference for making sense of it. An analysis of that rose and what it does and means in this text at hand, by consequence, relies upon other texts' uses of the rose. In terms of the Barthesian interest in mythologies, moreover, should that word/ image participate in the construction of a broader "myth" and ideology—as the rose does with notions of passion and love, infused as they are with ideologies of masculinity, femininity, and heterosexuality—the deeper, ideological meanings of the text at hand will also have been fashioned, in part, outside this text's own borders.

Bakhtin notes poetically that any speaker is "a respondent to a greater or lesser degree, [...] not, after all, the first speaker, the one who disturbs the eternal silence of the universe."[3] And Kristeva therefore concludes that no text is a point of fixed meaning. It is instead always also an intersection of other texts, "a mosaic of quotations; any text is the absorption and transformation of another."[4]

Intertextual theory was soon exported to media and cultural studies. Tony Bennett and Janet Woollacott's *Bond and Beyond* (1987), in particular, remains the most foundational work on intertextuality in media. Bennett and Woollacott examine the case of James Bond, fascinated by how Bond moved between novels, films, advertisements, merchandise, and more, carrying meaning—or at least residue of meaning—with him. His case, they argue,

> throws into high relief the radical insufficiency of those forms of cultural analysis which, in purporting to study texts "in themselves," do radical violence to the real nature of the social existence and functioning of texts in pretending that "the text itself" can be granted an existence, as a hypostasised entity, separated out from the always variable systems of inter-textual relations which supply the real conditions of its signifying function.[5]

Every time we encounter Bond, he and the text in which he appears are rich with meanings created in other texts. And while Bennett and Woollacott focused on Bond, they saw this process alive throughout media, as images, characters, words, and sounds always move across texts, such that the singular text "is never 'there' except in forms which it is also and always other than 'just itself,' always-already humming with reading possibilities which derive from outside its covers."[6] Or, as John Fiske, another key theorist of the media text, noted, intertextuality provides "ghost texts" that haunt the text at hand "like the ghost image on a television set with poor reception."[7]

While intertextuality has been theorized as part of analyzing text-audience relationships, and while one is most likely to find it used to discuss (as below) homage, allusion, references, parody, pastiche, and textual citation, it has also been discussed by scholars examining production and political economy. Eileen Meehan wrote of Batman's "commercial intertext,"[8] interested in how producers offered a rich web of intertexts in order to appeal to a broad and varied audience. John Caldwell has also written on intertextuality as industrial strategy in television, illustrating how the "postmodern" style that many associate with intertextual **pastiche** (playful or artistic citation with no commentary or editorializing implied), and that rose to prominence in the 1980s, is often driven by industrial imperatives.[9] Certainly, in today's media industries environment of synergy, convergence, and transmedia, content producers have reaped considerable profits by telling stories across platforms, recycling or "rebooting" stories and characters, adding sequels and prequels, citing other texts widely, and extending the lives of texts into other texts for financial reasons. Contemporary media culture gives us intertextuality in hyperdrive.

Today, one can find a wide range of intellectual projects conducted under the name of intertextuality, some of which will be discussed shortly. Ultimately, the key teaching of intertextuality is that the text is never closed. "Close" reading was always performed with the idea that the analyst could reach a point of complete understanding of the text. But since intertextuality envisions texts as always bumping into each other, whether forcefully or gently, on purpose or accidentally, and as transferring meaning in the process, intertextuality regards both the production of meaning and our interpretation of it as projects that never truly end. Intertextuality may be frustrating, inasmuch as it disallows us the comfort of ever dictating that this is unequivocally what a text means, and inasmuch as its more chaotic elements seemingly defy study. But there are many ways in which intertextual criticism can be practiced. And the reward is precisely that openness: an intertextual reading could always find more meaning than an Arnoldian close textual analyst allows, but it also encourages us to think in Barthesian fashion about how powerful texts with powerful meanings come to be and how they can be combatted, their meanings never secure, always at risk of intertextual disturbance.

Doing Intertextual Scholarship

The task for the scholar working with intertextuality is to move beyond the simple act of noting that an intertext is present (after all, intertexts are always present) to instead study what that intertextuality *does* to meaning. Intertextuality is a system of bridges between texts, but what we, as scholars, need to know is what meanings and audiences travel over these bridges, or how and why the bridges were constructed.

One could start by looking into **allusions**, **homage**, and **references**, moments when a text clearly invokes another text. For obvious examples, one could watch any episode of *The Simpsons* or *Family Guy* (FOX, 1999–), both of which regularly cite other texts to create humor. Entire sequences in the former mimic famous scenes from movies, as when Bart's act of stealing his father's spare change jar apes Indiana Jones' acquisition of a Peruvian golden idol. Names may be intertextual, too, as with the Simpsons' hometown of Springfield, an allusion to and play on *Father Knows Best*'s (CBS, 1954–55, 1958–60; NBC, 1955–58) iconic town, or as when *Bridget Jones's Diary* (2001) introduces us to Mr. Darcy, his name pulled directly from *Pride and Prejudice* (1813). Sounds and music can be used intertextually: the above-mentioned Indiana Jones scene in *The Simpsons* is accompanied by John Williams' famous soundtrack, and many texts introduce similarly iconic songs or sounds to gesture outside the text. Or entire plots riff off, or outright copy, others, as in the prominent examples of *Clueless* (1995) and *O Brother, Where Art Thou* (2000), homages to Jane Austen's *Emma* (1815) and Homer's *Odyssey* respectively, or with the obvious examples of outright remakes. But all texts learn and show their lineage from other texts, and thus an intertextual analysis might involve charting these influences. *Star Wars* (1977) and its franchise, for instance, brim with intertextual cues: Han Solo's costume labels him immediately as a gunslinger from a Western; the Jedi's honor code, use of lightsabers, and Eastern sounding names (Obi-Wan Kenobi, Qui-Gon Jinn) reference samurais and samurai films; *Star Wars*' plot is drawn from Akira Kurosawa's *Hidden Fortress* (1958); Princess Leia's name and white dress invoke fairy tale princesses; and so forth.

Stars and other prominent production personnel are always-already intertextual, too, carrying with them the resonance of past roles. At times, these connections may be actively used by creators, as when Colin Firth was cast as the aforementioned Mr. Darcy in the *Bridget Jones' Diary* film, when Firth was famous for his role as Darcy in the *Pride and Prejudice* miniseries (BBC1, 1995). Television shows sometimes playfully nod to their stars' former roles, as when an episode of *Scandal* (ABC, 2012–) is titled "Molly, You in Danger, Girl," using *Ghost*'s (1990) famous quote to pose danger from yet another character (*Scandal*'s president) played by Tony Goldwyn. Less gimmicky, actors are regularly hired with past roles and associations in mind. Liam Neeson, therefore, has played multiple noble father figures from many franchises,

including Qui-Gon Jinn, Zeus, Aslan, and Ra's al Ghul. Other actors' histories as likeable heroes are similarly tapped on a regular basis by Hollywood, so that we might expect Will Smith or Julia Roberts, for example, to immediately garner an audience's good graces even before they utter a word in a new script. Authors, too, encourage intertextual readings, as similar types of characters may appear across their work (e.g., the petite action heroine in Joss Whedon's work, or the hipster millennial in Lena Dunham's work). But we should also expect to find random, less intended resonances, as any actor's or production personnel's past work can frame future roles, or vice-versa if we watch them "out of order."

In all of the above cases, the challenge is to ascertain the value or effect of the intertextual link. Most prominently, intertextuality works to set expectations and create meaning via shortcut: casting Will Smith as a good guy allows a director to quickly establish his character, as an audience can be expected to like him from the outset. Allusions and references might also tell us something about a text's pretensions, and about how it would like audiences to classify it: by referencing Westerns, samurai films, and fairy tales, *Star Wars* invites us to make sense of it as an amalgam of these genres. Indeed, **genre** is itself a key mode of intertextuality.[10] When we encounter elements that invoke a particular genre, we are immediately invited to import the expectations of that genre. In the case of *Star Wars*, therefore, the fairy tale allusions suggest the presence of a moral binary, with good and evil characters. The Western and samurai film allusions, meanwhile, promise a battle and noble hero figures. Since both genres regularly posit lone figures against a vast system, moreover, we expect a particular type of hero. Ideologically and mythologically, too, these genres' investment in individualism, in moral binaries, in the battle of the individual versus the strange Other, and in traditional models of masculinity and femininity are all invoked.

However, expectations are not always invoked to be followed; rather, they may be invoked to be challenged. The *Law and Order* franchise occasionally cast comedians such as Stephen Colbert, Robin Williams, Chevy Chase, and Martin Short as bad guys precisely so that audiences wouldn't expect them to be bad guys. Of course, though, if one is familiar with the show's mechanics—itself an intertextual knowledge of past episodes and stories—one soon expects that any guest star is the bad guy! Princess Leia, too, is no fairy tale princess, so although her name and dress immediately invoke fairy tale dynamics, her early dialogue to Governor Tarkin that "I should have expected to find you holding Vader's leash. I recognized your foul stench when I was brought on board" announces her as distinctly unprincesslike. In cases such as these, the intertext ushers in an expectation that hovers over a text in order to draw attention to the text's deviation from it. By contrast, though, Han Solo and the Jedi fit expectations for Western gunslingers and samurai quite neatly. We can therefore ask questions about how this confluence of intertexts—some treated reverentially, some playfully, some challenged—creates not just expectations but meaning. In particular, we might use intertexts to analyze *Star Wars*' gender politics, wherein we are actively encouraged to read Leia as denying the dainty, victimized femininity of fairy tale princesses, yet, or perhaps because, she is still in a very male world full of gunslingers, samurai, and other classic tropes of "real masculinity." How then, we should ask, do *Star Wars*' intertexts set the table for the film's own contribution to the perpetuation, or not, of gendered myths?

Sometimes, as in *Star Wars*, this intertextual drama occurs implicitly. In other instances, as in **parody**, we will see an explicit play with textual or generic structures. Parody, it should be noted, is regularly used incorrectly in popular parlance, to mean any combination of humor and intertextuality. However, this is mere pastiche, for parody exists only when a text constructs an intertextual bridge to another text or genre to make fun of it. Thus, for instance, when *Family Guy* introduces us to Cookie Monster as a junkie, playing off his penchant for addiction, there is humor and an intertext, but very likely not parody. (I discuss the small possibility that it is parody later). Neither *Sesame Street* (NET, 1969–70; PBS, 1970–) nor children's programming is likely under attack. By contrast, when *The Daily Show* (Comedy Central, 1996–) invokes the format, look, and style of the news, it most definitely does so to attack the news. A *Daily Show* cast member, for instance, will appear on screen, wearing a suit, speaking as do the news' experts, and a chyron below introduces them as Senior Black Person Expert. Here, the show visually and aurally references the news and its techniques (newsvoice, everyone with impressive-sounding titles, expensive set, discussion at the table or via satellite) but mocks them: the lunacy that anyone could be a Senior Black Person Expert encourages us to question the credentials of all news guest "experts," and the inevitably absurd commentary offered by the commentator is funnier because offered in newsvoice, but in a way that aims to dispel the magic of newsvoice.

In *Watching with The Simpsons: Television, Parody, and Intertextuality*, I talk of parody as **critical intertextuality**.[11] Using *The Simpsons* as case study, I chart how intertextuality is harnessed to attack not only a genre but its ideology. Thus, *The Simpsons* regularly lampoons expected norms of the family sitcom—father Homer does *not* know best, for instance, as instead the family's little girl, Lisa, can best be counted upon to solve problems. Suburbia, meanwhile, is no longer the ideal, enlightened place that it is in countless other sitcoms; instead, it is a place of ignorance and parochialism. Yet since the family sitcom was so closely articulated to conservative family values and to patriarchal ideologies of men who do and know things and women who watch adoringly from the kitchen, *The Simpsons*' attack on this genre amounts to an attack on those values and ideologies. Rather than simply show a different type of family, its parody works through constantly invoking the expected generic norm only to remind viewers that it is breaking from it. The show invites us to take its newly offered suspicion of family sitcom bliss over the intertextual bridge to other shows that we may have watched or that we may yet watch, so that when we encounter a TV wife who is only too happy to stay in the kitchen while her husband and son rule supreme, we are "watching with *The Simpsons*" and its critique, invited to cast doubt upon the present show's realism *on its own turf* rather than simply while watching *The Simpsons*. Parody has regularly been written of as "parasitic," inasmuch as it crosses intertextual bridges and exports its critique to other host bodies.

Another way to use intertextuality is to examine what Raymond Williams called televisual **flow**, seeing how a set of successive programs and ads interact with each other.[12] Scheduling has long been an industrial art of sorts, and even in an age of DVRs and streaming, channels still pay close attention to which show goes when in the schedule, and creators regularly blame (sometimes spuriously, sometimes accurately) their show's place in the schedule for failure. When a channel creates a programming schedule, it tries to create meaningful connections that will carry audiences and viewing predispositions across intertextual bridges. Comedy has regularly been programmed in "blocks," for instance, so that the general mood of levity and mirth created by the first show in the block carries over to the next. By contrast, sandwiching a hard-hitting crime drama between two goofy comedies might seem in especially poor taste. Even within comedy blocks, though, tone and style matter, so that one usually sees multi-camera sitcoms scheduled together.

A discussion of flow and scheduling inevitably opens doors to thinking about intertextuality and audiences, and intertextuality as production strategy. For all the fame that the term "flow" has enjoyed in television studies, remarkably few studies have tried to chart it, to see which audiences cross bridges and with what meanings. Thus, we can point to isolated instances, whereby crafty advertisers twin products, and sometimes even ad style, with shows in ways that seem well designed to improve the success of the ads. Or we might think of occasional disjunctures, when ads interact oddly or rudely with the program. But more work could and should be done to track *who* flows from text to ad and text to text and to find specific forms of flow. Though analysts have put relatively little time into examining flow, producers are regularly trying to game the system to use it to their advantage. Intertextual bridges are constructed with the goal of enticing particularly desirable audiences to cross them. Advertisers similarly must consider what types of customers they want and where to find them in the television schedule, then embed their ads in those texts' ad breaks. And on a larger scale, over and beyond flow, intertextual ties are often created to call out to and hail particular audiences, as with *Family Guy*'s plethora of 1980s and '90s youth culture references yet dearth of earlier references, clearly a way to call out especially to those in their fifties, forties, or thirties, while making the show harder for older audiences to appreciate. Flow and juxtaposition are not just televisual, either, as one might also think of the considerable effort put into deciding upon campaign songs by politicians eager to create intertextual bridges that hail specific types of voters. And thus another key way of using intertextual analysis is to see how producers call out to specific audiences via specific intertexts.

A considerable risk exists, however, in assuming that all intertextuality is purposeful, organized, and contained. Intertextuality can and should be studied as ordered, but it is also a remarkably chaotic process, as is evident any time one changes channels and sees odd connections develop between the two programs. Moreover, almost every single bridge discussed above may be denied or used differently by yet other audiences. Despite my assertion that *Family Guy*'s Cookie Monster-as-junkie joke is mere pastiche, some audiences may read this as a parodic attack on children's shows' development of addictive (viewing) behavior. Should one have engaged in a queer reading of the Western, seeing its overwhelmingly male cast replete with stories of male bonding as homoerotic,

Han Solo's invocation of the Western gunslinger may immediately code him as queer. Liam Neeson's past roles as Qui-Gon Jinn, Aslan, and Oskar Schindler may code him as benevolent, paternal, and heroic to many, but viewers more familiar with his roles as Zeus and Ra's al Ghul may instead immediately be suspicious of his reckless mischief or outright evil. Or one may not see or know the bridge at all: surely plenty of viewers of *Star Wars* or *O Brother, Where Art Thou* have been entirely unaware of the references to *Hidden Fortress* and *The Odyssey* respectively, or may not even know the intertexts. On one hand, such instances call for intertextual analysis to be careful rather than declare *possible* meanings to be *definitive* meanings. Such instances also require that audience research be used to make specific conclusions, as intertextuality assures that different audiences will see different things. We all have different textual histories, meaning, in turn, that no text will ever be the same for two people. On the other hand, though, since functionally we will often want to talk with one another as though it is the "same" text (as, for instance, when someone asks if you've seen a specific movie or television show), intertextuality invites us to consider how meaning is organized and disciplined in ways that allow us to merge our respective versions into something we can all discuss.

Paratextuality

One such organizing and disciplining force, and another form of intertextuality on which the remainder of this chapter will focus, is **paratextuality**. A **paratext**, as defined by Gérard Genette, is any entity that surrounds a work of art and is in some way subservient to that work or serves as a reference to and indicator of that work.[13] Writing about books, Genette included elements appended to the work itself, such as the cover, prefaces, and afterwords, yet allowed for typeface or paper stock to serve a paratextual function, too. But he also considered elements not appended to the work, such as reviews, ads for the book, and other commentary upon it. Any of these could be removed and the *work* would ostensibly stay the same. However, the old adage that we should not judge a book by its cover reflects the degree to which covers are not value neutral, and they certainly do carry the potential to change how we read a *text*. Applying Genette's work on books to the media world writ large, many things count as paratexts, from title sequences, "previously on" or "next week on" segments before and after television shows, and closing credits, to DVD bonus materials, trailers, posters, ads, reviews, fan productions, publicity, ancillaries, licensed games, licensed merchandise and clothing, and more. Most of these materials are regularly discursively denied status as standalone texts, hence them not usually counting to critics as bona fide "intertexts" (though in truth, if an individual or group regards something as a text, it is a text). But they are fundamentally intertextual inasmuch as they similarly gesture towards and seek to frame or reframe our understanding of other texts. Arguably as parasitic as parody, paratexts often exist solely or largely to inflect meanings of the text.

Genette wrote of paratexts as the "threshold of interpretation," often focusing on what elsewhere I have called **entryway paratexts**,[14] those that we encounter before the work itself. Here, the power of the paratext is most obvious, for at the "threshold" of the text, meaning is already being created. Lisa Kernan, for example, offers a wonderful set of analyses of movie trailers, examining how they regularly introduce us to characters, plots, style, *mise-en-scène*, tone, and genre.[15] If we subsequently decide to watch this movie, we will therefore have a whole slew of expectations and a preliminary understanding of the film before it even begins. Indeed, if we have decided to see the movie, it is likely in part because of our interest in and engagement with what the trailer has told us. In short, the interpretive process has already begun—the *text* has started—before we encounter the work. To further illustrate the importance of paratexts such as trailers, though, consider the case of someone who sees the trailer but decides definitively not to watch the movie. How have they made such a judgment? The text that the trailer has begun to conjure for them is not one with which they wish to engage further, but they will walk away from the trailer with a sense of what the movie is, with a reaction (albeit negative) to it, and perhaps even an ability to articulate clear reasons why they are disinterested in the movie. If, as analysts, we now wish to ask that Barthesian question of what a text is doing in the world, we must consider this person who saw the trailer yet not the movie as someone who is interacting with the text. Think here of how any hit movie has its detractors and critics, consisting not just of those who watched and hated it but of those who saw an ad and were turned off. If we ask what place that movie has in society, we must acknowledge the paratext as having played a constitutive, important role in creating the text as many people know it. For this reason, and contra Genette who saw paratexts as separate from the text, paratexts are separate from the *work*, but always part of the *text* in that Barthesian sense of the activation of the work in society with an audience.

Take the case of the iconic poster for *Jaws* (1975), which depicts a lone woman swimming at sea, oblivious to the fact that a massive great white shark whose mouth is as wide as her body is long is about to gobble her up. In italics, the poster notes that this is "The terrifying motion picture from the terrifying No. 1 best seller." It clearly suggests a horror film, therefore, but also offers us an experience of that horror. One is invited to imagine the position of this poor, oblivious woman whose violent death is imminent. We see the shark, but cannot do anything, and thus the poster also offers an experience of helplessness—all we can do is watch. It taps into fears that potentially many viewers would have of "what lies beneath," and as a simple image of imminent destruction of life, it signals clearly what to expect from the film. Should the image have failed to do this, the repetition of "terrifying" underlines the dominant affect. The poster suggests, too, that Jaws will be the film's central character, or at least the one who matters; after all, the only other character to whom it introduces us is not long for this world. And yet the artfulness of the image twinned with the invocation of a "No. 1 best seller" as source material promises quality, not a B movie bloodfest. For the film to be based on a book suggests that the film will offer more than just visual spectacle (though the image promises us that too), and it invites us to expect a decent plot that might have earned the novel its place on a best-seller list. (In passing, we might note the degree to which the invocation of the novel shows how regularly paratexts network intertexts, recommending that we see the text at hand in terms of other, specific intertexts).

Since paratexts aim to direct our reading, viewing, and listening in particular ways, they demand close and careful study. The key questions we as analysts should ask are, How does this frame the text, and what does it tell us about it? What hopes or expectations does it establish, and how might those establish specific ways of interacting with that text? (Does it suggest the text will be fun, for instance? Does it suggest it will be deep and meaningful or light and frivolous?) Who does it invite as an audience, who does it shunt away, and how does it aim to position its various types of audiences? (Does it announce itself as a text for men or for women, for instance? Does it propose different ways for adults or children to view it?) What basic themes and deeper meanings does it propose? And, importantly, what kind of politics—if any—does it propose? (Does it suggest a patriarchal or feminist worldview? A capitalist one?) We might also ask further questions about audience, too, inquiring, for instance, into who is likely to encounter this paratext and hence how powerful it is likely to be, communicating to whom. Or when audiences have created the paratexts themselves (as with fan fiction or fan art), what powers do they have to sway textual meaning, and for whom? And multiple other questions might be asked about production cultures: Who created the paratext? Who commissioned it? Why? Did the work's ostensible "authors" have any authorship rights over the paratext (and if not, what does this say about the division of authorship amongst other creative personnel)?

All of these questions can and should be asked of **in medias res paratexts** as well, those that we encounter not at an "entryway" but after having consumed (part of) the work. Director or cast commentary tracks on DVD bonus materials, for instance, alongside interviews, podcasts, and personal blogs allow production personnel a chance to inflect how audiences make sense of particular scenes or of the entire text. Many fan productions are spaces in which audiences can inflect a text's meanings, focusing on the aspects of the text that they love most, perhaps amplifying and concentrating them, while downplaying, erasing, or outright attacking elements of a text that they dislike. *In medias res* paratexts may also be sites for the significant expansion of what a text is, who it is for, and what it does, as boardgames or videogames, for example, may allow a different mode of interaction with the textual world, as transmedia extensions continue a story or focus on a specific character, and as multiple paratexts may move the text outwards to a wider or simply another audience. If entryway paratexts establish textual rules and initiate the text, *in medias res* paratexts may at times allow new rules to be written and extensions or expansions to be added, while at other times they will serve as spaces for the reinforcement of specific rules and meanings.

Because they are encountered after a text has begun, *in medias res* paratexts should be studied for what, if any, role they have in repurposing the text or keeping it as it is. Do these paratexts work as invitations to do something new and different with the text, or as stern rejections of some textual play? Frequently this question will have political undertones, as paratexts will negotiate the political life of a text. Take, for instance, a brief segment of the cast commentary track for *Lord of the Rings: The Fellowship*

of the Rings (2001) in which Ian McKellen speaks of encouraging Sean Astin and Elijah Wood to (unknowingly) include a queer undertone to a particularly warm and touching scene between their characters Sam and Frodo. Here, McKellen in effect invites viewers to adopt a queer reading and see Sam and Frodo as gay. While few of the studio's or director's paratexts surrounding *Lord of the Rings* ever explicitly shut down a queer reading, few explicitly invited it. On one hand, therefore, McKellen's invitation—and by extension New Line's invitation, for the company could easily have decided not to include this comment on the DVD—stands to inflect the text for some readers, and to acknowledge and endorse a reading engaged by other readers. This invitation came after-the-fact, too, for many audiences who had long been writing fan fiction that queered Sam, Frodo, and others, and hence were already playing the paratextual game. On the other hand, however, McKellen's invitation is somewhat buried, almost two hours into one of four commentary tracks on a DVD full of bonus materials, not emphasized on a poster or in an interview with *Entertainment Weekly*. A full analysis of this paratext, therefore, would need to wrestle both with what McKellen "does" to the text, and whom he does it to and for.

While the above is an example of paratexts *opening* a text, we might also look at countless instances of paratexts aiming to *close* them. Robert Brookey and Robert Westerfelhaus examine the case of the *Fight Club* (1999) DVD, whose bonus materials aim to render deviant and improper a queer reading of the film, even when the film is steeped in homoeroticism.[16] Paratexts, in short, will regularly play a key role in determining, redetermining, and predetermining what politics a text has *or is allowed to have* in popular culture. The work may say one thing, but the paratexts are part of the text, and they may ultimately hold more sway in saying something else, or they may be key in amplifying what that work had to say. A paratextual analysis aims to track what paratexts do or might do to a text. Thus, whether we care primarily about the *work*, and want to see what is tampering with it, or about the *text*, and want to see how much meaning is generated outside the work, paratextual analysis can complement and transform close textual analysis.

Case Study: Paratextual Pre-Views

In writing "Television Pre-views and the Meaning of Hype,"[17] I was trying to highlight the role that paratexts play in beginning the interpretive process from the outset. I wrote it at a time when few scholars were using the language of paratexts, and hence when their importance had not been widely acknowledged. However, since we are all hopefully aware of the importance of advertisements and branding, I used this analogy as a way of conceiving of paratextual power. Ad campaigns are designed to give meaning to their products, but if this is a truism when discussing ads for toothpaste or a new car, I suggest that it is no less the case with media texts. Paratexts will similarly construct meanings wholesale before the item of media has arrived. Towards this end, I studied an ad campaign in the New York subway system and online for a new television show, *Six Degrees* (ABC, 2006), and a much-circulated extended trailer for another new television show, *Studio 60 on the Sunset Strip* (NBC, 2006–07).

Instead of repeating here the argument of the piece, I use it to consider how to do paratextual analysis and to consider the article's blindspots. First, one must find the paratexts, a perhaps deceptively simple step to which we will return shortly. But an important part of finding a paratext is finding something *worth studying*. Paratexts are everywhere, but your analysis will be banal unless it has a point. The great challenge in finding paratexts for analysis then lies in asking which paratexts are playing a constitutive, transformative, or defensive/

maintenance role in the text's construction of meaning. In this case, I saw the ad campaigns for both shows as constituting that meaning, establishing what the texts were about and how to make sense of them, hailing specific audiences, performing and creating textual identity. *Six Degrees*, for instance, did so by invoking women's magazine or "which *Sex and the City* character are you?"-style quizzes (see Figures 17.1 and 17.2) to propose a genre of young, urban romance. Other studies, though, may instead focus on paratexts that seem to challenge, edit, or shift the text's overall meaning, or on paratexts that aim to discipline the text's overall meaning, working against transformation.

Indeed, while this article aims largely to situate the existence and importance of paratexts, on one hand it does little to study the politics of paratextuality, whereas many paratextual analyses will be interesting precisely because they examine how the paratext determines, predetermines, or redetermines a text's politics. Jimmy Draper, for instance, has written of how the press surrounding *American Idol* (FOX, 2002–16) interacted with the show to frame its prospects for queer politics.[18] On the other hand, my article is also limited inasmuch as it looks at one paratext or group of paratexts per text, when in fact we should expect paratexts to be battling each other in some cases. Here, I'd pose the case

Figure 17.1 Ads for *Six Degrees* on the New York City subway

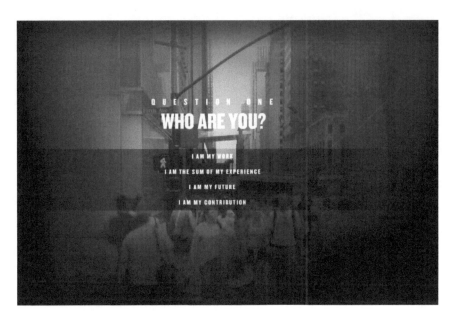

Figure 17.2 Screen grab from *Six Degrees'* pre-premier website

of *Mad Men*'s (AMC, 2009–15) feminism, which is powerfully situated by some paratexts, yet nowhere to be seen in Banana Republic's tie-in ad campaign, and actively trounced in many photo shoots of the show's female cast members. Thus, as complex as such a process may be, paratextual analysis could also take the form of examining how various paratexts and the work itself interact with each other, and to what end. To do so would require a consideration that is muted in my article, in examining to whom different paratexts talk. Paratexts don't talk to everyone, as audience members will usually only find a limited set of all the available paratexts, and as some paratexts are designed to seek out specific types of audiences by employing language and images that may speak preeminently to men, women, young people, the wealthy, or so forth; *Six Degrees'* subway and online ads, for instance, employed a vibrant purple color scheme and the language of women's magazine quizzes to hail young women. Some audiences are also more or less welcome to produce their own paratexts and hence to play around with the text and its meanings. Some forms of paratextual analysis could go well beyond what I did in this article by conducting a network analysis, working out how an entire field of paratexts and audiences interact, and exploring how paratexts work to exclude certain audiences from a potential market while ensuring others' presence in the audience.

Moreover, since many paratexts are ephemeral (my article, for instance, is one of the lone public records of the New York subway ads for *Six Degrees*), consideration of the temporality of varying paratexts is vital. Historical research is especially tricky, therefore, as the act of finding paratexts may prove remarkably difficult. If we wanted to compare *Six Degrees'* subway campaign to other subway ads from the same time, where would we find them now? When paratexts are lost to time, when they are actively destroyed or buried, or when they are saved for posterity and easily accessible, we are invited to ask another set of questions about textual politics, namely about whose interests are served by various paratexts dying or remaining. Finding "official" paratexts will often be easier than finding fan paratexts, which must often lay low for fear of litigation because of alleged copyright infringement, but they may prove no less important in framing the text, and thus analysts must actively seek them out, rather than just—as did my article—consider paratexts that seek out the analyst and audience. Also, though the study of paratexts easily lends itself to consideration of text and audience, they are wonderful windows into production culture research, too, as we may use them to observe moves made by production personnel to control a text, to contest other personnel's versions of the text, or to engage in specific branding exercises. In this case, who made the ad, with what information and direction from the producers, and what did they hope to achieve with the campaign? Such questions could be asked of the advertisers who devised the campaign, their answers telling us not just about *Six Degrees* but the place of advertising in media industries in general.

Another set of questions one could ask beyond those of the article is about the spatial location of paratexts. As the article notes, the subway ad campaign was restricted to New York City and Los Angeles, inviting us to consider how *Six Degrees* was marketed differently to residents of and visitors to these cities than to others, or perhaps even of the marketing purpose and value of situating such gimmicks only in New York City or Los Angeles in hopes that they will be reported upon by others elsewhere. But we could use a larger, global frame and ask how these two shows or others were marketed to the rest of the world. Media studies has shown increasing interest in the global moves of texts and, at times, surprise in how differently some texts are interpreted in different countries. We should expect paratexts to play a notable role in the transformation of texts across borders or across regions within any given nation. Illuminating how and why any given text is marketed differently is an implicitly paratextual study, and a fruitful one.

Conclusion

This chapter has argued that texts are always open and, consequently, that they are always open to being changed. Intertextual and paratextual analysis are ways to track this ongoing flow of meaning, to see what meanings precede the work, what meanings transform it later on, and what, if any, role they play in shifting or reinforcing the aesthetic or ideological place of that text. "Close textual analysis" is (ironically) just the preview or trailer for the more challenging act of ascertaining meaning, an act that requires the examination of intertextuality and paratextuality. As noted above, though, attention to intertextuality and paratextuality could—and hopefully *will* in future work—transform how we study production cultures, the role of the archive and how textual memory works, how audiences interact with texts, how they work via algorithms and variable interfaces, how global meanings are managed, and more. And intertextuality and paratextuality invite us scholars, artists, and citizens to realize that all texts are temporal beings subject to alteration; we can and should study and analyze their temporality and their current meanings, but we can and should also consider ways to intervene in the

intertextual, paratextual flow of meaning-making, to repurpose, correct, and ameliorate texts.

Notes

1. Roland Barthes, "From Work to Text," in *Image/Music/Text*, trans. Stephen Heath (New York: Hill and Wang, 1977), 157 (emphasis in original).
2. Valentin Volosinov, *Marxism and the Philosophy of Language*, trans. Ladislav Metejka and IR Titunik (London: Seminar, 1973), 27, 36, 70.
3. Mikhail Bakhtin, *Speech Genres and Other Late Essays*, trans. Vern McGee, ed. Caryl Emerson and Michael Holquist (Austin: University of Texas Press, 1986), 69.
4. Julia Kristeva, "Word, Dialogue, and Novel," in *Desire in Language: A Semiotic Approach to Literature and Art*, trans. Thomas Gora, Alice Jardine, and Leon Roudiez, ed. Leon Roudiez (Oxford: Basil Blackwell, 1980), 66.
5. Tony Bennett and Janet Woollacott, *Bond and Beyond: The Political Career of a Popular Hero* (London: MacMillan, 1987), 6–7.
6. Ibid., 90–91.
7. John Fiske, "Moments of Television: Neither the Text nor the Audience," in *Remote Control: Television, Audiences, and Cultural Power*, ed. Ellen Seiter, Hans Borchers, Gabriele Kreutzner, and Eva-Maria Warth (New York: Routledge, 1989), 66.
8. Eileen Meehan, "'Holy Commodity Fetish, Batman!': The Political Economy of a Commercial Intertext," in *The Many Lives of the Batman: Critical Approaches to a Superhero and His Media*, ed. Roberta Pearson and William Uricchio (London: BFI, 1991), 47–65.
9. John Caldwell, *Televisuality: Style, Crisis, and Authority in American Television* (New Brunswick: Rutgers University Press, 1995).
10. See Chapter 16 in this volume.
11. Jonathan Gray, *Watching with The Simpsons: Television, Parody, and Intertextuality* (New York: Routledge, 2006).
12. Raymond Williams, *Television: Technology and Cultural Form* (London: Fontana/Collins, 1974).
13. Gérard Genette, *Paratexts: Thresholds of Interpretation*, trans. Jane Lewin (Cambridge: Cambridge University Press, 1997).
14. Jonathan Gray, *Show Sold Separately: Promos, Spoilers, and Other Media Paratexts* (New York: New York University Press, 2010), http://openaccessbooks.nyupress.org/details/9780814731956/.
15. Lisa Kernan, *Coming Attractions: Reading American Movie Trailers* (Austin: University of Texas Press, 2004).
16. Robert Brookey and Robert Westerfelhaus, "Hiding Homoeroticism in Plain View: The *Fight Club* DVD as Digital Closet," *Critical Studies in Media Communication* 19, no. 1 (2002): 21–43.

17. Jonathan Gray, "Television Pre-Views and the Meaning of Hype," *International Journal of Cultural Studies* 11, no. 1 (2008): 33–49.

18. Jimmy Draper, "*Idol* Speculation: Queer Identity and a Media-Imposed Lens of Detection," *Popular Communication* 10, no. 3 (2012): 201–16.

Further Reading

Brooker, Will. "Living on *Dawson's Creek*: Teen Viewers, Cultural Convergence, and Television." *International Journal of Cultural Studies* 4, no. 4 (2001): 456–72.

Harries, Dan. *Film Parody*. London: BFI, 2000.

Hutcheon, Linda. *A Theory of Adaptation*. Revised edition. New York: Routledge, 2013.

Jenkins, Henry. *Convergence Culture: Where Old and New Media Collide*. New York: New York University Press, 2006.

Kompare, Derek. "Publishing Flow: DVD Box Sets and the Reconception of Television." *Television and New Media* 7, no. 4 (2006): 335–60.

Meinhof, Ulrike and Jonathan Smith, eds. *Intertextuality and the Media: From Genre to Everyday Life*. Manchester: Manchester University Press, 2000.

Scott, Suzanne. "Repackaging Fan Culture: The Regifting Economy of Ancillary Content Models." *Transformative Works and Cultures* 3 (2009). Accessed February 28, 2018, http://journal.transformativeworks.org/index.php/twc/article/view/150/122.

18.
STARDOM AND CELEBRITY
Suzanne Leonard and Diane Negra

As has been widely noted (though not widely analyzed) Donald J. Trump's 2016 election to the U.S. presidency rested in significant ways on the foundation built by his reality television (and to a lesser extent his tabloid) stardom. Trump's rise to political power thus strikingly illustrates that the study of celebrity—and particularly its operations, cycles, and outcomes—is vitally necessary in assessing the ideological investments and political economies of contemporary culture. As his election proved, the skills needed to build an ardent base of enthusiastic acolytes echo those demanded of contemporary stars: notions of authenticity and accessibility often outweigh other perceived assets or liabilities.

Trump's election and ensuing presidency also confirm the dominance of social media technologies, tools that have ineluctably shifted the landscape of stardom, celebrity, and entertainment. In Trump's case, this development is most visible in his fondness for Twitter rants at obscure hours, a means of communication that has been linked to his feted "relatability" but should also be understood as indexing new expectations for celebrities to operate in accessible modalities. Notable features of the contemporary fame environment include a pronounced rise in the interface between celebrities and their publics accompanied by hopes/fantasies/expectations of a dialogic connectivity, a proliferation in communities of celebrity consumption, and a greater role for celebrities in the circulation and modulation of social affect.

This chapter tracks the development of star and celebrity studies as a subset of the broader fields of media and cultural studies, pointing out the way in which stardom shapeshifts from a mark of distinction to a form of discourse that renders celebrities accessible, knowable, and perhaps most saliently, "ordinary."

While a history of media stardom is vast and would encompass early examples ranging from "Biograph Girl" Florence Lawrence to animal Internet celebrities like "Lil Bub" and "Grumpy Cat," our survey here will necessarily be more modest. At the same time, it sheds light on the fact that stars' lives, bodies, conversations, and public appearances consistently serve to arbitrate cultural norms, mores, and anxieties. Stars and celebrities consistently promote and seem to verify longstanding and long-cherished narratives of nationhood: in the case of the United States, "celebrities have always helped perpetuate narratives of meritocracy, class mobility, and opportunity."[1] To illustrate the perseverance of this narrative, even in a landscape where the possibilities for class ascension are alarmingly scarce, the chapter closes with a reflection on our study of Bethenny Frankel, a former reality series star turned entrepreneur and media mogul. Thanks to her meteoric rise from ordinary working woman to branding guru, Frankel is an apt example of the way celebrity identities are created, negotiated, managed, and maintained in the contemporary media ethos.

A central insight arising from the early "wave" of intellectual inquiry into the cultural functions of stardom is that **star personae** are "always intertextual and syncretic" (in Richard deCordova's phrasing) sustaining a "coherent continuousness" over and above individual roles and appearances.[2] This formulation was foundational in the development of **star studies**, and this chapter will point to aspects of such seminal scholarship in order to establish the key insights of the field. Additionally, it is imperative that a study of the intellectual practices in this area account for the fact that a central shift has taken place, what we loosely frame as a transition from star studies to celebrity studies. Whereas traditional scenarios of stardom (with its promises of being spontaneously discovered) appeal to fantasies of upward mobility, the study of celebrity requires grappling with the broad breakdown of meritocratic ideologies and influences of neoliberal governmentality that indelibly shape celebrity's wider contemporary cultural meanings. While stars are typically figured as extraordinary, celebrity typically hinges on notions of accessibility and authenticity. Unpacking the distinctions between stardom and celebrity, our discussion investigates the notion of persona as text and the situatedness of celebrity meanings within social history.

Organizationally, this chapter tracks the emergence of stardom as a subject of academic inquiry within media studies and cultural studies and then moves to the more contemporary analysis of celebrity in an environment often characterized as more turbulent and hyperconsumerist and less talent-centered than other periods. During the height of the studio era, film studios carefully groomed and trained actors—arguably, the first "stars"—as properties over long periods of time. Elizabeth Taylor, for instance, was for years known as MGM's "most dutiful daughter," as evidenced by the fact that "she went to school in the Culver City Studio, held her birthday parties on MGM's sound stages, and even met her first dates and husbands through studio publicists," according to Aida Hozic.[3] Such behaviors were consistent with the historical period in which her stardom proliferated: studios in the 1940s were well-oiled machines where star images were manufactured through authorized biographies and staged publicity events, and symbolically verified and legitimated by screen roles.[4]

Twenty-first century celebrity, by contrast, often appears more disposable, less dignified and rooted in flimsier and more superficial modes of identity. In the nearly twenty years since Mary Flanagan took note of the ways that "the cinematic star as a culturally produced body has evolved into a digital star system in which signifiers, identities and bodies themselves are called into question," the online universe has proliferated a range of digital celebrity modes whose modus operandi may not be fully explicable within these earlier theoretical parameters.[5] Recognizing that, as Su Holmes and Sean Redmond assert, "Celebrity is key to the way the social world organizes and commodifies its representations, discourses and ideologies, sensations, impressions, and fantasies,"[6] we assess not only the ways in which the Internet and the proliferation of reality television forms have provided impetus for

celebrity discourse but also the monetization of public knowledge about celebrities and new relations between celebrity, neoliberal subjectivity, and self-branding. The Kardashian brand is perhaps the apotheosis of this new turn, as signaled by the family's relentless and indefatigable efforts to fashion an aspirational intimacy with their fans "not only through their televisual omnipresence and array of self-fashioning products, but through social media."[7] Embracing what Alison Hearn terms a "monetization of being,"[8] the Kardashians' personal life (which doubles as their business) testifies to the new regimes of mandatory disclosure and transparency that epitomize celebrity in the age of social media. Whereas a film like *Lisa Picard is Famous* (2000) might once have satirized the fame-seeking behavior of a single individual, a more recent offering like *Ingrid Goes West* (2017) depicts the widespread mobilization of "followers" as social (and potentially commercial) resources that bring about a wholesale alteration of the concept of renown.

In an ever more fragmented media environment, celebrities whose signification is deeply meaningful for some audiences may remain wholly unknown to others. A notable element of the contemporary landscape, meanwhile, is the association of low-status celebrities with the cultural phenomenon of "hate-watching," which entails the close tracking of media texts in order to savor the pleasure of disliking them. At the same time, cultural tides can turn against celebrities who breach protocols of sensitivity, with lasting effects. Racist, sexist, and homophobic comments indelibly tarnished the reputations of a number of twenty-first century stars, including *Seinfeld*'s (NBC, 1989–98) Michael Richards, actor/director Mel Gibson, comedian Daniel Tosh, and *Duck Dynasty* (A&E, 2012–17) star Phil Roberston, all of whom were widely castigated for fomenting and promoting discrimination. "More and more issues of diversity and inclusion serve as the backdrop of celebrity scandal, tearing down established stars caught uttering bigoted speech," observes Russell Meeuf.[9] Discourses about stars often serve as litmus tests for what constitutes acceptable attitudes, whether this means unveiling a changing cultural norm, or highlighting the perseverance of longstanding ideals.

Intellectual History of the Concept

Many of the modes and mechanisms of contemporary celebrity originate in the pre-history of film, television, and digital media. Though celebrity is commonly theorized as the by-product of a twentieth- and twenty-first-century media culture, Brenda Weber usefully points out that "in the centuries before our own, celebrity was experienced with no lesser intensity."[10] The rise in variation and visibility of the concept of celebrity should nevertheless be traced to the advent of print cultures—particularly mass-market publications such as books, pamphlets, newspapers, and magazines—which burgeoned in the nineteenth and early twentieth centuries. Along with vaudeville, theater, and human-interest journalism, these incipient mass entertainment industries democratized the concept of celebrity and highlighted personality as a structuring principle. Whereas, prior to this period, fame was anchored by the perception that celebrities were special, different, and distinguished by achievement or birthright, according to historian Charles Ponce de Leon, a twentieth-century turn democratized the concept as more widely available to anyone in the public eye. Journalists also began investigating a subject's "real self," a strategy undergirded by the belief that the seat of personhood lies in one's private life. Valorizations of self-expression and behind-the-scenes investigations of public figures were thus newly identified as crucial components of celebrity. As Ponce de Leon argues,

> critics must accept that celebrity is intimately related to modernity—that this unique way of thinking about public figures, which differs so dramatically from the hagiographic discourse of fame, is a direct outgrowth of developments that most of us regard as progressive: the spread of a market economy and the rise of democratic, individualistic values.[11]

Debates over the amount, extent, and handling of self-disclosure in star discourse will, in turn, provide a throughline for this chapter's investigation of the development of stardom and celebrity as critical methodologies.

The consistently shifting boundary between "exceptionalism" and "ordinariness" presents a related and consistent tension in the discipline, a negotiation that underscores stars' persistently unstable appeal. Stars' commonplace qualities counterbalance their ability to serve as aspirational figures, and their position with respect to this dichotomy often indexes their commercial value. Silent-film star Mary Pickford, for instance, offered up a "girl-next-door" image in her life and in films like *Poor Little Rich Girl* (1917), a presentation deftly anchored by her wholesome femininity

and whiteness, notes Sean Redmond.[12] This image was also buttressed by her celebrated romance with and marriage to Douglas Fairbanks Jr.—the pair are roundly considered to be Hollywood's first celebrity couple. What this representation belied, however, were the adulterous circumstances that began Pickford and Fairbanks' romance, as well as "Little Mary's" (as she was often termed) position as a savvy businesswoman who well understood her commodity value to Paramount Studios. With Fairbanks, Charlie Chaplin, and D.W. Griffith, she ultimately helped to found United Artists, an independent studio that challenged the distribution dominance of her former employer.[13]

Stars designated as "ordinary" (readily evident in the phraseology of entertainment magazine *US Weekly*'s "Stars: They're Just like Us") typically enjoy a greater sense of connection with their publics, an effect film critic Richard Schickel calls "the illusion of intimacy."[14] Manifold advantages attend those well-poised to create such an illusion, and deCordova argues that controlling knowledge of film stars and positing them as morally upstanding individuals in line with American values helped to establish and consolidate the power of the studio system in its formative years. Supposedly "behind-the-scenes" investigations (a generic convention of early publicity periodicals like *Photoplay*), where stars spoke about their desire to protect their personal lives, homes, and families, helped to discourage the perception that stars were out of touch or elitist and reassure audiences of their adherence to wholesome virtues. The provision of access to stars' lives (they were, for example, often photographed in their homes) was nevertheless routinely balanced with a need to maintain a star's glamorous image.

The public also plays an integral role in helping to foster, support, and extend stardom and celebrity. According to Joshua Gamson, "celebrity culture is at once a commodity system, an industry, a set of stories, and a participatory culture. The commodity at stake is embodied attention."[15] This attention can take a number of forms, including attendance at stars' events and appearances; mimicking their styles and looks; consuming the products they promote; reading promotional and gossip materials; tracking their appearances; commenting on them in online forums, on fan sites, and via social media; and conversing about them either in person or virtually with other interested audiences. Film scholars in particular have been concerned with the idea of **audience** identification with stars, asking not only which stars draw audience investments but also what form such investments take, as Matt Hills investigates in Chapter 15. Because the question of how publics consume star images circumscribes what a star "means" or signifies, researching audience identification with stars has constituted a subset of the field of star studies. In her study of how British female audiences responded to female movie stars during and after World War II, for example, Jackie Stacey finds that

> Many forms of identification involve processes of transformation and the production of new identities combining the spectator's existing identity with her desired identity and her reading of the star's identity [. . .] If we take audiences as a starting point for understanding the consumption of stars, the active and productive elements of the star-audience relationship begin to emerge.[16]

The preponderance of consumer products associated with stars, particularly their clothes, accessories, cars, and homes, likewise modeled a transition from a producer to a consumer economy during the early twentieth century, a period coterminous with cinema's rise in visibility. "Consumption, as signified by stars, became the most visible mark of success for the striving 'new' middle class," observes Sumiko Higashi, "and involved not only acquiring goods but transforming selves."[17] The advent of a consolidated film industry in the 1920s, alongside the emergence of the New Woman as economically savvy proto-feminist, catapulted the image of the independent woman into high visibility. This star type has had enormous staying power throughout the twentieth and twenty-first centuries, and will prove important to our case study of Bethenny Frankel. Associations between celebrity and consumer culture and, specifically, the way in which stars' lives were positioned to encourage not only consumption as a habit of viewing but also the act of purchasing goods and services remain a cornerstone of celebrity study. As P. David Marshall argues, stars provide pedagogical instruction on selfhood, hence "Celebrity taught generations how to engage and use consumer culture to 'make' oneself."[18] Put differently, the discipline attends to the fact that star performances model and encourage specific desires and behaviors for men and women alike. A basketball star like Michael Jordan illustrates, for instance, how an exemplary figure of black masculinity could be appropriated to serve the interests of a wide range of commercial brands (foremost among them Nike). A film like *Space Jam* (1996), which satirizes *and* furthers

the web of commercial branding in which Jordan became enmeshed, depicts the complex way in which Jordan came to be presented as both racially specific and racially transcendent.

Analysis of the ways in which stars ground ancillary consumption of material goods, stage lifestyling scenarios, and generally foster regimes of capitalist desire constitutes an important subset of scholarly work in this area. In an early and influential account, Charles Eckert goes so far as to suggest that early Hollywood,

> drawing upon the resources of literature, art and music, did as much or more than any other force in capitalist culture to smooth the operation of the production-consumption cycle by fetishising products and putting the libido in libidinally invested advertising.[19]

The spectrum of scholarship in this area runs from Jane Gaines and Charlotte Herzog's investigation into the craze for knock-off dresses of the kind worn by Joan Crawford in *Letty Lynton* (1932) to Simon Dixon's contention that star homes be read as "ambiguous ecologies," customarily conceptualized and presented in magazine layouts as showcases for the preferred meanings of the star and "a theatre for the display for living,"[20] to Rebecca L. Epstein's argument for a more recent re-positioning of the star as a fallible consumer whose fashion choices are to be raked over by a public whose fundamentally critical role displaces the more adulatory relations of the past.[21] Pamela Church Gibson has relatedly pinpointed a transition in the relationship between fashion and celebrity culture, noting that whereas films used to exist as fashion showcases, nowadays that function is served by "press and Internet coverage of the stars' outfits and their personal lives, together with their commercial deployment within the 'fashion system,' in fashion features and advertising campaigns."[22] Arguably this shift is well captured in the "Stars: They're Just Like Us" feature we allude to above in which celebrities are customarily spotted consuming chain-brand goods and services.

The twenty-first century has also witnessed the rise of the star-turned-female-lifestyle expert, who in turn peddles a series of products synergized to her brand—notable examples include Gwyneth Paltrow, whose Goop brand promotes "cutting edge wellness advice," and Jessica Alba, whose Honest Company sells non-toxic, eco-friendly household products. These stars' use of social media to engage their publics (and promote their products) may be seen to up the (techno-consumerist) ante on fantasies of affiliation, engagement, and communication between celebrities and their publics as social media facilitate the creation of what Elizabeth Ellcessor deems "star texts of connection."[23]

Of course, the interrelations between celebrity culture and other facets of consumerism should not be simplistically conceptualized. People do not necessarily buy products simply because stars promote them. As Linda Mizejewski notes in her study of *It Happened One Night* (1934), Clark Gable was attributed with the commercial power to devastate the men's undershirt industry after he partially disrobed in one scene of the film and it became clear that he was not wearing any such garment. Yet this widely cited anecdote was an urban legend; no sales falloff in fact took place, and we might best understand the durability of this (inaccurate) account as a way of articulating the star power of Gable and the mass appeal of the film's erotic economy.[24] The cliché that a star has insured a particular body part for which they are well known operates as a similar attempt to materialize/financialize the often-ephemeral power of celebrity charisma. Stars who intentionally align themselves with specific consumables can also endure significant backlash, if, for example, a product fails to cohere with a larger brand signature, or the public feels that the promotion is false or forced. We take up this notion specifically in our investigation of Frankel, who jumpstarted a trend whereby women appearing on Bravo's *Real Housewives* (2006–) franchise attempted to use their appearances to shill products tethered to the concept of aspirational femininity. Whereas Frankel's products were highly consistent with her brand image—and the issues that seemed to matter in what was imagined to be her "real life"—other housewives were castigated for the lack of subtlety or coherence in their marketing efforts.

Stardom and Celebrity in Film, Television, and New Media

Since the discipline's location in the realm of media studies specifically, scholars of stardom and celebrity have grappled to determine the extent to which stars' images are produced by their works, their lives, or crucially, the overlaps and interactions between them. Typically, stars' significance was rooted in their casting, though a star's "real life" is typically more deterministic in curating their star image than any one specific acting role. According to deCordova, "with the star, the actor became the character in a narrative quite separable from his or her work in any film."[25] Stars remain at once inside and outside their mediatized roles as "characters," and Richard Dyer's landmark contribution to the field has been to emphasize the paratextual aspects that make the "star-as-person" indistinguishable from the "star-as-performer." Dyer coined the term **star image** to explain this concept, and pointed out the need to study ancillary texts associated with stars, as Jonathan Gray describes in Chapter 17. As Dyer writes, "a star image is made out of media texts that can be grouped together as promotion, publicity, films, and criticism and commentaries."[26] He later expanded this definition to include, "everything that is publicly available" about stars, such as "the promotion of those films and of the star through pin-ups, public appearances, studio hand-outs and so on, as well as interviews, biographies and coverage in the press of the star's doings and 'private' life."[27] Dyer also situated stars as "social types" such as the "rebel" or the "independent woman," but recognized that star images register as more complex, contradictory, and in his words, polysemous, than a single type would indicate. Star types work in conjunction with specific reception communities, and in his study of Judy Garland as a gay icon, Dyer identifies "ordinariness, androgyny, and camp," as aspects of Garland's image that were homologous with gay male culture. "Garland works in an emotional register of great intensity," he argues, "which seems to bespeak equally suffering and survival, vulnerability and strength, theatricality and authenticity, passion and irony," qualities that resonated particularly with gay men.[28]

While studies like Dyer's and deCordova's, as well as investigations such as Charles Maland's *Chaplin and American Culture: The Evolution of a Star Image*, Adrienne McLean's *Being Rita Hayworth*, and Rutgers University Press's *Star Decades* series, *Movie Stars from the 1910s to the 2000s* (10 volumes in total), have tended to focus on classical film stardom within a wider cultural milieu, different but related issues came to the fore when the discipline approached television stardom. From its inception, television was typically placed in a subordinate cultural position vis-à-vis film, such that

> the dominant tendency in star studies has been to denigrate the stature of television stardom, to argue that television does not actually produce stars of the complexity, depth, and cultural value that film does, largely because of the medium's lesser cultural status and its essential familiarity and intimacy,

explains Christine Becker.[29] Scholars have, however, challenged this assumption, a debate that again turns on the concept of the "ordinary." In *Hitch Your Antenna to the Stars: Early Television and Broadcast Stardom*, Susan Murray suggests that during the medium's earliest eras, a television star's ordinariness was in fact a calculated strategy: positioning stars as natural and authentic helped to court viewers and to ensure that star pitches for various products were seen as genuine. Television stars were also beholden to networks and sponsors in a more multi-varied way than film stars since they were bound not only to a network but also to a specific sponsor:

> Instead of conforming to the more uniform aims of a single studio, which only sold movies and related merchandise, the television star was required to advertise a product while also representing the textual and industrial strategies of a television network.[30]

Becker relatedly contends that "a plethora of decentralized and sometimes conflicting sites of authority competed to depict and define [television] stars: networks, sponsors, talent agents, gossip columnists, television critics, and even the stars themselves."[31]

Such industrial shifts serve as an important backdrop against which to understand the transition from stardom to celebrity in the discipline. "Whereas the film celebrity plays with aura through the construction of distance, the television celebrity is configured around conceptions of familiarity," attests Marshall.[32] Though this is a somewhat reductive account (given what we have been arguing about how film stars have historically negotiated tensions between appearing ordinary and extraordinary), television's impact on the discipline should not be underestimated, nor should we forget the enormous changes ushered in during the twenty-first century by an increasingly convergent media culture. Ellcessor notes that

> Internet celebrity is founded even more firmly on illusions of intimacy, expressed not so much in terms of television's regularity as through perceived access to private, backstage behavior. Internet-based fame depends on the authenticity of a star's self-representation and on the notion of intimacy, experienced through the possibility of interaction rather than through simple familiarity.[33]

Observing such alterations, Gamson concludes that "the economic push to make people known for themselves rather than for their actions remains at the heart of the now-decentralized star system: as sales aids, celebrities are most useful if they can draw attention regardless of the particular context in which they appear. Name recognition in itself is critical for commerce."[34] Christine Geraghty makes a related claim as she parses the meaning of what she terms the "star-as-celebrity," noting that "the term celebrity indicates someone whose fame happens outside the sphere of their work and who is famous for having a lifestyle."[35] As these sentiments suggest, stars serve as their own image purveyors to an increasing extent, complying with neoliberal regimes that mandate autonomy and self-determinism.

We contend that the contemporary convergent environment largely intensifies the predispositions of earlier cycles of celebrity production wherein media forms were more discrete. A similar argument has been advanced by Sue Collins in analyzing what she deems "dispensable" reality celebrity and finding that "by reminding audiences of what they are not, dispensable celebrities reaffirm the star system."[36] Nevertheless, a gap arguably exists in theorizing the multiple modes of celebrity at play in the highly stratified contemporary field. As television is increasingly graded according to rubrics of "quality" and "schlock," the artistic credibility of stars associated with prestige television—*Mad Men*'s (AMC, 2007–15) Jon Hamm, for instance, or *Girls*' (HBO, 2012–17) creator and star Lena Dunham—may now be as high or higher than that of film stars, an unprecedented development. Gamson has argued, meanwhile, that "For reality TV, ordinariness becomes a credential for stardom, not its antithesis."[37] While this seems largely to be the case, it is also clear that fame is facilitated and arbitrated by a set of new gatekeepers such as Simon Cowell, Perez Hilton, Ryan Seacrest and Kris Jenner, inheritors, to some extent, of the roles once played by Hollywood gossip columnists Louella Parsons and Hedda Hopper. Moreover, even the most banal forms of celebrity are zealously multi-platformed to maximize their commercial value. When Ashleigh Butler danced with her dog Pudsey to win the sixth season of *Britain's Got Talent* (ITV, 2007–) in 2012, this event proved only the opening salvo in a commercial onslaught that would come to include television and theater appearances and, in 2014, the feature film *Pudsey: The Movie*.

As we articulate in our case study, the advent of reality television, and particularly its valorization of self-commodification and self-branding, has proven an indispensable pillar for understanding the functioning of stardom and celebrity in the twenty-first century. In such realms, selling oneself replaces being "discovered," notions of talent are no longer as conceptually fixed, and qualities such as scrappiness and determination trump talent. At the same time, celebrities who earn their fame via reality vehicles—and who seek to capitalize on them by appearing in multiple other media forms—are often subject to accusations of "overexposure" in a fame environment which regularly contrasts the low status of reality celebrity with the artistry and craft attributed to the stars of "quality TV." As infotainment and celebrity gossip edge out more conventional newsmakers, celebrities embody the pressures of a cutthroat media marketplace. Specifically, their images and appearances are used to forge commercial alignments between the news media, magazine and online industries, and the promotional needs of major entertainment organizations. In star and celebrity discourse, a public persona is increasingly expected to serve as a multiply leveraged commercial asset.

Another distinct element of contemporary celebrity culture is its imbrication in celebrations of economic and social privilege with older stigmas regarding class warfare, inequality, and conspicuous consumption in notable retreat. In this vein, reality genres highlight forms of celebrity emphatically associated with self-interest, economic competition and, often, social mistrust. Laurie Ouellette has persuasively argued, for instance, that the authoritarian persona of Judge Judith Scheindlin of television's *Judge Judy* (syndicated, 1996–) grounds a franchise whose key ideological function is "to instruct TV viewers how to detect and avoid the risks that certain individuals are shown to represent."[38] A significant swathe of reality television is therefore organized around the project of "designing out" exterior markers of inequality, using fashion, appearance, and home beautification to lacquer class, race, or sexual distinctions, argues Jayne Raisborough.[39] The widespread neoliberal notion that it is possible to will one's way up the social-class hierarchy has arguably, and paradoxically, intensified its appeal in the face of overwhelming evidence to the contrary, and celebrity discourses have, if anything, only strengthened this ideology's vice grip. In a study of what they term "austere meritocracy," the authors of *Celebrity, Aspiration, and Contemporary Youth* conclude that British youth must act as though they live in a meritocracy, a belief system they shore up with "an intensified emphasis on 'hard work,' 'optimism,' and 'resilience' and a policing of relationships to consumption through discourses of 'un/deserving wealth' and 'thrift.'"[40]

Arguably this anti-democratic turn—which nevertheless works to privilege a status hierarchy of the "deserving"—recharges the necessity for the study of celebrity power in defining and testing normative citizenship roles. A recent wave of scholarship that considers the politicization of gender, class, race, and ability in the personae of celebrities highlights a key tension. On the one hand—and particularly as it relates to women—celebrity discourse tends to remain mired in troublesome gender logics, buttressing sexist, ageist, and classist ideals, and valuing what Su Holmes and Diane Negra have called "the security of female typology."[41] On the other hand, recent visibilities of formerly marginalized groups in celebrity culture can seem to indicate a more democratized social field marked by greater diversity. Meeuf's work on celebrities whose bodies render them outside cultural norms on the basis of their obesity, disability, race and ethnicity, or transgender status, appears at first glance to suggest the proliferation of a culture of inclusion. Yet, Meeuf argues that their potentially threatening differences are assuaged in a flattening process intrinsic to middle-class gender expression.[42]

No doubt, new scholarship in this area will continue to address itself to a celebrity environment in which bids for fame proliferate through the still-evolving protocols of social media. In an important account, Alice E. Marwick has explored how "the mindset and practices of micro-celebrity are made possible by social media technologies, which enable average people to gain the audiences of traditional celebrities."[43] Marwick defines **micro-celebrity** as a "state of being famous to a niche group of people, but it is also a behavior: the presentation of oneself as a celebrity regardless of who is paying attention."[44] Micro-celebrity, self-branding, and the promotional terrain of forms such as Facebook, LinkedIn, Instagram, and Twitter give rise to crucial questions regarding the corporatization of sociality that will need further exploration.

Case Study: Bethenny Frankel as Postfeminist Entrepreneur

Our article, "After Ever After: Bethenny Frankel, Self-Branding and the 'New Intimacy of Work,'" focuses on the fame of reality celebrity Bethenny Frankel, a media mogul who appeared in a variety of television offerings in the early twenty-first century including: *The Apprentice: Martha Stewart* (NBC, 2005); *The Real Housewives of New York* (Bravo, 2008–10); *Bethenny Getting Married?* (Bravo, 2010); *Bethenny Ever After*

(Bravo, 2010–12); and *Bethenny* (syndicated, 2012–14), finally returning to *The Real Housewives of New York* in 2015. Frankel was also a prolific author during this period, penning a novel entitled *Skinnydipping* (2012) and a variety of self-help books, including *A Place of Yes: 10 Rules for Getting Everything You Want Out of Life* (2011) and *I Suck at Relationships So You Don't Have To* (2015). Perhaps even more saliently, Frankel established herself as a formidable female entrepreneur, clustering a series of diet, exercise, and food products under her name including most famously, Skinnygirl Margarita, a brand that was sold to Beam Suntory (the parent company for Jim Beam) for a reported $100 million in 2011. (This feat also landed her on the cover of *Forbes*.) Thanks to what may be termed her overexposure, Frankel was the subject of a variety of media write-ups, including magazine cover stories and articles, interviews, photographs, and appearances in online celebrity gossip sites, paratexts which often doubled as promotional materials for her lucrative brand.

The majority of the aforementioned paratexts come into focus in our case study, which argues that Frankel's rise as a reality star-turned-lifestyle celebrity speaks to the dictates of hyper-entrepreneurialism, relentless self-commodification, and niche marketing in the early twenty-first-century television economy. Frankel was a fitting subject for our investigation not only because of her wide exposure but also because we were concerned with the way that her personal and professional trajectory confirms neoliberal conflations of market and intimacy realms. Whereas reality celebrity tends to be thought of in ephemeral terms, Frankel's story (much like that of the Kardashian celebrity empire) bespeaks a fundamental shift in contemporary labor economies. What Mark Andrejevic refers to as "the work of being watched" was in ample supply in Frankel's biography, as evidenced by her willingness to up the intimacy ante in each successive iteration of her reality television career.[45] Whereas her initial televised appearances scripted her as part of an ensemble cast, she pulled ahead of her fellow reality stars by earning her own show, *Bethenny Getting Married?* in 2010. As we discuss, it was a personal rather than professional milestone that earned Frankel this spot: namely, her willingness, while in the second and third trimesters of a pregnancy, to share with viewers her harried attempts to plan a wedding in six weeks, and to expose her stress and frustration during what is typically mythologized as a zenith experience of heterosexual women's lives. Frankel's raw exposure of her marital (and eventually maternal) stresses

continued to organize her television career, a situation we generalize to suggest that in current affective economies, women, in particular, are both rewarded and simultaneously chastised for turning their personal lives into money-making endeavors. Frankel's symbolic punishments (a divorce and the cancellation of her talk show) hence existed in tension with her seemingly unstoppable professional ascendance, a situation that highlighted the gendered pressures that attend this stage of capitalist self-production.

The success of Frankel's brand in a variety of platforms (television, print, online) is emblematic of the transmedia potentials of reality television stardom and the increasingly convergent nature of media celebrity. Yet, for all the richness and value of existing accounts, new theoretical models are still needed to make sense of the fame modes of the post-stardom era. As discussed, star and celebrity studies have historically been interested in the vagaries of self-disclosure, attending to the question of who controls this exposure and the shifting parameters concerning the appropriate amount, scale, and commercial value of such revelations. Understanding the implications of Frankel's rise necessitates acknowledgment that under neoliberal regimes, self-commodification has tipped into an everyday requirement—in short, the question is less about how much a celebrity will disclose but rather in what format confessional gestures will best maximize brand exposure. The masterful synergy between Frankel's life and her myriad "products" (we use this term loosely) presents a successful example of how one can utilize convergent media potentials to accomplish such ends. Since we published our article, Frankel has continued to be a poster woman for savvy self-branding, and she retains access to the use and promotion of the name Skinnygirl. A *New Yorker* profile of Frankel noted that by 2015 the Skinnygirl label had been attached to over 100 products, and, in a 2016 article titled "Skinnygirl, Fat Wallet," *Forbes* again diagrammed how masterfully Frankel's licensing deals benefit her bottom line.[46]

A subtextual contention of this chapter and our study of Frankel is that gender remains a salient organizing category for studies of both stardom and celebrity. This recognition indelibly informs our case study, for instance, when we discuss the fact that Frankel's signature Skinnygirl brand perfectly encapsulates the pressures and potentials of postfeminist subjecthood. By locating a source of women's power in her body, the brand makes an aspirational and troubling association between thinness and desirability, yet, in typically postfeminist terms, suggests this designation is under a woman's control. Relatedly, despite Frankel's commercial success, her celebrity remains plagued by the insecurities that are reported as continually dogging female stars as well as ordinary women, particularly an inability to "balance it all." While epitomizing a successful example of aggressive self-branding, Frankel illustrates an ambivalent neoliberalism and an anxious postfeminism, concretized in the blame attributed to her for her failed marriage and the cancellation of her eponymous talk show.

Reviewing Frankel's status as a figure who focalizes convergent media potentials serves to underscore the strengths and weaknesses of our study. On the one hand, we were able to analyze how Frankel's rise on the Bravo television network spoke to developments in niche marketing, cross-promotion, and segmented televisual markets. As an elite lifestyle network that typically features successful female entrepreneurs, Bravo was a fitting platform on which Frankel's brand could take shape, and we talk in some detail about the fit between her image and the network that cultivated it. One omission in this aspect of the study, however, is that we spent very little time on how Frankel's online presence (including her website) buttressed her brand efforts. We were also unable to ascertain the extent to which her visibility in unauthorized materials (such as celebrity gossip sites) dialogued with the more scripted promotional venues. Relatedly, though we attempted to investigate specifically what aspects of her attributed personality may have fueled this popularity, we were not able to obtain this evidence, short of anecdotal reportage that Bravo selected her for her own show based on this appeal. Since the publication of our article, this research has been attempted. In an intriguing audience study, Kavita Ilona Nayar examined two online fan forums in which audiences of *Bethenny Getting Married?* and *Bethenny Ever After* commented on what Nayar calls Frankel's "transformation into a branded self," a transformation that Nayar ties to the Beam Suntory deal.[47] While audiences varied in their responses to and perceptions of Frankel, those who tended to be her strongest supporters—labeled by Nayar as "brand ambassadors"—comment on how Frankel seems emotionally relatable because of her willingness to share her struggles with work and family. Nayar writes, "The vindication of Frankel's branded self is made even more enjoyable by her emotional labor on the reality television show, and audiences recognize this performance as a 'gift' she has given them."[48] According to Nayar, audiences see Frankel's brand as a work in progress and identify with her authenticity and willingness to showcase her vulnerabilities.

Another prospect for future development would be to fully situate Frankel within a larger network of female celebrity "lifestyle experts," such as Gwyneth Paltrow, whose saturation in a variety of female-centered markets ensures their lasting celebrity viability. Such a comparison raises questions about celebrity legacies—we note that Paltrow's familial inheritance (she is the daughter of actress Blythe Danner and film producer/director Bruce Paltrow) positions her as a sort of Hollywood royalty, standing in contradistinction to Frankel's more scrappy populist appeal. Paltrow's enduring relevance nevertheless highlights the persistence and centrality of concepts like aura and glamour to the study of Hollywood stardom and contemporary celebrity, even as reality regimes tend to privilege ordinariness and authenticity over exceptionalism.

Frankel also shared close ties with mentor Ellen DeGeneres, yet Frankel's foray into the talk show realm was not well received. DeGeneres retains a coveted position in the female mediascape, and her enduring success as a talk show host seems attributable to a folksy style that disguises her show's status as a platform for flogging a variety of media brands and products. The structuring logics of DeGeneres' show are thus framed as social and generous while Frankel's signify as individualistic. Finally, evaluating the place of the female lifestyle expert in such contexts repeats earlier points we make here about how stars have historically helped to channel libidinal and affective energies, and we remain curious about the tangible effects that celebrity influences have on the materiality of everyday women's lives.[49]

One of the most interesting components of Frankel's signification is that she conforms to relatively few of the conventional criteria for female "likeability"; while her activities and enterprises attract keen interest and a considerable amount of commercial loyalty, it may well be the case that she inspires little of the adulation or even regard conventionally associated with celebrity role models. In this respect, she serves as a useful example of the new affective parameters of a celebrity field in which goodwill for public figures appears to be significantly diminished. Among the most popular forms of celebrity discourse in recent years has been "Mean Tweets," a stock segment on *Jimmy Kimmel Live!* (ABC, 2003–) and avidly re-consumed on YouTube, in which celebrities read insulting and cruel tweets about themselves, often though not always, in a deadpan style.

In their trenchant analysis of the culture of celebrity schadenfreude Jo Littler and Steve Cross link increasingly common expressions of delight in celebrity misfortune to an "autistic economic culture" and provocatively speculate that schadenfreude "works to express irritation at inequalities but not to change the wider rules of the current social system."[50] We would contend that celebrities like Frankel play an important role in the cultural dynamics Littler has elsewhere deemed "meritocracy as plutocracy."[51] In significant ways, her life story incorporates "meritocracy's validation of upper-middle class values as norms to aspire to and its rendering of working-class cultures as abject."[52] Thus our case study here seeks to underscore the necessity of regularly linking scholarly work to the dynamics of great and growing inequality that characterize Western democracies and the heightened consumption of celebrity discourse under surveillance capitalism. In generating this account, we are struck by the cataclysmic reach of celebrity platforms, the increasingly convergent nature of media celebrity and the imperative to grapple with how a proliferation of "no holds barred" access to stars has transformed the notion of twenty-first-century celebrity from earlier models. At a time when neoliberal marketization runs rampant, the critical task of analyzing how celebrity systems promote exemplary and iconic individualism seems particularly urgent.

Notes

1. Russell Meeuf, *Rebellious Bodies: Stardom, Citizenship, and the New Body Politics* (Austin: University of Texas Press, 2017), 19.
2. Richard deCordova, *Picture Personalities: The Emergence of the Star System in America* (Champaign: University of Illinois Press, 2001).
3. Aida Hozić, "Hollywood Goes on Sale; or, What Do the Violet Eyes of Elizabeth Taylor Have to Do with the Cinema of Attractions?" in *Hollywood Goes Shopping*, ed. David Desser and Garth S. Jowett (Minneapolis: University of Minnesota Press, 2000), 206, 205.
4. For an overview of the ways that stars were considered studio owned-and-operated commodities until the 1950s, see Joshua Gamson, "The Assembly Line of Greatness: Celebrity in Twentieth-Century America," *Critical Studies in Mass Communication*, Vol. 9 (1992): 1–24.
5. Mary Flanagan, "Mobile Identities, Digital Stars, and Post-Cinematic Selves," *Wide Angle* 21 no. 1 (1999): 78.
6. Su Holmes and Sean Redmond, "Editorial: A Journal in Celebrity Studies," *Celebrity Studies* 1, no. 1 (2010): 1.
7. Alice Leppert, "Keeping Up with the Kardashians: Fame-Work and the Production of Entrepreneurial Sisterhood," in *Cupcakes, Pinterest, Ladyporn: Feminized Popular Culture in the Early 21st Century*, ed. Elana Levine (Champaign: University of Illinois Press, 2015), 217.
8. Alison Hearn, "Producing 'Reality': Branded Content, Branded Selves, Precarious Futures," in *A Companion to Reality Television*, ed. Laurie Ouellette (Malden: Wiley-Blackwell, 2014), 438.
9. Meeuf, Rebellious Bodies, 13.
10. Brenda Weber, *Women and Literary Celebrity in the Nineteenth Century: The Transatlantic Production of Fame and Gender* (London: Ashgate, 2012), 15.
11. Charles Ponce de Leon, *Self Exposure: Human Interest Journalism and the Emergence of Celebrity in America, 1890–1940* (Urbana and Chicago: University of Illinois Press, 2002), 4.
12. Sean Redmond, "The Whiteness of Stars: Looking at Kate Winslet's Unruly White Body," in *Stardom and Celebrity. A Reader*, eds. Su Holmes and Sean Redmond (London: Sage, 2007), 263–74.
13. Complicating matters still further, as Gaylyn Studlar has argued, is the fact that "The star persona of 'Little Mary' was produced in ubiquitous representations intended to represent innocence but implicated in a sexualized gaze fixed on the screen fiction of the girl-child played by a woman." *Precocious Charms: Stars Performing Girlhood in Classical Hollywood Cinema* (Berkeley: University of California Press, 2013), 49.
14. Richard Schickel, *Intimate Strangers: The Culture of Celebrity* (Chicago: Ivan R. Dee, 2000).
15. Joshua Gamson "The Unwatched Life Is Not Worth Living: The Elevation of the Ordinary in Celebrity Culture," *PMLA* 126, no. 4 (2011): 1062.
16. Jackie Stacey, "Feminine Fascinations: Forms of Identification in Star-Audience Relations," in *Feminist Film Theory*, ed. Sue Thornham (New York: New York University Press, 1999), 208.
17. Sumiko Hagashi, "Vitagraph Stardom: Constructing Personalities for 'New' Middle Class Consumption," in *Reclaiming the Archive: Feminism and Film History*, ed. Vicki Callahan (Detroit: Wayne State University Press, 2010), 265.
18. P. David Marshall, "The Promotion and Presentation of the Self: Celebrity as Marker of Presentational Media," *Celebrity Studies* 1, no. 1 (2010): 36.
19. Charles Eckert, "The Carole Lombard in Macy's Window," in *Stardom: Industry of Desire*, ed. Christine Gledhill (London & New York: Routledge, 1991), 39.
20. Simon Dixon, "Ambiguous Ecologies: Stardom's Domestic Mise-en-Scène," *Cinema Journal* 42, no. 2 (2003): 96.
21. Rebecca L. Epstein, "Sharon Stone in a Gap Turtleneck," In *Hollywood Goes Shopping*, eds. David Desser and Garth S. Jowett (Minneapolis: University of Minnesota Press, 2000), 200.

22. Pamela Church Gibson, *Fashion and Celebrity Culture* (London: Bloomsbury, 2012), 53.

23. Elizabeth Ellcessor, "Tweeting @feliciaday: Online Social Media, Convergence, and Subcultural Stardom," *Cinema Journal* 51, no. 2 (2012): 46–68.

24. Linda Mizejewski, *It Happened One Night* (Malden: Wiley-Blackwell, 2010), 96.

25. deCordova, *Picture Personalities*, 99.

26. Richard Dyer, *Stars* (London: BFI Publishing 1998), 60.

27. Richard Dyer, *Heavenly Bodies: Film Stars and Society* (London and New York: Routledge, 2004), 2.

28. Ibid., 151.

29. Christine Becker, "Televising Film Stardom in the 1950s," *Framework: The Journal of Cinema & Media* 46, no. 2 (2005): 5–21.

30. Susan Murray, *Hitch Your Antenna to the Stars: Early Television and Broadcast Stardom* (New York, Routledge, 2005), xi.

31. Becker, "Televising Film Stardom in the 1950s."

32. P. David Marshall, *Celebrity and Power: Fame and Contemporary Culture* (Minneapolis: University of Minnesota Press, 1997), 119.

33. Ellcessor, "Tweeting @feliciaday," 51.

34. Joshua Gamson, "The Assembly Line of Greatness: Celebrity in Twentieth-Century America," *Critical Studies in Media Communication* 9 (1992): 13.

35. Christine Geraghty, "Re-examining Stardom: Questions of Texts, Bodies, and Performance," in *Reinventing Film Studies*, eds. Christine Gledhill and Linda Williams (London: Arnold, 2000), 187.

36. Sue Collins, "Making the Most out of 15 Minutes: Reality TV's Dispensable Celebrity," *Television & New Media* 9, no. 2 (2008): 104.

37. Gamson, "The Unwatched Life Is Not Worth Living," 1065.

38. Laurie Ouellette, "'Take Responsibility for Yourself': *Judge Judy* and the Neoliberal Citizen," in *Reality TV Remaking Television Culture*, eds. Susan Murray and Laurie Ouellette (New York: New York University Press, 2004), 242.

39. Jayne Raisborough, *Lifestyle Media and the Formation of the Self* (New York: Palgrave MacMillan, 2011), 7.

40. Heather Mendick, Kim Allen, Laura Harvey and Aisha Ahmad, *Celebrity, Aspiration, and Contemporary Youth: Education and Inequality in an Era of Austerity* (London: Bloomsbury, 2018).

41. Su Holmes and Diane Negra, "Introduction," *In the Limelight and Under the Microscope: Forms and Functions of Female Celebrity*, eds. Su Holmes and Diane Negra (New York, Continuum, 2011), 8. See also chapters by Alice Leppert and Julie Wilson ("Living *The Hills* Life: Lauren Conrad as Reality Star, Soap Opera Heroine, and Brand") and Anna Watkins Fisher ("We Love This Trainwreck!: Sacrificing Britney to Save America") in that volume.

42. Meeuf, *Rebellious Bodies.*

43. Alice E. Marwick, *Status Update: Celebrity, Publicity & Branding in the Social Media Age* (New Haven: Yale University Press, 2014), 115.

44. Ibid., 114.

45. Mark Andrejevic, *Reality TV: The Work of Being Watched* (Lanham: Rowman & Littlefield, 2003).

46. Madeline Berg, "Skinnygirl, Fat Wallet: How Bethenny Frankel Earns More Than Any Other Real Housewife," *Forbes*, November 16, 2016, accessed March 9, 2018, www.forbes.com/sites/maddieberg/2016/11/16/skinnygirl-fat-wallet-how-bethenny-frankel-earns-more-than-any-other-housewife/#31bd5b056311.

47. Kavita Ilona Nayar, "You Didn't Build That: Audience Reception of a Reality Television Star's Transformation from a Real Housewife to a Real Brand," *Journal of Popular Culture* 48 no. 1 (2015): 3–16.

48. Ibid., 8.

49. For a work that looks at such materiality in the context of online fan labor, see Laurie Ouellette and Julie Wilson, "Women's Work: Affective Labour and Convergence Culture," *Cultural Studies* 25, no. 4–5 (2011): 548–65.

50. Jo Littler and Steve Cross, "Celebrity and Schadenfreude: The Cultural Economy of Fame in Freefall," *Cultural Studies* 24, no. 3 (2010): 395.

51. Jo Littler, "Meritocracy as Plutocracy: The Marketing of 'Equality' Under Neoliberalism," *New Formations: A Journal of Culture/Theory/Politics* 80–81 (2013): 52–72.

52. Ibid., 55.

Further Reading

Allen, Robert C. "The Role of the Star in Film History." In *Film History: Theory and Practice.* 172–89. New York: Alfred A. Knopf, 1985.

Banet-Weiser, Sarah. *Authentic: The Politics of Ambivalence in a Brand Culture.* New York: New York University Press, 2012.

Cashmore, Ellis. *Celebrity/Culture.* Abingdon, Oxon: Routledge, 2006.

Grindstaff, Laura. "Just Be Yourself – Only More So: Ordinary Celebrity in the Era of Self-Service Television." In *The Politics of Reality Television*, edited by Marwan M. Kreidy and Katherine Sender, 44–57. London: Routledge, 2011.

Guthey, Eric, Timothy Clark, and Brad Jackson. *Demystifying Business Celebrity.* London: Routledge, 2009.

Johnson, Robin. "The Discreet Charm of the Petite Celebrity: Gender, Consumption and Celebrity on *My Super Sweet 16.*" *Celebrity Studies* 1 no. 2 (2010): 203–15.

Maland, Charles. *Chaplin and American Culture: The Evolution of a Star Image.* Princeton: Princeton University Press, 1991.

McLean, Adrienne. *Being Rita Hayworth: Labor, Identity, and Hollywood Stardom.* New Brunswick: Rutgers University Press, 2004.

McLean, Adrienne and Murray Pomerance, eds. *Movie Stars from the 1910s to 2000s.* New Brunswick: Rutgers University Press, 2012.

Miller, Toby. *Cultural Citizenship: Cosmopolitanism, Consumerism and Television in a Neoliberal Age.* Philadelphia: Temple University Press, 2006.

Negra, Diane. *Off-White Hollywood: American Culture and Ethnic Female Stardom.* New York: Routledge, 2001.

Negra, Diane and Su Holmes. "Going Cheap? Female Celebrity in Reality, Tabloid and Scandal Genres." Special Issue of *Genders* 48 (2008). Accessed October 22, 2017. www.colorado.edu/genders/.

Redmond, Sean. "Intimate Fame Everywhere." In *Framing Celebrity*, edited by Su Holmes and Sean Redmond, 27–43. London: Routledge, 2006.

Redmond, Sean and Su Holmes, eds. *Stardom and Celebrity: A Reader.* Los Angeles and London: Sage, 2007.

Senft, Theresa. "Microcelebrity and the Branded Self." In *A Companion to New Media Dynamics*, edited by John Hartley, Jean Burgess, and Axel Bruns, 345–54. Malden: Wiley-Blackwell, 2013.

Studlar, Gaylyn. *This Mad Masquerade: Stardom and Masculinity in the Jazz Age.* New York: Columbia University Press, 1996.

Turner, Graeme. *Understanding Celebrity.* London: Sage, 2004.

Turner, Graeme. *Ordinary People and the Media.* London: Sage, 2010.

Wilson, Julie. "Stardom, Sentimental Education, and the Shaping of Global Citizens." *Cinema Journal* 53 no. 2 (2014): 27–49.

19.
CULTURAL GEOGRAPHY
Victoria E. Johnson

Where and how do we see **geography**—images of place and representations of place-identity—in film and media? Here are some examples: An iconic headline in the entertainment industry trade magazine, *Variety*, notes of 1930s film audiences, "Sticks Nix Hicks Pix." Almost three-quarters of a century later, a Fox TV series that portrays lush beach scenes and the glamorous lives of mansion-dwelling, surfboarding, sports-car driving teens, is considered responsible for a significant influx of global tourism to Southern California's "The OC." Cable networks Outdoor Life and RFD-TV market to expressly different **demographics** or intended audiences than Bravo and Sundance Channel. Rutgers University notes that its applications for admission in 2015 went up by 12 percent following its entry into the Big Ten athletic conference, whose sports telecasts gave the university added weekly exposure to an estimated one million households. Cell phone apps such as "I Heart Radio" enable connection to far-flung radio stations regardless of one's actual location, while apps like Feastly or Party With a Local allow travelers to live like locals when visiting a new city. From 1930s film distribution business concerns, to broadcast and cable TV narrative address and market strategies, to handheld, mobile technologies' appeals to authenticity, each of these examples demonstrates geography's importance when thinking about the media industry, its texts, and their reception contexts and uses. Each example points to geography as a key cultural concept with real social power that has economic and political ramifications offscreen.[1]

Geography, both real and symbolic, is **capital**—it accrues and confers material and social power. Geographic capital is **structural**—as seen in "market expansion and development and definitions of consumer demography."[2] In the above examples these include distinctions made between film markets (distribution to "hicks" in the "sticks" vs. urban audiences), or in the expansion of networks along existing corridors of commerce and trade (whether broadcast and cable or broadband and fiber-optic), or in the differentiation of Outdoor Life's advertisers (e.g., Bass Pro Shops) from those on Bravo (e.g., IKEA). Geography is also **symbolic** capital, "expressed through aesthetic distinctions and presumptions regarding audience disposition or 'tastes.'"[3] Symbolic capital is expressed in formal properties of texts and in their address to an imagined audience ("hicks" and hunters vs. "city" folks and hipsters).

Most typically, however, film, broadcast, and digital media have been theorized and historicized through frames of temporality and *placelessness* rather than those of geographic locale and embeddedness. Film audiences are often presumed to share a uniform viewing experience regardless of screening venue. Radio's and TV's sounds and images are often imagined to travel through the "ether" to seamlessly connect cross-continental mass audiences and to transport those viewers to events outside of their homes. Contemporary discussions of TV as a streaming medium and descriptions of new media's mobility beyond the boundaries of the living room via laptop, tablet, or phone imagine them to be **space-binding** technologies characteristic of networking and the expansion of national and global markets. But film and media are always received by viewers who are located in specific places. Film and media texts imagine specific settings and connect their audiences to the locales at which each was produced. Thus, film and media studies must think about specificities of place to examine the active work that is required to imagine visual culture as "placeless," and, further, to consider what investments and whose interests "placeless" mythologies serve.

Cultural geography is thus an interdisciplinary, critical, analytical framework that intersects with other analyses of social subjectivity that are historically central to modern film studies and foundational to television and digital media studies: race, gender, sexuality, generation, and class. Thinking geographically attends to questions of context and social power in which the text is one element of a broader chain of discourses that are historically contingent and representative of shifting relations of power. The interdisciplinarity of cultural geography coheres through the types of questions that are posed regarding historical context, subjectivity, and power. These questions are characteristic of **cultural studies** approaches in critical communication studies, American studies, social history, gender studies, critical race theory, and critical legal studies.[4] This chapter focuses on humanistic approaches to cultural geography in film and media studies as they depend upon methodologies and lines of inquiry developed in varied national contexts. Specific examples of cultural geographic work in film and media studies are, here, limited to those from U.S. scholarship focusing on U.S. industry, texts, and context.

Critical Prerequisites for Thinking Geographically

In the humanities, there are two primary traditions of critical thinking about media, place, and identity informing work on cultural geography in U.S. film and media studies. Each of these traditions laid a foundation for scholarship whose emphasis is history "from below," writing the history and experience of everyday life in a diversity of contexts into film and media studies. The two primary traditions to which I refer are the **Chicago School of Social Thought,** which emerged between World War I and World War II at the University of Chicago in the United States, and British Cultural Studies, which is particularly identified with the **Birmingham Centre for Contemporary Cultural Studies** of the 1960s–1990s in Britain.

In the United States, the era of industrialization and cross-continental expansion coincided with the birth of film and the emergence of broadcasting. On the heels of the Progressive era (1890–1920), in this emergent mass media environment, a group of scholars affiliated with the University of Michigan and

later with the University of Chicago posed questions regarding the "transformations created by the turn from an agricultural to an industrial society, from the rural and small to the urban and large."[5] This group included, among others, Robert Park, James Dewey, George Mead, Georg Simmel, Charles Cooley, Thorstein Veblen, and Walter Lippmann. Dewey, in particular, argued that, in the U.S. context, as the expanse of frontier began to close, there was as yet no shared culture, particularly in more rural regions distant from cultural, economic, and industrial hubs. Given this, Dewey proposed that "[w]hat tradition is to the rest, communication is to us: the process and resource through which we constitute ourselves and the little world we inhabit."[6]

The Chicago School thinkers and their students moved away from studying communication as propaganda or communication's "effects," toward conceiving of communication as a site of struggle through which social life itself was imagined, negotiated, and produced. Here, culture is a *process*. With questions of class struggle, the group included questions of place, race, religion, ethnicity, although not, as yet, gender.[7] The studies that emerged from the Chicago School largely focused on particularities of community-formation and the media's role in defining these communities both to themselves and to others. By conceiving of communication media as sites of *local* struggle and interpretation, these scholars provided space for differentiated voices within the communication process and included reception context and varying experiences of media "messages" in scholarly analysis.

Notably, alternate contemporary approaches to communication emerging from the Chicago School—particularly that of the **Frankfurt School** scholars in exile—instead emphasized that media were governed by a **spatial bias** that prioritized questions of control via messages that emanated from one place to address a shared audience, simultaneously, with uniform results. Frankfurt School thinkers, including Theodor Adorno and Max Horkheimer, wrote from the experience of having watched Fascist, totalitarian, and Nazi regimes successfully mobilize mass audiences in the interests of the State, via film, radio, and print media. In the U.S. context, they warned that with industrialization's ability to transform previously artisanal products into reproducible formulae, standardization of culture would, by extension, standardize *thought* and thus neuter critical awareness and the diversity of public voices requisite to democratic functioning.[8]

There are important threads that conjoin these divergent sets of approaches from the Chicago School and foreshadow—if not provide the foundation for—the post-World War II critical labor of the Birmingham Centre for Contemporary Cultural Studies and British Cultural Studies scholarship there and elsewhere. Each "branch" of the Chicago School presumed that communication media were *cultural* artifacts; each proposed that *popular*, commercial media were important to analyze and to take seriously as sites of ideological production and circulation; and each assumed that, typically, media circulate in a *national* context as key contributors to broader social discourse regarding national "ideals" and questions of regional/local/community "difference" by which these ideals are thrown into relief.

Upheavals in British society of the immediate post-World War II years, including an increasing democratization of education simultaneous to increased availability of popular media and ensuing concerns regarding "Americanization," challenged traditionally classed, raced, and gendered proscriptions on student enrollment and curricular design, leading to a revolutionary break with past theories of culture and its scholarly analysis. With the institution of the Centre for Contemporary Cultural Studies (CCCS) in 1964, Raymond Williams, Richard Hoggart, and Stuart Hall became identified as the "British Group." Significantly, each of these figures in CCCS's emergence came from backgrounds which were in some way—whether because of their rural, working-class, and/or racial identity—"marginal to the centers of English academic life."[9] This claim to theory from the **periphery** underscored the group's method and focus on everyday practice and interpretation of popular media, especially by or within rural and working-class populations.

However, cultural studies' professed commitment to speak from, of, and to the "margins," was initially somewhat paradoxical. This work attended to previously ignored working-class subcultures—including a groundbreaking focus on youth as active subjects, through which sites of identification such as fashion and music were now included as objects of study. However, many of the early studies of subculture were focused primarily on white, male, working-class subcultural activity.[10] This was not lost on the "Birmingham Feminists," whose Women's Studies Group (including Dorothy Hobson and Charlotte Brunsdon) began to rigorously examine female youth fandoms, as well as women's television viewing and novel-reading habits, in order to assess the significance and power of "women's" genres. This "turn" to analysis of gendered subjectivity helped to ally work in Britain with emergent work in gender studies, feminist geography, and feminist film and media studies that were, increasingly, moving away from the *Screen* theory model of textual and psychoanalytic analysis and toward studies of texts in the context of their reception, the active production of subjectivity, and increasing scholarly attention to "histories from below." Crucial to subsequent film and media studies incorporating cultural geography were these scholars' understanding that the domestic sphere is not an apolitical space, isolated from the "real" social world, but, is, rather, an explicitly gendered, politicized, socially structured space. As Daphne Spain argues, "'Gendered spaces' separate women from knowledge used by men to produce and reproduce power and privilege."[11] However, these scholars also paid new attention to the ways in which popular cultural forms—especially those conventionally categorized as "women's genres"—do not necessarily only reinforce patriarchy or simply reproduce structures in dominance, but may, indeed, offer liberating possibilities or encourage a politics of empowerment instead of marginalization. Thinking in cultural geographic terms is thus encouraged and, arguably, demanded by the critical turns in post-structuralism and cultural studies toward analysis of subjectivity and cultural power. Geographic identity becomes a critical term in the cultural imagination and struggle over who and *where* count within a particular historic moment and national context.

Consider the contemporary mythologies of "red states" and "blue states" in the United States' electoral political landscape. While voting patterns themselves tend to be broadly purple on a county-by-county basis, the stark, primary color maps of the states imply both a reductive legibility to complicated issues and a field of relations or chain of vivid, iconic associations that then define a place, its people, and their dispositions. For example, Texas's "redness" is **articulated** through a chain of powerful, historic, contextually specific iconography (cowboy hats, six-guns, wide-open ranch lands, longhorns) that connotes individualism, ruggedness, and self-sufficiency. Imagining such qualities to be at home in red Texas disallows "blue" states from representing these same ideals. However, this cuts both ways: the values ascribed to "red" Texas as "naturally" occurring there do not include, for instance, associations of Texas-ness with "high" culture (the symphony, art museums, ballet) or refinement in either lifestyle or educational realms.

We logically understand that such qualities are not exclusive to "blue" coastal "elites," but—particularly during national election cycles in the United States— "red" and "blue" identifications begin to appear historically ratified, deeply held, and true.

Our subjectivity—gendered or geographic—is not inherent *to* us; it is the product of various social institutions to which we are "subject." **Social institutions** help form us and define our identities to ourselves and others. Some of the most important of these include, for example, family, media, education, religion, and politics. Through these we are also the product of social constructs of geography, gender, class, race, and sexual identity. The "subject" is, then, a very conflicted entity. Just as there are contradictions between the institutions in a society, there are also contradictions within the subject. We can consider how this might be the case when thinking of the shifting relations and identifications that occur between one's identity as a professional at work and the different position one may occupy in relation to one's family. For example, you may be the boss at work and act and be treated accordingly, but remain the "baby" of the family when home for holiday celebrations and the like. One identification confers a sense of the self as occupying a position of responsibility and control, while the other may suggest that one assumes a more subordinate role. Both roles seem "natural" to us and definitive of "who" we are though both are social constructions.

While individual **subjectivity** is a contradictory mix of confirming and conflicting identities, social institutions try to manage this conflict. Film, television, and other cultural institutions work to construct an ideal subject position which we are invited to occupy and, if we do, we are rewarded with the ideological pleasure that is provoked when we experience the "reward" that occurs when the meanings of the text and our sense of the world synch up, producing "common sense" pleasures of recognition. Film and media scholars explicitly interested in analysis of these cultural phenomena through geographic frames do so by focusing on **practices in context** rather than on the centrality or primacy of the text.

New Cinema History

Typically, film scholars have approached the geographic in two primary ways: through analysis of on-screen representation *of* place and through analysis of spectating practice *in* place. The first approach has been practiced via studies of the representation of specific places on film (e.g., "city cinemas") and through theories adapted from literary studies, such as those that analogize the cinema spectator with the "*flaneur*."[12] The second approach is often referred to by its practitioners as "**new cinema history**." New cinema history focuses on viewing context over analysis of the film text itself in order to address regional distinctiveness, often highlighting ways that cinema audiences interpret films and interact with them in a counterintuitive manner to producers' or critics' expectations.

Prior to the intervention of new cinema history, the predominant paradigm for thinking about cinema's growth and standardization was the **modernity thesis**. According to Kathryn Fuller-Seeley, "Cinema in the 'modernity thesis' seems to transform viewers and their culture, the surrounding theaters and streets, into a vast, skyscrapered, fragmented, rapid-paced urban milieu."[13] Such an **urban bias** evacuates the actual *unevenness* of distribution practices and the diversity of viewing contexts and communities of cinemagoers. By embracing the modernity thesis as an analytical frame and urbanity as analog for cinema itself, most work in film studies has privileged an imagined white, middle-class, and city-dwelling audience that reflects the economic, social, and political ranking of cinema's spectators, theaters, and communities in ways that reward dominant viewing and exhibition practices.

To try to counter this bias, scholars such as Barbara Ching, Gerald Creed, Henry Jenkins, Richard Maltby, Melvyn Stokes, and Robert C. Allen propose that the spectator's primary relationship with filmgoing has not been with individual films but with the social experience of going *to* the movies in a particular context, as part of a community often characterized by significant regional differences.[14] Notably, as Jenkins' history of vaudeville makes clear, "rustic," "hinterland" locales *also* impacted the Broadway or Hollywood product, rebutting the notion of a **one-way flow** of culture from the metropolitan center to the rural periphery. Scholars such as Mary Carbine have also significantly nuanced understandings of urban audiences and filmgoing practices themselves. She complicates the **embourgeoisiement thesis** by analyzing how working-class and immigrant audiences "tactically" consumed films, incorporating Hollywood's constructions "into specifically African American cultural practices."[15] Mass-cultural venues are, thus, *not* necessarily forces of homogenization but, potentially, sites for distinctive community expression.

Jacqueline Stewart's *Migrating to the Movies* further challenges film history's lack of attention to the fact that the Great Migration was historically analogous with the rise of cinema. Thus, where cinema did take shape as an urban institution, Stewart asks how the growth of African American communities directly impacted its development, representational practices, and communal significance. While Stewart reconstructs viewing practices of African Americans in Chicago's South Side Black Belt, she also underscores that this was *not* a homogeneous viewing community. Stewart thus emphasizes "the notion of overlapping public spheres," which allows for examination of "how Black interactions with the cinema were intimately related to other institutions, activities, and discourses that were prevalent in Black urban communities during the first two decades of the twentieth century."[16] Most recently, Paula Massood has contributed to this growing body of site-specific cinema study in her examination of Harlem's role in imagining and constructing African American identity—both in production culture and cinematic representation—from film's inception to the present.[17]

Broadcast and Digital Media: The National "Ideal" and Persistence of the Local

U.S. studies of broadcast media through cultural geographic frames are conjoined by a guiding presumption that U.S. television, in particular, remains broadly *national* in its institutional identity (business practices, economic organization, imagined audience) and cultural resonance (as the most-engaged-with media in American life on a daily basis and as the central site wherein the nation imagines itself and struggles over its conflicting and competing ideals). How are "national" ideals, in fact, dependent upon contrast with local "difference" for their definition? How were radio and television's growth and standardization characterized by rather more staggered and uneven adoption than uniform, national availability?[18] How does the symbolic or representational imagination of place on national TV have real social ramifications and power, beyond the TV screen?

Cultural geographic concerns were largely implicit in early scholarly work on U.S. broadcast media. Emerging in the late 1980s, this work was most concerned to examine the "essential" properties of the medium—particularly as they contrasted with that which was presumed to define Hollywood cinema. As with the Birmingham Feminists, U.S. feminist scholars embraced study of the politics of everyday life particularly by examining "women's genres" (e.g., soap opera, talk shows) and the pleasures they provided their viewers, who were often presumed to be housewives. This work on radio and TV as representational realms encouraged later scholars to extend such questions of representation to analyses of broadcast media's symbolic geographies. Such questions might ask, for example, what explains the fascination of the 1960s rural sitcoms at the same moment as the Kennedy-era's expressed New Frontier ideals and the space race; or, to what end did *The Goldbergs* alter recognizably Jewish cultural references from its radio broadcasts to its more suburban television adaptation?[19]

A second tradition definitive of U.S. radio and television studies more explicitly relates to place by analyzing the radio console (or, later, transistor) and TV set (and, now, mobile device) as *material* objects in intersection with other social institutions and imperatives regarding subjectivity, technological design, and cultural "norms." Lynn Spigel's foundational *Make Room for TV* opened the way for such work, with its careful reconstruction of a postwar milieu into which television was introduced that encouraged *all* Americans—regardless of race, class-affiliation, sexual identity, or geographic locale—to identify with and to internalize the consumer habits of middle-class, white suburbanites and accompanying architectural, material, and gendered domestic ideals.[20] Spigel primarily uses women's magazines of the era to explore a discursive context that encouraged and rewarded fealty to a revived "Victorian" domestic logic of a woman's "place," consistently busy in the home while also appearing in "appropriately" gendered attire and repose. Such struggles extended to the "man of the house" in his need to negotiate post-work "couch potato" relaxation and to exhibit a new, masculine, "handyman" suburban competency around the yard and garage. For Spigel, the place of TV within the home is fraught with broader social dilemmas regarding definitions of the family and gendered behavioral ideals that extend outside the home to the broader public sphere.

This public sphere is where Anna McCarthy and Jon Kraszewski, in particular, extend Spigel's work by studying TV's important role as it is integrated "into the social rhythms and material life of spaces *outside* the home."[21] McCarthy's *Ambient Television* examines TV's everyday presence in venues ranging from stores and airports to waiting rooms, food courts, and public art installations to examine "the ways in which the audiovisual and material forms of TV blend with the social conventions and power structures of its locale."[22] For both Kraszewski and McCarthy, a key site of TV-in-public is the tavern or sports bar, which each sees as a locale where televised sports help to mediate social ties and facilitate community identity across sometimes fraught class lines. Kraszewski studies Pittsburgh Steeler fans—displaced from their Pennsylvania roots to suburban Texas due to far-flung job opportunities, as they gather to watch Steeler games with fellow fans in Fort Worth. This work acknowledges the trauma and lack of control that accompany post-2000s transformations in labor and the economy for which football "watch parties" provide some temporary regional reconnection and salve. And yet, within this microcosm of "shared" community, Kraszewski finds the reconstitution of social tensions from back home, even if sports fandom ultimately overrides these.[23]

Current scholarship on digital media from film and media studies (including film, television and its digital extensions, the Internet, computing, videogaming, and mobile devices, such as cell phones) has also furthered questions of place, geography, subjectivity, and power. Much of the strongest work on these issues has focused on the media industries and their economic, labor, and environmental practices—all of which challenge notions of "new" media as inherently "placeless," borderless," or "global." While much digital media scholarship replicates early "mass" media theories on the potential space-binding, placeless "ideal" of neoliberal individualism, enhanced mobility, and finance capital fluidity, a significant subset of film and media scholars see digital media as extensions and, sometimes, concentrations of prior media forms' economic, social, and political structures and relations. Scholars including Vicki Mayer, Serra Tinic, and John Caldwell, for example, challenge us to critically examine the local realities of media production and labor relations in site-specific analyses (examining New Orleans' or Vancouver's own specific hierarchies and production "ecologies," or studying the ramifications of "off-shoring" CGI sequences in Hollywood blockbusters).[24] Others, such as Nicole Starosielski, Jennifer Holt, and Patrick Vonderau, have examined media geographies as having *ecological* as well as political, infrastructural impacts.[25] Further, studies of handheld media's locative capabilities examine the tension between interactivity and data-mining that is central to navigation apps, underscoring that "[g]overnmentality and self-expression are not opposed but reciprocally confirming."[26]

But, how might we get more specific about the above approaches to consider popular media in cultural geographic terms? Below, I offer a case study of a chapter from my book, *Heartland TV: Prime Time Television and the Struggle for U.S. Identity*. I hope that this example demonstrates each of the critical components addressed above: that geography is capital—of both the structural and the symbolic kind—and that the concept of the "Heartland" was mobilized, at a particular historic **conjuncture** to reimagine regional borders for a national TV audience as part of a broader discursive appeal to specifically raced, gendered, and classed understandings of place-identity, its political valences, and its economic and cultural worth. The chapter explores a critical conjuncture in the national imagination as this "rewriting" of the Heartland as a newly "calm" and desirable space within the turbulence of the 1970s represented a momentary and inherently unstable reworking of the **regional myth**.

Case Study—"'You're Gonna Make It After All!'"

Heartland TV examines the history and use-value of the concept of the U.S. "Heartland" Midwest as it appeared simultaneous to the rise of broadcasting in America and as it has been reworked at critical moments in U.S. social, political, and cultural history from the postwar era to the early 2000s. The book thus writes regionalism's role back into U.S. TV history by considering it as a network infrastructure and market development strategy; a network promotional, branding appeal; a key consideration in broadcast regulatory policy; an aesthetic style and mode of address evidenced in programs; and a critical element in the imagination and judgment of television's audience. Beyond the case study discussed here, other chapters in my book examine how broadcast policymakers wrote regional mythologies into the laws that defined and governed radio and TV; ways in which overtly regional, Heartland address in prime-time programming was seen to run contrary to New Frontier national and internationally looking ideals; and, the book considers contemporary controversies regarding sexual identity and its expression in prime time, focusing on the displacement of fears regarding, particularly, lesbianism onto concerns about the Midwest as irrevocably "square" space.

"'You're Gonna Make It After All!' The Urbane Midwest in MTM Productions' 'Quality' Comedies," examines a significant revision of the Heartland myth, following its relatively stable imagination from the end of World War II through the 1960s. The chapter analyzes MTM program texts (*The Mary Tyler Moore Show* [CBS, 1970–77], *The Bob Newhart Show* [CBS, 1972–78] and *WKRP in Cincinnati* [CBS, 1978–82]) in intersection with industrial discourses of the period (including policy changes that encouraged targeting of new audience demographics), critical discourses (by which TV critics singled out MTM comedies and their stars for their "quality"), and popular discourses about the Midwest as a newly *idealized* region (as seen, particularly, in the pages of popular magazines such as *Time*). This period evinces a marked shift from representations of the Heartland that had coalesced to imagine the region to be singularly rural, white, middle class, politically inflexible, conservative, doggedly isolationist, and out of touch with the broader world.

Significantly, however, just as Midwestern cities from Cleveland and Detroit to Chicago and St. Louis were struggling with deindustrialization and urban uprisings over structural injustices in housing, wages, and social and civic services, media, industry, and civic discourses all began to excise or write these locales *out* of the perceptual region of the Midwest. In other words, if urban America of the 1970s was, increasingly, presumptively Black, working class, and politically charged, a revised version of the Heartland myth needed to be willed into existence in order to carve out an imaginary "safe" space and site of idealized **equilibrium** for the new decade. Thus, the Heartland became "integral to popular imagination of national restoration in the 1970s" that envisioned "a new American Middle—one populated by urbane 'squares' who had 'somehow ... fended off the sixties.'"[27]

The chapter thus examines "equilibrium" as a geographic concept (epitomized by the 1970s Midwest Heartland), a political concept (status-quo calm vs. "extremes" or revolutionary action), an industrial concept (via, particularly, CBS's cultivation of a new, younger demographic audience for its "quality" series), and a cultural concept (associating "common sense" square-ness with self-awareness, modesty, gentility, and good taste). Close textual analysis of the title sequences from each season of *The Mary Tyler Moore Show* evidence the lead character's transformation—ideally analogous to that of much of the program's target audience—from shy but determined small-town secretary to independent, fashionable, mobile, urbane exemplar of "The Good Life in Minnesota."[28] Close analysis is also undertaken of the comic conceits and character types across each of the three MTM series to illustrate

specific narrative and formal properties by which MTM Productions' "stars, settings, and program aesthetics and address were explicitly analogized with the Midwest and midwesternness as the 1970s locus of a liberal humanist equilibrium ... and consensus 'good taste.'"[29] Notably, "equilibrium" appeals did not end with the conclusion of MTM series' run in prime time: Indeed, this "sensibility" has been reenergized via Heartland tourism, invigorated particularly post-9/11 and in partnership with TV Land and the civic locales of MTM series, which continue to position Minneapolis, in particular, "as a site of public liberation and private self-actualization."[30]

What should be underscored here is that revising the Heartland to be a site of "equilibrium" is really about *raced* identity and the region's "redefinition" for the 1970s. The realities of African American populations and activism in the Midwest in this period were consciously, actively excised in the name of an imagined "white" "middle." Thus, the *geographic*, here, is the conceptual terrain that licenses or appears to enable a disavowal and *displacement* of race from the region. Such disavowal all the more powerfully underscores what George Lipsitz theorizes to be the "possessive investment in whiteness" and its "invisibility."[31] Frequent popular and critical discursive references to the 1970s Heartland as calm, solid, characterized by sobriety, hard work, and high civic tradition evacuated of political concerns all explicitly construct the 1970s Heartland as simultaneously pastoral and urbane but resolutely *not* urban and, implicitly (in the main), idealize a *white* "universal" subject.

For this chapter, I used four categories of primary materials to build the discursive network or web through which I could "read" appeals to or expressions of the Heartland and from which I could identify patterns of consistent association of the Midwest *as* Heartland in a fundamentally revised mythology for the 1970s. I examined the formal and narrative properties of the MTM series themselves to identify "urbane" aural and visual appeals to CBS's new, desired demographic. Within episodes, key comedic conceits or tropes emerged (humility always wins, at home; outsiders to this Heartland home must be deflated and/or expelled) that reinforced *externally* circulating publicity about the series' creators, stars, and MTM's "quality" logics in the period (especially as contrasted with Lear and Yorkin's Tandem Productions). Such publicity was gleaned from popular press, trade industry press, and archival interviews with MTM Productions' casts and staffs. Popular press materials examined here included major United

States magazines and newspapers to construct a broader sense of the nationally circulating debates and emerging consensus regarding political and cultural transitions of the 1970s and the ways in which these cast the Heartland into a newly desirable status. In the context of the Watergate era, President Nixon's resignation, civil rights, women's rights, and anti-war activism, such coverage of *Mary Tyler Moore's* Minnesota as a state that "works" seemed particularly significant. Such cover stories were synchronous with and, often, included reference to MTM's "good taste." Together, industrial, textual, popular press, and broader social discourses create a field within and through which the Heartland and its political and cultural *value* were constructed at the end of the 1960s through the 1970s.

The key secondary literature upon which the chapter depends comes from regional studies, particularly James Shortridge's scholarship on the actively shifting conceptual borders of the Midwest after World War II. Complementary to this work, the chapter is dependent upon Raymond Williams' conceptualization of "selective tradition" as the process whereby some elements of a prevailing myth remain powerfully explanatory (e.g., the Heartland as pastoral site of All-American values) even as revisions selectively alter the myth for a particular historic conjuncture and political valence (e.g., the conscious excising of Detroit, Chicago, St. Louis, and other cities from the perceptual framework of the Midwest, allowing the idealized, mythic Heartland to remain "untouched" by 1970s urban "strife" and, fundamentally, to be recuperated as white space). My argument also clearly depends on work from critical race theory and critical legal theory (as regards whiteness as property), particularly that of George Lipsitz and Herman Gray. A third key theoretical field the chapter depends upon comes from TV studies' body of work on "quality TV" and MTM Productions, in particular, as exemplar of such. To consider Mary Tyler Moore and Bob Newhart as icons of "representative mediocrity," I draw on Constance Penley's and Richard Dyer's scholarship on star personae.[32] Finally, the chapter depends on archival and industry documents regarding civic promotional campaigns for Minneapolis and as regards the broader economic phenomenon of Heartland tourism.

As with all work, after the fact, other possibilities for its research or further exploration become apparent. As regards particular questions of cultural geography, there are several possible gaps in the existing work that might be productively reconsidered.

Though the chapter specifically focused on nationally available discourses about MTM and the Midwest in the 1970s, this emphasis broadly disallowed much analysis, understanding, or reconstruction of actual viewer sensibilities about these rhetorics and/or any regional or local contradictions to the myth of "equilibrium." Similarly, the lack of any archival study of MTM Productions' scripts or production notes allows that the most "polished," and arguably uniform, way of talking about these series and their settings stands as *the* history—a history that was, no doubt, somewhat more contentious "in house."

It would, likewise, be interesting to have comparative market data for ratings and viewing demography of these series. Such information often provides evidence for series' popularity that may contradict the intended "ideal" address or presumed viewership. For example, though *The Lawrence Welk Show* (ABC, 1955–71 and syndicated, 1971–82) was routinely dismissed by critics and even its own network for its "clodhopper charm," its highest ratings were earned outside of the Midwest, in Boston and Philadelphia. So, if viewer demographics for MTM shows proved to be more Southern or more rural than anticipated, for example, that might lead to some recontextualization of industrial and critical discourses regarding CBS's "turn to relevance" and its imagined "ideal" demographics.

Finally, though the chapter explicitly focuses on Midwest-set MTM half-hour sitcoms from the 1970s, MTM Productions also had "coastal" sitcoms and hour-long, urban, Los Angeles-set dramas during these years that challenge the style of comedy and appeal of the three shows featured in my case study. Three of these series were spin-offs from *The Mary Tyler Moore Show* itself: the New York City-set *Rhoda* (CBS, 1974–78), the San Francisco-set *Phyllis* (CBS, 1975–77), and the Los Angeles-set *Lou Grant* (CBS, 1977–82). Beyond these spin-offs, I would add MTM's *The White Shadow* (CBS, 1978–81), which explicitly examined race relations and class struggles at "Carver" High School in South Central Los Angeles. How might MTM's broader history of production in the 1970s diverge from "urbane Midwest" series to encourage additional questions of place, race, and quality TV?

Identifying possible gaps, omissions, or areas for expansion in one's work leads to thinking about opportunities to pursue further work on the cultural geographic aspects of film, broadcast, and digital media. I hope that the above has offered a compelling rationale to raise questions of geography to a shared level of attention to those categories of identity and capital relations with which it crucially intersects and which it critically informs (including race, class, gender, sexuality, and generation). How does our "common sense" understanding of geographic identity and its value shape our assumptions about demography and social and political worth? At the opening of this chapter, I recalled *Variety*'s famous headline about "Hicks" not being interested in the rural-themed films that were being targeted to them. Why should this have taken distributors by surprise? How do continued, persistent industry references, such as "flyover" (states, audiences, texts) engage geographic mythologies in not just imagining but, in fact, structuring a nation in which regionalism continues to powerfully differentiate market, social, and political values—explicitly welcoming some participants but actively dissuading and excising others? Are there media that—in spite of our increasingly handheld, personalized delivery devices—still appeal to a broadly *national* community of shared experience? Why might this still be desired?

A native Californian student of mine once claimed, "You know, in Kansas, they think reality TV is really real." This student was attempting to bolster her own critical capital by using "Kansas" as a broad term for naïveté. Cultural geography does the work to investigate why she *would* believe that film and media audiences in Kansas—not to mention scholar-students living there—would be any less critically savvy and aware than those on either coast. Such continued imagination of the U.S. Midwest as a region marked by simple, pastoral naïveté is particularly striking given that the language now commonly used to describe new media technology depends upon rural references as a strategy that effectively displaces its material realities (including infrastructure and labor) as well as its ecological ramifications. For example, companies speak of server "farms" rather than unsightly warehouses, and the "cloud" is the soft, dreamy, welcoming expanse of our collected digital lives, rather than a cold, metallic digital matrix or grid.

The current moment seems paradoxical: on the one hand, for those with streaming media access at home or who have the ability to travel with connected technologies, media are now ostensibly more truly "global" than ever before (especially in the notoriously parochial United States); on the other hand, those same mobile devices (phones, tablets, etc.) are capable of tracking and addressing us at the site of our most intimate local experiences. Foregrounding *geography* as a key determinant in media's development, standardization, accessibility, address, and use keeps social power and its strategic functions at the core of media studies.

Notes

1. George McCall, "Sticks Nix Hicks Pix," *Variety*, July 17, 1935, 1, 51. On The OC and tourism to Orange County, CA, see Richard Chang, "'The O.C.': Show Put Region on the Map," *Orange County Register*, Feb. 18, 2007. Accessed February 26, 2018. www.ocregister.com/2007/02/18/the-oc-show-put-region-on-the-map/.

   On Rutgers University applications, see Keith Sargeant, "Rutgers Enrollment Chief Says Applications Are On the Rise," *NJ.com*, March 30, 2015. Accessed February 26, 2018. www.nj.com/rutgersfootball/index.ssf/2015/03/rutgers_enrollment_chief_says_applications_are_up.html. For the local appeal of apps, see Alyson Krueger, "Apps for Encounters of the Local Kind," *The New York Times*, April 7, 2015. Accessed February 26, 2018. www.nytimes.com/2015/04/12/travel/apps-for-encounters-of-the-local-kind.html.

2. Victoria E. Johnson, *Heartland TV: Prime Time Television and the Struggle for U.S. Identity* (New York: New York University Press, 2008), 6.

3. Ibid.

4. Such grounding questions are, here, definitive of the humanities-based, multi-disciplinary approaches to cultural geography described in this chapter. This differentiates the work in film and media studies presented here from approaches common to the social-scientific-based discipline of human geography and from much of the work definitive of scholars whose primary academic association is the Association of American Geographers. Analyses of human geography and geographic studies from such venues date from the 1800s in the U.S. social sciences with strong roots in "hard" sciences and work with geographic information systems. There are productive intersections across this work. However, this chapter focuses on scholarship that identifies as "film and media studies" through cultural geographic approaches, rather than as geographic studies with film and media as its "text."

5. James Carey, "The Chicago School and the History of Mass Communication Research," in *James Carey: A Critical Reader*, eds. Eve Stryker Munson and Catherine A. Warren (Minneapolis: University of Minnesota Press, 1997), 29.

6. Ibid., 27.

7. Ibid., 32.

8. See, for example, Theodor W. Adorno, *The Culture Industry: Selected Essays on Mass Culture* (New York: Routledge, 1990).

9. Lawrence Grossberg, *Cultural Studies* (New York: Routledge, 1992), 12.

10. See, for example, Stuart Hall and Tony Jefferson, eds. *Resistance Through Rituals* (New York: Harper Collins, 1976); or, Dick Hebdige, *Subcultures: The Meaning of Style* (New York: Routledge, 1979).

11. Daphne Spain, *Gendered Spaces* (Chapel Hill: University of North Carolina Press, 1992), 3.

12. See, for example: Giuliana Bruno, *Streetwalking on a Ruined Map: Cultural Theory and the City Films of Elvira Notari* (Princeton: Princeton University Press, 1993); David Clarke, ed., *The Cinematic City* (New York: Routledge, 1997); Anne Friedberg, *Window Shopping: Cinema and the Postmodern* (Berkeley: University of California Press, 1993).

13. Kathryn H. Fuller-Seeley and George Potamianos, "Introduction: Researching and Writing the History of Local Moviegoing," in *Hollywood in the Neighborhood*, ed. Kathryn Fuller-Seeley (Berkeley: University of California Press, 2008), 5.

14. See, for example, Barbara Ching and Gerald W. Creed, eds., *Knowing Your Place: Rural Identity and Cultural Hierarchy* (New York: Routledge, 1997); Henry Jenkins, *What Made Pistachio Nuts? Early Sound Comedy and the Vaudeville Aesthetic* (New York: Columbia University Press, 1992); Richard Maltby, Melvyn Stokes, and Robert C. Allen, eds., *Going to the Movies: Hollywood and the Social Experience of Cinema* (Exeter: University of Exeter Press, 2007).

15. Mary Carbine, "The Finest Outside the Loop: Motion Picture Exhibition in Chicago's Black Metropolis, 1905–1928," *Camera Obscura* 23 (May 1990): 11, 12.

16. Jacqueline Najuma Stewart, *Migrating to the Movies: Cinema and Black Urban Modernity* (Berkeley: University of California Press, 2005), 12.

17. Paula J. Massood, *Making a Promised Land: Harlem in 20th Century Photography and Film* (New Brunswick: Rutgers University Press, 2013).

18. For a critical analysis of radio in these terms, see Alexander Russo, *Points on the Dial: Golden Age Radio Beyond the Networks* (Durham: Duke University Press, 2010); and Michele Hilmes, ed., *NBC: America's Network* (Berkeley: University of California Press, 2007).

19. See, for example, Lynn Spigel, "From Domestic Space to Outer Space: The 1960s Fantastic Family Sitcom," in *Welcome to the Dreamhouse: Popular Media and Postwar Suburbs* (Durham: Duke University Press, 2001), 107–40; Michael Curtin, *Redeeming the Wasteland: Television Documentary and Cold War Politics* (New Brunswick: Rutgers University Press, 1995); and George Lipsitz, "The Meaning of Memory: Family, Class, and Ethnicity in Early Network Television Programs," in *Private Screenings: Television and the Female Consumer*, eds. Lynn Spigel and Denise Mann (Minneapolis: University of Minnesota Press, 1992), 71–109.

20. Lynn Spigel, *Make Room for TV: Television and the Family Ideal in Postwar America* (Chicago: University of Chicago Press, 1992).

21. Anna McCarthy, *Ambient Television: Visual Culture and Public Space* (Durham: Duke University Press, 2001), 2.

22. Ibid.

23. Jon Kraszewski, "Pittsburgh in Fort Worth: Football Bars, Sports Television, Sports Fandom, and the Management of Home," *Journal of Sport & Social Issues* 32, no. 2 (2008): 139–57.

24. Vicki Mayer, *Below the Line: Producers and Production Studies in the New Television Economy* (Durham: Duke University Press, 2011); Serra Tinic, *On Location: Canada's Television Industry in a Global Market* (Toronto: University of Toronto Press, 2005); John Caldwell, *Production Culture: Industrial Reflexivity and Critical Practice in Film and Television* (Durham: Duke University Press, 2008).

25. Nicole Starosielski, *The Undersea Network* (Durham: Duke University Press, 2015); Jennifer Holt and Patrick Vonderau, "'Where the Internet Lives': Data Centers as Cloud Infrastructure," *Signal Traffic: Critical Studies of Media Infrastructures*, eds. Lisa Parks and Nicole Starosielski (Urbana: University of Illinois Press, 2015), 71–93.

26. Heidi Rae Cooley, *Finding Augusta: Habits of Mobility and Governance in a Digital Era* (Hanover: Dartmouth College Press, 2014), 78. See also, Mark Andrejevic, *iSpy: Surveillance and Power in the Interactive Era* (Lawrence: University Press of Kansas, 2007); and Tiziana Terranova, "Free Labor: Producing Culture for the Digital Economy," in *The Media Studies Reader*, ed. Laurie Ouellette (New York: Routledge, 2013), 331–49.

27. Johnson, *Heartland TV*, 112.

28. Ibid., 118.

29. Ibid., 125.

30. Ibid., 134.

31. George Lipsitz, *The Possessive Investment in Whiteness: How White People Profit from Identity Politics* (Philadelphia: Temple University Press, 1998).

32. See Constance Penley, "Spaced Out: Remembering Christa McAuliffe," *Camera Obscura* 29 (Winter 1992): 178–213; and Richard Dyer, *Stars* (London: British Film Institute, 1998).

Further Reading

Classen, Steven D. *Watching Jim Crow: The Struggles Over Mississippi TV, 1955–1969*. Durham: Duke University Press, 2004.

D'Acci, Julie. *Defining Women: The Case of Cagney and Lacey*. Chapel Hill: University of North Carolina Press, 1994.

Gray, Herman. "Television, Black Americans, and the American Dream." In *Television: The Critical View*, edited by Horace Newcomb, 176–87. New York: Oxford University Press, 1994.

Hall, Stuart. *The Hard Road to Renewal: Thatcherism and the Crisis of the Left*. London: Verso, 1988.

Hall, Stuart and Paddy Whannel. *The Popular Arts*. Boston: Beacon Press, 1964.

Hilmes, Michele. *Network Nations: A Transnational History of British and American Broadcasting*. New York: Routledge, 2012.

———, ed. *Radio Reader: Essays in the Cultural History of Radio*. New York: Routledge, 2002.

Johnson, Victoria E. "The Persistence of Geographic Myth in a Convergent Media Era." *Journal of Popular Film and Television* 38, no. 2 (2010): 58–65.

Kraszewski, Jon. "Country Hicks and Urban Cliques: Mediating Race, Reality and Liberalism on MTV's *The Real World*." In *Reality TV: Remaking Television Culture*, edited by Susan Murray and Laurie Ouellette, 179–96. New York: New York University Press, 2004.

Lipsitz, George. *How Racism Takes Place*. Philadelphia: Temple University Press, 2011.

McDowell, Linda. *Gender, Identity and Place: Understanding Feminist Geographies*. Minneapolis: University of Minnesota Press, 1999.

Morley, David. *Home Territories: Media, Mobility and Identity*. London: Routledge, 2000.

Newcomb, Horace and Paul M. Hirsch. "Television as a Cultural Forum." In *Television: The Critical View*, edited by Horace Newcomb, 455–70. New York: Oxford University Press, 1987.

Nye, David E. *Electrifying America: Social Meanings of A New Technology*. Cambridge: MIT Press, 2001.

Oren, Tasha. "Reiterational Texts and Global Imagination: Television Strikes Back." In *Global Television Formats: Understanding Television Across Borders*, edited by Tasha Oren and Sharon Shahaf, 366–81. New York: Routledge, 2012.

Ouellette, Laurie. *Viewers Like You? How Public TV Failed the People*. New York: Columbia University Press, 2002.

Ouellette, Laurie and James Hay. *Better Living Through Reality TV*. Malden: Blackwell, 2008.

Pascucci, Ernest. "Intimate (Tele)visions." In *Architecture of the Everyday*, edited by Steven Harris and Deborah Berke, 38–54. Princeton: Princeton Architectural Press, 1997.

Pertierra, A.C. and Turner, Graeme. *Locating Television: Zones of Consumption*. London: Routledge, 2013.

Rivero, Yeidy M. *Broadcasting Modernity: Cuban Commercial TV, 1950–1960*. Durham: Duke University Press, 2010.

Russo, Alexander. *Points on the Dial: Golden Age Radio Beyond the Networks*. Durham: Duke University Press, 2010.

Spigel, Lynn and Jan Olsson, eds. *Television After TV: Essays on a Medium in Transition*. Durham: Duke University Press, 2004.

Williams, Mark, ed. "U.S. Regional and Non-Network Television History." Special issue, *Quarterly Review of Film and Video* 16, no. 3–4 (1997): 221–28.

Williams, Raymond. *The Country & The City*. New York: Oxford University Press, 1973.

Zelinsky, Wilbur. *The Cultural Geography of the United States: A Revised Edition*. Englewood Cliffs: Prentice Hall, 1992.

Zukin, Sharon. *Landscapes of Power: From Detroit to Disney World*. Berkeley: University of California Press, 1991.

20.
NATIONAL/TRANSNATIONAL/GLOBAL
Shanti Kumar

Overview

It is now commonplace in media studies to state that media are global. But what does it mean to be global? How do we analyze the role that globalization plays in the production, distribution, and consumption of media around the world? Let's begin with a few media examples that could be considered global in different ways. First, consider a spectacular global sporting event like the Cricket World Cup match held on March 29, 2015 in Melbourne, Australia, which was broadcast live into millions of homes simultaneously via television and the Internet across international boundaries and time zones. Next, take the globalization of the *Idols* format of reality television, inspired by a New Zealand reality show called *Popstars* (TV2, 1999), and first produced as a British reality TV show *Pop Idols* (ITV, 2001–03) that in turn was adapted over several years to create many different national versions such as *American Idol* (FOX, 2002–16), *Canadian Idol* (CTV, 2003–08), and *Indian Idol* (SET, 2004–present) as well as regional versions such as *Latin American Idol* (SET, 2006–09) and *Arab Idol* (MBC, 2011–present). Finally, look at how Psy's "Gangnam Style" music video— inspired by, and a parody of the very trendy Gangnam district in Seoul, South Korea—spread rapidly around the globe in 2012 to become the first viral sensation to get over a billion views on YouTube.

To discuss globalization in these very different examples of different types of media from different parts of the world in the same way would obviously require a vast overgeneralization. If globalization means different things to different people in different places at different times, then how can we analyze these differences that constitute global media? This chapter outlines the different ways in

which globalization has been examined in the fields of international communications and global media studies. It provides an overview of the wide range of scholarship that has critically interrogated concepts such as the "national," "transnational" and "global" in media studies using the following frameworks: (1) nationalism and transnationalism, (2) cultural imperialism and cultural globalization, and (3) the "global village" and deterritorialization. Finally, this chapter introduces the methodological framework of "process geography" for critically evaluating the dynamic relationality of global, national, and local media in specific contexts, and it describes a case study from the author's research on the process geography of globalization by drawing on an essay titled "Regional Cinemas and Globalization in India."[1]

Nationalism and Transnationalism

In global media studies, scholars often view media as expressions of national cultures. In an essay titled, "The Fixity of the Nation in International Media Studies," Divya McMillin critically examines the reasons why the nation-state is considered a cohesive unit of analysis.[2] Drawing on John Breuilly's demarcation of common approaches used by scholars to study nation-states and nationalisms, McMillin outlines four methodological perspectives.[3] They are (1) the nationalist approach in which the nation traces its identity back to some originary myths about premodern cultural histories, symbols, and memories; (2) the Marxist approach that critiques nationalism as modern ideology that emerges in relation to the upheavals caused by industrial capitalism in eighteenth-century Europe; (3) the psychological approach wherein the nation is seen as a modern response to an innate psychological need among humans to organize themselves into large collectives based on proto-nationalist or tribal desires to associate with others who share similar attributes such as skin color, language, or religion; and (4) the communications approach that explains how diverse groups of people can create and sustain a sense of community that transcends their many differences through a process of communication.

A very influential framework in the communications approach for analyzing the relationship between media and nationalism in modern societies is derived from Benedict Anderson's well-known book, *Imagined Communities*.[4] Anderson defines **imagined communities** as groups of people dispersed across time and space who do not meet each other face to face, but imagine themselves as part of the same community. For example, Anderson shows how a group of very diverse people dispersed across time and space in any given place can read a story in a newspaper or a magazine and feel an imagined sense of connectedness with other readers of the same story. Anderson argues that collective imaginations of nations as communities were facilitated by the rise of what he called **print-capitalism** in Europe and in European colonies in Asia, Africa, and the Americas during the Industrial Revolution. The confluence of printing technologies with the rise of industrial capitalism, Anderson argues, played a crucial role in the mass production and consumption of shared languages and cultural histories among an emergent group of middle-class readers of mass media like newspapers and magazines.

While Anderson's formulation of "imagined communities," has been enormously influential in global media studies, it has been criticized for many shortcomings. In *Provincializing Europe*, Dipesh Chakrabarty faults Anderson for unquestioningly locating the origins of all nationalist imaginations in Europe and for describing the spread of nationalism in the colonial world largely in relation to European discourses of modernity, industrialization, and capitalism. Chakrabarty also criticizes Anderson for celebrating the power of print-capitalism to create a collective sense of national identity and for ignoring the ways in which marginalized groups can resist such collective imaginations or imagine alternative ways of creating communities within and beyond the nation.[5] Another strand of critique comes from media scholars who argue that Anderson's use of print-capitalism as a historical framework is highly problematic for analyzing the more contemporary discourses of electronic capitalism. In *Modernity at Large,* Arjun Appadurai

reworks Anderson's concept of imagined communities and coins the term "imagined worlds" to describe how in an age of globalization, electronic media like radio, television, and the Internet can easily cross national and international borders and instantaneously reach audiences beyond the nation.[6] However, in a polemically titled essay, "Television and the Nation: Does this Matter Any More?" Graeme Turner contends that reports of the death of the nation-state in electronic capitalism are greatly exaggerated.[7] Answering the rhetorical question in the subtitle of his essay with an emphatic "yes," Turner reminds readers that television broadcasting (i.e., reaching a mass audience) has always been central to the operation of the public sphere in modern nation-states. To Michael Curtin's critique that the nation-state may no longer be a "sufficient site"[8] for analyzing the role of media in global contexts, Turner responds that the nation still remains an unavoidable site.

Turner concedes that the centrality of the nation-state and the dominance of national broadcasting in the public sphere have been challenged by globalization and the rise of narrowcasting technologies like cable and online and digital media that fragment the national audiences into niche segments. But he cautions against hasty announcements of the "end of broadcasting" because he finds that there are certain areas, such as live events, sports, and national celebrations, in which broadcasting remains the most widely available national medium. Also, there are always occasions where nation-states need to address all their citizens collectively. Therefore, Turner opines that there will always be room for national broadcasting systems in most countries. Finally, Turner argues that the everydayness of broadcasting and the ways in which television has become ingrained in the daily rituals of the viewing public's individual and collective lives would suggest that the national model of broadcasting will remain a powerful and viable option in the near future.

Echoing Turner's sentiments, John Sinclair uses the telenovela genre as a case study to support his argument about the persistence of national broadcasting in Latin America.[9] The national model of broadcasting persists in Latin America, Sinclair suggests, due to the enormous popular appeal of telenovelas that have historically been produced and consumed in very national contexts. Surveying the history of and the current growth strategies for globalization of major Latin American media corporations, Sinclair finds that national broadcasters such as Brazil's TV Globo, Mexico's Televisa, Venezuela's

Venevision, and Argentina's Telefe depend in different ways on the success of the telenovela genre in their respective national markets as they attempt to move beyond broadcasting and into global markets and digital platforms. Therefore, Sinclair concludes, at least from the perspective of media in Latin America, we are not yet in a post-broadcasting era.

Similarly, the question of the nation has also been at the center of the debates about the globalization of cinema around the world. As Stephen Crofts points out, the term **national cinema** has traditionally been used to refer to cinematic cultures and industries that are not Hollywood.[10] Crofts outlines different varieties of national cinemas such as European and Third World entertainment cinemas, Anglophone cinemas beyond Hollywood, state-controlled and state subsidized cinemas, and regional cinemas. As Crofts argues, the "national cinema" framework has been a particularly useful methodological tool in film studies for giving voice to the diverse cinematic traditions that exist and flourish between, betwixt, and beyond the globally dominant Hollywood. However, one of its key limitations is that U.S. cinema is almost never described as a national cinema. As a result, many scholars in global media studies have called for the **de-Westernization** of media studies by embracing more transnational methodologies that are not centered on the U.S. nation-state. This type of scholarship is evidenced by the recent spate of books with titles such as *De-Westernizing Media Studies, De-Westernizing Film Studies, De-Westernizing Communication Research*, and *Internationalizing Internet Studies: Beyond the Anglophone Paradigm*.[11]

At the same time, scholars within the traditions of U.S. media studies and American studies have called for a **New Americanism** that moves away from an exclusive focus on the nation-state as a unit of analysis. For example, the influential book series on "New Americanists" from Duke University Press edited by Donald E. Pease Jr. seeks to "displace the preconstituted categories and master narratives of an earlier American studies."[12] Indicative of the "new Americanist" turn in American studies are titles from the series such as *Trans-Americanity* by José David Saldívar, *Hemispheric Imaginings* by Gretchen Murphy, *Virtual Americas* by Paul Giles, *Black Empire* by Michelle Ann Stephens, and *The Futures of American Studies* edited by Robyn Wiegman and Donald E. Pease.[13] In media studies, the work of scholars like Michele Hilmes in *Network Nations: Transnational History of American Broadcasting*, Timothy Havens in *Black Television Travels: African American Media*

around the Globe, Ramon Lobato in *Shadow Economies of Cinema: Mapping Informal Film Distribution* and Neil Campbell in *The Rhizomatic West: Representing the American West in a Transnational, Global Media Age* are particularly noteworthy of this mode of scholarship.[14] These media scholars have advanced a valuable methodological framework for displacing naturalized categories and master narratives of earlier American media studies and for historicizing the always-already transnational/global trajectories of U.S. media industries and cultures.

Cultural Imperialism and Cultural Globalization

To counter Eurocentric and U.S.-centric master narratives implicit in Western histories of nationalism, many scholars in the fields of international communications and media studies have defined globalization in terms of an unequal set of economic relations between Western "centers" and non-Western "peripheries." For example, influenced by the world systems theory of Immanuel Wallerstein, media scholars like Herbert I. Schiller, Fred Fejes, and Oliver Boyd-Barrett argued that the world had reached a new stage of **cultural imperialism** with the rise of transnational media corporations that spread American media and culture around the globe after World War II.[15] Similarly, Ariel Dorfman and Armand Mattelart,[16] in *How to Read Donald Duck*, provided a scathing critique of the power of Disney comic books to disseminate American cultural values and capitalist ideologies in Latin America by creating a dependency among Latin American audiences for U.S. media products.

Writing in the early 1970s, Dorfman and Mattelart found that Disney—both the man and the company—used comic books, cartoons, and animated films to create a "common sense" view of the modern world in which the primary source of wealth is always the creativity of the Western bourgeoisie, which gives them the advantage to succeed in global capitalism. For example, in their close textual analyses of comic books featuring the international adventures of Donald Duck with Huey, Dewey, and Louie in Latin America, Africa, and Asia, Dorfman and Mattelart argue that Disney represented cultures of the Global South as decrepit ruins of past civilizations. In these comics, the ancient treasures of the civilizational ruins in Asia, Africa, and Latin America are shown to be easily available for exploitation by adventurous and enterprising Western explorers like Donald and his young nephews. Therefore, Dorfman and Mattelart argue, Disney's adventure narratives produced a radical break between the present-day inhabitants of the Global South and the supposed annihilation of their civilizational ancestors. Thus disconnected from their cultural pasts, the young consumers of Disney comics in the Global South read the adventure stories of Donald Duck and his nephews not as fantasy tales but as instructions for how to live in a world dominated by the excesses of capitalist consumer culture emanating from Hollywood. In spite of providing a seemingly compelling critique of the global power of American media like Disney comics, there are many limitations of the cultural imperialism and dependency theories proposed by Marxist scholars like Schiller, Dorfman, Mattelart, and many others. In response to these limitations, media scholars in the theoretical traditions of cultural globalization have advanced several critiques to reframe the debate over the cultural power of media around the world.

In his well-known books, *Cultural Imperialism* and *Globalization and Culture*, John Tomlinson defines **cultural globalization** as a methodology for interrogating the leading role that culture plays in making life meaningful in the various dimensions of globalization like politics, economics, technology, and language. He critiques the cultural imperialism theorists for assuming that the economic power of global capitalism can be equated with its cultural effects in diverse local contexts and for arguing without any empirical evidence that those effects are felt uniformly by people around the world. Secondly, Tomlinson finds it curious that cultural imperialism theories that seek to critique Western dominance emerge from a rather Western-centric notion of culture that is based in stereotypical characterizations of non-Western cultures as being pure in their traditional authenticity and unspoiled by any previous contact with other outside cultures. Finally, Tomlinson argues that the cultural imperialism thesis fails to account for the creative power of audiences to resist the domination that can occur in even the most exploitative contexts of imperialism.[17]

In a powerful rebuttal of the cultural imperialism thesis, Tamar Liebes and Elihu Katz in their book, *The Export of Meaning: Cross-Cultural Readings of Dallas*, analyze the diverse responses of audiences in Israel (and later in Japan) to argue that cultural differences play an important role in the interpretation of globally distributed American television shows like *Dallas* (CBS, 1978–91).[18] Similarly, Ien Ang in her pioneering study *Watching Dallas* demonstrates how female television viewers in the Netherlands often made alternative meanings of the dominant cultural codes embedded in the globally distributed American television show *Dallas* and thus asserted their own sense of identity, difference, nationality, and transnationality.[19]

In an article published in 2007 titled "Television Fictions Around the World," Ang looks back at, and updates, her early critique of cultural imperialism outlined in *Watching Dallas* to examine how the television melodrama has evolved around the world in the wake of *Dallas*.[20] Ang argues that after the massive global success of *Dallas*, the soap opera format was adopted by many national television industries around the world. The result was what Ang calls the glocalization of the TV melodrama genre. A neologism coined by Roland Robertson, **glocalization** has been used in media studies to refer to how media formats travel around the world through a process where the format and the formula are standardized globally, but production of narrative content is always specific to local contexts.[21]

As examples of glocalization, Ang mentions the soap opera *Yearnings* (1990) shown on China's national broadcasting service CCTV, the hybrid genre of Ramadan television serials produced in Egypt (and later in other parts of the Islamic world), and Hindu mythological epics like *Ramayan* (1987–88) and *Mahabharat* (1988–90) telecast by the Indian national network Doordarshan. In each of these cases, Ang finds that the glocalization of TV melodrama was made possible not only by embracing the generic conventions of *Dallas*, but also by adapting the genre to the specific national context by incorporating culturally specific content that would resonate with the cultural sensibilities of the national audiences. Therefore, Ang argues that glocalization of television fictions around the world must be understood in terms of the relationship between the proliferation of global formats (such as *Dallas*), the diversity of local variations (various versions of *Dallas* in different national contexts), and the cultural specificity of content in each context.

To understand the central role of cultural context in the glocalization of TV melodramas, Ang compares the rise of Japanese "trendy" dramas with the rise of the hybrid "dramedy" genre in U.S. prime-time schedules in the 1990s. Situating these transformations in relation to the show *Dallas*, Ang recalls how in *Watching Dallas* she outlined two different ways in which viewers identified with the melodramatic texts of the soap opera genre: (1) affective mode of pleasure—the emotional pleasure of viewers who take melodrama seriously, and (2) ironic pleasure—the pleasure of viewers who like to poke fun at and thus neutralize the emotional pleasures of melodrama. While viewers in the first category derive pleasure in being swept away by the emotional highs and lows of the narrative, viewers in the second category derive pleasure by claiming distance from the emotional excess by knowingly telling themselves and others, "I love watching it *because* it is so bad."[22]

In the United States, soap operas like *Dynasty* (ABC, 1981–89) and TV melodramas that followed *Dallas* tried to replicate this formula for success. Although *Dallas* and *Dynasty* belonged to the same soap opera genre, *Dynasty* tried to differentiate itself from *Dallas* in some important ways. While *Dallas* drew on conventions of melodrama to connect with the affective modes of pleasure of its viewers, *Dynasty* tried to set itself apart by poking fun at melodramatic conventions, and at itself, by using irony, parody, exaggeration, and outlandish excess (and thus presenting itself as a more self-reflexive than *Dallas*). By the 1990s, Ang argues, the affective mode of pleasure in taking melodrama seriously had become "uncool" in American prime-time television, and the ironic pleasure of poking fun at one's own emotional identification with melodramatic excess had become "trendy" and "cool." The result was the rise of a new hybrid genre of "dramedy" that combined elements of drama and comedy. Some of the popular shows in the United States that Ang lists as part of the dramedy trend include *Moonlighting* (ABC, 1985–89), *Melrose Place* (FOX, 1992–99), *Ally McBeal* (FOX, 1997–2002), *Sex and the City* (HBO, 1998–2004), and *Desperate Housewives* (ABC, 2004–12).

During the same period in the 1990s in East Asia, however, Ang finds that viewers were being swept away by a new genre called "trendy" dramas. Unlike the ironic mode of engagement preferred by the producers of U.S. dramedies, the makers of trendy dramas—first in Japan and then in Korea—invoked melodrama's emotional realism to focus on high-quality youth-oriented serials that showcased romantic relations among young professionals in modern, stylish, and gorgeous contemporary urban settings. Ang argues that the popularity of Japanese trendy dramas like *Tokyo Love Story* (Fuji Television, 1991) and Korean dramas like *Winter Sonata* (KBS2, 2002) can be attributed to their ability to attract a new generation of viewers in East Asia by using the emotional realism of melodrama to represent the tensions between modernity and tradition in the everyday lives of urban youth.

By highlighting the two very different trajectories in the evolution of the melodrama genre after

Dallas—ironic dramedies in the United States and trendy dramas in East Asia—Ang demonstrates how cultural context is a crucial factor in media production, circulation, and consumption in different parts of the world. Therefore, Ang concludes, the different trajectories of dramedy in the United States and trendy drama in East Asia provide compelling evidence in favor of theories of hybridity in cultural globalization. For Ang, **hybridity** is best defined as the linkage between the global and the local using terms such as "glocalization."

The long-standing debates between theories of cultural globalization and cultural imperialism about categories such as "global," "local," "national," etc. have been extremely influential in international communications and global media studies for revealing the many diverse trajectories of uneven media flows around the world. Moreover, the cultural globalization and cultural imperialism perspectives have been instrumental in providing much-needed correctives to the overly optimistic picture of globalization painted by technological enthusiasts, who drawing on Marshall McLuhan, see mass media as the harbingers of an idyllic "global village."[23]

The Global Village and Deterritorialization

Written in the midst of the Cold War between the United States and the Soviet Union, McLuhan's vision of uniting the world into a **global village** emerged from his utopian faith in the power of new media technologies such as satellites, transoceanic cables, and television networks to cross boundaries and increase international and intercultural communication. McLuhan's concept of the "global village" captivated public imagination and became a popular metaphor for understanding the crucial role media play in the process of globalization. McLuhan attained a celebrity status in North American popular culture, was featured on cover pages of leading magazines like *Newsweek,* and was headlined in influential newspapers like *The New York Times* as the prophet of a new global order.[24] But McLuhan was also roundly criticized by leading media scholars of the time, such as Raymond Williams, for being too eager to celebrate the power of technological forms to effect positive social change, and for being completely ahistorical in his analysis of globalization.[25] Williams argued that McLuhan's catchy slogans like "the medium is the message" failed to highlight how dominant social authorities can and do always select and control how new technologies operate in the world. At the same time, Williams argued, McLuhan's other slogans like "the medium is the massage"[26]—which claimed to reveal how media extend the human sensorium—could not account for how media audiences can and do always challenge the power of new media technologies and transform the communicative practices of those technologies in society.

In more recent times, however, the "global village" metaphor has been revived by media scholars and journalists to emphasize the growing power of digital, mobile, and social media technologies to connect places, people, and communities around the world while also circumventing the authority of nation-states and transnational corporations in the information age. Titles such as *McLuhan's Global Village Today: Transatlantic Perspectives*, *From Rural Village to Global Village: Telecommunications for Development in the Information Age*, and *Digital McLuhan: A Guide to the Information Millennium* are indicative of this (re)turn to McLuhan in global/digital media studies in the twenty-first century.[27] For example, in *Digital McLuhan*, Paul Levinson argues that McLuhan's "global village" was not a fundamentally flawed concept as his critics argued, but instead was an idea way ahead of its time. During McLuhan's time, the simultaneity of global communications that electronic media such as satellites and radio and television broadcasting could provide was based largely on one-way transmissions between senders and receivers. Thus, Levinson argues that the electronic villagers in McLuhan's global village were passive consumers who could only eavesdrop on other people's communications and media interactions. Levinson claims that in the digital age, McLuhan's vision of the "global village" has been more fully realized because technologies such as the Internet enable people around the world to interact with each other instantaneously in real time, thus opening up the possibilities for more democratic participation and autonomous communication.[28]

Although media scholars like Levinson are very optimistic about the power of digital technologies to realize McLuhan's ideals, they cautiously posit their visions for a new "global village" as possibilities in the future, given the enormous inequalities of power relations that still exist in our world today. However, in more popular accounts of the so-called global technological revolution, there is an unbridled enthusiasm for, and an unflinching faith in, the power of new technologies to erase global inequities and to solve age-old problems that earlier generations could

not. Examples of such works include the writings of Thomas Friedman in books such as *The World is Flat* and *The Lexus and the Olive Tree*[29] and the corporate-strategy guru Kenichi Ohmae in his books, *The Invisible Continent* and *The Next Global Stage*.[30]

According to Robert McChesney, "cheerleaders" of globalization like Friedman are fundamentally wrong in proclaiming the dawn of a new "golden age" for the human race where digital technologies, democracy, and capitalism will inevitably undermine and overthrow oppressive regimes around the world.[31] McChesney argues that the celebratory rhetoric of the "golden age" of globalization is highly misleading because it is ideologically overcoded in favor of transnational corporate interests. In order to critically interrogate the ongoing transformations of the world's media systems, McChesney prefers the term **neoliberalism** instead of the utopian visions of the "global village."

McChesney defines neoliberalism in terms of a set of national and international policies that calls for the primacy of the marketplace in all social affairs with minimal countervailing force from either nation-states or civil society. The ideology of neoliberalism calls for the corporate privatization of areas that are or were historically in the "public" domain—such as media, education, health care, social welfare, or even international warfare. The dominance of neoliberal ideologies in the twenty-first century is aptly indicated by the generalized shift from public broadcasting—which was the dominant form of media worldwide in the twentieth century—to private, commercial media systems in areas such as broadcasting, satellite and cable technologies, wired and wireless telephony, the Internet and digital media. As many media historians have argued, before the 1980s, national media systems around the world were dominated by mostly domestically owned radio, television, and newspaper industries, either as public media systems or as a mix of public/private media systems.[32]

However, since the 1980s, and particularly after the end of the Cold War, there has been a growing trend towards transnational ownership of media systems by private corporations. The result, McChesney argues, has been the rise of a "global oligopoly" of transnational media corporations. The defining trait of the global oligopoly is its ability to expand into the farthest reaches of the world without any significant competition or opposition. According to McChesney, the oligopoly functions through a two-tiered global media system. In the first tier are a handful of transnational media corporations mostly based in the United

States, such as Disney, Comcast, Viacom, Sony, NewsCorp, and Time-Warner. The second tier is constituted by regional media powerhouses or national corporations that control niche markets such as Dow Jones, Gannett, and Knight-Ridder in North America; Pearson, Reuters, and Reed Elsevier in Europe; Mexico's Televisa, Brazil's Globo, Argentina's Clarin, and Venezuela's Cisneros Group in Latin America, and so on. All these companies have aggressively embraced strategies for the consolidation of ownership through the vertical and horizontal integration of their media assets and infrastructures.

While many of the tier-two companies are also seeking markets in areas traditionally dominated by the tier-one corporations, McChesney finds that there is hardly any competition in the global media system because the tier-one corporations often collaborate or have joint-ventures with the tier-two companies. Moreover, both tier-one and tier-two corporations have extensive ties to global investment banks, and they all depend on the same transnational advertising companies and sponsors for their revenues. McChesney argues that the central role of advertising as the driving force in contemporary global media reveals why convergence cannot be defined solely in technological terms, but must be understood in terms of the converging commercial interests of global, regional, national media corporations that are all seeking greater synergy through economies of "scale." Therefore, McChesney argues that the ideologies of neoliberalism bear a striking similarity to—and have a complex relationship with—earlier forms of cultural imperialism.

McChesney's theorization of neoliberalism as a new form of Western imperialism has been critiqued by media scholars like Michael Keane and Michael Curtin in a manner reminiscent of the critique of the cultural imperialism thesis by scholars of cultural globalization like Tomlinson and Ang discussed earlier in this chapter. In a much-cited essay titled "Once Were Peripheral," Keane critiques the theory of neoliberal global media systems advanced by McChesney for being too "American-centric."[33] Keane's main objection is that these American-centric critiques of neoliberalism see emerging media capitals in peripheral—or once-peripheral—regions such as East Asia merely as cheap "off-shore" locations for Western media industries centered predominantly in the United States. Keane, however, finds that the binary division of the world in terms of "core" and "peripheries" or the "West" and the "rest" is now inadequate and outdated. Instead, he calls for the recognition of the role of regional

media capitals in globalization from the perspective of media producers and consumers in these once-peripheral locations.

The reason for the shift toward regional media capitals, Keane claims, is that a new model of globalization has emerged as a result of four key changes in our world from the mid-1970s to the late 1990s. The first is the increased role of intellectual capital in the service sector and the informational economy as a result of the trend toward digitization in production processes and the computerized networking of communication and information exchange in industrial practices and social relations. The second change that Keane refers to is the rapid growth of international collaborations and co-productions between the traditionally dominant media centers in North America and Western Europe and "once peripheral" locations such as East Asia. As an example, Keane describes how international collaborations in Hong Kong, which functions as a nexus between dominant media capitals of the East and the West, helped enhance the media capacity in the East Asian region and helped the growth of once-peripheral media industries in South Korea and Taiwan.

The third key change, Keane argues, is the growing interdependence between nations in the global informational economy. The digitization and deterritorialization of production practices along with the growing mobility of capital and labor practices have enabled—or even required—nations to cooperate with each other to sustain and profit from the global networks of communication and information exchange. These global networks are, of course, not equally available or accessible to all nations, and the exchange of information and capital around the world is hardly egalitarian or democratic. However, the growing interdependence between nations has meant that the efficient control of global networks through coordinated polices of risk management (such as international trade agreements or intellectual property laws) have become the essential prerequisites for national organizations and transnational corporations to ensure stability of profits in the twenty-first century.

The fourth and final change that Keane outlines in his analysis of media capacity in East Asia is the emergence of new players in the global economy. Keane outlines five categories through which the new centers of financial and creative activity in East Asia are increasing their media capacity: (1) deterritorialization of a world factory model (where the multiplier effect of low-cost outsourcing in local companies provides the potential for the creation of high-value creative industries); (2) mimetic isomorphism (where local companies are able to illegally clone global TV formats and film formulas with great success in the short term, but get entangled in legal problems with the international intellectual property regime in the long term); (3) cultural technology transfer (where local companies enter into legal agreements on international co-productions with globally renowned franchises through the sharing of intellectual property); (4) niche breakthroughs (where distribution of local productions through multiple channels on multiple platforms transform niche films like *Hero* (2004) or *House of Flying Daggers* (2004) into global hits); and (5) creative industry clusters (where the creation of hi-tech film cities or information parks enable local players in smaller towns and cities to compete with regional and global players). Keane draws on Curtin's concept of **media capitals** to argue that the above-mentioned changes in the global economy have contributed to the growth of new centers of financial and creative activities in cities like Hong Kong, Cairo, and Mumbai. According to Curtin, media capitals are places where things come together in dual senses of the word "capital" both as a geographic center of activity and as a concentration of resources, reputation, and talent.[34] Arguing that a media capital is a nexus or a switching point, Curtin demonstrates how the media production and consumption practices in cities like Chicago, LA/Hollywood, and Hong Kong occur at intersections of complex, global economic, social, and cultural flows.

The complex dynamics of globalization that media scholars like Keane and Curtin map out in their analyses of media capitals and flows have been most famously theorized by Appadurai as disjuncture and difference in the global cultural economy.[35] For Appadurai, globalization does not refer to the linear transmission of communication from a powerful (Western or American) sender to a relatively powerless (non-Western) receiver in international affairs, but to a complex, overlapping, and non-isomorphic set of deterritorialized cultural flows. To describe this emerging order of **deterritorialization**, Appadurai maps five dimensions of cultural flows consisting of ethnoscapes, mediascapes, technoscapes, financescapes, and ideoscapes. According to Appadurai, **ethnoscapes** refer to the movement of people as workers, tourists, students, immigrants, refugees, and others. **Technoscapes** refer to technologies that move at high speeds across traditionally impervious boundaries. **Financescapes** refer to rapid movements of capital on a global scale. **Mediascapes**

refer to both the global media that enable electronic transmission of information and to the variety of images that are available to audiences as resources for cultural imagination. **Ideoscapes** are also "concatenations of images" but are defined more explicitly as political. Appadurai uses the suffix "-scape" to describe how the world can appear rather stable like a landscape when seen from a particular perspective in spite of disjuncture and difference within and across the various flows of globalization.

Since the publication of Appadurai's groundbreaking text in the 1990s, much has been written about how media production and consumption have become more decentered in a deterritorialized cultural economy, and how audiences are experiencing global cultures as "imagined worlds" built around a dynamic set of disjunctive but overlapping global-scapes. For instance, Michael Hardt and Antonio Negri have characterized the current state of deterritorialization in our world in terms of the concept of **Empire**.[36] For Hardt and Negri, Empire differs from earlier forms of imperialism where imperial (European) powers exerted their sovereign authority over far-flung colonies through a centralized command structure. In the Empire of the twenty-first century, Hardt and Negri argue, imperial power is no longer centralized in a sovereign (European) authority, but is instead exerted through more diffused global networks of nation-states, transnational corporations, informational networks, supranational institutions, nongovernmental organizations, and a multitude of informal, collective interests. Therefore, Hardt and Negri advocate a move beyond binary categories such as the West and the rest, the global and the local, the center and the periphery, and call for a rhizomatic approach to engage more productively with the deterritorialized and deterritorializing power of Empire.

The **rhizome** of globalization that Hardt and Negri draw on, is a concept developed by Gilles Deleuze and Felix Guattari in their pathbreaking book, *A Thousand Plateaus*.[37] The rhizome, for Deleuze and Guattari, refers to a type of root system that grows horizontally from the middle and thus has no organizing center or a fixed point of origination. Hardt and Negri argue the contemporary moment of globalization is rhizomatic in that there are no longer centralized sovereign powers like nation-states. The modern form of sovereignty, they argue, has become more diffused in the decentered network structure of media technologies like the Internet, the deterritorialized corporate organization of transnational media industries, and the transversal connections among supranational agencies, such as the European Union or the World Trade Organization.

Highlighting the tension between the opposing frameworks of deterritorialization and territorialization in the discipline of film studies, Will Higbee and Song Hwee Lim, argue that the use of "transnational" to signify the rhizomatic spaces of globalization may not be an entirely unproblematic strategy, compared to earlier frameworks that may have problematically worked within the territorial confines of categories such as the "national."[38] For them, the term "transnational" still privileges the space of the nation-state (or at least the need/desire to overcome the nation-state framework) and thus marginalizes the rich diversity of cultural and geographic descriptors that could be used to describe the spaces of globalization. Examples of such alternative descriptors include geographical categories like regions, localities, and borders, and cultural processes like migration, exile, and hybridity. Higbee and Lim provide three alternative descriptors that have been used in film studies to overcome the national/transnational binary in globalization: (1) national borders as limits for transnationalism; (2) diasporic, exilic, and postcolonial cultures; and (3) regional formations.

National cinema, Higbee and Lim argue, remains a useful framework if the national is defined not as the origin of but as a limit for transnationalism. In other words, transnationalism although global, is not a limitless phenomenon because national governments can use cultural regulations, laws, and policies to limit the transnational flows of cinema. Higbee and Lim argue that the major drawback of this approach is that a focus on the nation's limiting powers could potentially obscure the political, economic, and ideological imbalances that national governments can create and manipulate across and within borders, and it could ignore the politics of difference in issues of migration and diaspora that are central to transnational flows in the contemporary world. The second perspective in transnational cinemas that Higbee and Lim outline is the study of diasporic, exilic, and postcolonial cultures that critique the Eurocentric biases of the theoretical constructs of nationalism and transnationalism by analyzing representations of cultural identity as fluid, dynamic, and hybrid. For Higbee and Lim, a potential limitation of this approach is that the diasporic, exilic, or postcolonial perspectives are often marginal to the hegemonic culture and thus may have fairly limited influence on the mainstream. Although the lack of access to mainstream culture

is not deemed inherently problematic in any way, Higbee and Lim wonder if this lack works against the stated political goals of marginal cinemas to intervene in and alter hegemonic ideologies. The third perspective on transnationalism that Higbee and Lim describe requires a shift from the transnational to "regions" that share a common cultural heritage and/or geo-political boundaries. Higbee and Lim argue that examples of such "regions" are Chinese cinema and Nordic cinema. However, Higbee and Lim suggest that the term "transnational" may be inadequate to define these regional cinemas, and they prefer "supranational Chinese" cinema and "regional Nordic" cinema.

Case Study: The Process Geography of Regional Cinemas in India

In my article, "Regional Cinemas and Globalization in India,"[39] I engage in an extensive debate with Crofts' discussion of "national cinema/s" and Higbee and Lim's analysis of terms such as "national," "transnational," "supranational," and "regional." While I do not entirely disagree with Higbee and Lim's analysis, I argue that there is a fundamental problem with their understanding of "regions" around the world purely in terms of "traits" such as common cultural heritage and shared geographic boundaries. In doing so, I argue, they propagate what Appadurai has identified as the dominant paradigm in the study of areas and regions that takes "a particular configuration of apparent stabilities for permanent associations between space, territory and cultural organization."[40] For instance, I explain that when histories of Indian cinema are written in terms of the perceived stability of traits such as dominant languages, traditions, values, and physical borders within the nation-state, regional cinemas are relegated to sub-national status, even though such "regions" have always been supra-, trans-, and pan-national as well.

As a student of Indian cinema, I have always found neat categorizations like global, national, local, and regional to be inadequate for analysis because Indian film industries and cultures have been hybrid right from the beginning. However, the history of Indian cinema has been dominated by a nationalist desire among filmmakers, fans, and scholars alike to create coherent narratives that can neatly coincide with the hegemonic ideologies of the modern nation-state. For example, in nationalist narratives of Indian cinema, the term "Bollywood" is increasingly being used as a buzzword to describe all aspects of commercialized Indian popular culture in diverse arenas such as film, television, music, and fashion. While Bollywood as buzzword serves as a convenient branding category for the mass production, distribution, and consumption of commercialized popular culture in India and in the Indian diaspora, it ignores a range of non-commercial and parallel media industries in Hindi, such as documentary filmmaking and experimental art. At the same time, the term Bollywood does not adequately capture the diversity of media industries and cultures that thrive in a variety of regional languages in India. Therefore, in my research on regional cinemas in India, I have always tried to find sites that do not fit easily into one or another convenient category, and, thus, provide insights into the very complex, multidimensional histories and geographies of Indian cinema.

To foreground the multidimensional sites of "regional" cinemas as simultaneously national, global, transnational, local, and regional, I turn to Appadurai's argument about shifting our research methodologies away from "trait geographies" to "process geographies." As Appadurai defines them, **process geographies** enable us to map "significant areas of human organization as precipitates of various kinds of action, interaction and motion—trade, travel, pilgrimage, warfare, proselytization, colonization, exile and the like."[41] Appadurai writes,

> Regions are best viewed as initial contexts for themes that generate variable geographies, rather than as fixed geographies marked by pre-given themes. These themes are equally "real", equally coherent, but are results of our interests and not their causes. The trouble with much of the paradigm of area studies as it now exists is that it has tended to mistake a particular configuration of apparent stabilities for permanent associations between space, territory and cultural organization. These apparent stabilities are themselves largely artifacts of: the specific trait-based idea of "culture" areas; a recent Western cartography of large civilizational landmasses associated with different relationships to "Europe" (itself a complex historical and cultural emergent); and a Cold-War based geography of fear and competition in which the study of world languages and regions in the United States was legislatively configured for security purposes into a reified map of geographical regions.[42]

Drawing on Appadurai's call to shift our research methodologies away from trait-based geographies to

process geographies, I examine the national, transnational, global, local, and regional flows of media in film cities, such as Ramoji Film City (RFC) in Hyderabad and Innovative Film City (IFC) in Bengaluru in South India. Film cities like RFC and IFC provide filmmakers from anywhere in the world the opportunity to make an entire film from pre-production to post-production in a one-stop studio that provides multiple outdoor locales and diverse indoor settings. In addition to being state-of-the-art media production centers, RFC and IFC are major tourist attractions, which provide visitors access to a variety of picturesque gardens, entertainment parks, and tours of production studios.

I argue that film cities—many of which are located in "regional" film production centers in India—are the most visible manifestations of a process geography that is redefining the "regional" cinemas of India by showcasing their simultaneously global, national, local, transnational, and "subnational" status in Indian cinema. I foreground the hybrid mediascapes produced at RFC and IFC to underscore the creative ways in which film cities in India are mapping a new process geography of cultural production and consumption. I argue that film cities like RFC and IFC are very good case studies for understanding the changing realities of the global entertainment industry, where connections between older trait geographies of place are being re-imagined in terms of newer process geographies of mediation, mobility, travel, and tourism.

Conclusion

This chapter describes the different ways in which globalization has been examined in the fields of international communications, film studies, and global media studies. In doing so, it provides a broad overview of some of the major theoretical frameworks and methodological considerations for the study of media in terms of concepts like nationalism, transnationalism, and globalization. It explores why the concept of the "nation" has been, and in some ways continues to be, the predominant category for understanding media in international contexts. It also discusses how media scholars from different theoretical perspectives have used concepts like transnationalism, cultural imperialism, cultural globalization, and deterritorialization to critique the unquestioning acceptance of the nation as the de facto unit of analysis in media studies. Finally, this chapter uses the case study of regional cinemas in India to highlight the dynamic relationality of global, national, and local media in specific contexts through a methodological perspective defined as "process geography."

As media industries and cultures around the world are increasingly becoming more interconnected, the traditional methods of demarcating media into neat categories like global, national, local, and regional are becoming less viable in media studies. Therefore, this chapter concludes that it is now essential for scholars in media studies to discard old trait-based categories that divide the world into neat but empirically suspect compartments, and move toward more dynamic frameworks that focus on the process geographies of globalization as a multidimensional phenomenon.

Notes

1. Shanti Kumar, "Regional Cinemas and Globalization in India," in *Global Communication: New Agendas in Communication*, ed. Karin G. Wilkins, Joseph D. Straubhaar, and Shanti Kumar (New York: Routledge, 2014), 83–99.
2. Divya C. McMillin, *International Media Studies* (Malden: Blackwell, 2007).
3. John Breuilly, *Nationalism and the State* (Chicago: University of Chicago Press, 1994).
4. Benedict Anderson, *Imagined Communities: Reflections on the Origin and Spread of Nationalism* (London: Verso, 1991).
5. Dipesh Chakrabarty, *Provincializing Europe: Postcolonial Thought and Historical Difference* (Princeton: Princeton University Press, 2000).
6. Arjun Appadurai, *Modernity at Large: Cultural Dimensions of Globalization* (Minneapolis: University of Minnesota Press, 1996).
7. Graeme Turner, "Television and the Nation: Does this Matter Any More?" in *Television Studies After TV: Understanding Television in the Post-Broadcast Era,* ed. Graeme Turner and Jinna Tay (New York: Routledge, 2009), 54–64.
8. Curtin, "Media Capital: Toward the Study of Spatial Flows," *International Journal of Cultural Studies* 6, no. 2 (2003): 202–28; 271.
9. John Sinclair, "Latin America's Impact on World Television Markets," in *Television Studies After TV,* ed. Graeme Turner and Jinna Tay, 141–48.
10. Stephen Crofts, "Reconceptualizing National Cinema/s," *Quarterly Review of Film and Video* 14, no. 3 (1993): 49–67.
11. James Curran and Myung-Jin Park ed., *De-Westernizing Media Studies* (New York: Routledge, 2000); Saër Maty Bâ and Will Higbee, ed., *De-Westernizing Film Studies* (New York: Routledge, 2012); Georgette Wang ed., *De-Westernizing Communication Research: Altering Questions and Changing Frameworks* (New York:

Routledge, 2011); Gerard Goggin and Mark McLeland ed., *Internationalizing Internet Studies: Beyond the Anglophone Paradigm* (New York: Routledge, 2008).
12. Donald E. Pease, series editor, "Overview," New Americanists Series, Duke University Press, accessed January 14, 2016, www.dukeupress.edu/Catalog/ProductList.php?viewby=series&id=43.
13. José David Saldívar, *Trans-Americanity: Subaltern Modernities, Global Coloniality, and the Cultures of Greater Mexico* (Durham: Duke University Press, 2011); Gretchen Murphy, *Hemispheric Imaginings: The Monroe Doctrine and Narratives of U.S. Empire* (Durham: Duke University Press, 2005); Michelle Ann Stephens, *Black Empire: The Masculine Global Imaginary of Caribbean Intellectuals in the United States, 1914–1962* (Durham: Duke University Press, 2005); Paul Giles, *Virtual Americas: Transnational Fictions and the Transatlantic Imaginary* (Durham: Duke University Press, 2002); Robyn Wiegman and Donald E. Pease ed., *The Futures of American Studies* (Durham: Duke University Press, 2010).
14. Michele Hilmes, *Network Nations: A Transnational History of American Broadcasting* (New York: Routledge, 2012); Timothy Havens, *Black Television Travels: African American Media Around the Globe* (New York: New York University Press, 2013); Ramon Lobato, *Shadow Economies of Cinema: Mapping Informal Film Distribution* (New York: Palgrave McMillan, 2012); Neil Campbell, *The Rhizomatic West: Representing the American West in a Transnational Global Media Age* (Lincoln: University of Nebraska Press, 2008).
15. Immanuel Wallerstein, *The Capitalist World-Economy* (Cambridge: Cambridge University Press, 1979); Herbert I. Schiller, "Not Yet the Post-Imperialist Era," *Critical Studies in Mass Communication* 8, no. 1 (1991): 13–28; Fred Fejes, "Media Imperialism: An Assessment," *Media Culture* 3, no. 3 (1981): 281–89; Oliver Boyd-Barrett, "Media Imperialism: Towards an International Framework for the Analysis of Media Systems," in *Mass Communication and Society,* ed. James Curran and Michael Gurevitch (London: Edward Arnold, 1977), 116–35.
16. Ariel Dorfman and Armand Mattelart, *How to Read Donald Duck: Imperialist Ideology in the Disney Comic* (New York: International General, 1975).
17. John Tomlinson, *Globalization and Culture* (Cambridge: Polity Press, 1999); John Tomlinson, *Cultural Imperialism: A Critical Introduction* (London: Continuum, 1991).
18. Tamar Liebes and Elihu Katz, *The Export of Meaning: Cross-Cultural Readings of Dallas* (Cambridge: Oxford University Press, 1993).
19. Ien Ang, *Watching Dallas: Soap Opera and the Melodramatic Imagination* (New York: Routledge, 1989).
20. Ien Ang, "Television Fictions Around the World: Melodrama and Irony in Global Perspective," *Critical Studies in Television* 2, no. 2 (2007): 18–30.

21. Roland Robertson, "Glocalization: Time-Space and Homogeneity-Heterogeneity," in *Global Modernities*, ed. Mike Featherstone, Scott Lash and Roland Robertson (London: Sage Publications, 1995), 25–44.

22. Ang, "Television Fictions," 21.

23. Marshall McLuhan, *Understanding Media: The Extensions of Man* (New York: McGraw Hill, 1964).

24. "The Message of Marshall McLuhan," *Newsweek*, March 6, 1967, cover page; Richard Kostelanetz, "Understanding McLuhan (in part)," *The New York Times*, January 29, 1967, accessed July 18, 2013, www.nytimes.com/books/97/11/02/home/mcluhan-magazine.html.

25. Raymond Williams, *Television, Technology and Cultural Form* (New York: Schoken Books, 1975).

26. Marshall McLuhan and Quentin Fiore, *The Medium is the Massage* (New York: Bantam, 1967).

27. Carmen Birkel, Angela Krewani, and Martin Kuester, ed. *McLuhan's Global Village Today: Transatlantic Perspectives* (New York: Routledge, 2014); Heather E. Hudson, *From Rural Village to Global Village: Telecommunications for Development in the Information Age* (New York: Routledge, 2011); Paul Levinson, *Digital McLuhan* (New York: Routledge, 1999).

28. Levinson, *Digital McLuhan*.

29. Thomas Friedman, *The World is Flat: A Brief History of the Twenty-first Century* (New York: Farar, Strauss and Giroux, 2005); *The Lexus and the Olive Tree: Understanding Globalization* (New York: Farar, Strauss and Giroux, 1999).

30. Kenichi Ohmae, *The Next Global Stage: Challenges and Opportunities in Our Borderless World* (Philadelphia: Wharton School Publishing, 2005); *The Invisible Continent: Four Strategic Imperative of the New Economy* (New York: Harper Collins, 2001).

31. Robert McChesney, "Global Media, Neoliberalism and Imperialism," in *Monthly Review* 52, no. 10 (2001), accessed December 16, 2001, http://monthlyreview.org/2001/03/01/global-media-neoliberalism-and-imperialism/.

32. Please see Chapter 10 on political economy in this book. Also, see David Croteau and William Hoynes, *The Business of Media: Corporate Media and the Public Interest* (Thousand Oaks: Sage Publications, 2006); Erik Barnouw and Patricia Aufderheide, *Conglomerates and the Media* (New York: New Press, 1997); Edward Hermann and Robert W. McChesney, *Global Media: The New Missionaries of Global Capitalism* (New York: Continuum, 2004).

33. Michael Keane, "Once Were Peripheral: Creating Media Capacity in East Asia, *Media Culture Society* 28, no. 6 (2006): 835–55

34. Michael Curtin, "Media Capital."

35. Arjun Appadurai, *Modernity at Large*.

36. Michael Hardt and Antonio Negri, *Empire* (Cambridge: Harvard University Press, 2000).

37. Gilles Deleuze and Felix Guattari, *A Thousand Plateaus: Capitalism and Schizophrenia* (Minneapolis: University of Minnesota Press, 1987).

38. Will Higbee and Song Hwee Lim, "Concepts of Transnational Cinema: Towards a Critical Transnationalism in Film Studies," *Transnational Cinemas* 1, no. 1 (2010): 7–21.

39. Kumar, "Globalization of Regional Cinemas in India."

40. Arjun Appadurai, "Globalization and the Research Imagination," *International Social Science Journal* 51, no. 160 (1999): 232.

41. Ibid.

42. Ibid.

Further Reading

Artz, Lee. *Global Entertainment Media: A Critical Introduction*. Malden: John Wiley and Sons, 2015.

Chopra, Rohit and Radhika Gajjala, eds. *Global Media, Culture, and Identity: Theory, Cases, and Approaches*. New York: Routledge, 2012.

Lull, James. *Media, Communication, Culture: A Global Approach*. Cambridge: Polity Press, 2000.

Mirrlees, Tanner. *Global Entertainment Media: Between Cultural Imperialism and Cultural Globalization* (New York: Routledge, 2013).

Wise, MacGregor J. *Cultural Globalization: A Users' Guide*. Malden: Blackwell, 2008.

21.
HISTORY AND HISTORIOGRAPHY
Michael Kackman

What makes media history different from other modes of critical analysis? After all, historical scholarship can employ most of the methodologies in this collection, from studies of representation or ideology to analyses of policy, visual style, or stardom. In many respects, scholars engage with past phenomena much as we do those in the present. We ask who is involved, and to what effect. We ask questions about cultural contexts, about economics, or about politics. We inquire about meaning, or about aesthetics, or we might try to understand how different audiences might respond to a particular film or television program.

Take, for example, the popular CBS series *I Love Lucy* (1951–57). One could ask any number of very different kinds of questions about the show, and indeed historians and critics have done so for decades. One common place to start is with institutions and industries, and consider the profitable gamble taken by the show's producers and stars, Lucille Ball and Desi Arnaz, who convinced CBS to support their plans to move production to Los Angeles and shoot the series on film; in so doing, they helped to revolutionize the television industry.[1] But who was really the agent of Desilu's success? Was it Desi Arnaz, generally recognized at the time as the company's visionary leader, or was that a gendered presumption that overlooked Ball's role? After all, she continued to lead the company after the couple's divorce, and oversaw the development of such series as *Mission: Impossible* (CBS, 1966–73) and *Star Trek* (NBC, 1966–69). Another candidate is Jess Oppenheimer, whom Miranda Banks credits with inventing the role of the TV writer-producer.[2] Or perhaps, as Peter Kovacs has recently argued, we're overlooking the powerful influence of tobacco giant Philip Morris, which not only sponsored *I Love Lucy*, but built its entire early 1950s corporate strategy around the series.[3]

Corporate maneuvers, however, are not the only entry points to understand the show historically. We might consider visual aesthetics and the role of cinematographer Karl Freund, whose career spanned from German Expressionism (including shooting Fritz Lang's 1927 masterpiece *Metropolis*) to an Academy Award for *The Good Earth* (1937) before he developed an innovative three-camera film system for *I Love Lucy*. Or, we might, as Yeidy Rivero has, place the show in a history of the circulation of genres and formats globally; *I Love Lucy* was, after all, the source of an unauthorized Cuban television adaptation in 1953, and was an important influence on Cuban television.[4]

Or, for that matter, we might consider Lucille Ball, the star. We might explore her brush with the House Committee on Un-American Activities during the Red Scare, or her early years with the RKO film studio. And while today we instantly—and perhaps only—read Lucille Ball as the character Lucy Ricardo, Alex Doty has argued that much of the complexity of the show's humor rested on its play with her earlier glamorous star persona. Despite her bumbling, grasping hunger for attention and success, Lucy Ricardo was, according to Doty, "constantly on the verge of becoming deconstructed by the movie-vaudeville performer who played her."[5] For Doty, this tension between the movie star and the screwball was absolutely central to the show's pleasures. Patricia Mellencamp, on the other hand, turns to Freud to explore slightly different tensions in the show—those between woman as object and subject of humor, and between humor's power to liberate and to contain.[6] Moving beyond academia, we might also consider the bizarre ill-conceived bronze statue in Lucille Ball's hometown, or references to the show in filmmaker Todd Haynes' reverie on childhood fantasy in his short film *Dottie Gets Spanked* (1993). There are many Lucys.

Each of these approaches—like hundreds of other histories of the show, its stars, and their impact—is rooted in methodologies that can be used to explore more proximate phenomena. The challenge of writing historically is not so much one of learning a distinct methodology, then, but one of managing the paradoxes of temporal distance. The vast, unfolding past is irretrievably gone, a foreign country in which we will always be tourists—and yet in some ways we know more about the past than those who inhabited it. None of us were in the room when Ball, Arnaz, and the executives of CBS negotiated the terms of their relationship, yet we know not only that the subsequent show was a commercial success but that it helped pioneer new modes of television production and distribution. We may not be sure how Ball developed her persona of the hobbled housewife who yearns for something more, but we can place her in the context of postwar women's employment, and see in her longing to escape the bounds of domesticity flickers of what Betty Freidan, more than a decade after *Lucy*'s premiere, called the "problem that has no name."[7] And yet, despite the confidence with which we might connect *I Love Lucy* to the women's liberation movement or to the emergence of the Hollywood television production system of the network era, there is no ultimate test of our historical claims that is not itself an historical narrative. We can never conclusively check our work by going back to the data, for there is always other data, located in other archives and experiences, that can be expressed in different kinds of narratives.

None of this, however, is to suggest that the difficulty of making conclusive arguments about the past means that all historical claims are equally valid. Rather, it is simply to say that, despite the enormous cultural and political power of historical writing, history is, in Keith Jenkins' phrase, plagued by **epistemological fragility**.[8] That is, history has an essential, but ultimately tenuous, relationship to the past that it purports to explain. In confronting a past that is never fully knowable—both because there is always more past than we will ever be able to explore, and because we can never visit it to corroborate our arguments—Jenkins calls for circumspection on the part of historians, and better critical reading strategies

by those who read historians' work. Fundamentally, we must recognize that history doesn't *describe* the past; it *narrates* it.

It's easy to overlook history's fragility, in part because we have a long tradition of granting enormous authority to historical narrative. We often treat historical representation—whether that of a film like Steven Spielberg's *Lincoln* (2012) or that of Doris Kearns Goodwin's book *Team of Rivals* on which it depends—as transparently descriptive.[9] At most, we might question the indexical relationship between a particular claim and the past (was Mary Todd Lincoln really mentally ill?), but we rarely engage in a more substantive discussion of how we know what we know about such a person, or of how they are represented in such texts. Following Jenkins, we might inquire not only into what kinds of evidence might be available about Mrs. Lincoln and her health, but about what "mental health" even meant in nineteenth-century America. We might ask how her character functions in a narrative centered on Lincoln's moral decision-making, or consider the possibility that Goodwin, Spielberg, and screenwriter Tony Kushner might be making presumptions about family relationships and political management styles that are more reflective of our contemporary society than they are of Washington, DC, circa 1865.

Those kinds of questions are less about the past than they are about historical evidence and narration. In other words, they are questions about **historiography**—the critical study of historical research and argumentation. Although our culture is suffused with historical representations—from memoirs, scrapbooks, and popular films to professional/scholarly histories influenced by virtually every discipline in the academy—our critical literacy about how those histories are written is woefully underdeveloped. Most of us are better equipped to engage critically with the narrative strategies of *Citizen Kane* or *Breaking Bad* than we are those of a typical historical essay. Fortunately, though, some of the same analytical tools that help us make sense of popular storytelling forms are useful for the study of historical writing. Just as films and novels have characters, precipitating conflicts, underlying tensions, and ideological problematics, so, too, do nonfiction histories; and as in fictional entertainment, those elements are deployed by historians to make meaning out of the raw material of the past. This chapter thus aims not to explain the past, but to draw attention to the techniques that media historians use to imbue the past with meaning.

Intellectual Foundations: The History of History

Few historians today would claim that their work is simply the neutral, scientific describing of reality. There remains, however, considerable debate about how confident historians ought to be about their truth claims, and how generalizable their arguments might be. Even a fairly traditionalist historian like John Lewis Gaddis, for example, might aspire to the epistemological confidence of a scientist, but he recognizes not only that it's extraordinarily difficult to bend the chaos of human behavior to fit anything remotely as predictable as a true scientific law, but also that scientists themselves aren't nearly as confident as they once might have been.[10] Where someone like Gaddis diverges from most of the humanists in this book is his residual confidence that somehow history is better, more sturdy, more reliable. In that, he isn't much different from a graduate school colleague of mine, a political historian who once leaned over his wire-rimmed glasses and intoned gravely, "Really, history is the physics of the humanities."

One of the focal points of debates about the knowability of the past has been **causality**: What does it mean to claim that one event was precipitated by another? Approached from a literary perspective, a causal argument might be understood essentially as a series of rhetorical claims, buttressed by evidence but ultimately made compelling via narrative **tropes**: recognizable rhetorical patterns and figures of speech (e.g., psychologically complete characters taking rational actions in the face of identifiable pressures). But even then, it seems crucial to distinguish between immediate and more distant causes. Marc Bloch invokes, as a thought experiment, a mountaineer who has fallen from a cliff (discussions of historiography are littered with imaginary corpses).[11] Should we attribute his death to poor footwear? Bad training? Perhaps the plate tectonics that created the mountains? Or simply gravity? Of course, what we most naturally say is that he slipped; we choose the proximate cause, both because it is coherent and because it has the most immediate explanatory power.

But how are we to weigh between immediate and distant causes? Surely, there must be something other than narrative convention—essentially genre—to give explanatory force to a particular interpretation. Arguing against dominant modes of historiography that skewed heavily toward biography and top-down accounts of political leaders and movements, Bloch and fellow French historian

Lucien Febvre in 1929 formed the journal *Annales d'histoire économique et sociale*. The *Annalistes*, as they came to be known, argued for a historiography not of political leaders, but of society. By focusing on deep social structures, demography, and economics, they laid the foundations of **social history**. Building on the emerging social sciences of sociology and political science, they sought to understand the *longue durée*—the big picture, contextualized within the sensibilities (or *mentalités*) of an age.

Though they would likely dismiss it as overly deterministic, the *Annaliste* impulse to understand social transformation economically and structurally resonated with the nineteenth-century Marxist principle of **historical materialism**. For Marx and his co-author Friedrich Engels, historical materialism was not a literary or rhetorical trope; it was akin to a natural law. Eulogizing Marx, Engels claimed:

> Just as Darwin discovered the law of development of organic nature, so Marx discovered the law of development of human history: the simple fact—hitherto concealed by the overgrowth of ideology—that mankind must first of all eat, drink, have shelter and clothing, before it can pursue politics, science, art, religion, etc.; that therefore the production of the immediate material means of subsistence and consequently the degree of economic development attained by a given people or during a given epoch form the foundation upon which the state institutions, the legal conceptions, art, and even the ideas on religion, of the people have been evolved, and in light of which they must, therefore, be explained.[12]

Marxist historiography shaped the ways that historians understood the relationship between individuals and social forces—what in sociology comes to be articulated as a tension between **structure** and **agency**. Do underlying social forces determine the conditions and possibilities of historical change, or is individual action more prominent? What structural conditions enable certain kinds of agency, for certain people, and not others?

The *Annalistes* and Marxists weren't the only voices calling for a historiography that sought to understand the social forces and sensibilities of entire nations. In the late nineteenth century, Herbert Baxter Adams helped to articulate the foundations both of U.S. historiography and political science. His student Frederick Jackson Turner became famous for the "frontier thesis," which argued that the history of western expansion had left an indelible stamp on the American psyche, producing a people who were fiercely independent and violent but also generous, adventuresome, and self-sufficient.[13] The frontier thesis of "rugged individualism" was enormously influential in historical scholarship throughout the early twentieth century. It shaped the political rhetoric of presidents like Franklin Roosevelt and John F. Kennedy, and it remains a potent political ideology today. Turner also laid some of the key foundations of what is now called American studies, characterized in its early years by an effort to explain that which was distinctively emblematic of the American character, using methods that mixed literary and political history. Turner would eventually be characterized more often as an artifact of self-congratulatory U.S. mythmaking, but the field's ongoing conversations about, and trenchant critiques of, American exceptionalism remain an important influence on media historiography.[14]

The broad movement toward social history in the mid-twentieth century also opened up new lines of inquiry into previously dismissed arenas of social activity. Once we shift our attention away from a narrow understanding of agency, leadership, and historical change, other social experiences and people come into view. It's no coincidence that some of the early Marxist historians turned to the organized labor movement—they did so not only in a political gesture of solidarity with workers, but also as a historiographic and methodological intervention and a refutation of a "great man" conception of heroic leadership. Even more transformative was the emergence of women's history, which insisted not only on the significance of particular women as historical actors, but also drew attention to the invisible labor of women in the family and the workplace, and charted how gender has operated as a key mechanism of political power. Gerda Lerner, in particular, was central to the development of feminist historiography from the 1960s to 1980s, both through her primary scholarship and her insistence on developing a new set of methodological tools that would better serve women's history.[15] By 1989, the inaugural issue of *Gender and History* argued for what we would now recognize as an intersectional methodology that grappled with the differential experiences of women of different races, nationalities, and socioeconomic classes, the historical study of masculinity, and a comparative international approach to gender.[16]

The layers of historiographical complexity prompted by these successive waves of revision from the 1960s through the 1980s made it increasingly difficult to conceive of the social as a coherent object, or even arena, of analysis. Where once the *Annalistes* sought to develop an omniscient historiography, it became increasingly difficult to imagine such a task without glossing over significant differences in human experience and valorizing one particular form of human subjectivity: white, heterosexual, wealthy, able-bodied, and male. Moreover, across the humanities and social sciences, scholars began to turn toward **cultural contextualism** as a key concern. Anthropologist Clifford Geertz argued in 1973 that cultural practices were important acts of expression and meaning-making, and he advocated "thick description" as a tool for accessing the production of those meanings.[17] Raymond Williams, leading scholar of the British cultural studies tradition, theorized **cultural materialism**, a critical approach that blended close reading of representations, careful contextualism regarding social and political forces, and attention to the processes by which subordinated peoples negotiate meaning and power in everyday life.[18] Williams' concept of "structures of feeling" seems to evoke the *Annalistes'* interest in the spirit of an age—but Williams sought to replace broad generalizations about entire societies with close readings of specific cultural struggles. Williams noted that communities, ideologies, and identities are always in flux, riven by conflicts between residual, dominant, and emergent structures of feeling.[19]

The historiographic impact of this "cultural turn" is difficult to overstate. What emerges by the 1980s and 1990s is a new model of **cultural history**, partly based on earlier modes of social history, but infused with new tools and theories. Whereas social history aims to explain societies—including such things as economic practices, civic structures, and institutions—cultural history turns toward symbolic practices and representations, material artifacts, and everyday life. In their study of James Bond intertexts, Tony Bennett and Janet Woollacott suggest a vague but productive heuristic phrase, the "**cultural surround**"—the mix of discourses, ideologies, texts, artifacts, and practices that envelop and inform any site of cultural activity. For Bennett and Woollacott, a particular artifact doesn't stand alone, and neither does a particular individual. Instead, text and reader are always mutually constitutive, held together in what they call a **reading formation**.

The reader is conceived not as a subject who stands outside the text and interprets it any more than the text is regarded as an object the reader encounters. Rather, text and reader are conceived as being co-produced within a reading formation.[20]

In practice, social and cultural history share many overlapping concerns, and many historians use both approaches. In *Homeward Bound: American Families in the Cold War Era*, for example, Elaine Tyler May turns to conventionally "social" evidence, including housing and banking policies as well as longitudinal social science research conducted in the 1950s and 1960s. At the same time, though, she reads advertisements, popular films, memoirs, and other cultural ephemera. The resulting book both documents the economic and social forces that impinged on families of the period, but also maps the kinds of material and symbolic resources through which such families understood their own identities and those around them.[21]

One of the more compelling historiographic shifts of cultural history is a rethinking of questions of **scale**. By relocating analysis away from leaders and the institutions they created, and instead toward (initially) larger social forces and (subsequently) the practices of everyday life, cultural historians have had to rethink causality and the explanatory power of any particular piece of evidence. If our interest is in, say, Lucille Ball as a studio executive, we could reasonably claim that a particular corporate memo represented her intentions and could be said to generate a series of historical effects. We know, after all, that she said "yes" to *Star Trek*. But if we're interested in *I Love Lucy* as a cultural touchstone, what counts as evidence? What does one anecdote about a group of friends reenacting the scene of Lucy and Ethel panicking on the chocolate assembly line *mean*? If I mimic their boss in that scene, swagger into the kitchen while someone is making dinner, and bellow "Let 'er roll!", I'm clearly demonstrating something about the ongoing cultural life of the show . . . but *what*, exactly?

Renaissance historian Carlo Ginzburg helped address this problem of scale by advocating what he calls **microhistory**, which he uses to characterize the analysis of small details which illuminate larger fields or conditions. Ginzburg positioned his approach specifically against the comprehensive aspirations of the *Annalistes*, and also against what he calls the "total history" of nineteenth-century literary realism. Ginzburg's interest in details doesn't lead him to search for a "typical" example (the part that stands

in, metonymically, for the whole), and he rejects what he calls Leo Tolstoy's "grand and intrinsically unrealizable project": the novelist's "conviction that a historical phenomenon can become comprehensible only by reconstructing the activities of all the persons who participated in it."[22] Ginzburg also rejects the micro as causal, which is akin to seeking that one butterfly whose flapping wings set off a chain reaction that sank the Spanish Armada and ushered in three centuries of British imperial power. Instead, Ginzburg seeks to explain the **exceptional normal**: moments that reveal the structuring conditions which produced them. Such examples might help us get beyond simply chronicling (and thus reproducing) systems of norms, and instead allow us to talk about **normalization**: the processes of conflict and negotiation by which norms emerge.

One small example conducive to this approach might be the Fox television network's awkward roll-out of the 2002 Joss Whedon space-western *Firefly*. Fox launched the show with an atypical episode with little character development, plucked out of serial narrative order, because they intended to promote it as an episodic action series on Friday nights. The show was a misfire, failing to reach the audience Fox sought, while also frustrating fans of Whedon's character-driven earlier work (particularly *Buffy the Vampire Slayer* [WB, 1997–2001; UPN, 2001–03]). *Firefly*'s cancellation is neither typical nor causal, but it might be an example of the exceptional normal. Its failure sheds light on network marketing strategies on the cusp of the streaming era, on audience and industry expectations regarding genre and authorship, and on our understanding of television narrative form in that period.

The shift toward cultural history has been particularly enriched by the distinct skills of media scholars. It is axiomatic within media studies that different forms—whether film, television, games, or other media—are not simply sites of discourse, convenient containers of ideologies and representations; instead, they are rule-governed systems with long institutional and industrial histories, and complex formal languages. Although some film scholars are skeptical about what they call "symptomatic interpretation" (i.e., reading films as emblematic of cultural conditions or ideologies), no one is likely *better* equipped to situate film and other media in their cultural environs than those with a deep training in the history and contexts in which those forms developed.[23] And for those who consider themselves to be both scholars of a particular medium and more broadly historians of culture, the media we study are important within a particular historical moment precisely *because* of their formal qualities, their distinct cultural status, and their unique conditions of production and reception.

Regardless of methodology, the choices historians make in *pursuing* research are deeply intertwined with the choices they make in *presenting* it. That's because historians' narrative choices exist in a dynamic relationship with their search for evidence. It doesn't seem a particularly radical observation that the kind of evidence we find—a fan letter, a CEO's memo about an acquisition, an FCC policy document, or an interview with a star—drives our choices about how to tell a story. But Hayden White reminds us of the inverse: that our presumptions and interests (audience studies, political economy, star studies, etc.) lead us to seek out particular information in the first place, and to see it as meaningful and probative. Only then can such information be **emplotted**—inscribed into a causal narrative in which certain pieces of information are made representative of larger patterns. Narrative, White writes,

> is more than a mode of explanation, more than a code, and much more than a vehicle for conveying information. It is not a discursive strategy or tactic that the historian may or may not use, according to some pragmatic aim or purpose. It is a means of symbolizing events without which their historicality cannot be indicated.[24]

This isn't to say, as some skeptics might, that somehow White is claiming that all meaning is arbitrary, even fictional. Even outside our current era of "alternative facts" and "fake news," that's a chilling thought. Absolute rationality and total epistemological confidence, however, are clearly impossible—and there is nothing quite so tyrannical as a regime that claims complete sovereignty over all knowledge. Perhaps it's not so much that the past is unknowable, but, simply, that knowledge is hard. And unstable. In short, history is much like the other humanist tools we use to render the world knowable: it is incomplete, partial, and subject to continual revision, which is not such a terrible place to be. After all, an incomplete conversation is one which we can join.

The Practice of Media History: Modes of Media Historiography

It would be impossible, even were this chapter to fill this entire book, to offer a comprehensive survey of the historiographic strategies of media historians. There are too many approaches, too many side conversations, and too many companion disciplines and methods. Instead, I want to use this brief space to sketch a few potential pathways through some modes of historical media scholarship, and profile some work that helped to shift the conversation by asking new questions or seeking out new materials. The examples I discuss here are admittedly narrow, focusing on the different ways in which historiographies of industries, institutions, and audiences emerged around U.S. film and television. There are always more questions, and more histories. New technologies, new forms, and new contexts invite new historiographies; some of the most dynamic of these come from the critical interventions of cultural studies, postcolonialism, critical race studies, and feminist critiques, because insights from those areas have demanded that we rethink structuring historical principles—of nations, identities, and communities. My aim here is to invite a larger inquiry into how these works characterized their objects of study, their evidence, and their implicit or explicit theorization of the medium or media in question.

"History" and "theory" are mutually constitutive ways of apprehending media forms. Media histories always make inferences about the nature of the medium, and theory is always historical, both in the sense that it makes implicit claims about the past and in the sense that it emerges in a particular intellectual and historical context. When video game scholars turned to ludology (as Matthew Payne and Nina Huntemann explain in Chapter 25), they sutured the new medium into the history of play; that gesture both theorizes and historicizes the medium.

Given its international origins, film historiography has long been complexly international. In the United States, though, scholars have long grappled with the medium's commercial development. The crisp modern cover of Benjamin Hampton's comprehensively titled 1931 book *A History of the Movies* tells readers,

> The first complete survey of the most romantic development in American business. Here is the whole story of the movies through the three and a half decades of their existence—what they are, what they do, and what they mean to millions of Americans and to the world at large.[25]

We now smile at its ambition, but these historiographic frames would pervade U.S. film scholarship for decades: questions of corporate strategy, film language, and audiences. Lewis Jacobs' 1939

The Rise of the American Film even more overtly captures the tensions implicit in the field: "Primarily the motion picture is a great popular art and, as such, concerns the art-student first, but it is also the concern of the historian and the sociologist."[26] The characterization at the heart of this sentence—"popular art"—would shape decades of film scholarship. At the same time film scholars were articulating cinema's distinctive aesthetic properties, historians sought to reconcile the industry's commercial imperatives with the products of that industry: art that was paradoxically unattributable to a single artist. (It's worth noting that at the emergence of television studies in the 1970s, scholars once again reached for this distinctive phrase to capture and reconcile the dynamic relationship between commerce and aesthetics.[27]) What was necessary was a new kind of theory, and a new kind of historiography.

It's thus not surprising that one of the most productive tensions within historical film scholarship of subsequent decades was that between industrial structures and authorship. Although critical debates moved well beyond Andrew Sarris' advocacy of French *auteur* theories, inquiry into whether and how a creative artist might articulate a distinct voice within and through the Hollywood film industry would influence a great deal of historical scholarship—not just by scholars seeking to corroborate (or refute) Sarris' claims or chart the medium's distinct aesthetic voices, but as part of an overall exploration of how the industrial process generated aesthetically coherent products.[28] Very broadly, this historiographic generalization might be understood as an exploration of questions of structure and agency, or perhaps agency through structure. Much of the scholarship that followed was rooted in archival industry research, which formed the basis of work like Tino Balio's multivolume history of United Artists, or Tom Schatz's *Genius of the System* (which relocated creative agency away from directors and toward the studios' star/genre system).[29] A similarly fundamental question shaped 1985's *The Classical Hollywood Cinema: Film Style & Mode of Production to 1960*, which lays the foundations for what David Bordwell would come to call **historical poetics**—an attempt to explain the relationship between particular aesthetic and narrative strategies and their conditions of production.[30]

Film historiography was never only concerned with Hollywood, of course, even in the United States, and industry-focused research was not its only tool. Important scholarship also insisted that we should attend to exhibition. Tom Gunning famously argued that pre-1906 films should be understood not as proto-narratives but as wondrous spectacles that were pleasurable to audiences because of their manipulation of time, space, and vision. This "cinema of attraction," as he first called it, was not a teleological step on the road to industrial narrative filmmaking, but a distinct period when cinema should be understood in the context of magic, spiritualism, and new forms of visuality. In Chapter 16 in this volume, Amanda Ann Klein provides yet another reading, using the inherently historical frameworks of genre studies to find new patterns of meaning in these films.[31]

Disagreements in film historiography between those who attempted to explain historical audiences through psychoanalytic theories of spectatorship and those who advocated empirical historical exhibition research were often contentious, but helped lead to some productive work in both directions.[32] In *An Everyday Magic*, Annette Kuhn pulled the research challenge into the center of the conversation, exploring through ethnography how people remembered their own life experiences through their experiences as cinema viewers. And Jackie Stacey directly confronted the tensions between theorized and empirical audiences, blending theories of spectatorship with analysis of historical diaries of film-viewing practices and more recent reflections from women about their film viewing in the 1940s and '50s.[33] Augmenting those research methodologies, Jacqueline Stewart has used historical research about African-American film exhibition practices to illuminate black civic life,[34] while Barbara Wilinsky considers how small theaters contributed to the development of a postwar arthouse cinema culture that would powerfully shape our understanding of independent and international film, and influence exhibition practices for decades.[35] In each of these cases, the difficulty of accessing historical audiences becomes an opportunity to rethink research tools and, eventually, to rethink how we understand the relationship between cinema and its various audiences and communities.

Scholarship in the history of broadcast media follows something of a similar trajectory of ostensible objects—industries, the texts they produce, and the audiences that engaged with them—but much of the time in very different historiographic and theoretical frames. The historiography of broadcast media is profoundly shaped by their use of public airwaves, their subsequent characterization as sites of federal regulatory control, their presence in the home, and their capacity to rearticulate civic relationships via their distinct claims on public and private life. One result of this has been a historiography of publicness and nationhood, including approaches

from mass communication and from cultural studies. Robert McChesney's *Telecommunications, Mass
Media, and Democracy*, a political economic history
of the struggles over radio licensing in the United
States, articulates broadcast media as nationally
bounded and regulated institutions that are central to civil society. Methodologically, this leads
McChesney to archival sources that represent those
public claims, such as hearings and political speech.[36]
Susan Douglas' influential account of the pre-history
of network radio is similarly rooted in questions
of publicness, with a mix of sources that reference
similar arenas of civic debate, but also the everyday
culture of wireless amateurs, who made radically different claims on the new medium.[37] Consider, also,
Michele Hilmes' *Radio Voices: American Broadcasting,
1922–1952*, which turns toward the affective bonds
and cultural experiences around which a national
community coheres.[38] Hilmes draws inspiration not
from American political economy but from theories of
nationhood and identity, feminist cultural history, and
critical race scholarship; her objects of study include
the women and African-Americans whose voices and
cultures were systematically exploited and marginalized in the development of normative national radio
programming.

Questions of publicness echo through Anna
McCarthy's *Citizen Machine*, for example, which
shows how networks, nonprofit foundations, and corporate "sponsor-citizens" articulated television as a
technology of governance, while Evan Elkins turns
toward the microhistorical, documenting a failed
attempt by former NBC president Pat Weaver to
develop a fourth television network that would better serve the public good.[39] And scholars like Aniko
Bodroghkozy, Steven Classen, and Allison Perlman
have used a variety of archival and ethnographic
methods to reconstruct public crises on and around
television as a civic institution.[40]

The cultural turn in general, and the development
of British cultural studies in particular, were essential
to the development of television historiography, in
part because they contributed new ways of thinking
about television audiences and the spaces in which
the medium was used. Television's ubiquity, everydayness, and low cultural status made it an important
site of early cultural studies work, and feminist television studies added both critical energy and new
methodological tools. The scholarship associated
with Console-ing Passions media studies conferences
in the early 1990s, in particular, often explored questions of domesticity and the often-dismissed, and
feminized, audiences of soap opera and other "low"

television. Lynn Spigel's *Make Room for TV* forcefully
argued for the mutually constitutive forces of 1950s
television and postwar suburbanization, and developed new research tools to understand the marketing
of television technologies and to assess their integration into the home. In a similar methodological vein,
but focusing on a different medium, popular music
scholar Keir Keightley's research on masculinity and
mid-century hifi culture showed how these new technologies mediated gender identities and changing
discourses of domestic space.[41]

Media historians' work has also been heavily
influenced by approaches loosely clustered under the
umbrella of the history of technology. Originally a disciplinary companion to the history of science, research
in this area has addressed a wide range of research
objects and scales of analysis, from the micro to the
epochal, articulating methodologies that were attentive to the particularities of the industries they charted,
but which also engaged to varying degrees with questions of popular culture. Carolyn Marvin's influential
When Old Technologies Were New, for example, not
only maps the emergence of new systems of communication that "annihilated space and time," but also
theorized a technological historiography that focused
not on devices, but on their users. Marvin argues,

> The early history of electric media is less the
> evolution of technical efficiencies in commu-
> nication than a series of arenas for negotiating
> issues crucial to the conduct of social life; among
> them, who is inside and outside, who may speak,
> who may not, and who has authority and may
> be believed. ... Here, the focus of communica-
> tion is shifted from the instrument to the drama
> in which existing groups perpetually negotiate
> power, authority, representation, and knowl-
> edge with whatever resources are available. New
> media intrude on these negotiations by providing
> new platforms on which old groups confront one
> another.[42]

Important differences remain, however, in how
media historians approach questions of technology. It's worth considering two different histories
of emergent technologies of the 1920s and 1930s:
Scott Higgins' history of Technicolor and Philip
Sewell's history of early experimental television.[43]
Higgins opens a window into the specialized world
of color theorists and cinematographers, with an
emphasis on new tools and aesthetic opportunities
that transformed Hollywood studio production and
cinematic language. Sewell, by comparison, is more

invested in detours, dead-ends, and missed opportunities. Higgins' richly detailed technical history maps the relatively internal processes by which studios adopted color, while Sewell veers outward, tracing a cultural debate about distance, vision, and simultaneity. Neither approach is right or wrong; they simply ask different questions, which leads them to different materials, and to different conclusions.

While these works are in some sense emblematic of their disciplinary contexts, it would be a mistake to conclude that these different methodologies are inherent to the media object in question. A relatively new approach, **media archaeology**, brings a vast range of media objects and practices into its purview—from magic lanterns to the imaging technologies on drone aircraft—aiming to understand the emergence of new (or even imaginary) media technologies.[44] Media archaeology is currently more closely associated with film studies and art history than with television studies, though for scholars working in this area the choice of object is less important than their curiosity about how technological change is enmeshed in new epistemologies and desires.

All media scholarship, historical or otherwise, speaks to questions within and across disciplines.

So, too, for the wide range of historical projects not treated here—from star studies and questions of geography to those involving representation, distribution, and transmediation. The larger challenge, both for students and professional scholars, is to assess how and why particular modes of research place their objects of analysis in particular theoretical and/or historiographic frames. Some scholars are quite generous and show their work—they clearly explain why and how they're framing their questions, and explain why those questions lead them to certain types of evidence. Others are less overt and presume more background orientation on the part of the reader. But regardless, it is worth repeating an essential observation by Hayden White: These choices of evidence and narrative are not coincidental, or arbitrary. Instead, they shape the very search for the past, and make historical argument possible.

Case Study: Children's Westerns, Transmediation, and the Origins of Global TV

The project at the heart of my case study began with a paragraph in another historian's book.

Figure 21.1 Hopalong Cassidy and one of his millions of young admirers, shown on the cover of Chevrolet's *Friends Magazine*, August 1950

Christopher Anderson's *Hollywood TV* shows how Warner Bros. extracted every last bit of utility out of older properties, particularly as they shifted production to television. He wrote that the "process of recycling occurred throughout the studio system, most literally when studios used the same costumes, props, and scenery in movie after movie. . . . Warner Bros. took this approach to the extreme, recycling screenplays—and even footage—with abandon."[45] Intrigued, I wrote a mediocre paper speculating about reused footage in low-budget children's television Westerns. Eventually, while working on another project, I discovered the papers of William Boyd, star and eventual producer of *Hopalong Cassidy* (NBC, 1949–54) at the University of Wyoming American Heritage Center, and I was hooked. Boyd had played Hoppy in dozens of "B" theatrical films, and, on the cusp of the television era, had purchased both the older films he had starred in and all rights to the character and stories. After re-editing the films for television, Boyd produced dozens of new episodes and built a merchandising and licensing empire that not only established precedents that would become familiar strategies by the Walt Disney Company and other major corporations, but which also laid the foundations for global television syndication. My article "Nothing on But Hoppy Badges" is the result of this research.[46]

I started with an interest in reruns, but merchandising and global syndication became central to the project. In over 100 cubic feet of paper records, I found reams of television sales data, but also quite a lot of information about promotional appearances and product licensing, which suggested that Boyd had built an international syndication empire by the mid-1950s, much earlier than most historians of media globalization had documented. My earlier research on spy shows and the Cold War had led me to some fascinating evidence that the producers of *Mission: Impossible* (CBS, 1966–73) had edited scripts to avoid offending international audiences; at the time, that seemed very early evidence of the impact of global sales on U.S. television production practices.[47] But the *Hopalong Cassidy* example was not only more than a decade earlier, it was incredibly robust. Particularly in a climate in which fellow media scholars were developing new insights about **transmediation**—the exploitation of intellectual property across multiple media forms—my research documented practices that we had often assumed became commonplace only later. This project also contributes to a growing body of work that shows that some of the most influential changes in television industry practices came from relative outsiders, rather than the dominant networks and studios.

The article I published doesn't contain much analysis of the television series itself. I largely left

Figure 21.2 Newspaper ads and inserts exhorted young fans to drink Hoppy-branded milk and to come to visit him on his promotional tours (undated promotional flyer, c.1951, from the collection of the author)

out questions of textual form—ironically the aspect of "recycling" that initially captured my interest. The project would likely have been enriched with more detail about the programs themselves, as well as more on the circumstances of reception in the wide range of countries where *Hopalong Cassidy* was sold. In my subsequent research, I've looked at the global distribution of other children's Westerns (particularly *The Cisco Kid*), but enormous gaps remain in what we know about global television distribution during this period. Though archival materials can be plentiful for particular programs, it can be difficult to triangulate between different programs and international contexts, particularly given the spotty archiving of early distribution records and the vastly different contexts of television development worldwide. I'm also continuing to work to expand my own literacy in television industries and forms internationally, from a robust body of scholarship about British television to new work on lesser known television systems, such as Anikó Imre's research on Eastern European TV during the Cold War.[48] The more I understand about these different local contexts, the more nuanced claims I can make about how U.S. series fit in. Mostly, this project exposed how little we know about international television in this period; there's clearly more work to do.

Conclusion: The Future of Media History?

Without a doubt, the biggest opportunities and challenges looming for media historians are related to the digital transformation of our media culture and of our media archives. Online resources have been enormously helpful in opening up access to new historical materials. Commercial streaming has provided access to programs once thought to be lost entirely, and libraries and archives have been working hard to digitize research materials that once required physical presence for access, including paper archives, celluloid film and videotape, and microfilm. Their work has been supplemented by a thriving orphan film movement that seeks to preserve abandoned works and non-commercial and personal films, through sites like TexasArchive.org and the NYU Orphan Film Symposium. What was once an immense private collection of ephemeral films (including governmental propaganda, training films, and other non-commercial materials) are now accessible publicly at archive.org, which also hosts the web history search tool the Internet Wayback Machine. The Vanderbilt Television News Archive, which once required slow and expensive searches and videotape transfers, is now accessible digitally through many university libraries. Those interested in the history of fan magazines and technical journals that have never been indexed by conventional libraries, in government documents related to media cases, or in out-of-print media scholarship will be amazed at the materials freely available at MediaHistory Project.org. And while media historians have for years hoarded (and shared) poor-quality dubs for research and teaching clips, YouTube now contains a vast, if idiosyncratic, compendium not only of commercial materials but also of home videos and other ephemera that provide a growing archival record of everyday life in a digital world. Archivists are working hard at developing new preservation strategies, based not on creating a single centralized repository but on the principle that Lots of Copies Keeps Stuff Safe (www.lockss.org). Lots of copies also make research materials more accessible.

And yet ... digital materials are in many ways even more fragile than analog media, because they are so dependent on specific hardware platforms to be played. The problem is even more acute for historians of video games and computer systems: When was the last time you saw a functioning Apple II personal computer or a Commodore 64? The last VHS player will eventually die—to say nothing of Betamax, ¾" HiMatic, or 2" commercial video tape players. Commercial digital restorations of older texts can be a boon, but they may not be exact reproductions; when Paramount restored *Star Trek: The Original Series* (CBS, 1966–69), they substituted new "improved" special effects. Lots of old TV series are syndicated on cable channels in heavy rotation; many of these are missing scenes, though, because they've been trimmed to make room for more commercials, or have different soundtracks due to licensing issues. Like archaeological artifacts taken from a dig, digital access can create at least as many problems as it solves. The unavailability of a clean HD transfer of the original *Star Wars* trilogy frustrated fans for years, which led to a creative solution: the most faithful versions of these films come not from Lucasfilm/Disney, but from "despecialized" fan edits downloadable from the darker corners of the Internet ... at least until a cease-and-desist letter shuts them down entirely. Digital distribution has extended access to some materials, but digital copyright protection can make scholarly fair use very difficult, while non-digitized material in studio catalogs and private collections becomes ever more invisible. And where will we go for the Netflix streaming archive?

As with most matters related to digital media, there are no absolutes. The shift to digital documents and email means that there will never be another paper corporate archive to match the NBC papers held at the University of Wisconsin (itself the only paper archive collection of a major U.S. television network). That is a loss to researchers, but there may yet be other opportunities. Corporations guard some data more jealously than ever, but when they do become available, researchers in computational linguistics have developed new search tools that use email databases to map corporate behavior and decision-making, which may make the opaque processes of the media industries at least occasionally more visible.[49] Digital tools have added to researchers' toolkits in other ways, too; in Chapter 27 in this collection, Miriam Posner shows how data mapping and visualization tools can be used historically to reveal interconnections within creative communities that might otherwise go unnoticed.

As we continue to grapple with each of these shifts, some pieces of the past will slip away, and others will come into view. Some of the losses will be terrible, others never noticed, which is terrible in its own way. I've spent most of this chapter arguing that historians' presumptions and narrative frameworks guide them to particular kinds of data. The reverse is true, as well. New kinds of information will lead to new conversations, for, just as narrative shapes evidence, evidence also shapes narrative—and there's always more past to discover.

There's always more present, too. The basic tools of historiography—questioning evidence, pondering causality and consequence, introspection about the representativeness of our examples, circumspection about the theoretical inclinations and narrative tropes that guide our inquiry, an eye for cultural and political contexts, and critical empathy for those we study—are invaluable across a wide range of scholarly modes. The historical imagination is ultimately less about the past than it is a kind of relationship toward knowledge: it is that vigorously reflective process by which we try to think the present historically.

Notes

1. Thomas Schatz, "Desilu, *I Love Lucy*, and the Rise of Network Television" in *Making Television: Authorship and the Production Process*, eds. Robert J. Thompson and Gary Burns (New York: Greenwood, 1990), 117–35.

2. Banks, Miranda J. "*I Love Lucy*: The Writer-Producer," in *How to Watch Television*, eds. Jason Mittell and Ethan Thompson (NYU Press, 2013), 244–252.

3. Peter Kovacs, "Big Tobacco and Broadcasting, 1923–1960: An Interdisciplinary History," Ph.D. diss., University of Texas at Austin, 2017.

4. Yeidy M. Rivero, *Broadcasting Modernity: Cuban Commercial Television, 1950–1960* (Durham: Duke, 2015).

5. Alexander Doty, "The Cabinet of Lucy Ricardo: Lucille Ball's Star Image," *Cinema Journal* 29, no. 4 (1990): 15.

6. Patricia Mellencamp, "Situation Comedy, Feminism and Freud: Discourses of Gracie and Lucy," in *Studies in Entertainment: Critical Approaches to Mass Culture*, ed. Tania Modleski (Bloomington: Indiana, 1986), 80–95.

7. Betty Friedan, *The Feminine Mystique* (New York: Norton, 1963), 15.

8. Keith Jenkins, *Rethinking History* (New York: Routledge, 2003), 13.

9. Doris Kearns Goodwin, *Team of Rivals: The Political Genius of Abraham Lincoln* (New York: Simon & Schuster, 2005).

10. John Lewis Gaddis, *The Landscape of History: How Historians Map the Past* (New York: Oxford, 2002).

11. Marc Bloch, *The Historian's Craft: Reflections on the Nature and Uses of History and the Techniques and Methods of Those Who Write It* (New York: Vintage, 1953), 157.

12. Paul Blackledge, *Reflections on the Marxist Theory of History* (Manchester: Manchester University Press, 2006), 32.

13. Frederick Jackson Turner, *The Significance of the Frontier in American History* (New York: Cornell, 1956).

14. For example, see Henry Nash Smith, *Virgin Land: The American West as Myth and Symbol* (Cambridge: Harvard, 1950); David M. Wrobel, *The End of American Exceptionalism: Frontier Anxiety from the Old West to the New Deal* (Kansas, 1992); Lucy Maddox, ed., *Locating American Studies: The Evolution of a Discipline* (Johns Hopkins, 1999); and Amy Kaplan and Donald E. Pease, eds., *Cultures of United States Imperialism* (Duke, 1993).

15. Gerda Lerner, *The Creation of Patriarchy* (New York: Oxford, 1986) and *The Majority Finds Its Past: Placing Women in History* (Durham: University of North Carolina, 1979). See also the widely cited Joan W. Scott, "Gender: A Useful Category of Historical Analysis," *The American Historical Review* 91, no. 5 (1986): 1053–75.

16. See, in particular, Evelyn Brooks Higginbotham, "Beyond the Sound of Silence: Afro-American Women in History," *Gender & History* 1, no. 1 (1989): 50–67.

17. Clifford Geertz, *The Interpretation of Cultures* (New York: Basic, 1973), 3–30.

18. Raymond Williams, *Problems in Materialism and Culture: Selected Essays* (London: Verso, 1980).

19. Raymond Williams, *Marxism and Literature* (New York: Oxford, 1977), 128–35.

20. Tony Bennett and Janet Woollacott, *Bond and Beyond: The Political Career of a Popular Hero* (London: Routledge Kegan & Paul, 1987), 64.

21. Elaine Tyler May, *Homeward Bound: American Families in the Cold War Era* (New York: Basic, 1988).

22. Carlo Ginzburg, "Microhistory: Two or Three Things That I Know about It," trans. John Tedeschi and Anne C. Tedeschi, *Critical Inquiry* 20, no. 1 (1993): 32.

23. David Bordwell, *Making Meaning: Inference and Rhetoric in the Interpretation of Cinema* (Cambridge: Harvard, 1989).

24. Hayden White, *The Content of the Form: Narrative Discourse and Historical Representation* (Johns Hopkins, 1990), 54.

25. Benjamin Bowles Hampton, *A History of the Movies* (New York: Ayer Company, 1931).

26. Lewis Jacobs, *The Rise of the American Film: A Critical History* (New York: Harcourt, Brace, 1939), 4.

27. Horace Newcomb, *TV: The Most Popular Art* (New York, Doubleday, 1974).

28. Andrew Sarris, *The American Cinema: Directors and Directions, 1929–1968* (New York: Da Capo Press, 1969).

29. Tino Balio, *United Artists: The Company Built by the Stars* (Madison: Wisconsin, 1976); Thomas Schatz, *The Genius of the System: Hollywood Filmmaking in the Studio Era* (New York: Pantheon, 1988).

30. David Bordwell, Janet Staiger, and Kristin Thompson, *The Classical Hollywood Cinema: Film Style & Mode of Production to 1960* (New York: Columbia, 1985); David Bordwell, "Historical Poetics of Cinema," in ed. R. Barton Palmer, *The Cinematic Text: Methods and Approaches* (New York: AMS Press, 1989), 369–98.

31. Tom Gunning, "The Cinema of Attraction: Early Film, Its Spectator, and the Avant-Garde," *Wide Angle* 8, no. 3–4 (1986): 63–70.

32. Robert C. Allen, "From Exhibition to Reception: Reflections on the Audience in Film History," *Screen* 31, no. 4 (1990): 347–56, and "Relocating American Film History: The 'Problem' of the Empirical," *Cultural Studies* 20, no. 1 (2006): 48–88.

33. Annette Kuhn, *An Everyday Magic: Cinema and Cultural Memory* (New York: IB Tauris, 2002); Jackie Stacey, *Star Gazing: Hollywood Cinema and Female Spectatorship* (New York: Routledge, 1994).

34. Jacqueline Najuma Stewart, *Migrating to the Movies: Cinema and Black Urban Modernity* (Berkeley: University of California, 2005).

35. Barbara Wilinsky, *Sure Seaters: The Emergence of Art House Cinema* (Minneapolis: University of Minnesota, 2001).

36. Robert W. McChesney, *Telecommunications, Mass Media, and Democracy: The Battle for the Control of U.S. Broadcasting, 1928–1935* (New York: Oxford, 1995).

37. Susan J. Douglas, *Inventing American Broadcasting, 1899–1922* (Baltimore: Johns Hopkins, 1989).

38. Michele Hilmes, *Radio Voices: American Broadcasting, 1922–1952* (Minneapolis: University of Minnesota, 1997).

39. Anna McCarthy, *The Citizen Machine: Governing by Television in 1950s America* (New York: New York University Press, 2013); Evan Elkins, "'The Kind of Program Service All the People Want': Pat Weaver's Failed Fourth Network," *Historical Journal of Film, Radio and Television* 35, no. 1 (2015): 179.

40. Aniko Bodroghkozy, *Equal Time: Television and the Civil Rights Movement* (Urbana: University of Illinois, 2012); Steven D. Classen, *Watching Jim Crow: The Struggles over Mississippi TV, 1955–1969* (Durham: Duke, 2004); Allison Perlman, *Public Interests: Media Advocacy and Struggles Over U.S. Television* (New Brunswick: Rutgers, 2016).

41. Keir Keightley, "'Turn It Down!' She Shrieked: Gender, Domestic Space, and High Fidelity, 1948–59." *Popular Music* 15, no. 2 (1996): 149–77.

42. Carolyn Marvin, *When Old Technologies Were New: Thinking About Electric Communication in the Late Nineteenth Century* (New York: Oxford, 1990), 4–5.

43. Scott Higgins, *Harnessing the Technicolor Rainbow: Color Design in the 1930s* (Austin, TX: University of Texas Press, 2007); Philip W. Sewell, *Television in the Age of Radio: Modernity, Imagination, and the Making of a Medium* (New Brunswick, NJ: Rutgers University Press, 2014).

44. Jussi Parikka, *What Is Media Archaeology?* (New York: Wiley, 2013).

45. Christopher Anderson, *Hollywood TV: The Studio System in the 1950s* (Austin: University of Texas, 1994), 181.

46. Michael Kackman, "Nothing on but Hoppy Badges: *Hopalong Cassidy*, William Boyd Enterprises, and Emergent Media Globalization," *Cinema Journal* 47, no. 4 (2008): 76–101.

47. Michael Kackman, *Citizen Spy: Television, Espionage, and Cold War Culture* (Minneapolis: University of Minnesota, 2005).

48. Imre, Anikó. *TV Socialism* (Durham: Duke, 2016).

49. Nathan Heller, "What the Enron E-mails Say About Us," *The New Yorker*, July 24, 2017.

Further Reading

Allen, Robert Clyde, and Douglas Gomery. *Film History: Theory and Practice.* Hodder & Stoughton, 1985.

Bentley, Michael, ed. *Companion to Historiography.* New York: Routledge, 2006.

Cook, James W., Lawrence B. Glickman, and Michael O'Malley, eds. *The Cultural Turn in US History: Past, Present, and Future.* University of Chicago, 2012.

Elsaesser, Thomas. *Film History as Media Archaeology: Tracking Digital Cinema*. Amsterdam University Press, 2016.

Foner, Eric. *Who Owns History?: Rethinking the Past in a Changing World*. New York: Macmillan, 2002.

Godfrey, Donald G., ed. *Methods of Historical Analysis in Electronic Media*. New York: Routledge, 2006.

Iggers, Georg G., Q. Edward Wang, and Supriya Mukherjee, *A Global History of Modern Historiography*. London: Taylor & Francis, 2016.

Lerner, Gerda. *Why History Matters: Life and Thought*. New York: Oxford, 1998.

22.
PRODUCTION
Timothy Havens

Overview

The study of how media texts get made and who stamps their authorial imprint on them goes by many names—"production studies," "media industry studies," "cultural industry studies," and "production of culture" studies, to name a few. The methods span **administrative** research, which is conducted by or for industry sponsors; **interpretive** work that seeks to understand why various production activities function as they do; and **critical** research that addresses the following theoretical questions: What role does the production and dissemination of media play in the constitution of individual and group identities? How do changes in technology alter media production and its social significance? What is the impact of the industry on the diversity of media output? And what is the industry's impact on the creative autonomy of workers?

Production studies run the gamut from amateurs who make and distribute media in their free time to multinational conglomerates that earn billions of dollars per year from high-budget projects. As such, the field is highly diverse and fragmented in its approaches and intellectual commitments. Nevertheless, production research tends to be either sociological in its orientation, methods, and objects of study, or historical, as distinct from political-economic inquiry, which is covered in Chapter 10 of this volume. Production scholars tend to treat media creators and workers in various occupations as cultural interpreters, whose understanding of the purposes of media, the needs of audiences and communities, and the potentialities of the prevalent technology shape the content of the media they produce in profound ways that can be studied, understood, and theorized.

Moreover, scholarship in this area tends to transcend any particular medium, seeking to pay as much attention to trends and practices that span different media as to those that are medium-specific. This tendency arises from the recognition that industries involved in symbol-production, which covers all of the media industries, often face similar regulatory environments and economic realities. Since the 1990s, a wave of technological convergences among traditionally distinct media industries and the consolidation of different media companies into large conglomerates have reinforced this tendency to study cross-media industry practices and developments.

General agreement exists among scholars that digital production and distribution technologies, consolidation of ownership, and the globalization of labor markets, programming markets, and media corporations have all deeply altered media production; debate centers on the impact of these changes. Some observers see decreased autonomy, increasing standardization, and the growing exploitation of labor around the world, and others argue for greater creative freedom and content diversity due to digitization and fragmentation of media distribution.

Intellectual Roots

The intellectual roots of media production studies trace from four related yet distinct traditions: ethnography and cultural studies, auteur studies, critical theory, and organizational sociology. In many ways, the study of media production can be traced back to the 1951 publication of Hortense Powdermaker's **ethnography** of filmmaking in the United States, *Hollywood: The Dream Factory*.[1] Ethnography is a research technique that involves careful, extended observations of a particular culture and interviews with informants, aiming at "thick descriptions" of complicated human activities.[2] While authorship had been important in literary studies since at least the beginning of the twentieth century (see Chapter 9 in this volume), what Powdermaker's research brought to the fore was the relationship between capitalism and culture—or commerce and art, to use her terms. This consideration remains at the heart of contemporary media production studies, as does the relationship between self-expression and technology.

Powdermaker insisted that art and commerce were inherently incompatible and used interviews and observations collected from more than a year of ethnographic work in Hollywood to argue that commerce straight-jacketed creative workers in the industry as well as the films they produced. In the immediate wake of Powdermaker's study, and somewhat contrary to her findings, film scholars studying cinemas other than Hollywood introduced the notion of "auteurism" to explain the authorial control and vision that they witnessed in non-studio films, especially French New Wave cinema. Unlike films created in the studio system, which seemed to have no particularly distinct voice, French film theorists and producers at the time used the concept of the auteur to carve out a space for creative freedom in film production. Auteur theory holds that, much like literary authors, the directors of films are in control of the production process and that they stamp their unique signatures on every film they direct. Scholars working from this perspective seek to identify the signature elements of films by particular directors, as well as how those directors navigate the organizations that they work within to achieve those visions. Similar scholarship takes place outside of film studies as well, on television producers, game designers, musicians, and others.

While critics of auteur theory often caricature the approach as naïve because it ignores the collective nature of much of media production, proponents of the approach often see the auteur more as an ideal for creatives within the media industries to aim for, rather than a manifest reality. Still, developments in the humanities disciplines in the 1960s, spurred on by Roland Barthes' essay "Death of the Author"[3] and Michel Foucault's "What is an Author?"[4] led to a substantial shift away from examining authors as the sources of cultural texts, instead focusing on texts themselves or on readers/audiences as the primary creators of meaning. In this perspective, an author is essentially an assembler of cultural fragments that predate the creation of any text, and the potential meanings of the text exceed any creative individual's ability to control them.

The shift in humanities scholarship from authorship to texts and audiences led to a lacuna in media production studies for much of the 1960s and 1970s. In the 1980s, some feminist cultural studies scholars, who had written a great deal on women's popular genres and their fans, turned their attention to studying soap opera production. Dorothy Hobson's study of the British soap opera, *Crossroads*, for instance, brought an ethnographic approach to studying both the production and the reception of soap operas, showing how feminine culture was dismissed in both realms as inferior to masculine culture.[5] This method entails observing media productions and interviewing creative workers in order to understand how the production process works, and what the implications of these inner workings are for the production of social identities, especially gender. Though infrequent through the 1980s and 1990s, this approach has become more refined and pronounced in the 2000s, as evidenced by Elana Levine's identification of five factors shaping a production culture that need to be investigated by production scholars: production restraints, the production environment, production practices and routines, the production of content, and the role of the audience in the production process.[6] These different areas of investigation continue to shape cultural studies of production to this day.

Another vein of humanistic inquiry into media production comes from production histories that explore how certain industrial changes can foster, rather than impede, creativity and artistic vision.[7] In some ways, these approaches are similar to auteur theory approaches, except that they locate the conditions for creativity not in the individual artists but rather in the intersections between artistic vision and industrial conditions. While Powdermaker's groundbreaking research emphasized the domineering tendencies of capitalist culture industries over creative artists, production histories often seek to theorize the contradictions and lapses within the industry where creativity might flourish. Studies of specific production studios have expanded to cover a range of different media organizations and production contexts, from Avi Santo's examination of the merchandising of the *Lone Ranger* franchise to Adam Abraham's study of the animation house UPA, the creators of the Mr. Magoo character, to Jean-Jacques Jura and Rodney Norman Bardin II's history of the silent film studio, Balboa Films.[8] All of this scholarship is anchored by historical research in company archives, journalistic reports, and examinations of the cultural output of the organizations, in an effort to establish (a) what is innovative about the cultural output and (b) what conditions led to those innovations.

A third root of contemporary production studies comes from the book chapter "The Culture Industry: Enlightenment as Mass Deception" by Max Horkheimer and Theodor W. Adorno, which has attracted a number of scholarly adherents and detractors.[9] Horkheimer and Adorno argued that the industrialization of cultural expression leads to a banal form of middle-brow culture that destroys human imagination and stunts critical thought. In the United States, a generation of sociologists took Horkheimer and Adorno to task for their simplistic understanding of how the cultural industries actually work. Doing what sociologists do best, these researchers sought to identify the social organization of the media industries, their process and routines, and the roles and hierarchies we find in these organizations. The purpose was to discover how these industries function and why they function as they do. Richard Peterson and David Berger, for instance, found in their study of popular music that the commercial music industry neither homogenizes music nor "gives listeners what they want," but that periods of concentration and de-concentration of ownership are correlated with more or less diversity of content. Moreover, the organizational structure of the industries and the opportunities and risks of the markets are what explain the cycles of concentration and fragmentation of ownership.[10] Training their analytic lens on labor in Hollywood filmmaking, Paul Weiss and Robert Faulkner sought to demonstrate how the specificity of film production helped create conditions where freelance, craft labor was the most efficient organization of that labor market.[11]

Rooted in organizational sociology, the scholarship in this area, which came to be known as production of culture scholarship, is decidedly functionalist, designed, as one of its founding figures writes, as a "depoliticized exploration of what Adorno . . . had earlier characterized as the industrialization of high culture."[12] Production of culture studies recognize that the cultural industries share several formal features, including the need to employ and manage creative workers, the constant search for new talent and new content, and the highly unpredictable nature of popular success. Scholars in this tradition seek to understand how the organizational features and practices of the industry shape the products that the cultural industries produce. In a similar vein, sociology of news research looks at the structures and practices of the newsroom, particularly those that impact the independence of journalists, their objectivity, and the identification and selection of news stories.

In addition to production of culture scholarship, several critical scholars also draw on critiques of the Horkheimer and Adorno chapter, in particular the work of the French sociologist Bernard Miège.[13] Miège distinguished between publishing, written press, and flow industries in order to identify the different degrees of cultural homogenization evident in distinct industries. In industries that follow the logics of publishing industries—the creation of isolated works for purchase by individual consumers—a great deal of product differentiation exists. At the other end of the spectrum, the demands of industries that work like the written press, including newspapers, magazines, and blogs, do not produce discrete cultural products, but rather a series of related products that are purchased regularly. The result of this industrial organization is that written press industries tend to produce fairly standardized fare.

The impact of Miège's scholarship was largely limited to Europe, while U.S. media industry scholarship primarily proceeded in the production of culture vein. However, the work of Joseph Turow stands out as one of the lone voices of critically informed media industry studies in the 1970s and 1980s, in particular his **power roles** theory.[14] Defining power as the capacity to withhold needed resources from another organization, Turow developed a typology of thirteen distinct power roles within the media industries, including producers, investors, authorities, patrons, linking pins, distributors, exhibitors, and the public, to name a few. Rather than an all-pervasive and indistinct form of capitalism infusing every aspect of the media industries, as in the Horkheimer and Adorno chapter, Turow's method of analysis is able to explain how conflicts, disagreements, and differences play out among the organizations involved in making media, even when all of them operate as profit-making entities.

Major Modes and Terminology of Media Production Studies

Contemporary media production studies scholarship continues to get published in most of the subfields mentioned above. In addition, the following types of critical media production studies have developed.

Creative Industries Studies

Research conducted in this vein is often practical in its conclusions, much like the production of culture scholarship described above, even as creative industries work is informed by a critical commitment to increasing media diversity and creative autonomy. In particular, work on the creative industries typically seeks to advise national policymakers on the possibilities and best practices for developing local, commercial media industries. Typically, this scholarship takes places outside the major media centers, in locales such as Australia and Denmark. John Hartley's anthology of essays, *Creative Industries*, and Richard Caves' analysis of the economics of creative enterprises, *Creative Industries: Contracts between Art and Commerce*, were central to the development of this area of scholarship.[15] Both books link what they see as changes in the global economy, particularly the growth in industries based upon producing and distributing symbolic goods, such as games and computer software, with specific policy and industry recommendations about how particular cities and nations can become centers of creative work. As such, this scholarship examines economic reports, industry innovation models, and policy initiatives. Luciana Lazzeretti's edited volume, *Creative Industries and Innovation in Europe*, is a case in point, using a comparative approach to examine the best practices available for European locales seeking to build their capacity in the creative global economy.[16] Because of its focus on helping to cultivate commercial media industries, creative industries scholarship is sometimes critiqued for being too friendly toward political and economic elites.

Critical Media Industry Studies/ Production Studies

Both of these forms of media industry scholarship stem from cultural studies of production, described above, and explore the production, distribution, and exhibition of media culture. Production studies is most closely aligned with the work of John Thornton Caldwell, particularly his book *Production Culture*, which examines how we should study contemporary Hollywood's production practices, especially in an era when, as Caldwell notes, production workers are increasingly savvy about exaggerating their own pedigrees in order to secure good press.[17] As an antidote to this tendency, Caldwell advocates analyzing

trade workers and the cultures they inhabit, interviewing film and television workers, observing production spaces, and conducting economic and industry trade journals research. Importantly, given the challenges of getting straight answers from practitioners, he advocates using all of these methods to "cross-check" information and scholarly interpretations of industry practices and developments.

Critical media industry studies was introduced in a journal article of the same name written by Timothy Havens, Amanda Lotz, and Serra Tinic.[18] The difference between this perspective and production studies scholarship is really only one of emphasis: While production studies tends to focus on creative workers in the media industries, critical media industry studies tends to cast a somewhat broader net, researching business executives, distributors, merchandisers, and others (although production studies do sometimes address these players as well).

Cultural Industry Studies

This area of research stems from Miège's response to Horkheimer and Adorno's "Culture Industry" chapter, discussed above, as well as a critical political economy of media perspective (see Chapter 10). Most scholars working in cultural industry studies are located in the United Kingdom and trace a lineage to critical political economy of the media. As such, they tend to be primarily interested in how commercial media limit the creative freedom and autonomy of artists and craftspeople, even as they see media capital as producing "complex, ambivalent, and contested" working conditions and cultural outputs.[19] Methodologically, the tools that cultural industry studies researchers use are similar to those of production studies and critical media industry studies. The difference between the approaches, instead, is usually one of emphasis: whereas the former tend to emphasize those moments when media organizations limit creativity and diversity of output, the latter often emphasize opportunities for resistance and creative freedom.

Independent Production Studies

A good deal of scholarship, particular within film studies, has looked at alternative organizational forms and how they enable the production of unique cultural products, commonly referred to as **independent** films, which are those produced outside the Hollywood studio system. In the 1970s and 1980s, feminist film scholars including Laura Mulvey and Jacqueline Bobo sought to discover, valorize, and encourage the unique filmmaking practices of feminist and Black filmmakers.[20] For their part, queer film scholars like Richard Dyer and Julianne Pidduck brought critical attention to independent LGBT films.[21] Beyond film studies, scholars of popular music such as Simon Frith have long understood independent labels as part of the larger culture of music production.[22] These early studies of feminist, minority, and LGBT media primarily focused on media texts, not their productions, except under the rubric of auteur theory.

In addition to independent media producers, amateurs and fans have always made media outside the purview of formal media organizations. The study of amateur production developed in the 1980s and 1990s. One of the most notable examples is Henry Jenkins' study of fan culture related to the *Star Trek* franchise and how fans wrote fiction that reimagined characters and storylines to better fit their own social positions and perceptions of the characters.[23] As both an observer and a participant in *Star Trek* fan culture, Jenkins was able to gain access to conventions, reunions, and fan materials, and he could describe in detail how and why fans of the television series and films create fan culture. In a similar vein, Mary Celeste Kearney examined how teenage girls have been engaged in reworking dominant media portrayals of gender and sexuality since the 1960s and continue to do this work of reimagining themselves through media productions that often fly under the radar of the dominant media and the popular press.[24] Because of the non-mainstream nature of much of girl-produced media, Kearney relied on interviews with creators, personal and professional networks, and alternative media outlets to understand how these forms of amateur and independent media get produced and consumed, and what they mean to the girls involved in the culture.

With the growth in digital production and distribution due to the roll-out of broadband Internet access in the United States and the developed world, amateur cultural production has flourished. For some observers, these new forms of production and distribution, as well as the expansion of funding possibilities like crowdsourcing, offer some of the most innovative and important aspects of media production today. Because much of this activity takes place outside the formal economies and organizations involved in corporate media production, the focus of scholarship about amateur and do-it-yourself cultural production typically examines questions of individual and community identity production through the process of media production. Vicki Mayer, for instance, explores how nonprofit Mexican American video producers in San Antonio, Texas, in the late 1990s worked to produce different conceptualizations of Mexican Americans as subjects of media representation and as citizens of the United States.[25]

Technologies of Media Production

A good deal of the technical study of the technologies of media production is limited to engineering journals, user handbooks, and textbooks on how to operate equipment. However, critical scholars over the years have turned their attention to careful analysis of the impact of particular technologies on textual aesthetics and ideologies. This kind of research requires the researcher to understand the technologies of media-making as thoroughly as they understand aesthetics and culture, and most of the analytical work involves making compelling connections between technological function, aesthetic elements, and cultural practice. Caldwell, for instance, has examined a number of digital editing techniques in the television industry and their capacity to mark certain kinds of texts as "trash" or quality.[26] Similarly, Leo Enticknap seeks to understand how major developments throughout the history of film production have influenced the style and aesthetics of cinema.[27]

Cultural Economy Approaches

Also growing out of the British cultural studies tradition, in particular the emphasis on cultural roots of economic practices and the importance of ethnographic observation as a method, this approach looks quite broadly at the symbolic tools, from paper and pen to computer code, that get employed in commercial industries and how they shape the economics of those industries. Although media industries are among those researched, the approach aims to include a much broader research agenda, as indicated by the chapters in the book *Cultural Economy* (2002), which address computer software in manufacturing industries, the performance of identity in scientific labs, and the role of aesthetics in creating economic value in the music industry.[28] This form of scholarship brings together researchers in economic sociology, media and cultural studies, and science and technology studies. However, since the early years of the 2000s, the approach has been somewhat overshadowed by the turn to creative industry studies discussed above.

Main Issues in Production

Across all of these modes of analysis, a consistent set of issues and terms tends to get deployed. The main issues include **concentration of ownership**, technological change, and globalization. Concentration of ownership refers to the shrinking number of multinational corporations that control the majority of media profits in the United States and abroad. Typically, these conglomerates own production, distribution, and exhibition companies across all types of media and in all parts of the world. Perhaps the best-known chronicler of this trend has been Ben Bagdikian, whose measurements of market concentration reveal that, in the twenty-first century, only five corporations controlled the vast majority of media in the United States, down from twenty-five companies in the 1980s.[29]

The growing concentration of ownership in the media industries was spurred by **deregulation** of those industries by national governments around the world in the 1980s and 1990s. While many nations had strict controls on media industries throughout the twentieth century, those industries successfully lobbied to have them removed, first in the United States and the United Kingdom and later across Europe and Asia, with the help of the U.K. and U.S. governments. Simultaneously, many nations privatized their media systems, most of which, outside the Western Hemisphere, had been publicly funded until the 1990s. Consequently, a global system of private, commercially driven, multimedia organizations has developed worldwide, many of which are owned or co-owned by a small number of transnational firms. In addition to globalization and privatization, the media industries have been rocked in recent decades by the growth of digital production, distribution, and exhibition, which has created new revenue streams, caused old streams to dry up, introduced new competitors, eliminated old ones, and generally upended a good deal of the business.

The analysis of large-level, systemic developments in regulation, technology, and the economy generally fall under the purview of political economy approaches to media. Media production scholars tend to focus instead on the autonomy of media workers who are employed by these globally integrated digital media companies and the diversity (or lack thereof) of content that these companies produce. Susan Baker and David Hesmondhalgh, on the one hand, found through interviews across the media industries that economic pressures in the industry and the increasing casualization of the workforce led creative workers to devote more and more time to networking and fundraising, and less and less time to autonomous creative activities. Regarding diversity of content, on the other hand, Ron Becker has shown how the technological and economic changes related to post-network television gave rise to an explosion of gay characters on television in the 1990s, even as those forces also delimited the range of gay characters in terms of gender, race, and class.[30]

Some media production scholars have identified broad, industry-wide trends associated with issues of worker autonomy and diversity of media content. Justin Wyatt identifies a particular type of media product—the "high concept" film or television series—that can be easily explained to studios and networks, as well as the general audience, and helps with marketing and **synergies** across media conglomerates and products. Synergies are opportunities for cross-promotion and media development designed to drive fans of a particular media product toward other media products that share similar characters and storylines. Wyatt used his prior status as an industry executive to gain access to how executives talk and think, and linked this terminology to broader patterns in the industry of consolidation and synergy.

Beyond concentration of ownership, several researchers have examined the impact of globalization on autonomy and diversity. Toby Miller and his colleagues, for example, suggest that globalization and digitization have led to a "New International Division of Cultural Labor," in which highly-skilled creative work is located primarily in the well-to-do Western nations, while media workers elsewhere are generally left unskilled, underpaid, and vulnerable.[31] On the contrary, Michael Curtin notes that numerous creative media centers have sprung up around the world, most of which are integrally linked with transitional markets. He developed the concept of "media capitals" in order to explain the forces of creative migration, financial concentration, and distributive reach that global cities today must possess in order to achieve the status of a media capital.[32] Meanwhile, Henry Jenkins, Sam Ford, and Joshua Green have coined the term **spreadable media** to identify, among other things, the kind of media content that is likely to receive extensive circulation today across media platforms.[33] In this perspective, the technological environment encourages certain kinds of textual practices, while discouraging others. Among these are **convergent media**, which refers to the way in which digital media environments erase boundaries between fans, texts, and producers.[34]

Finally, Derek Johnson explores the development of **franchising** in contemporary media industries, where certain stories and characters get leveraged across multiple media platforms and numerous iterations in order to develop synergies among popular media.[35] For instance, Marvel Worldwide comic book characters such as Wolverine and Spiderman attract viewers to films based on these characters, while the films drive fans back to the comic books, as well as numerous other media including games, TV shows, and novels. Adopting a production studies or critical media industry studies perspective, Johnson explores the impact of franchising on both textual diversity and the autonomy of creative workers working within franchises.

In addition to scholarship centered on creative autonomy and textual diversity, some researchers look at how large-scale systemic developments like deregulation and concentration of ownership filter down into day-to-day industry practices and strategies. Turow, for instance, has extensively chronicled how the marketing and advertising industries have come to collect more and more digital data on consumers and to produce increasingly precise profiles of consumers' behaviors, tastes, social networks, and more. Amanda Lotz, meanwhile, examines the technological and economic changes taking place in the American television industry in order to map out the new revenue streams, business practices, technological implements, and textual possibilities of contemporary television.[36]

Finally, working from the observation that digitization has opened up new opportunities for the production, funding, and circulation of alternative and amateur media, several scholars of new media production have begun exploring these possibilities, their limitations, and the ways in which they challenge conventional practices in industrial media production studies. Axel Bruns has argued that, rather than a strict division between producers and consumers of media, digital media spaces are characterized by an ongoing, interactive process of "produsage," in which media content is consistently changed and updated with direct fan consultation.[37] **Produsage** is a new form of participatory culture, in which voices that were marginalized or excluded from mass media in the past can now gain access. Digital video spaces like YouTube, in particular, offer the opportunity for user-generated content to be produced and circulated outside of the demands of the commercial media industries. At the same time, these amateur media spaces have an economy of their own, where reputation leads to

increased viewership, subscriptions, and "likes." As commercial media owners like Google have taken over ownership of sites like YouTube, they have been able to parlay contributor's reputations into advertising dollars, blurring the distinction between amateur and professional media producers.

Collaborative forms of produsage have flourished in recent years, in particular among groups traditionally excluded from or stereotyped by mass media. Many scholars who study these production practices make outreach to creative communities a central part of their methodology, creating a feedback loop between media production and scholarship *about* media production that has largely been absent in U.S.-based media production research. Mary Gray's *Out in the Country*, for instance, demonstrates how LGBT youth living in rural America utilize digital media to participate in global-local alliances of production and consumption that give participants meaning, identity, and needed resources.[38] In a similar vein, Aymar Jean Christian has shown how the Internet creates opportunities for queer media producers and producers of color to create television and video content that is both profitable *and* provides settings, stories, characters, and aesthetic choices that rarely appear in conventional mass media.[39] Christian is both a creator and a scholar of web television series that feature Black and LGBT themes and characters, who sees his role as a chronicler and curator of this content, as well as a creator and a critic. He not only publishes interviews with creators working in this medium, but also created a forum for making and funding web series projects in the Chicago area, Open TV. In this way, Christian is a good example of a new breed of production scholar who critiques and produces, but also engages the creative community more broadly by trying to find ways to nurture and fund new talent.

Case Study: Minority Television in a Global, Post-Network Era

The case study that I want to discuss as an example of production studies comes from my book chapter entitled "Minority Television Trade as Cultural Journey: The Case of New Zealand's *bro'Town*."[40] The chapter examines the global circulation of an animated New Zealand series, trying to tease out how the logics of contemporary global media trade permit the worldwide circulation of culturally specific minority television, when most models of global media assume that widely circulated content has to be culturally nonspecific and universal.

The book chapter falls most clearly into the critical media industries perspective, as described above: it examines media industry practices through a combination of sources, including trade-journal and online research into which foreign channels bought the series and why, interviews with the series' producers, promotional materials provided by the producers, and textual analysis of the series. Ultimately, the chapter seeks to examine the impact of global commercial media on diversity of media content—in this instance, a particular moment in which the industry permits the production and circulation of diverse media content. In order to make this argument, I cite a good deal of secondary literature that discusses the impact of globalization and commercialization on the diversity of television content, particularly arguments about the disappearance of cultural specificity in globally circulated texts.

The major claim of my chapter is that recent, post-network developments in global television have provided the opportunity for culturally specific, minority television programming to circulate worldwide. Specifically, niche channels have prompted programmers to rethink the television viewer's willingness to confront difference, confusion, and complexity, which has led to a growing perception that viewers are willing to embark on a "cultural journey" when they encounter foreign programming. I begin by analyzing an episode from the series *bro'Town* in order to demonstrate how the humor, the characters, the speech, the setting, and the storyline mark the series as distinctly Polynesian-New Zealand. While White New Zealanders and foreigners can understand much of the series, they also inevitably miss out on many of the cultural allusions and much of the humor. In addition, the political stance of the episode is undoubtedly pro-Polynesian minority and anti-White majority. Next, I look at the thirteen foreign markets that purchased the series and find three different kinds of buyers: those from "culturally proximate" markets that have a large Polynesian audience and produce very little of their own programming, for whom it makes good economic sense to import a cheaper foreign series; those from international, youth-oriented channels far from New Zealand; and those from channels that specifically target minority or indigenous viewers in different parts of the world, including the Canadian Aboriginal People's Network.

The study next looks at prevalent attitudes about the series and its global success among industry insiders, particularly Fox Latin America, which purchased rights to the series and programmed it. By examining debates about how and whether to translate specific Polynesian terms into Spanish, it became clear that these executives were thinking about audiences in ways that global television executives typically do not. In particular, they were talking about audiences being on a "cultural journey" when they watch television, willing to encounter different cultures and to struggle to understand difficult words and jokes. I knew from earlier interviews I had conducted with executives that this was very different than the typical image of viewers as people who do not want anything challenging on the small screen and flip the channels when they encounter something they don't understand or need to think about.

Finally, then, my chapter argues that this image of the viewer as being on a "cultural journey" is an emerging way of thinking about audiences that differs from conventional thinking in which viewers are attracted to "universal themes" in imported programming. Moreover, I argue this new way of thinking stemmed directly from the fact that these executives had to rely a lot on imported programming and were trying to figure out the tastes of youth audiences, rather than an adult or a family audience. On a theoretical level, the case is significant because it demonstrates that media globalization and cultural homogenization need not go hand-in-hand. On a practical level, it also shows television producers, particular minority producers, that numerous sales outlets for their products might exist around the world.

Although I believe that my chapter does hit on a potentially emerging way of thinking about television programs and audiences among television executives that has the potential to facilitate the production and circulation of global minority television, the essay does have its limitations. The chapter does not, for instance, explore how widespread the industry lore about "cultural journeys" is; instead, the evidence of a shift in industry discourse about minority programming comes from email exchanges among *bro'Town*'s producer, buyer, and distributor, as well as trade journal research. The argument would benefit from case studies of other series that exhibit extensive minority cultural content and that have succeeded in selling abroad. More opportunity to interview program merchants and translators around the world would have given a clearer index of how widespread the discourse of "cultural journeys" truly is.

One of the main obstacles that I faced in collecting additional examples is simply the lack of access to globally-circulated minority texts that do not originate from within U.S. culture. While *bro'Town* happened to find its way onto the upper reaches of my digital satellite service, the vast majority of non-U.S. minority television content is rarely aired in the United States. While streaming services have opened up access to much of the world's television content, accessing it still often requires the technical skills necessary to establish virtual private network (VPN) tunnels. Even more fundamentally, though, the lack of *awareness* of non-American minority television content and lack of language skills can be basic barriers to studying the global circulation of minority television programming. For those U.S. series that primarily target racial and ethnic minorities, such as *Chappelle's Show* (Comedy Central, 2003–06), I knew it would be difficult to get access to interviews with distributors, in particular. This is a growing concern for those of us who study media production, which is why a good deal of research in the area has shifted to smaller productions and non-U.S. productions.

Future Research

The explosion of streaming media services in the second decade of the twenty-first century has upended a good deal of settled scholarly beliefs about media economics, regulations, markets, distribution, production, and consumption. Jade Miller and Brian Larkin, for instance, have examined the role of informal media exhibition and distribution in the global popularity of Nollywood videofilms, which are low-budget movies produced in Nigeria and exported around the world.[41] As broadband Internet access becomes more widespread and robust, it facilitates the sharing of high-quality video content and brings to the center of production studies the relationship between formal and informal media economies. One of the primary reasons that this relationship is so central is that informal and small-scale distribution networks create the possibility for numerous groups that have traditionally been excluded from the commercial media industries to produce, circulate, and consume media content that they find relevant. At the same time, the more we consume, share, and comment online, the more we subject ourselves to surveillance by commercial interests and the national security state.

The predicament of the digital media revolution strikes at the core of many issues in production studies. How do we understand cultural difference and survival in a borderless cyberspace? How do culture and power interact in an era of fragmentation and surveillance? How do we evaluate the increased visibility and autonomy of individuals and communities of all kinds with the increased possibilities for exploitation this visibility makes possible? These are the fundamental questions that will drive production studies in the years to come.

Notes

1. Hortense Powdermaker, *Hollywood, The Dream Factory: An Anthropologist Looks at the Movie-Makers* (Boston: Grosset & Dunlap, 1950).
2. Clifford Geertz, *The Interpretation of Cultures* Vol. 5019 (New York: Basic Books, 1973).
3. Roland Barthes, *Image-Music-Text*, trans. Stephen Heath (New York: Hill & Wang, 1977).
4. Michel Foucault, "What Is an Author?" in *Michel Foucault: Aesthetics, Method, and Epistemology*, ed. James D. Faubion, trans. Robert Hurley, et al. (New York: The New Press, 1998), 205–22.
5. Dorothy Hobson, *"Crossroads": The Drama of a Soap Opera* (London: Metheun, 1982).
6. Elana Levine, "Toward a Paradigm for Media Production Research: Behind the Scenes at *General Hospital*," *Critical Studies in Media Communication* 18, no. 1 (2001): 66–82.
7. Tino Balio, *United Artists: The Company Built by Stars* (Madison: University of Wisconsin Press, 1976); Jane Feuer, Paul Kerr, and Tise Vahimagi, *MTM: Quality Television* (London: BFI Press, 1983); Thomas Schatz, *The Genius of the System: Hollywood Filmmaking in the Studio Era* (New York: Pantheon Books, 1988).
8. Avi Santo, *Selling the Silver Bullet: The Lone Ranger and Transmedia Brand Licensing* (Austin: University of Texas Press, 2015); Adam Abraham, *When Magoo Flew: The History of Animation Studio UPA* (Middletown: Wesleyan University Press, 2012); Jean-Jacques Jura and Rodney Norman Bardin II, *Balboa Films: A History and Filmography of the Silent Film Studio* (Jefferson: McFarland & Co., 2009).
9. Max Horkheimer and Theodor W. Adorno, *Dialectic of Enlightenment*, trans. John Cumming (New York: Continuum, 1987).
10. Richard A. Peterson and David G. Berger, "Cycles in Symbol Production: The Case of Popular Music," *American Sociological Review* (1975): 158–73.
11. Paul R. Weiss and Robert R. Faulkner, "Credits and Craft Production: Freelance Social Organization in the Hollywood Film Industry, 1964–1978," *Symbolic Interaction* 6, no. 1 (1983): 111–23.
12. Paul M. Hirsch, "Culture Industries Revisited," *Organization Science* 11 (2000): 356–61.
13. Bernard Miège, *The Capitalization of Cultural Production* (New York: International General, 1987).
14. Joseph Turow, *Media Systems in Society: Understanding Industries, Strategies, and Power* (New York: Longman, 1997).

15. John Hartley, ed., *Creative Industries* (London: Blackwell Publishing, 2005); Richard E. Caves, *Creative Industries: Contracts between Art and Commerce* (Cambridge: Harvard University Press, 2000).

16. Luciana Lazzeretti, ed., *Creative Industries and Innovation in Europe: Concepts, Measures and Comparative Case Studies* (New York: Routledge, 2012).

17. John Thorton Caldwell, *Production Culture: Industry Reflexivity and Critical Practice in Film and Television* (Durham: Duke University Press, 2008).

18. Timothy Havens, Amanda D. Lotz, and Serra Tinic, "Critical Media Industry Studies: A Research Approach," *Communication, Culture, Critique* 2 (2009): 234–253.

19. David Hesmondhalgh, *The Cultural Industries*, 2nd edition (London: Sage, 2012).

20. Laura Mulvey, *Visual and Other Pleasures* (London: Palgrave Macmillan UK, 1989); Jacqueline Bobo, ed., *Black Women Film and Video Artists* (New York: Routledge, 1998).

21. Richard Dyer and Julianne Pidduck, *Now You See It: Studies in Lesbian and Gay Film* (London: Routledge, 2003).

22. Simon Frith, *Performing Rites: On the Value of Popular Music* (Cambridge: Harvard University Press, 1998).

23. Henry Jenkins, *Textual Poachers: Television Fans and Participatory Culture* (London: Taylor & Francis, 1992).

24. Mary Celeste Kearney, *Girls Make Media* (New York: Routledge, 2006).

25. Vicki Mayer, *Producing Dreams, Consuming Youth: Mexican Americans and Mass Media* (New Brunswick: Rutgers University Press, 2003).

26. John Thornton Caldwell, *Televisuality: Style, Crisis, and Authority in American Television* (New Brunswick: Rutgers University Press, 1995).

27. Leo Enticknap, *Moving Image Technology: From Zoetrope to Digital* (London: Wallflower Press, 2005).

28. Paul du Gay and Michael Pryke, eds., *Cultural Economy: Cultural Analysis and Commercial Life* (London: Sage, 2002).

29. Ben H. Bagdikian, *The New Media Monopoly* (Boston: Beacon Press, 2004).

30. David Hesmondhalgh and Sarah Baker, *Creative Labour: Media Work in Three Cultural Industries* (London: Routledge, 2010); Ron Becker, *Gay TV and Straight America* (New Brunswick: Rutgers University Press. 2006).

31. Toby Miller, Nitin Govil, John McMurria, Ting Wang, and Richard Maxwel, *Global Hollywood 2* (London: BFI Publishing, 2008).

32. Michael Curtin, *Playing to the World's Biggest Audience: The Globalization of Chinese Film and TV* (Berkeley: University of California Press, 2007).

33. Henry Jenkins, Sam Ford, and Joshua Green, *Spreadable Media: Creating Value and Meaning in a Networked Culture* (New York: New York University Press, 2013).

34. Henry Jenkins, *Convergence Culture: Where Old and New Media Collide* (New York: New York University Press, 2006).

35. Derek Johnson, *Media Franchising: Creative License and Collaboration in the Culture Industries* (New York: New York University Press, 2013).

36. Amanda Lotz, *The Television Will Be Revolutionized*, 2nd edition (New York: New York University Press, 2015); Joseph Turow, *The Daily You: How the New Advertising Industry Is Defining Your Identity and Your Worth* (New Haven: Yale University Press, 2011).

37. Axel Bruns, *Blogs, Wikipedia, Second Life, and Beyond: From Production to Produsage* (New York: Peter Lang, 2008).

38. Mary L. Gray, *Out in the Country: Youth, Media, and Queer Visibility in Rural America* (New York: New York University Press, 2009).

39. Aymar Jean Christian, "Video Stars: and Indie Entrepreneurs: Marketing Marginality in New Media Economies," in *Intersectional Internet: Race, Sex, and Culture Online*, ed. Andre Brock (New York: Peter Lang, 2014), 78–94.

40. Timothy Havens, "Minority Television Trade as Cultural Journey: The Case of New Zealand's *bro'Town*," in *Watching While Black: Centering the Television of Black Audiences*, ed. Beretta Smith-Shomade (New Brunswick: Rutgers University Press, 2012) 232–46.

41. Jade L. Miller, *Nollywood Central* (New York: Palgrave Macmillan, 2016); Brian Larkin, *Signal and Noise: Media, Infrastructure, and Urban Culture in Nigeria* (Durham: Duke University Press, 2008).

Further Reading

Anthropology

De Boer, Stephanie. *Co-Producing Asia: Locating Japanese-Chinese Regional Film and Media*. Minneapolis: University of Minnesota Press, 2014.

Lukács, Gabriella. *Scripted Affects, Branded Selves: Television, Subjectivity, and Capitalism in 1990s Japan*. Durham: Duke University Press, 2010.

Moeran, Brian, ed. *Asian Media Productions*. Honolulu: University of Hawai'i Press, 2001.

Creative Industry Studies

Flew, Terry. *Creative Industries: Culture and Policy*. London: Sage, 2012.

Flew, Terry. *Global Creative Industries*. Indianapolis: John Wiley & Sons, 2013.

Hartley, John, Jason Potts, Stuart Cunningham, Terry Flew, Michael Keane, and John Banks, eds. *Key Concepts in Creative Industries*. Thousand Oaks: Sage, 2012.

Jones, Candace, Mark Lorenzen, and Jonathan Sapsed, eds. *The Oxford Handbook of Creative Industries.* Oxford: Oxford University Press Handbooks, 2015.

Potts, Jason. *Creative Industries and Economic Evolution.* North Hampton: Edward Elgar Publishing, 2011.

Cultural Industry Studies

Fitzgerald, Scott Warren. *Corporations and Cultural Industries: Time Warner, Bertelsmann, and News Corporation.* New York: Lexington Books, 2011.

Oakley, Kate, and Justin O'Connor, eds. *The Routledge Companion to the Cultural Industries.* New York: Routledge, 2015.

Saha, Anamik. *Race and the Cultural Industries.* London: Polity Press, 2017.

Critical Media Industry Studies/ Cultural Industry Studies

Curtin, Michael, Jennifer Holt, and Kevin Sanson, eds. *Distribution Revolution: Conversations about the Digital Future of Film and Television.* Oakland: University of California Press, 2014.

Curtin, Michael, and Kevin Sanson. *Precarious Creativity: Global Media, Local Labor.* Oakland: University of California Press, 2016.

Elkins, Evan. *Locked Out: Regional Restrictions in Digital Entertainment Culture.* New York: New York University Press, 2018.

Holt, Jennifer, and Alisa Perren, ed. *Media Industries: History, Theory, and Method.* Oxford: Wiley-Blackwell, 2008.

Levine, Elana, ed. *Cupcakes, Pinterest, and Ladyporn: Feminized Popular Culture in the Early Twenty-First Century.* Urbana: University of Illinois Press, 2015.

Morris, Jeremy. *Selling Digital Music, Formatting Culture.* Berkeley: University of California Press, 2015.

Sociology

Bielby, Denise, and C. Lee Harrington. *Global TV: Exporting Television and Culture in the World Market.* New York: New York University Press, 2008.

Deuze, Mark. *Media Work.* Malden: Polity, 2008.

Gitlin, Todd. *Inside Prime Time.* London: Routledge, 1983.

Hirsch, Paul. "Processing Fads and Fashions: An Organization-Set Analysis of Cultural Industry System." *American Journal of Sociology* 77 (1972): 639–59.

Moeran, Brian, and Jesper Strandgaard Pedersen, eds. *Negotiating Values in the Creative Industries: Fairs, Festivals and Competitive Events.* Cambridge: Cambridge University Press, 2011.

Peterson, Richard A., and Narasimhan Anand. "The Production of Culture Perspective." *Annual Review of Sociology* 30 (2004): 311–34.

Independent Production Studies

Holmlund, Christine, and Justin Wyatt, eds. *Contemporary American Independent Film: From the Margins to the Mainstream.* New York: Routledge, 2004.

Kruse, Holly. *Site and Sound: Understanding Independent Music Scenes.* Vol. 1. New York: Peter Lang, 2003.

Langlois, Andrea, and Frédéric Dubois. *Autonomous Media: Activating Resistance & Dissent.* Montreal: Cumulus Press, 2005.

Ortner, Sherry B. *Not Hollywood: Independent Film at the Twilight of the American Dream.* Durham: Duke University Press, 2013.

Rascaroli, Laura, Gwenda Young, and Barry Monahan, eds. *Amateur Filmmaking: The Home Movie, the Archive, the Web.* New York: Bloomsbury Academic, 2014.

PART III

EMERGENT AND CHALLENGING OBJECTS

23.
POPULAR MUSIC
Norma Coates

Popular music studies is much like **popular music**. Popular music contains many different genres, for example hip-hop, pop, and rock, while popular music scholars approach it from many disciplines and with many methodologies. Fans feel strongly about "their" music, and scholars advocate fiercely for their approach to popular music studies. Popular music and popular music studies are challenging, meaningful, and vibrant. Popular music refracts and reflects our culture and society, as well as our individual identities, desires, and sense of ourselves. Accordingly, popular music studies enables us to understand why and how popular music means so much to so many—as culture, as part of an industry, as music, as entertainment, as history, and more.

Popular music studies takes two very different forms in academia. Within music schools, faculties, and departments, popular music is defined by what it is not, **classical music**, also called **Western art music**. Classical music was long privileged as high culture in and out of the academy; consequently, popular music was ignored or dismissed. That has changed, as more musicologists focus their attention on popular music. **Popular musicologists** attend to the **textual** and **formal** aspects of "the music itself" using techniques adapted from the study of classical music. They may, for example: focus on the written scores of popular songs or a body of work employing the technical tools of musical notation and music theory; produce diagrams analyzing a performer's oeuvre; or study the formal musical and lyrical techniques used to craft songs. Others study how recordings are shaped in the studio by musicians working in tandem with producers and engineers.

This chapter focuses on another way of conceptualizing and studying popular music, asserting that popular music is much more than its formal and technical aspects, or the notes and lyrics, of "the music itself." Popular music studies, in this mode, is interested in how popular music works in and as culture and how it is mobilized socially, individually, and within and across media to make meaning. Popular music scholars in the humanities and social sciences are broadly concerned with the industrial production, circulation, and consumption of popular music and the myriad forms of and practices within these and other categories.

These two approaches to popular music studies can and do overlap. Some popular musicologists include cultural analysis in their studies, and many popular music scholars in the humanities and social sciences discuss how music works using the technical language of musical analysis. The difference lies in whether the researcher treats popular music as musical object or cultural signifier.

Intellectual History

Popular music studies is an evolving field; what follows is a snapshot of major moments in its development. Popular song lyrics first drew the attention of communication scholars in the 1950s who used content analysis, a social science methodology, to explore contemporary American values as reflected in the lyrics of pop songs. Popular music scholar Martin Cloonan locates the seeds of what would become popular music studies in the rise of popular youth music of the 1960s, specifically the global success of the Beatles.[1] Their music, including song lyrics, was analyzed by distinguished classical musicologists including Wilfred Mellers, and discussed in prestigious newspapers and journals using the language of classical music analysis.[2]

Popular song lyrics drew the attention of sociologist Donald Horton, among others, before the advent of rock and roll in the mid-1950s.[3] Literary critics began to scrutinize the "poetic" language of rock lyrics, for example those of Bob Dylan, beginning in the mid-1960s using theories and methods developed within their field.[4] **Lyrical analysis** was and is useful but limited in its utility. Unlike poetry, popular music lyrics can rarely stand on their own. A popular song's meaning is often conveyed as much by its sound and arrangement as by its lyrics. Unlike poetry, song lyrics might seem to mean one thing when read but something entirely different when heard.

Cultural studies, developed and practiced by a group of neo-Marxist sociologists at the Birmingham Centre for Contemporary Cultural Studies (CCCS) in the mid-1970s, is a foundation of popular music studies. Cultural studies legitimized the academic study of popular and lived culture. CCCS researchers initially focused on the everyday politics of class by studying post-World War II working-class youth **subcultures** in Great Britain. They sought to understand how and why Teddy Boys, Rockers, Mods and other "spectacular subcultures" used everyday items such as clothes and music to express their difference from their working-class parents and to signal their resistance to the dominant culture. *Resistance Through Rituals: Youth Subcultures in Post-War Britain* (1975) collected the initial working papers of the group. The volume established some of the methodological and intellectual investments that enabled and shaped popular music studies.[5]

CCCS scholar Dick Hebdige's influential *Subculture: The Meaning of Style*, initially published in 1979, combined theoretical insights from the sociology of deviance, semiotics, and structuralism to closely examine how race and class, among other things, were deeply structured and made visible as subcultural style.[6] His discussion of postwar subcultures focused primarily upon punk as it emerged in mid-1970s Great Britain. Hebdige linked the postwar migration of West Indians to Great Britain and the proximity of black and white youth in that era, to the subsequent influence of reggae music and culture on the punk subculture and its stylistic and musical manifestations.

By the late 1970s and early 1980s, **popular music criticism**, especially **jazz** and **rock journalism**, had created a common language for thinking

and writing about popular music, deployed in jazz magazine *Downbeat, Crawdaddy, Rolling Stone*, and *Creem* in the United States, and *New Musical Express* and *Melody Maker* in Great Britain. Simon Frith, a rock critic and sociologist of culture, was the first to take a critical sociological stance toward popular music as a cultural object itself, not only as an element of a subculture. His 1979 monograph, *The Sociology of Rock*, established the cultural significance of the "outside" elements of popular music, including its industry, audiences, creators, performances, and imbrication in the concept, not just chronological age, of youth.[7] In *Performing Rites*, published in 1996, Frith grappled with ideas of taste and perceptions of the value of popular music through explorations of genre, rhythm, identity, and performance in order to understand how music makes meaning, for whom, and why.[8] Frith was among the first to approach popular music as an industrial product, theorize the impact of copyright on popular music, thickly describe live performance, provoke debates about the relationship between rock music and television, and discuss sexuality in popular music. Any research project or paper in popular music studies should begin with a check to see what Frith has written about the topic.

By 1990, popular music studies was established enough to warrant its first major anthology. *On Record: Rock, Pop & the Written Word*, edited by Frith and cultural studies scholar Andrew Goodwin, collected articles that influenced the field and provided a snapshot of popular music studies at that moment, emphasizing subcultures, scenes, creativity, musical analysis, industrial organization, sexuality, and fandom.[9] The volume remains a valuable resource and a document of an emerging field at the moment when new intellectual movements would further extend its methodological and analytical investments.

Post-structuralism, a form of radical critique that emerged out of **structuralism**, was taken up in the academic humanities, including popular music studies, in the 1980s and 1990s. Like structuralism, post-structuralism views all human activity as constructed, not natural. Post-structuralism eschews the idea that cultures are governed by deep structures that organize and order all content, asserting instead that origins and foundations do not exist. Meaning is therefore unstable and subjectivity decentered. Post-structuralism is keenly interested in how knowledge is produced and naturalized as "truth." It is therefore concerned with history and the relationship of an era's dominant belief systems to the constitution of knowledge.

Consequently, for cultural studies and related areas of inquiry such as popular music studies, class was no longer the privileged modality of analysis. Scholars trained in post-structuralism raised questions of identity, including sexuality, race, gender, and ethnicity in their research. Queer theory, postcolonial studies, critical race studies, media studies, and more developed as theoretical frameworks in the wake of post-structuralism. Popular music scholars influenced by post-structuralism denaturalized taken-for-granted aspects of popular music, including but not limited to the association of whiteness in music with intellect and blackness with the body; questions of identity and performativity; and the gendering or racialization of genres and audiences.

New theoretical paradigms of the 1990s inspired new ways for popular music scholars to conceptualize rock music, and brought scholarly attention to the specificities of other genres, notably hip-hop, pop, country music, and heavy metal, as well as the popular music of non-Anglophone countries. A rich history of scholarship on African American music was acknowledged, with particular attention to the rise of hip-hop culture, music, and associated practices, including breakdancing and graffiti writing. Feminist approaches to popular music, energized by the rise of gay and lesbian studies in the 1980s, critiqued the gendered norms of popular music performance, production, consumption, and discourse.[10] The 1990s and 2000s saw a turn toward a cultural industries approach that has resulted in attention to cultural labor and production rather than a strict political economic analysis of the music industries. During the same period, historiographers adopted post-structuralist methods that revised popular music history; recovered audiences and performers that were marginalized or ignored in conventional narratives; explored the history of different genres, not just rock; and revealed gendered and raced motivations behind taken-for-granted aspects of popular music.

In 1981, cable channel MTV introduced young American audiences to the short clips long used to promote songs on television in Great Britain and the occasional American variety program. The initial "24-hour flow" on MTV of what became known as **music videos** caught the attention of film and literary scholars, in particular E. Ann Kaplan, author of the first book-length study of music video, *Rocking Around the Clock: Music Television, Postmodernism, and Consumer Culture*. Kaplan and others assessed the impact of postmodernism on visual aesthetics, social,

and cultural life without discussing the music of music video.[11] Goodwin's *Dancing in the Distraction Factory* brought the focus back to music arguing, among other things, that listeners already formed pictures in their minds when listening to music (synaesthesia), and the quick editing cited as disorienting and postmodern by film and literary scholars often followed the beat of the music.[12] Scholars who explored music video helped bring issues of identity, especially gender, race, and sexuality, into popular music scholarship. Foundational work in this vein includes Robert Walser's study of representations of masculinity in heavy metal video and Lisa Lewis' exploration of femininity in "female address video," each analyzing music video from the 1980s.[13]

Other scholars approached the aesthetics of music video, studying it as a new form of visual storytelling. Using techniques derived from film studies, paying attention to visual elements such as mise-en-scène, editing, cinematography, and overall style, film scholars, notably Carol Vernallis, established the study of music video as an adjunct to traditional film studies as well as an important stream within popular music studies.[14] Music video scholarship is often adapted to national and generic contexts, and increasingly, to new technologies such as YouTube, which permits users to consume, produce, remix, and talk back to music videos.

Popular music scholars apply methodologies and concepts from media, radio, television, film, and American studies to television music beyond music video. Historical studies by Norma Coates, Murray Forman, and others scrutinized the long-standing engagement between the music and television industries in the promotion, performance, and circulation of popular music.[15] The global "Idol" television phenomenon has been studied from a variety of methodological and disciplinary perspectives.[16] Popular music scholars increasingly explore popular music in television narrative and branding, and television's role in "breaking" new artists and providing another revenue stream to established artists.

Scholars of performance and theater studies have contributed insights about live performance, as well as the performative role of the performer off stage to popular music studies. Philip Auslander combined performance studies, the insights of sociologist Erving Goffman about the presentation of the self, and popular music genre studies to construct a framework for analyzing popular music performers as musical personae, subject to genre and audience expectations. More recently, Auslander and others, notably David Shumway, have applied insights from celebrity and star studies on the increasingly complicated terrain of music and media stardom.[17]

Modes and Terminology

Popular music studies is radically interdisciplinary, its object constantly evolving and changing. Popular music scholars often employ methodologies and approach their research from the perspective of their home disciplines, some of which, like American studies or media studies, are already interdisciplinary. Research questions about popular music objects dictate the methodologies and theoretical approaches used to answer them. Accordingly, modes of inquiry are often combined. A popular music historiographer, for example, might combine discourse analysis of fan magazines from the 1960s with scholarship and insights from audience studies to historicize female fan practices; a popular music ethnographer might interview the members of a scene or subculture to map its racial politics; or a popular music political economist might examine and theorize the impact of streaming on the livelihoods of older musicians. While it is difficult to provide a definitive accounting, the modes introduced below organize much of the extant scholarship in popular music studies.

Production of Popular Music

Popular music was traditionally the product of **cultural industries** and interrogated by scholars since the 1940s.[18] Simon Frith's 1987 article, "The Industrialization of Rock," delivered an important insight: music is the end-product, not the beginning, of an industrial process. Frith's reversal of the common sense about musical creation and production continues to inform the study of popular music industries and the production of popular music.[19] Even today, when more and more production is done in home studios, artists still rely upon some sort of cultural intermediary—be it a publisher, online vendor such as Bandcamp or iTunes, Spotify and other streaming services, YouTube, social media, or a record label—to ensure that their music is heard.

Popular music scholars explore the popular music industries from several analytical and methodological perspectives. **Political economy** focuses on the construction and exploitation of audiences, markets, and artists by large and small corporate entities in pursuit of maximum profit.[20] Keith Negus and David Hesmondhalgh, among others, apply a **cultural**

industries approach, rooted in cultural studies and cultural sociology to explore contradictions within the specific conditions of cultural industries.[21] This approach highlights tensions between production and consumption, symbol creators (musicians and artists), information and entertainment, and historical variations in the social relations of cultural production. Matt Stahl, Leslie Meier, Bethany Klein, and Devon Powers are among scholars who scrutinize the conditions of **cultural labor** in the music industries, currently and historically, combining concepts and methodologies from media studies, cultural sociology, contract law, and copyright law.[22]

Regulation and Policy

Government regulation and policy have an impact upon the music industries and the production, distribution, and consumption of music. Regulation and policy are not the same but sometimes have similar results. Copyright law and policies exemplify that dynamic. **Copyright** is defined in most countries as intellectual property, increasingly owned by media conglomerates, and deployed to criminalize the behavior of consumers as well as producers and artists who construct music using samples. The recording industry has long railed against piracy, conflating large-scale recording reproduction with individual file-sharing and downloading. Kembrew McLeod and Pete DiCola analyze the impact of copyright legislation on the creation of music that samples previously recorded work, while Joanna Demers explores the impact of copyright legislation and policy on musical creativity in general.[23] Other scholars attend to the revenue streams afforded to artists and other industry players, or the global distribution and reproduction of popular music.[24]

International, national, state, regional, and local **policy** around popular music production, sales, and consumption is a long-standing concern within popular music studies. For example, Lilian Radovac and Jennifer Stoever examine local noise regulations and their historical role in disciplining musical styles and audiences and members of ethnic and racial groups.[25] Other scholars explore the role of politics and policy in preserving national musical cultures given the global reach of American music industries and artists.[26]

Censorship, through legal or extralegal means, is a form of regulation and as such a subject of keen interest to popular music scholars. The history of popular music is rife with attempts to control it. Youth-oriented genres, including rock and roll, hip-hop, and pop, have spawned calls for censorship.[27] Music censorship beyond North America is an active and fertile site of scholarly exploration.[28]

Technology

For popular music studies, **technology** means more than just the equipment used to create and record popular music. The history of popular music technology is not only about change but about cultural norms, assumptions, and values mapped onto new technologies as they are envisioned, developed, marketed, and consumed. Technological developments such as radio in the 1920s, the Walkman mobile device in the 1980s, and the Internet in the 2000s have had a profound impact on the economics and structure of music industries, the invention of musical instruments and playback formats, what is produced, who music is produced for, the distribution of music, and new modes and practices of consumption.[29]

For example, values, ideological assumptions, gendered, and racialized meanings are encoded into the design of instruments and equipment attached to them. Mavis Bayton, for example, asserts that the design of electric guitars reinforces cultural norms of "appropriate" masculine and feminine practices.[30] Similarly, Mary Anne Clawson explores how gender norms are reiterated and reinforced by attaching gendered associations to the electric bass and to the adolescent creation of rock bands, while Tara Rodgers amplifies the voices of women electronic music producers and composers.[31] Steve Waksman's study of the electric guitar includes an incisive analysis of the racialized and gendered meanings of Jimi Hendrix and his guitar style.[32] The use of samplers and software tools to "compose" music is a site of much debate over what constitutes making and performing music. As recorded music becomes more digital, popular music studies research assesses the cultural impact of new technologies on artists and audiences, as well as the economic impact of the corresponding new distribution and royalty models on musicians.[33]

Genre

Genre refers to categories or types, and ways of organizing production and facilitating consumption. Popular music scholars study the musical styles and material practices of specific genres. For example, heavy metal, as both music and scene, is the object of several influential studies that examine how the genre constructs its culture and vice versa.

As complex cultural objects, musical genres are full of assumptions and connections. They are more than the formal characteristics of musical composition and performance, of formats devised to assemble audiences for radio stations, or the organization of playlists offered by streaming services. Franco Fabbri was the first popular music scholar to theorize the role of genre in popular music, postulating its operation under a set of socially constructed and accepted rules: formal and technical, semiotic, behavioral, social and ideological, and commercial and juridical.[34] Fabbri's framework informs subsequent work by other popular music scholars, including Frith, Fabian Holt, and David Brackett.[35] Genre "rules" are not hard and fast, but are sets of expectations shared by performers and audiences that contribute to the meaning of genres. Popular music scholars also study single genres; important studies include Deena Weinstein's exploration of Heavy Metal and Dave Laing's analysis of 1970s punk rock.[36]

Creativity

Creativity is central to popular music, and takes many forms, including song and lyric writing, record production, performance, arranging, and directing music videos. Creativity is treated as a practice or set of practices subject to social, cultural, generic, industrial, and other constraints and expectations. For example, popular music scholars might analyze the sound of a particular musical object not for its timbral qualities but for its cultural impact, reflection, or resonance.

Popular music studies attends to the cultural politics inherent in creativity using varied methodological perspectives. Frequently, as in scholarship by Mary Anne Clawson, Rebekah Farrugia, and Joseph Schloss, creativity is deeply imbricated with gendered and racialized approaches to technology.[37] Ruth Finnegan underscores the importance of music-making by amateurs in the everyday life of individuals and communities.[38] More critically, cultural sociologist Jason Toynbee convincingly argues that musical creativity at any historical moment is constrained by social location, markets, industrial practices, cultural norms, and other factors.[39]

Audiences and Consumption

Audiences do much more with popular music than passively consume products created by professional musicians. Popular music scholars study the different ways in which audiences engage with popular music, from solo or mobile listening, to group listening in various settings, to the arena stage.

Popular music fandom has intrigued scholars for decades. Initial studies portrayed fandom as anti-social behavior. For example, teenage girls who screamed at pop stars were called deviant or mentally ill. Fandom is now studied in more productive ways. Ethnographers interview subjects about their listening habits and affective relationships with particular artists or genres.[40] Scholars, notably Tia Denora, explore how music creates meaning for individuals and groups in daily life.[41] Daniel Cavicchi and other historians reconstruct historical modes of fandom and practices by examining fanzines, fan club correspondence and ephemera, personal recollection, newspaper and magazine accounts, and other primary sources.[42] Andy Bennett is among those studying aging and popular music.[43] New media, particularly online social networks, are an active site of scholarly inquiry into the changing nature of fandom and the increasingly interactive relationships between musicians and their audiences, and fans and each other.[44]

Identity

There are (at least) two major modes of thinking about **identity** in popular music studies. Scholars have explored popular music's role in **identity formation**, especially but not only amongst youth.[45] For example, we embody our musical affinities via hairstyles and colors or body modification. We dance, play along, and sing our favorite songs in the shower. We wear t-shirts bearing the names and logos of our favorite bands in order to say something about ourselves to others.

A second way of thinking about identity is influenced by post-structuralism and the subsequent development of new theoretical tools including queer theory, critical race studies, sexuality studies, ethnic studies, postcolonial studies, and disability studies. This deep stream of scholarship examines the impact of social and cultural norms, political ideologies, discourse, popular culture more broadly, and other influences on identity roles, hierarchies, performativity, and other aspects of popular music.[46]

Recent work in popular music studies approaches identity and identities as **intersectional**. Intersectional theory accepts that identity is multiple and pays close attention to the unequal privileging of some bodies over others. Scholars explore topics

such as the ability of white female performers to draw upon their raced privilege to restore their image, or the struggles for visibility of African American female artists who are doubly marginalized for their African American-ness, their femininity, and, sometimes, their presence in a genre in which they do not "belong."[47]

Subcultures, Scenes, and Communities

In sociological theory, a **subculture** is a "deviant" offshoot of the larger common culture. Those affiliated with subcultures incorporate sets of rules, codes, and stylistic preferences into systems of signification. Affinities for particular music genres were found to be important parts of the signifying systems of the subcultures studied by the CCCS in the 1970s. Further research refined and extended subcultural theory. For example, Sarah Thornton's 1996 monograph *Club Culture: Music, Media and Subcultural Capital* applied sociologist Pierre Bourdieu's mapping of categories of capital to the rave subculture in Great Britain to conceptualize **subcultural capital,** aesthetic hierarchies, and significations within subcultures.[48]

Will Straw's influential article "Systems of Articulation, Logics of Change: Scenes and Communities in Popular Music" differentiated **scenes** from subcultures, broadly defining a "scene" as a group of people with a shared affinity in musical taste or practices, such as the transnational and translocal heavy metal and electronic dance music (EDM) scenes.[49] A scene may be local, referring to a musical activity in a bounded locality, be it a borough (e.g., Brooklyn), a city, even a nation.[50] Or, scenes may be virtual, with participants separated geographically but unified through, for example, fan clubs, publications of various types, festivals, conventions, and, more recently, spaces on the Internet and on social media.

History and Historiography

Popular music historians use archival documents, primary sources such as newspapers, magazines, trade journals, interviews, liner notes, set lists, catalogs, and many other kinds of ephemera, as well as secondary sources. Scholars glean historical material from biographies, journalism, recordings, and archival repositories of the records, papers, and ephemera of performers, journalists, recording companies, and fans. Rock history has conventionally stood in for popular music history, told and repeated in narratives that privileged rock above other genres. That is rapidly changing, as popular music historians influenced by cultural studies, including Karl Hagstrom Miller, Bernard Gendron, Diane Pecknold, and Lisa Rhodes recover and recuperate missing and marginalized genres, audiences and performers, and write more inclusive and expansive industrial histories.[51]

Popular Music and Media

Popular music is both a form of media and intensely mediated. It often circulates through other media, including **radio**, **television**, **film**, televised and online **music video**, and **streaming** services. Popular music is an integral part of visual media. It can serve as a compiled score for a narrative film or a distinctive underscore for television programming. As a cultural object, popular music is the subject of countless documentaries and fictional film and television treatments. Documentaries, in particular, provide visual renderings of the history, performers, and major events in popular music.[52] Or, as in the case of the recent *20 Feet from Stardom*, documentaries recover hidden or secret histories of popular music and its production.

Scholars actively study popular music's historical and contemporary engagements with radio, film, television, and now the Internet and social media sites such as YouTube.[53]

There are rich opportunities for the study of popular music and visual media beyond film and television. The intersection of game music and popular music is a developing area for cultural analysis, especially to augment a growing body of musicological research into game scoring and gameplay.[54]

Published media, including newspapers, magazines, liner notes, press releases, blogs, web sites, and music criticism, contribute to the cultural conception of popular music. What is written about popular music, how it is written, what it assumes, and who it is written about are just some of the ways in which published discourse influences popular music cultures.[55]

Popular music scholars now approach music video from many perspectives, including genre studies, political economy, cultural studies, queer theory, film studies, feminism, and postcolonialism. Some of this work is available in two notable anthologies, *Medium Cool: Music Videos from Soundies to Cellphones* and *Music/Video: Histories, Aesthetics, Media.*[56]

Performance and Stardom

Performance has multiple meanings for popular music scholars. One is the actual art of performing and presenting music on stage, from the smallest club to the 60,000-seat arena.[57] Popular music scholars study, among other things, aspects of dress, costuming, stage design, lighting, dance, musicianship, interaction with other band members, and engagement with and of the audience in various venues and spaces. They also study how **stardom** is performed off- as well as onstage, as popular music performances do not conclude at the end of a set, but rather continue in interviews, fan interactions, websites, publications, fanzines, marketing materials, blogs, and other sites that create, reinforce, and circulate cultural meaning. **Stars** drive profit making in the industry and contribute to the meanings that audiences and cultural interlocutors (for example, journalists) make and circulate about popular music.[58]

Making Meaning

Popular music, its performers, and its audiences are multifarious and diverse. There is no overarching **ideology** of popular music. That popular music is closely tied to **youth** continues to have a place in the popular imagination, although that place is less stable as genres, performers, and audiences age. Critics, academics, and some performers may apply particular ideologies to popular music, but fans and audiences might not care about them. Meanings that audiences make from popular music vary by genre: for example, pop music might signify fun or escape to its audiences, while heavy metal might signify a lifestyle, affect, or world view.

Nevertheless, notions of **authenticity** continue to play an outsized role in critical discourse and culture, and are often imbricated with perceptions of **taste**.[59] Notions of authenticity, derived from meanings attributed to folk music, modernism, and the romantic ideal of the artist as an individual striving to present his (gender intentional) truth, took hold in the 1960s as performers, critics, and audiences sought to differentiate rock music from what was considered more blatantly commercial music. Keir Keightley draws upon sociologist Pierre Bourdieu's insights about distinction and taste to claim that ideas about authenticity are a compass by which critics and consumers navigate the popular music mainstream.[60] The ideological assumptions bundled under the term "***rockism***" continue to inflect critical discourse about all popular music today, although that influence is waning. Moreover, authenticity signifies differently in different genres.[61] For example, hip-hop authenticity is related to the performer's relationship to her or his community, place of origin, or experience. Authenticity has another, more populist and, sometimes, conservative meaning to fans and performers of country music. Ultimately, authenticity may reside in the listener's affective response to a piece or genre of music.

Case Study: Girls and Women and Rock Culture in the 1960s and Early 1970s

Rock music was my obsession as a child and teenager growing up in the seventies and well into my adult years. My affective relationship to it is not as intense as it once was, but it remains powerful enough that I made the study of popular music my career. Upon entering graduate school in order to study popular music, what I subconsciously intuited after years of tamping down my enthusiasm and hiding my opinions and knowledge about music, especially around men, was that women were not truly afforded a place in rock culture. That realization came in the 1990s when, despite the increased presence of women in bands, and the success of individual female performers, women were marginalized in more subtle ways. Female fans were still categorized as groupies, teenyboppers, or rock chicks (a designation usually applied to gorgeous glamorous girlfriends of rock stars), and female artists were "Women Who Rock" or "Angry Young Women." Did men not rock? Were young male rockers not angry? Why were female performers regarded differently than their male counterparts?

My article, "Teenyboppers, Groupies, and Other Grotesques: Girls and Women and Rock Culture in the 1960s and early 1970s," turned these questions around to ask how masculinity became naturalized and women marginalized or subservient to men in rock culture and its discursive formations in the 1960s.[62] I identified and examined two sites: critical and mainstream reaction to "teenybopper television" of the 1950s and 1960s and their female audiences; and discourse about teenage girls and women in *Rolling Stone* magazine in the late 1960s, especially its notorious "Groupies" issue. I was not interested in performing textual analyses of the television programs under consideration, but in what was said about them by contemporary critics in mainstream newspapers and in hindsight by rock critics as they developed an ideologically inflected interpretation of rock history.

My primary materials consisted of rock and trade journalism and television programs. I used articles in *Rolling Stone* magazine and *Crawdaddy*, the self-appointed first magazine of serious rock criticism, to examine how early rock critics talked about women, teenagers, and music. I also paid attention to the number of articles about women and rock music; to a scholar, omissions sometimes speak louder than inclusions. There was scant rock criticism available before 1966 in the United States, so I included reviews and articles from trade journals, particularly *Variety* and *Billboard*, to observe how mainstream ideas about television, music, and audiences might have influenced later rock criticism. Although I do not provide textual analysis of television programs in the article, I did watch as many episodes of *The Monkees* and *The Partridge Family* as I could in the pre-YouTube, pre-reissue, pre-streaming days of the late 1990s and early 2000s.

Secondary literature enabled me to build a theoretical framework for my analysis and to inform my revision of popular music orthodoxy. I employed several theoretical tools. Literary theory, particularly Peter Stallybrass and Allon White's Bakhtin-inspired theorization of "low Others" and "displaced abjection," allowed me to theorize the necessity of women and teenyboppers for stabilizing heterosexual masculinity in rock musical and culture.[63] Andreas Huyssen's aesthetic theory, particularly his identification of "mass culture as woman," supported my argument that television was "low culture" and therefore on the wrong side of a binary relationship with more "serious" culture.[64] Although not specifically cited in my references, feminist and gender theory permeates the article, particularly the post-structuralist gender theory of Judith Butler.[65] The tool employed to dissect and examine rock criticism was Foucauldian discourse analysis, with a particular interest in discursive formation and the power of discursive regimes to form and condition the "truth."[66] I consulted formative works of popular music studies to ascertain the impact of 1960s rock criticism on the academic analysis of popular music. Sheryl Garratt's feminist study, "Teenage Dreams" helped me consider alternative ways of viewing the relationship of women to music.[67] Feminist and media histories of the 1960s further grounded my historiography.

This combination of research materials, background reading, and theoretical framework led me to several conclusions. First, for decades, there were essentially two ways to imagine the relationship of women to rock music, either as teenyboppers or as groupies. Both were negative, marginalizing, and hard to transcend. Second, rock critics applied modernist aesthetics to their discussion and analysis of rock music, thereby erasing female presence and subjectivity. Third, the ideology of authenticity, so important to rock critics and culture, marked women as outsiders. Television was feminized and deemed inauthentic and commercial in relation to rock music. Fourth and finally, femininity was marginalized in rock in the 1960s. The result was a small array of mostly subservient roles for women and girls and, in a few select cases, the elevation of a few rock star girlfriends to more exalted status as "rock chicks." Other ways of imagining women as participants in rock culture were foreclosed.

A single essay cannot cover everything important or interesting about a topic, so my article offers abundant opportunities for further research. The study is U.S.-centric and does not explore how national differences in the press, audience, and music scenes might affect my conclusions. Race and sexuality need more consideration, as my article defaults to white heteronormativity. Since I wrote the article, much more source material is available. Textual analysis of complete episodes of *The Monkees* television program and digitized copies of magazines and newspapers from the era could further support, or complicate, claims made in the article. Close readings of magazines directed to teen and female readers could result in different conclusions.

Into the Future

Popular music studies is an exciting and expanding field with an international community of scholars, several journals, and many annual conferences. The biannual meeting of the International Association of Popular Music Studies and the annual meetings of national branches showcase the wide range of interdisciplinary research undertaken by scholars whose disciplinary homes are in the "traditional" humanities and social sciences. Recent trends in the field include expanding the scope of popular music studies from its foundational focus on Anglophone youth music of the post-World War II era. For example, scholars are remapping popular music studies by focusing upon the cultural specificities and histories of popular music outside of the Anglophone sphere and studying historical popular music, such as the prodigious output of Tin Pan Alley songwriters in the first half of the twentieth century. Other active areas of research include the impact of new technologies, new players, and concomitant policies on the production, distribution, and reception of popular music globally; revisionist historical work that troubles or refutes standard narratives; complex explorations of intersectional identities

in the production, performance, and consumption of popular music; attention to age and aging; the development and study of popular music pedagogies; and studies of the production and consumption of genres that are little-known, under-researched, or, like modern pop, previously under-valued.

Exciting intersections with other fields, some emerging and some established, chart the future of popular music studies. Insights from sound studies, philosophy, transgender studies, and disability studies are all informing scholarship by established scholars and current graduate students in the field.[68] Scholars will need to continue to pay close attention to the impact of new modes of production, distribution, and consumption on the livelihoods of music creators, and the impact of algorithmic culture on music and music consumers. The impact of changes in both the form and content of popular music, music's intersections with other types of media, and the ongoing effect of new digital technologies will drive scholarship in the future.

Notes

1. Martin Cloonan, "What is Popular Music Studies? Some Observations," *British Journal of Music Education* 22, no. 2 (2005): 77–93.
2. Wilfred Mellers, *Twilight of the Gods: The Beatles in Retrospect* (New York: Viking Press, 1974).
3. Donald Horton, "The Dialogue of Courtship in Popular Song" *American Journal of Sociology* 62, no. 2 (1956): 569–78.
4. See Michael Gray, *Song and Dance Man: The Art of Bob Dylan* (London: Hutchinson, 1976).
5. Stuart Hall and Tony Jefferson, *Resistance Through Rituals: Youth Subcultures in Post-War Britain* (London: Hutchinson, 1976).
6. Dick Hebdige, *Subculture: The Meaning of Style* (London: Methuen, 1979).
7. Simon Frith, *The Sociology of Rock* (London, Constable, 1978).
8. Simon Frith, *Performing Rites: On the Value of Popular Music* (Cambridge: Harvard University Press, 1996).
9. Simon Frith and Andrew Goodwin, *On Record: Rock, Pop & the Written Word* (New York: Pantheon Books, 1990).
10. See, for example, Sheila Whiteley, ed., *Sexing the Groove: Popular Music and Gender* (London: Routledge, 1997); Mavis Bayton, *Frock Rock: Women Performing Popular Music* (Oxford: Oxford University Press, 1998); Marian Leonard, *Gender in the Music Industry: Rock, Discourse and Girl Power* (Aldershot, UK: Ashgate, 2007); and Sherrie Tucker, *Swing Shift: "All-Girl" Bands of the 1940s* (Durham, NC: Duke University Press, 2000).

11. E. Ann Kaplan, *Rocking Around the Clock: Music Television, Postmodernism, and Consumer Culture* (New York: Methuen, 1987); John Fiske, "MTV: Post-Structural Post-Modern," *Journal of Communication Inquiry* 10, no. 1 (1986): 74–79.

12. Andrew Goodwin, *Dancing in the Distraction Factory: Music Television and Popular Culture* (Minneapolis: University of Minneapolis Press, 1992).

13. Lisa A. Lewis, *Gender Politics and MTV: Voicing the Difference* (Philadelphia: Temple University Press, 1990); Robert Walser, *Running with the Devil: Power, Gender, and Madness in Heavy Metal* (Hanover: University Press of New England, 1993).

14. Carol Vernallis, *Experiencing Music Video: Aesthetics and Cultural Context* (New York: Columbia University Press, 2004).

15. See, for example, Norma Coates, "Excitement is Made, Not Born: Jack Good, Television, and Rock and Roll," *Journal of Popular Music Studies* 25, no. 3 (2013): 301–25; Murray Forman, *One Night on TV is Worth Weeks at the Paramount* (Durham: Duke University Press, 2012); Paul Fryer, "'Everybody's on Top of the Pops': Popular Music on British Television 1960–1985," *Popular Music and Society* 21, no. 2 (1997): 71–89.

16. See Katherine Meizel, *Idolized: Music, Media, and Identity in American Idol* (Bloomington: Indiana University Press, 2011).

17. Philip Auslander, *Glam Rock: Gender and Theatricality in Popular Music* (Ann Arbor: University of Michigan Press, 2006); David R. Shumway, *Rock Star: The Making of Musical Icons from Elvis to Springsteen* (Baltimore: Johns Hopkins University Press, 2014).

18. See Theodor Adorno with George Simpson, "On Popular Music," *Zeitschrift für Sozialforschung* 9, no. 1 (1941): 17–48. Also in Frith and Goodwin, eds., *On Record*, 301–14.

19. Simon Frith, "The Industrialization of Popular Music," in *Popular Music and Communication*, ed. James Lull (Newbury Park: Sage, 1987), 53–77.

20. See Steve Chapple and Reebee Garofalo, *Rock 'n' Roll Is Here to Pay: The History and Politics of the Music Industry* (Chicago: Nelson-Hall, 1977); Jacques Attali, *Noise: The Political Economy of Music*, trans. Brian Massumi (Minneapolis: University of Minneapolis Press, 1984); Reebee Garofalo, "From Music Publishing to MP3: Music and Industry in the Twentieth Century," *American Music* 17, no. 3 (1999): 318–54; and Chapter 10 in the present volume.

21. See David Hesmondhalgh, "Post-Punk's Attempt to Democratize the Music Industry: The Success and Failure of Rough Trade, *Popular Music* 16, no. 3 (1997): 255–76; Keith Negus, *Producing Pop: Culture and Conflict in the Popular Music Industry* (New York: Routledge, Chapman and Hall, 1992).

22. See Matt Stahl, *Unfree Masters: Popular Music and the Politics of Work* (Durham: Duke University Press, 2013); and Bethany Klein, Leslie Meier, and Devon Powers, "Selling Out: Musicians, Autonomy, and Compromise in the Digital Age, *Popular Music and Society* 40, no. 2, (2017): 222–38.

23. Kembrew McLeod and Peter DiCola, *Creative License: The Law and Culture of Digital Sampling* (Durham: Duke University Press, 2011); Joanna Demers, *Steal This Music: How Intellectual Property Law Affects Musical Creativity* (Athens: University of Georgia Press, 2006).

24. See Kembrew McLeod, *Owning Culture: Authorship, Ownership and Intellectual Property Law* (New York: Peter Lang, 2001); Simon Frith and Lee Marshall, eds. *Music and Copyright,* 2nd ed. (Edinburgh: Edinburgh University Press, 2004).

25. Jennifer Stoever, "Splicing the Sonic Color-Line: Tony Schwartz Remixes Postwar Nueva York," *Social Text* 28, no. 1 (2010): 59–85; Lilian Radovac, "The 'War on Noise': Sound and Space in La Guardia's New York," *American Quarterly* 63, no. 3 (2011): 733–60.

26. See Krister Malm and Roger Wallis, *Media Policy and Music Activity* (New York: Routledge, 1992); and Ryan Edwardson, *Canadian Content: Culture and the Quest for Nationhood* (Toronto: University of Toronto Press, 2008).

27. See Martin Cloonan and Reebee Garofalo, eds., *Policing Pop* (Philadelphia: Temple University Press, 2003); Linda Martin and Kerry Segrave, *Anti-Rock: The Opposition to Rock'n'Roll* (New York: Da Capo Books, 1993).

28. See Michael Drewett and Martin Cloonan, eds., *Popular Music Censorship in Africa* (Aldershot: Ashgate, 2006).

29. See Steve Jones, *Rock Formation: Music, Technology, and Mass Communication* (Newbury Park: Sage, 1992); Paul Théberge, *Any Sound You Can Imagine: Making Music / Consuming Technology* (Hanover: University Press of New England for Wesleyan University Press, 1997).

30. Mavis Bayton, "Women and the Electric Guitar," in Whiteley, ed., *Sexing the Groove*, 99–114.

31. Mary Ann Clawson, "Masculinity and Skill Acquisition in the Adolescent Rock Band," *Popular Music* 18, no. 1 (1999): 99–114; Tara Rodgers, *Pink Noises: Women on Electronic Music and Sound* (Durham: Duke University Press, 2010).

32. Steve Waksman, *Instruments of Desire: The Electric Guitar and the Shaping of Musical Experience* (Cambridge: Harvard University Press, 2001).

33. See Jeremy Wade Morris, *Selling Digital Music, Formatting Culture* (Berkeley: University of California Press, 2015).

34. Franco Fabbri, "A Theory of Musical Genres: Two Applications," *Popular Music Perspectives* 1 (1982): 52–81.

35. Fabian Holt, *Genre in Popular Music* (Chicago: University of Chicago Press, 2007); David Brackett, *Categorizing Sound: Genre and Twentieth-Century Popular Music* (Oakland: University of California Press, 2016).

36. Deena Weinstein, *Heavy Metal: The Music and Its Culture*, rev. ed. (Chicago: Da Capo Press, 2000); Dave Laing, *One Chord Wonders: Power and Meaning in Punk Rock* (Milton Keynes: Open University Press, 1985).

37. Mary Ann Clawson, "When Women Play the Bass: Instrument Specialization and Gender Interpretation in Alternative Rock Music," *Gender and Society* 13, no. 2 (1999): 193–210; Joseph Schloss, *Making Beats: The Art of Sample-Based Hip-Hop* (Middletown: Wesleyan University Press, 2004); Rebekah Farrugia, *Beyond the Dance Floor: Female DJs, Technology, and Electronic Dance Music* (Bristol: Intellect, 2012).

38. Ruth Finnegan, *The Hidden Musicians: Music-Making in an English Town* (Cambridge: Cambridge University Press, 1989).

39. Jason Toynbee, *Making Popular Music: Musicians, Creativity and Institutions* (London: Arnold, 2000).

40. See Nancy Baym, "The New Shape of Online Community: The Example of Swedish Independent Music Fandom," *First Monday* 12, no. 8 (2007), http://dx.doi.org/10.5210/fm.v12i8.1978; Daniel Cavicchi, *Tramps Like Us: Music & Meaning Among Springsteen Fans* (New York: Oxford University Press, 1998).

41. Tia DeNora, *Music in Everyday Life.* (Cambridge: Cambridge University Press, 2003); Susan D. Crafts, Daniel Cavicchi, and Charles Keil, *My Music: Explorations of Music in Daily Life* (Middletown: Wesleyan University Press, 1993).

42. Daniel Cavicchi, *Listening and Longing: Music Lovers in the Age of Barnum* (Middletown, CT: Wesleyan University Press, 2011).

43. Andy Bennett, *Music, Style, and Aging: Growing Old Disgracefully?* (Philadelphia: Temple University Press, 2013); Nick Stevenson, "Talking to Bowie Fans: Masculinity, Ambivalence, and Cultural Citizenship," *European Journal of Cultural Studies* 12, no. 1 (2009): 79–98.

44. See Jeremy Wade Morris, "Artists as Entrepreneurs, Fans as Workers," *Popular Music and Society* 37, no. 3 (2014): 273–90; Nancy Baym, "Connect with Your Audience! The Relationship Labor of Connection," *The Communication Review* 18, no. 1 (2015): 14–22.

45. See Sue Wise, "Sexing Elvis" in Frith and Goodwin, eds., *On Record*, 390–98.

46. See Whiteley, ed., *Sexing the Groove*; Matthew Bannister, *White Boys, White Noise: Masculinities and 1980s Indie Guitar Rock* (Aldershot: Ashgate, 2006);

Tricia Rose, *Black Noise: Rap Music and Black Culture in Contemporary America* (Hanover: Wesleyan University Press, 1997); and Allison McCracken, *Real Men Don't Sing: Crooning and American Culture* (Durham: Duke University Press, 2015).

47. Daphne A. Brooks, "'This Voice Which is Not One': Amy Winehouse Sings the Ballad of Sonic Blue(s)face Culture," *Women & Performance: A Journal of Feminist Theory* 20, no. 1 (2010): 37–60; Maureen Mahon, "Listening for Willie Mae 'Big Mama' Thornton's Voice: The Sound of Race and Gender Transgressions in Rock and Roll." *Women and Music: A Journal of Gender and Culture* 15, no. 1 (2011): 1–17, doi: 10.1353/wam.2011.0005.

48. Sarah Thornton, *Club Cultures Music, Media and Subcultural Capital* (Hanover: Wesleyan University Press, 1996).

49. Will Straw, "Systems of articulation, logics of change: communities and scenes in popular music," *Cultural Studies* 5, no. 3 (1991): 368–88.

50. See Barry Shank, *Dissonant Identities: The Rock 'n' Roll Scene in Austin, Texas* (Hanover: Wesleyan University Press, 1994); Sara Cohen, *Rock Culture in Liverpool: Popular Music in the Making* (Oxford: Oxford University Press on Demand, 1991).

51. See Bernard Gendron, *Between Montmartre and the Mudd Club: Popular Music and the Avant-Garde* (Chicago: University of Chicago Press, 2002); Karl Hagstrom Miller, *Segregating Sound: Inventing Folk and Pop Music in the Age of Jim Crow* (Durham: Duke University Press, 2010); Diane Pecknold, *The Selling Sound: The Rise of the Country Music Industry* (Durham: Duke University Press, 2007); Tim Lawrence, *Love Saves the Day: A History of American Dance Music Culture, 1970–1979* (Durham: Duke University Press, 2003); and Lisa Rhodes, *Electric Ladyland: Women and Rock Culture* (Philadelphia: University of Pennsylvania Press, 2005).

52. See Robert Edgar, Kirsty Fairclough-Isaac, and Benjamin Halligan, eds., *The Music Documentary: Acid Rock to Electropop* (New York: Routledge, 2013).

53. See Eric Weisbard, *Top 40 Democracy: The Rival Mainstreams of American Music* (Chicago: University of Chicago Pres, 2014); Jeff Smith, *The Sounds of Commerce: Marketing Popular Film Music* (New York: Columbia University Press, 1998); James Deaville, ed., *Music in Television: Channels of Listening* (New York: Routledge, 2011).

54. K.J. Donnelly, William Gibbons, and Neil Lerner, eds., *Music in Video Games: Studying Play* (New York: Routledge, 2014).

55. See Steve Jones, ed., *Pop Music and the Press* (Philadelphia: Temple University Press, 2002).

56. Roger Beebe and Jason Middleton, eds. *Medium Cool: Music Videos from Soundies to Cellphones* (Durham: Duke University Press, 2007); Gina Arnold, Daniel Cookney, Kirsty Fairclough, and Michael Goddard, eds., *Music/Video: Histories, Aesthetics, Media* (New York: Bloomsbury Academic, 2017).

57. See Philip Auslander, "Performance Analysis and Popular Music: A Manifesto," *Contemporary Theatre Review* 14, no. 1 (2010): 1–13; Wendy Fonarow, *Empire of Dirt: The Aesthetics and Rituals of British Indie Music* (Middletown: Wesleyan University Press, 2006).

58. See Cathy Schwichtenberg, *The Madonna Connection: Representational Politics, Subcultural Identities and Cultural Theory* (Boulder: Westview Press, 1993).

59. Carl Wilson, *Let's Talk about Love: A Journey to the End of Taste* (New York: Continuum, 2007).

60. Keir Keightley, "Reconsidering Rock" in *The Cambridge Companion to Pop and Rock*, Simon Frith, Will Straw, and John Street, eds. (Cambridge: Cambridge University Press, 2001), 109–42.

61. See Miles Park Grier, "'Said the Hooker to the Thief': 'Some Way Out' of Rockism," *Journal of Popular Music Studies* 25, no. 1 (2013): 31–55.

62. Norma Coates, "Teenyboppers, Groupies, and Other Grotesques: Girls and Women and Rock Culture in the 1960s and early 1970s," *Journal of Popular Music Studies* 15, no. 1 (2003): 65–94.

63. Peter Stallybrass and Allon White, *The Politics and Poetics of Transgression* (Ithaca: Cornell University Press, 1986).

64. Andreas Huyssen, *After the Great Divide: Modernism, Mass Culture, Postmodernism* (Bloomington: Indiana University Press, 1986).

65. Judith Butler, *Gender Trouble: Feminism and the Subversion of Identity* (New York: Routledge, 1990).

66. Michel Foucault, *The Archaeology of Knowledge and The Discourse on Language,* trans. A. M. Sheridan Smith (New York: Vintage Books, 2010).

67. Sheryl Garratt, "Teenage Dreams" in Frith and Goodwin, eds., *On Record*, 399–409.

68. See Jennifer Stoever, *The Sonic Color Line: Race and the Cultural Politics of Listening* (New York: New York University Press, 2016); Robin James, *Resilience and Melancholy: Pop Music, Feminism, Neoliberalism* (Winchester: Zero Books, 2015); George McKay, *Shakin' All Over: Popular Music and Disability* (Ann Arbor: University of Michigan Press, 2013).

Further Reading

Bennett, Andy, and Steve Waksman. *The SAGE Handbook of Popular Music*. Los Angeles: Sage Reference, 2015.

Born, Georgina, and David Hesmondhalgh. *Western Music and its Others: Difference, Representation, and Appropriation in Music*. Berkeley: University of California Press, 2000.

Chang, Jeff. *Can't Stop Won't Stop: A History of the Hip-Hop Generation*. New York: St. Martin's Press, 2005.

Gottlieb, Joanne, and Gayle Wald. "Smells Like Teen Spirit: Riot Grrrls, Revolution and Women in Independent Rock." In *Microphone Fiends: Youth Music, Youth Culture*, edited by Andrew Ross and Tricia Rose, 250–74. New York: Routledge, 1994.

Grossberg, Lawrence. *We Gotta Get Out of This Place: Popular Conservatism and Postmodern Culture*. New York: Routledge, 1992.

Hennion, Antoine. "An Intermediary between Production and Consumption: The Producer of Popular Music." *Science, Technology, & Human Values* 14, no. 4 (1989): 400–24.

Keightley, Keir. "Long Play: Adult-Oriented Popular Music and the Temporal Logics of the Post-War Sound Recording Industry in the USA." *Media, Culture & Society* 26, no. 3 (2004): 375–91.

Neal, Mark A., and Forman, Murray. *That's the Joint!: The Hip-Hop Studies Reader*. New York: Routledge, 2004.

Shumway, David. "Watching Elvis: The Male Rock Star as Object of the Gaze." In *The Other Fifties: Interrogating Midcentury American Icons*, edited by Joel Foreman, 124–43. Urbana: University of Illinois Press (1997).

24.
NEW MEDIA
Madhavi Mallapragada

New media studies as developed through critical and cultural studies perspectives represent a dynamic and burgeoning field of enquiry within communication and media studies. **New media**, popularly understood, refers to digital, virtual, interactive, multimedia forms as well as the communication practices they engender. Starting roughly in the 1980s, digitization and computerization became increasingly central to mass communication and media. This shift not only created "new" media but also transformed existing media of the twentieth century, notably print, radio, film, and television. The phrase "new media studies" today functions as an umbrella term that encapsulates the study of objects/units of analysis that are, on the one hand, distinct in form and function—a website is different from a YouTube video—but, on the other, bring to the fore overlapping (if not similar) themes, issues, and concepts such as online self and sociality, virtual communities, network culture, digital capitalism, immaterial labor, and participatory culture practices. Cultural studies of new media, which is the broad intellectual framework of this chapter, have roughly since the mid-1990s developed a series of theoretical and methodological questions, debates, and frameworks that seek to (a) critically understand the nature, types, practices, and implications, of new media texts, industries, users, their dispersion, and regulation; (b) locate and evaluate the significance of new media cultures in the transformation of everyday life and our social world (inclusive of the economic, cultural, ideological domains); and (c) reflect on and respond to the ethical and political dimensions of living in an ever-expanding and intensifying network culture, where the latter is closely aligned with the perpetuation of the market logics of neoliberal forms of capitalism.

Global developments in the second half of the twentieth century, namely the rise and growth of network computing and, relatedly, the development of software to enhance human interactions via computers, fundamentally altered the communication terrain and heralded the shift from the electronic to the digital age. The successful implementation, in 1969, of packet switching—a mode of data transmission in network communication where messages are broken into small packets (of information), to be sent across the network and reassembled into their original sequence at the destination point—and the official adoption, in 1983, of TCP/IP (Transmission Control Protocol/Internet Protocol)—a fundamental protocol governing computer networking—are key developments leading to the emergence of the **Internet** and the **World Wide Web** as media and communication technologies in the 1980s and 1990s.

The Internet is a global network of interconnected computers that communicate with each other as a result of an evolving set of technical protocols and communication standards built around TCP/IP. The World Wide Web Consortium (W3C), the primary standards organization for the World Wide Web, describes the latter as "an information space in which the items of interest, referred to as resources, are identified by global identifiers called Uniform Resource Identifiers (URI)."[1] Tim Berners-Lee, also known as the "inventor of the Web," wrote the Web's primary specifications, the URL (Uniform Resources Locators/Identifiers), HTTP (Hypertext Transfer Protocol), and (Hypertext Markup Language) in 1989. **Hypertext**, refers to a text displayed on the computer screen that contains hyperlinks to other texts. By clicking on the hyperlink, a user can access the referenced documents, which in turn can contain hyperlinks to other associated documents. Webpages written in HTML, the foundation language layer of the Web, hence engender a space where information can be displayed, retrieved, stored, and accessed in a nonlinear, nonsequential pattern based on associative linkages. The popularization of the Web, however, is linked to its easier access following the introduction of the web browser, a software application with a graphical user interface that retrieves and presents information (URLs) from the Web at the click of the mouse/touch of the button. The world's first popular web browser, Netscape Navigator was released in 1994. A decade later, in 2004, the social networking service, Facebook was launched and the term, "**Web 2.0**," referring to an interactive, user-generated, content-based, collaborative, and interoperable Web, was popularized.[2]

In the first ten or so years of the Web (the time period referenced by the retronym Web 1.0), the relationship between new media and ideas of cultural practice, community, commerce, communication, time, space, and identity emerged as key intellectual concerns. While these issues continue to shape our collective concerns around new media, they have also been transformed in the wake of new layers of meanings and implications attached to ideas of interactivity or participatory culture since the increased popularity of social media and mobile technologies since 2004.

The following sections offer the reader an overview of the main issues, debates, interventions, and challenges, both theoretical as well as methodological, that have emerged within the field of new media studies. The information presented in these sections and the works referenced are not organized around a chronological logic, so, works published in the mid-1990s may be cited alongside a more recent work from the 2010s. The goal of these sections is both to convey when (in terms of historical time) a certain issue or theme came to the fore within the field as well as to historicize emerging issues within a broader context. It is to see, for example, that contemporary debates over capital, labor, and global reproduction of systemic inequities via new media industries (Facebook "Free Basics" colonialism debacle, Googleopoly, Apple sweatshops in Asia) have a lot in common with the late 1990s–early 2000s postcolonial, critical race, and feminist scholarship around the imperial, colonial, and patriarchal logic shaping the cultural imagination (the Internet as "Electronic frontier") and material realities of the Internet and Web as "social" technologies.[3] Or to see that concerns over dynamic and evolving web content and the need to archive data

before it disappears emerged in the 1990s over webpages that were "here today gone tomorrow" (leading technology journalists to ponder, where do websites go when they die?) and that those concerns seem to be at the core of ongoing conversations about Twitter as "notoriously" difficult to research. Seeing overlaps, acknowledging antecedents while simultaneously paying close attention to the specific and the emergent have been intellectual goals that cultural studies work, in media studies at large (and not just new media studies), has long advocated.

Theoretical and Methodological Debates in New Media

The emergence of new media as an object of media research brings a distinct set of theoretical and methodological concerns to the fore. At the same time, as new theories and methods are articulated to the field, existing theories and methods from cultural studies and media studies are drawn in and rearticulated to the new context of research and study.

Real Life and Virtual Realities: Early Dichotomies

With the popular use of computer-mediated communication in the 1990s, the dichotomy of **real life versus virtual life**, commonly represented as RL vs. VR, entered the popular lexicon and naturally found its way into intellectual debates over the transformation of life and the everyday in the age of the Internet. The tension over the "real" and the "virtual" emerged in part because of the popular representations of the Internet as a space that transcends time, place, and materiality. The now iconic, "On the Internet, nobody knows you're a dog," cartoon was published by the *New Yorker* in 1993, and is representative of the utopian narratives about the liberating potential of the Internet.[4] Of course, liberation, as science fiction narratives in literature and film from the 1980s onwards had been reinforcing, had something to do with transcending the body ("the meat") and losing oneself in the data-sphere (the immaterial system). The explosion of virtual environments based on digital texts, visuals, and simulated objects—for example, bulletin board system chat rooms, webpages, digital games—resulted in a great deal of scholarly attention to the textual and symbolic layers of disembodiment, role play, and performance attached to virtual interactions in turn advancing ideas such as the immateriality of the Web, the disembodiment of virtual travel, and the play and freedom associated with anonymity, as well as the symbolic nature of the online. Essays published across several readers and edited collections through the first decade of the Web focused on textual analysis, semiotics, and tracing Western postmodernist and post-structuralist philosophical epistemologies of notions of virtual time and space in their examination of new media texts.[5]

While these writings introduced a new set of terms, such as virtual body, virtual identity, cyber selves, and virtual gender, and opened up new ways to theorize subjectivity (its formation and negotiation), scholars have also noted the limitations, if not dangers, of researching and representing the online as an immaterial text in a symbolic order of digital signs. To some extent, the trend towards philosophical interpretations, textual readings, and semiotic analyses in the early writings about the Internet can be viewed within a larger crisis of the idea of embodiment/bodies online. As David Holmes notes in the introduction to his edited book, *Virtual Politics: Identity and Community in Cyberspace*, with the users' bodies offline but their words or interactions online, a method such as ethnography appeared to be extremely challenging to employ.[6] This crisis of where the body lies in relation to the digital realm and how to study it required not just a creative rethinking of what a new media ethnography would look like but, more urgently, a rethinking of the nature of the body (and relatedly, the "real") and the "virtual."

Sherry Turkle's books *The Second Self: Computers and the Human Spirit* and *Life on the Screen* represent some of the early ethnographies of computer usage among children and teenagers. While producing more psychological and sociological accounts rather than media studies ethnographies, Turkle's methods of on-site observation, questionnaires, and one-to-one follow-up interviews allowed her to build her larger theoretical argument that there is "life on the screen." Turkle's studies demonstrated that how we relate to computers is not separate from our real selves and bodies but rather increasingly relevant to how we think and feel about ourselves.[7] Holmes' aforementioned volume is one of several books published in the late 1990s/early 2000s that argued for recognizing the materiality and historical relevance of the "virtual." Such books argued that we must historicize and contextualize how the "virtual" as disembodied or not really material was always a part of the imaginations around the "real," even as we focus on how electronic and digital environments complicate existing conceptualizations of the "real." Patricia Wise

contextualizes this insight by pressing feminist analyses of the concept of the "virtual" against universalist, masculinized claims to the "real." Her key argument is that women are always already virtual in male-centric narratives of technology because their presence is an afterthought, if not erased, much like the "virtual" is represented in Western rational thought as something outside the "real."[8] More broadly, the epistemological crises over what is real and what is virtual in early debates in Internet studies also cleared the space for acknowledging that bodies matter online, but that only some bodies have the power and access to migrate online (to be seen, represented, and catered to), while others don't. As we will see in the section on cultural difference later in this chapter, feminist, critical race, postcolonial, and queer theorizations of the characteristics and cultures of new media complicate the one-dimensional framing of the "real" and "virtual" as a switch that is on or off at the moment of logging in or logging out (leading to equally vexing online–offline characterization).

Characteristics of New Media

The formal features of new media became important to describe, understand, and define as Internet and Web research increasingly implied diverse objects of study. The aesthetics, visual culture, and display and interactive features were diverse as were the producers of the online content. *The New Media Reader, New Media: A Critical Introduction, The New Media Theory Reader, Digital Cultures: Understanding New Media*, and *The New Media and Technocultures Reader* are some of the volumes that have discussed the characteristics of new media.[9] *New Media: A Critical Introduction* highlights five key aspects of new media, namely, digitality, hypertextuality, interactivity, virtuality, and dispersal. Although initially used in the context of the hypertextual Web, the concept of hypertext has had other notable applications, such as reading the interactive and storytelling conventions of computer games as a form of electronic hypertext.[10] **Interactivity** foregrounds a couple of different aspects of new media culture. One, it refers quite simply to the ability to interact with the digital text (for instance, using graphical interfaces, typing in URLs, clicking on website links); two, it refers to a mode of participation in the read–write culture engendered by social media platforms and user-generated content whereby, users not only "read" digital content but "write" into it through practices such as adding, editing, and remixing to create new, altered, or derivative content. **Dispersal** refers to the fragmentation of media production, circulation, and distribution in network economies. Many of the writings on this topic also critically elaborate on the ideological connotations of "new" in "new media" as "cool," "efficient," "developed," and "relevant"—an ideology they note needs to be understood in relation to market forces and cultural imaginaries. Think of the digital capitalist market's role in establishing the notion that we need the latest technology or we will be left behind; or the cultural capital associated with having the latest digital gadgets; or the fact that the digital divide is most commonly understood as the separation of those who have access to computers and those who don't (instead of reading the divide as a more recent and expansive expression of systemic sociocultural economic disparities in society).

The dynamic nature of the Web expressed through constantly updated web content and hyperlinks also represents a challenge. Scholars have discussed it in terms of impermanence and instability of the materials of the Web, be it disappearing webpages (e.g., the millions of personal homepages that were lost when hosting site Geocities was shut down in the United States in 2009), or the constantly changing look and identity of a site such as YouTube (where the videos featured on the main page change based on current trends and popularity).[11]

The Politics of Cultural Difference in New Media

Questions of **difference** and the cultural politics of social relations as they emerged through the representational, aesthetic, discursive, economic, and institutional contexts of the Internet and Web were brought to the fore early on in the field, even as things were still being figured out methodologically. An early volume in new media studies, *Wired Women: Gender and New Realities in Cyberspace*, explored topics such as the masculinized spaces of premier technology magazine *Wired*, harassment in online forums, the gendered aesthetics of women's personal homepages, the **gendered code** of "hard" and "soft" ware.[12] Anthologies such as *Processed Lives: Gender and Technology in Everyday Life* and *Virtual Gender* explored the ways in which gender norms get coded or disrupted through women's experiences with computing machines.[13] While Laura Miller called attention to the patriarchal ideology underpinning concerns over making the "Net" safe for women and children, Michele White drew on feminist theorizations of the gaze to argue that the textual features of the game, LambdaMOO

(multi-user object-oriented), "perpetuate the dominant cinema's scripting of male subjects who control and look upon female objects."[14] Feminist scholarship, over the years, has also expanded the frame in which to consider the question of gender vis-à-vis digital cultures. Documenting the presence of women's networks online, foregrounding women as early adopters and creators of digital technologies, highlighting the radical, feminist, or resistant uses of the Internet, researching women's roles as producers of online content and networks, and noting the ambivalence and "liberation" afforded by the inclusion of the computer in the domestic space of the home represent some of the many themes discussed.[15]

Postcolonial, critical race, and queer theorizations advanced **intersectional analyses** of new media and called for greater attention to the structures of race, class, sexuality, nationalism, and language in examinations of the textual, discursive, and institutional contexts of the Web.[16] In the mid-to-late 1990s, Arturo Escobar, Guillermo Gómez-Peña, and Vinay Lal, among several others, brought postcolonial theorizations of "empire," "development," and **electronic "frontier"** to illuminate the Western and imperializing tendencies in the governance of the Web (for example, English being the predominant language of an imagined "global" Web or the colonial imaginary at the heart of the spatial metaphor of the frontier).[17] Anna Everett's study of African American and African diasporic participation in the early years of the Internet and the Web, Radhika Gajjala's ethnography of South Asian diasporic women's online networks, and Lisa Nakamura's interrogation of racializing visual codes in narratives about digital culture across media (film, video games, websites) all notably demonstrated that, to unpack new media's complex and diverse settings, one needs to not just include formerly marginalized groups (such as diasporic or racial minority groups), but simultaneously interrogate how dominant approaches to core issues in new media are inscribed by ideologies of race, gender, class, and nationalism.[18] For instance, Everett's study illuminates how Black people's participation is erased from dominant narratives of early adopters of technology, while Nakamura problematizes the bias in new media research to study Asian Americans predominantly as consumers, and not producers, of new media.[19]

Queer theorizations have similarly made a case for unpacking heterosexist and Eurocentric assumptions about the social role and function of online spaces, in turn foregrounding the need for materially grounded research on sexualities in new media contexts.[20] Similarly, studies of new media in diasporic contexts have argued for bringing theories of nationalism and migration to bear on the study not just of immigrant groups online but also of dominant paradigms in web studies.[21] For instance, how can theories of nationalism and Euro-American centrism help us better understand the fact that it is often assumed that if a website does not carry a country code in its URL, it is most likely a U.S.- or U.K.-based website? Or, how might we use diaspora studies' theorization of "home" and "homeland" to explore narratives of virtual belonging and categories such as the homepage and the smart home?[22] Such interventions at large, have been aimed at disrupting normative understandings of new media: what they are, how they look, and what function they fulfill. They can also be understood as rigorous efforts to reexamine the dominant paradigms that have shaped the field of new media studies. A notable collection in this regard is *Internationalizing Internet Studies: Beyond Anglophone Paradigms*, which argues that

> it is necessary for Internet Studies to take greater account of developments in the non-Anglophone world and to qualify the conception of the Internet as a 'global' technology with increased recognition of its very local histories and cultures of use.[23]

Network and Digital Cultures

Another body of literature has emerged over the past two decades around network and digital cultures, where the critical focus of the interventions is related to locating the politics of network and digital culture within the structures of late capitalist societies and the emergent forms of neoliberal capitalism and globalization. Within that framework, scholars have considered what kinds of politics, forms of subjectivity, and new patterns of power, control, and resistance are being shaped in **network cultures**, in turn bringing issues relating to labor, biocapital, and anti-war and anti-capitalist activism to the fore. Citing the shift of capital relations from an industrial to a digital economy, Tiziana Terranova highlights immaterial labor as an outcome of the turn towards intellectual labor and gift economies.[24] Using the examples of chat, fan fiction, newsletters, and mailing lists, Terranova argues that, while for users and fans there might be pleasure associated with such forms of online cultural production, we cannot overlook the fact that their "free labor" generates monetary value

in the digital economy.[25] Like Terranova, Jodi Dean interrogates the politics of ideologies of creativity and participation in Web 2.0 cultures.[26] She advances the theory of "communicative capitalism," the exploitation of communication by neoliberal market forces, to explain what, in her observation, is a greater emphasis on communicating about social change through social networks rather than organizing and participating in activism.

Other scholars have also discussed the potential of new media for mobilizing activists, reimagining social justice work, and bringing about social change.[27] While early debates included thinking about **online activism** vis-à-vis offline activism, recent conversations have focused on recognizing how access to and participation in new and social media spaces can in fact be a critical part of the process and mechanisms by which social justice work is carried out. In *Tactical Media*, Rita Raley examines the hacktivist tactics of electronic civil disobedience (a social justice movement that participates nonviolently in the information wars by jamming information flows), critical interactive digital arts projects (such as Black Shoals: Stock Market Planetarium, a real-time visualization of the global stock exchange markets), and role-playing games with a social agenda (such as Turista Fronterizo where players virtually cross the San Diego–Tijuana border, which involves role playing "stock" characters such as the illegal migrant, the drug dealer, and the businessman).[28] Raley argues that such social justice projects critique neoliberal globalization and market forces but do so not by being oriented "toward the grand, sweeping, revolutionary event; rather they engage in a micropolitics of disruption, intervention, and education."[29] Matt Ratto and Megan Boler offer the frame of "DIY Citizenship" to grasp the diverse ways in which users of social media are repurposing the tools and practices of social media platforms to enact and perform a type of political participation.[30] A particularly dynamic area of ongoing research is "hashtag activism," wherein scholars are paying close attention to the potential and challenges of practices such as microblogging (blogging with instant messaging) in the age of mobile phones and social media platforms such as Twitter and Tumblr.[31] That said, it has also been pointed out that design features such as Facebook's bi-directional design (you and I both need to agree to be friends) versus Twitter's unidirectional design (we can "follow" someone who is not following us) need to be analyzed further for their role in creating asymmetrical ties in the forms of sociality shaped by social networking sites.[32]

Historicizing the New

At the outset, critical histories of new media seek to arrest, disrupt, and ultimately overthrow the uncritical and utopian emphases on the unprecedented, unique, and radical newness of media culture in the age of computers. One might wonder for how long Web media (29 years old as of 2018) will continue to be discussed within the "new media" category. While it is true that a host of new categories and subfields (network culture, online media, digital culture, social media) have complicated the conversation about current media in productive and insightful ways, it is also the case that the notion of "new," with all its theoretical baggage, continues to shape our academic enquiry (and, in turn, our pedagogy and curricula). Over the past two decades, a robust body of scholarship has attended to the "new" in new media by calling out the implicit biases and erasures in such a framing while simultaneously rerouting the inquiry around the uniqueness of digital media through contextualized, historically situated analyses of so-called "old" and current media. The critical histories of new media discussed in books, such as *The Language of New Media*, *Old Media, New Media*, and *The Long History of New Media: Technology, Historiography and Contextualizing Newness*, foreground how many of the communicative forms, textual and industrial practices, and patterns of usage as well as the role and function of the media technologies have antecedents in media and technological cultures that preceded the Internet and the Web.[33]

Web History, arguably the first edited anthology of its kind, considers historical overlaps between past and present versions of the Web while pointing to possibilities for the Web of the future.[34] Noting that the Web "is now at an age at which it may be time to address its past," Niels Brügger makes a case for greater clarity and rigor in analytical frames to examine the Web; even he recommends keeping definitions of the Web flexible and open-ended (given overlaps between the Internet, the Web, and social media).[35] The book foregrounds the following five analytical strata: "the web as a whole, the web sphere, the individual website, the individual webpage and the individual textual web element on the webpage."[36] While an example of a history of the Web as a whole would be a history of globally relevant standards (such as URL), a history of a web sphere would involve a history of websites organized around a similar theme or event. In the collection, one of the essays discusses the historical evolution of the

BBC news website from 1997–2010 by noting four distinct time periods that mark the website's shifting look and strategies, while another one, focusing on the individual textual element of advertisements, offers a historical overview of the latter's changing trends, aesthetics, and politics of placement on the webpage at large. Another set of key issues raised by this collection relates to **archiving** and writing histories with existing web archives. Whether one is referring to robust archives like the Internet Archive's **Wayback Machine** or a smaller-scaled personal or community archive, web historians need to be attentive to the fact that a given archived page is only a partial snapshot of a site that is dynamic (all the updates can never be fully captured and some moving images cannot be captured). Relatedly, the act of archiving a website requires many strategic decisions, such as "how far from the start URL the archiving is to continue."[37] Hence, those conducting web histories have to theoretically engage the practice and politics of re-construction that is at the heart of the archived web document.

Jay Bolter and Richard Grusin's *Remediation: Understanding New Media*, which I draw on for my case study discussed later in this chapter, focuses on historical genealogies of digital and virtual technologies as well as the older forms of mediation through the photograph, the painting, film, and television.[38] The authors propose **remediation** as a theoretical framework for studying new media. Remediation theory argues for a relationship of repurposing and refashioning between so-called old and new media. The authors further argue that remediation in the digital age is organized around the dual and contradictory logic of "immediacy and hypermediacy."[39] Simply put, our new media culture is shaped by a simultaneous impulse to erase the process of mediation to create immediacy (where we look through the computer at a live event, much like live TV), as well as to accentuate the process of mediation to create hypermediacy (where we look at the computer and become aware of its mediation through the act of having multiple windows open on a computer screen). The concept of remediation can be productively applied to recognize traits and trends across mediums while noting what elements get framed as "old" and what is given the cultural capital of "new." *Remediation* demonstrates the importance of keeping concerns over historical continuities and ruptures, multiple temporalities-spatialities, and a resignification of social and economic relations at the front and center of the enquiry into new media cultures.

José van Dijck's **historiography,** published more than a decade after Bolter and Grusin's work, speaks to the continued relevance of such an approach. In *The Culture of Connectivity: A Critical History of Social Media*, José van Dijck historically contextualizes the rise of social media by looking at the interrelationship of technology, design, business models, governance, sociality, and ideology in creating a media ecology of connective media (his case studies include Twitter, Flickr, YouTube, Facebook, and Wikipedia).[40] By foregrounding the constitutive nature of that interrelationship (where, for example, design features such as open-source software in turn foster a sharing culture), van Dijck's historiography also reflects on the future challenges to connectivity culture as social media companies, once tradition-breaking start-ups (the "new") increasingly appear to be following the corporate business model of big media companies and monopolies of the past (the "old").

Debates over New Media Research and Research Methods

In cultural studies, concerns of theory and method are difficult to separate. New media scholarship raising theoretical concerns (such as the tendency towards ahistoricism in analyzing the latest, newest, most current media) is also essentially a commentary on the need for more informed methodologies (such as, new media historiography). That said, several books and anthologies published in the field have focused explicitly on the issue of research methods in new media. In early anthologies, such as *Doing Internet Research: Critical Issues and Methods for Examining the Net*, the key framework is grappling with the new "online" context for communication practices.[41] Both quantitative and qualitative methods are discussed, and the essays deal with both the practical and conceptual rethinking of communication and media research methods in light of the new media turn. For instance, if quantitative data analysis needed to be recalibrated to understand "data" in cyberspace, the formulation and traits of a community needed to be revisited to understand how to identify and explore community formations online.[42] *Internet Communication and Qualitative Research* exemplifies the shift in attention from online media as object of study and research site to online media as research tool and data collection site.[43] The book discusses the advantages of doing research online (for instance, it gives the researcher access to hard-to-reach groups or places; online surveys are cost-effective and can be time-effective)

while also pointing to potential areas of caution (the researcher needs to maintain confidentiality, ensure informed consent agreement is in place, and observe ethical practices in data collection and storage).

Among qualitative methods, ethnography (see Chapter 14 in this volume) has offered both tools and challenges to studying new media contexts. Christine Hine's *Virtual Ethnography* and Robert Kozinet's *Netnography*, the latter focusing on social media, develop the argument that **virtual ethnography** as method can help one understand the online environment in a more complex, fleshed-out, "lived experience" way but also can help us recast the core assumptions (about place, time, space) and practices (entering the "site," observing the participants) that have been traditionally associated with the ethnographic "field."[44] In *Virtual Methods* and *Internet Inquiry: Conversations about Method*, among other issues, the scale and scope of data collection and interpretation in the age of social media are also discussed.[45] As new media sites are dynamic, mobile, and always connected to other sites of media, deliberations on method have also turned to developing models—the web as a sphere, using maps to visualize online activity—that would help researchers determine boundaries for their study, justify why some media links are included and not others, and explain how the scope of accessible data shaped the research questions.[46]

Speaking of accessible data, **big data,** or what Lev Manovich calls "big social data," has raised some new practical and, arguably, more significant, theoretical and epistemological concerns over media research ethics, the rigor of method, and the nature and politics of research.[47] As anyone who has researched a platform like Twitter or Facebook knows, the sheer amount of data available as well as the "dispersed" nature of the data can be intimidating to work through. For example, given that there are roughly 6,000 tweets per second and 500 million tweets in any given day, how does one go about studying "what is trending," and how can one collect tweets relating to a particular hashtag? While these kinds of concerns relate to logistical challenges and to developing methods to collect, process, and aggregate large sets of information, there is another concern that relates to the methods and tools that social media companies have generated in part to enable users and researchers to access their data.[48] Facebook and Twitter, for example, have made their search and streaming **APIs** (Application Programming Interface, or a set of tools for building software applications) accessible and **open-source** (the source code is made freely available to the public for use, modification and distribution).[49] Using other open-source tools and programming scripts that would decode, visualize, and filter the big data (such as Gawk, Gephi), researchers are able to harvest and analyze specific data from social network sites. When social networks offer their own data-mining toolkits such as Twitter's official archive **yourTwapperkeeper**, which allows you to archive all tweets with a particular hashtag, or **TwChat**, which keeps a log of all your tweets, there is an interesting tension that emerges. As Jean Burgess and Axel Bruns note, on the one hand, many of the "scholarly possibilities [of studying the social and cultural dynamics of social media] would remain latent if it were not for the widespread availability of Open APIs for social software (including social media) platforms."[50] Yet, on the other hand, we cannot overlook the fact that these APIs are technical specifications calibrated to yield particular search results. The criteria for determining those search results are constantly evolving in the new media ecology, which, as van Dijck reminds us, is increasingly shaped by regulatory as well as business concerns.[51] These emergent tensions in the field of new media research will have broader implications for the methodologies used in media and cultural studies.

Case Study: The Remediation of Religion in Digital Culture

Given my research interests, which are at the intersections of new media, diaspora, and transnational cultures, I have been very fascinated by the mobilizing of new media technologies for everyday informal as well as public institutionalized forms of communication by Indian immigrants living in the United States. One particularly significant area that drew my attention was the prolific presence and growth of Hindu temple websites catering to diasporic Indians in the United States. In my article, "Desktop Deities: Hindu Cultures, Online Cultures and the Politics of Remediation" (2010), I focus on three "types" of Hindu temple websites that I argue could be categorized as such based on a close evaluation of their textual, institutional, and discursive character.[52] The three types are (1) the Hindu temple site, which functions as the virtual homepage for a physical temple located in a specific geographical location in the United States; (2) the commercial puja (ritual services) site, which essentially is in the business of "selling" ritual services and "divine blessings" (typically called prasad) for a

fee; and (3) virtual temples online that bear no direct link to a physical temple and in fact argue for the virtuality of the Hindu religious tradition. My primary sources were four websites, HTA.org, the homepage of the Hindu temple of Atlanta, Georgia (example of the first type); e-saranam.com and e-prarthana.com, both India-based sites and arguably the world's leading sites in commercial Hindu services (example of the second type); and vmandir.com, a site that reimagines the idea of the Hindu temple as a solely virtual environment (example of the third type). The different ways in which these three categories of Hindu religion online spoke to the interactions between the virtual cultures of new media and the virtual dimension of the spiritual experience that undergirds religion (and its institutionalized forms) appealed to me as a critical site for doing research in ways that could offer insights into not just new media but also diasporic cultures.

My research questions were the following: What online practices shape the three different types of Hindu temple sites? Given the significance of temples and image culture (of anthropomorphic deities, saints, and symbols) in the Hindu tradition, and the virtual, hypertextual, interactive, and symbolic features of online media, how do these two cultures (temples and online) interact with one another? And relatedly, what might we learn from such interactions about the evolving politics of place, time-space, and the "virtual" (sacred)?

To answer these questions, I drew on Bolter and Grusin's theoretical framework of remediation (discussed in the previous section) and brought their arguments about the old refashioning itself in the new and the new incorporating elements of the old to bear on the specific tradition of Hindu representations of the sacred—be it an image, text, place, or time-space. My argument in the article is this: Hindu temple websites are repurposing "older" media forms, such as photographs of deities, Hindu calendar art, analog sacred texts and temple books, and audio tapes of religious discourse, through their textual and discursive practices of representing online temples. Likewise, aspects of digital media such as hypertextual connectivity, virtual forms of dis/embodiment and im/materiality, and mobile flows of capital and culture are deployed to pay service to place-centric, embodied, and material practices shaping Hindu temple cultures. In this remediation of Hindu representational forms and material practices with new media ideologies and practices, both Hindu temples and new media as cultural forms are reinvented as "desktop deity cultures."

I conducted close textual and discursive analyses of the four primary websites for this study. I used the theoretical framing of hypertext as associative linkages to select particular links for a more thorough analysis, while summarizing other elements of each page that were not central to my theoretical focus. For example, given my theoretical emphases on historically produced understandings of the role of sacred image and presence as lived experience, I discussed hta.org's "archive" section in great detail and argued for understanding the archive as a strategic production of a collective memory that may or may not have been shared in the first instance (as many of the images were from either private cameras or of events where the public was not present). For my secondary materials, I drew from a wide variety of interdisciplinary sources. New media theories of the hypertextual site, the interactive image, and the visual and mobile aesthetics of a webpage helped me examine the textual organization and spatial economy of the webpages. But to unpack the specific meanings associated with sacred image, text, and symbol and their circulation on the Hindu websites, I drew from the fields of South Asian visual culture, sociology, and anthropology. Scholarship at the intersection of religious studies and new media studies gave me the language to historically consider the "virtual" as a category of the "real" (through the domain of the religious experience) and not solely tied to digitally mediated environments. Lastly, by simultaneously considering the insights of scholars who have paid attention to the cultural politics of religion and nationalism in Indian digital diasporic settings and those who have considered transnational (and immigrant-engendered) flows within a framework of global capitalism and commodity culture, I was able to connect the e-commerce business model and the transnational capital flows undergirding the e-ritual sites to the commodification of "culture" in and through network cultures in the age of digital capitalism.

Given the limitations of time and resources, for this study, I did not conduct any ethnographic studies of U.S. users of these sites, nor was I able to interview or talk to the people behind the India-based ritual service business. I think both these "gaps" present fresh opportunities to update this study. In particular, talking to Hindu immigrants who use these services might help push the conversation about public/ private mediated spaces of belonging and cultural production among U.S. racial/ethnic minorities in productive ways. Similarly, doing a closer analysis of the multiple U.S.–India networks of human capital

and capital networks that are brought together in the e-ritual business can help complicate the conversations about labor, work, and revenue in digital culture.

Conclusion

It has become quite commonplace in the academy to respond very enthusiastically to "new media" research, be it while considering graduate students for admission, interviewing faculty, or expanding the direction of a department. Institutional reasons aside (where universities, often functioning as academic markets, need to be seen as embracing the digital turn fully and unequivocally), as media researchers we are acutely aware that whether we care about print, radio, cinema, or television, a new media connection to our object of study is almost unavoidable. This leads to the predicament whereby all media research appears to be new media research. Additionally, when we consider that the Web has been around for more than a quarter of a century, we must wonder whether the term "new media" carries more baggage and less use value these days. As the preceding sections have sought to highlight, new media studies is not just the study of a new technological medium but rather a field of intellectual enquiry that is, and historically has been, invested in a particular cluster of theoretical ideas, methodological issues, themes, and relations that in some form or shape are concerned about the evolving relationship between computer-generated media cultures and the social, cultural, political world. Let us take a tricky example to expand on this point. If we were to study television fandom online, we must ask ourselves, is the study going to focus on something related to the interactions between popular culture and online spaces or might it focus on using the case study to reinvigorate debates about "television after TV"? Asking such questions as "Is my work going to help us understand television better or online media better?" is not an exercise in prescriptive research or an anti-disciplinary move. It is, rather, a thoughtful approach to an increasingly convergent media culture that, while appearing seamless, interoperable, and even democratizing in much of our interactions with it, is, in fact, undergirded by economic systems and institutional structures that have multiple different trajectories and motivations for the business they are in—to create markets, produce capital, and mobilize power. Making some critical distinctions across and within media can help ground our research so that more insightful analyses can follow.

Notes

1. "Architecture of the World Wide Web," Volume One, *W3C*, last modified December 15, 2004, accessed October 22, 2017, www.w3.org/TR/webarch/.

2. Tim O'Reilly, "What is Web 2.0: Design Patterns and Business Models for the Next Generation of Software," *O'Reilly*, September 30, 2005, accessed October 22, 2017, www.oreilly.com/pub/a/web2/archive/what-is-web-20.html.

3. See for example, Subhashish Panigrahi, "Millions of Indians Slam Facebook's Free Basics App," *Global Voices Advox*, December 29, 2015, accessed October 29, 2017, https://advox.globalvoices.org/2015/12/29/millions-of-indians-slam-facebooks-free-basics-app/; Kathleen E. McLaughlin, "Silicon Sweatshops: Apple Supply Chain Workers in Asia Fall Ill Again," *Public Radio International*, March 4, 2011, accessed October 29, 2017, www.pri.org/stories/2011-03-04/silicon-sweatshops-apple-supply-chain-workers-asia-fall-ill-again; Dahlia Lithwick, "Google-oply: The Game No One But Google Can Play," *Slate*, January 29, 2003, accessed October 29, 2017, www.slate.com/articles/news_and_politics/jurisprudence/2003/01/googleopoly_the_game_no_one_but_google_can_play.html. The metaphor of the "electronic frontier" was introduced and popularized in the scholarly writings of the 1990s, notably, by John Perry Barlow, founding member of the Electronic Frontier Foundation as well as Howard Rheingold, author of *Virtual Community: Homesteading on the Electronic Frontier* (Reading: Addison-Wesley, 1993).

4. See, John Perry Barlow, "A Declaration of the Independence of Cyberspace," *Electronic Frontier Foundation*, February 8, 1996, accessed October 5, 2017, www.eff.org/cyberspace-independence, and Rheingold, *Virtual Community*, for examples of utopian narratives.

5. An indicative, and certainly not exhaustive, list of such writings includes: Mark Dery, ed., *Flame Wars: The Discourse of Cyberculture* (Durham: Duke University Press, 1994); Steven G. Jones, ed., *CyberSociety: Computer-Mediated Communication and Community* (Thousand Oaks: Sage, 1995); David Porter, ed., *Internet Culture* (New York: Routledge, 1997); Sarah Kiesler, ed., *Culture of the Internet* (Mahwah: Lawrence Erlbaum, 1997); Pierre Levy, *Becoming Virtual: Reality in the Digital Age*, trans. Robert Bononno (New York: Plenum, 1998); N. Katherine Hayles, *How We Became Posthuman: Virtual Bodies in Cybernetics, Literature and Informatics* (Chicago: University of Chicago Press, 1999); Barbara M. Kennedy and David Bell, eds., *The Cybercultures Reader* (London: Routledge, 2000); David Gauntlett, ed., *Web.studies: Rewiring Media Studies for the Digital Age* (London: Arnold, 2000); Geoff King and Tanya Krzywinska, *Science Fiction Cinema: From Outerspace to Cyberspace* (London: Wallflower Press, 2000); Don Idhe, *Bodies in Technology* (Minneapolis: University of Minnesota Press, 2002); Ken Hillis, *Digital Sensations: Space, Identity, and Embodiment in Virtual Reality* (Minneapolis: University of Minnesota Press, 1999).

6. David Holmes, ed., *Virtual Politics: Identity and Community in Cyberspace* (London: Sage Publications, 1997), 6–7.

7. Sherry Turkle, *The Second Self: Computers and the Human Spirit* (New York: Simon and Schuster, 1984), and *Life on the Screen: Identity in the Age of the Internet* (New York: Touchstone, 1995).

8. Patricia Wise, "Always Already Virtual: Feminist Politics in Cyberspace," in *Virtual Politics*, ed. David Holmes, 179–96.

9. Noah Wardrip-Fruin and Nick Montfort, eds., *The New Media Reader* (Cambridge: MIT Press, 2003); Martin Lister, Jon Dovey, Seth Giddings, Iain Grant, and Kieran Kelly, *New Media: A Critical Introduction* (London: Routledge, 2003); Robert Hassan and Julian Thomas, *The New Media Theory Reader* (Maidenhead: Open University Press, 2006); Glen Creeber and Royston Martin, *Digital Cultures: Understanding New Media* (Maidenhead: Open University Press, 2009); Seth Giddings and Martin Lister, eds., *The New Media and Technocultures Reader* (Abingdon: Routledge, 2011).

10. See Noah Wardrip-Fruin and Pat Harrigan, eds., *First Person: New Media as Story, Performance and Game* (Cambridge: MIT Press, 2004).

11. Several essays in *Web History*, edited by Niels Brügger (New York: Peter Lang, 2010) explore these themes.

12. Lynn Cherny and Elizabeth Reba Weise, eds., *Wired Women: Gender and New Realities in Cyberspace* (Seattle: Seal Press, 1996).

13. Jennifer Terry and Melodie Calvert, eds., *Processed Lives: Gender and Technology in Everyday Life* (London: Routledge, 1997); Eileen Green and Alison Adam, eds., *Virtual Gender: Technology, Consumption and Identity* (London: Routledge, 2001).

14. Laura Miller, "Women and Children First: Gender and the Settling of the Electronic Frontier," in *Resisting the Virtual Life: The Culture and Politics of Information*, eds., James Brook and Ian A. Boal (San Francisco: City Lights, 1995), 49–57; Michele White, "Visual Pleasure in Textual Places: Gazing in Multi-User Object-Oriented World," in *Virtual Gender*, eds., Green and Adam (124–49), 144.

15. Judy Wajcman, *TechnoFeminism* (Cambridge: Polity, 2004); Mary Frank Cox, Deborah G. Johnson, and Sue V. Rosser eds., *Women, Gender and Technology* (Urbana-Champaign: University of Illinois Press, 2006); Melissa Gregg, *Work's Intimacy* (Cambridge: Polity Press, 2011); essays published in *Ada: A Journal of Gender, New Media and Technology* from 2012–present, accessed February 25, 2018, http://adanewmedia.org/.

16. See Chapter 8 in this volume.

17. Arturo Escobar, "Welcome to Cyberia: Notes on the Anthropology of Cyberculture," in *Cyberfutures: Culture and Politics on the Information Superhighway*, eds., Ziauddin Sardar and Jerome R. Ravetz (New York: New York University Press, 1996), 111–37; Guillermo Gómez-Peña, "The Virtual Barrio @ The Other Frontier (or The Chicano interneta)," *Pochanostra*.com, July 1997, accessed October 22, 2017, www.pochanostra.com/antes/jazz_pocha2/mainpages/page1.htm; Vinay Lal, "North American Hindus, the Sense of History, and the Politics of Internet Diasporism," in *Asian America. Net: Ethnicity, Nationalism and Cyberspace*, eds., Rachel Lee and Sau-ling Cynthia Wong (New York: Routledge, 2003), 98–138.

18. Anna Everett, *Digital Diaspora: A Race for Cyberspace* (Albany: State University of New York Press, 2009); Radhika Gajjala, *Cyberselves: Feminist Ethnographies of South Asian Women* (Walnut Creek: AltaMira Press, 2004); Lisa Nakamura, *Digitizing Race: Visual Cultures of the Internet* (Minneapolis: University of Minnesota Press, 2008).

19. See Everett, *Digital Diaspora*, 19–32; Nakamura, *Digitizing Race*, 171–201.

20. See Chris Berry, Fran Martin, and Audrey Yue, eds., *Mobile Cultures: New Media in Queer Asia* (Durham: Duke University Press, 2003); Mary Gray, *Out in the Country: Youth, Media and Queer Visibility in Rural America* (New York: New York University Press, 2009).

21. Andoni Alonso and Pedro. J. Oiarzabal, eds., *Diasporas in the New Media Age: Identity, Politics, and Community* (Reno: University of Nevada Press, 2010); Myria Georgiou, *Diaspora, Identity and the Media: Diasporic Transnationalism and Mediated Spatialities* (Cresskill: Hampton Press, 2006).

22. David Morley, *Home Territories: Media, Mobility and Identity* (London: Routledge, 2000).

23. Gerard Goggin and Mark McLelland, eds., *Internationalizing Internet Studies: Beyond Anglophone Paradigms* (New York: Routledge, 2008), 12.

24. Tiziana Terranova, "Free Labor: Producing Culture for the Digital Economy," *Social Text* 18, no. 2 (2000): 33–58, accessed February 25, 2018, http://web.mit.edu/schock/www/docs/18.2terranova.pdf, and *Network Culture: Politics for the Information Age* (London: Pluto Press, 2004).

25. Terranova, "Free Labor," 36–38.

26. Jodi Dean, *Blog Theory: Feedback and Capture in the Circuits of Drive* (Cambridge: Polity Press, 2010).

27. Martha McCaughey and Michael Ayers, *Cyberactivism: Online Activism in Theory and Practice* (New York: Routledge, 2003).

28. Rita Raley, *Tactical Media* (Minneapolis: University of Minnesota Press, 2009).

29. Raley, *Tactical Media*, 1.

30. Matt Ratto and Megan Boler, eds., *DIY Citizenship: Critical Making and Social Media* (Cambridge: MIT Press, 2014).

31. For example, see André Brock 2012, "From the Blackhand Side: Twitter as a Cultural Conversation," *Journal of Broadcasting & Electronic Media* 56, no. 4 (2012): 529–49; Mia Fischer, "#Free_CeCe: The Material Convergence of Social Media Activism," *Feminist Media Studies* 16, no. 5 (2016): 755–71.

32. I am drawing on Nicole B. Ellison, Cliff Lampe, Charles Steinfield, and Jessica Vitak, "With a Little Help from My Friends: How Social Network Sites Affect Social Capital Processes," in *A Networked Self: Identity, Community and Culture on Social Network Sites* ed., Zizi Papacharissi (New York: Routledge, 2011), 140–41; José van Dijck, "Tracing Twitter: The Rise of a Microblogging Platform," *International Journal of Media and Cultural Politics* 7, no. 33 (2011): 333–48.

33. Lev Manovich, *The Language of New Media* (Cambridge: MIT Press, 2001); Wendy Hui Kyong Chun and Thomas Keenan, eds., *Old Media, New Media: A History and Theory Reader* (New York: Routledge, 2006); David W. Park, Nicholas W. Jankowski, and Steve Jones, eds., *The Long History of New Media: Technology, Historiography and Contextualizing Newness* (New York: Peter Lang, 2011).

34. Niels Brügger, ed., *Web History* (New York: Peter Lang, 2010).

35. Brügger, "Web History, an Emerging Field of Study," in *Web History*, 1.

36. Ibid., 3.

37. Ibid., 7.

38. Jay David Bolter and Richard Grusin, *Remediation: Understanding New Media* (Cambridge: MIT Press, 2000), 20–51.

39. Ibid., 5.

40. José van Dijck, *The Culture of Connectivity: A Critical History of Social Media* (Oxford: Oxford University Press, 2013).

41. Steve Jones, ed., *Doing Internet Research: Critical Issues and Methods for Examining the Net* (London: Sage, 1999).

42. See for instance, Fay Sudweeks and Simeon J. Simoff, "Complementary Explorative Data Analysis: The Reconciliation of Quantitative and Qualitative Principles," in Jones, *Doing Internet Research*, 29–56; Jan Fernback, "There is a There: Notes towards a definition of Cybercommunity," in Jones, *Doing Internet Research*, 203–20.

43. Chris Mann and Fiona Stewart, *Internet Communication and Qualitative Research: A Handbook for Researching Online* (London: Sage, 2000).

44. Christine Hine, *Virtual Ethnography* (London: Sage, 2000); Robert V. Kozinets, *Netnography: Doing Ethnographic Research Online* (London: Sage, 2010);

45. Christine Hine, ed., *Virtual Methods: Issues in Social Research on the Internet* (Oxford: Berg, 2005); Annette N. Markham and Nancy K. Baym, eds., *Internet Inquiry: Conversations about Method* (London: Sage, 2009).

46. I am drawing on Martin Dodge, "The Role of Maps in Virtual Research Methods," in Hine, *Virtual Methods*, 113–28; and Steven M. Schneider and Kirsten A. Foot, "Web Sphere Analysis: An Approach to the Studying Online Action," in Hine, *Virtual Methods*, 157–70; Nancy Baym, "Question Six: What Constitutes Quality in Qualitative Internet Research?" in Markham and Baym, *Internet Inquiry*, 173–90.

47. Lev Manovich, "Trending: The Promises and the Challenges of Big Social Data," *Manovich*, April 28, 2011, accessed November 10, 2017, http://manovich.net/index.php/projects/trending-the-promises-and-the-challenges-of-big-social-data.

48. Alex Bruns and Jean Burgess, "Researching News Discussion on Twitter: New Methodologies," *Journalism Studies* 13, no. 5–6 (2012): 801–14.

49. Andrew Leonard, "Open Season," *Wired*, May 1, 1999, accessed November 10, 2017, www.wired.com/1999/05/open-source-2/.

50. Jean Burgess, Axel Bruns, "Twitter Archives and the Challenges of 'Big Social Data' for Media and Communication Research," in *M/C Journal* 15, no. 5 (2012), accessed January 23, 2016, www.journal.media-culture.org.au/index.php/mcjournal/article/viewArticle/561.

51. van Dijck, *The Culture of Connectivity*.

52. Madhavi Mallapragada, "Desktop Deities: Hindu Temples, Online Cultures and the Politics of Remediation," *South Asian Popular Culture* 8, no. 2 (2010): 109–21, doi: 10.1080/14746681003797955.

Further Reading

Chun, Wendy Hui Kyong. *Control and Freedom: Power and Paranoia in the Age of Fiber Optics*. Cambridge: MIT Press, 2008.

Goggin, Gerard and Mark McLelland, eds. *The Routledge Companion to Global Internet Histories*. New York: Routledge, 2017.

Herman, Andrew and Thomas Swiss, eds. *The World Wide Web and Contemporary Cultural Theory*. New York: Routledge, 2000.

Jenkins, Henry. *Convergence Culture: Where Old and New Media Collide*. New York: New York University Press, 2008.

Nakamura, Lisa and Peter A. Chow, eds. *Race After the Internet*. New York: Routledge, 2012.

25.
GAMES AND GAMING
Matthew Thomas Payne and Nina B. Huntemann

Introduction: "The Play's the Thing"[1]

Video games are enigmatic by design. They are challenging objects of study because they have been purposefully engineered to withhold; they are computational sphinxes, created to tease money, time, and energy from those daring to engage their algorithmic riddles. Simply put, video games are "desire machines."[2] Take, for example, the first popular incarnation of video games, your typical coin-operated arcade game. Housed inside a wooden cabinet adorned with spirited artwork crafted to attract the wandering eye, this technical curiosity calls out to passers-by. It invites them, for only a coin or two, to interact with the characters, narratives, and puzzles hidden within its lines of code. It welcomes its pay-to-play adventures: "Player 1, press start." It holds out hope to those bested by its wily programming: "Insert coin to continue." And it welcomes: "Player 2, enter your initials," so their performance might stand the test of time (or until it's unplugged). No longer confined to the arcade, video games continue to manufacture desire, luring us in with quick plays during the morning commute or long, late-night raids with friends. As the experiential product of a computational text and a user's playful disposition, gameplay is an elusive concept that is fragile, fleeting, but fun. Gameplay is *why* people play non-electronic and digital games. And it is **gameplay**, perhaps more than any other single formal structure or design element, that is the primary analytic focus of game studies.

We both teach university courses about video games in departments focused on communication and culture to students who intend to pursue careers in film and television production or journalism. Our students are familiar with thinking about media as texts worth scrutinizing, and many are accustomed

to applying critical and cultural theories to popular entertainment. And yet, they will question the academic rigor of a games course. Students confess to owning a variety of gaming devices and having multiple titles installed on their mobile phones and tablets. And yet, they are often quick to exclaim, "I am not a gamer" and assume that only hardcore players deserve such an identity label. While some class assignments require students to create games, we both stress in our syllabi and on the first day that our classes are *not* design courses. Still, students worry that their inability to program games means that they cannot be properly critical of them. This nexus of skepticism, performance anxiety, and technophobia is a challenging, but also, we think, an inspiring, pedagogical springboard from which to introduce students to the serious work of critical gameplay analysis.

Gathering up a methodological inventory and tracing the theoretical lineages of video games and gaming is a tricky business. Like many disciplines or research areas oriented around a medium, **game studies** is fraught with definitional ambiguity, not the least of which is the basic question, "What is a game?" Furthermore, relative to established medium-specific disciplines, namely television and film studies, game studies is an emerging field still working through its growing pains. Game scholars continue to ask, what exactly constitutes our object(s) of inquiry? Is there a foundational set of epistemological questions? And, what theoretical lenses are best for understanding the particularities of the medium?

We believe that these open questions and fuzzy boundaries are not to be feared, but represent exciting opportunities for conducting innovative research. The study of games thus far has benefited from its interdisciplinarity, as scholars from numerous traditions have found their way to games via media studies, psychology, political science, anthropology, computer science, education, etc. This intellectual influx has enriched the study of games as much as it has complicated its nascent disciplinary identity. For games are never just games; they are also rules, and they are culture. Thus, like the other media forms examined throughout this anthology, video games are bound up in popular contestations for social power. This chapter outlines how scholars have endeavored to make sense of games as an expressive cultural form, and how game studies is well-positioned not just to shine a light on the meaningfulness of gameplay but to make contributions to critical media studies generally.

Historical Foundations: Theorizing Play

Because games provide players with interactive affordances and new media experiences that differ from that of radio, film, and television, the study of games demands that scholars attend to these medium-specific differences. A useful point of departure from the various approaches discussed in this collection is the notion of **play**. While most media may be consumed in playful ways—writing fan fiction that expands a fictional universe (see Chapter 15), crowdsourcing clues and solutions to complex narratives (see Chapter 3), creating and donning cosplay costumes of favorite anime characters, or remixing popular music—play is an existential prerequisite for the video game experience.

The historical foundations of game studies are located in play theory and the study of pre-electronic games. The work of Dutch cultural historian Johan Huizinga (1872–1945) and French sociologist Roger Caillois (1913–1978) figure prominently in the prehistory of game studies. Both theorists contributed substantial ideas regarding the importance of play in culture and society. Huizinga's most famous and relevant work to game studies is *Homo Ludens*, first published in 1938, in which he argues that play is a formative element of culture, not merely a byproduct of it.[3] He points to the acts of play observable in animals as a primary, socializing force of many species, and finds play evident in various aspects of human society, including law, war, art, and philosophy. An idea from *Homo Ludens* that became a central—although contested—concept in game studies was his description of the **magic circle** that separates the game world from the rest of the social world. Huizinga argued that a magic circle is formed when participants freely engage with the system of rules

that constitute the game, accepting that what occurs within the magic circle has no influence or bearing on what exists outside of it. The border drawn by Huizinga's magic circle between play and the rest of social reality is a source of debate within play theory and is problematic for critical game studies, given its emphasis on investigating the symbolic connections between fantastic game worlds and everyday life. As will be discussed further below, critical game studies situates gaming within broader cultural environs that determine the kinds of games that can be played, as well as the meanings that players forge while in the throes of gameplay.

In emphasizing the importance of play to the formation of culture, Huizinga saw evidence of play everywhere in the world. He wished for play to be taken seriously, but as a result of this expansive application of play, he offered less insight toward distinguishing different manifestations of it. This is where Caillois' contribution to game studies is most helpful. In his 1958 book *Les Jeux et Les Hommes*, Caillois builds upon Huizinga's definition by proposing a play typology organized by the primary goal of each form: competition, imitation, chance, and sensation.[4] Popular games in these categories include basketball (competition), charades (imitation), roulette (chance), and merry-go-round (sensation). Caillois further suggests that these forms exist on a spectrum between **paidia** (unstructured, free-form play) and **ludus** (structured, rules-based play). For example, playing with wooden blocks is a form of free play. Where and how the blocks are placed is limited only by the weight, size, and shape of each block and one's imagination. The purpose of play may be to build the tallest structure or make the most stable shape, but more often than not there is no specific, universal goal. In contrast, chess is a highly structured form of play, governed by rules for where, when, and how players can move the pieces, all of which are oriented by the goal of capturing the opponent's king. While there may be many achievable paths toward this goal, all possibilities are delimited by the game's rules.

Caillois' typology and play spectrum are useful insofar as they provide basic characteristics from which to differentiate between "playing" and "playing a game." However, like many typologies of complex social systems and behavior, Caillois' categories fail to capture the complexity and wonderment of the play experience. Moreover, video and computer games can exemplify multiple play forms at once, while migrating back and forth on the paidia–ludus spectrum. Imagine, for example, how a "sandbox"-style game like *Grand Theft Auto* (*GTA*) complicates Caillois' typology. The *GTA* games are designed to provide players with opportunities to roam around with no particular objective other than, perhaps, exploration and experimentation. Or, the player can engage in the game's central narrative by completing a linear path through a series of missions. At times, *GTA* adheres to more ludic play while at other moments it exhibits the characteristics of paidia. In either case, the player is always restricted by the game's programming, itself a system of rules, and hardware, which imposes creative limitations of a different sort.[5]

The difficulty in defining the experience of play and/or recognizing when behavior is or is not playful underscores the complexities of studying human behavior. Folklorist, education scholar, and play theorist Brian Sutton-Smith embraced this ambiguity and advocated against any universal definition of play.[6] Instead, he proposed that play, while present in most human societies and animal species, required scholars to consider its cultural specificities. He acknowledged the cognitive function of play in child development, such as in the influential work of Jean Piaget, but argued that the existence of certain types of play, the pervasiveness of particular games, and their attendant meanings can be traced to society's dominant values and belief systems.

While playing a game, existing power structures may be imposed or undermined, and dominant ideologies enforced or challenged. This idea has been a productive concept for critical game studies and supports the notion discussed below that games can be a persuasive platform. As demonstrated in this chapter's case study of *Spec Ops*, playing a video game may not have immediate material consequences outside of its virtual world, but engagement with a game's symbolism and play mechanics can inspire players to imagine that another world is possible, just as games can reveal the unquestioned assumptions and ideological foundations that guide and structure our lives.

Intellectual History: It's *How* You Play the Game

The emergence of a discipline, especially one that is born from a contemporary object, is often defined by what it is not. In the case of game studies, the contrast most often drawn is against the intellectual traditions associated with media studies. Any book written about contemporary media would be incomplete without an accounting of video games. However, while many of the approaches featured in this collection are applicable to the study of games—and, indeed, we point to those connections below—the form's qualities have ushered in a critical lexicon that attends to those particularities. At the most general level of abstraction, we can define video games as: interactive, rule-based structures, facilitated by computational systems that are most typically mediated by screens. Below we highlight key modes of analysis and terminology that have most significantly shaped game studies to date.

Researchers typically approach video games from one of two dominant perspectives, each with its own particular concerns: social scientists focus on behavioral and psychological issues, asking, "What do video games do to people?" while humanists are concerned with meaning-making, asking, "What do people do with video games?" Motivated by concerns over the behavioral influence of arcade games on children in the 1970s, the school shootings and violence debates around games like *Doom* in the 1990s, and moral panics associated with the diffusion of new media generally, U.S. empiricism from the media effects tradition has defined a significant body of social science games scholarship. This contrasts with the formalist tradition described below. The humanist turn in game studies begins in the late 1990s, specifically with the publication of two central books in 1997: Espen Aarseth's *Cybertext*, which explores the structural functions of interactive text, and Janet Murray's *Hamlet on the Holodeck*, which asks if and how storytelling changes with the arrival of new media technologies. These two books and the perspectives of their authors generated two competing frameworks—"**ludology**" and "**narratology**"—that shaped the early intellectual history of game studies.

In *Hamlet on the Holodeck*, Murray wondered what new narrative forms computers would make possible, referencing the historical example of the novel as a form of storytelling made possible only after the arrival of the printing press.[7] To explore this question, she examined examples of hypertext, interactive chat, and video games, applying narrative theory to her analysis. She concludes that computers and other interactive, computational formats will expand the possibilities of narrative expression.

In *Cybertext*, Aarseth is concerned with the tasks that readers must complete in order to engage a nonlinear text, like a hyperlinked work of fiction.[8] The process of turning the page and scanning one's eye across a printed text, Aarseth argues, requires a trivial amount of work from the reader. His critique of Murray and so-called narratologists comes from his emphasis on the work required for engaging nonlinear versus linear forms, which he argues cannot be understood from a narrativist approach. Instead, he contends that new modes of analysis are needed. In either case, both narratology and ludology privilege the form of a text over its representational contents.

Electronic games and computational media are fundamentally different from analog media because they are procedural in nature: designed as a set of executable instructions or rules advanced through human interaction. In order to study games, then, it is necessary for scholars to play games and experience the system under investigation. This can be a daunting undertaking since many games require twenty or more hours to play through. It is also possible to "finish" a game's narrative but not experience all of its narrative possibilities, visit all of its realms, or interact with all of its characters, objects, and side missions. Further complicating matters, persistent and massively multiplayer online (MMO) games like *EVE Online* do not have a definitive end, and the gameplay experience differs considerably with the presence or absence of other players. As a result, the researcher must approach the game not as a static object, but as a dynamic system that generates emergent and unexpected actions.

Analyzing video games as a system of actions is a central concern of digital media scholar Alexander Galloway. In his 2006 book *Gaming: Essays on Algorithmic Culture*, Galloway outlines a classification of actions in games that includes gameplay as well as cheats, hacks, and bugs.[9] Galloway's approach provides a more precise vocabulary for understanding what happens in games, and he considers the potential real-world political consequences of in-game actions. Not only do games simulate and model real-world processes with increasing fidelity, but games also provide the spaces within which we experiment with new social possibilities. This is most recognizable in games about contemporary war, which Galloway argues are less about giving the player a sense of control over the ambiguities and uncertainties of war, and more about a new form of ideological manipulation: the perception of agency within a new system of command and control. However, for every control system governed by rules there is the potential for hacks and chaos, and in the conclusion of *Gaming*, Galloway explores the possibility of subversive strategies through what he calls "**countergaming**."

Similarly to Galloway, game designer, critic, and scholar Ian Bogost also privileges the systems of a game over its classic representational elements (image, text, sound). In *Persuasive Games*, which builds upon the concept of **procedurality**, Bogost argues that a game's meaning comes from a player's interaction with the game's processes or computational procedures. Furthermore, these procedures represent a new form of rhetoric whose "arguments are made not through the construction of words or images, but through the authorship of rules of behavior."[10] Like other forms of persuasion, procedural rhetoric can reinforce existing power structures, but they can also confront and alter these structures (political countergames). In the 2003 game *September 12th: A Toy World*, for example, gameplay invites a player to launch missiles at terrorists in a crowded village. With each "successful" hit the player also destroys homes and kills civilians. Civilians who are killed in the strikes re-appear as terrorists who have become radicalized by the martial intervention. This process repeats until militants overrun what is left of the village. This countergame uses recognizable game rules and mechanics to make the simple point that violence begets violence, and no "win state" in the War on Terror is possible.

While the attention to the procedurality of interactive media is a unique lens through which to examine games, critical analysis must also attend to the representational, contextual, and industrial components that constitute and color gameplay experiences. Jesper Juul, a former "pure" ludologist who once argued that the representation of a game was irrelevant to understanding gameplay, has amended his position. Video games, Juul now contends, are a half-real medium that fuses rule-based systems *and* fictional worlds.[11] Games are played in the real world, but players accomplish wins or losses inside of imaginary places, performing the rules as make-believe characters. So, while two games may be functionally similar, using the same mechanics and programming code, representational differences will fundamentally affect the player's experience.

As literary and media studies have established, consumption of a text is not a passive process, but requires active participation from the reader/viewer who works to decode the meanings of a text encoded by its producers. Games presuppose active participation. The player must press start to begin, and often a game will not progress without actions taken by the player. Decoding a game is, quite literally, to understand the programming code as it manifests in the rules of the game. Interacting with a game, however, is not necessarily bound by the rules of a game. Players frequently exploit the rules and hack the code to their advantage. Mia Consalvo's exploration of cheating in games reveals how players avail themselves of cheat codes, strategy guides, and walkthroughs in order to experience the game on their own terms.[12] Players engage with, create, and trade in paratextual materials, building their expertise or social gaming capital and negotiating the meaning of their gameplay in relation to an industry and culture that enables, reveres, regulates, and disdains cheating.

The role of cheating in gameplay illustrates the importance of broadening an analysis of games beyond the game itself. Gaming and its many connected behaviors are part of participatory culture that has characterized the use and consumption of digital media.[13] For example, some players document their gameplay and record humorous commentaries in "Let's Play" videos using widely available screen capture software. These videos are entertaining critiques of games and game culture, but their popularity is also evidence of the expansive reach of ludic content.[14]

Another arena that demonstrates the pervasive, cultural influence of gameplay as well as its growing market value is the professionalization of electronic sports competitions. Online connectivity and access to ample bandwidth transformed a once niche activity into an international phenomenon. Sociologist T.L. Taylor's ethnographic study of the rise of e-Sports documents the transformation of gameplay competitions from regional video game arcade contests and local-area network tournaments, to a multimillion dollar industry with organized teams, corporate sponsors, live broadcast events, and an international audience of fans.[15] Through her analysis of e-Sports, Taylor addresses larger social and cultural concerns, including notions of labor and leisure, the influence of money on sports, the gendered construction of games and technology, the future of broadcast entertainment, and the challenges faced by subcultures as they move into the mainstream.

The transformation of video gameplay into broadcasted competition, from single-screen viewing into a spectator sport, represents a further commercialization of gameplay. But in widening an *interactive* experience for one into a *viewing* experience for many, e-Sports also signals the continued **remediation** of video games as a cultural form. Coined by Jay David Bolter and Richard Grusin to refer to the historical processes by which newer media are constantly building on and modifying pre-existing media, remediation is the "mediation of mediation."[16] Indeed, it is perhaps a telling sign of our postmodern times that games being played in e-Sports leagues contain visual

and aural elements borrowed from film and television (such as narrative "cut-scenes," non-interactive story sequences) to make them more compelling experiences. These games are then broadcast to audiences as a live televised sporting event would be, effectively fusing cinematic, televisual, and computational elements into a single media product. Furthermore, remediation possesses a "double logic" whereby it simultaneously draws attention to its own practices and hides its own artifice. Like most games, *Spec Ops* reveals the contradictory traits of hypermediacy and immediacy. For example, the game gives players information regarding their weapons and ammo using a heads-up display (hypermediacy), which allows for more precise control, even as it withholds additional narrative prompts that would otherwise guide players' choices (immediacy). *Spec Ops*, as it will be discussed presently, also generously borrows elements from multimedia war entertainment, serving as a useful reminder that researchers ought to put game studies into a wider dialogue with media and communication studies whenever possible.

Case Study: *Spec Ops: The Line*

Spec Ops: The Line makes for a fascinating case study in critical gameplay analysis because it is a duplicitous title that teases the player throughout its campaign with the promise of mission success—a moment that never truly materializes.[17] Indeed, with each "level complete" comes additional narrative confusion and tactical missteps, which beget more complications for the seemingly cursed mission. *Spec Ops* effectively inverts the standard social contract between video game and player. Instead of enjoying a sense of mastery of the game's operational logic and growing an empathetic bond with the player's hero-avatar by "leveling up" their combat abilities, this game makes it clear that enjoying any sense of control in war, even a fictional one, is a dangerous illusion. *Spec Ops* is an engaging game to be sure, as is evidenced by the voluminous praise from journalists and fans. However, it does not necessarily make for a fun experience, putting it at considerable odds with the overwhelming majority of video games on the market. One does not win at *Spec Ops* so much as one endures it.

The game's design studio, Yager Development, updated Joseph Conrad's *Heart of Darkness* for the twenty-first century's War on Terror. *Spec Ops* puts the player in the role of U.S. Army Captain Martin Walker who is searching for the missing soldiers of the 33rd Battalion (aka "the Damned 33rd") who lost contact with military command after the city of Dubai, U.A.E. was nearly erased by monstrous sandstorms. Taking equal inspiration from Francis Ford Coppola's *Apocalypse Now* (itself greatly indebted to Conrad's haunting novella about post-colonial power), Captain Walker and his two Delta Force teammates search for Colonel John Konrad, the commanding officer of the Damned 33rd who became disillusioned and abandoned his post along with his battalion. The player's mission goes from bad to worse as Walker's exploration of the city's ruins produces evidence that contradicts the right-eousness of their "search and rescue" mission as well as Walker's mental stability. Walker's refusal to change course even after committing war crimes makes the player culpable in the horrors that befall his team and Dubai's hapless citizens.

Spec Ops' fairly conventional gameplay mechanics and its level design are fused to narrative and diegetic elements foreign to the popular military shooter genre. The narrative's downward spiral critiques the ideological pleasures of military entertainment writ large while simultaneously admonishing players seeking to lose themselves in the mythological canards of mediated warfare. *Spec Ops*, like the liminal state of play generally, is and is not what it purports to be. That is, the game's form and its content exist in a state of dialectical tension. Formally speaking, the game is a third-person military shooter where the player scrambles for advantageous firing positions to outflank, outmaneuver, and outgun the enemy threats level after level. In this regard, the game is exceedingly ordinary. However, because none of these tactical victories result in any lasting, positive outcomes for the player's team, the game's cultivation of displeasure makes it one of the cultural industries' first mainstream anti-war shooter games.

One of the primary attractions of video games is that the choices a player makes structure their experience. But player actions always unfold within a delimited field of play established by designers' choices. For example, the player can fight Walker's opponents using different weapons and battlefield tactics. However, they cannot freely explore Dubai in whatever manner they choose (e.g., they cannot backtrack, skip levels, select their own dialogue). It is therefore imperative that game studies incorporate into its analyses extra-textual sources that provide a fuller picture of how a game was realized, and how a studio's creative personnel (level designers, producers, writers, artists, programmers, etc.) are themselves constrained by institutional structures and commercial imperatives. Fortunately for game studies, there is no shortage of gaming blogs, developer videos, postmortems, social media, and other materials that can enrich analyses. The *Spec Ops* study benefits from access to critic and designer commentary, just as it benefits from an awareness of how the game compares to others within the popular shooter genre. This *Spec Ops* study treats critic and designer commentaries as important paratextual materials that shape players' experiences of the game, and it contextualizes the game within broader industry design practices by situating it within the popular shooter genre.

Figure 25.1 The player discovers American soldiers who have been tortured and killed (*Spec Ops: The Line*, 2K Games, 2012)

Methodologically, it is essential to know how a game is situated generically within a larger field of cultural production to determine whether its aesthetic choices and textual contours are typical, atypical, or lie somewhere in between. *Spec Ops'* Middle Eastern locale and its basic "cover and fire" combat system are clearly derivative of other post-9/11 shooters. But players who trek beyond the game's initial, tutorial-style levels will see that this is not another jingoistic bro-romp through some sandy, military hotspot. *Spec Ops'* true experiential mission is revealed gradually through its punishing narrative and its hyper-aware mode of address (more on these points shortly). Player-scholars can appreciate the radicalness of the Yager Development team only if they know the design rules that comprise the broader textual constellation of the military shooter. Thus, it behooves researchers to familiarize themselves with the title being scrutinized *and* its marketplace contemporaries to get a sense of the textual expectations affecting a given genre.

Because textual genres cohere both from within *and* from without, a game's implied social contract is evident in its design and is previewed paratextually in its promotional materials.[18] Gameplay trailers, magazine advertisements, developer interviews, and other producer-sponsored materials showcase marketers' varied strategies for selling the public on a game's attractions, while framing how said game should be interpreted. Holistically contextualizing and historicizing gameplay demands that player-scholars immerse themselves (repeatedly) in a game, examine its contemporaries, and track how supporting paratexts serve as preemptive frames of meaning for gameplay. Accordingly, the primary research materials for the *Spec Ops* study discussed here include a close examination of its single-player game mode, a survey of published interviews conducted with the Yager Development team, and the author's personal experience with first- and third-person shooter video games. Putting these varied materials into a critical dialogue enables one to connect digital games to broader cultural concerns and social forces. In the case of *Spec Ops*, the critique born of the disjunction between its generic form and its dystopic content is aimed squarely at the military-entertainment complex.

Spec Ops vs. the Military-Entertainment Complex

Following the lead of critical communication scholars like Roger Stahl, Nick Dyer-Witheford, and Greig De Peuter, the case study discussed above draws on two relatively distinct literatures: media and war scholarship, and video game studies. Fusing these areas enables the researcher to establish that shooters are emblematic products of the military-entertainment complex, before arguing why *Spec Ops'* deviation from that formulaic script is significant. What follows is a brief overview of the key terms and concepts that informed the writing of the *Spec Ops* essay.

President Eisenhower's "military-industrial complex," or the nexus of power and influence between defense contractors, the military, and congressional lawmakers following World War II, became a prime target for criticism when its power was most evident during the height of the Vietnam War. By contrast, the "**military-entertainment complex**" is primarily a post-Cold War phenomenon that describes the network of government, defense, and entertainment interests that collaborate on the production and distribution of a range of commercial and noncommercial cultural goods that paint the United States' wars, its military policies, and its service personnel in a positive light. *Spec Ops* critiques the military-entertainment complex's cultural output by transforming its banal war play into critical play. As the case study explains, "banal war" describes combat imagery and war reportage that has become disaffecting through repetition.[19] Banal war media normalize martial conflicts by making these presumptive inevitabilities entertaining, and video war games have been especially successful at engineering pleasurable, if normative, means for interacting with American Empire.[20]

But instead of embracing the mainstream design truism that a game's story and its system of play should exist in a harmonious relationship, we argue that *Spec Ops* takes the opposite tack to engender a state of **critical play**. According to game scholar and game designer Mary Flanagan, critical play means crafting "play environments or activities that represent one or more questions about aspects of human life . . . characterized by a careful examination of social, cultural, political, or even personal themes that function as alternatives to popular play spaces."[21] *Spec Ops* engages in a veritable "bait and switch" over the course of its single-player campaign, trading the shooter's standard hegemonic pleasures of power and control for an affecting dissonance that highlights the disquieting contradictions that necessarily come with playing shooters. That is, while gamers combat waves of enemies in a hellish Dubai, *Spec Ops* is at war with its gamers—daring them to reflect on what it means to pleasurably play war.

But while the medium holds out the promise for advancing rhetorical claims and fostering consciousness-raising experiences, there are no guarantees that games will engender such moments. In fact, there are economic, industrial, and cultural pressures that actively foreclose critical elements from appearing in mainstream commercial titles. Game designers and producers must therefore make a special effort to integrate such elements and mechanics into their titles if they wish to facilitate these revelatory moments. Like Murray and Bogost, Flanagan too sees mediated and non-mediated games as expressive social technologies that can either reinforce or challenge reigning cultural mythologies.

The very existence of *Spec Ops* proves that, despite the economic and political advantages possessed by those interested in projecting the mythology of an indefatigable and omnipresent U.S. military presence, the medium remains a difficult one to control because it is predicated on experimentation, discovery, and play. Given the technical contingencies of the gaming apparatus, the vicissitudes of its play contexts, and the liminal state of the gameplay experience, we argue that it is crucial that scholars attend carefully to how gaming experiences emerge from specific player–text interactions and how antecedent social practices like design and marketing shape these encounters. Remaining attentive to the ways social practices are imbricated in the video game's algorithmic form *and* in the circuits of culture that swirl around it reminds gamer-scholars that ephemeral "magic circles" of play often serve material interests.

Dispelling with Realism: A Gameplay Analysis of Spec Ops

This case study argues the following: Although commercial military-themed video games produced after the September 11, 2001 terrorist attacks largely celebrate America's War on Terror as a grave but politically necessary undertaking, *Spec Ops: The Line* runs counter to this trend by deploying "ludonarrative dissonance" as a means of critiquing the attractions of military shooters. Coined by game designer Clint Hocking, **ludonarrative dissonance** describes the potential disagreement between a game's narrative and its operations as a gaming system.[22] In the case of *Spec Ops*, the game's shooter format and its dystopian, anti-war content are at irreconcilable odds. The genre asks players to lose themselves in a military fantasy while the narrative and mode of address repeatedly break that spell. The disquieting dissonance that *Spec*

Ops engenders is not a consequence of poor design, but is rather a pointed rejoinder to the design strategies that shooters utilize to mask over the experiential gap between playing a game and taking lives.

Spec Ops' ludonarrative dissonance is achieved principally through (1) its visual handling of the Dubai game space and the Walker avatar; (2) its intertextual references to popular war media; and (3) its real and imagined opportunities for player interaction. *In toto*, the creation of discord and disidentification rather than immersion and escapism generate a sense of distance that questions the illusion of realism that all military shooters trade in, but one that few acknowledge.

Representation

Dubai and Walker function as allegorical proxies for the U.S.-led War on Terror and the player's symbolic participation in, and tacit support of, militainment. The once-opulent city of Dubai, presented in *Spec Ops* as a veritable graveyard of Western excess, stands in as another disastrous consequence of the wars in Iraq and Afghanistan. The Americans did not cause the sandstorms afflicting the city; however, their military-helmed humanitarian aid only increased the suffering of the civilians trapped there. Moreover, Captain Walker eventually comes to resemble the city itself, with each firefight and questionable decision leaving the player's avatar more visually ravaged. By the game's end, the non-descript, white everyman hero has been transformed into a monstrosity—from commanding his teammates with cool confidence, to hurling hoarse expletives at enemies. The player's third-person view of Walker offers a dramatic vantage point for witnessing this game-long metamorphosis, and for reflecting on how it differs from most shooters when it comes to representing the "Other."

The practice of "Othering" in games is predicated on establishing stark divides between the forces of good (i.e., the player) and evil (i.e., the AI-controlled opposition)—a divide that *Spec Ops* purposefully conflates and collapses. In military shooters, the enemy is most often depicted as fundamentally different than the player's character. They are a different color, speak a different language, subscribe to a different ideology, or worship a different god. But in *Spec Ops* the player must face down waves of English-speaking U.S. soldiers who perceive Walker and his two compatriots as the real threat to the citizens of Dubai. Fighting American soldiers and inadvertently killing unarmed Middle

Easterners caught in the crossfire begs the question, just who is the real enemy here? Walker is initially an empty vessel for the player's projection of power. However, this military fantasy becomes a nightmare as Walker emerges as the very monster that he was charged with bringing to justice. It is Walker—the player's own character and proxy—who is effectively "Othered" by the game's end.

Visual documentation is a key asset for making sense of the level design and avatar (de)construction in *Spec Ops*. Gamer-scholars should, as a practical research recommendation, consider complementing their detailed notes about characters, level design, and dialogue with screen grabs. Because Walker's mission spans eight to nine hours for a single play-through, screen grabs become incredibly useful for collecting one's thoughts about how the narrative is visually reinforced through its spatial and character constructs. In fact, over the course of the game's levels, the captured screen images become a visual travelogue chronicling Dubai's crumbling state and Walker's horrific transformation.

Intertextuality

Spec Ops contains numerous allusions to popular war entertainment, and the essay argues that the game's intertextuality serves at least two purposes. First, the Yager Development team uses intertextuality to prove that it is familiar with the cultural milieu of combat fare. For example, the game's soundtrack abounds with music tracks associated with Vietnam War media:

Deep Purple's "Hush," Martha and the Vandellas' "Nowhere to Run," and Jimi Hendrix's "Star Spangled Banner." Similarly, the game's collectible awards—called "achievements" on the Xbox and "trophies" on the PlayStation—which are earned for specific in-game accomplishments, are named after combat films (e.g., *Deer Hunter, Apocalypse Now*), recruiting slogans (e.g., Army of One, Be All You Can Be), and war novels (e.g., *A Bridge Too Far, A Farewell to Arms*).

However, the second, more remarkable use of intertextuality allows the game to alternatively erect and then puncture the diegetic fourth wall by deploying elements that situate *Spec Ops* firmly within the realm of militainment, only to reveal these choices *as* choices—in effect, transforming intertextuality into self-referentiality. The interstitial loading screens between levels, for instance, tease the player with rhetorical questions and sardonic quotes: "Can you even remember why you came here?" "To kill for entertainment is harmless," and "The U.S. military does not condone the killing of unarmed combatants. But this isn't real, so why should you care?" By alternating between moments of immersion and alienation (or Brechtian distanciation),[23] *Spec Ops* functions as a kind of meta-commentary on the rote design practices that shooter games typically pursue in cultivating their delimited sense of military realism.[24]

One of the persistent methodological challenges of tracking media intertextuality is the critic's ability to recognize a text's "winks and nods." Keeping detailed field notes and screen captures certainly helps in this regard, but these are imperfect methods for

Figure 25.2 The game forces the player to kill fellow American soldiers with incendiary rounds of white phosphorous that burn them alive (*Spec Ops: The Line*, 2K Games, 2012)

identifying references. Ultimately, spotting or deciphering allusions depends on being literate with a medium, a genre, and/or a textual universe. Further complicating matters, gaming literacy demands (at least) one additional skill: namely, the performative ability to uncover all those elements that are squirreled away in an interactive world (e.g., "Easter eggs" and unlockable achievements). Indeed, even if gamer-scholars have mastered a game, it does not necessarily mean that they will have explored or discovered all that it has to offer. Gameplay completion, in other words, *cannot* be the standard by which gameplay methodology ought to be judged. Rather, gamer-scholars should instead aim to be as comprehensive as possible by filling in their performative shortcomings with the extra-textual resources mentioned above (e.g., blogs, FAQs, interviews, walkthrough videos).

Agency

Finally, *Spec Ops* achieves its meta-commentary on the illusionary nature of player agency in games by presenting a universe that seemingly needs military intervention (e.g., Dubai's citizens need saving, Konrad should be brought to justice) but where the suffering only increases as the player pushes on. That is, the game reinforces its ludonarrative dissonance by *only* rewarding players' choices with disastrous consequences. There are, to be clear, no "good" decisions that result in a successful mission; conducting multiple play-throughs bears this out. In lieu of rewarding players for experimentation and ingenuity as most games do, *Spec Ops* punishes them for continuing their military misadventure despite growing evidence that they should put the controller down. The tacit promise of meaningful ludic action is but a specter, forever out of reach; the game is a fantastic exercise in futility. As the essay observes, the "freedom" at the heart of *Spec Ops* is summarized nicely by one of its loading screen's title cards (which is borrowed, uncredited, from Jean-Paul Sartre): "Freedom is what you do with what's been done to you."

Some of the most interesting insights about the game's engineering of alienation are found in long-form interviews with and postmortems by the Yager Development team. Across a wealth of online media, *Spec Ops'* writers and producers discuss the process of refining the game with aggravated play-testers, explaining how they set out to create something different for an over-populated shooter market that tends to reproduce the same tired form of military realism. The analytic benefit of including extra-textual sources in a gameplay analysis is that they can reveal the conditions and expectations under which game development happens. For instance, *Spec Ops'* multiplayer mode is forgettable and uninspired. But the reason why this under-produced gameplay mode was included at all is because the publisher, 2K Games, refused to distribute a shooter that did not have a multiplayer setting, believing that its omission would unduly limit sales. This is obviously not something that a researcher could surmise based on gameplay alone. And just as gameplay represents a rule-bounded playground, production histories and developer reports remind researchers that the

Figure 25.3 The player discovers that the civilians their team was trying to save have become "collateral damage," having been burned alive by the player's incendiary weapons (*Spec Ops: The Line*, 2K Games, 2012)

creation of these fictional freedoms are likewise constrained by extant industrial structures and production cultures. The unrelenting deconstruction of shooters' pleasures across *Spec Ops'* narrative campaign forces a reconsideration both of the cultural values guiding the creation of realism in mainstream militainment and of one's relationship to worldly violence. And herein, concludes the essay, lies the game's larger consciousness-raising potential.

Methodological Blind Spots

Even gameplay analyses that strive for comprehensiveness by uniting close readings of textual elements with industry discourse and production trends, such as developer interviews and genre conventions, invariably have their methodological blind spots. Gameplay's fleeting experiential nature and the basic functional contingencies of the object of study make the phenomenon of mediated play fantastically difficult to secure. How much playtime, for example, must gamer-scholars log before they can write authoritatively about a game? What happens if the researcher lacks the skill to advance even after repeated attempts? How should one handle games with branching storylines and multiple playable characters? How many times or how much time must one play before gaining the confidence to stake definitive knowledge claims about such a mercurial artifact? How does downloadable content that extends the playability of games complicate attempts to bracket off gameplay for analysis? What about procedurally generated worlds that change each time the game is launched, games that rely on user-created content, or games that are only multiplayer affairs? How do these variables change the research tack?

The *Spec Ops* case study is not without its methodological shortcomings. For example, the textual analysis does not examine the multiplayer mode. In fact, it was set aside out of analytical convenience because its conventional design muddies the argument that *Spec Ops* is an anti-war shooter. This begs the question, can one rightly call *Spec Ops* a radical game if it contains a gameplay mode that is anything but?

The essay also leans heavily on developer interviews to present a more complete picture of the thinking that went into its creation. However, the creatives at Yager Development and its publisher 2K Games are professionals who have a clear stake in authoring and authorizing their own versions of its production history. Given the precarious nature of

work in the cultural industries, researchers should remember that working professionals might have ulterior motives when presenting their takes on a game's development.

The essay's focus on the intertextuality and conventions of shooters necessarily limits its argumentative scope. Largely ignored in the case study are those popular culture texts that utilize satire and irony to critique mediated warfare. There is no discussion of the films *Dr. Strangelove* or *Three Kings*, or the web-based **machinima** series, *Red versus Blue*.[25] And besides fleeting mention in the conclusion, Hollywood films and TV series that second-guess U.S. interventionism with darker, "gallows humor" are likewise set aside (e.g., *Full Metal Jacket*, *Platoon*, *Generation Kill*). Focusing on shooters at the exclusion of other war media may give the false impression that there is little to learn from other forms of militainment.

Conclusion: Leveling Up? Game Studies after Gameplay

The *Spec Ops* case study was selected for discussion here, in part, because it demonstrates how multiple methods brought to bear on several sources of primary material (gameplay design, production histories, and genre expectations) can create a critical dialogue in order to deeply engage a single game text as well as to make larger, cultural claims. Military shooters not only share representational tropes and design practices, but they also demonstrate how political, cultural, and economic forces give shape to, and are represented in and by, those same algorithmic artifacts. The textual disjunction of *Spec Ops'* generic form and its dystopic content enables its critique to extend beyond the world of gaming to the wider post-9/11 military-entertainment complex. Critical gameplay analysis, in other words, demands that critics account for the form and for the content of games to establish how social power is articulated as an opportunity for play.

Given the medium-specific challenges posed by games and the limitations of this case study, what are the research opportunities moving forward? Does gameplay analysis represent the limit of game studies? Or, posed differently, what else might game studies teach us about how social power is mediated by and through these playthings? Since game studies is a relatively new field, fruitful scholarship is needed in cognate humanistic fields to arrive at more informed gameplay analyses. For example, a thorough examination of the industrial processes involved in producing, publishing, and distributing a video game would be invaluable towards understanding the production contexts within which games are made. Important strides are also being made in game history, as scholars engage in media archeology and determine how historiography will inform their reclamation projects of lost games and gaming cultures of yesteryear.[26]

Game studies is a relatively new scholarly endeavor, but its research goals are not. There is the temptation within media studies to periodize it as an academic novelty belonging to the new century, following the course set by television studies in the late twentieth century and film studies before it. But while video games represent new objects of study, the human activity of gameplay does not. We have been playing games as a species for as long as we have been using language; in fact, most of us played games like "peek-a-boo" well before uttering our first words. Critical game studies makes the case for the cultural significance of actions too frequently dismissed as mere "play" but which speak volumes about the game worlds we choose to inhabit and the corporal world we must endure. Through the purposeful consideration of games and gameplay, critical game studies advances the ongoing human quest to understand who we are, what we fear and desire, and why we play.

Notes

1. William Shakespeare, *The Tragedy of Hamlet, Prince of Denmark*, 15th ed. (New York: Penguin Group, 1987).
2. Tanya Krzywinska, "The Strange Case of the Misappearance of Sex in Video Games," in *Computer Games and New Media Cultures: A Handbook of Digital Game Studies*, eds. Johannes Fromme and Alexander Unger (Dordrecht: Springer, 2012), 158.
3. Johan Huizinga, *Homo Ludens: A Study of the Play-Element in Culture* (Boston: Beacon Press, 1955).
4. Roger Caillois, *Man, Play and Games*, trans. Meyer Garash (Glencoe: The Free Press of Glencoe, Inc., 1961).
5. Electronic games are programs executed on computational systems (platforms), which are a result of software and hardware design. The capabilities of a platform will significantly influence the design and development of a game. Software studies is concerned with the social and cultural influence of software programs, while platform studies investigates the relationship between software and hardware system. Both of these approaches complement the study of games. For an example of a platform analysis of a video game system, see: Nick

Montfort and Ian Bogost, *Racing the Beam: The Atari Video Computer System* (Cambridge: MIT Press, 2009). On software studies, see Chapter 26 in this volume.
6. Elliott M. Avedon and Brian Sutton-Smith, *The Study of Games* (New York: John Wiley & Sons, 1971).
7. Janet Murray, *Hamlet on the Holodeck: The Future of Narrative in Cyberspace* (New York: Simon and Schuster, 1997).
8. Espen Aarseth, *Cybertext: Perspectives on Ergodic Literature* (Baltimore: Johns Hopkins University Press, 1997).
9. Alexander R. Galloway, *Gaming: Essays on Algorithmic Culture* (Minneapolis: University of Minnesota Press, 2006).
10. Ian Bogost, *Persuasive Games: The Expressive Power of Videogames* (Cambridge: MIT Press, 2007), 29.
11. Jesper Juul, *Half-Real: Video Games Between Real Rules and Fictional Worlds* (Cambridge: MIT Press, 2005), 1.
12. Mia Consalvo, *Cheating: Gaining Advantage in Videogames* (Cambridge: MIT Press, 2007).
13. Henry Jenkins, *Convergence Culture: Where Old and New Media Collide* (New York: New York University Press, 2006).
14. In 2014, one of the most popular content creators on YouTube was Swedish gamer Felix "PewDiePie" Kjellberg. His collection of Let's Play videos has attracted more than 28 million subscribers.
15. T.L. Taylor, *Raising the Stakes: E-Sports and the Professionalization of Computer Gaming* (Cambridge: MIT Press, 2012).
16. Jay David Bolter and Richard A. Grusin, *Remediation: Understanding New Media* (Cambridge: MIT Press, 2000), 55.
17. Yager Development, *Spec Ops: The Line*, Xbox 360, 2K Games, 2012.
18. For further insights on the utility of using genre theory and paratexts in critical media analysis, see Chapters 16 and 17, respectively, in this anthology.
19. Nicholas Mirzoeff, *Watching Babylon: The War in Iraq and Global Visual Culture* (New York: Routledge, 2005).
20. See Nick Dyer-Witheford and Greig De Peuter, *Games of Empire: Global Capitalism and Video Games* (Minneapolis: University Minnesota Press, 2009); Nina B. Huntemann and Matthew Thomas Payne, "Online Games and Militarism," in *The International Encyclopedia of Digital Communication and Society, Vol. III*, ed. James Ivory and Aphra Kerr (New York: Wiley-Blackwell, 2015), 828–34; Roger Stahl, *Militainment, Inc.: War, Media, and Popular Culture* (New York: Routledge, 2010).
21. Mary Flanagan, *Critical Play: Radical Game Design* (Cambridge: MIT Press), 6.
22. Clint Hocking, "Ludonarrative dissonance in *BioShock*: The problem of what the game is about," *Click Nothing: Design from a long time ago* (blog), October 7, 2007,

accessed February 25, 2018, http://clicknothing.type
pad.com/click_nothing/2007/10/ludonarrative-d.html.

23. German dramatist Bertolt Brecht would frequently rup-
ture the fantasy illusion of his stage performances by
acknowledging the artifice of the performance space
and its social rules. His goal was to provoke the audience into reflecting on the unquestioned conventions of
theater.

24. See Matthew Thomas Payne, "Marketing Military
Realism in *Call of Duty 4: Modern Warfare*," *Games &
Culture* 7, no. 4 (2012): 305–27.

25. "Machinima," a portmanteau of "machine" and "cinema," typically refers to the practice of editing video
game footage into new narratives. For more on this
fusion of game performance and digital storytelling,
see Henry Lowood and Michael Nitsche, eds., *The
Machinima Reader* (Cambridge: MIT Press, 2011).

26. Mark J.P. Wolf, ed., *Before the Crash: Early Video Game
History* (Detroit: Wayne State University Press, 2012).

Further Reading

Fullerton, Tracy. *Game Design Workshop: A Playcentric
Approach to Creating Innovative Games*, 3rd edition.
Boca Raton: CRC Press, 2014.

Huntemann, Nina B. and Matthew Thomas Payne, eds.
*Joystick Soldiers: The Politics of Play in Military Video
Games.* New York: Routledge, 2010.

Jones, Steven. *The Meaning of Video Games: Gaming and
Textual Strategies.* New York: Routledge, 2008.

Kline, Stephen, Nick Dyer-Witheford, and Greig de Peuter.
*Digital Play: The Interaction of Technology, Culture, and
Marketing.* Montreal: McGill-Queen's University Press,
2003.

Mäyrä, Frans. *An Introduction to Game Studies.* Thousand
Oaks: Sage Publishing, 2008.

Payne, Matthew Thomas. *Playing War: Military Video Games
after 9/11.* New York: New York University Press, 2016.

Ruberg, Bonnie and Adrienne Shaw, eds. *Queer Game Studies.*
Minneapolis: Minnesota University Press, 2017.

Salen, Katie and Eric Zimmerman. *Rules of Play: Game Design
Fundamentals.* Cambridge: MIT Press, 2004.

Suits, Bernard. *The Grasshopper: Games, Life, and Utopia*, 3rd
edition. Peterborough: Broadview Press, 2014.

Sutton-Smith, Brian. *The Ambiguity of Play.* Cambridge:
Harvard University Press, 2001.

Wolf, Mark J. P. and Bernard Perron, eds. *The Video Game
Theory Reader.* New York: Routledge, 2003.

26.
SOFTWARE
Eric Freedman

Why Software Studies?

In a 2012 ad campaign for the iPhone 4S, actress Zooey Deschanel stands inside her retro chic bathroom, wearing pink pajamas. She apparently hears rainfall, and with her iPhone in hand asks Siri for confirmation: "Is that rain?" As Siri begins to answer the prompt, Deschanel steps toward a pair of French casement windows, pauses, and peers through the glass. As the physical signs of precipitation are well within Deschanel's line of sight, her prompt hardly requires the procedural mechanics of Apple's software agent; this act of translation, of turning an analog impulse into a digital signpost seems like an unnecessary detour. To state things more succinctly, the answer is obvious, and yet this advertisement seems to trivialize (or simply naturalize and humanize) the role of **software** (task-oriented computer programs) in everyday life, which perhaps makes the subject of this chapter, the matter of software studies, not so obvious. The goal of this chapter is to "locate" software; for software is a rather challenging "non-object" (given its relative immateriality) that is nonetheless central to contemporary cultural experience.

The field of software studies seeks to lift the theoretical haze surrounding software.[1] The rise of **algorithmic culture** and the degree to which, in contemporary media space, computation informs most machines of projection make this an important critical cornerstone of contemporary media studies.[2] Software is not simply a tool, it is also a structuring transaction, actuated with little debate or understanding, and difficult to tackle alongside an informed textual or industrial analysis of any media form; yet software is the media and the context of convergence culture. Software is everywhere and

nowhere; reflecting on its fluidity and its omnipresent nature, Adrian Mackenzie suggests that software is a "multidimensional and mutating object of analysis."[3] Studies of new media, when they are informed by the legacies of film and television criticism and the preconditions of early apparatus theory (a critical model that emerged in the 1970s to suggest the mechanics of representation—production and reception—have ideological weight), are commonly inattentive to the formative nature of software. Visuality must be reconceptualized in a culture vastly transformed by computerization, where our notion of the screen must be expanded (or excavated) to understand the interpolative power of software and its algorithms.

To illustrate how software studies can lead to deeper explorations in critical media studies, this chapter explores and expands upon my previous analysis of the development and deployment of Siri (the case study essay discussed below) to examine the parallel organizing influence of video game engines (among them, Unity and Unreal). The personal assistant and the video game engine are built on similar assumed relations between operators (consumers) and machines (devices), in both instances codifying communication, action, and expression through the operations of software and hardware (information systems). While our engagements with video game engines are far less familiar than our attachments with Siri, game engines have been used by a wide array of industries to contour play, educate, train, and shape our perception of the world.

This chapter begins with an overview of the key concepts in software studies and traces the critical origins of the field, as well as related paths of inquiry including video game studies and platform studies (which places software in its hardware context).

It surveys the historical connections between media and computing technologies and considers the critical and practical intersections between software and everyday life. The chapter emphasizes the importance of understanding programming and code, and developing computational literacy.

The chapter moves on to summarize the most influential approaches to software studies, considering software as an object of analysis but also framing software studies as a discipline—a critical lens for analyzing contemporary digital culture. The chapter pays particular attention to those critical models that understand coding as a transformative practice, forging new social, economic, and industrial relations, and opening up new modes of play and expression. Code and data, and software and hardware, interact as a discursive construct shaped by history, culture, industry, and technology.

Cultural Histories

We live in a software culture, which we can begin to approximate first by gathering together our everyday software and then expanding our scope outward to consider the toolsets that impact our lives, even if they are beyond our reach: search engines, social media systems, mapping applications and global positioning systems (GPS), blogging platforms, instant messaging clients, online shopping portals and their offline warehouses, assemblies and distribution systems, aeronautical and military systems, platforms that allow the writing of new software (including APIs— application programming interfaces), and game engines. We may differentiate between software programs (applications) and software environments (application contexts—for example, within an operating system, as part of a database system, or framed by a suite of development tools); between common-use software that connects industries and user groups (technologically integrated market sectors) and software deployed in micro-industrial contexts (such as Amazon's inventory management system, and middleware deployed in peer-to-peer architectures for systems integration). Collectively, these reference points produce a sense of computational ubiquity that is lived and material, and may be broadly framed as part of increasingly complex information space, of context-aware, data-rich connections between software and the physical world.[4] We should differentiate between software and **code**; software represents one set of fixed relations for what is otherwise a context-free set of abstractions, while code refers to the written programming statements and compiled instructions of a computer language. Software allows us to consider code as a material practice, as one possible design of organized computation—a formal community of agents.[5] Mackenzie notes that code allows us to understand the relative mutability and stasis associated with software; it pushes us to reconsider traditional studies of new media that treat internal data structures as static formalizations of attributes that can simply be read.[6] In this chapter I hold onto both terms—software and code—as my goal is to isolate and unlock the contingencies of the former by speaking to the expressive possibilities of the latter.

Software studies is an interdisciplinary field that emerged over the last decade, as a creative and critical approach to the theories and practices of computing—to understand the core yet under-examined role of software in culture and society. Software can shape subjectivity, social agency, politics, and aesthetics; and it is produced, activated, theorized, and re-inscribed by computer scientists, engineers, hackers, consumers, artists, technologists, philosophers, entrepreneurs, and industrialists. The limits of participatory culture, where tech-savvy consumers are also empowered producers, are tethered to the relative openness of coded architectures; as software applications become more complex, their scripts become more specialized and inevitably de-democratized. At the same time, new programming languages such as Apple's Swift have begun to recolonize the terrain, setting new standards for open-source environments.

As a critical corrective, software studies examines the specific nature of software (the medium) and its infrastructural position in everyday life (its context). The first Software Studies Workshop was held at the Piet Zwart Institute, Rotterdam in 2006, followed by a second convening at the University of California, San Diego, in 2008. These gatherings brought together key academic voices in the field and led to the development of the Software Studies book series at MIT Press. Software studies has continued to gain traction within educational circles as core curricula have opened up to include information and computational literacy (and liberal arts fields have expanded to embrace the digital humanities) and beyond the academy as the labor market has revived skills-based initiatives in high-tech fields including software programming, mobile application development, data analysis, and user experience design. These two impulses have foregrounded to varying degrees the material layer of software (as a matter of

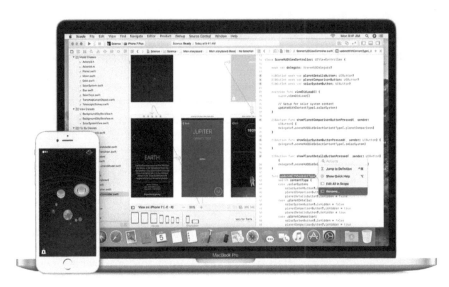

Figure 26.1 Apple offers a full suite of development tools as part of its design, build and deploy software ecosystem (https://developer.apple.com/develop/)

language and engineering) and its ideological layer (as an instrumental part of social formations).

Software is at the center of our global economy, culture, social life, and, increasingly, our politics; it lies at the heart of various institutional operations that need control mechanisms, data management, and assessment tools, from social service agencies to hospitals to universities (Jenzabar and Canvas are two common systems used in higher education) to scientific research labs, corporate retailers, and municipalities (which deploy a number of digital tools for mapping, data visualization, and data-driven decision making, including ArcGIS). Online social network sites such as Facebook have their own structural logics that map the fundamental premises of sociality. Software undergirds contemporary systems of representation, communication, organization, and interaction; software is the substrate and context of media. Every software program has distinct architectures of coding, scripting, and programming that govern basic linguistic processes, the specificity of contextual actions, and the implications of device control. We may understand the impact of software on material culture, but what methodology do we use to scrutinize the immaterial layer of code?

Software studies does not simply map the techniques of critical media studies onto software objects; it calls for us to consider the transformative nature of digital technologies (and not simply digital media) across visual and aural culture; software studies cuts

across radio, film, television, video games, mobile, and other media forms and environments. Software studies situates digital technologies in their cultural contexts as part of broader emerging media and information ecosystems, examines specific artifacts of code and their operations (a strand of inquiry often referred to as critical code studies), elevates the industrial labors of programmers and the machinations of programming languages, and outlines the contours of the technological imagination. Software studies can be focused on code, language, network, environment, interface, and design (while the study of computing systems—a series of unique relations between hardware and software—is commonly considered platform studies). Software studies consistently links the technical considerations of software to economic, political, cultural, and ideological concerns, and connects software as an object, material, and medium to software practice.

It is helpful to frame the data transformation that takes place during coding as a meaningful act and not simply a technical feat of software engineering. The aim is to connect theory to praxis, and algorithm to action to material outcome. We see the end result of this process in the content-delivery services provided by Amazon, Netflix, and other digital distributors, and the algorithms these service providers use to produce communities of interest—online recommendations steered by artificial intelligence. These recommendation engines are produced by a mathematical process. The artifacts are the net result of collaborative filtering, sorting large volumes of data into groups with shared affinities, and the whole operation is the result of a synergy between science and entertainment. Engineers have been firmly brought into the fold of the contemporary media industries. Media technologies and computing technologies have always experienced a close affinity, and both are central to modern mass societies. If we want to understand contemporary techniques of control, communication, representation, vision, writing, and interaction, our analysis cannot be complete until we consider the layer of software. If we ignore this critical blindspot, we are in danger of always dealing only with "outputs"—the all too obvious artifacts of media studies—rather than the programs and socially contoured industrial processes that produce these outputs. The ability to generate, organize, manipulate, and disseminate data, though part of the developmental trajectory of computer programming, has a much broader impact, influencing how we process the world around us. Computational space has become part of lived space (we live in an interface culture), and, in an era of pervasive computing, it is easy to lose sight of the social and political consequences of our companion technologies.

Software studies confronts the tension between our understanding of computers as technologies of visibility (of seeing, connecting, and acting across a network or within a rich field of possibility—our experience living in an Internet of Things where any device can be connected and seamless data flow can be used to build smart cities) and the opaqueness of their internal operations. The tension is invoked yet under-examined in a culture affected so broadly by computerization, and so fluidly connected. Wendy Chun notes: "The computer—that most nonvisual and nontransparent device—has paradoxically fostered 'visual culture' and 'transparency.'"[7] We evidence the former in the sheer volume of digital images that are shared across networks, while the latter, transparency, is the net effect of immediacy, of total information access, and of the combined work of database systems (where consumers are "known" by Google, Facebook, Amazon, their cable companies, and other agencies in the business of commercial surveillance and consumptive desire), artificial intelligence, and interface design to produce unobstructed transactional engagements, effortlessly linking inputs and outputs without calling attention to the language of software.

To study software is to understand any interface as a mediating environment that cannot be untethered from the more obviously critically inflected signposts of content or the subtler trails of core technologies that transform space, place, and time into data points; an interface stands between these foreground and background layers of narrativity and the engine. We may understand this, as Alexander Galloway points out, as a layer model, with mathematical logic at its core. An interface is an intentionally designed set of relations that serve as the nexus of the embodied production of social space. An interface is a second-order process. Google, for example, would like to be our primary lens on the world, through its networks, applications, and devices; the company's interlinked Nest products (camera, thermostat, doorbell, alarm) provide perspective on a home's well-being while recording and revealing our interactions with domestic space through a series of visual and aural cues—the alarm speaks and glows, the thermostat produces images of green leaves, the doorbell detects and records. Similarly, Lyft and Uber have translated location-based data into a new ridesharing economy, where the experience of travel is quantified (time and distance) and qualified (value and merit) through the markers of their respective interfaces; neighborhoods are reduced to coordinates. Mapping marks a movement from description (and the actual experience of the terrain) to prescription; the mechanics of data-centric mapping produce a stagnant concretization of travel. Our interactions with these products do not penetrate to their deepest layer: software. The software that drives these products is a primary process that remains invisible and inaccessible to consumers; our awareness of software is raised only when these networked systems seek to update themselves.

As we are presented with new imaging technologies, we are offered new ways of organizing the visual field. Such new patterns and structures may find opposition in the cultures and traditions (the social contexts) that ground them. Yet Herbert Marcuse warns: "In advanced capitalism, technical rationality is embodied, in spite of its irrational use, in the productive apparatus."[8] Freeing up computation and freeing up culture requires a cooperative interaction that makes sense of the complexity of everyday life without an inflexible dependence on predetermined laws of engagement (or programs); yet technological rationality is driven toward efficiency. Our common apps are personal utilities. Both Lyft and Tinder (a location-based mobile dating app that connects mutually interested users through swiping gestures), for example, are symptomatic of a results-driven database culture. They change the way we see and are seen; they channel our autonomous self-interest (to be somewhere or with someone) through data-driven location-based interfaces that can be understood more broadly as willful identification with an apparatus (translating ourselves and others into data points). If code and data, and software and hardware, interact as a discursive construct and contract, their applications and outcomes may provide some useful lessons in understanding to what degree individuality is compromised by the general computational codes and filters of industrially sanctioned technological forms.

Software Studies and Media Studies

Software studies teaches us that computer programming and code are not value neutral. Software studies reveals how space and place, engagement, and subjectivity can be contoured by the disciplinary logics of computerization and algorithmic manipulation. To understand the ideological implications of new technologies, media studies must attend to the architectures of hardware and software. Software studies can produce new critical analyses of film and television in an age of networked digital media, where encryption, compression, and delivery inform our analyses of screen culture. While we may readily access the ideological value of the varied objects that emerge from the repurposing of new technologies, we need to pay equal attention to the "immaterial" practices that birth such arrangements. This is the focus of software studies. What we may also discover along the way is the inherent value of procedural and systems literacy, as we become aware of the role of software in socio-cultural relations and its position as a protocol for control. From a progressive ideological vantage point, the study of software opens us up to the possibility of free expression in a landscape of normative, stable, and centrally developed interfaces that erase the open operation of code and the performative nature of (programming) language. We may conclude that code is not deterministic—code is affected by social, political, economic, and emotional processes.

Software studies uses and develops cultural, theoretical, and practice-oriented approaches to build critical, historical, and experimental accounts of (and interventions with) the objects and processes of software. It considers how software reformulates the processes, ideas, institutions, and objects of contemporary culture and society around their closeness to algorithmic description and action. Software studies broadly explores the histories of computational

cultures, drawing from the intellectual histories and resources of computing, yet working reflexively beyond any particular disciplinary boundary, such as media studies or the computer sciences, to explore more purposefully the possible entanglements across otherwise siloed academic environments. As a valuable lesson in contemporary media studies, software studies works across theory and practice, objects and flows, and examines the construction of information space. Software studies speaks to assumed demarcations between the complexity of code, the simplicity of interfaces, and the matter-of-factness of objects; while interfaces are designed to efface the complexity of code, code in itself is more often about simplifying the technical procedures of social life, fostering models of unquestioning value and exchange, filtering and aggregating, finding affinities and translating inquiries into simplified binaries. Franco "Bifo" Berardi suggests, "Compatibility and consistency and syntactic exactness are the conditions of operational functionality of code."[9] Programming languages depend on precise sets of rules; statements need to connect. Yet code is a technological construct emerging within a localized industrial context; it is a language borne of a particular moment, and as with any language, as with any semiotic act, it institutes limits.[10] Any discussion of new media must exceed simply talking about the technological apparatus or technological events; every instance of new media is at its foundation a multiply determined development—a process wherein technology is deeply embedded with other agents. As with the basic tenets of apparatus theory in other media forms (cinema, for example), any significant study must formulate a relation between technological and social agents. Looking backward to Stephen Heath's work in *Questions of Cinema,* we must remember to hold together "the instrumental and the symbolic."[11]

Software studies can serve as a bridge between the sciences and the humanities, and as a productive inroad into more nuanced fields of inquiry such as game studies and the digital humanities. While software studies may seem grounded in the computer sciences, it has particular attachments to media studies. Software studies may be aligned with the study of political economy, as software is requisite to the emergence of a networked information economy. More broadly, software studies may be aligned with industrial analysis. The commercial shaping of software and standards serves the interests of a series of industries looking to protect their intellectual properties; those protections are challenged by the very nature of their digitally encoded cultural products (such as audio files). The Digital Millennium Copyright Act and the attack on peer-to-peer file-sharing services is an obvious example of the importance of software and the tenuous status of open-source development; open-source development is a free software approach grounded in a nonproprietary model based on shared effort, made possible through Web-based hosting services such as GitHub that facilitate distributed source code management and co-creative application development. Software undergirds all of visual and aural culture in the digital age, and an understanding of the mechanics, imperatives and regulations of software can deepen our critical engagement with a wide array of objects and industries. The critical importance of this line of inquiry is that algorithms act transversally on both humans and machines—though statements of machinic discourse, their effects are broad and real.[12]

The Intellectual History of Software Studies

Lawrence Lessig has made clear that code is a part of the regulatory process, although it is differentially applied.[13] We often forget the evolutionary nature of technological practices; focusing too much on ontological considerations, we fail to culturally situate the medium—which is a critical part of more precise media criticism. Networked communication is a dense mimetic thicket; researchers at Bell Labs understood this as early as 1948, when they began to explore fundamental problems of communication across circuitry—the discord between the semantic aspects of communication and the problems of engineering. "A Mathematical Theory of Communication," published by Claude Shannon in the 1948 issue of the *Bell System Technical Journal*, reads potential communiqués in statistical and logarithmic terms—transposing communication into numerical probabilities and signal-to-noise ratios. The birth of computer culture in the 1950s was largely about solving the language problem; the decade was marked by significant inroads in computer language development and artificial intelligence that would lay the groundwork for subsequent research in human-centered interface design and automatic problem solving.

There have been a number of intellectual efforts to secure the relevancy of code objects such as software. Lev Manovich has taken an ontological approach, outlining the intrinsic properties of software objects and programmable media.[14] Lessig has focused on the commodity value of code.[15] Theorists such as Mackenzie have attended to the machinations of labor (and the production of identity and subcultural formations) associated with the work of hackers, programmers, and those bound up in the consumption of their knowledge capital.[16] Each of these frameworks considers code at a particular juncture, and collectively they suggest code is a continuum— a site of negotiations involving commodity production, organizational life, technoscientific knowledge, and industrially-aligned geopolitical territorialization. Code carries power relations, distributes agency, shapes communication, contours personhood, and organizes everyday life. Yet code readily disappears behind functional surfaces. Software has often been theorized in the context of associated hardware, and in the broader flows of new forms of social interaction that may be regulated by program and code; however, software is not a singularity, nor does it necessarily reside in a bounded location. Software exists within and across networks of information, although we are most commonly aware of its presence on our mobile devices and personal computers.

New media theorist Friedrich Kittler characterizes the cultural problem and importance of code by suggesting, "Programming languages have eroded the monopoly on ordinary language and grown into a new hierarchy of their own."[17] Code evades perception; as it reaches from simple operations into complex languages, it also moves through several distinct assemblies, passing from the fluid production framework of programmers to the relatively fixed mechanisms of hardware controls. The programmer invariably steps out of the equation, leaving the program to run on its own; as code evades our cognition (which is code by design—it enables us to act), it also appears to write itself and conceals its constitutive limits.

The intellectual traditions of software studies emerge from a number of theorists and practitioners engaged with the field of interactive computation, including Vannevar Bush (who conceived of the Memex in 1945—a storage device aligned with the principles of associative indexing that serves as a precursor to modern hypertext) and Douglas Engelbart (who debuted the oNLine System in 1968 as part of a call to building collaborative knowledge-sharing environments). To borrow Engelbart's phrase, these efforts collectively served to "augment the human intellect," to connect human and machine-based logic, and required the study of natural-language processing and reasoning. These affinities extend to Mark Weiser's research on ubiquitous computing at

Xerox PARC (Palo Alto Research Center) beginning in the 1980s, with its emphasis on the convergence of computational space and lived space. Taken together, these efforts set the stage for modern efforts in augmented reality that have transformed the world into a datascape—a series of densely locked information layers. The critical work needed to unravel contemporary media space can be traced to the efforts of Matthew Fuller and the gathering of the Software Studies Workshop in Rotterdam in 2006; the project's stakeholders sought to mend the gaps in the study of computational media and culture by attending to the materiality of software and staking out new paths of scholarly inquiry.

Case Study: Applied Software Studies

In my case study on networked bodies, "Technobiography: Industry, Agency and the Networked Body," I consider how subjectivity may be increasingly understood as a series of encounters with technology; in essence, it is written through and shaped by them.[18] We see this in the life of smart objects that record our personal preferences and recognize us, and we see this in the type of fluidity we expect in our engagements with new technologies.[19] My research on technobiography is a way of making material the bridge between algorithms and outcomes, and attending to the computational layer of things; my goal is to shed light on the ideological machinations of new media industries. As such, I am following up on the fundamental proposition of the Rotterdam workshop, and of software studies in general, that software is a valuable object of study. My analysis pulls together histories of technology and the associated fundamentals of computer science, related scientific studies and their literatures, as well as a broad range of artifacts (including corporate press releases and advertising campaigns) that punctuate the landscape of applied material innovation. I weave together these primary and secondary materials across a number of case studies to illustrate the complex relays between science, technology, industry, and culture, and to highlight several key pressure points between personal agency and industrial design—relations that are circumscribed by the historical, technical, and material conventions of industry. What is to be gained from studying software? If the goal is to understand the ideological trappings of new technologies, and our operational limits as citizen-consumers, we must understand the architectures and pipelines of hardware and software development. To do so, we must

be equipped with the requisite technological literacies, and we must know how to position our readings of software within a meaningful critical frame—one that is reflexive and not merely procedural, mechanistic, or pseudo-scientific, and one that may not follow the familiar outlines of media studies.

The term "**technobiography**" calls on us to understand how we are situated within social relations that inherently involve engaging with information technologies and to consider to what extent our lives may be mapped through our encounters with technology. I am interested in how our technological dependencies may be driven by industry—how Apple, for example, humanizes its products, fostering personal attachments with new communication frameworks such as Siri. Or how Nike runners may see themselves as a data trail—the company's shoe-based biometric devices give athletes insight into their well-being. These deeply felt relationships we develop with technology are structured by private-sector research, and these material practices bridge the work carried out in research laboratories with the popular deployment of parallel technologies in the commercial sector. As they do so, they bridge multiple media forms and object lessons, and are a comfortable entry point to media studies in an era marked by continued convergence.

Siri, the human-like personal assistant Apple has embedded in its mobile devices, lies at the center of my case study. The personal attachments we develop with Siri are structured by underlying algorithms linking semantic intent to information retrieval (in effect translating natural language into data acquisition) and are the product of years of defense-sponsored research on speech recognition and artificial intelligence at Menlo Park, California-based SRI International. The technology was developed as part of the CALO (Cognitive Assistant that Learns and Organizes) project, an initiative launched by SRI in 2003 with $22 million in startup funds from the Defense Advanced Research Projects Agency (DARPA). A complex set of artificial intelligence insights run behind the app. A chain of machine-learning, natural-language processing, and Web-search algorithms translate each consumer query and effectively transform the iPhone into a body with a spatial awareness and a sense of intent. Years of research and development have been channeled into fixed material relations that forge symbiotic attachments between the software and the user. With a mobile device such as the iPhone, these algorithms can be tethered to the contextual awareness of GPS location reading and end-user preferences to transform the search engine into a *do*[i] engine. Most locative prompts, such as asking Siri for directions (driving, walking, or riding on public transit), can be used to illustrate this point (while also revealing the hermetic nature of an iPhone ecosystem that intuitively opens Apple Maps rather than Google Maps).

As a nonprofit research and development center doing contract research for the government and other clients, SRI has focused on the conceptual and practical relations between science, technology, and communications since its founding as the Stanford Research Institute in 1946. A notable event in the institute's history was a public lecture by Douglas Engelbart on December 9, 1968.[20] He and his research colleagues from the Augmentation Research Center presented a live public demonstration of the collaborative computer-based system, NLS (oNLine System), they had been working on since 1962. Engelbart's tech-laden lecture was the public debut of many innovations, including the computer mouse, hypertext, object addressing and dynamic file linking, and shared-screen collaboration involving two persons at different sites communicating over a network with an audio-visual interface. The session featured the computer-based, interactive, multi-console display system being developed at SRI under the sponsorship of ARPA, NASA, and RADC (Rome Air Development Center), and was readily situated as part of a contemporaneous research agenda that suggested interactive computer aids could augment intellectual capability.

During his address, Engelbart took what at first seemed a rather humorous digression: "Let me go to a file that I prepared just after my wife called me and said, 'On the way home will you do a little shopping for me?'" But he proceeded by readily contextualizing the conversational fragment: he organized his shopping list into a series of numbered statements, and illustrated how the system can reorder the terms according to the logic of commerce—the layout of the grocery store—as he grouped the list's produce items. He also visualized his to-do list as a line diagram that crudely traced his route home, with stops at the library, the drugstore, the market, and other destinations; the data set became a task-oriented vector and a formal abstraction of agency within a personalized geography. Engelbart's demonstration can be situated as a necessary moment in the development of computer culture and the doctrines of commodity fetishism; the success of new technologies can be correlated in part with the relative openness of their semantic intent, and their ability to foster new and deeply felt personal relationships.

Looking back at Siri's pre-history, the challenge to the CALO team (and for SRI to bring its innovation to market) was explaining the core architecture of its cognitive agent—the belief-desire-intention (BDI) framework that structures the mental state of the agent and plays an important role in determining its goal-oriented behaviors.[21] Trust is necessary to any successful private- to public-sector migration. The team determined that providing transparency into the system's reasoning and execution was key to establishing trust, to aligning the mental states of agent and consumer, both in their latent and active relations.[22] The goal was to perfect the symbiotic attachments between the software and the user, and transparency seemed to be a necessary foundation for what would become a relatively calm technology. Translating the lessons of transparent BDI-based task processing into popular terms structured into natural-language voice commands, Apple suggests, "Siri not only understands what you say, it's smart enough to know what you mean. And Siri is proactive, so it will question you until it finds what you're looking for."[23]

One difficulty in deciphering these systems is that in today's culture industry, the cultural and the industrial are often coterminous, and the reverse engineering of algorithmic manipulation demands that programmers understand what end users are doing.[24] At the same time, consumers are acutely aware of the fetishistic logic framing their engagement with smart devices—that these relations are governed by interrelated forms of technical transcoding. Software is dynamic and performative—the dynamic outputs of real-time computation driven by our interaction with rule-based systems. Program code is complex and not obviously meaningful, especially outside the context of its associated libraries that may exist across multiple virtualized spaces and in multiple forms (the script, the database). Program structure does not have a singular correlation with end-user experience. Instead, we need to focus on the transactional nature of code, interface, device, content, and user, and the role of software in larger media ecologies. Siri embodies the principles of postindustrial capital, as a body at once localized (at our fingertips) and dispersed (comingled with the data cloud). This desiring (search) engine is part of a productivity suite and, as such, runs antithetical to any experimental and potentially subversive practice that might interfere with the structures and desires of capitalism; Siri may invoke the agentive concept of "becoming," but its value is based on the reliability (the completeness) of its executable code and the certainty of its tasks and outcomes—the imperatives of syntactic exactness. The indeterminacy of Siri's application, which speaks to the user's desire, is matched by the determinacy of its innate mechanics, which speaks to the commercially driven mandates of programming and design. Siri's response to any question is the product of machine learning enabled by end-user data, a localized dynamic cache, and a neural network.

My challenge throughout this analysis is connecting code to action or intent; as distributed material practices are messy, they defy orderly structural analysis. While I can situate Siri as a rule-based system, I cannot continuously monitor the proprietary advances in artificial intelligence that are changing its codebase and modifying its operations. Siri continues to advance as part of the broader landscape of machine learning (as conversational and facial recognition converge). It is far easier (and perhaps more satisfying for some) to examine the evolution of our quotidian negotiations with Siri (an ego-driven series of transactions and actions) than it is to examine the roots and the evolution of Siri's semantic intent.

The Lessons of Software Studies

The questions of identity politics raised by traditional screen studies (questions about representation, spectatorship, narrative form, and cultural context) cannot be satisfactorily mapped onto the material relations embodied by interactivity without understanding the coded mechanics of agency and the various industrial discourses that drive interactive architectures. We need to tackle the coded rules of engagement that are a fundamental part of the industrial processes of development and fabrication. We must move beyond the surface, taking a multilevel approach without losing the image or object. We need to read across image, interface, and interaction, and examine the industrial frameworks that contour our technobiographic practices of work and play.

Siri is a powerful inflection point to illustrate the pervasive yet under-examined role of software in the culture at large. Yet Siri is one of many informatic systems. Since writing about Siri, I have expanded my research to consider other software artifacts, all of which can be opened up to highlight the deep cultural dependencies between organic and inorganic actors and the all-too-common critical rift between surface and substrate. As one final object lesson that may help media scholars tease out those relations, consider the

relative absence of analytical work on video game engines. As with Siri, the game engine, as an object of critical inquiry, can be used to illustrate the synthetic power of computing and the instrumentality of code. Engine development took root in the early nineties and fostered a well-defined separation between core software components and functionalities (such as rendering, physics, collision detection, audio systems, scripting, and artificial intelligence) and game specific content (the art assets and rules of play). Engine development built on the already-extant separation of source code from assets and resources (data). The engine is a data-driven architecture, while a game contains hard-coded logic or special-case code to render specific types of assets. The game engine can be best understood as a foundation, though the engine itself can be subdivided between runtime components (the subsystems required when a game is executed) and a tool suite (for digital content creation) that suggest even more deeply bifurcated fields of production and analysis.

The game industry is not simply a sum total of its software enterprises and its serialized intellectual properties; it is also an arena of hardware and software development and licensing. Brand names are not simply attached to game franchises, but also to engines that govern the physics-based properties of characters and, by extension, those players who read and engage them. With most engines, success is measured by the naturalness of the relations across engine, asset, controller, character, and player. The proprietary game engine is illusive; beyond the editor environment, it is pure code (although some engine editors feature integrated visual scripting tools to foster collaboration between artists, designers, and programmers). For developers, game engines create a series of fixed relations but also present a necessary mechanical order. Game engines make the process of development more economical, but the need for rapid development and cross-platform deployment that engines answer also presents a trade-off between order and control, and freedom and possibility. The writing of an engine requires that larger development teams work through the idiosyncratic approaches (to writing code) of individual programmers to arrive at a common codebase. The engine allows the insertion of an infinite variety of assets that may perform the same way; the engine provides the syntax and produces the relative openness of the game universe. The engine controls the soft and hard physics, determines the relative utility of exploration, and emits the signals of agency—the engine determines the relative impact (and realness) of our (avatar's) presence on the world we inhabit, and the general push is toward realism in effect and affect. The ongoing industrial migrations of game engines (across entertainment forms, 3D imaging, prototyping and manufacturing, scientific visualization, architectural rendering, cross-platform mixed reality, and within the military) suggest they have broad power for organizing the cultural field. In a multi-million-dollar deal with game developer Crytek, Amazon licensed the CryEngine in 2015 as a codebase for its own proprietary Lumberyard engine; the company's goal was to expand the Amazon Web Services ecosystem by consolidating a suite of products and services for video game developers (tools for building, hosting, and livestreaming).[25]

Several of the major 3D authoring tools, including Unreal and Unity, and their respective parent companies, have had a significant impact on contemporary visual culture, and, for this area of my research, they provide a useful entry point to consider the technical and ideological power of game engines. NASA undertook its first initiative with Unity in 2008, using the proprietary engine to develop the "Cassini at Saturn Interactive Explorer" (CASSIE), a project to showcase the agency's mission to Saturn, which began in 1997 with the launch of the Cassini-Huygens satellite. Engineers at NASA's Jet Propulsion Lab took real mission data from the spacecraft to build an interactive game-like environment using Unity. The CASSIE expedition tracks the satellite over a portion of its mission, following its movement and maneuvers, and tracing the path laid out by mission scientists and navigators.

In 2009, NASA launched "Eyes on the Earth 3D." Developed using Unity's browser-based visualization technology, the application displays the location of all of NASA's currently operating Earth-observing missions in real time. These missions constantly monitor our planet's vital signs, such as sea-level height, the concentration of carbon dioxide in our atmosphere, global temperatures, and the extent of sea ice in the Arctic. Widening its scope, in 2011, NASA launched "Eyes on the Solar System," an interactive Web-based tool that allows users to experience missions in real time (and to travel through time). The tool is populated with NASA data dating back to 1950 and projected to 2050.

NASA released its first mission simulator game *Moonbase Alpha* in 2010 (built on the Unreal Engine 3) and its second *NetworKing* in 2011 (built on the Unity Web Player). Both educational games illustrate NASA's commitment to foster reform in STEM (science, technology, engineering, and math) teaching and learning, and signal the currency of software as a tool to shape human knowledge and experience.

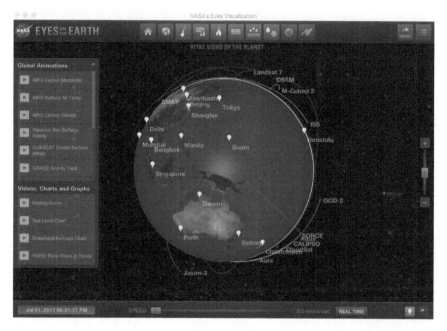

Figure 26.2 NASA's Eyes on the Earth displays the locations of all of the agency's currently operating Earth-observing missions in real time and invites viewers to add a number of global surface and atmospheric layers

In 2011, Unity announced a partnership with the U.S. military. The company's press release promotes the broad potential and comprehensive benefit of its proprietary engine: "Today's announcement means that Unity can be used to create and deploy task management trainers, virtual worlds, situational awareness trainers, cultural awareness trainers, medical trainers and various other serious game applications for the US Army and Air Force."[26]

Unity's client list is extensive, and includes a vast net of media companies, including Disney, Microsoft, Warner Brothers, and Electronic Arts, and corporate customers such as Coca-Cola. Its development tools have been adopted by large and small media production studios, educational institutions, students, and hobbyists seeking turnkey solutions for interactive 3D content creation and publishing. Unity-based content can be found across platforms—the Web, mobile, game consoles, and other media-rich environments. What is touted as a democratizing vision of interactive 3D technology is also a closed communications network—a content-creation suite, digital content marketplace, and distribution service—bridging multiple industrial sectors. Game engines are now multifaceted tools; BMW has advanced its vehicle prototyping with the Unreal Engine, as the automobile manufacturer folds mixed-reality systems into its vehicle development process.

To unpack this circuit of relations is to begin the arduous yet important task of turning a critical eye toward examining the ideology of hardware and software, by tracing the seamless migration of particular applications that can be deployed for entertainment or militarized or called into action within the sciences. Geographically based game tools such as NASA's "Eyes on the Earth 3D" and "Eyes on the Solar System" transform each landscape into a playable interface, drawn from a database into a nexus of several complex interactions foundational for the production of embodied space in locative and map-based media. As graphically oriented displays of space, NASA's Unity projects are merely single permutations of distinct data sets; and the sum of interface and database cannot be separated from its cultural layer, its contextual markers, and its historical and psychosocial dimensions. Sites evolve and their evolution—their adaptive dynamism—is consistent with an understanding of technologies as transformative tools. The NASA project (a sum total of its serialized intellectual properties) is accompanied by its own discursive regime that promotes and makes commonsense its message.

This guidance against entropy is a common feature of all engines, many of which are designed to produce knowable space. An engine not only shapes the characters, the field of play, and the environmental mechanics; it also shapes the consumer's interaction by contouring the visual and physical experience. In this latest ideological permutation of the digital age, "immaterial" core technologies are used to reorganize the terrain. The game engine is a type of abstract core technology that, while it may exert its own personality through telltale traces of its various abilities and features (the "machinic embodiments" of nondiegetic code mechanics), is mostly unlinked from the end-user experience layered within it.

Many independent game developers, in the pursuit of efficiency, have no choice but to tie their intellectual properties to the systematized writing associated with one of several proprietary game engines. There are a broad range of engines and development environments beyond Unity and Unreal, including entry-level tools, such as Twine and GameMaker. The latter have been celebrated for their accessibility. Twine is a free, open-source browser-based tool that requires only basic HTML; and GameMaker is primarily a 2D engine that features a drag and drop system, a proprietary scripting language (GML), and a fairly deductive build process of rooms, objects, and pre-built script events. More significantly, for queer game artists, the simpler mechanics of Twine and GameMaker seem to facilitate qualities such as empathy, community, and communicative openness. But we need to avoid understanding even the value of game engine choice in such binary terms. Freedom, expressivity, and multivocality are in every case delimited by software mechanics, and Twine communities don't commonly intersect with Unity communities—creating a set of linguistic (and perhaps class-based) barriers between those who have been taught to code (Unity is part of most academic interactive media programs) and those who have not. Engine choice is commonly driven by language choice and proficiency; most Unity developers write code in C# and most Unreal developers write in C++ (or marry C++ with Blueprint, the engine's visual scripting system). The affordances (and relative complexities) of programming languages parallel the affordances of their engines.

I continue to study software systems, even though I have shifted my attention from Siri to video game engines. And while I am consistently drawn to projects that can shed light on the governing influence of algorithmic culture, each new case study invites new research questions. In my conversations with independent game studios (and developers), my main line of inquiry has been focused on engine choice—understanding the decisions driving engine choice, adoption and development per studio and per project, and the distinct impact of engine choice and versioning on programmers and artists. These teams may have decidedly different mindsets, skill sets, and workflows, but they must work with complementary toolsets (and vocabularies) as part of the game development pipeline.

Closing Thoughts: On Software and Society

By studying software, we are unlocking our ability to be mindful of the manner in which closed design and deployment systems push human agency toward technocentric certitude; by studying software we are getting to know technologies as causal influences in the social trajectories of individuals and their developmental pathways. We should position systems literacy (making sense of complex information systems) alongside other media literacies, and we should expand the application of political economy to weave together the social, individual, cultural, technological, and industrial forces that shape new media. From this critical vantage point, we might also examine several contemporary software practices: the open data movement (the goal of which should be to develop informed, networked publics), and a recent educational movement aimed at teaching children to code (the goal of which should be to develop the forms of digital literacy that are required to understand, interrogate, and thrive in a convergent media environment marked by increasing opaqueness and privatization). We should demand algorithmic accountability (journalists have firsthand experience with the debilitating power of no-fault syndication algorithms).

Code is the new horizon for media studies. We are living in a machine-readable world that can be acted on by software, independent of human control. The power of code is significant. Turning our attention away from information and communication technologies and their associated artifacts as things to be read or, perhaps, simply looking more deeply, software studies allows us to consider the role of code in setting transactional limits, to scrutinize the understated organizational power of code and to expose code as a constant in a changing formula of experienced social relations.

Notes

1. Matthew Fuller, "Introduction," *Software Studies: A Lexicon,* ed. Matthew Fuller (Cambridge: MIT Press, 2008), 4.
2. An algorithmic culture is one defined by informatic software systems. Computers, driven by mathematical imperatives, take on what is considered to be the traditional work of culture—classifying, organizing, locating, connecting—and produce new forms of human thought, expression, and interaction.
3. Adrian Mackenzie, *Cutting Code: Software and Sociality* (New York: Peter Lang, 2006), 2.
4. Patrice Roy, Bessam Abdulrazak, and Yacine Belala, "A Distributed Architecture for Micro Context-Aware Agents," *Procedia Computer Science* 5 (2011): 296–97.
5. Mackenzie, *Cutting Code*, 5.
6. Ibid., 6.
7. Wendy Hui Kyong Chun, "On Software, or the Persistence of Visual Knowledge," *Grey Room* 18 (Winter 2004): 27.
8. Herbert Marcuse, *One-Dimensional Man: Studies in the Ideology of Advanced Industrial Society* (Boston: Beacon Press, 1964), 22.
9. Franco "Bifo" Berardi, "Foreword: Debt, Exactness, Excess," *Speaking Code: Coding as Aesthetic and Political Expression,* ed. Geoff Cox (Cambridge: MIT Press, 2013), xii.
10. Ibid., xii.
11. Stephen Heath, *Questions of Cinema* (Bloomington: Indiana University Press, 1981), 227.
12. Andrew Goffey, "Algorithm," *Software Studies: A Lexicon,* ed. Matthew Fuller (Cambridge: MIT Press, 2008), 18.
13. Lawrence Lessig, *Code and Other Laws of Cyberspace* (New York: Basic Books, 1999), 30.
14. See, for example, Lev Manovich, *Software Takes Command* (New York: Bloomsbury, 2013).
15. See, for example, Lessig, *Code and Other Laws of Cyberspace.*
16. See, for example, Mackenzie, *Cutting Code.*
17. Friedrich Kittler, "There is No Software," *CTHEORY,* October 18, 1995, accessed February 25, 2018, www.ctheory.net/articles.aspx?id=74.
18. Eric Freedman, "Technobiography: Industry, Agency and the Networked Body," *Produsing Theory in a Digital World: The Intersection of Audiences and Production in Contemporary Theory,* ed. Rebecca Ann Lind (New York: Peter Lang, 2012), 51–68.
19. Eric Freedman, *Transient Images: Personal Media in Public Frameworks* (Philadelphia: Temple University Press, 2011), 78.
20. *1968 "Mother of All Demos" with Doug Engelbart & Team (1/3),* YouTube video, 34:45, from a lecture recorded at the Fall Joint Computer Conference in San Francisco

on December 9, 1968, posted by "Doug Engelbart Institute," March 12, 2017, accessed July 5, 2017, www.youtube.com/watch?v=M5PgQS3ZBWA.

21. Anand S. Rao and Michael P. Georgeff, "Modeling Rational Agents within a BDI-Architecture," *Proceedings of the Second International Conference on Principles of Knowledge Representation and Reasoning (KR'91),* eds. James Allen, Richard Fikes, and Erik Sandewall (San Mateo: Morgan Kaufmann, 1991), 473.

22. Deborah L. McGuinness, Alyssa Glass, Michael Wolverton, and Paulo Pinheiro da Silva, "Explaining Task Processing in Cognitive Assistants That Learn," *Technical Report SS-07-04: Proceedings of the AAAI 2007 Spring Symposium on Interaction Challenges for Intelligent Assistants* (Menlo Park: AAAI Press, 2007), 85.

23. Apple, "Apple—iPhone 4S—Ask Siri to help you get things done," 2011, accessed December 19, 2011, www. apple.com/iphone/features/siri.html (site now revised).

24. Alexander R. Galloway, "Language Wants to be Overlooked: On Software and Ideology," *Journal of Visual Culture* 5, no. 3 (2006): 318.

25. With its 2017 acquisition of Body Labs, a 3D body-modeling startup, Amazon expanded its investments in artificial intelligence; the company's interest in avatar-based technologies is part of a broader visual communications and e-commerce strategy.

26. Unity Technologies, "Unity Development Platform and Web Player Certified by the US Army and Air Force," *Marketwire*, May 9, 2011, accessed November 29, 2014, www.marketwired.com/press-release/unity-development-platform-and-web-player-certified-by-the-us-army-and-air-force-1511958.htm.

Further Reading

Bush, Vannevar. "As We May Think." *The Atlantic Monthly* (July 1945): 101–18.

Dourish, Paul. *The Stuff of Bits: An Essay on the Materialities of Information.* Cambridge: MIT Press, 2017.

Engelbart, Douglas C., and William K. English. "A Research Center for Augmenting Human Intellect." *AFIPS Conference Proceedings of the Fall Joint Computer Conference* 33 (December 1968): 395–410.

Fuller, Matthew. *Behind the Blip: Essays on the Culture of Software.* New York: Autonomedia, 2003.

Kitchin, Rob, and Martin Dodge. *Code/Space: Software and Everyday Life.* Cambridge: MIT Press, 2011.

Licklider, J. C. R. "Man–Computer Symbiosis." *IRE Transactions on Human Factors in Electronics* (March 1960): 4–11.

Nelson, Theodor H. "A File Structure for the Complex, the Changing, and the Indeterminate." *Association for Computing Machinery: Proceedings of the 20th National Conference* (1965): 84–100.

Shannon, Claude E. "A Mathematical Theory of Communication." *The Bell System Technical Journal* 27 (July, October 1948): 379–423, 623–56.

Turing, Alan M. "Computing Machinery and Intelligence." *Mind: A Quarterly Review of Psychology and Philosophy* 59, no. 236 (1950): 433–60.

Weiser, Mark. "The Computer for the 21st Century." *Scientific American* (September 1991): 94–104.

27.
DIGITAL HUMANITIES
Miriam Posner

Digital humanities, a relative newcomer to the media scholar's toolkit, is notoriously difficult to define. Indeed, a visitor to www.whatisdigitalhumanities. com can read a different definition with every refresh of the page. Digital humanities' indeterminacy is partly a function of its relative youth, partly a result of institutional turf wars, and partly a symptom of real disagreement over how a digitally adept scholar should be equipped. Most digital humanities practitioners would agree that the digital humanist works at the intersection of technology and the **humanities** (which is to say, the loose collection of disciplines comprising literature, art history, the study of music, media studies, languages, and philosophy). But the exact nature of that work changes depending on whom one asks. This puts the commentator in the uncomfortable position of positing a definition that is also an argument.

For the sake of coherence, I will hew here to the definition of digital humanities that I like best, which is, simply, the use of digital tools to explore humanities questions. This definition will not be entirely uncontroversial, particularly among media scholars, who know that the borders between criticism and practice are quite porous. Most pressingly, should we classify scholarship on new media as digital humanities?

New media scholarship is vitally important. But a useful classification system needs to provide meaningful distinctions among its domains, and scholarship on new media already has a perfectly good designation, namely new media studies (as outlined in Chapter 24 in this volume). So in my view, the difference between digital humanities and scholarship about digital media is praxis: the digital humanities scholar employs and thinks deeply about digital tools as part of her argument and research methods.

Can one produce digital humanities scholarship about new media? Absolutely, if the use of digital tools to research, compose, or disseminate one's work is an integral part of one's argument. But one can also produce nondigital humanities work about digital media. With Steven Jones, I recognize that "some topics and approaches simply live at the fractally uncertain border between the two fields" of digital humanities and media studies. (Video game and software studies come to mind; see Chapters 25 and 26 of this volume.) Nevertheless, I am relatively stern, compared with some other digital humanities scholars, about where I draw the line.[1]

For all its brevity, this definition of digital humanities emphasizes several crucial aspects of the field: hands-on engagement with digital tools and a focus on the humanities question at stake. Moreover, with my use of the word "explore," rather than "answer," I mean to emphasize that humanities questions do not tend to have cut-and-dried answers. The conscientious digital humanist, then, uses technology in her work not to draw definitive conclusions about her source material but to open new possible ways of looking at it.

Why might a media scholar be interested in digital humanities methods? First, digital technology makes it possible to incorporate audio and visual material directly into media scholarship, meaning that the media scholar can produce an argument in conversation with the object of her study, rather than describing in words a work the reader might never see. Curtis Marez, for example, enriches his 2013 multimedia essay on Cesar Chavez's video collection with annotated film clips, audio, and photographs.[2] Digital humanities methods also make it possible to examine shots from many works at the same time, as Lev Manovich does in his examination of shot length and frame composition in the films of Dziga Vertov.[3] Third, deep engagement with digital technology can help media scholars lay bare, and thus more intimately understand, the mechanisms of the media they study. For example, Laila Shereen Sakr both studies media archives and maintains one, in the form of the R-Shief system for storing social media content.[4] Finally, digital technology presents many possibilities for **deformance**, a term devised by Jerome McGann and Lisa Samuels to describe a digital humanities practice of purposely distorting a work in order to illuminate aspects of it the reader might not otherwise have noticed.[5] Nicholas Rombes engages in deformance when he bases his critical arguments solely on frames pulled from a film's 10-, 40-, and 70-minute marks, rather than the entire film.[6]

Tara McPherson, in a 2009 essay, offers the "multimodal scholar" as an archetype for the digital humanist. This new breed of scholar "brings together databases, scholarly tools, networked writing, and peer-to-peer commentary while also leveraging the potential of visual and aural media that so dominate contemporary life."[7] McPherson's multimodal scholar does not assume that the result of her work will be the monograph or the journal article; instead, she considers a palette of strategies and chooses those that best suit her argument and audience. The result might be an interactive web-based database, as it is in Katherine Hayles's experimental article "Narrating Bits" (which is itself about databases).[8] Or it might be a video essay like Catherine Grant's "All That Pastiche Allows," which juxtaposes clips from Todd Haynes's *All That Heaven Allows* with Douglas Sirk's *Far from Heaven*.[9] The multimodal scholar is at ease with a panoply of media, and composes, using digital technology, in the mode that fits her scholarly goals.

As one might expect of a relatively new field, digital humanities scholars have no shortage of debates, both within the field and with scholars in other disciplines. In fact, to the extent that there is a textbook for digital humanities classes, it is probably 2012's *Debates in the Digital Humanities* (and its subsequent annual volumes).[10] Some of these debates can be summarized by the title of a 2011 paper by the digital humanities scholar Stephen Ramsay: "Who's In and Who's Out."[11] As I explain below, digital humanities has attracted a great deal of institutional attention recently. This has sharpened what might once have been fairly abstract debates about the nature of the field into animated struggles over grants, jobs, space, resources, and institutional investment.

One of the most pressing of these battles is over where digital humanities ends and new media studies begins, which I have already discussed. A similar battle rages over whether digital humanities scholars have been insufficiently attentive to the great volume of digital work taking place within the field of composition and rhetoric.[12] Meanwhile, scholars increasingly ask why digital humanities prizes those technical skills valorized by Silicon Valley (programming, data analysis, machine learning) while tending to dismiss those methods by which women, people of color, and activist communities often forge meaning (social media activism, video production, multimedia composition).

This last debate points to one of the most cutting criticisms of digital humanities: that it constitutes a naively positivist refuge from cultural studies, critical race theory, postcolonial theory, and other scholarly methods designed to surface the concerns of marginalized communities.[13] Indeed, Scott Weingart's annual examination of the papers and posters accepted to the field's major annual conference (called simply "Digital Humanities") has shown that works on text analysis, data mining, and history far outnumber papers on cultural studies or media studies.[14] Noting that digital humanities' rise to prominence corresponds roughly with Gayatri Spivak's 2003 *Death of a Discipline*,[15] David Golumbia writes, "Digital humanities as a *politics* has overtaken (though by no means displaced) another, to my mind, much more radical politics, one that promised a remarkable, thoroughgoing, and productive reconsideration of the foundations of scholarly research."[16]

Equally troubling, digital humanities has very real problems with racial diversity and gender representation in its scholarly community. While no comprehensive data has been assembled about the race, gender, and international backgrounds of digital humanities practitioners, almost everyone agrees that this lack of diversity is a pressing problem. "I had never experienced a stronger sense of being racially/ethnically other," writes the Chicana scholar Annemarie Perez of attending digital humanities panels at the 2012 Modern Language Association Convention. "The rooms, crowded to bursting, were visibly, notably white spaces."[17] Thanks to the willingness of scholars like Perez to share their stories, and to initiatives like the African American History, Culture, and Digital Humanities program at the University of Maryland, race is now more frequently a topic of conversation within the field—but certainly not frequent enough.[18] Also like many fields, digital humanities has a decently balanced mix of genders among its practitioners, but its leadership tends to skew white and male. In a speech at the Digital Humanities 2015 conference in Sydney, Australia, the film scholar Deb Verhoeven excoriated the conference committee for an opening night consisting entirely of speeches by men: "When was the last time you saw seven consecutive women get up at a DH conference and speak about anything other than gender?"[19]

These problems are coming to light now partly because digital humanities is expanding beyond a relatively insular group of scholars and into domains like media studies, ethnic studies, women's studies, and cultural studies. And since these fields have powerful methods and critiques of their own, there is some evidence that as digital humanities makes its way into these spaces, the field itself is being meaningfully transformed. Groups like #transformDH, FemTechNet, HASTAC, and #dhpoco have pushed digital humanities scholars to scrutinize their methods and the field's composition, and scholars trained in critical and ethnic studies have been vocal in advocating for more radical forms of scholarship and criticism. It seems likely that the field that emerges from the debates of the current moment will be profoundly different from the field of a few decades ago.

History

Many histories of digital humanities trace the field's emergence to Roberto Busa, an Italian Jesuit scholar who, beginning in 1949, built a concordance (an index of the appearance of every word) of the writings of St. Thomas of Aquinas with the assistance of computers supplied by IBM.[20] In the following decades, a number of scholars followed Busa's lead, producing concordances, authorship analyses, and linguistic studies with the aid of punch-card and paper-tape mainframe computers. *Computers and the Humanities*, the first journal in what was then called "humanities computing," launched in 1966, and the first major international humanities computing conference was held in 1970.[21] (The name "digital humanities" is of relatively recent vintage. It came into wide use only with the 2004 publication of *A Companion to Digital Humanities*—chosen, according to John Unsworth, one of the book's editors, only as a compromise with the book's publisher, who wanted to call the book *A Companion to Digitized Humanities*.[22])

As academic computing centers increased in number and resources in the 1970s and 1980s, the popularity of humanities computing—then focused almost exclusively on texts—grew, too. The widespread availability of the personal computer during the 1980s and 1990s brought computer-assisted research into the purview of the individual scholar, and 1987 saw the launch of the Text Encoding Initiative (TEI), a major international effort to standardize the way that **scholarly editions** (authoritative, deeply researched collections of documents) are encoded. The TEI, scholarly editing, and linguistic projects would dominate humanities computing for some time to come.

The early 1990s saw the development of large archival and digitization projects, many of which incorporated both text and images. The Institute for Advanced Technology in the Humanities (IATH) at the University of Virginia, helped to galvanize the next wave of activity. Founded in 1992 (and subsidized, like Busa's work, by IBM), IATH helped give rise to a number of landmark projects, including Valley of the Shadow, a hypertext archive documenting two communities during the American Civil War; the Rossetti Archive, which juxtaposed the writings and paintings of Dante Gabriel Rossetti; and the Walt Whitman Archive, an online scholarly edition of Whitman's work.[23]

Meanwhile, film and media scholars experimented with laserdiscs, computers, and video-capture hardware. Stephen Mamber, at Georgia Tech and UCLA, experimented with computational analysis of film as early as 1989, producing Digital Hitchcock (which synchronized storyboards of *The Birds* (1963) with footage from the film) and 3D mockups of filmic space.[24] Other important early to mid-1990s media studies digital projects include Marsha Kinder's 1994 CD-ROM companion to *Blood Cinema*, her book on Spanish film; and Lauren Rabinowitz's *The Rebecca Project* CD-ROM (1995), on Hitchcock's *Rebecca* (1940).[25] A 1998 special issue of the journal *Postmodern Culture* was dedicated to the computational analysis of film, with essays on Evans Chan, Stanley Kubrick, Dziga Vertov, and *Singin' in the Rain*. (1952).[26]

As the 1990s and early 2000s progressed, Internet speeds increased, making it easier to share large files online. This helped spur the creation of ambitious multimedia projects like Labyrinth, an interactive narrative experiment led by Marsha Kinder, in 1997; and *Vectors*, an important, experimental multimedia cultural studies journal, in 2005. This period also gave rise to a burst of activity in geospatial analysis, 3D modeling, and digital tools purpose-built for humanities scholars. In media studies, theorist-practitioners like Lev Manovich and N. Katherine Hayles brought large-scale database, interface, and image analysis to a wider audience of scholars.[27]

By the late 2000s, digital humanities had hit the big time, institutionally speaking. The Alliance of Digital Humanities Organizations, formed in 2005, held its first international conference in 2006.[28] CenterNet, an international network of digital humanities centers, launched in 2007, and now counts more than 100 digital humanities centers among its members.[29] In 2008, the National Endowment for the Humanities launched the Office of Digital Humanities, which awards grants for digital humanities projects. "No DH, no interview," wrote the *Chronicle* columnist William Pannapaker, reflecting not so much the reality of the academic job market in the humanities as the general sense that digital humanities is now ubiquitous, volatile, and impossible to ignore.[30]

Most histories of digital humanities emphasize its origins in textual analysis, but in fact film scholars have conducted research with computers virtually from the moment it became possible to do so. Moreover, surely the field's lineage has changed as the field itself has changed. We now classify video essays under the digital humanities heading, for example. But aren't they more properly an outgrowth of the ciné-essay than of Roberto Busa's concordance? This isn't to say that video essays are not digital humanities; but it is to say that the existence of video essays should force us to recognize influences on digital humanities other than Busa and his punch cards. Do wildly experimental projects like *Vectors* have more in common with the TEI, or with multimedia art of the late 1990s? Surely expressive programming languages, like processing, have more to do with software art than they do with corpus linguistics. "What Is Digital Humanities and What's It Doing In English Departments?" asks Matthew Kirschenbaum's widely cited essay on the origins of the field.[31] But what happens to digital humanities when it is not in English departments? A broader history of the field, one that looks not to Busa for its origins but to media art or to documentary production, might suggest some possibilities for lively, engaging scholarship that takes image, audience, and immersion seriously.

Major Modes and Terminology

To the newcomer (and even the not-so-newcomer) the range of projects classed as digital humanities can be baffling to the point of exasperation. DHCommons, the closest thing to a comprehensive repository of digital humanities projects, lists 759 projects, divided into thirty-six categories of "research objects" (everything from "text-bearing objects" to "virtual research environments").[32]

With experience, one can tease out meaningful patterns from this apparent chaos. I do this in two ways: by sorting a given project into one or a few categories, and then by applying a three-part heuristic device to reverse-engineer it. I start here with an account of the most commonly encountered types of digital humanities projects. This is not an exhaustive list, nor is it meant to be prescriptive. But understanding that maps and data visualizations are two possible end-states for a digital humanities project can get one surprisingly far in understanding (and even replicating for oneself) the mechanisms of a digital project.

First, a digital project might include a **digital exhibit or archive**: a collection of objects (like documents, recordings, or other artifacts) that have been described, catalogued, and made retrievable in digital form. Documenting Ferguson, for example, based at Washington University in St. Louis, gathers media produced by St. Louis community members following the shooting death of Michael Brown in 2014.[33] Media scholars have also created **databases** as a form of digital scholarship: These are collections of data, made retrievable through some kind of interface. Yuri Tsivian's Cinemetrics Database, for example, collects the shot lengths of thousands of films and television shows.[34] Scholarly editions are collections of important documents, edited and annotated to show important features such as variations among editions. Specialists in scholarly editing have devised a language (the Textual Encoding Initiative, discussed above) specifically for this purpose. The Agrippa Files, based at the University of California, Santa Barbara, provides a carefully edited presentation of pages from William Gibson's *Agrippa (a book of the dead)* along with an emulation of the digital poem that accompanied it.[35]

Many digital projects incorporate **maps**: representations of geographic space that display information tied to place. Going to the Show, for example, based at the University of North Carolina, documents 1,300 movie venues across North Carolina.[36] For many media scholars, **multimedia narratives** have natural appeal: These are article- or book-length works enhanced with images, sound, and video. Erin B. Mee's "Hearing the Music of the Hemispheres," for example, incorporates audio and video in its discussion of Maria Chavez's performance art piece *Music of the Hemispheres*.[37] The genre of **data visualization** is familiar to anyone who has looked at election results or basketball scores: These are images produced by assigning visual attributes to data. Frederic Brodbeck's Cinemetrics project (not to be confused with Tsivian's Cinemetrics Database) uses information drawn from films to create visual "fingerprints" to represent important information about them.[38]

For many people, digital humanities is closely associated with textual analysis (sometimes called distant reading). Both of these terms really refer to an assortment of different methods, all of which use algorithms to uncover patterns within large bodies of texts. For example, Eric Hoyt, Kevin Ponto, and Carrie Roy's "Visualizing and Analyzing the Hollywood Screenplay with ScripThreads" uses a custom-built tool called ScripThreads to analyze narrative features of screenplays.[39] In recent years, media scholars have increasingly embraced the digital **video essay** (sometimes called the **visual essay**, **videographic essay**, or **audiovisual essay**). This mode allows the scholar of the moving image to perform her critique on video. "Bergman Senses," published by the journal of videographic criticism *[in]Transition* exemplifies this mode of digital scholarship.[40] Media scholars have also engaged in the construction of **three-dimensional objects** and **virtual-reality environments**. Jentery Sayers, for example, has produced three-dimensional reconstructions of obsolete media technologies as part of an effort to understand their material features.[41] Finally, media scholars have created **digital games**—interactive, rules-based works that incorporate a goal—in order to explore and convey ideas. For example, *Speculation*, created by Patrick Jagoda, is an alternate reality game that deals with digital media and finance capital.[42]

For all the field's variety, one can pull apart and analyze most digital humanities projects by separating them into three layers: **sources**, **processing**, and **presentation**.[43] "Sources" are those materials that form the basis of the study at hand. "Processing" refers to the work of translating those sources into machine-readable data. The "presentation" is the face the project presents to the viewer. Each of these layers is formed as the result of many human decisions, and each of these decisions affects the argument and epistemological orientation of the project as a whole.

It is helpful here to examine a few examples. Elif Akcali's "Ceylan's Women" is a five-minute video essay that presents a series of shots of female characters from the films of Nuri Bilge Ceylan.[44] The sources, then, are Ceylan's films. Here, we might pause to ask some of the same questions we might have asked if Akcali had presented us with a conventional journal article: Why investigate Ceylan's films? Does Akcali

include all of her films in her investigation, and if not, what are her criteria for the films' selection? Next, we can observe that Akcali's has processed these films by cutting them into shots of a few seconds' duration, isolating only those moments in which women look at, or are looked at by, another character. Why has Akcali done this? In cutting the shots to this length, have we lost other important information? Is the trade-off worthwhile? Finally, Akcali has presented her sources: she has edited these shots into a five-minute video, grouping them thematically according to mood and supplying a soundtrack. Why a video? How would this project have been different if she had prepared a database or a collage of still images? What effect do the sequence and the soundtrack have on the final project? Taken as a whole, does the project succeed in making a coherent and defensible argument?

This method also works for radically different projects. Jennifer Terry's "Killer Entertainments" (designed by Raegan Kelly) introduces viewers to combat videos shot by soldiers in Iraq and Afghanistan.[45] Its interface confronts the viewer with three videos that play simultaneously. Keywords and snippets of context periodically drift upwards as the videos play. To understand "Killer Entertainments" as a work of scholarship, one can start with the sources: How did Terry choose these videos? Why these videos? At the layer of processing, one might ask how she's edited them, sorted them into categories, and altered them from the form in which she found them. Finally, it becomes clear that Terry's most significant intervention is at the level of presentation. Why the three-screen arrangement? How would this project have been different if Terry had sorted the videos into a searchable database or edited them into a single long video? Why has Terry chosen to provide so little context for these videos? Taken as a whole, does the project tell us something we didn't know? Is it coherent, and does it do justice to its source material?

No layer of a digital project will ever be discrete; in fact, the longer one scrutinizes any given layer, the harder it becomes to draw boundaries around it. The aim of this exercise, however, is not to produce hard-and-fast schematics for digital projects but to think systematically about each part of what might otherwise appear to be a black box.

Case Study: Oscar Micheaux's Network

An example from my own work will show not only how blurry each layer of digital humanities is in practice but also how many critical decisions a human being must make in the course of composing any digital project. The case study describes not a final product but the beginning stages of a project that eventually resulted in a collaboration with students, a website, an article, and two exhibitions (discussed below). Here, I discuss a pilot exploration I conducted with some data about Oscar Micheaux's cast lists, including how it suggested some questions that I eventually explored alongside my students.

Oscar Micheaux (1884–1951), the pioneering Black American filmmaker, wrote, produced, and directed films primarily for Black audiences on the segregated film circuit. In total, he made about thirty-seven films between 1918 and 1948, articulating a distinct aesthetic characterized by elliptical storylines and temporal discontinuity.

Reading an essay by Sister Francesca Thompson on the Lafayette Players (the Black theater troupe from which Micheaux and other directors drew many of their actors), I was struck by the richly interconnected, mutually constitutive community Thompson evoked.[46] I wondered to what extent this described the cast of Micheaux's films. Is it possible that these closely connected groups of actors had an unacknowledged influence on Micheaux himself? Since only three of Micheaux's twenty-two silent films survive, the historian has to make the most of every piece of evidence that does remain from the period, as discussed in Chapter 21 in this collection. What might Micheaux's cast lists yield if subjected to digital methods of analysis?

Of course, digital methods aren't the only way I could have undertaken this study. I could, for example, have relied on close readings of cast lists and primary and secondary literature. But since I have some experience with digital methods of analysis, I knew that computational methods might allow the researcher to perform operations on networks—such as calculations of centrality or edge-density—that could suggest avenues of inquiry that might not be apparent from conventional forms of inquiry.

The case study that follows, then, is a very particular kind of digital humanities project: network analysis drawn from structured data. There are, as I have outlined, many other kinds of digital projects. Some of them, like digital maps and databases, draw heavily on the spreadsheet-intensive data-management techniques I describe below. Others, like text analysis, video essays, and multimedia narratives, require fewer considerations of metadata and more skill with sound and images. But no matter the specific method

she uses, the digital scholar must ask herself the same set of questions: What sources am I using? How will I get them into a format a computer can read? And how will I present them to an audience?

The narrative I present builds toward a set of questions rather than a fully developed argument, but this, I've found, is typical of digital humanities projects. A digital humanities project only rarely proceeds from data to conclusion, the way a lab experiment might; instead, it often moves from supposition to provocation and then back to the sources themselves. The process, of course, is messy, inefficient, and often frustrating. But then so are most modes of criticism.

Sources

I began this inquiry just as a "traditional" media scholar might: with a set of questions, and by determining which works I would consider in this investigation. I decided to focus on Micheaux's silent films, on the logic that Micheaux's shift to sound in 1931 might have disrupted the circles of interrelated actors I hope to uncover. If this line of inquiry proved fruitful, I decided, I would extend the investigation into Micheaux's sound period. This left me with twenty-two films—at least it seemed to. Various sources give different versions of Micheaux's work. I decided to hew to the most widely cited filmography of Micheaux, that contained in Pearl Bowser, Jane Gaines, and Charles Musser's *Oscar Micheaux and His Circle.*[47]

Any decision about where to circumscribe the object of one's study will be unsatisfactory on some level. For example, why limit myself to Micheaux, if my object is to understand how Black screen actors circulated in networks? Perhaps expanding my scrutiny to include Micheaux's contemporaries would have given me a more accurate picture of where these people traveled. But the more I considered other possible networks, the more this project seemed doomed never to get off the ground. Better, I decided, to start with a more manageable network, and move from there to an expanded view, if the method of analysis seemed promising.

Processing

It is not hard to find cast lists of Micheaux's films, but finding lists in formats that a computer can process—that is to say, as data—is harder than almost anyone ever thinks it is. In fact, obtaining and cleaning data is often the most time-consuming (and frustrating) part of any digital humanities project.

As a starting point, I used the programming language Python to automatically gather data about Micheaux's films from the Progressive Silent Film List (PSFL), the web-based list of silent-era filmographies. The result was a spreadsheet that stored the cast list in rows and columns, with one row per film. The neat rows of the spreadsheet, however, mask some unresolved ambiguity within this data. Some of this inconsistency is clearly the result of mistakes. The cell that contains "and Sylvester Jenkins," for example, shouldn't contain the word "and." These problems are easy enough to clean up.

But some of kinds of ambiguity in the data are harder to resolve. What about "[?] Lorenzo McClane or Lorenzo McLane?" for example? Which is it? On the PSFL, both variants can coexist without a problem. For this name to become useful *data*, however, I need to pick one. If my spreadsheet contained both Lorenzo McLane and Lorenzo McClane, how could I show how many films this actor—assuming he is one actor—appeared in?

Conveniently, one can query other databases to find the "official" versions of particular kinds of data. These lists of accepted terms are called authorities, and they exist for many different domains. Art historians, for example, might use the Getty's Art & Architecture Thesaurus, while astronomers might reference the Astronomy Thesaurus. But these authority files, like human beings, are fallible, and mistakes and biases within the authority files can easily propagate through the datasets that reference them. For example, the Library of Congress's name authority files offer only three options for gender: male, female, or not known. But as others have observed, this method of describing gender violates many of the tenets of queer and feminist theory, which see gender as neither binary nor stable.[48]

I know all of this, but, as is becoming obvious, computers demand not abstract knowledge but concrete decisions. Indeed, the entire process of turning information *as I find it* into data *as a computer can read it* is a series of decisions that change the nature of that information in fundamental ways. When people talk about "data-cleaning," this is really what they mean: imposing human-authored rules on information that, in its present state, doesn't conform to them.

Presentation

This stage of digital humanities research often performs a dual function: it allows the scholar to bring hidden patterns to the surface of the data and, ideally,

to present those patterns as part of an argument. This method of presentation needn't be a chart or graph, per se. I could, for example, produce a table that simply offers values in tabular form. It's easy enough, though, to move from a table to a simple bar chart—thus shifting one's scholarship into the realm of data visualization. This mode of presentation, in which numeric values computationally generate graphical forms, relies on humans' abilities to perceive color, shape, and position in order to demonstrate meaningful patterns within data.

Here, a few words of caution will have to stand in for the reams of advice on creating truthful and accurate data visualizations.[49] It is exceedingly easy to create misleading data visualizations. It often surprises my students to learn that there are no *laws* that dictate how numerical values should be bound to graphical renderings; we rely only, astoundingly, on convention to understand how one data point relates to another. Visualizations, then, can with impunity be blatantly misleading, such as those that truncate the scale of a Y-axis or pack more than 100 percent into a pie chart.

But they can also mislead in more subtle ways. Every form of data visualization carries with it a certain set of ideological assumptions, such as that dates can be divided discretely into years (as opposed to, say, seasons, generations, or memories), or that an actor's appearance or nonappearance in a film is the only meaningful index of her involvement. It takes a great deal of practice and skill to decode these assumptions, and our ability to deconstruct graphs and charts falls far short of their ubiquity and persuasiveness in our moment of "big data." It often strikes me as odd that humanists have largely ceded responsibility for conceptualizing visualizations to statisticians and visualization designers, who have a very different understanding of information than people in other disciplines. This, in fact, might itself be an argument for creating data visualizations, or helping students to do so: it is one way to make it abundantly clear that "objective" data visualizations simply don't exist.

Nevertheless, I hope to demonstrate that visualizations can in fact help us to understand information in meaningful ways, if only by pointing the researcher back to further avenues of exploration. When I started this investigation, I was interested in relationships, so I turned to network analysis, an area of scholarship that scrutinizes the way that entities connect with each other. Network diagrams demand a certain configuration of data: each entity must be one of only two (at most) categories; in this case "actors" and "films." The cast lists, then, must

Table 27.1 Actors and films, prepared for a network diagram

The Homesteader	Charles D. Lucas
The Homesteader	Evelyn Preer
The Homesteader	Iris Hall
The Homesteader	Inez Smith
The Homesteader	Vernon S. Duncan
The Homesteader	Charles S. Moore
The Homesteader	Trevy Wood
The Homesteader	William George

be reorganized into two columns, one containing the film titles and the other the name of each actor who appeared in the film.

Each row of this table represents a relationship of actor to film. Importing a table like this one into network-visualization software—in this case Gephi—creates a diagram that looks impressive but is, unfortunately, illegible (see Figure 27.1).

The entire network presented in this way *does* show who appeared in which film, but the network is too large for anyone to make sense of it without

additional filtering. Part of the problem is that we have two kinds of things, actors and films, in our diagram, meaning it's a bimodal graph. In general, it's easier for people to make sense of a one-mode, or unimodal, graph, which contains only one kind of thing. What would happen, I wonder, if my graph showed only actors, or only films?

To get to this next stage, as is so often the case, I have to do some additional data manipulation. A truncated version of my list of actors and films currently looks something like Table 27.2.

By representing only the relationships among actors, on the one hand, and only the relationships among films, on the other, I can transform my two-mode table into two separate one-mode graphs (see Tables 27.3 and 27.4).

Table 27.2 A two-mode network table

The Homesteader	Charles D. Lucas
The Homesteader	Evelyn Preer
The Homesteader	Iris Hall
The Homesteader	Inez Smith

Figure 27.1 The entire network of actors appearing in Micheaux films. The gray lines, or edges, indicate a relationship

Table 27.3 A truncated one-mode network table for actors

Charles D. Lucas	Evelyn Preer
Charles D. Lucas	Iris Hall
Charles D. Lucas	Inez Smith
Evelyn Preer	Iris Hall
Evelyn Preer	Inez Smith
Inez Smith	Iris Hall

By organizing the data this way, I've lost some crucial information: namely, the films that form the context for actors' relationships in the first table, and the actors that bind the films together in the second. But I've gained some useful insight, such as that *Within Our Gates* (1920) and *The Brute* (1920) share four actors in common, while *Within Our Gates* and *The Conjure Woman* (1926) share only one. My network graphs take on additional clarity, too. Figure 27.2 helps to show that *When Men Betray* and *The Wages of Sin* share the most actors in common, with *The Wages of Sin* and *The Broken Violin* a close second. In fact, most of Micheaux's films share only one or two actors—but they all, interestingly, share at least one. The network diagram also suggests (though it doesn't prove) possible relationships. It's much more likely, for example, that an actor who appeared in *When Men Betray* would be familiar with the company of *The Wages of Sin* than with that of *The House Behind the Cedars*.

A network diagram of the actors' relationships proves less immediately legible. Again, we have too many nodes to visually untangle. By leaning on methods drawn from network analysis, however, I can begin to break this mass of nodes into smaller clusters

of information. Gephi, the software I'm using, allows me to apply a **community detection algorithm** to the graph. This particular algorithm, called the Louvain method, measures the density of edges (the lines that indicate relationships between entities) and clusters together those entities that are densely connected (Figure 27.3).[50] Applying this algorithm to the network reveals seven distinct clusters. A closer look reveals that two actors seem to serve a bridging function, connecting at least four separate communities: A.B. De Comathiere and Evelyn Preer (Figure 27.4).

As I continue to inspect this network diagram, I notice something else that intrigues me. If I **weigh** each edge—that is, assign it a numerical value—according to how many times each pair of actors has appeared together, I can see which sets of actors are bound by "heavy" edges. Highlighting these highly weighted edges (Figure 27.5) appears to show two discrete clusters of actors, each of which is composed of actors who tended to appear with each other in films. If I create a new network diagram (Figure 27.6), this one containing only actors who co-appear in more than three films, I can see that there are indeed two disconnected clusters of actors within Micheaux's body of work. The first, composed of Evelyn Preer, E.G. Tatum, Lawrence Chenault, and Mattie Wilkes, appeared in Micheaux films between 1918 and 1927, with the bulk of appearances around 1922. The second, consisting of Ardella Dabney, Ethel Smith, Gertrude Snelson, Katherine Noisette, Lorenzo Tucker, and William A. Clayton, Jr., appeared in Micheaux films only after 1928, beginning with *The Broken Violin*.

I would hesitate to say anything definitive about any of these findings without further research, but it

Table 27.4 A truncated one-mode network table for films

Film 1	Film 2	Number of overlapping actors
Within Our Gates	The Brute	4
Within Our Gates	The Symbol of the Unconquered	1
Within Our Gates	The Gunsaulus Mystery	2
Within Our Gates	Deceit	1
Within Our Gates	Son of Satan	1
Within Our Gates	Birthright	2
Within Our Gates	The Conjure Woman	1
Within Our Gates	The Spider's Web	1
The Brute	The Symbol of the Unconquered	2
The Brute	The Gunsaulus Mystery	3
The Brute	Deceit	3
The Brute	Son of Satan	2
The Brute	Birthright	3

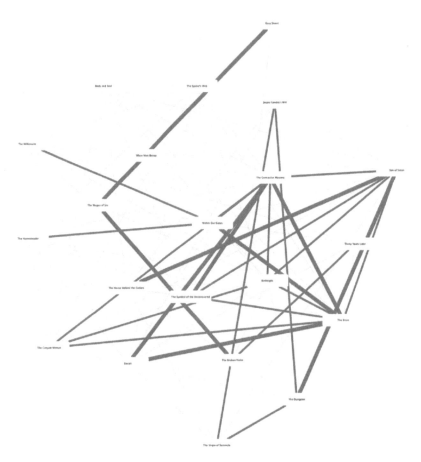

Figure 27.2 A one-mode diagram of films' relationships to each other, as measured by the number of actors who appear together. Thicker lines indicate a larger number of shared actors

strikes me as noteworthy that the center of gravity for Micheaux's casts seems to have shifted around 1927. What accounts for this shift in personnel? The diagrams I've created here don't offer any definitive answers, but they do point toward interesting questions that I might not have arrived at on my own: Did something happen around 1927 to change which actors tended to appear in Micheaux's films? What relationships did the actors have with each other? Turning these questions into presentable work would take additional research, both conventional and digital, and in the final product, the network diagrams themselves may play a small role. But by directing my analysis through a series of systematic steps, this project has nudged me toward findings that might otherwise have eluded me.

As this example demonstrates, "digital" humanities is actually human in the extreme. My graphs might resemble scientific diagrams, but contingency enters this process countless times: in the gathering, cleaning, and ordering of data; in the algorithms with

which that data sorted and arranged; and in the visual forms it ultimately takes. It is critically important that the digital humanist recognize and acknowledge that contingency. In my view, this divided knowledge—that the algorithm can offer useful surprises, but that humans, not machines must ultimately generate insight—is the hallmark of a digital humanist.

In the end, this relatively small experiment evolved into a much larger and more ambitious set of projects. UCLA Library Special Collections holds the George P. Johnson Negro Film Collection, a large archive of clippings, photographs, and publicity material related to the Black film industry from 1916 until Johnson's death in 1977. Working with the Johnson collection and with other primary and secondary sources, my students and I assembled a comprehensive database of every silent-era race film and company we could find, along with every person who worked in the industry. Our work is presented on a website, along with network analysis, maps, and narratives discussing our findings. We also published an

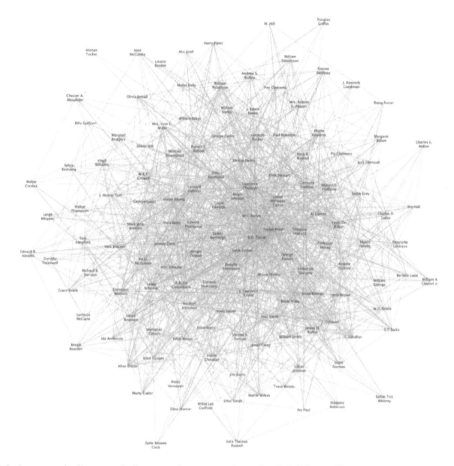

Figure 27.3 A one-mode diagram of all actors who appeared together in Micheaux films

article discussing our findings in *Moving Image*. That work, in turn, led to two separate exhibitions, which my students and I curated: The Industry of Uplift, presented at the UCLA Young Research Library from May to September 2017; and Center Stage: African American Women in Silent Race Films, at the California African American Museum, from June 28 to October 15, 2017.[51]

Conclusion

The field of digital humanities moves quickly and unpredictably—so much so that simply keeping up with developments in the field is a major challenge for many initiates. Moreover, the variety of technologies and methods in use is daunting enough to drive one, in bleaker moments, to despair. It is important to remember, however, that no single person can be an expert on everything; it is much more common for digital humanists to find a corner of the field that suits their scholarly goals

(videographic criticism, for example, or network analysis) and develop expertise there.

But is it still possible, then, to refer to digital humanities as any kind of unified "method"? How can digital humanists speak to each other if their tools are so disparate? Answers here will certainly vary, but I believe that digital humanities remains a field with some structural integrity. As I have discussed above, digital humanities projects, no matter how different they appear, are composed of the same fundamental layers. And digital humanities scholars must help each other learn to interrogate each layer with increasing levels of rigor and sophistication. The fundamental questions that animate digital humanities, beyond all of the fiddling with algorithms and databases, are simply, what should the humanities scholar's relationship with technology be? Where do humanism and digital technology collide? And where might the intersection of the two produce ideas that—like any good scholarship—show us some kind of beauty, meaning, and order to the world?

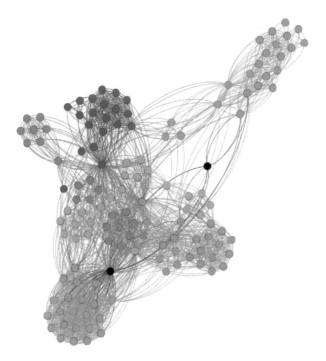

Figure 27.4 Evelyn Preer and A.B. De Comathiere (darkest spots) appear to bridge multiple communities

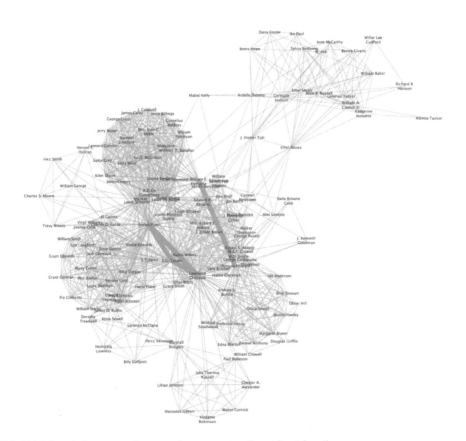

Figure 27.5 Thick lines indicate sets of actors who appear together at least four times

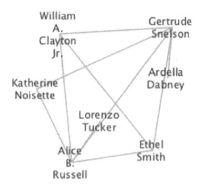

Figure 27.6 Filtering the network diagram so that it shows only actors who co-appeared three or more times reveals two separate sets of actors

Notes

1. For other takes on this question, see Jamie Henthorn, ed., "What Are the Differentiations and Intersections of Media Studies and the Digital Humanities?," *In Media Res*, May 29, 2013, accessed February 25, 2018, http://mediacommons.futureofthebook.org/question/what-are-differentiations-and-intersections-media-studies-and-digital-humanities; Kathleen Fitzpatrick, "Humanities, Done Digitally," in *Debates in the Digital Humanities*, ed. Matthew K. Gold (Minneapolis: University of Minnesota Press, 2012), 12–15; Moya Z. Bailey, "All the Digital Humanists Are White, All the Nerds Are Men, but Some of Us Are Brave," Journal of Digital Humanities, March 9, 2012, accessed February 25, 2018, http://journalofdigitalhumanities.org/1-1/all-the-digital-humanists-are-white-all-the-nerds-are-men-but-some-of-us-are-brave-by-moya-z-bailey/; Johanna Drucker, "Theory as Praxis: The Poetics of Electronic Textuality," *Modernism/Modernity* 9, no. 4 (2002): 683–91, accessed February 25, 2018, https://doi.org/10.1353/mod.2002.0069.

2. Curtis Marez, "Cesar Chavez's Video Collection," *American Literature* 85, no. 4 (2013), accessed February 25, 2018, http://scalar.usc.edu/nehvectors/curtis-marez/index.

3. Lev Manovich, "Visualizing Vertov," *Russian Journal of Communication* 5, no. 1 (2013): 44–55, https://doi.org/10.1080/19409419.2013.775546.

4. Laila Shereen Sakr, "R-Shief: A Media System for Research," n.d., accessed January 13, 2016, http://r-shief.org/.

5. Lisa Samuels and Jerome McGann, "Deformance and Interpretation," *New Literary History* 30, no. 1 (1999): 25–56.

6. Rombes, Nicholas. "10/40/70: *The Fury* (1978)." *IndieWire: Press Play*, April 11, 2012, accessed March 8, 2018, http://blogs.indiewire.com/pressplay/10-40-70-the-fury.

7. Tara McPherson, "Introduction: Media Studies and the Digital Humanities," *Cinema Journal* 48, no. 2 (2008): 119–23, accessed February 25, 2018, https://doi.org/10.1353/cj.0.0077.

8. Katherine Hayles, "Narrating Bits: Encounters between Humans and Intelligent Machines," *Vectors* 1 (Winter 2005), accessed February 25, 2018, www.vectorsjournal.org/projects/index.php?project=6.

9. Catherine Grant, *All That Pastiche Allows*, 2012, accessed February 25, 2018, https://vimeo.com/40242698.

10. Matthew K. Gold, ed., *Debates in the Digital Humanities* (Minneapolis: University of Minnesota Press, 2012).

11. Stephen Ramsay, "Who's In and Who's Out," 2011, accessed March 8, 2018, https://web.archive.org/web/20160106025925/http://stephenramsay.us/text/2011/01/08/whos-in-and-whos-out/.

12. See, for example, Cheryl Ball, "The Asymptotic Relationship Between Digital Humanities and Computers and Writing" (Emory University Writing Program Lecture

Series, Emory University, February 5, 2015), accessed February 25, 2018, http://ceball.com/2015/09/04/the-asymptotic-relationship-between-digital-humanities-and-computers-and-writing-emory-university/.

13. Stephen Brier, "Where's the Pedagogy? Teaching and Learning in the Digital Humanities," in *Debates in the Digital Humanities*, ed. Matthew Gold (Minneapolis: University of Minnesota, 2012), 390–401.

14. Scott Weingart, "Submissions to DH2016 (Pt. 1)," *The Scottbott Irregular*, December 7, 2015, accessed February 25, 2018, www.scottbot.net/HIAL/index.html@p=41533.html.

15. Gayatri Chakravorty Spivak, *Death of a Discipline* (New York: Columbia University Press, 2003).

16. David Golumbia, "Death of a Discipline," *Differences* 25, no. 1 (2014): 159–60, https://doi.org/10.1215/10407391-2420033.

17. Annemarie Perez, "Lowriding Through the Digital Humanities," in *Disrupting the Digital Humanities*, ed. Dorothy Kim and Jesse Stommel, 2016, accessed February 25, 2018, www.disruptingdh.com/lowriding-through-the-digital-humanities/; Tara McPherson, "Why Are the Digital Humanities So White?," in *Debates in the Digital Humanities*, ed. Matthew K Gold (Minneapolis: University of Minnesota Press, 2012), 139–60.

18. On the African American History, Culture, and Digital Humanities Initiative, please see http://mith.umd.edu/aadhum, accessed February 25, 2018.

19. Deb Verhoeven, "Has Anyone Seen a Woman?" July 2, 2015, accessed November 12, 2017, https://vimeo.com/144863312.

20. See, for example, Matthew G. Kirschenbaum, "What Is Digital Humanities and What's It Doing in English Departments?" *ADE Bulletin* 150 (2010): 55–61; Susan Hockey, "The History of Humanities Computing," in *Companion to Digital Humanities*, ed. Ray Siemens, John Unsworth, and Susan Schreibman, Blackwell Companions to Literature and Culture (Oxford: Blackwell Publishing Professional, 2004), accessed February 25, 2018, www.digitalhumanities.org/companion/; Anne Burdick, Johanna Drucker, Peter Lunenfeld, Todd Presner, and Jeffrey Schnapp, *Digital_Humanities* (Cambridge: MIT Press, 2012).

21. Hockey, "The History of Humanities Computing."

22. Cited in Kirschenbaum, "What Is Digital Humanities?" 2–3.

23. Institute for Advanced Technology in the Humanities, "Projects" (University of Virginia, n.d.), accessed February 25, 2018, www.iath.virginia.edu/projects.html.

24. Matthew Mirapaul, "They'll Always Have Paris (And a Scholarly Web Site)," *The New York Times*, March 18, 2002, sec. Movies, accessed February 25, 2018, www.nytimes.com/2002/03/18/movies/arts-online-they-ll-always-have-paris-and-a-scholarly-web-site.html; Robert

Kolker, "Digital Media and the Analysis of Film," in *Companion to Digital Humanities*, ed. Susan Schreibman, Ray Siemens, and John Unsworth, Blackwell Companions to Literature and Culture (Oxford: Blackwell Publishing Professional, 2004), accessed February 25, 2018, www.digitalhumanities.org/companion/.

25. Marsha Kinder, "Blood Cinema" (Los Angeles: Cine Discs, 1994); Lauren Rabinowitz, *The Rebecca Project* (New Jersey: Rutgers University Press, 1995).

26. Robert Kolker, ed., "Special Issue on Film," *Postmodern Culture* 8, no. 2 (1998).

27. N. Katherine Hayles, *My Mother Was a Computer: Digital Subjects and Literary Texts* (Chicago: University of Chicago Press, 2005); Lev Manovich, *The Language of New Media* (Cambridge, MA: MIT Press, 2002).

28. The Alliance of Digital Humanities Organizations, "About," ADHO, n.d., accessed February 25, 2018, http://adho.org/about.

29. centerNet, "About," n.d., accessed February 25, 2018, http://dhcenternet.org/about.

30. William Pannapacker, "No DH, No Interview," *The Chronicle of Higher Education*, July 22, 2012, accessed February 25, 2018, http://chronicle.com/article/No-DH-No-Interview/132959/.

31. Kirschenbaum, "What Is Digital Humanities and What's It Doing in English Departments?"

32. "Projects," in *DHCommons*, 2011, accessed November 12, 2017, http://dhcommons.org/projects; Luise Borek, Quinn Dombrowski, Jody Perkins, and Christian Schöch, "TaDiRAH - Taxonomy of Digital Research Activities in the Humanities," 2014, accessed February 25, 2018, https://github.com/dhtaxonomy/TaDiRAH.

33. Rudolph Clay, Shannon Davis, Chris Freeland, Jadia Ghasedi, Sonya Rooney, Andrew Rouner, Rebcca Wanzo, and Micah Zeller, *Documenting Ferguson* (St. Louis: Washington University in St. Louis, 2014), accessed February 25, 2018, http://digital.wustl.edu/ferguson/.

34. www.cinemetrics.lv/database.php (accessed February 25, 2018).

35. Alan Liu, Paxton Hehmeyer, James J. Hodge, Kimberly Knight, David Roh, and Elizabeth Swanstrom, ed., *The Agrippa Files* (Santa Barbara: University of California, Santa Barbara, 2006), accessed February 25, 2018, http://agrippa.english.ucsb.edu/.

36. Robert Allen, Natasha Smith, Elise Moore, Adrienne MacKay, Kevin Eckhardt, and Cliff Dyer, ed., *Going to the Show: Mapping Moviegoing in North Carolina* (Chapel Hill: University of North Carolina, 2007), accessed February 25, 2018, http://docsouth.unc.edu/gtts/.

37. Erin B. Mee, "Hearing the Music of the Hemispheres," *TDR: The Drama Review* 57, no. 3 (2013), accessed February 25, 2018, http://scalar.usc.edu/anvc/music-of-the-hemispheres/index.

38. Frederic Brodbeck, *Cinemetrics*, 2011, accessed February 25, 2018, http://cinemetrics.fredericbrodbeck.de/.

39. Eric Hoyt, Kevin Ponto, and Carrie Roy, "Visualizing and Analyzing the Hollywood Screenplay with ScripThreads" 8, no. 4 (2014), accessed February 25, 2018, www.digitalhumanities.org/dhq/vol/8/4/000190/000190.html.

40. Thomas Elsaesser, Anne Bachmann, and Jonas Moberg, "Bergman Senses," *[in]Transition*, February 2014, accessed February 25, 2018, http://mediacommons.futureofthebook.org/intransition/2014/02/28/bergman-senses-thomas-elsaesser-anne-bachmann-and-jonas-moberg-2007.

41. Jentery Sayers, "Why Fabricate?" *Scholarly and Research Communication* 6, no. 3 (2015), accessed February 25, 2018, http://src-online.ca/index.php/src/article/view/209.

42. Patrick Jagoda, N. Katherine Hayles, and Patrick LeMieux, *Speculation*, 2012, accessed February 25, 2018, www.patrickjagoda.com/projects/speculation.

43. The heuristic that follows uses my own terms to refer to a tripartite method of understanding digital humanities projects outlined in Johanna Drucker and David Kim, "Introduction to Digital Humanities | Concepts, Methods, and Tutorials for Students and Instructors," 2013, accessed February 25, 2018, http://dh101.humanities.ucla.edu/.

44. Elif Akcali, "Ceylan's Women: Looking | Being Looked At," *[in]Transition* 2, no. 3 (2015), accessed February 25, 2018, http://mediacommons.futureofthebook.org/intransition/2015/08/05/ceylans-women-looking-being-looked.

45. Jennifer Terry, "Killer Entertainments," *Vectors Journal of Culture and Technology in a Dynamic Vernacular* 3, no. 1 (2007), accessed February 25, 2018, http://vectors.usc.edu/projects/index.php?project=86.

46. Sister Francesca Thompson, "From Shadows N Shufflin' to Spotlights and Cinema: The Lafayette Players, 1915–1932," in *Oscar Micheaux and His Circle: African-American Filmmaking and Race Cinema of the Silent Era*, ed. Pearl Bowser, Jane Gaines, and Charles Musser (Bloomington: Indiana University Press, 2001), 19–33.

47. Musser, Charles, Corey K. Creekmur, Pearl Bowser, J. Ronald Green, Charlene Regester, and Louise Spence, "An Oscar Micheaux Filmography," in *Oscar Micheaux and His Circle: African-American Filmmaking and Race Cinema of the Silent Era*, ed. Pearl Bowser, Jane Gaines, and Charles Musser (Bloomington: Indiana University Press, 2001), 228–77.

48. Amber Billey, Emily Drabinski, and K.R. Roberto, "What's Gender Got to Do with It? A Critique of RDA Rule 9.7," *Cataloging and Classification Quarterly* 52, no. 4 (2014): 412–21.

49. Two of the works I find most useful on "conventional" data visualization are Nathan Yau, *Data Points: Visualization That Means Something* (Indianapolis: Wiley & Sons, 2013); and Alberto Cairo, *The Truthful Art: Data, Charts, and Maps for Communication* (Berkeley: New Riders, 2016). In recent years, digital humanists have theorized and experimented with humanities-inflected visualization strategies. On this, see, Johanna Drucker, *Graphesis: Visual Forms of Knowledge Production*, MetaLABprojects (Cambridge: Harvard University Press, 2014); Johanna Drucker, "Humanities Approaches to Graphical Display," *Digital Humanities Quarterly* 5, no. 1 (2011), accessed February 25, 2018, http://digitalhumanities.org/dhq/vol/5/1/000091/000091.html; Lauren F. Klein, "The Image of Absence: Archival Silence, Data Visualization, and James Hemings," *American Literature* 85, no. 4 (2013): 661–88, https://doi.org/10.1215/00029831-2367310.

50. Vincent D. Blondel, Jean-Loup Guillaume, Renaud Lambiotte, and Etienne Lefebvre, "Fast Unfolding of Communities in Large Networks," *Journal of Statistical Mechanics: Theory and Experiment* 10 (2008), 1–12, https://doi.org/10.1088/1742-5468/2008/10/P10008.

51. Marika Cifor, Shanya Norman, William Lam, Hanna Girma, Karla Contreras, Monica Berry, Aya Grace Yoshioka, and Miriam Posner, *Early African American Film: Reconstructing the History of Silent Race Films, 1909–1930* (Los Angeles: University of California, Los Angeles, 2016), accessed February 25, 2018, http://dhbasecamp.humanities.ucla.edu/afamfilm/; Marika Cifor, Hanna Girma, William Lam, Shanya Norman, and Miriam Posner, "Tracing a Community of Practice: A Database of Early African-American Race Film," *The Moving Image* 17, no. 2 (2017); "The Industry of Uplift: Silent Race Film, The Lincoln Motion Picture Company, and George P. Johnson" (Los Angeles: University of California, Los Angeles, May 1, 2017), accessed February 25, 2018, www.library.ucla.edu/events/industry-uplift-silent-race-film-lincoln-motion-picture-company-george-p-johnson; "Center Stage: African American Women in Silent Race Films" (Los Angeles: California African American Museum, October 28, 2017), accessed February 25, 2018, https://caamuseum.org/exhibitions/2017/center-stage-african-american-women-in-silent-race-film.

Further Reading

Histories and Definitions of Digital Humanities

Berry, David. "The Computational Turn: Thinking About the Digital Humanities." *Culture Machine* 12 (2011). www.culturemachine.net/index.php/cm/article/viewDownloadInterstitial/440/470.

Schreibman, Susan, Raymond George Siemens, and John Unsworth. *A New Companion to Digital Humanities*. Hoboken: Wiley & Sons, 2016. https://doi.org/10.1002/9781118680605.

Media Studies and/versus Digital Humanities

Hayles, N. Katherine. *How We Think: Digital Media and Contemporary Technogenesis*. Chicago: University of Chicago Press, 2012.

Hoyt, Eric, and Acland Charles R. *The Arclight Guide to Media Studies and Digital Humanities*. Sussex: REFRAME, 2016.

Parikka, Jussi. "Archives in Media Theory: Material Media Archaeology and Digital Humanities." In *Understanding Digital Humanities*, edited by David M. Berry, 85–104. New York: Palgrave Macmillan, 2012.

Ross, Michael, Manfred Grauer, and Bernd Freisleben. *Digital Tools in Media Studies: Analysis and Research: An Overview*. Bielefeld; New Brunswick: Transcript Verlag, 2009.

Sayers, Jentery, ed. *Routledge Companion to Media Studies and Digital Humanities*. New York: Routledge, 2016.

Noteworthy Digital Humanities/Media Studies Projects and Publications

Anderson, Steven, Holly Willis, Philip Ethington, Tara McPherson, Eric Loyer, and Anna Helm. *Critical Commons*. University of Southern California, 2008–present. www.criticalcommons.org/.

Dawes, Brendan. *Cinema Redux*, 2014. www.brendandawes.com/projects/cinemaredux.

Flueckiger, Barbara. *Timeline of Historical Film Colors*. University of Zurich, 2011–present. http://zauberk lang.ch/filmcolors/.

Hughes, Kit, Eric Hoyt, Derek Long, Kevin Ponto, and Tony Tran. "Hacking Radio History's Data: Station Call Signs, Digitized Magazines, and Scaled Entity Search." *Media Industries* 2, no. 2 (2015). www.mediaindustries journal.org/index.php/mij/article/view/128.

[in]Transition Journal of Videographic Film & Moving Image Studies, 2014–present. http://mediacommons.future ofthebook.org/intransition/.

Kuhn, Virginia. "The Rhetoric of Remix." *Transformative Works and Cultures* 9 (2012). http://journal.transforma-tiveworks.org/index.php/twc/article/view/358/279.

Maltby, Richard, Dylan Walker, and Mike Walsh. "Digital Methods in New Cinema History." In *Advancing Digital Humanities: Research, Methods, Theories*, edited by Katherine Bode and Paul Longley Arthur, 95–112. New York: Palgrave MacMillan, 2014.

Manovich, Lev. "Visualizing Vertov." *Russian Journal of Communication* 5, no. 1 (2013): 44–55. https://doi.org/10.1080/19409419.2013.775546.

Mittell, Jason. "Caption Mining at the Crossroads of Digital Humanities & Media Studies." *Just TV*, November 30, 2012. https://justtv.wordpress.com/2012/11/30/caption-mining-at-the-crossroads-of-digital-humanities-media-studies/.

Verhoeven, Deb, Alwyn Davidson, Alex Gionfriddo, James Verhoeven, and Peter Gravestock. "Turning Gigabytes into Gigs: 'Songification' and Live Music Data." *Academic Quarter* 9 (Autumn 2014): 151–63.

Verhoeven, Deb, Mike Walsh, Richard Maltby, and Kate Bowles. *CAARP: Cinema and Audience Research Project*, 2014–present. http://caarp.edu.au/.

CONTRIBUTORS

Cynthia Baron is a Professor in the Department of Theatre and Film at Bowling Green State University. She is author of *Denzel Washington* (BFI, 2015) and *Modern Acting: The Lost Chapter of American Film and Theatre* (Palgrave Macmillan, 2016). She is co-author of *Reframing Screen Performance* (University of Michigan Press, 2008) and *Appetites and Anxieties: Food, Film, and the Politics of Representation* (Wayne State University Press, 2014). She is co-editor of *More Than a Method* (Wayne State University Press, 2004) and founding editor of *The Projector: A Journal on Film, Media, and Culture*. She is co-author of *Acting Indie: Aesthetics, Industry, and Performance* (Palgrave, 2018) and Bowling Green State University Research Professor of Excellence for 2017–20.

Ron Becker is Associate Professor in the Department of Media, Journalism, and Film and director of the Comparative Media Studies Program at Miami University in Oxford, Ohio. He is the author of *Gay TV and Straight America* (Rutgers, 2006) and co-editor of *Saturday Night Live and American Television* (Indiana University Press, 2013). His work has appeared in *The Television Studies Reader, Queer TV: Theories, Histories, Politics; The Great American Makeover: Television, History and Nation; Television and New Media; Reading the Bromance: Homosocial Relationships in Film and Television;* and *Queer Studies in Media and Popular Culture*.

Mary Beltrán is Associate Professor of Radio-Television-Film and an affiliate of Mexican American & Latina/o Studies and Women's and Gender Studies at the University of Texas at Austin. She is the author of *Latina/o Stars in U.S. Eyes: The Making and Meanings of Film and TV Stardom* (University of

Illinois Press, 2009) and co-editor of the anthology *Mixed Race Hollywood* (New York University Press, 2008). Her new book in progress is titled *Bronzing the Box: Latina/o Images, Storytelling, and Advocacy in U.S. Television.*

Patrick Burkart is a Professor of Communication at Texas A&M University. He is the author of *Pirate Politics: The New Information Policy Contests* (2014, MIT Press), *Music and Cyberliberties, Digital Music Wars: Ownership and Control of the Celestial Jukebox* (with Tom McCourt, 2006, Rowman & Littlefield), and *Popular Communication, Piracy, and Social Change* (co-edited with Jonas Andersson Schwarz) (2017, Routledge). He also serves as co-editor-in-chief of *Popular Communication: The International Journal of Media and Culture.*

Jeremy G. Butler is Professor of Creative Media at the University of Alabama and has taught television, film, and new media courses since 1977. To support his television courses, he created the textbook *Television: Visual Storytelling and Screen Culture*—now in its fifth edition (Routledge, 2018). He wrote *Television Style* (Routledge, 2010), edited the anthology *Star Texts: Image and Performance in Film and Television* (Wayne State University Press, 1991), and published articles on *Mad Men, ER, Roseanne, Miami Vice, Imitation of Life,* soap opera, the sitcom, and other topics in publications such as *Cinema Journal, Journal of Film and Video,* and *Screen.*

Cynthia Chris is Associate Professor in the Department of Media Culture at the College of Staten Island, City University of New York. She is the author of *Watching Wildlife* (University of Minnesota

Press, 2006), co-editor (with Sarah Banet-Weiser and Anthony Freitas) of *Cable Visions: Television Beyond Broadcasting* (New York University Press, 2007) and (with David Gerstner) of *Media Authorship* (Routledge, 2013), and former co-editor (with Matt Brim) of *Women's Studies Quarterly*, 2014–16. Her next book is *The Indecent Screen: Regulating Television in the Twenty-First Century.*

Norma Coates is Associate Professor with a joint appointment in the Don Wright Faculty of Music and the Faculty of Information and Media Studies at the University of Western Ontario. Her publications include articles about gender and popular music, sound studies, and transmedia engagements with music. She is a past officer of IASPM-US, and is active in the Sound Studies Special Interest Group of the Society for Cinema and Media Studies. She serves on the Executive Board of Console-ing Passions: International Conference on Television, Video, Audio, New Media and Feminism.

Eric Freedman is Professor and Dean of the School of Media Arts at Columbia College Chicago. He is the author of *Transient Images: Personal Media in Public Frameworks* (Temple University Press, 2011). His most recent essays include "Resident Racist: Embodiment and Game Controller Mechanics" and "Technobiography: Industry, Agency and the Networked Body." Dr. Freedman serves on the editorial board of the *Journal of e-Media Studies*, and holds a Ph.D. from the School of Cinematic Arts at the University of Southern California.

Rosalind Gill is Professor of Social and Cultural Analysis, at City, University of London. Her work focuses on questions related to feminism and postfeminism, neoliberalism and subjectivity, sexuality and intimacy, and cultural and creative work. She is author or editor of ten books, including *Gender and the Media* (Polity Press, 2007), *Gender and Creative Labour* (Blackwell, 2015), and *Mediated Intimacy: Sex Advice in Media Culture* (Polity, 2017). She is currently writing a book for Duke University Press on "The Confidence Cult."

Jonathan Gray is Professor of Media and Cultural Studies at University of Wisconsin, Madison. He is author of *Show Sold Separately: Promos, Spoilers, and Other Media Paratexts* (New York University Press, 2010), *Watching with "The Simpsons": Television, Parody, and Intertextuality* (Routledge, 2006), *Television Entertainment* (Routledge, 2008), and (with Amanda D. Lotz) *Television Studies* (Polity, 2012). He is also

co-editor of *Keywords in Media Studies* (New York University Press, 2017), *A Companion to Media Authorship* (Blackwell, 2013), *Satire TV: Politics and Comedy in the Post-Network Era* (New York University Press, 2009), and *Fandom: Identities and Communities in a Mediated World* (New York University Press, 2017, second edition).

Mary L. Gray is a Senior Researcher at Microsoft Research and Fellow at Harvard University's Berkman Klein Center for Internet and Society. She maintains a faculty position in the School of Informatics, Computing, and Engineering with affiliations in Anthropology, Gender Studies, and the Media School, at Indiana University. Mary studies how technology access, material conditions, and everyday uses of media play out in people's lives. Her books include studies of queer youth political action, media access and queer identities in rural America, and, most recently, the meaning of work among people producing data for a living in on-demand gig economies.

Timothy Havens is a Professor of Communication Studies, African American Studies, and International Studies at the University of Iowa, where he also serves as Chair of the Department of Communication Studies. He is the author of *Black Television Travels: African American Media Around the Globe* (New York University Press, 2013) and *Global Television Marketplace* (British Film Institute Publishing, 2006), co-author (with Amanda D. Lotz) of *Understanding Media Industries* (Oxford University Press, 2011, 2016), and co-editor (with Aniko Imre and Katalin Lustyik) of *Popular Television in Eastern Europe Before and Since Socialism* (Routledge, 2012). He is also a former Fulbright Scholar to Hungary.

Matt Hills is Professor of Media and Film at the University of Huddersfield, where he is also co-Director of the Centre for Participatory Culture. Matt is co-editor on the "Transmedia" book series for Amsterdam University Press, and has written six sole-authored monographs, starting with *Fan Cultures* (Routledge, 2002) and coming up to date with *Doctor Who: The Unfolding Event* (Palgrave, 2015). He has also published more than a hundred book chapters or journal articles on media fandom, audiences and cult film/TV. Amongst other projects, Matt is working on a follow-up to his first book, entitled *Fan Studies.*

Michele Hilmes is Professor Emerita at the University of Wisconsin-Madison, where she taught media studies for more than twenty years. Her books include *Hollywood and Broadcasting: From Radio to Cable* (University of Illinois Press, 1990), *Radio Voices: American Broadcasting 1922–1952* (University of Minnesota Press, 1997), *Network Nations: A Transnational History of British and American Broadcasting* (Routledge, 2011), and *Only Connect: A Cultural History of Broadcasting in the United States* (Cengage Learning, 2011, third edition). She is co-editor of *The Radio Journal: International Studies in Radio and Audio Media*. In March 2017, she received the Distinguished Career Achievement Award from the Society for Cinema and Media Studies.

Nina B. Huntemann is Director of Academics and Research at edX, a nonprofit online education provider founded by Harvard University and the Massachusetts Institute of Technology. She is the co-editor of the anthologies *Global Gaming: Production, Play and Place* (Palgrave, 2013) and *Joystick Soldiers: The Politics of Play in Military Video Games* (Routledge, 2010).

Victoria E. Johnson is Associate Professor in the Department of Film and Media Studies and the Department of African American Studies at the University of California, Irvine. Her research and publications examine questions of place, race, and community in popular U.S. media and sports culture. Her *Heartland TV: Prime Time Television and the Struggle for U.S. Identity* (New York University Press, 2008) was the Society for Cinema and Media Studies' Katherine Singer Kovács book award winner in 2009. Her book *Sports Television* is forthcoming with Routledge.

Michael Kackman is Associate Teaching Professor in the Department of Film, Television, and Theatre at the University of Notre Dame, where he teaches courses in the history and criticism of U.S. television, Cold War cultural history, nationhood and political culture, and history and memory practices in everyday life. He is the author of *Citizen Spy: Television, Espionage, and Cold War Culture* (University of Minnesota Press, 2005), and co-editor of *Flow TV: Television in the Age of Media Convergence* (Routledge, 2010).

Mary Celeste Kearney is Director of Gender Studies and Associate Professor of Film, Television, and Theatre at the University of Notre Dame. She is author of *Girls Make Media* (Routledge, 2006) and *Gender and Rock* (Oxford, 2017). She is editor of

The Gender and Media Reader (Routledge, 2011) and *Mediated Girlhoods: New Explorations of Girls' Media Culture* (Peter Lang, 2011), as well as co-editor (with Morgan Blue) of *Mediated Girlhoods'* second volume (Peter Lang, 2018). She is academic editor of the book series Routledge Research in Gender, Sexuality, and Media, and serves on the boards of several academic journals.

Bill Kirkpatrick is Associate Professor of Media Studies in the Communication Department at Denison University. His publications include articles in *Communication, Culture, and Critique*; *Critical Studies in Media Communication*; *Television & New Media*; *Radio Journal*; the *International Journal of Communication*; and several anthologies. He is co-editor (with Elizabeth Ellcessor) of *Disability Media Studies* (New York University Press, 2017), an anthology bringing media studies and disability studies into dialog; he is also completing a monograph on early U.S. radio and the medical profession.

Amanda Ann Klein is Associate Professor of Film Studies in the English Department at East Carolina University. She is the author of *American Film Cycles: Reframing Genres, Screening Social Problems, & Defining Subcultures* (University of Texas Press, 2011) and co-editor of the anthology *Multiplicities: Cycles, Sequels, Remakes and Reboots in Film & Television* (University of Texas Press). She is currently working on a book manuscript about MTV reality programming and youth identity politics. Her scholarship has appeared in *Quarterly Review of Film and Video*, *Jump Cut*, *Flow*, *Antenna*, *Salon*, and *The New Yorker*.

Shanti Kumar is an Associate Professor in the Department of Radio-Television-Film at the University of Texas-Austin. He is the author of *Gandhi Meets Primetime: Globalization and Nationalism in Indian Television* (University of Illinois Press, 2006), and the co-editor of *Global Communication: New Agendas in Communication* (Routledge, 2014), *Television at Large in South Asia* (Routledge, 2012), and *Planet TV: A Global Television Reader* (New York University Press, 2003). He has published book chapters in edited anthologies and articles in journals such as *BioScope*, *Jump Cut*, *Popular Communication*, *South Asian Popular Culture*, *Quarterly Review of Film and Video*, and *Television and New Media*.

Suzanne Leonard is Associate Professor of English at Simmons College, and co-coordinator of the college's interdisciplinary minor in Cinema and Media

Studies. She is co-editor (with Yvonne Tasker) of *Fifty Hollywood Directors* (Routledge, 2015), as well as author of *Fatal Attraction* (Wiley-Blackwell, 2009) and *Wife, Inc.: The Business of Marriage in the Twenty-First Century* (New York University Press, 2018).

Jessa Lingel is an Assistant Professor at the Annenberg School of Communication at the University of Pennsylvania. She received her Ph.D. in communication and information from Rutgers University. She has an MLIS from Pratt Institute and an MA from New York University. Her first book, *Digital Countercultures and the Struggle for Community*, was published in 2017 by the MIT Press, and she is currently working on a second book that examines peer-to-peer online marketplaces.

Madhavi Mallapragada is Associate Professor in the Department of Radio-Television-Film at the University of Texas at Austin. She is the author of *Virtual Homelands: Indian Immigrants and Online Cultures in the United States* (University of Illinois Press, 2014). She has also published articles in *Television and New Media, Communication, Culture & Critique, New Media and Society,* and *South Asian Popular Culture.* Mallapragada is working on a new book, *Race and Ethnicity in U.S. Media Industries,* and teaches courses in new media, Asian American popular culture, media and diaspora, and race and media industries.

Daniel Marcus is Professor of Communication and Media Studies at Goucher College in Baltimore, Maryland. He is the author of *Happy Days and Wonder Years: The Fifties and the Sixties in Contemporary Cultural Politics* (Rutgers University Press, 2004) and co-editor (with Selmin Kara) of *Contemporary Documentary* (Routledge, 2016). He writes and teaches on documentary, alternative media, television history, and media and politics.

Todd McGowan teaches theory and film at the University of Vermont. He is the author of *Only a Joke Can Save Us: A Theory of Comedy* (Northwestern University Press, 2017), *Capitalism and Desire: The Psychic Cost of Free Markets* (Columbia University Press, 2016), *Enjoying What We Don't Have: The Political Project of Psychoanalysis* (University of Nebraska Press, 2013), *The Real Gaze: Film Theory After Lacan* (State University of New York Press, 2007), *The Impossible David Lynch* (Columbia University Press, 2007), and other works.

Jason Mittell is Professor of Film & Media Culture and American Studies at Middlebury College. He is the author of *Genre & Television: From Cop Shows to Cartoons in American Culture* (Routledge, 2004), *Television & American Culture* (Oxford University Press, 2009), *Complex Television: The Poetics of Contemporary Television Storytelling* (New York University Press, 2015), *The Videographic Essay: Criticism in Sound and Image* (with Christian Keathley; caboose books, 2016), *Narrative Theory and* Adaptation (Bloomsbury, 2017), and co-editor (with Ethan Thompson) of *How to Watch Television* (New York University Press, 2013). He is a Fellow at the Peabody Media Center.

Ted Nannicelli teaches at The University of Queensland in Australia. He is the author of *A Philosophy of the Screenplay* (Routledge, 2013) and *Appreciating the Art of Television: A Philosophical Perspective* (Routledge, 2017), as well as co-editor of *Cognitive Media Theory* (Routledge, 2014) and editor of *Projections: The Journal for Movies and Mind.*

Diane Negra is Professor of Film Studies and Screen Culture and Head of Film Studies at University College Dublin. A member of the Royal Irish Academy, she is the author, editor, or co-editor of ten books including *What a Girl Wants?: The Reclamation of Self in Postfeminism* (Routledge, 2008) and *Extreme Weather and Global Media* (with Julia Leyda, Routledge, 2015). Her work in media, gender and cultural studies has been recognized with a range of research awards and fellowships, including an award from the Government of Japan and a Fulbright Scholarship. She is co-editor-in-chief of *Television and New Media.*

Matthew Thomas Payne is an Assistant Professor in the Department of Film, Television, and Theatre at the University of Notre Dame. He is author of *Playing War: Military Video Games after 9/11* (New York University Press, 2016) and is a co-editor of the anthologies *Flow TV: Television in the Age of Media Convergence* (Routledge, 2011) and *Joystick Soldiers: The Politics of Play in Military Video Games* (Routledge, 2010).

Miriam Posner is an Assistant Professor at the UCLA School of Information. She's also a digital humanist with interests in labor, race, feminism, and the history and philosophy of data. As a digital humanist, she is particularly interested in the visualization of large bodies of data from cultural heritage institutions, and the application of digital methods to the analysis of images and video. A film, media, and American studies scholar by training, she frequently writes on the application of digital methods to the humanities. She is at work on two projects: the first on what "data" might mean for humanistic research, and the second on how multinational corporations are making use of data in their supply chains.

Jacob Smith is Professor in the Department of Radio-Television-Film and Director of the MA in Sound Arts and Industries at Northwestern University. He has written several books, including *Vocal Tracks: Performance and Sound Media* (2008), *Spoken Word: Postwar American Phonograph Cultures* (2011), and *Eco-Sonic Media* (2015), all for the University of California Press, and has published articles on media history, sound, and performance.

INDEX